· Bartholomew ·

COMPACT WORLD ATLAS

·Bartholomew·

COMPACT WORLD ATLAS

Bartholomew
A Division of HarperCollins*Publishers*

Bartholomew
A Division of HarperCollins Publishers
Duncan Street, Edinburgh EH9 1TA

First published by Bartholomew 1991
Revised edition 1992

ISBN 0 7028 2100 4

Printed in Hong Kong

E/B5550

CONTENTS

viii-ix World Physical
x-xi World Political
xii-xiii World Time Zones
xiv-xv World Environment
xvi Key to Symbols

1 Arctic Ocean 1:40M
2-3 North America – Political 1:35M
4-5 Canada, West 1:15M
6-7 Canada, East 1:15M
8-9 USA, West 1:12·5M
10-11 USA, East 1:12·5M
12 USA, Alaska 1:10M
13 Canada Pacific 1:7·5M
14-15 Lower Canada, USA North-East 1:5M
16 Washington – New York – Boston 1:2·5M
17 USA, South-East 1:5M
18-19 USA, South-Central 1:5M
20 USA, Pacific NW 1:5M
21 USA, Pacific S 1:5M
22 San Francisco & Los Angeles 1:2·5M
23 Central Mexico 1:5M
24-25 Mexico & Central America 1:15M
26-27 Caribbean 1:10M

28 South America - Political 1:40M
29 South America, South 1:15M
30 South America, Central 1:15M
31 South America, NE 1:15M
32-33 South America, North 1:15M
34 Central Argentina 1:7·5M
35 South-East Brazil 1:7·5M

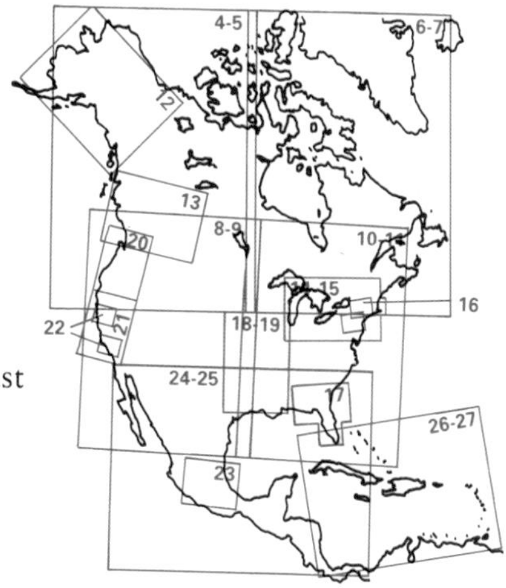

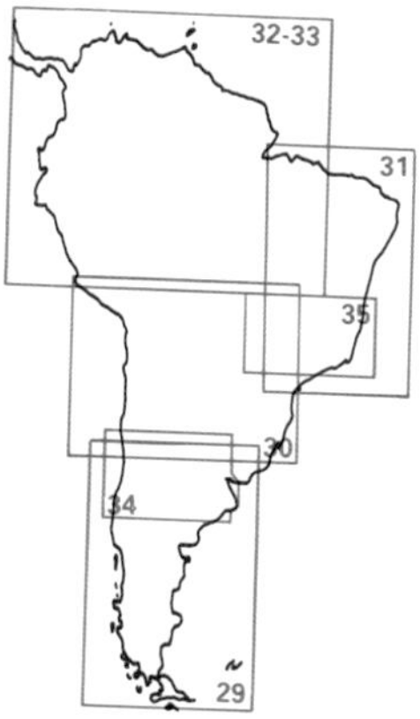

36-37 Europe – Political 1:16M
38-39 Scandinavia 1:7·5M
40-41 British Isles 1:5M
42-43 England & Wales 1:2·5M
44 Scotland, North 1:2·5M
45 Ireland 1:2·5M
46 Paris - Brussels – Ruhr 1:2·5M
47 Alps 1:2·5M
48-49 France 1:5M
50-51 Spain 1:5M
52-53 Italy 1:5M
54-55 The Balkans 1:5M
56-57 Germany & Austria 1:5M
58-59 East-Central Europe 1:5M
60-61 Central European Russia 1:10M
62 North Asia - Political 1:45M
63 Russian Federation, East 1:20M
64-65 Russian Federation, West 1:20M
66-67 South Asia – Political 1:40M
68-69 East Asia 1:20M
70-71 South-East Asia 1:20M
72-73 Central China 1:10M
74 Japan & Korea 1:10M
75 Central Japan 1:5M
76-77 Indo-China & Singapore 1:10M
78 Indonesia, Central 1:10M
79 Philippines 1:10M
80-81 Middle East 1:20M
82-83 India & West China 1:20M
84-85 India, NW & Pakistan 1:7·5M

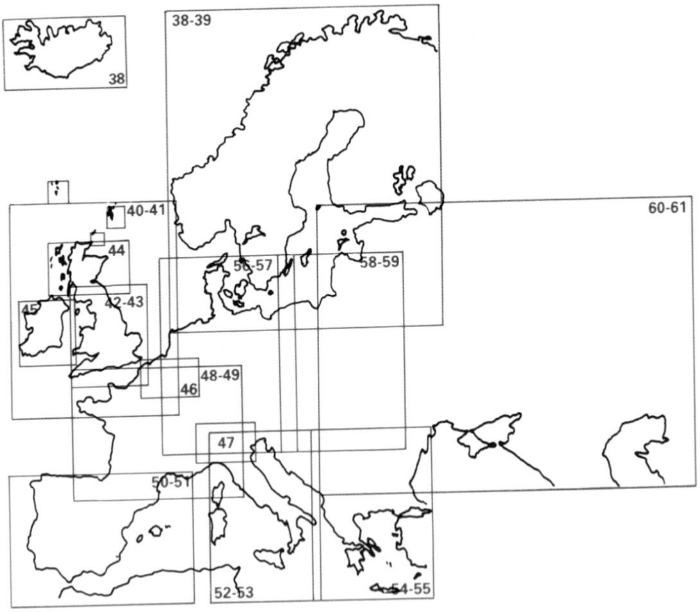

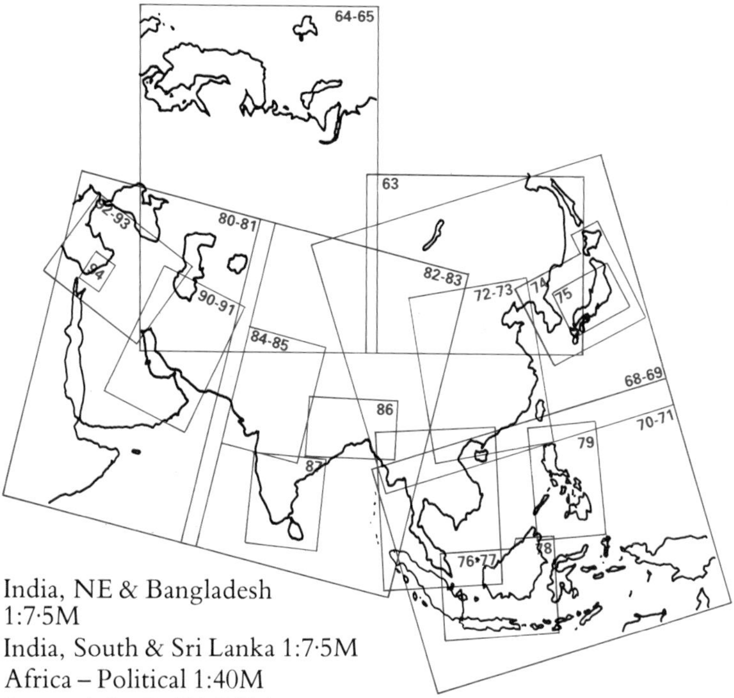

86 India, NE & Bangladesh 1:7·5M
87 India, South & Sri Lanka 1:7·5M
88-89 Africa – Political 1:40M
90-91 Iran and the Gulf 1:7·5M
92-93 Turkey, Syria & Iraq 1:7·5M
94 Israel & Lebanon 1:2:5M

95 Africa, North-East 1:15M
96-97 Africa, West 1:15M
98-99 Africa, Central 1:15M
100-101 Africa, South 1:15M
102-103 Atlantic Ocean 1:60M
104-105 Australasia 1:60M
106-107 Australia 1:20M
108-109 Australia, South-East 1:7·5M
110-111 New Zealand 1:5M
112 Antarctica 1:40M
Index

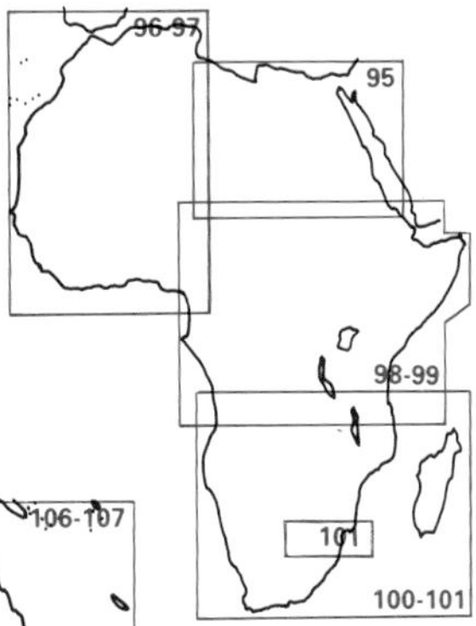

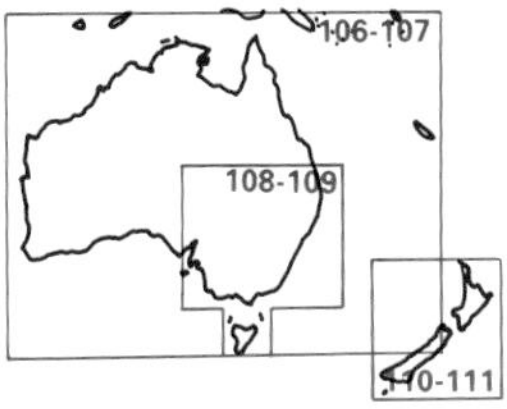

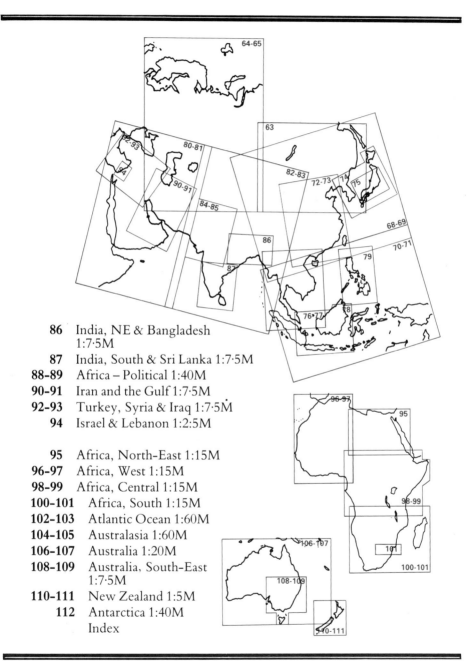

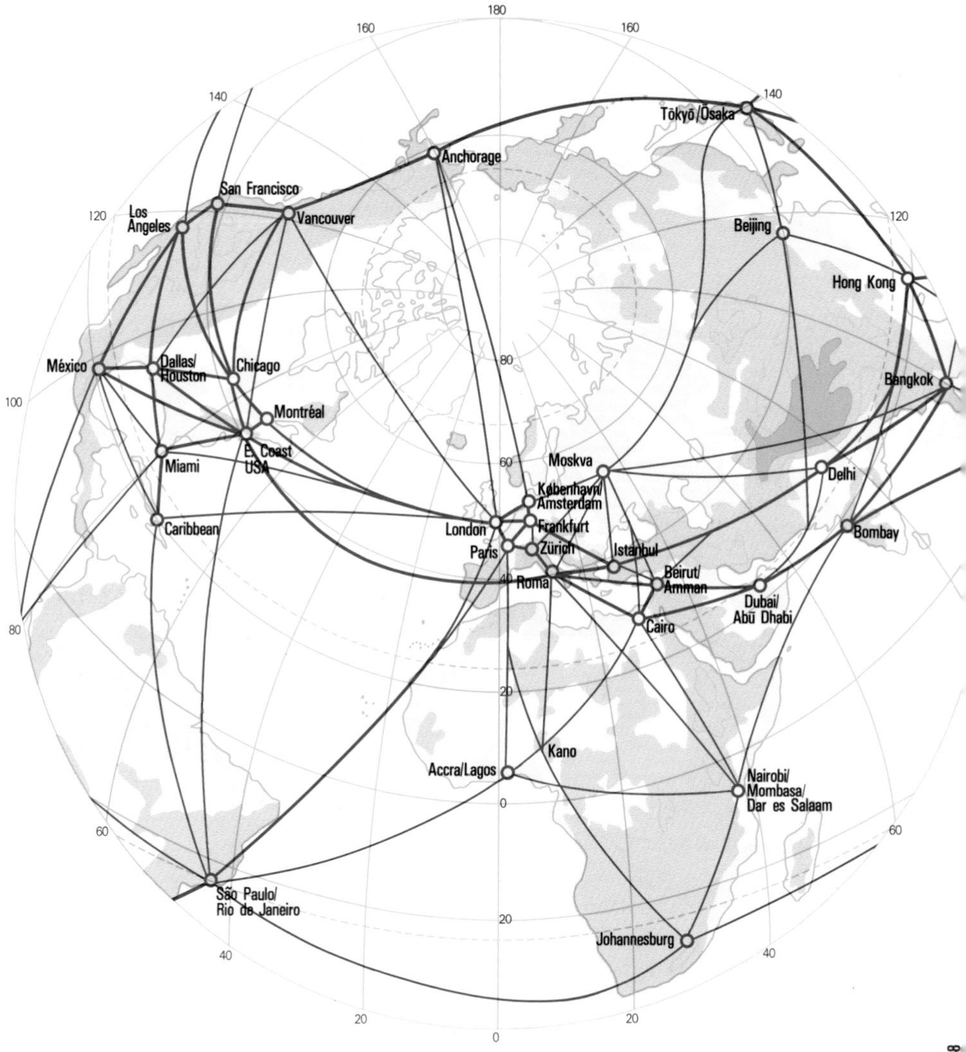
Anchorage
San Francisco
Vancouver
Los Angeles
México
Dallas/ Houston
Chicago
Montréal
E. Coast USA
Miami
Caribbean
Tōkyō/Ōsaka
Beijing
Hong Kong
Bangkok
Delhi
Bombay
Moskva
København/ Amsterdam
Frankfurt
London
Paris
Zürich
Istanbul
Roma
Beirut/ Amman
Dubai/ Abū Dhabi
Cairo
Kano
Accra/Lagos
Nairobi/ Mombasa/ Dar es Salaam
São Paulo/ Rio de Janeiro
Johannesburg
180
160
140
120
100
80
60
40
20
0

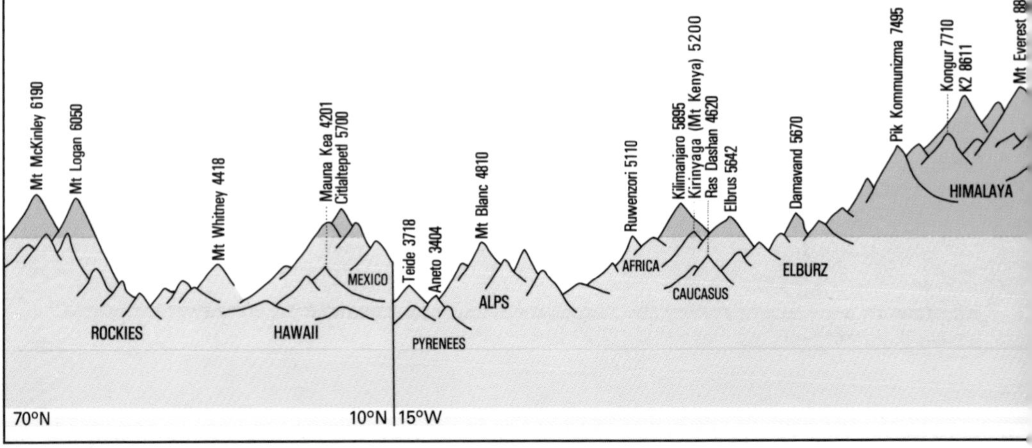
Mt McKinley 6190
Mt Logan 6050
Mt Whitney 4418
Mauna Kea 4201
Citlaltepetl 5700
Teide 3718
Aneto 3404
Mt Blanc 4810
Ruwenzori 5110
Kilimanjaro 5895
Kirinyaga (Mt Kenya) 5200
Ras Dashan 4620
Elbrus 5642
Damavand 5670
Pik Kommunizma 7495
Kongur 7710
K2 8611
Mt Everest 8848
ROCKIES
HAWAII
MEXICO
PYRENEES
ALPS
AFRICA
CAUCASUS
ELBURZ
HIMALAYA
70°N
10°N
15°W

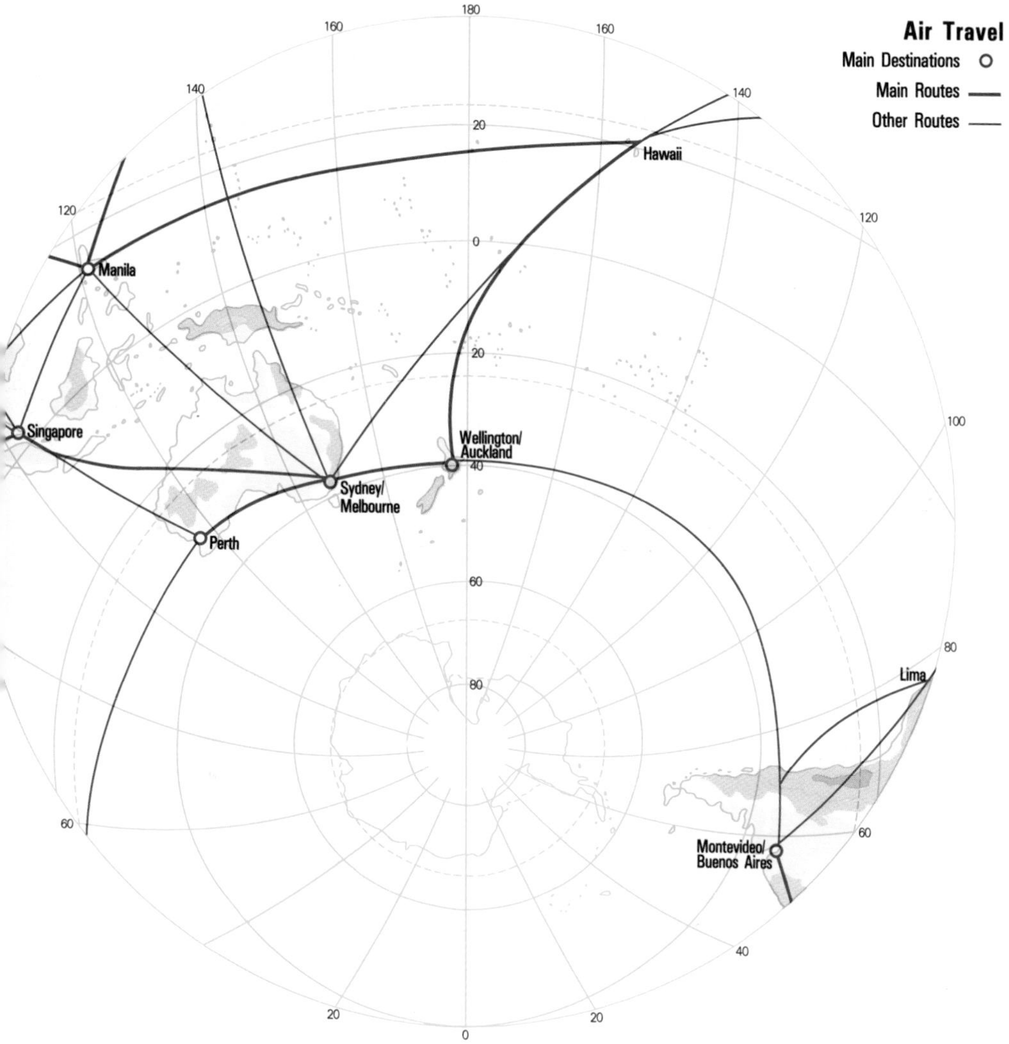
Air Travel
Main Destinations
Main Routes
Other Routes
Hawaii
Manila
Singapore
Wellington/
Auckland
Sydney/
Melbourne
Perth
Lima
Montevideo/
Buenos Aires
180
160
160
140
140
120
120
100
80
60
60
40
20
20
0
20
0
20
40
60
80

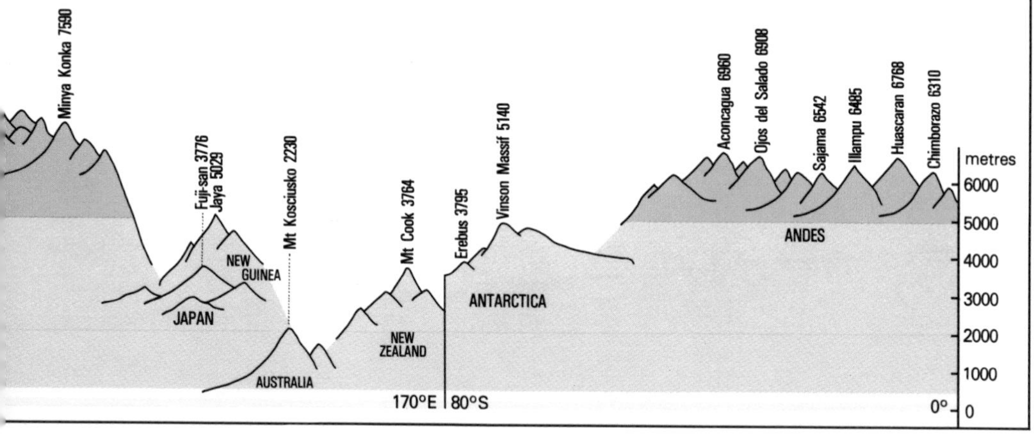
Minya Konka 7590
Fuji-san 3776
Jaya 5029
Mt Kosciusko 2230
Mt Cook 3764
Erebus 3795
Vinson Massif 5140
Aconcagua 6960
Ojos del Salado 6908
Sajama 6542
Illampu 6485
Huascaran 6768
Chimborazo 6310
NEW
GUINEA
JAPAN
AUSTRALIA
NEW
ZEALAND
ANTARCTICA
ANDES
170°E
80°S
0°
metres
6000
5000
4000
3000
2000
1000
0

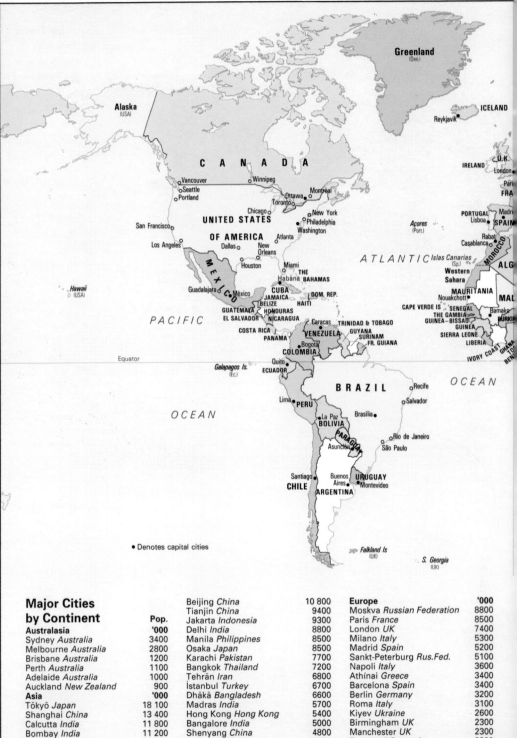

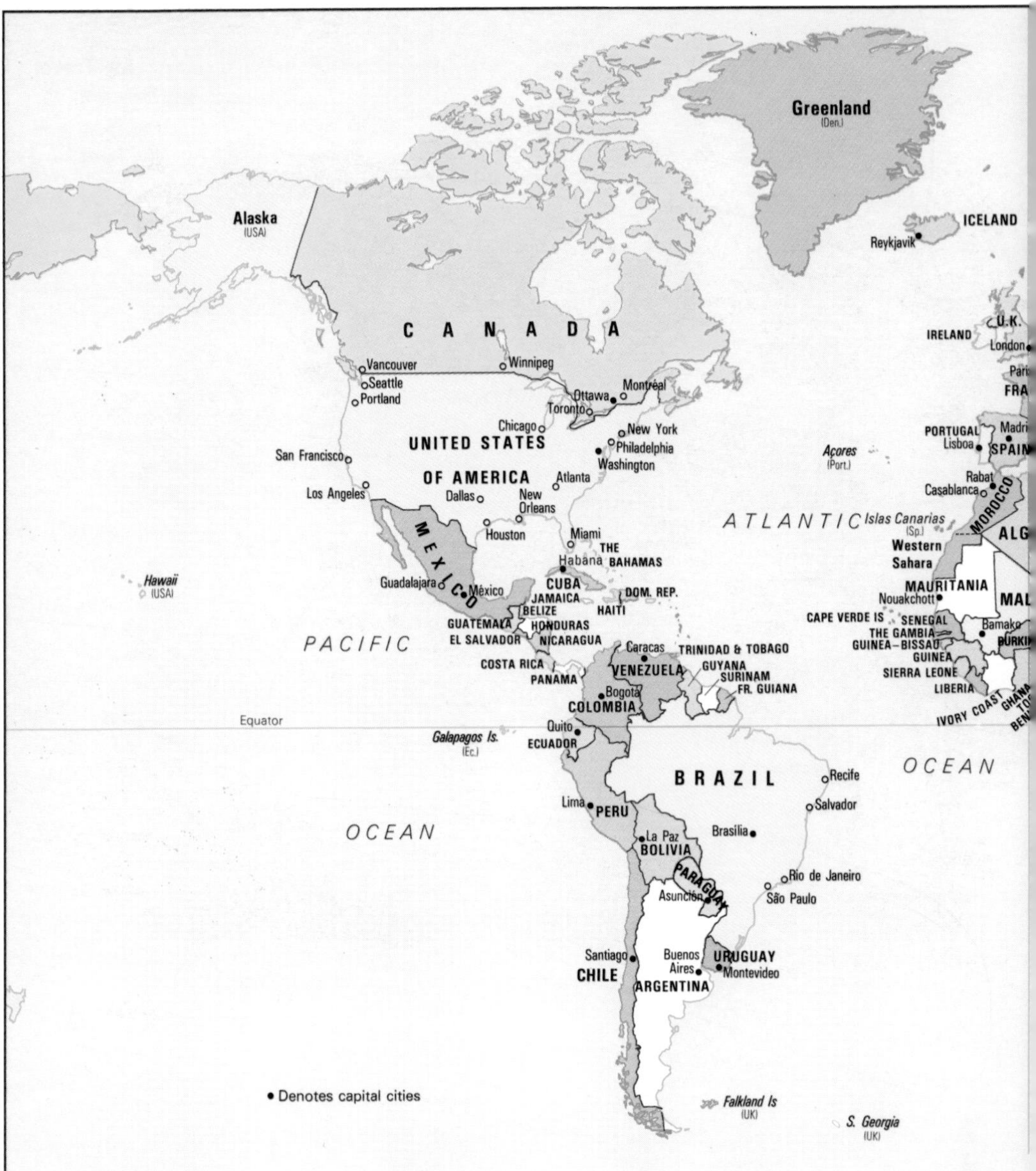

Major Cities by Continent

Australasia	Pop. '000
Sydney *Australia*	3400
Melbourne *Australia*	2800
Brisbane *Australia*	1200
Perth *Australia*	1100
Adelaide *Australia*	1000
Auckland *New Zealand*	900
Asia	**'000**
Tōkyō *Japan*	18 100
Shanghai *China*	13 400
Calcutta *India*	11 800
Bombay *India*	11 200
Sŏul *South Korea*	11 000
Beijing *China*	10 800
Tianjin *China*	9400
Jakarta *Indonesia*	9300
Delhi *India*	8800
Manila *Philippines*	8500
Osaka *Japan*	8500
Karachi *Pakistan*	7700
Bangkok *Thailand*	7200
Tehrān *Iran*	6800
İstanbul *Turkey*	6700
Dhākā *Bangladesh*	6600
Madras *India*	5700
Hong Kong *Hong Kong*	5400
Bangalore *India*	5000
Shenyang *China*	4800
Lahore *Pakistan*	4100

Europe	'000
Moskva *Russian Federation*	8800
Paris *France*	8500
London *UK*	7400
Milano *Italy*	5300
Madrid *Spain*	5200
Sankt-Peterburg *Rus.Fed.*	5100
Napoli *Italy*	3600
Athínai *Greece*	3400
Barcelona *Spain*	3400
Berlin *Germany*	3200
Roma *Italy*	3100
Kiyev *Ukraine*	2600
Birmingham *UK*	2300
Manchester *UK*	2300
Bucureşti *Romania*	2200

North and Central America	'000
México *Mexico*	20 200
New York *USA*	16 200
Los Angeles *USA*	11 900
Chicago *USA*	7000
Philadelphia *USA*	4300
Detroit *USA*	3700
San Francisco *USA*	3700
Toronto *Canada*	3500
Dallas *USA*	3400
Guadalajara *Mexico*	3200
Houston *USA*	3000
Monterrey *Mexico*	3000
Montréal *Canada*	3000
Washington *USA*	2900
Boston *USA*	2800

South America	'000
São Paulo *Brazil*	17 400
Buenos Aires *Argentina*	11 500
Rio de Janeiro *Brazil*	10 700
Lima *Peru*	6200
Santiago *Chile*	5000
Bogotá *Colombia*	4900
Caracas *Venezuela*	4100
Belo Horizonte *Brazil*	3600
Pôrto Alegre *Brazil*	3100
Recife *Brazil*	2500
Brasília *Brazil*	2400
Salvador *Brazil*	2400
Fortaleza *Brazil*	2100
Curitiba *Brazil*	2000
Guayaquil *Ecuador*	1700

Africa	'000
Cairo *Egypt*	9000
Lagos *Nigeria*	7700
Alexandria *Egypt*	3700
Kinshasa *Zaire*	3500
Casablanca *Morocco*	3200
Alger *Algeria*	3000
Cape Town *South Africa*	2300
Abidjan *Ivory Coast*	2200
Tarābulus *Libya*	2100
Adīs Ābeba *Ethiopia*	1900
Khartoum *Sudan*	1900
Dar es Salaam *Tanzania*	1700
Johannesburg *South Africa*	1700
Luanda *Angola*	1700
Maputo *Mozambique*	1600

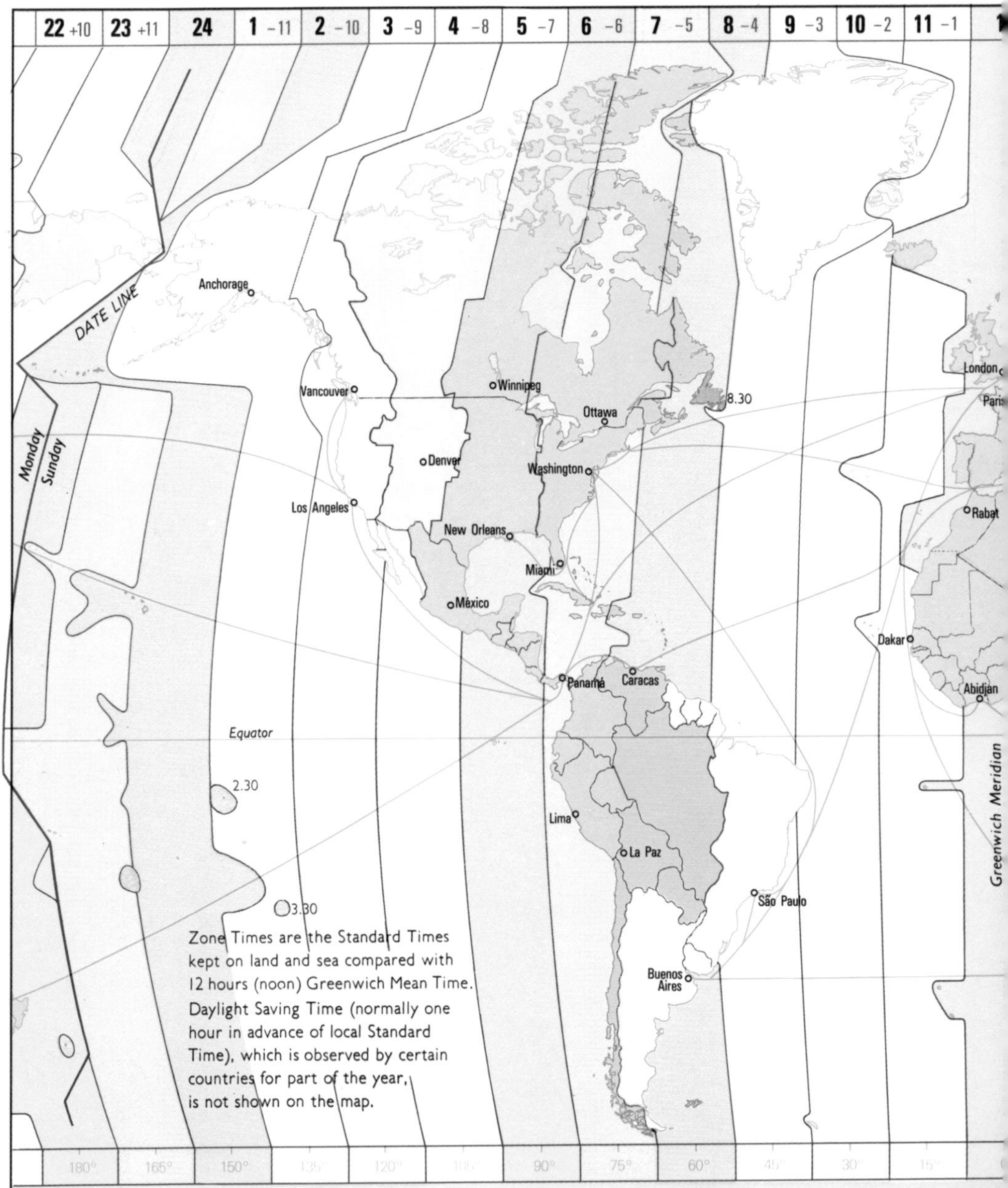

Zone Times are the Standard Times kept on land and sea compared with 12 hours (noon) Greenwich Mean Time. Daylight Saving Time (normally one hour in advance of local Standard Time), which is observed by certain countries for part of the year, is not shown on the map.

Journey Times

Sail (via Cape)
164 days

Steam (via Cape)
43 days

Steam (via Suez)
30 days

Supertanker
(via Cape)
28 days

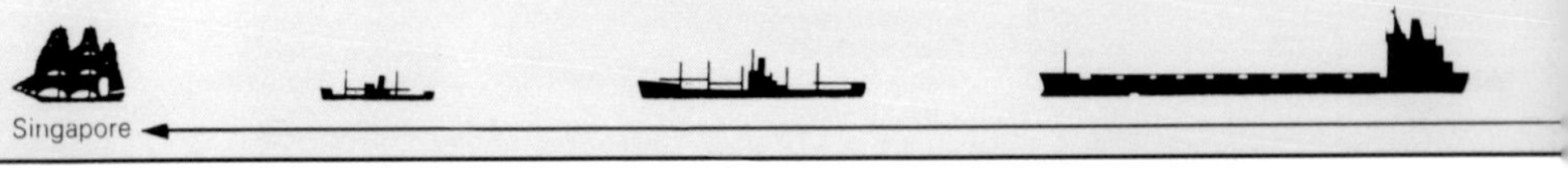

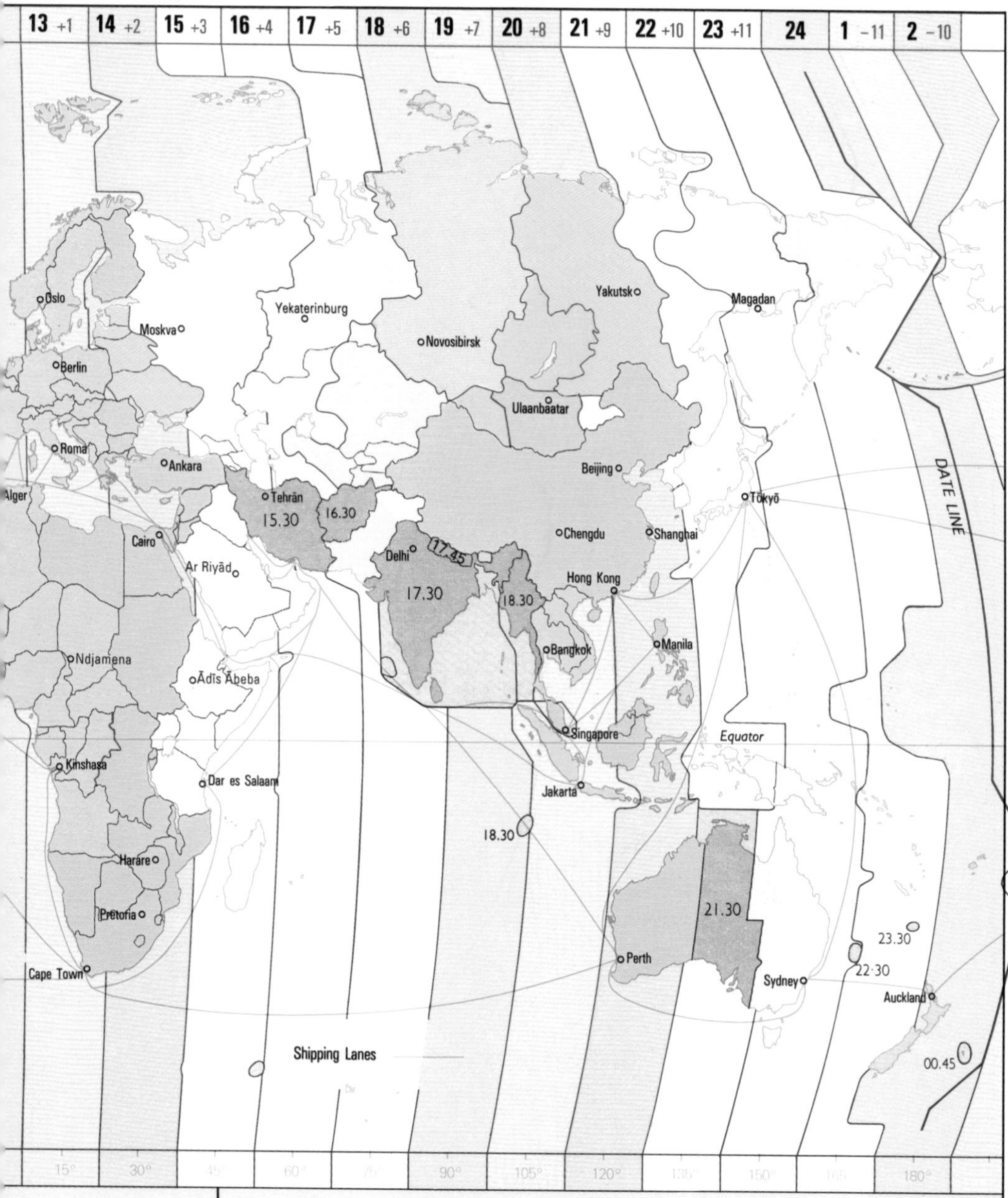
13 +1
14 +2
15 +3
16 +4
17 +5
18 +6
19 +7
20 +8
21 +9
22 +10
23 +11
24
1 −11
2 −10
Oslo
Moskva
Yekaterinburg
Novosibirsk
Yakutsk
Magadan
Berlin
Ulaanbaatar
Roma
Ankara
Beijing
Alger
Tehrān
15.30
16.30
Tōkyō
DATE LINE
Cairo
Delhi
17.45
Chengdu
Shanghai
Ar Riyād
Hong Kong
17.30
18.30
Ndjamena
Bangkok
Manila
Ādīs Ābeba
Singapore
Equator
Kinshasa
Dar es Salaam
Jakarta
18.30
Harare
21.30
Pretoria
23.30
Perth
22·30
Cape Town
Sydney
Auckland
Shipping Lanes
00.45
15°
30°
45°
60°
75°
90°
105°
120°
135°
150°
165°
180°

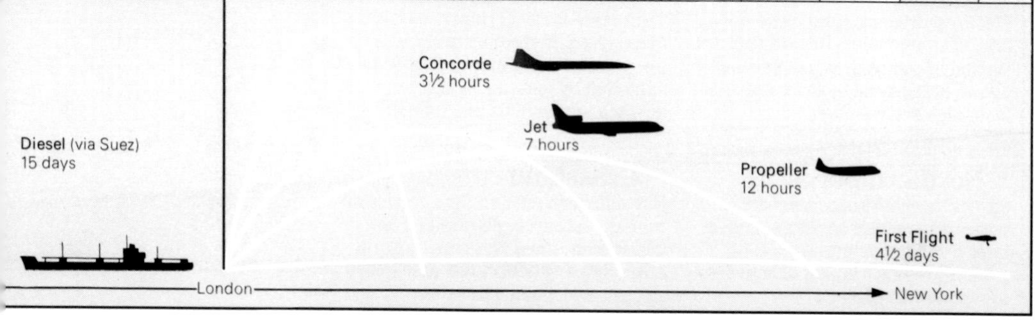
Concorde
3½ hours
Jet
7 hours
Diesel (via Suez)
15 days
Propeller
12 hours
First Flight
4½ days
London
New York

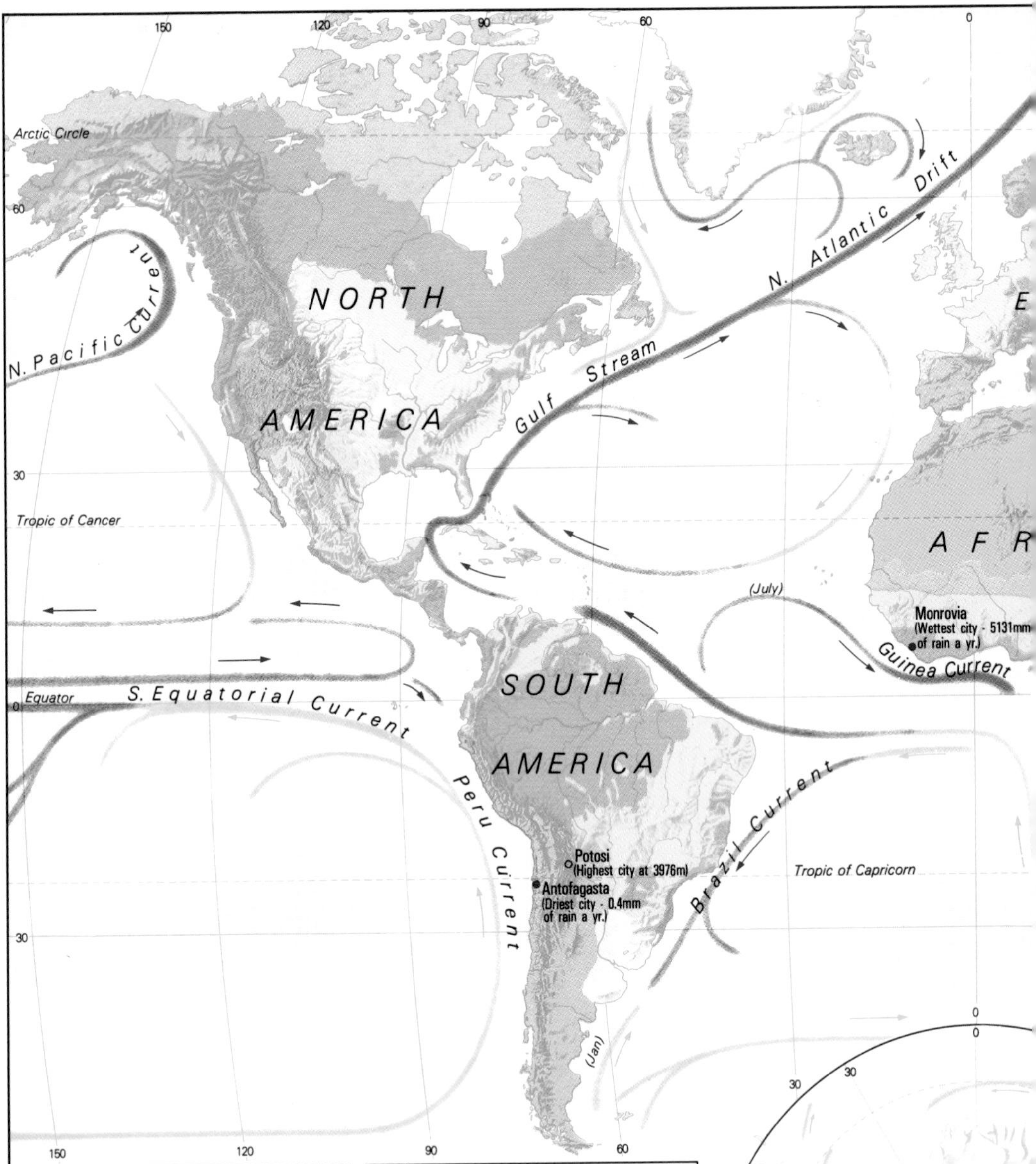

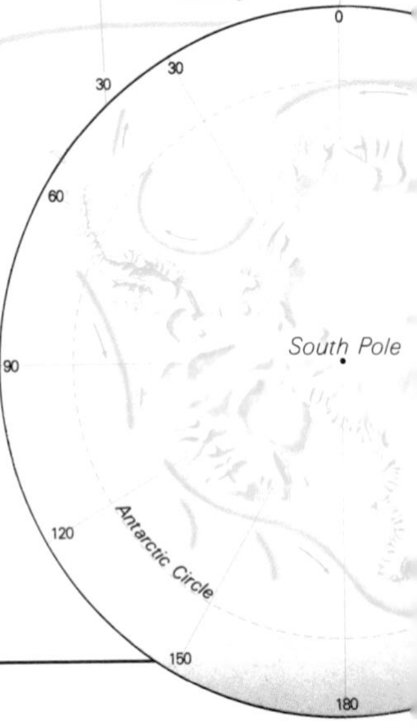

Tundra
Flat areas frozen over except during brief summers when flooding occurs. Habitat of compact, wind resistant plants; lichens and mosses: animals ; lemmings and reindeer.

Northern Forest
Extensive coniferous forest area where winters are severe, summers brief. Conifers include spruce, fir, giant redwoods. Habitat of beavers, squirrels and red deer.

Woodland and Grass
Temperate areas of richer soils, its forest characterised by deciduous trees - oak, beech, maple. Region most exploited by man for intensive farming, settlements and industry.

Grassland
Hot summers, cold winters, moderate rainfall. Vast area of grassland and 'black' soils. Ideal for growing grain crops, grazing beef cattle. Also called steppe, veld, pampas, prairie.

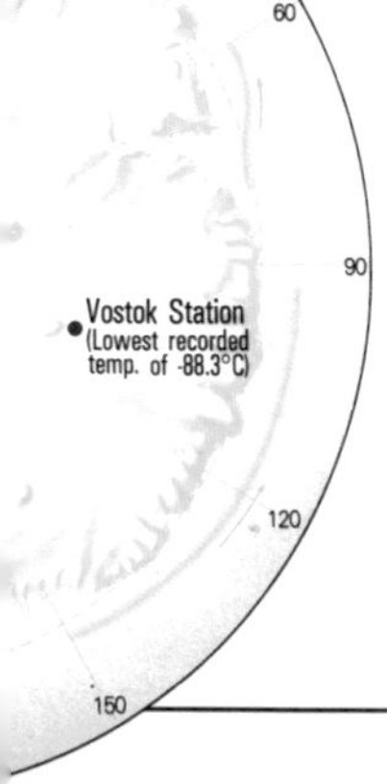

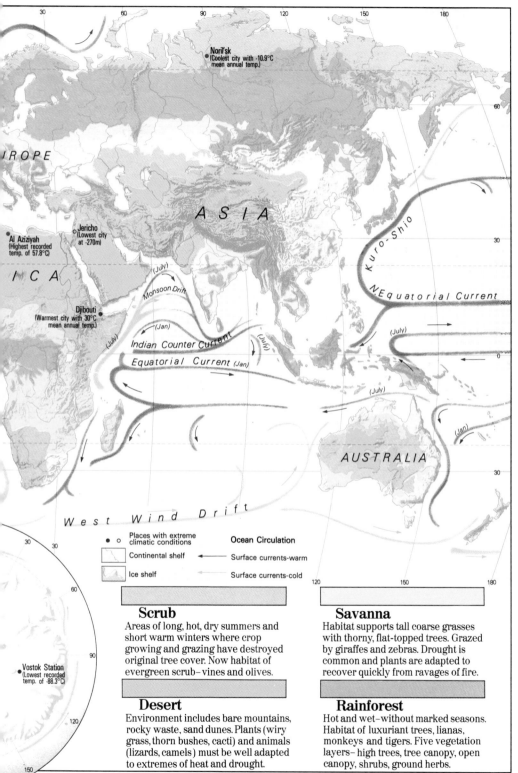

Scrub
Areas of long, hot, dry summers and short warm winters where crop growing and grazing have destroyed original tree cover. Now habitat of evergreen scrub– vines and olives.

Desert
Environment includes bare mountains, rocky waste, sand dunes. Plants (wiry grass, thorn bushes, cacti) and animals (lizards, camels) must be well adapted to extremes of heat and drought.

Savanna
Habitat supports tall coarse grasses with thorny, flat-topped trees. Grazed by giraffes and zebras. Drought is common and plants are adapted to recover quickly from ravages of fire.

Rainforest
Hot and wet–without marked seasons. Habitat of luxuriant trees, lianas, monkeys and tigers. Five vegetation layers– high trees, tree canopy, open canopy, shrubs, ground herbs.

BOUNDARIES

- International
- International under Dispute
- Cease Fire Line
- Autonomous or State/Administrative
- Maritime (National)
- International Date Line

COMMUNICATIONS

- Motorway/Under Construction
- Major/Other Road
- Under Construction
- Track
- Road Tunnel
- Car Ferry
- Main/Other Railway
- Under Construction
- Rail Ferry
- Rail Tunnel
- Canal
- International/Other Airport

LANDSCAPE FEATURES

- Glacier, Ice Cap
- Marsh, Swamp
- Sand Desert, Dunes
- Freshwater
- Saltwater
- Seasonal
- Salt Pan

OTHER FEATURES

- River/Seasonal
- Pass, Gorge
- Dam, Barrage
- Waterfall, Rapid
- Aqueduct
- Reef
- .217 ▲4231 Spot Height, Depth/Summit, Peak
- Well
- Oil/Gas Field
- Gas / Oil — Oil/Natural Gas Pipeline
- Gemsbok Nat. Pk — National Park
- ∴UR — Historic Site

LETTERING STYLES

CANADA	Independent Nation
FLORIDA	State, Province or Autonomous Region
Gibraltar (U.K.)	Sovereignty of Dependent Territory
Lothian	Administrative Area
LANGUEDOC	Historic Region
Loire *Vosges*	Physical Feature or Physical Region

TOWNS AND CITIES

Square symbols denote capital cities

New York	Major City
Montréal	City
Ottawa	Small City
Québec	Large Town
St John's	Town
Yorkton	Small Town
Jasper	Village
	Built-up-area

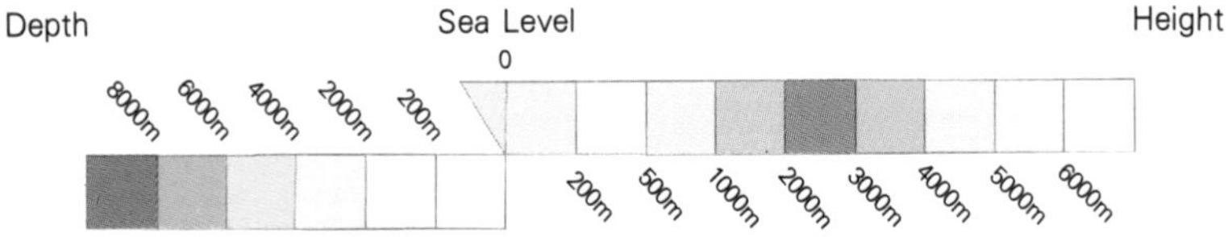

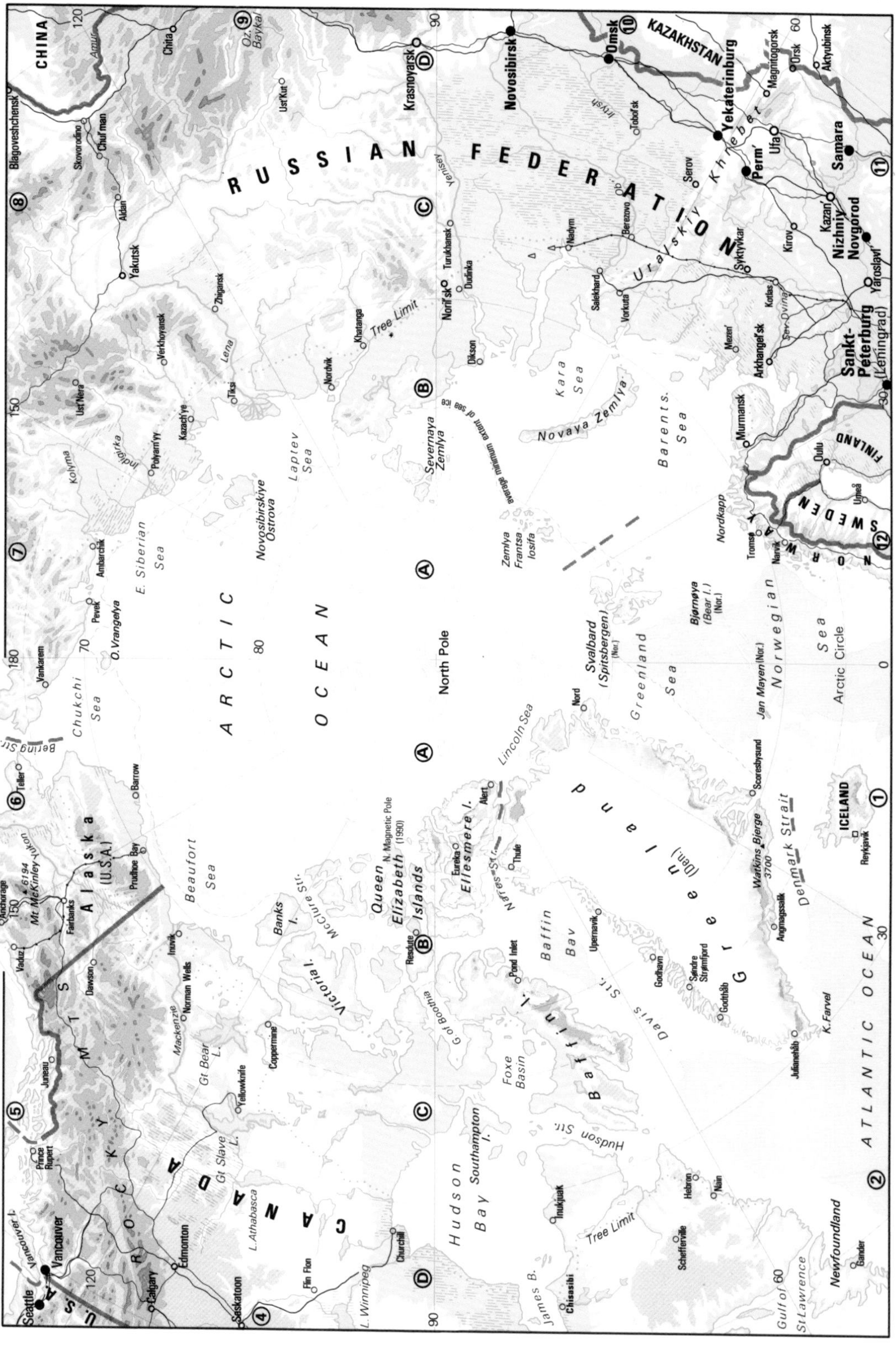
ARCTIC OCEAN
North Pole
RUSSIAN FEDERATION
CHINA
KAZAKHSTAN
FINLAND
SWEDEN
NORWAY
ICELAND
CANADA
Alaska (U.S.A.)
Greenland (Den.)
ATLANTIC OCEAN
Laptev Sea
Kara Sea
Barents Sea
E. Siberian Sea
Chukchi Sea
Beaufort Sea
Lincoln Sea
Greenland Sea
Norwegian Sea
Baffin Bay
Davis Str.
Hudson Str.
Hudson Bay
Foxe Basin
Denmark Strait
Bering Str.
Nares Str.
McClure Str.
G. of Boothia
Arctic Circle
Tree Limit
average minimum extent of sea ice
Severnaya Zemlya
Novaya Zemlya
Zemlya Frantsa Iosifa
Novosibirskiye Ostrova
O. Vrangelya
Svalbard (Spitsbergen) (Nor.)
Bjørnøya (Bear I.) (Nor.)
Jan Mayen (Nor.)
Queen Elizabeth Islands
N. Magnetic Pole (1990)
Ellesmere I.
Banks I.
Victoria I.
Baffin I.
Southampton I.
Newfoundland
ROCKY MTS
Ural'skiy Khrebet
Mt. McKinley 6194
Watkins Bjerge 3700
Oz. Baykal
Gt Bear L.
Gt Slave L.
L. Athabasca
L. Winnipeg
James B.
Gulf of St Lawrence
Vancouver I.
K. Farvel
Nordkapp
Lena
Yenisey
Ob
Irtysh
Amur
Indigirka
Kolyma
Mackenzie
Yukon
Sev. Dvina
Omsk
Novosibirsk
Krasnoyarsk
Yekaterinburg
Perm'
Ufa
Samara
Kazan'
Nizhniy Novgorod
Yaroslavl'
Sankt-Peterburg (Leningrad)
Arkhangel'sk
Murmansk
Mezen'
Kotlas
Syktyvkar
Kirov
Vorkuta
Salekhard
Nadym
Berezovo
Serov
Tobol'sk
Magnitogorsk
Orsk
Aktyubinsk
Chita
Ust'Kut
Blagoveshchensk
Skovorodino
Chul'man
Aldan
Yakutsk
Zhigansk
Verkhoyansk
Ust'Nera
Tiksi
Kazach'ye
Polyarnyy
Ambarchik
Pevek
Vankarem
Khatanga
Nordvik
Noril'sk
Dudinka
Turukhansk
Dikson
Oulu
Umeå
Tromsø
Narvik
Reykjavik
Nord
Scoresbysund
Angmagssalik
Julianehåb
Godthåb
Søndre Strømfjord
Godhavn
Upernavik
Thule
Alert
Eureka
Resolute
Pond Inlet
Barrow
Teller
Prudhoe Bay
Fairbanks
Anchorage
Vaduz
Dawson
Inuvik
Norman Wells
Coppermine
Yellowknife
Juneau
Prince Rupert
Vancouver
Seattle
Calgary
Edmonton
Saskatoon
Flin Flon
Churchill
Inukjuak
Chisasibi
Schefferville
Hebron
Nain
Gander
U.S.A.

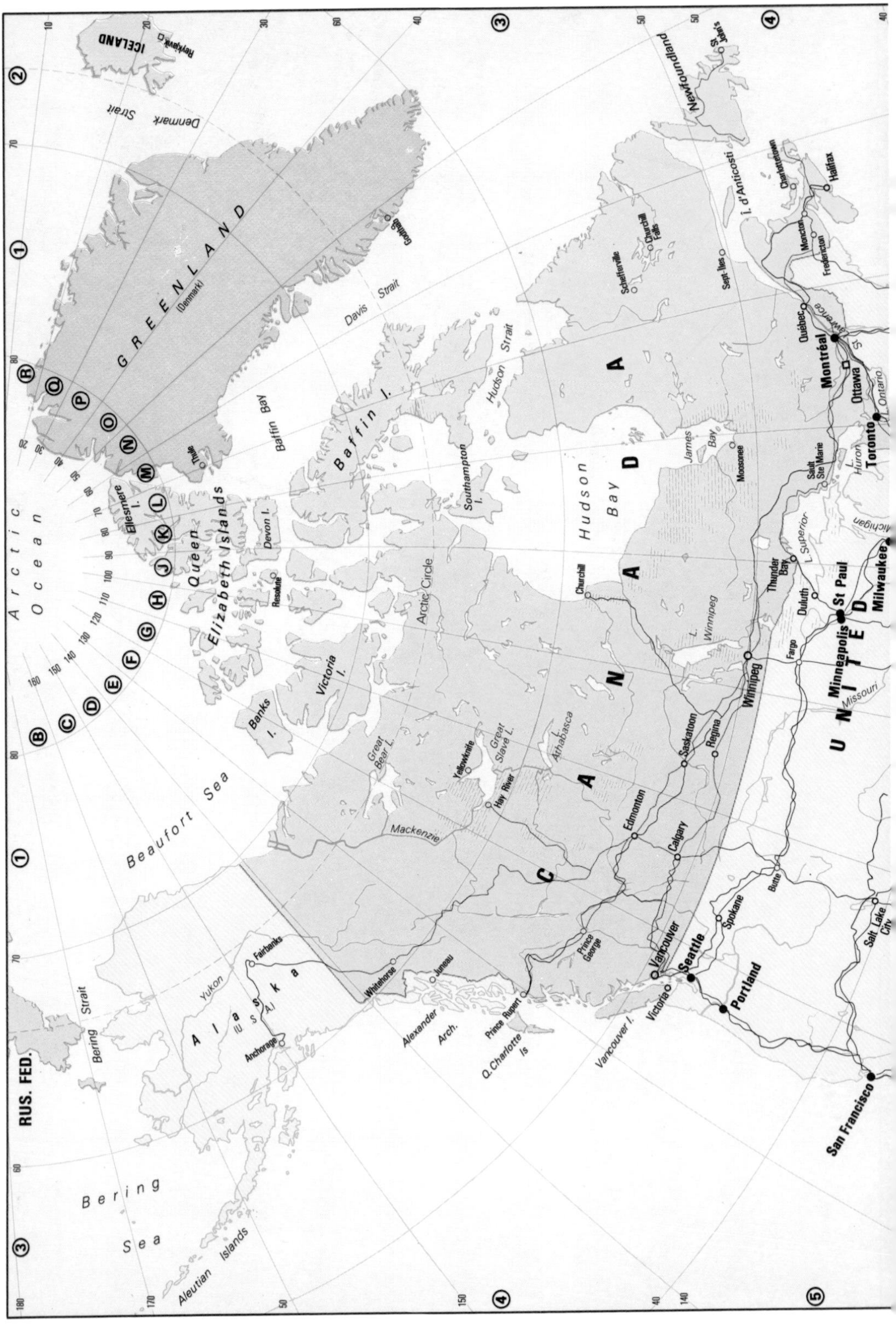
ICELAND
Reykjavik
Denmark Strait
GREENLAND
(Denmark)
Godthåb
Thule
Davis Strait
Baffin Bay
Baffin I.
Hudson Strait
Southampton I.
Hudson Bay
James Bay
Moosonee
Arctic Ocean
Ellesmere I.
Queen Elizabeth Islands
Devon I.
Resolute
Victoria I.
Banks I.
Arctic Circle
Beaufort Sea
Great Bear L.
Great Slave L.
Yellowknife
Hay River
Mackenzie
L. Athabasca
L. Winnipeg
Churchill
CANADA
Newfoundland
St. John's
I. d'Anticosti
Sept-Îles
Schefferville
Churchill Falls
Charlottetown
Halifax
Moncton
Fredericton
Québec
St Lawrence
Montréal
Ottawa
L. Ontario
Toronto
L. Huron
Sault Ste Marie
L. Superior
L. Michigan
Thunder Bay
Duluth
St Paul
Minneapolis
Milwaukee
Fargo
Missouri
UNITED
Winnipeg
Regina
Saskatoon
Edmonton
Calgary
Butte
Spokane
Salt Lake City
Prince George
Prince Rupert
Vancouver
Victoria
Vancouver I.
Seattle
Portland
San Francisco
Q. Charlotte Is
Alexander Arch.
Juneau
Whitehorse
Fairbanks
Anchorage
Alaska
(U S A)
Yukon
Bering Strait
Bering Sea
Aleutian Islands
RUS. FED.

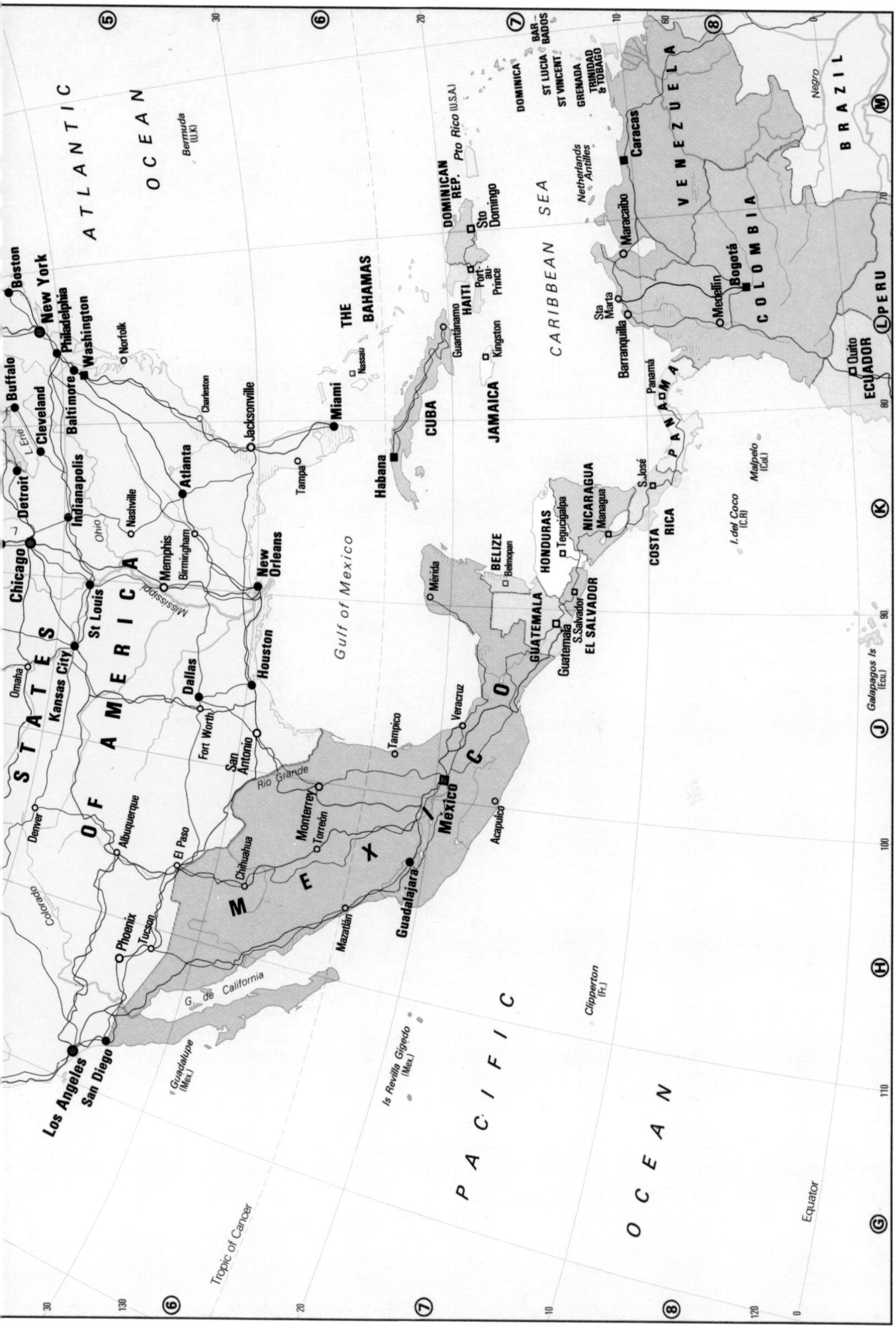

STATES OF AMERICA
Omaha
Chicago
Detroit
L. Erie
Buffalo
Boston
Cleveland
New York
Philadelphia
Baltimore
Washington
Los Angeles
San Diego
Denver
Colorado
Kansas City
Indianapolis
St Louis
Ohio
ATLANTIC
OCEAN
Bermuda (U.K)
Phoenix
Tucson
Albuquerque
Nashville
Norfolk
Mississippi
Memphis
Birmingham
Atlanta
Charleston
El Paso
Dallas
Fort Worth
Guadalupe (Mex.)
G. de California
Tropic of Cancer
MEXICO
Chihuahua
Rio Grande
San Antonio
Houston
New Orleans
Jacksonville
Tampa
Miami
Monterrey
Torreón
Mazatlán
Gulf of Mexico
Nassau
THE BAHAMAS
Is Revilla Gigedo (Mex.)
Tampico
Guadalajara
Habana
CUBA
Mérida
México
Veracruz
Acapulco
Guantánamo
HAITI
DOMINICAN REP.
Pto Rico (U.S.A.)
Port-au-Prince
Sto Domingo
JAMAICA
Kingston
BELIZE
Belmopan
PACIFIC
DOMINICA
GUATEMALA
Guatemala
HONDURAS
Tegucigalpa
S.Salvador
EL SALVADOR
CARIBBEAN SEA
ST LUCIA
BARBADOS
ST VINCENT
GRENADA
TRINIDAD & TOBAGO
Netherlands Antilles
Clipperton (Fr.)
NICARAGUA
Managua
Sta Marta
Barranquilla
Maracaibo
Caracas
OCEAN
COSTA RICA
S.José
Panamá
PANAMA
VENEZUELA
Medellín
Bogotá
COLOMBIA
I.del Coco (C.R)
Malpelo (Col.)
Equator
Negro
BRAZIL
Quito
ECUADOR
PERU
Galapagos Is (Ecu.)

1:35M
0 250 500 750 1000 1250 km
0 250 500 750mls

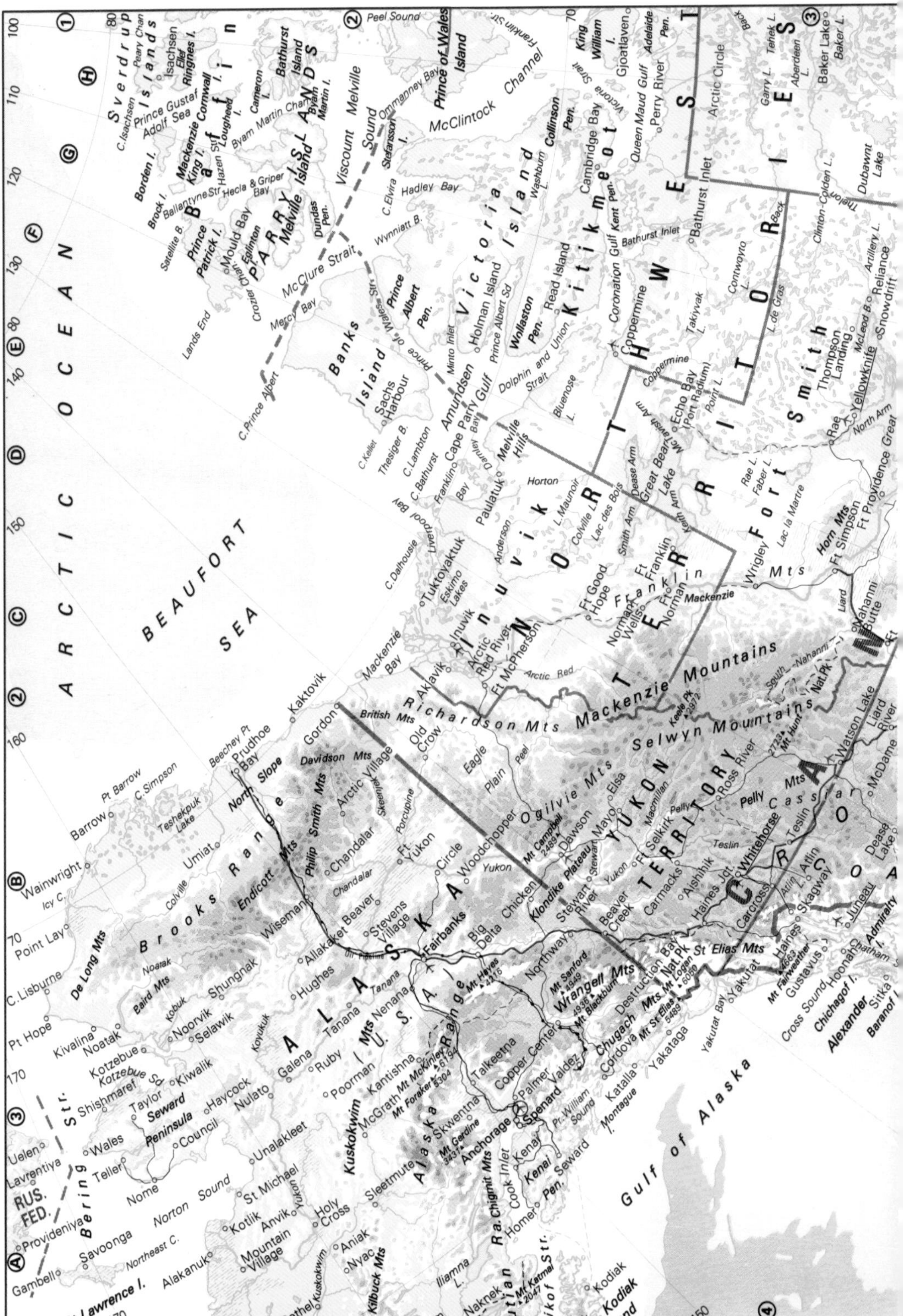
ARCTIC OCEAN
BEAUFORT SEA
Sverdrup Islands
PARRY ISLANDS
Banks Island
Victoria Island
Prince of Wales Island
McClintock Channel
Viscount Melville Sound
McClure Strait
Amundsen Gulf
Coronation Gulf
Queen Maud Gulf
Great Bear Lake
Mackenzie Mountains
Richardson Mts
Selwyn Mountains
Ogilvie Mts
Franklin Mts
Mackenzie Bay
YUKON TERRITORY
NORTHWEST TERRITORIES
Inuvik
Kitikmeot
Fort Smith
Tuktoyaktuk
Aklavik
Ft McPherson
Dawson
Whitehorse
Ft Simpson
Yellowknife
ALASKA
U.S.A.
Brooks Range
Alaska Range
Wrangell Mts
St Elias Mts
Chugach Mts
Kuskokwim Mts
Mt McKinley 6194
Mt Logan 6050
Mt St Elias 5489
Fairbanks
Anchorage
Juneau
Barrow
Prudhoe Bay
Nome
Kodiak Island
Seward Peninsula
Kenai Pen.
Norton Sound
Bering Str.
St Lawrence I.
Gulf of Alaska
RUS. FED.

1:15M

0 200 400 600 km
0 100 200 300 mls

GREENLAND (Denmark)
ICELAND
DENMARK STRAIT
DAVIS STRAIT
BAFFIN BAY
Labrador Sea
HUDSON STRAIT
Baffin Island
Foxe Basin
Foxe Channel
Keewatin
QUEEN ELIZABETH ISLANDS
PARRY ISLANDS
Devon Island
Ellesmere Island
Axel Heiberg Island
Sverdrup Islands
Lancaster Sound
Jones Sound
Somerset Island
Prince of Wales Island
Boothia Peninsula
Gulf of Boothia
Melville Peninsula
Southampton Island
Cumberland Sound
Cumberland Peninsula
Hall Peninsula
Meta Incognito Peninsula
Frobisher Bay
Cape Dorset
Resolute
Arctic Bay
Pond Inlet
Clyde
Igloolik
Repulse Bay
Coral Harbour
Chesterfield Inlet
Baker Lake
Rankin Inlet
Thule
Reykjavík
Akureyri
Godthåb
Jakobshavn
Upernavik
Angmagssalik
Kap Farvel
Arctic Circle
Melville Bugt
Nares Str.
Kane Basin
Amadjuak Lake
Nettilling Lake
Barnes Icecap
Kong Christian IX Land
Kong Frederik VI Kyst
Sdr. Strømfjord

1:15M
0 200 400 600 km
0 100 200 300 mls
HUDSON BAY
NEWFOUNDLAND
Labrador
CANADA
QUEBEC
ONTARIO
NOVA SCOTIA
NEW BRUNSWICK
PRINCE EDWARD I.
MAINE
NEW HAMPSHIRE
VERMONT
MASS.
CONN.
NEW YORK
MINNESOTA
WISCONSIN
MICHIGAN
ATLANTIC OCEAN
LAKE SUPERIOR
L. HURON
L. Ontario
L. Erie
L. MICHIGAN
Gulf of Saint Lawrence
James Bay
Ungava Bay
Nastapoka Islands
Belcher Is.
King George Is
Akimiski I.
Î. d'Anticosti
Cape Breton I.
Sable I.
Bay of Fundy
Long Island
Montréal
Québec
Ottawa
Toronto
Halifax
Boston
Providence
Hartford
Buffalo
Detroit
Milwaukee
Minneapolis
St Paul
Duluth
Thunder Bay
Sault Ste Marie
Sudbury
Timmins
Kapuskasing
Moosonee
Churchill
York Factory
Fort Severn
Big Trout Lake
Attawapiskat
Fort Albany
Chibougamau
Chicoutimi
Sept-Iles
Baie-Comeau
Rimouski
Gaspé
Fredericton
Saint John
Moncton
Charlottetown
Sydney
Corner Brook
St John's
Gander
Goose Bay
Churchill Falls
Labrador City
Schefferville
Kuujjuaq
Inukjuak
Kenora
Dryden
Syracuse
Rochester
Albany
Portland
Bangor
60
50
40
70
80
90

1:12.5M

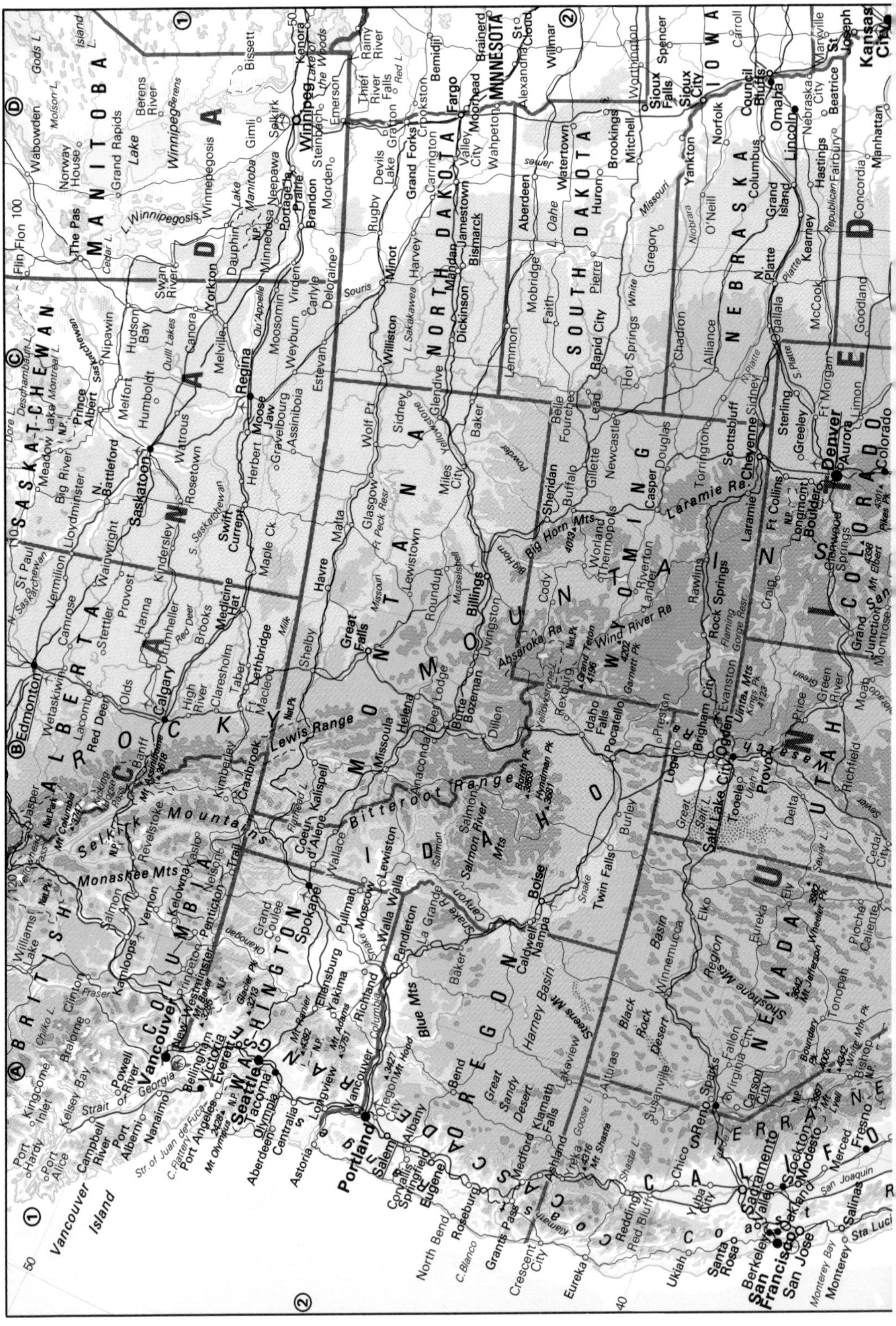
0 100 200 300 400 500 km
0 100 200 300 mls
BRITISH COLUMBIA
ALBERTA
SASKATCHEWAN
MANITOBA
CANADA
WASHINGTON
OREGON
IDAHO
MONTANA
WYOMING
NORTH DAKOTA
SOUTH DAKOTA
NEBRASKA
MINNESOTA
IOWA
COLORADO
UTAH
NEVADA
CALIFORNIA
UNITED STATES
ROCKY MOUNTAINS
CASCADE RANGE
SIERRA NEVADA
Vancouver Island
Winnipeg
Regina
Saskatoon
Edmonton
Calgary
Vancouver
Victoria
Seattle
Tacoma
Spokane
Portland
Salem
Eugene
Boise
Helena
Great Falls
Billings
Bismarck
Fargo
Pierre
Rapid City
Sioux Falls
Omaha
Lincoln
Cheyenne
Casper
Denver
Salt Lake City
Ogden
Provo
Reno
Sacramento
San Francisco
Oakland
San Jose
Fresno
Kansas City
Str. of Juan de Fuca
Lewis Range
Bitterroot Range
Selkirk Mountains
Monashee Mts
Big Horn Mts
Wind River Ra
Absaroka Ra
Laramie Ra
Uinta Mts
Salmon River Mts
Blue Mts
Black Rock Desert
Great Sandy Desert
Harney Basin
Great Salt L.
Lake Winnipeg
L. Winnipegosis
Lake Manitoba
Lake of the Woods
L. Sakakawea
L. Oahe
Ft Peck Resr
Flaming Gorge Resr

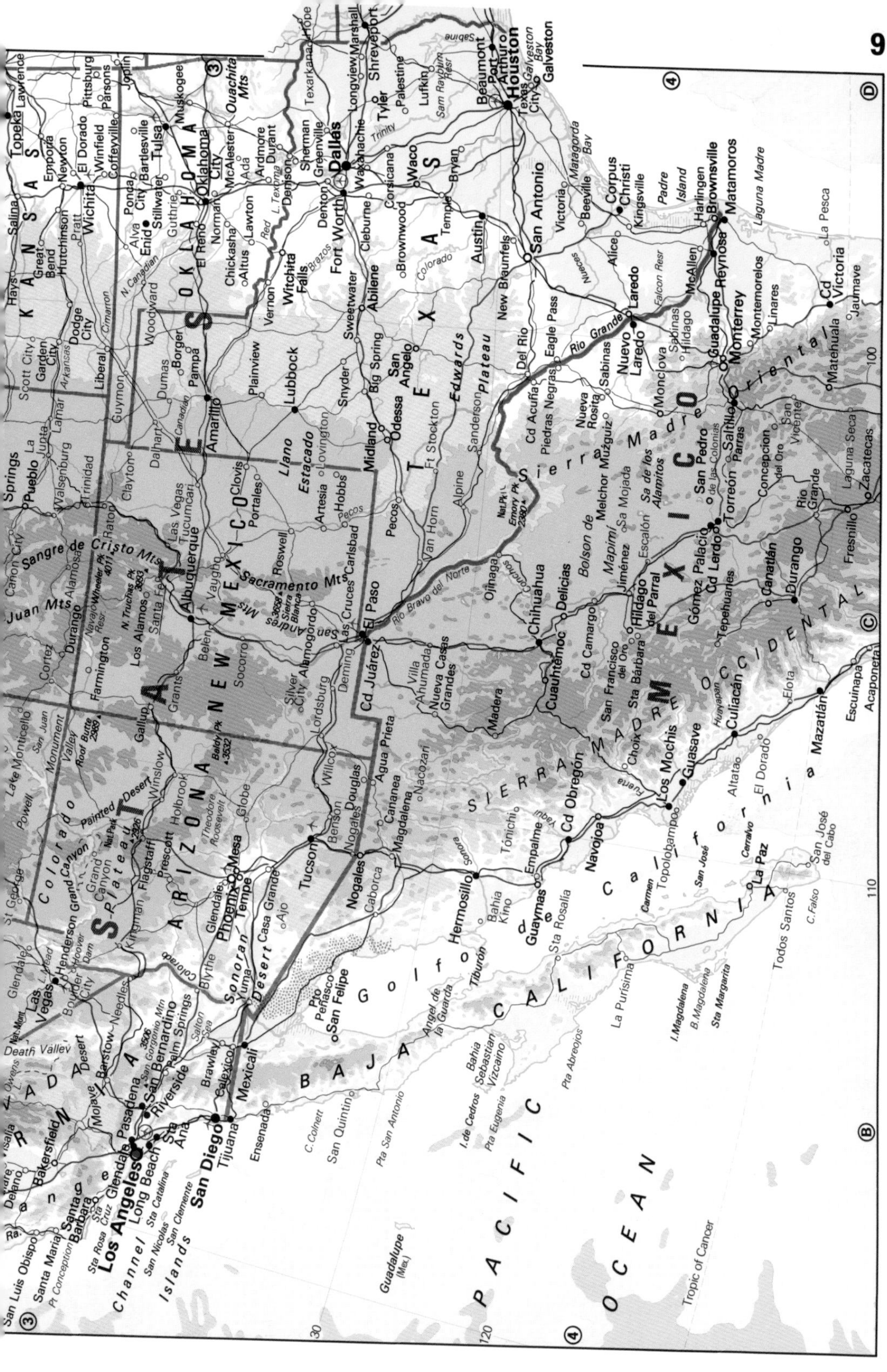
K A N S A S
O K L A H O M A
T E X A S
N E W M E X I C O
A R I Z O N A
S T A T E S
M E X I C O
PACIFIC
OCEAN
BAJA CALIFORNIA
Golfo de California
SIERRA MADRE OCCIDENTAL
Sierra Madre Oriental
Colorado Plateau
Sonoran Desert
Painted Desert
Mojave Desert
Death Valley
Llano Estacado
Edwards Plateau
Bolson de Mapimí
Sangre de Cristo Mts
Sacramento Mts
San Andres Mts
Ouachita Mts
Channel Islands
Tropic of Cancer
Topeka
Lawrence
Emporia
Newton
Wichita
Hutchinson
Salina
Great Bend
Hays
Dodge City
Garden City
Scott City
Liberal
El Dorado
Winfield
Coffeyville
Pittsburg
Parsons
Joplin
Tulsa
Muskogee
Bartlesville
Ponca City
Stillwater
Enid
Alva
Guthrie
Oklahoma City
Norman
El Reno
Chickasha
Lawton
Altus
McAlester
Ardmore
Durant
Woodward
Guymon
Amarillo
Borger
Pampa
Dumas
Dalhart
Lubbock
Plainview
Wichita Falls
Vernon
Denton
Dallas
Fort Worth
Sherman
Denison
Greenville
Waxahachie
Corsicana
Waco
Temple
Bryan
Austin
San Antonio
New Braunfels
Houston
Galveston
Texas City
Beaumont
Port Arthur
Tyler
Longview
Marshall
Shreveport
Texarkana
Hope
Palestine
Lufkin
Victoria
Corpus Christi
Beeville
Kingsville
Alice
Laredo
Nuevo Laredo
Eagle Pass
Del Rio
Cd Acuña
Piedras Negras
Brownsville
Harlingen
McAllen
Reynosa
Matamoros
Abilene
Sweetwater
Big Spring
San Angelo
Snyder
Midland
Odessa
Pecos
Van Horn
Ft Stockton
Alpine
Sanderson
El Paso
Cd Juárez
Las Cruces
Alamogordo
Roswell
Carlsbad
Hobbs
Artesia
Clovis
Portales
Tucumcari
Las Vegas
Santa Fe
Albuquerque
Los Alamos
Belen
Socorro
Grants
Gallup
Farmington
Silver City
Deming
Lordsburg
Raton
Trinidad
Walsenburg
Pueblo
Springs
Cañon City
Alamosa
Durango
Cortez
Monticello
Lamar
La Junta
Clayton
Phoenix
Mesa
Tempe
Glendale
Tucson
Nogales
Flagstaff
Prescott
Winslow
Holbrook
Globe
Kingman
Yuma
Douglas
Benson
Willcox
Casa Grande
Ajo
Las Vegas
Henderson
Boulder City
Needles
Barstow
Los Angeles
Long Beach
Pasadena
San Bernardino
Riverside
Palm Springs
Santa Ana
San Diego
Tijuana
Mexicali
Calexico
Brawley
Bakersfield
Santa Barbara
Santa Maria
San Luis Obispo
Ensenada
San Quintín
San Felipe
Pto Peñasco
Hermosillo
Guaymas
Empalme
Cd Obregón
Navojoa
Los Mochis
Topolobampo
Guasave
Culiacán
Mazatlán
Escuinapa
Acaponeta
Chihuahua
Delicias
Cuauhtémoc
Ojinaga
Nueva Casas Grandes
Madera
Hidalgo del Parral
Jiménez
Cd Camargo
Torreón
Gómez Palacio
Cd Lerdo
Durango
Saltillo
Monterrey
Monclova
Sabinas
Nueva Rosita
Linares
Montemorelos
Cd Victoria
Zacatecas
Fresnillo
La Paz
Sta Rosalía
San José del Cabo
Todos Santos
Cd Camargo
Caborca
Magdalena
Cananea
Agua Prieta
Rio Grande
Rio Bravo del Norte
Emory Pk 2380
Wheeler Pk 4011
Baldy Pk 3532
Sierra Blanca 3658
San Gorgonio Mtn 3506
Grand Canyon Nat Park
Gulf of Mexico
A
B
C
D
③
④
30
120
110
100

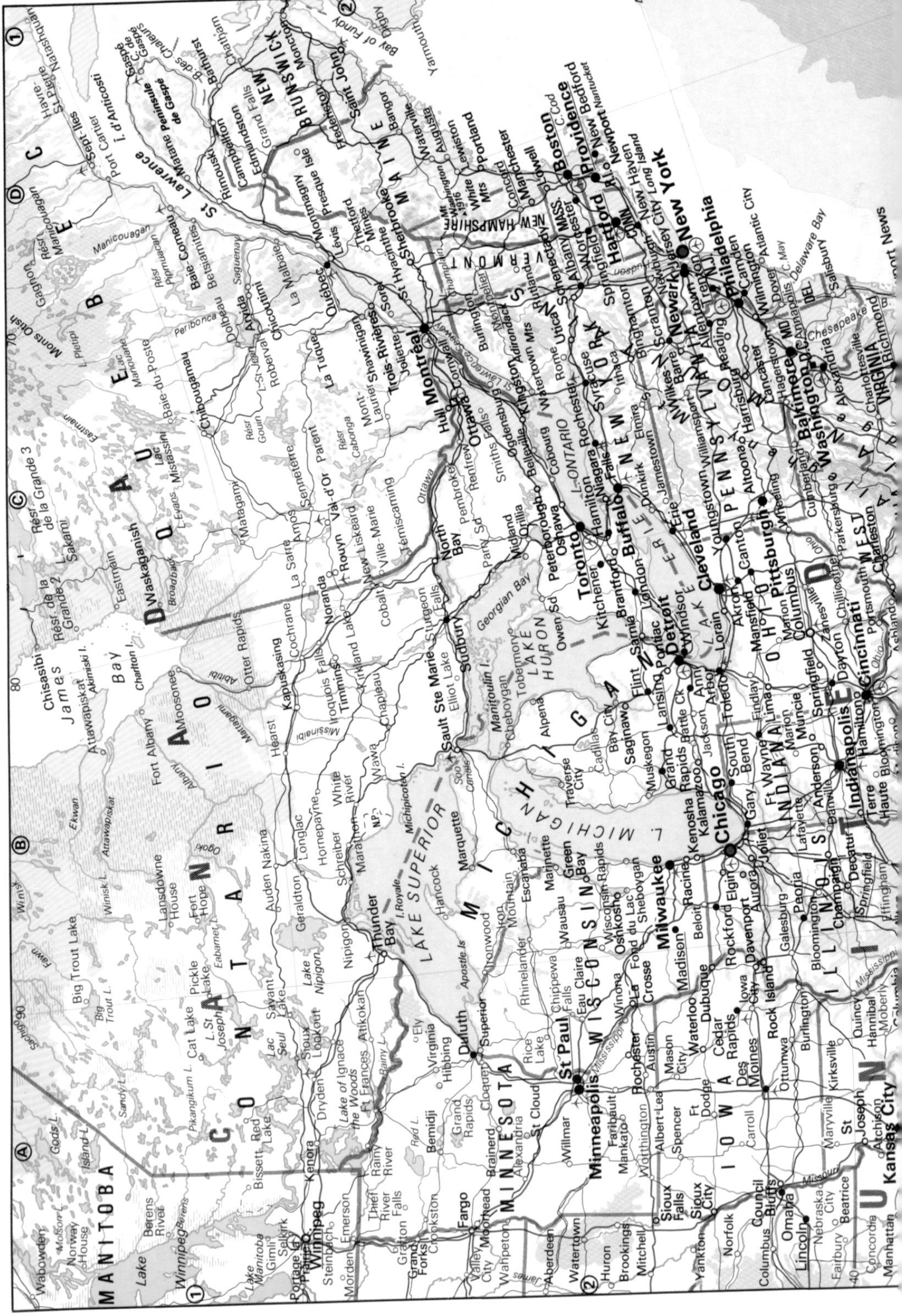
MANITOBA
ONTARIO
QUEBEC
NEW BRUNSWICK
MAINE
VERMONT
NEW HAMPSHIRE
NEW YORK
PENNSYLVANIA
OHIO
MICHIGAN
WISCONSIN
MINNESOTA
IOWA
ILLINOIS
INDIANA
LAKE SUPERIOR
L. MICHIGAN
LAKE HURON
L. ONTARIO
LAKE ERIE
James Bay
Georgian Bay
Bay of Fundy
Winnipeg
Thunder Bay
Duluth
Minneapolis
St Paul
Milwaukee
Chicago
Detroit
Cleveland
Pittsburgh
Toronto
Buffalo
Ottawa
Montréal
Québec
Boston
Providence
Hartford
New York
Philadelphia
Baltimore
Washington
Indianapolis
Cincinnati
Columbus
Kansas City
Omaha
Sault Ste Marie
Sudbury
Saint John

1:12.5M 0 100 200 300 400 500 km 0 100 200 300 mls

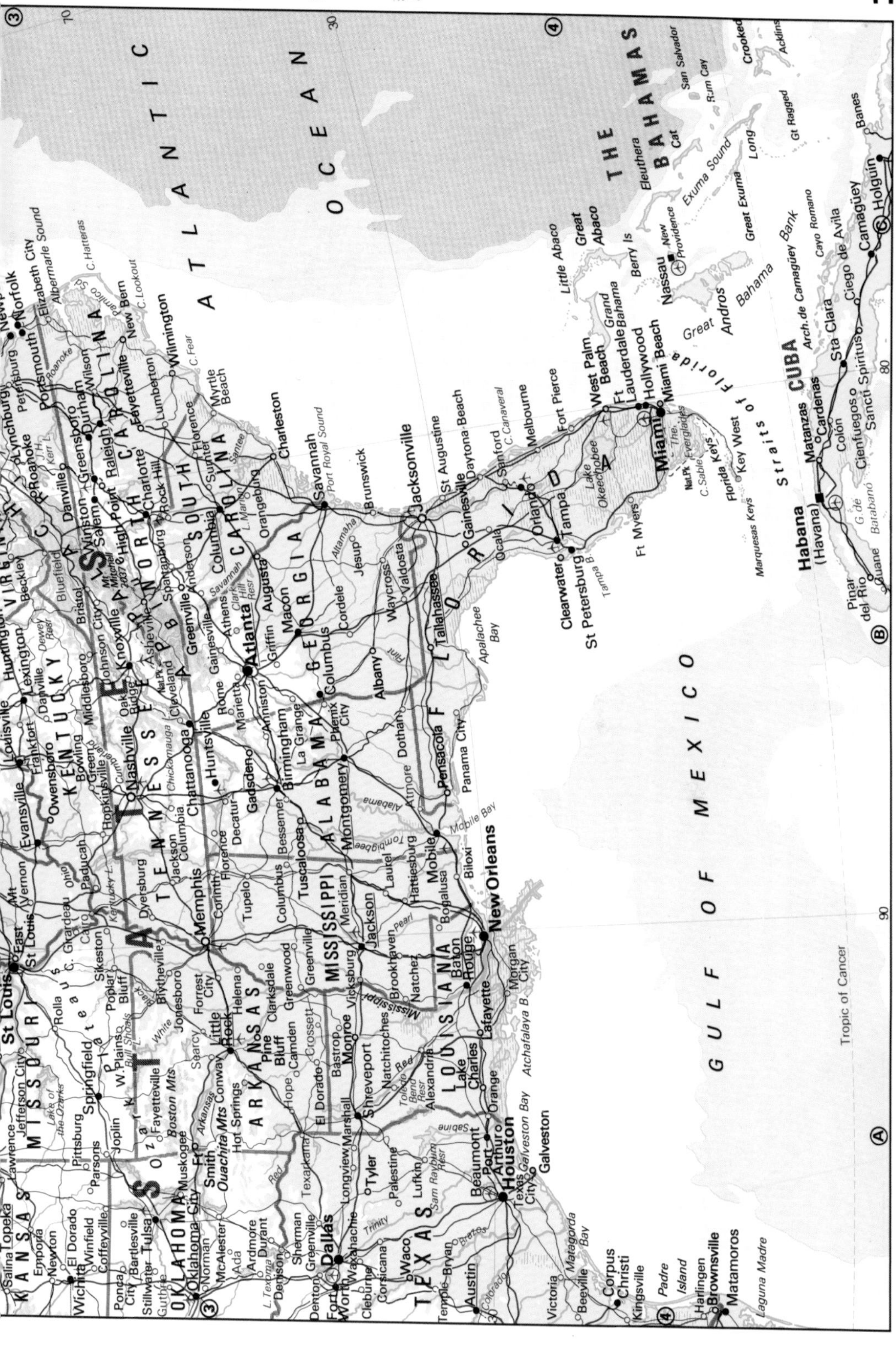

ATLANTIC OCEAN
GULF OF MEXICO
THE BAHAMAS
CUBA
Straits of Florida
KANSAS
MISSOURI
OKLAHOMA
ARKANSAS
TEXAS
LOUISIANA
MISSISSIPPI
ALABAMA
GEORGIA
FLORIDA
TENNESSEE
KENTUCKY
NORTH CAROLINA
SOUTH CAROLINA
St Louis
Memphis
Nashville
Atlanta
Jacksonville
Tampa
Miami
New Orleans
Houston
Dallas
Austin
Oklahoma City
Tulsa
Little Rock
Birmingham
Montgomery
Jackson
Charleston
Savannah
Charlotte
Raleigh
Norfolk
Habana (Havana)
Camagüey
Holguín
Nassau
Tropic of Cancer

1:10M

0 100 200 300 400 km
0 100 200 mls
Gulf of Alaska
Alexander Archipelago
Bristol Bay
Norton Sound
Kotzebue Sd
Seward Peninsula
Kuskokwim Bay
Mackenzie Mountains
Ogilvie Mountains
Wernecke Mountains
Richardson Mts
Philip Smith Mts
Endicott Mts
Baird Mountains
Brooks Range
Alaska Range
Chugach Mountains
Wrangell Mts
St Elias Mountains
Pelly Mountains
Kuskokwim Mountains
Kenai Peninsula
Cook Inlet
Kodiak I.
Baranof Island
Chichagof Island
Yukon
Porcupine
Tanana
Fairbanks
Anchorage
Juneau
Whitehorse
Dawson
Nome
Kotzebue
Bethel
Valdez
Cordova
Sitka
Skagway
Haines
Kodiak
Dillingham
McGrath
Tok
Eagle
Old Crow
Fort Yukon
Barrow
Arctic Circle
Mt McKinley 6194
Mt Foraker 5033
Mt Logan 6050
Mt St Elias 5489
Mt Blackburn 5036
Mt Sanford 4940
Trans Alaska Pipeline

1:7.5M 0 100 200 300 km
0 50 100 150 mls

BRITISH COLUMBIA
ALBERTA
WASHINGTON
IDAHO
MONTANA
COAST MOUNTAINS
ROCKY MOUNTAINS
Vancouver
Victoria
Calgary
Edmonton
Saskatoon
Prince George
Prince Rupert
Kamloops
Kelowna
Red Deer
Lethbridge
Medicine Hat
Jasper
Banff
Lloydminster
Ft McMurray
Dawson Ck
Ft St John
Cariboo Mts
Selkirk Mts
Purcell Mts
Monashee Mts
Queen Charlotte Sound
Vancouver I.
Str. of Georgia
Juan de Fuca Str.
Mt Robson 3954
Mt Waddington 4016

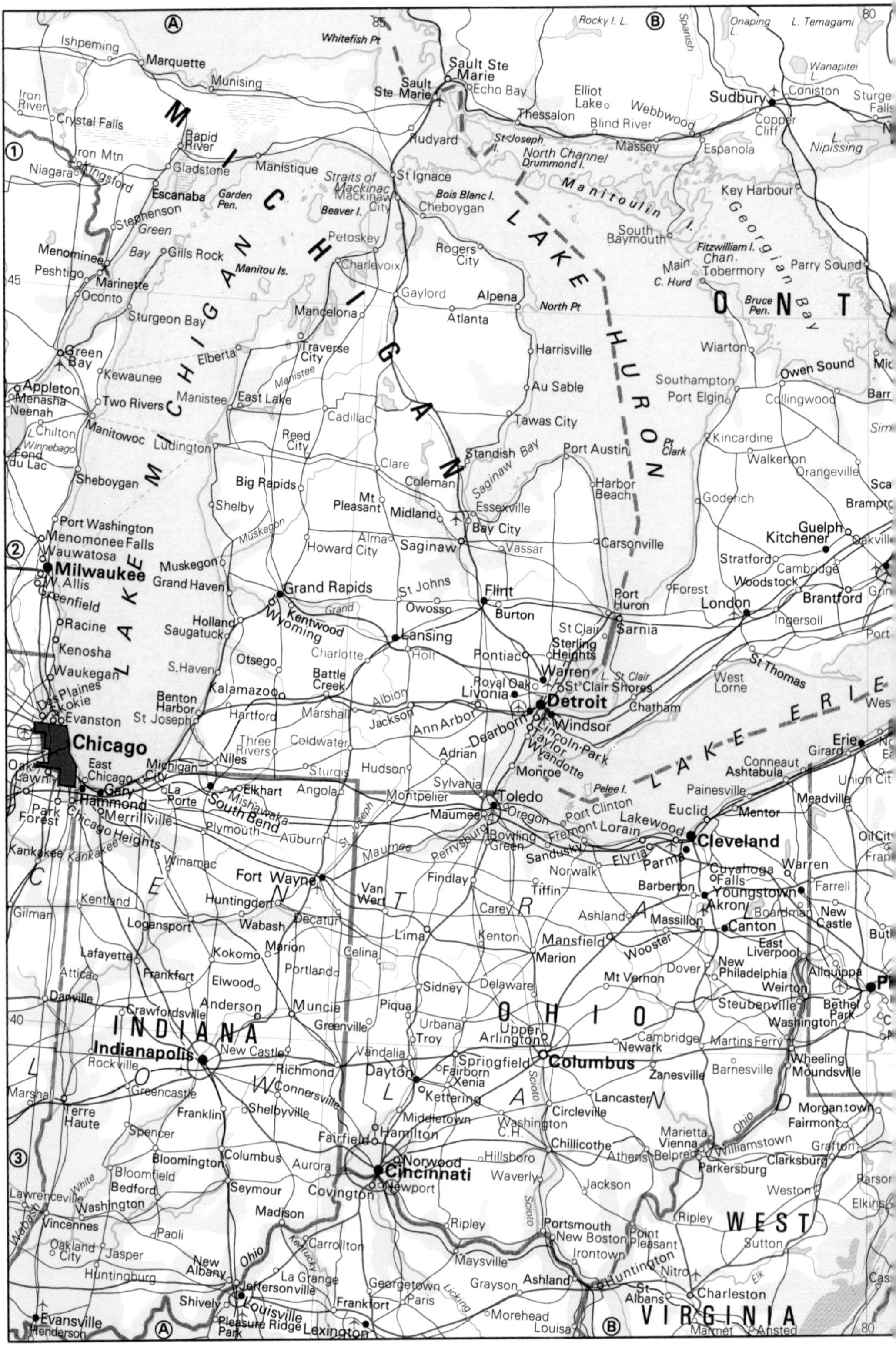
A
B
1
2
3
85
80
45
40
Rocky I. L.
Spanish
Onaping L.
L. Temagami
Wanapitei L.
Whitefish Pt
Ishpeming
Marquette
Munising
Sault Ste Marie
Sault Ste Marie
Echo Bay
Elliot Lake
Webbwood
Sudbury
Coniston
Sturgeon Falls
Iron River
Crystal Falls
Thessalon
Blind River
Copper Cliff
Rapid River
Rudyard
St Joseph I.
Massey
Espanola
L. Nipissing
Iron Mtn
Kingsford
Niagara
Gladstone
Manistique
North Channel
Drummond I.
Straits of Mackinac
St Ignace
Mackinaw City
Manitoulin I.
Key Harbour
Escanaba
Garden Pen.
Beaver I.
Bois Blanc I.
Cheboygan
Georgian Bay
Stephenson
Green Bay
MICHIGAN
LAKE HURON
Petoskey
Rogers City
South Baymouth
Fitzwilliam I.
Main Chan.
C. Hurd
Tobermory
Parry Sound
Menominee
Gills Rock
Manitou Is.
Charlevoix
Peshtigo
Marinette
Oconto
Gaylord
Alpena
North Pt
ONT
Bruce Pen.
Sturgeon Bay
Mancelona
Atlanta
Traverse City
Harrisville
Wiarton
Green Bay
Elberta
Owen Sound
Kewaunee
Manistee
Southampton
Appleton
Menasha
Neenah
Two Rivers
Manistee
East Lake
Au Sable
Port Elgin
Collingwood
Chilton
L. Winnebago
Manitowoc
Cadillac
Tawas City
Fond du Lac
Ludington
Reed City
Standish
Saginaw Bay
Port Austin
Pt Clark
Kincardine
Walkerton
Clare
Orangeville
Sheboygan
Big Rapids
Coleman
Harbor Beach
Goderich
Shelby
Mt Pleasant
Midland
Essexville
Bay City
Port Washington
Muskegon
Alma
Saginaw
Carsonville
Guelph
Kitchener
Menomonee Falls
Wauwatosa
Howard City
Vassar
Stratford
Cambridge
Milwaukee
W. Allis
Greenfield
Muskegon
Grand Haven
Grand Rapids
St Johns
Flint
Port Huron
Forest
Woodstock
Brantford
Owosso
Burton
London
Racine
Holland
Saugatuck
Kentwood
Wyoming
Grand
St Clair
Sarnia
Ingersoll
Lansing
Kenosha
Charlotte
Holt
Sterling Heights
Pontiac
Otsego
St Thomas
Waukegan
S.Haven
Battle Creek
Warren
L. St Clair
West Lorne
Royal Oak
St Clair Shores
Des Plaines
Skokie
Kalamazoo
Livonia
Detroit
Chatham
Benton Harbor
Albion
Evanston
Hartford
Marshall
Jackson
Ann Arbor
Windsor
St Joseph
Dearborn
Lincoln Park
Taylor
Wyandotte
LAKE ERIE
Chicago
Three Rivers
Coldwater
Adrian
Erie
Girard
Niles
Oak Lawn
East Chicago
Michigan City
Sturgis
Hudson
Monroe
Conneaut
Ashtabula
Gary
La Porte
Elkhart
Angola
Sylvania
Pelee I.
Painesville
Hammond
Mishawaka
Montpelier
Toledo
Park Forest
South Bend
Maumee
Oregon
Port Clinton
Euclid
Mentor
Meadville
Merrillville
Chicago Heights
Plymouth
Auburn
Bowling Green
Fremont
Lakewood
Lorain
Cleveland
Oil City
Kankakee
Kankakee
St Joseph
Maumee
Perrysburg
Sandusky
Elyria
Parma
Winamac
Findlay
Norwalk
Cuyahoga Falls
Warren
Fort Wayne
Van Wert
Tiffin
Barberton
Youngstown
Farrell
Kentland
Huntingdon
Carey
Akron
Boardman
New Castle
Gilman
Logansport
Wabash
Decatur
Ashland
Massillon
Canton
Lima
Kenton
Mansfield
Wooster
East Liverpool
Lafayette
Kokomo
Marion
Celina
Marion
Dover
New Philadelphia
Aliquippa
Attica
Frankfort
Portland
Elwood
Sidney
Delaware
Mt Vernon
Weirton
Danville
Anderson
Muncie
Piqua
Steubenville
Bethel Park
Crawfordsville
Greenville
Urbana
OHIO
Washington
INDIANA
Troy
Upper Arlington
Cambridge
Newark
Martins Ferry
Indianapolis
New Castle
Vandalia
Rockville
Richmond
Dayton
Springfield
Columbus
Wheeling
Moundsville
Zanesville
Barnesville
Fairborn
Xenia
Marshall
Greencastle
Connersville
Kettering
Lancaster
Terre Haute
Franklin
Shelbyville
Middletown
Circleville
Morgantown
Fairmont
Scioto
Spencer
Fairfield
Hamilton
Washington C.H.
Chillicothe
Marietta
Vienna
Belpre
Williamstown
Ohio
Bloomington
Columbus
Aurora
Norwood
Hillsboro
Athens
Grafton
Parkersburg
Clarksburg
Cincinnati
Bloomfield
White
Bedford
Seymour
Covington
Newport
Waverly
Jackson
Lawrenceville
Washington
Weston
Elkins
Wabash
Madison
Vincennes
Ripley
Ripley
WEST
Portsmouth
New Boston
Point Pleasant
Paoli
Carrollton
Kentucky
Oakland City
Jasper
Sutton
New Albany
Ohio
Maysville
Irontown
Huntington
Nitro
Elk
Huntingburg
La Grange
Jeffersonville
Georgetown
Licking
Grayson
Ashland
Charleston
Shively
Louisville
Frankfort
Paris
St Albans
Evansville
Henderson
Pleasure Ridge Park
Lexington
Morehead
Louisa
VIRGINIA
Marmet
Ansted

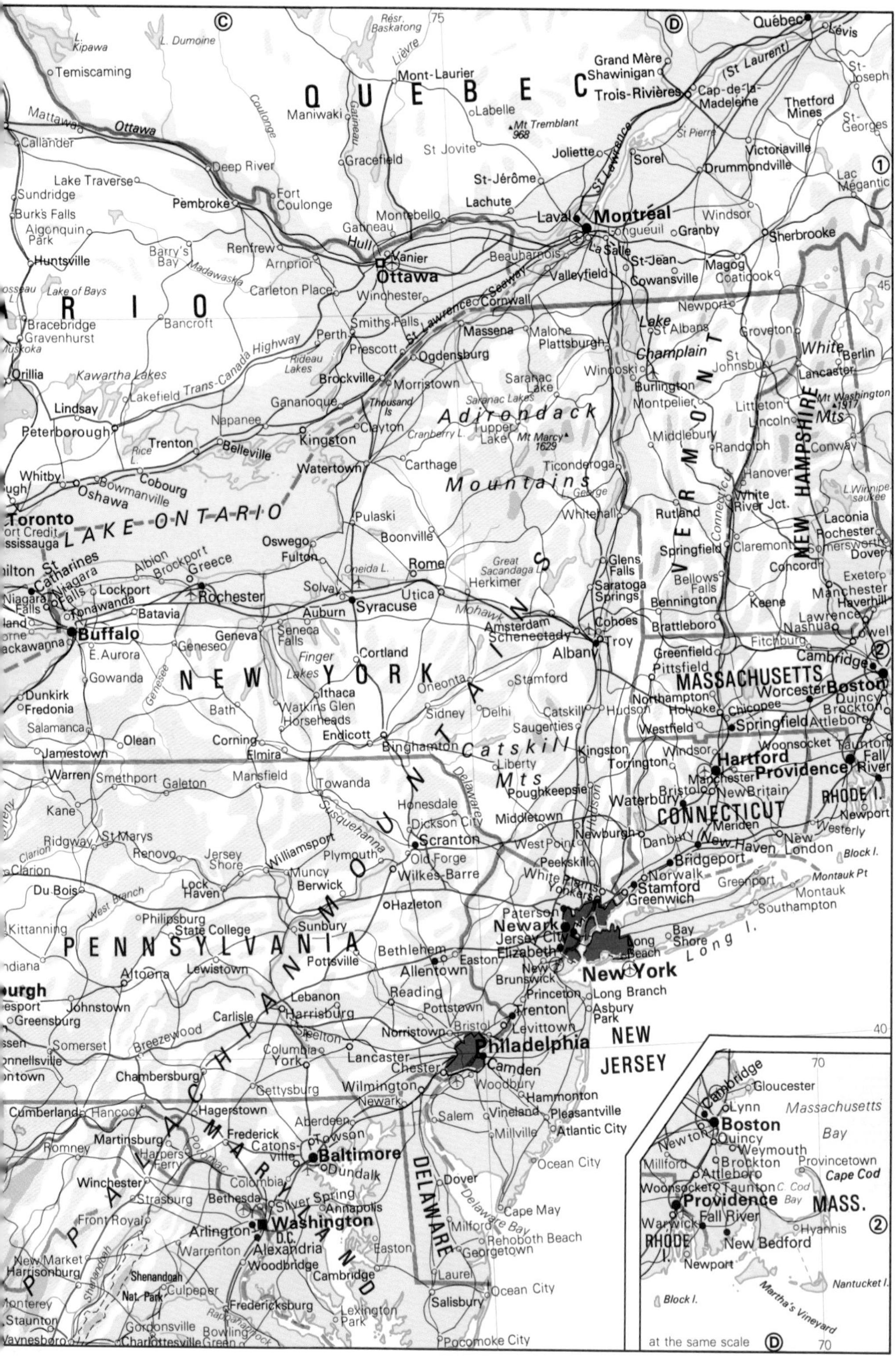
Q U E B E C
Québec
Lévis
Grand Mère
Shawinigan
Trois-Rivières
Cap-de-la-Madeleine
(St Laurent)
St-Joseph
Thetford Mines
St-Georges
Victoriaville
Drummondville
Lac Mégantic
Sorel
St Pierre
Joliette
St-Jérôme
St Lawrence
Lachute
Laval
Montréal
Longueuil
Granby
Windsor
Sherbrooke
La Salle
St-Jean
Magog
Coaticook
Cowansville
Beauharnois
Valleyfield
Cornwall
Seaway
St Lawrence
Mt Tremblant 968
Labelle
St Jovite
Mont-Laurier
Rés. Baskatong
Lièvre
Maniwaki
Gatineau
Gracefield
Montebello
Hull
Vanier
Ottawa
Winchester
Smiths Falls
Perth
Prescott
Ogdensburg
Brockville
Morristown
Massena
Malone
Plattsburgh
Newport
Lake Champlain
St Albans
Groveton
Winooski
Burlington
Montpelier
St Johnsbury
Berlin
White Mts
Lancaster
Mt Washington 1917
Littleton
Lincoln
Middlebury
Randolph
Conway
L. Kipawa
L. Dumoine
Temiscaming
Coulonge
Mattawa
Ottawa
Callander
Deep River
Lake Traverse
Sundridge
Pembroke
Fort Coulonge
Burk's Falls
Algonquin Park
Renfrew
Barry's Bay
Madawaska
Arnprior
Huntsville
Lake of Bays
Carleton Place
O N T A R I O
Bancroft
Bracebridge
Gravenhurst
Muskoka
Orillia
Kawartha Lakes
Trans-Canada Highway
Rideau Lakes
Lakefield
Lindsay
Napanee
Gananoque
Thousand Is
Peterborough
Rice L.
Trenton
Belleville
Kingston
Clayton
Adirondack Mountains
Saranac Lake
Saranac Lakes
Tupper Lake
Cranberry L.
Mt Marcy 1629
Watertown
Carthage
Ticonderoga
L. George
Whitehall
Whitby
Oshawa
Bowmanville
Cobourg
Toronto
Port Credit
Mississauga
LAKE ONTARIO
Pulaski
Boonville
Oswego
Fulton
Rome
Oneida L.
Great Sacandaga L.
Glens Falls
Saratoga Springs
St Catharines
Niagara Falls
Albion
Brockport
Greece
Lockport
Tonawanda
Rochester
Solvay
Syracuse
Utica
Herkimer
Mohawk
Amsterdam
Schenectady
Cohoes
Troy
Albany
Batavia
Auburn
Buffalo
Lackawanna
E. Aurora
Geneva
Seneca Falls
Geneseo
Finger Lakes
Cortland
Gowanda
N E W Y O R K
Ithaca
Oneonta
Stamford
Dunkirk
Fredonia
Genesee
Watkins Glen
Horseheads
Bath
Sidney
Delhi
Catskill
Hudson
Saugerties
Salamanca
Olean
Corning
Elmira
Endicott
Binghamton
Catskill Mts
Kingston
Jamestown
Warren
Smethport
Galeton
Mansfield
Towanda
Liberty
Poughkeepsie
Kane
Honesdale
Delaware
Susquehanna
Dickson City
Middletown
Newburgh
Scranton
West Point
Ridgway
St Marys
Renovo
Clarion
Jersey Shore
Williamsport
Plymouth
Old Forge
Wilkes-Barre
Peekskill
White Plains
Yonkers
Lock Haven
Muncy
Berwick
Du Bois
West Branch
Hazleton
Paterson
Newark
Jersey City
Elizabeth
Kittanning
Philipsburg
State College
Sunbury
P E N N S Y L V A N I A
Bethlehem
Pottsville
Easton
Allentown
New Brunswick
New York
Long Beach
Long I.
Altoona
Lewistown
Pittsburgh
Johnstown
Lebanon
Reading
Princeton
Long Branch
Asbury Park
Greensburg
Harrisburg
Pottstown
Trenton
Levittown
Carlisle
Breezewood
Somerset
Steelton
Norristown
Bristol
Philadelphia
NEW JERSEY
Columbia
York
Lancaster
Chester
Camden
Chambersburg
Woodbury
Gettysburg
Wilmington
Hammonton
Newark
Cumberland
Hancock
Hagerstown
Aberdeen
Salem
Vineland
Pleasantville
Frederick
Towson
Millville
Atlantic City
Martinsburg
Catonsville
Baltimore
Romney
Harpers Ferry
Potomac
Dundalk
Ocean City
Columbia
Winchester
Strasburg
Bethesda
Silver Spring
Annapolis
Dover
DELAWARE
Delaware Bay
Cape May
Front Royal
Arlington
Washington D.C.
Milford
Rehoboth Beach
Georgetown
Warrenton
Alexandria
Easton
New Market
Harrisonburg
Shenandoah
Woodbridge
Cambridge
Laurel
Shenandoah Nat. Park
Culpeper
Salisbury
Ocean City
Monterey
Fredericksburg
Rappahannock
Lexington Park
Staunton
Gordonsville
Bowling Green
Waynesboro
Charlottesville
Pocomoke City
M A R Y L A N D
A P P A L A C H I A N M O U N T A I N S
V E R M O N T
NEW HAMPSHIRE
Hanover
White River Jct.
L. Winnipesaukee
Laconia
Rutland
Connecticut
Rochester
Springfield
Claremont
Somersworth
Dover
Bellows Falls
Concord
Exeter
Manchester
Haverhill
Bennington
Keene
Lawrence
Nashua
Lowell
Brattleboro
Fitchburg
Greenfield
Cambridge
Pittsfield
MASSACHUSETTS
Boston
Worcester
Quincy
Northampton
Holyoke
Chicopee
Brockton
Westfield
Springfield
Attleboro
Woonsocket
Taunton
Windsor
Hartford
Providence
Fall River
Torrington
Manchester
New Britain
RHODE I.
Bristol
Waterbury
CONNECTICUT
Newport
Meriden
Westerly
Danbury
New Haven
New London
Block I.
Bridgeport
Norwalk
Montauk Pt
Stamford
Greenport
Montauk
Greenwich
Southampton
Bay Shore
45
40
75
Gloucester
Lynn
Massachusetts Bay
Newton
Weymouth
Milford
Provincetown
Cape Cod
Cape Cod Bay
MASS.
Hyannis
Warwick
New Bedford
Nantucket I.
Martha's Vineyard
at the same scale
70

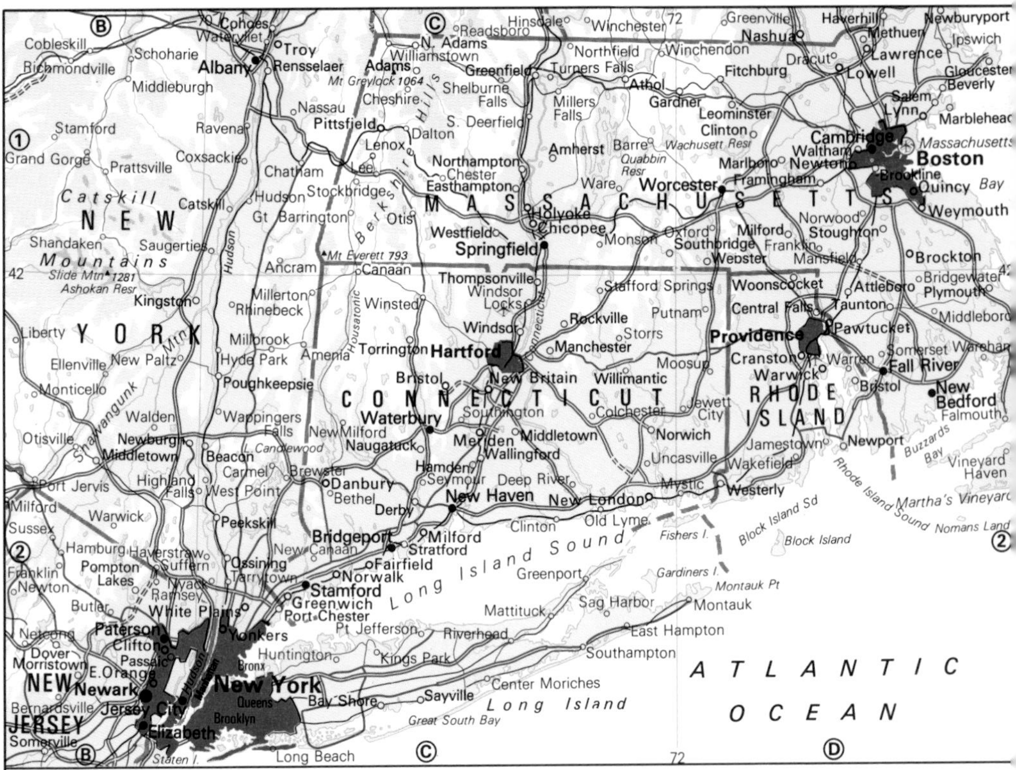

NEW YORK
Catskill Mountains
MASSACHUSETTS
CONNECTICUT
RHODE ISLAND
NEW JERSEY
Albany
Troy
Schenectady
Cohoes
Rensselaer
Kingston
Poughkeepsie
Newburgh
Middletown
Peekskill
White Plains
Yonkers
Paterson
Clifton
Newark
Jersey City
Elizabeth
New York
Bronx
Queens
Brooklyn
Staten I.
Long Island Sound
Long Island
Great South Bay
Long Beach
Pittsfield
Springfield
Holyoke
Chicopee
Worcester
Fitchburg
Nashua
Lowell
Lawrence
Haverhill
Cambridge
Boston
Quincy
Brockton
Fall River
New Bedford
Providence
Pawtucket
Cranston
Warwick
Newport
Hartford
New Britain
Waterbury
New Haven
Bridgeport
Stamford
Norwalk
Danbury
Meriden
Middletown
New London
Westerly
Block Island Sd
Block Island
Martha's Vineyard
Montauk Pt
Montauk
East Hampton
Southampton
Riverhead
ATLANTIC OCEAN

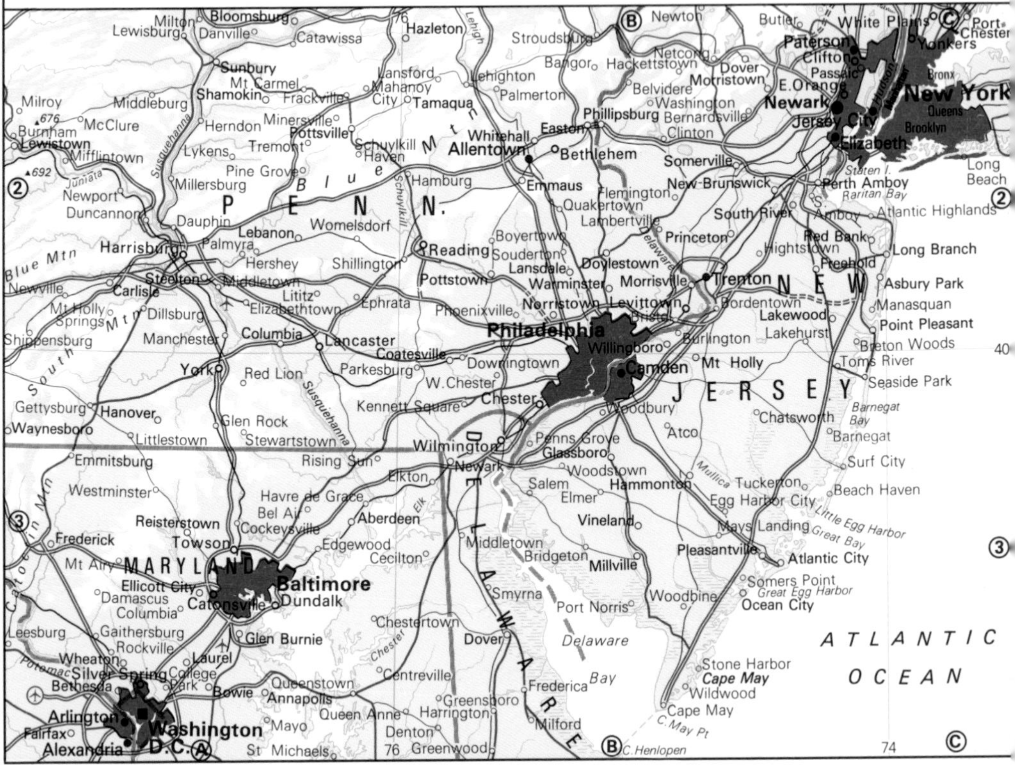

PENN.
NEW JERSEY
MARYLAND
DELAWARE
Hazleton
Allentown
Bethlehem
Easton
Reading
Lancaster
Harrisburg
York
Pottstown
Norristown
Philadelphia
Camden
Chester
Wilmington
Newark
Trenton
Princeton
New Brunswick
Perth Amboy
Paterson
Newark
Jersey City
Elizabeth
New York
Long Branch
Asbury Park
Lakewood
Toms River
Vineland
Millville
Atlantic City
Ocean City
Cape May
C. May Pt
C. Henlopen
Dover
Milford
Delaware Bay
Baltimore
Towson
Dundalk
Annapolis
Silver Spring
Bethesda
Arlington
Alexandria
Washington D.C.
Frederick
Hagerstown
Gettysburg
Hanover
ATLANTIC OCEAN

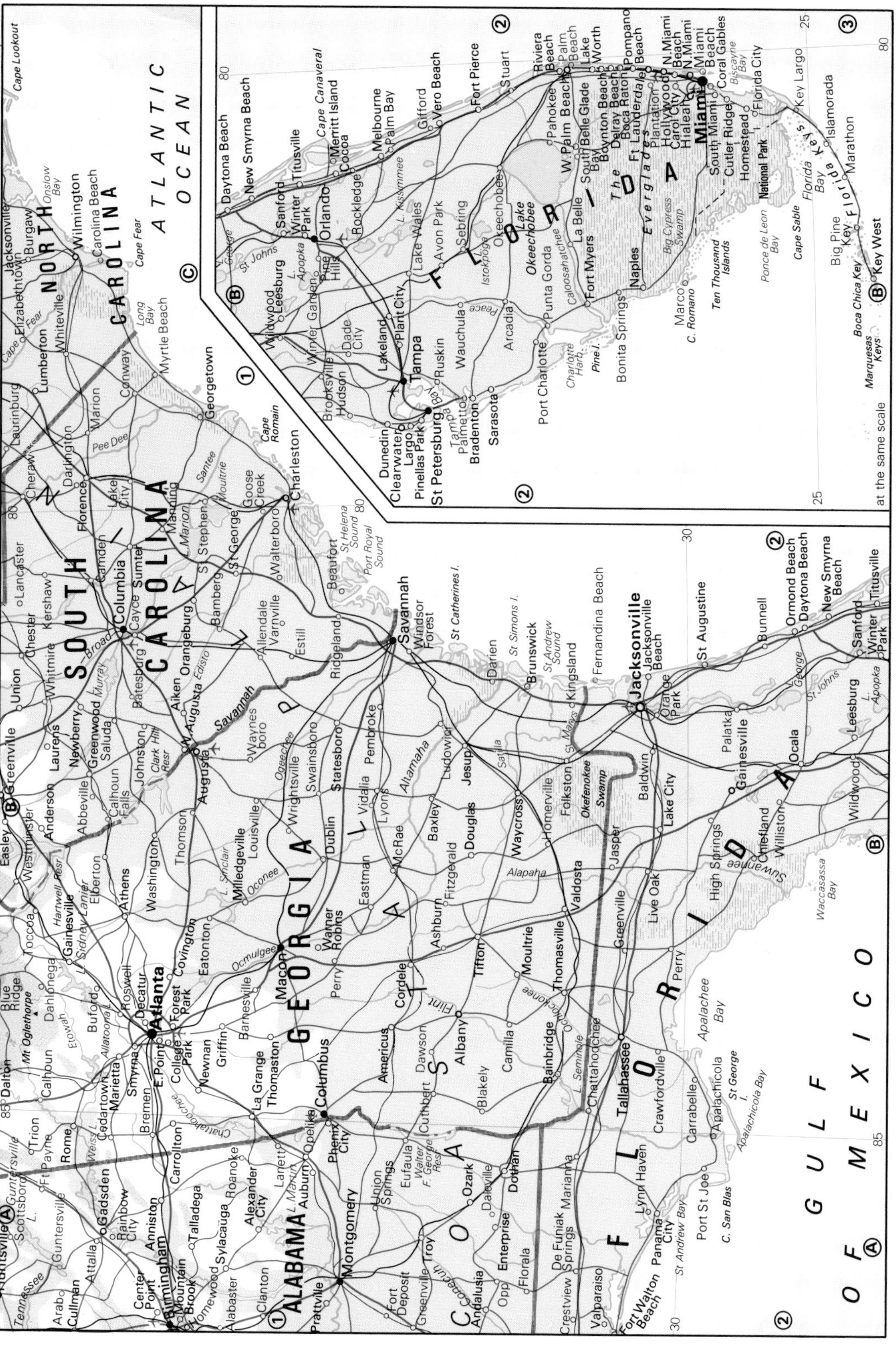
ATLANTIC OCEAN
GULF OF MEXICO
NORTH CAROLINA
SOUTH CAROLINA
GEORGIA
ALABAMA
FLORIDA
Cape Lookout
Jacksonville
Wilmington
Onslow Bay
Carolina Beach
Cape Fear
Long Bay
Myrtle Beach
Georgetown
Cape Romain
Charleston
Goose Creek
Columbia
Florence
Sumter
Orangeburg
Aiken
Augusta
Savannah
Beaufort
Brunswick
Jacksonville
Jacksonville Beach
Fernandina Beach
St Augustine
Ormond Beach
Daytona Beach
New Smyrna Beach
Titusville
Gainesville
Ocala
Tallahassee
Panama City
Apalachicola
Atlanta
Macon
Columbus
Albany
Valdosta
Montgomery
Birmingham
Dothan
Athens
Greenville
Okefenokee Swamp
Apalachee Bay
Orlando
Cape Canaveral
Tampa
St Petersburg
Clearwater
Sarasota
Fort Myers
Naples
Lake Okeechobee
West Palm Beach
Fort Lauderdale
Miami
Miami Beach
Homestead
National Park
Key Largo
Key West
Florida Keys
at the same scale

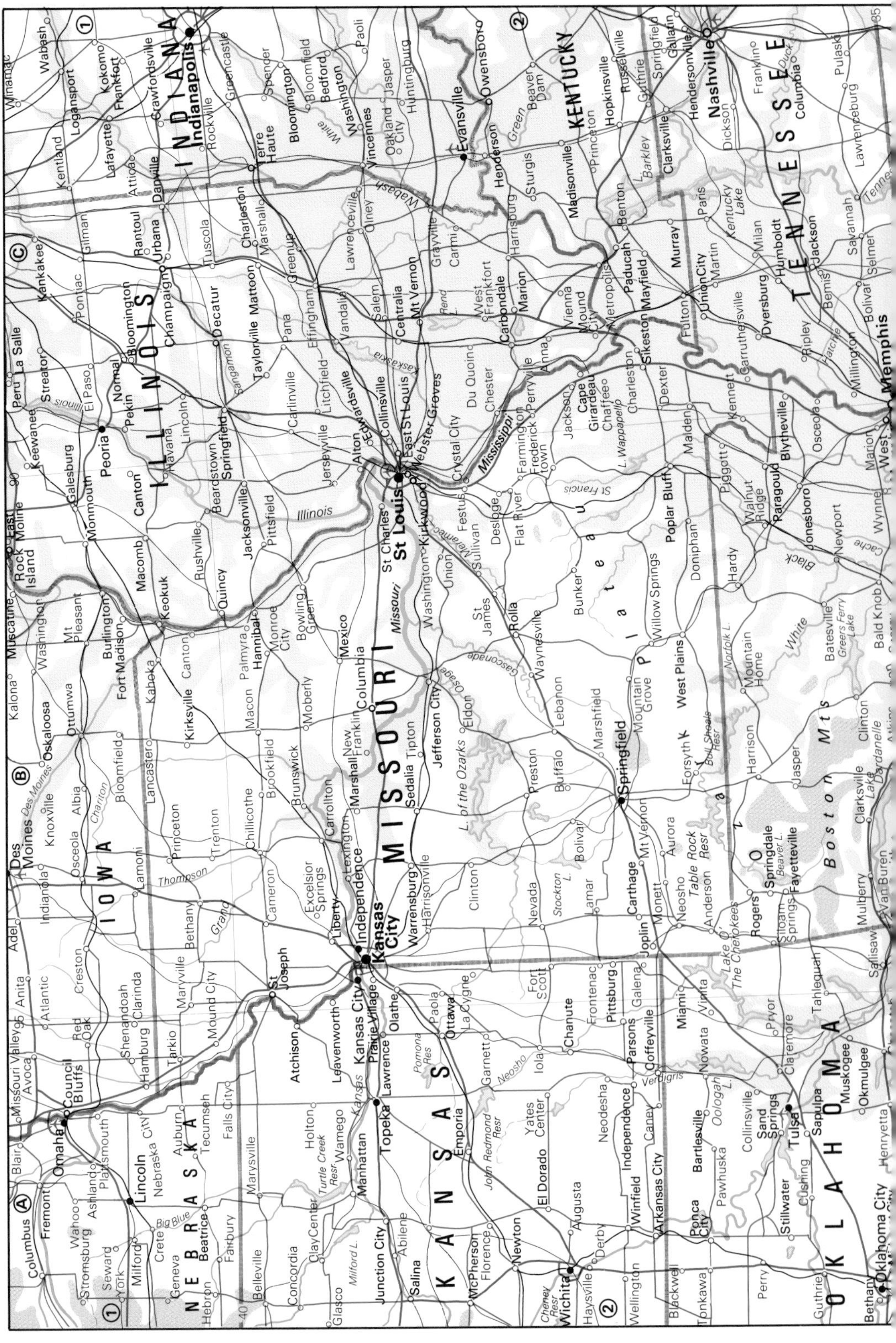
INDIANA
ILLINOIS
IOWA
MISSOURI
KANSAS
NEBRASKA
KENTUCKY
TENNESSEE
OKLAHOMA
Indianapolis
Evansville
Terre Haute
Bloomington
Vincennes
Peoria
Springfield
Champaign
Decatur
Quincy
St Louis
East St Louis
Kansas City
Independence
Jefferson City
Columbia
Springfield
Joplin
Topeka
Lawrence
Wichita
Salina
Emporia
Lincoln
Omaha
Council Bluffs
Des Moines
St Joseph
Nashville
Clarksville
Paducah
Memphis
Jackson
Tulsa
Oklahoma City
Bartlesville
Muskogee
Cape Girardeau
Rolla
Poplar Bluff
Ozark Plateau
Boston Mts
Mississippi
Missouri
Illinois
Wabash
Kansas
Arkansas City
Table Rock Resr
Lake of the Ozarks

1:5M

0 50 100 150 200 km

0 50 100 mls

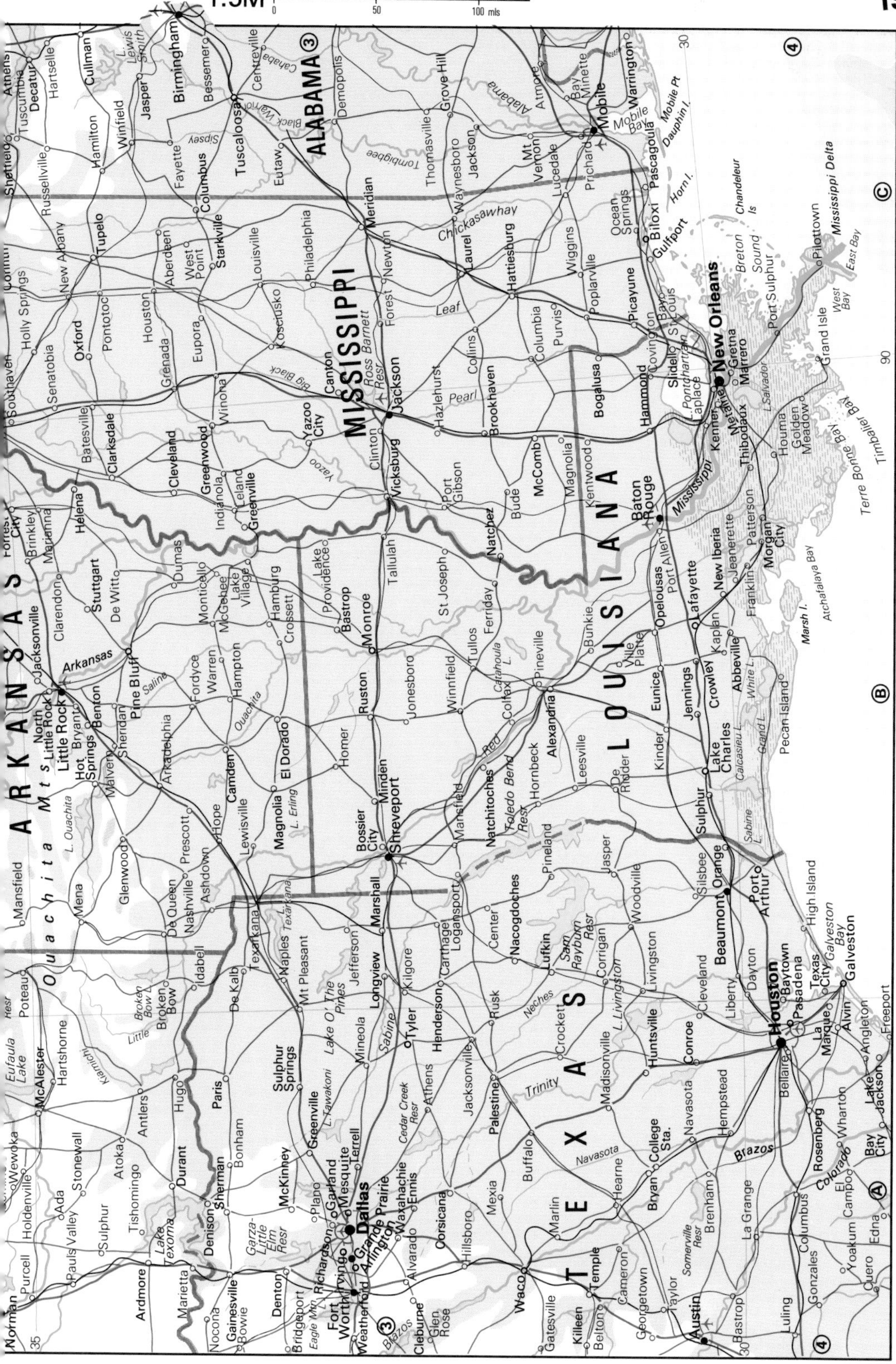

1:5M

0 50 100 150 200 km
0 50 100 mls

A B C
1 2
125 120 45

CANADA
WASHINGTON
OREGON
IDAHO
NEVADA
CALIFORNIA
COLUMBIA PLATEAU
CASCADE RANGE
COAST RANGE
OKANOGAN RA.

Parksville, Gibsons, Horseshoe Bay, Vancouver, Port Hammond, Mission City, Hope, Princeton, Okanagan Falls, Kettle, Castlegar, Salmo
Port Alberni, Nanaimo, Vancouver, New Westminster, Fraser, Agassiz, Skagit Mtn 2356, Keremeos, Oliver, Osoyoos, Grand Forks, Trail, Creston
Barkley Sd, Bamfield, Ladysmith, Cowichan, Chilliwack, Abbotsford, Blaine, 2627 Lakeview Mt, Metaline Falls, Bonners Ferry
Duncan, Sidney, Port Renfrew, Victoria, Esquimalt, Str. of Juan de Fuca, C. Flattery, San Juan Is, Anacortes
Ferndale, Bellingham, Mt Baker 3285, North Cascades Nat. Park, Ross L., Mt Logan 2733, Oroville, Tonasket, Kettle River Ra., Ione, Pend Oreille, Priest L., Colville
Burlington, Skagit, Concrete, Mt Vernon, Okanogan, Republic, Omak, Okanogan, Franklin D. Roosevelt Lake, Sandpoint
Port Angeles, Forks, Olympic Nat. Park, Mt Olympus 2428, Marysville, Everett, Snohomish, Glacier Peak 3221, Brewster, Columbia, Grand Coulee, Newport, Priest River, Pend Oreille L., Spirit Lake
Monroe, Edmonds, Bellevue, Seattle, Bremerton, Renton, Port Orchard, L. Chelan, Chelan, Banks L., Wilbur, Spokane, Coeur d'Alene, Medical Lake, Coeur d'Alene L., Cheney, Kellogg
Kent, Auburn, Tacoma, Snoqualmie Pass, Wenatchee, Ephrata, Odessa, Plummer, St Joe, St Maries
Shelton, Puyallup, Yakima, Moses Lake, Ritzville
Hoquiam, Grays Harb., Aberdeen, Olympia, Mt Rainier 4392, Mount Rainier Nat. Park, Ellensburg, Othello, Colfax, Potlatch
Willapa B., South Bend, Raymond, Centralia, Naches, Selah, Wenatchee, Pullman, Moscow, Kendrick
Chehalis, Winlock, Yakima, Eltopia, Snake
Cowlitz, C. Disappointment, Longview, Kelso, Toppenish, Sunnyside, Richland, Pasco, Dayton, Clarkston, Lewiston
Astoria, Rainier, Mt St Helens 2950, Mt Adams 3751, Kennewick, Walla Walla
Seaside, Woodland, Goldendale, Columbia, Umatilla, Blue Mountains, Grande Ronde
St Helens, White Salmon, Vancouver, Echo, Pendleton, Wallowa
Tillamook, Hillsboro, Portland, Camas, Hood River, The Dalles, Arlington, Enterprise, Riggins
Lake Oswego, Newberg, Gresham, Oregon City, Mt Hood 3427, John Day, La Grande, Hells Canyon, He Devil Mtn 2863
McMinnville, Woodburn, Mt Wilson 1707, Deschutes, Condon, Ukiah, Wallowa Mts, Sacajawea Pk 2997
Lincoln City, Salem, Stayton, Willamette, Spray, Baker
Newport, Corvallis, Albany, Idanha, Mt Jefferson 3199, Madras, Long Creek, Midvale
Yachats, Lebanon, Sweet Home, Dayville, Unity, John Day, Canyon City, Prineville, Weiser
Redmond, Eugene, Springfield, Three Sisters 3156, Bend, Payette, Ontario
Florence, Lowell, Cottage Grove, Brothers, Vale, Nyssa, Emmett
Reedsport, Oakridge, La Pine, Drewsey, Caldwell, Nampa
Umpqua, Coos Bay, Coos Bay, N. Bend, Oakland, Crescent, High Desert, Burns, Harney Basin, Crane, Malheur L., Snake
Roseburg, Myrtle Creek, Myrtle Point, Mt Thielsen 2799, Silver Lake, Harney L., Jordan Valley, Murphy
C. Blanco, Port Orford, Canyonville, Prospect, Crater L. Nat. Pk, Mt Scott 2721, Owyhee, Owyhee Mts
Gold Beach, Rogue, Wolf Creek, Grants Pass, Chiloquin, Steens Mtn
Mt McLoughlin 2894, Upper Klamath L., Bly, Valley Falls
Central Point, Medford, Ashland, Klamath Falls, Lakeview
Brookings, O'Brien, Warner Mts
Hornbrook, Dorris, Willow Ranch, Denio, Mc Dermitt
Pt St George, Crescent City, Clear L. Resr, Goose L., Upper L.
Yreka, Klamath Mts, Santa Rosa Ra.
Klamath, Klamath, Weed, Mt Shasta 4317, Mount Shasta, Canby, Middle Alkali L., Alturas, Black Rock Desert, Osgood Mts
Dunsmuir, Pit, Adin
Humboldt Bay, Eureka, Arcata, Shasta L., Burney, Winnemucca, Golconda, Humboldt
Fortuna, Weaverville, Project City, Rye Patch Resr, Imlay, Battle Mountain
C. Mendocino, Redding, Nat. Pk, Lassen Pk 3187, Eagle L., Susanville, Mt Tobin 2979

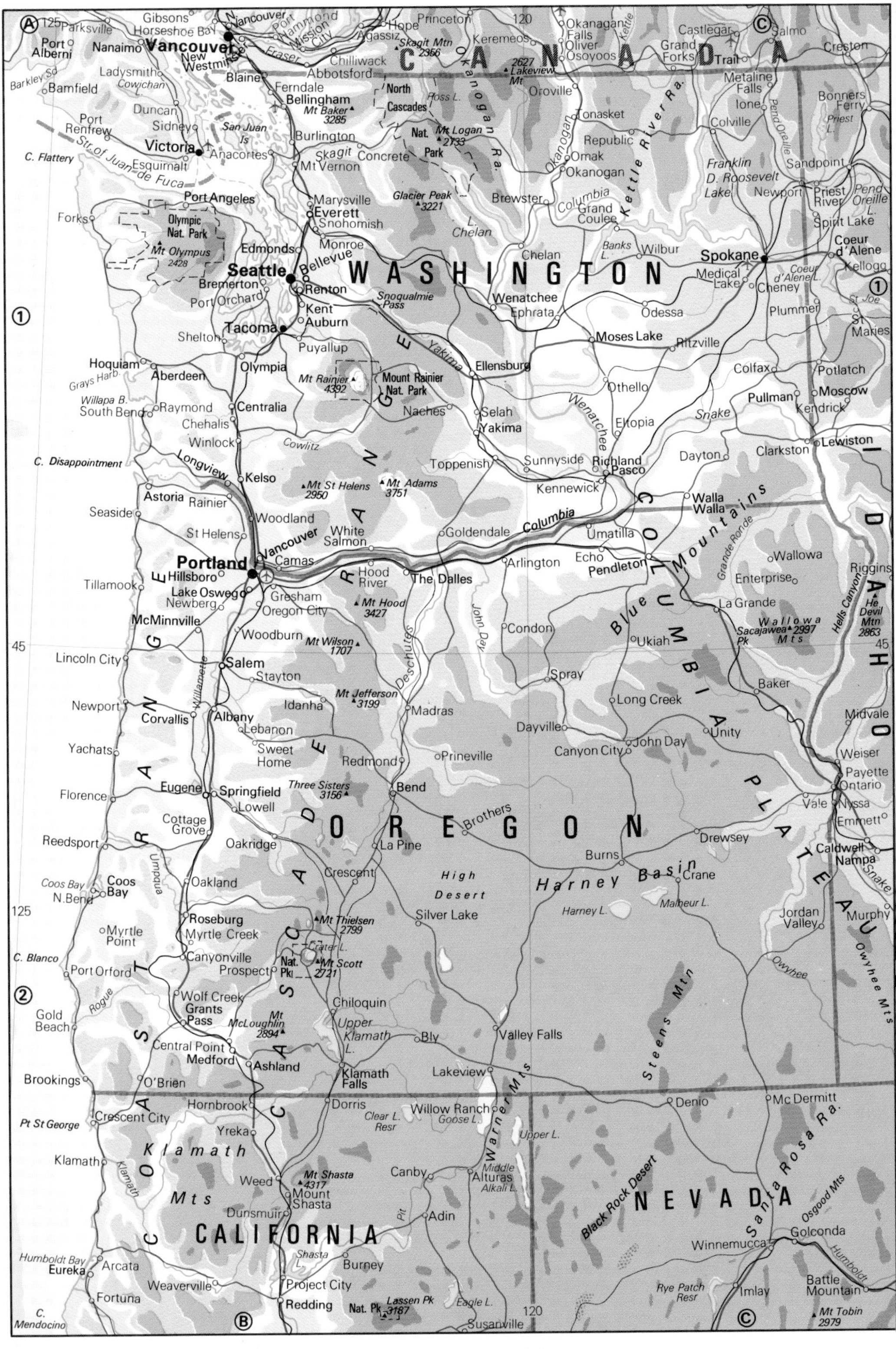

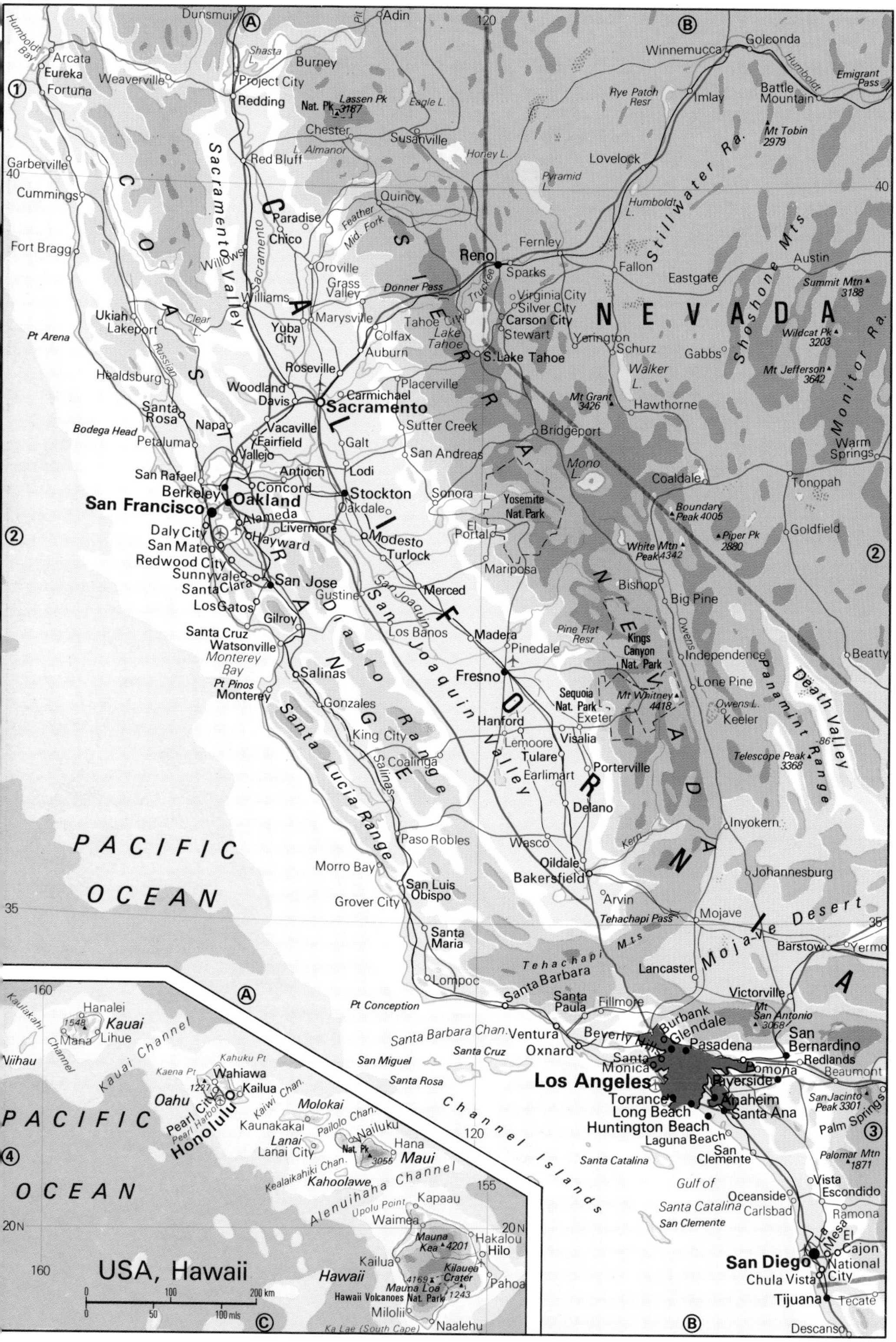
Humboldt Bay
Arcata
Eureka
Fortuna
Weaverville
Dunsmuir
Shasta L.
Project City
Redding
Burney
Adin
Pit
Nat. Pk
Lassen Pk 3187
Eagle L.
Chester
Susanville
L. Almanor
Honey L.
Red Bluff
Garberville
Cummings
Fort Bragg
Sacramento Valley
Sacramento
Paradise
Chico
Feather Mid. Fork
Quincy
Oroville
Grass Valley
Willows
Williams
Donner Pass
Ukiah
Lakeport
Clear L.
Pt Arena
Russian
Marysville
Yuba City
Colfax
Auburn
Tahoe City
Lake Tahoe
Truckee
Reno
Sparks
Fernley
Virginia City
Silver City
Carson City
Stewart
S. Lake Tahoe
Roseville
Healdsburg
Woodland
Davis
Sacramento
Carmichael
Placerville
Santa Rosa
Napa
Vacaville
Fairfield
Bodega Head
Petaluma
Vallejo
Galt
Sutter Creek
San Andreas
San Rafael
Antioch
Lodi
Berkeley
Concord
Oakland
Stockton
San Francisco
Alameda
Oakdale
Sonora
Yosemite Nat. Park
Daly City
Livermore
Modesto
El Portal
San Mateo
Hayward
Turlock
Redwood City
Mariposa
Sunnyvale
Santa Clara
San Jose
Merced
Los Gatos
Gustine
Gilroy
Santa Cruz
Los Banos
Madera
Watsonville
Monterey Bay
Pinedale
Fresno
Salinas
Pt Pinos
Monterey
Gonzales
King City
Hanford
Lemoore
Tulare
Visalia
Exeter
Sequoia Nat. Park
Kings Canyon Nat. Park
Pine Flat Resr
Coalinga
Earlimart
Porterville
Delano
Salinas
Santa Lucia Range
Diablo Range
San Joaquin Valley
San Joaquin
Paso Robles
Wasco
Oildale
Bakersfield
Kern
Morro Bay
San Luis Obispo
Arvin
Grover City
Tehachapi Pass
Santa Maria
Tehachapi Mts
Lompoc
Santa Barbara
Pt Conception
Santa Paula
Fillmore
Ventura
Oxnard
Santa Barbara Chan.
San Miguel
Santa Cruz
Santa Rosa
Channel Islands
PACIFIC OCEAN
C O A S T
S I E R R A
N E V A D A
C A L I F O R N I A
Winnemucca
Golconda
Humboldt
Emigrant Pass
Rye Patch Resr
Imlay
Battle Mountain
Mt Tobin 2979
Lovelock
Stillwater Ra.
Pyramid L.
Humboldt L.
Fallon
Eastgate
Austin
Shoshone Mts
Summit Mtn 3188
NEVADA
Wildcat Pk 3203
Yerington
Schurz
Gabbs
Walker L.
Mt Jefferson 3642
Monitor Ra.
Mt Grant 3426
Hawthorne
Bridgeport
Warm Springs
Mono L.
Coaldale
Tonopah
Boundary Peak 4005
Piper Pk 2880
Goldfield
White Mtn Peak 4342
Bishop
Big Pine
Owens
Independence
Beatty
Lone Pine
Mt Whitney 4418
Owens L.
Keeler
Panamint Range
Death Valley
-86
Telescope Peak 3368
Inyokern
Johannesburg
Mojave
Mojave Desert
Barstow
Yermo
Lancaster
Victorville
Mt San Antonio 3068
San Bernardino
Redlands
Beaumont
Burbank
Glendale
Pasadena
Beverly Hills
Santa Monica
Pomona
Los Angeles
Riverside
Torrance
Anaheim
Long Beach
Santa Ana
San Jacinto Peak 3301
Palm Springs
Huntington Beach
Laguna Beach
San Clemente
Santa Catalina
Gulf of Santa Catalina
San Clemente
Palomar Mtn 1871
Vista
Oceanside
Escondido
Carlsbad
Ramona
La Mesa
El Cajon
San Diego
National City
Chula Vista
Tijuana
Tecate
Descanso
120
40
35
(1) (2) (3) (4)
(A) (B) (C)
Kaulakahi Channel
Hanalei
1548
Kauai
Mana
Lihue
Niihau
Kauai Channel
Kahuku Pt
Kaena Pt
Wahiawa
1227
Kailua
Oahu
Pearl City
Pearl Harbor
Honolulu
Kaiwi Chan.
Molokai
Kaunakakai
Pailolo Chan.
Nailuku
Lanai
Lanai City
Nat. Pk
3055
Hana
Maui
Kealaikahiki Chan.
Kahoolawe
Alenuihaha Channel
Upolu Point
Kapaau
Waimea
Mauna Kea 4201
Hakalau
Hilo
Kailua
Kilauea Crater
Hawaii
4169
Mauna Loa
1243
Pahoa
Hawaii Volcanoes Nat. Park
Milolii
Ka Lae (South Cape)
Naalehu
PACIFIC OCEAN
160
155
20N
USA, Hawaii
0 100 200 km
0 50 100 mls

1:2.5M 0 25 50 75 100 km / 0 25 50 mls

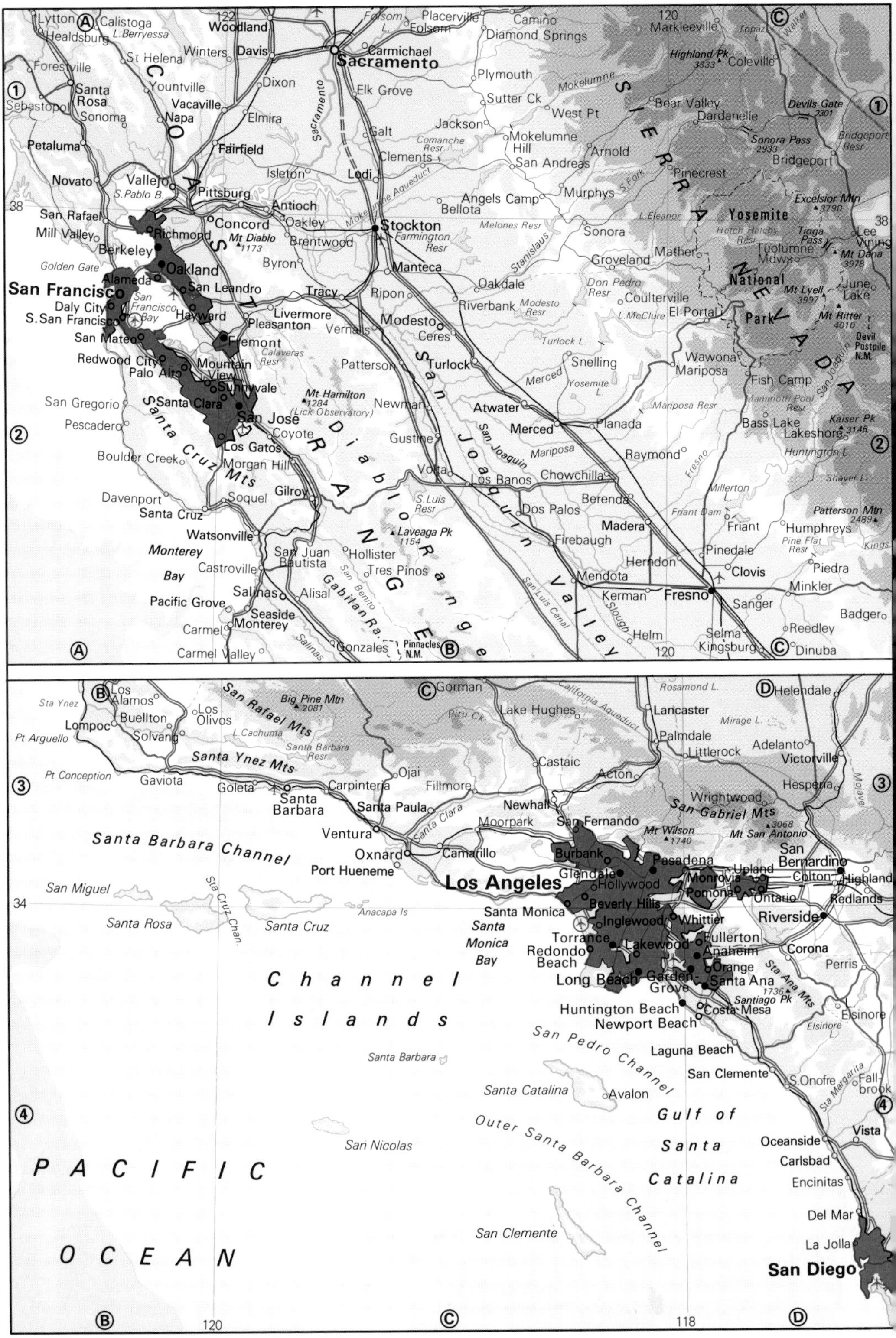

GULF OF MEXICO
SIERRA MADRE ORIENTAL
SIERRA MADRE DEL SUR
SIERRA MADRE DE OAXACA
JALISCO
NAYARIT
COLIMA
MICHOACÁN
GUANAJUATO
QUERÉTARO
HIDALGO
MORELOS
TLAXCALA
GUERRERO
OAXACA
VERACRUZ
PUEBLA
AGS.
San Luis Potosí
México
Guadalajara
Tlaquepaque
Tepic
Aguascalientes
León
Irapuato
Salamanca
Celaya
Querétaro
Morelia
Uruapan
Zamora
Toluca
Cuernavaca
Puebla
Tlaxcala
Pachuca
Jalapa
Veracruz
Córdoba
Orizaba
Oaxaca
Tehuantepec
Salina Cruz
Acapulco
Chilpancingo
Iguala
Taxco
Zihuatanejo
Lázaro Cárdenas
Colima
Manzanillo
Cd Madero
Tampico
Poza Rica
Tuxpan
Cd Guzmán
Tehuacán
Tuxtepec
Nev. de Toluca 4558
Vol. Citlaltepetl 5700
Popocatepetl 5450
Nev. de Colima 4330
L. de Chapala
Pto Marquéz
Pta S. Telmo
Pta Maldonado

A
B
110
100
30
20
10
2
3
4
San Diego
Tijuana
Ensenada
Mexicali
Brawley
Salton Sea
Colorado
Yuma
Phoenix
Mesa
Wickenburg
Baldy Peak 3532
Theodore Roosevelt L.
ARIZONA
Casa Grande
Tucson
Silver City
Lordsburg
Alamogordo
Las Cruces
El Paso
Cd Juárez
NEW MEXICO
Vaughn
Sa Blanca 3658
Sacramento Mts
Artesia
Roswell
Tucumcari
Clovis
Amarillo
Red
Plainview
Llano Estacado
Lubbock
Carlsbad
Midland
Big Spring
Snyder
Odessa
Pecos
Van Horn
San Angelo
Sweetwater
Abilene
Brownwood
Colorado
UNITED STATES
Chickasha
Lawton
El Reno
Oklahoma City
OKLAHOMA
Ardmore
Wichita Falls
L.Texoma
Durant
Brazos
Denison
Greenville
Fort Worth
Dallas
Corsicana
Waco
TEXAS
Edwards Plateau
Austin
New Braunfels
Houston
San Antonio
Del Rio
Cd Acuña
Eagle Pass
Piedras Negras
Victoria
Nueces
Beeville
Matagorda B.
Corpus Christi
Kingsville
Padre I.
Laredo
Nuevo Laredo
Falcon Resr
McAllen
Reynosa
Brownsville
Matamoros
Lag. Madre
Alpine
Emory Pk 2389
Rio Bravo del Norte
Rio Grande
Ojinaga
Sierra Madre Oriental
Nueva Rosita
Sabinas
Monclova
Bolson de Mapimí
Sa de los Alamitos
Sabinas Hidalgo
Monterrey
Guadalupe
Saltillo
Montemorelos
Torreón
Gómez Palacio
Concepción del Oro
Matehuala
Cd Victoria
Cd Madero
Tampico
Cd Valles
Lag. de Tamiahua
C.Rojo
Tuxpan
Poza Rica
Papantla
San Luis Potosí
Zacatecas
Fresnillo
Pto Peñasco
San Quintín
Pta Baja
Nogales
Douglas
Agua Prieta
Cananea
Caborca
Magdalena
Nacozari
Nuevo Casas Grandes
Hermosillo
Sonora
Tiburón
Angel de la Guarda
Baja California
Golfo de California
Cedros
Ba Sebastian Vizcaino
Pta Eugenia
Madera
Chihuahua
Cuauhtémoc
Delicias
Cd Camargo
Empalme
Guaymas
Yaqui
Sta Rosalía
Pta Abreojos
Ciudad Obregón
Navojoa
Fuerte
Choix
San Francisco del Oro
Hidalgo del Parral
Sta Barbara
Sierra Madre Occidental
MEXICO
Los Mochis
Topolobampo
Guasave
Huayapan
I.Magdalena
Ba Magdalena
I.Sta Margarita
Tropic of Cancer
Culiacán
Altata
El Dorado
Tepehuanes
La Paz
C.Falso
San José del Cabo
Canatlán
Durango
Mazatlán
Escuinapa
Acaponeta
Tuxpan
Las Tres Marías
Tepic
R.Gd de Santiago
Aguascalientes
Lagos de Moreno
León
Guadalajara
Ba de Banderas
C. Corrientes
Pto Vallarta
Ameca
L.de Chapala
Irapuato
Celaya
Querétaro
Ocotlán
Sahuayo
Zamora
Acámbaro
Pachuca
San Benedicto
Roca Partida
Revillagigedo (Mex.)
Clarión
Socorro
Autlán
Cd Guzman
Colima
Manzanillo
Tecomán
Morelia
Uruapan
México
Toluca
Apatzingan
P.del Infiernillo
Lázero Cárdenas
Ba de Petacalco
Cuernavaca
Taxco
Popocatepetl 5452
Puebla
Orizaba
Citlaltepetl 5699
Córdoba
Jalapa
Veracruz
Tehuacán
Tierra Blanca
Balsas
Iguala
Acatlán
Chilpancingo
Sierra Madre del Sur
Tecpan
Acapulco
Oaxaca
Ixtepec
Tehuantepec
Golfo de Tehuantepec
PACIFIC OCEAN
Clipperton I. (France)

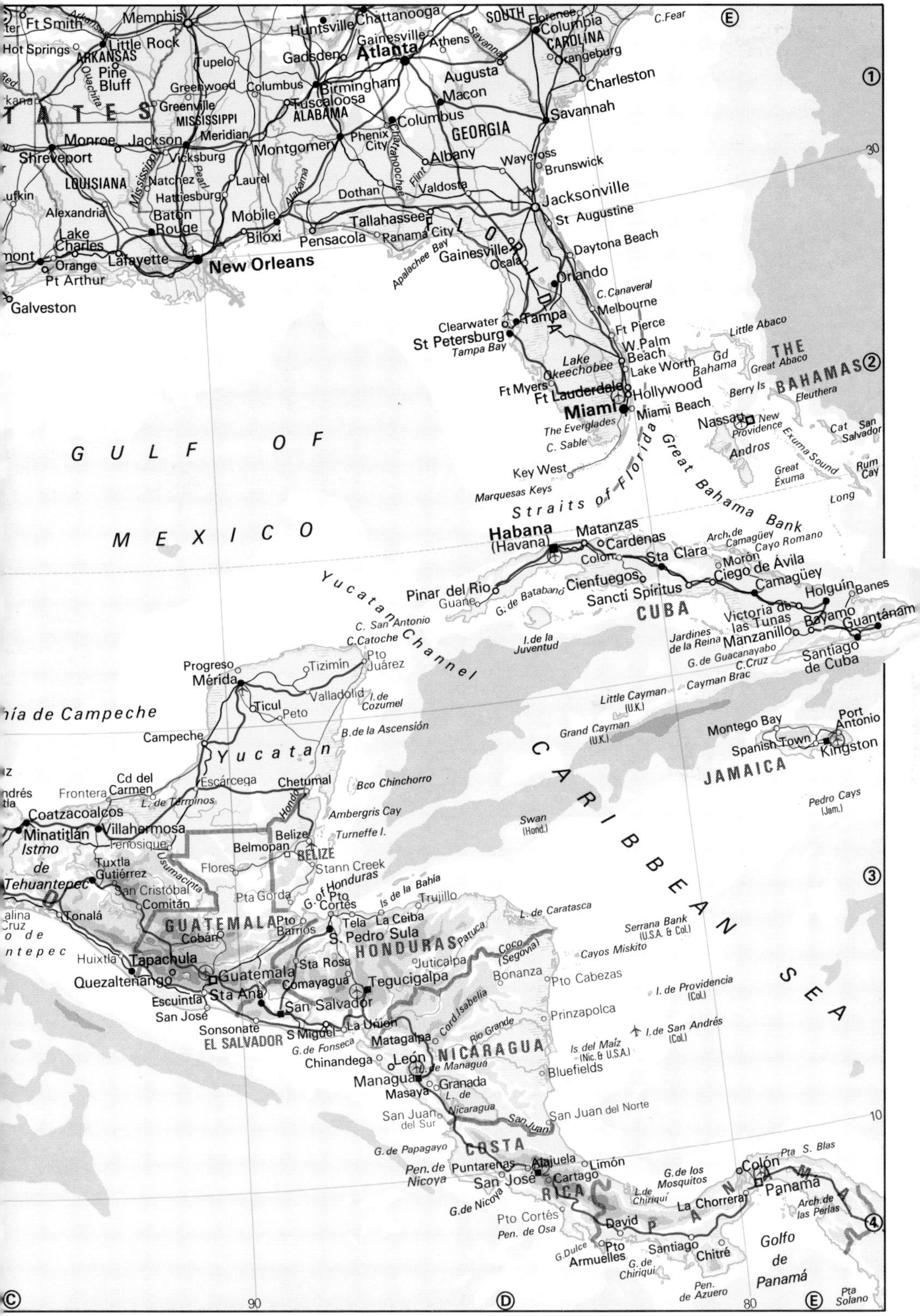
Ft Smith
Memphis
Chattanooga
SOUTH CAROLINA
Florence
Columbia
C.Fear
Hot Springs
Little Rock
ARKANSAS
Pine Bluff
Huntsville
Gainesville
Athens
Gadsden
Atlanta
Orangeburg
Tupelo
Augusta
Charleston
Greenwood
Columbus
Birmingham
Macon
Greenville
MISSISSIPPI
Tuscaloosa
ALABAMA
Savannah
Columbus
GEORGIA
Meridian
Monroe
Jackson
Shreveport
Vicksburg
Montgomery
Phenix City
Albany
Waycross
Brunswick
LOUISIANA
Natchez
Laurel
Hattiesburg
Dothan
Valdosta
Jacksonville
Lufkin
Alexandria
Baton Rouge
Mobile
Tallahassee
St Augustine
Lake Charles
Biloxi
Pensacola
Panama City
FLORIDA
Daytona Beach
Orange
Lafayette
New Orleans
Apalachee Bay
Gainesville
Ocala
Orlando
Pt Arthur
C. Canaveral
Galveston
Melbourne
Clearwater
Tampa
St Petersburg
Tampa Bay
Ft Pierce
Little Abaco
W.Palm Beach
Lake Okeechobee
Lake Worth
Gd Bahama
THE BAHAMAS
Great Abaco
Ft Myers
Ft Lauderdale
Hollywood
Berry Is
Eleuthera
Miami
Miami Beach
Nassau
New Providence
The Everglades
C. Sable
Andros
Exuma Sound
Cat
San Salvador
GULF OF MEXICO
Key West
Great Exuma
Rum Cay
Marquesas Keys
Straits of Florida
Great Bahama Bank
Long
Habana (Havana)
Matanzas
Cardenas
Arch.de Camagüey
Cayo Romano
Colón
Sta Clara
Morón
Ciego de Ávila
Camagüey
Yucatan Channel
Pinar del Rio
Guane
G. de Batabanó
Cienfuegos
Sancti Spíritus
Holguín
Banes
CUBA
C. San Antonio
C.Catoche
I.de la Juventud
Jardines de la Reina
Victoria de las Tunas
Bayamo
Manzanillo
Guantánamo
Pto Juárez
G. de Guacanayabo
Santiago de Cuba
C.Cruz
Progreso
Tizimín
Mérida
Cayman Brac
Valladolid
I. de Cozumel
Little Cayman (U.K.)
Ticul
Peto
Bahía de Campeche
B.de la Ascensión
Grand Cayman (U.K.)
Montego Bay
Port Antonio
Campeche
Spanish Town
Kingston
Yucatan
CARIBBEAN SEA
JAMAICA
Cd del Carmen
Escárcega
Chetumal
Bco Chinchorro
Frontera
L. de Términos
Pedro Cays (Jam.)
Coatzacoalcos
Hondo
Ambergris Cay
Minatitlán
Villahermosa
Belize
Turneffe I.
Swan (Hond.)
Istmo de Tehuantepec
Tenosique
Belmopan
BELIZE
Tuxtla Gutiérrez
Usumacinta
Flores
Stann Creek
San Cristóbal
G. of Honduras
Is de la Bahía
Comitán
Pta Gorda
Pto Cortés
Trujillo
Tonalá
GUATEMALA
Pto Barrios
Tela
La Ceiba
L. de Caratasca
Cobán
S. Pedro Sula
Serrana Bank (U.S.A. & Col.)
HONDURAS
Patuca
Coco (Segovia)
Huixtla
Tapachula
Cayos Miskito
Sta Rosa
Juticalpa
Quezaltenango
Guatemala
Bonanza
Comayagua
Tegucigalpa
Pto Cabezas
I. de Providencia (Col.)
Escuintla
Sta Ana
San Salvador
San José
Prinzapolca
Sonsonate
La Unión
Cord.Isabelia
EL SALVADOR
S Miguel
Rio Grande
I. de San Andrés (Col.)
G.de Fonseca
Matagalpa
NICARAGUA
Is del Maíz (Nic. & U.S.A.)
Chinandega
León
L. de Managua
Bluefields
Managua
Granada
Masaya
L. de Nicaragua
San Juan del Sur
San Juan
San Juan del Norte
G. de Papagayo
COSTA RICA
Pta S. Blas
Pen. de Nicoya
Puntarenas
Alajuela
Limón
G.de los Mosquitos
Colón
San José
Cartago
L.de Chiriquí
Panamá
PANAMA
G.de Nicoya
La Chorrera
Arch.de las Perlas
Pto Cortés
David
Pen. de Osa
Golfo de Panamá
G.Dulce
Pto Armuelles
Santiago
Chitré
G. de Chiriquí
Pen. de Azuero
Pta Solano
30
10
90
80
C
D
E
1
2
3
4

FLORIDA
Miami
Naples
Hollywood
Ft Lauderdale
Pompano Beach
Delray Beach
L.Worth
Palm Beach
Belle Glade
The Everglades
Florida Bay
Florida Keys
Key West
Marquesas Keys
Straits of Florida
Grand Bahama
Freeport
Marsh Harbour
Great Abaco
Dunmore Town
Eleuthera
Nicholl's Town
New Providence
Nassau
Andros
Great Bahama Bank
Kemps Bay
Cat
New Bight
San Salvador
Rum Cay
Great Exuma
Long
Deadman's Cay
Acklins
Mayaguana
Great Inagua
Lit. Inagua
Matthew Town
THE BAHAMAS
ATLANTIC
Tropic of Cancer
Cay Sal
Anguilla Cays
Habana
Guanabacoa
S.Antonio de los Baños
Güines
Matanzas
Pinar del Rio
G.de Batabano
Nueva Gerona
I.de la Juventud
(I.de Pinos)
Sagua la Grande
Santa Clara
Cienfuegos
San Juan 1156
Ciego de Avila
Morón
Arch. de Camagüey
Esmeralda
Nuevitas
Camagüey
CUBA
Victoria de las Tunas
Holguín
Banes
Jardines de la Reina
Sta Cruz del Sur
G.de Guacanayabo
Manzanillo
Turquino 2005
C.Cruz
Sagua de Tánamo
Palma Soriano
Baracoa
Guantánamo
Santiago de Cuba
Windward Passage
GREATER ANTILLES
Little Cayman
Cayman Islands (U.K.)
Cayman Brac
Grand Cayman
CAYMAN TRENCH
HAITI
Port-de-Pai
Cap-Haïtien
I.de la Gonâve
Anse d'Hainault
Massif de la Hotte
Les Cayes
Jacmel
Port-au-Prince
Montego Bay
Savanna la Mar
Mandeville
Blue Mtn Pk 2256
Port Antonio
Spanish Town
Kingston
JAMAICA
Jamaica Channel
Swan I. (Hond.)
Pedro Cays (Jam.)
CARIBBEAN SEA
S.Negril Point
Savanna la Mar
Brus Laguna
Lag.de Caratasca
Caratasca
HONDURAS
Cabo Gracias à Dios
Coco
Waspán
Cayos Mistiko
Puerto Cabezas
Bonanza
La Luz
Prinzapolca
Rio Grande
L.de Perlas
NICARAGUA
Bluefields
I.de Providencia (Col.)
I.de San Andres (Col.)
Is del Maíz (Nic. & U.S.A.)
San Juan del Norte
Sa Juan
Viejo
COSTA RICA
Alajuela
Heredia
Limón
San José
Cartago
Chirripo 3820
B.de Coronado
Palmar Sur
Volcán Barú 3477
L.de Chiriqui
G.de los Mosquitos
PANAMA
Panama Canal
Colón
Panamá
La Chorrera
Golfo del Darién
Ríohacha
Sta Marta
Barranquilla
Ciénaga
Soledad
Sabanalarga
5775
Sa Nevada de Sta Marta
Cartagena
Valledupar
Magdalena
S. Onofore
Plato
Sincelejo
El Banco
Catatumbo
COLOMBIA
85
80
75
25
20
15
10
1
2
3
4
5
A
B
C
G

1:10M 0 100 200 300 400 km 0 100 200 mls

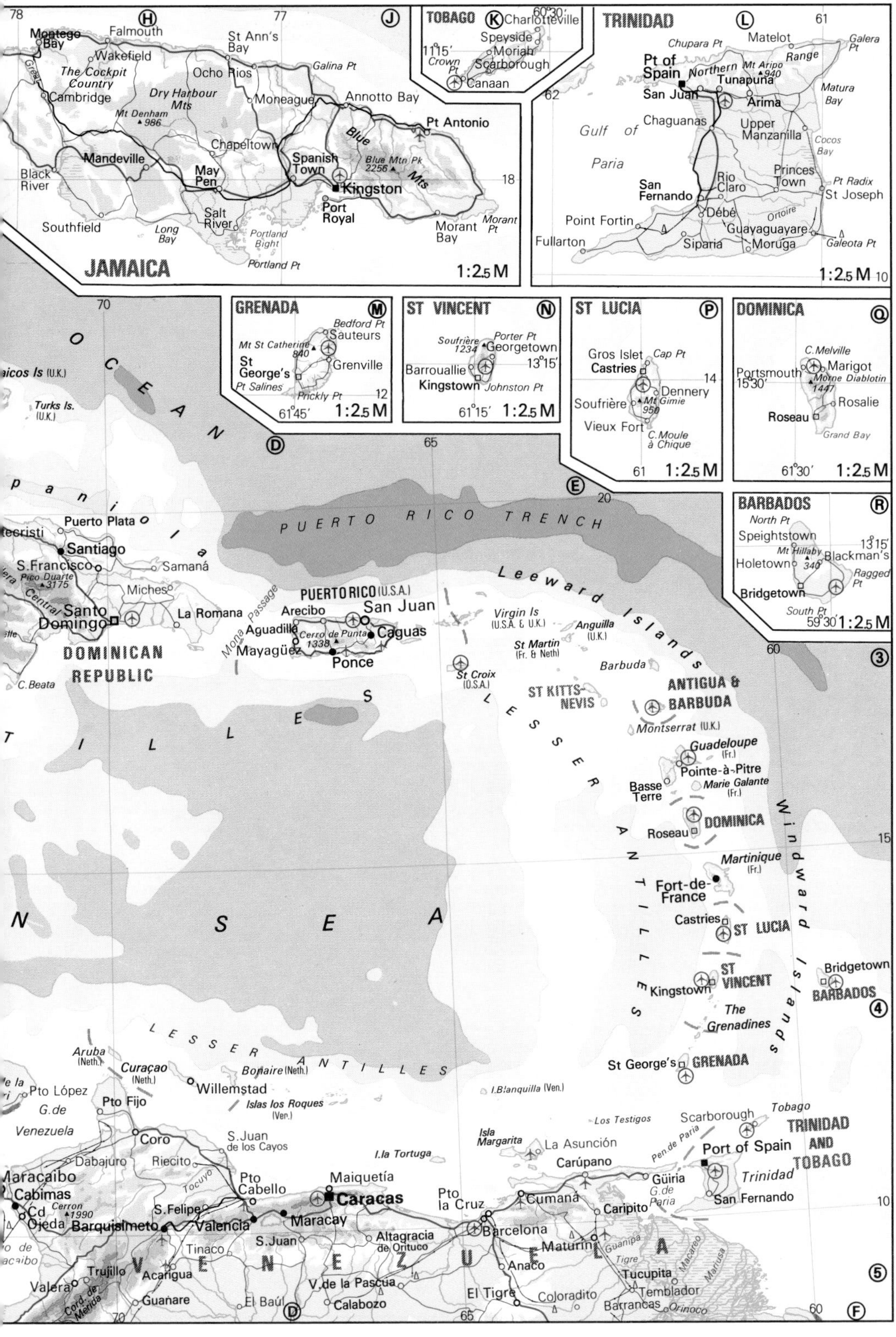

1:40M

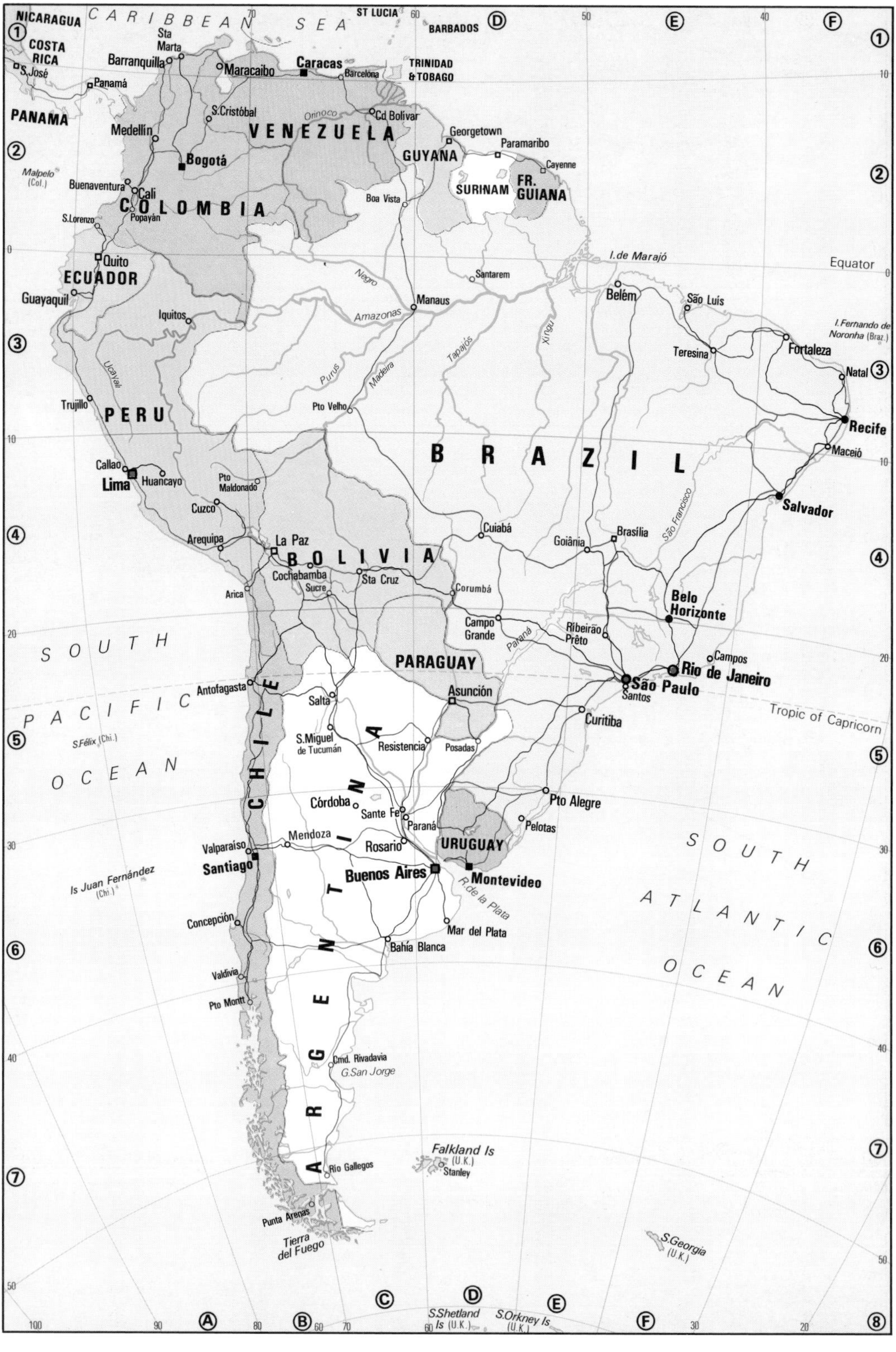
0 400 800 1200 1600 km
0 400 800 mls
CARIBBEAN SEA
NICARAGUA
COSTA RICA
S.José
Panamá
PANAMA
ST LUCIA
BARBADOS
TRINIDAD & TOBAGO
Sta Marta
Barranquilla
Maracaibo
Caracas
Barcelona
Orinoco
Cd Bolívar
S.Cristóbal
Medellín
VENEZUELA
Georgetown
Paramaribo
Cayenne
GUYANA
SURINAM
FR. GUIANA
Bogotá
Malpelo (Col.)
Buenaventura
Cali
Popayán
COLOMBIA
Boa Vista
S.Lorenzo
Quito
ECUADOR
Guayaquil
I.de Marajó
Equator
Santarem
Negro
Belém
São Luís
Manaus
Amazonas
Iquitos
Xingu
Tapajós
I.Fernando de Noronha (Braz.)
Fortaleza
Teresina
Natal
Ucayali
Purus
Madeira
Trujillo
Pto Velho
PERU
Recife
Maceió
BRAZIL
Callao
Lima
Huancayo
Pto Maldonado
Salvador
Cuzco
São Francisco
Cuiabá
Brasília
Goiânia
Arequipa
La Paz
BOLIVIA
Cochabamba
Sucre
Sta Cruz
Corumbá
Arica
Belo Horizonte
Campo Grande
Ribeirão Prêto
Paraná
SOUTH PACIFIC OCEAN
Campos
PARAGUAY
Rio de Janeiro
São Paulo
Santos
Antofagasta
Asunción
Salta
Tropic of Capricorn
Curitiba
S.Félix (Chi.)
S.Miguel de Tucumán
Resistencia
Posadas
CHILE
Pto Alegre
Córdoba
Sante Fe
Paraná
Pelotas
Mendoza
Valparaíso
Rosario
URUGUAY
Santiago
Buenos Aires
Montevideo
Is Juan Fernández (Chi.)
R.de la Plata
SOUTH ATLANTIC OCEAN
Concepción
Mar del Plata
Bahía Blanca
ARGENTINA
Valdivia
Pto Montt
Cmd. Rivadavia
G.San Jorge
Falkland Is (U.K.)
Stanley
Rio Gallegos
Punta Arenas
Tierra del Fuego
S.Georgia (U.K.)
S.Shetland Is (U.K.)
S.Orkney Is (U.K.)

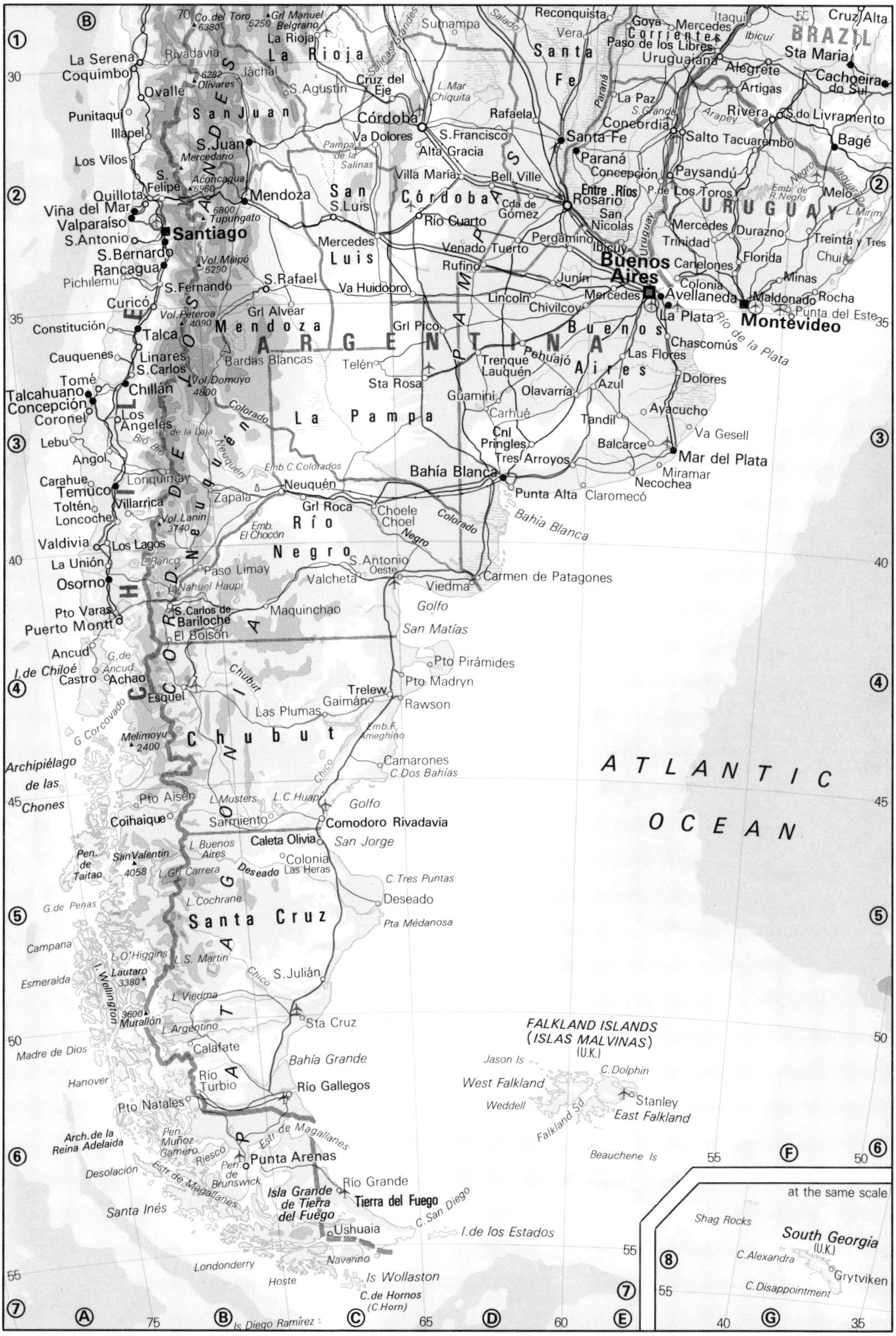
BRAZIL
ARGENTINA
URUGUAY
ATLANTIC
OCEAN
CHILE
ANDES
CORDILLERA DEL NEUQUÉN
PAMPAS
PATAGONIA
La Rioja
San Juan
Santa Fe
Córdoba
San Luis
Mendoza
La Pampa
Buenos Aires
Entre Ríos
Río Negro
Neuquén
Chubut
Santa Cruz
Reconquista
Goya
Corrientes
Mercedes
Paso de los Libres
Uruguaiana
Alegrete
Itaqui
Ibicuí
Cruz Alta
Sta Maria
Cachoeira do Sul
Artigas
Rivera
S.do Livramento
Bagé
Salto
Tacuarembó
Paysandú
Melo
Los Toros
Durazno
Mercedes
Trinidad
Florida
Treinta y Tres
Chuí
Canelones
Minas
Colonia
Maldonado
Rocha
Punta del Este
Montevideo
Río de la Plata
La Serena
Coquimbo
Ovalle
Punitaqui
Illapel
Los Vilos
S. Felipe
Quillota
Viña del Mar
Valparaíso
S.Antonio
Santiago
S.Bernardo
Rancagua
Pichilemu
S.Fernando
Curicó
Constitución
Talca
Cauquenes
Linares
S.Carlos
Chillán
Tomé
Talcahuano
Concepción
Coronel
Los Angeles
Lebu
Angol
Carahue
Temuco
Toltén
Villarrica
Loncoche
Valdivia
Los Lagos
La Unión
Osorno
Pto Varas
Puerto Montt
Ancud
I.de Chiloé
Castro
Achao
G.de Ancud
G. Corcovado
Archipiélago de las Chones
Pto Aisén
Coihaique
Pen. de Taitao
G.de Penas
Campana
Esmeralda
I. Wellington
Madre de Dios
Hanover
Pto Natales
Arch.de la Reina Adelaida
Pen. Muñoz Gamero
Riesco
Pen. de Brunswick
Punta Arenas
Desolación
Santa Inés
Estr. de Magallanes
Londonderry
Hoste
Navarino
Is Wollaston
C.de Hornos (C.Horn)
Is Diego Ramírez
Ushuaia
Isla Grande de Tierra del Fuego
Tierra del Fuego
Río Grande
C. San Diego
I.de los Estados
Co.del Toro 6380
Grl Manuel Belgrano 6250
Rivadavia
Jáchal
6282 Olivares
S.Agustín
Sumampa
Salinas Grandes
Salado
Vera
Cruz del Eje
L.Mar Chiquita
Rafaela
Paraná
La Paz
Concordia
S.Grande
Arapey
Va Dolores
S.Francisco
Alta Gracia
Santa Fe
Paraná
Concepción
Pampa de la Salinas
S.Juan
Mercedario
Aconcagua 6960
Mendoza
6800 Tupungato
Villa María
Bell Ville
Rosario
Cda de Gómez
San Nicolás
S.Luis
Río Cuarto
Pergamino
Ibicuy
Uruguay
Buenos Aires
Venado Tuerto
Mercedes
Rufino
Vol.Maipó 5290
S.Rafael
Va Huidobro
Junín
Lincoln
Chivilcoy
Avellaneda
La Plata
Grl Alvear
Vol.Peteroa 4090
Grl Pico
Pehuajó
Chascomús
Las Flores
Bardas Blancas
Telén
Trenque Lauquén
Sta Rosa
Dolores
Vol.Domuyo 4800
Guaminí
Olavarría
Azul
Colorado
Carhué
Tandil
Ayacucho
L.de la Laja
Bío Bío
Cnl Pringles
Va Gesell
Balcarce
Tres Arroyos
Mar del Plata
Emb.C.Colorados
Miramar
Bahía Blanca
Necochea
Lonquimay
Neuquén
Punta Alta
Claromecó
Zapala
Grl Roca
Choele Choel
Vol.Lanin 3740
Emb. El Chocón
Colorado
Bahía Blanca
Negro
L.Ranco
Paso Limay
S.Antonio Oeste
Carmen de Patagones
L.Nahuel Haupi
Valcheta
Viedma
S.Carlos de Bariloche
Maquinchao
Golfo San Matías
El Bolsón
Pto Pirámides
Pto Madryn
Chubut
Trelew
Gaimán
Rawson
Esquel
Las Plumas
Emb.F. Ameghino
Melimoyu 2400
Camarones
C.Dos Bahías
Chico
L.Musters
L.C.Huapí
Golfo San Jorge
Sarmiento
Comodoro Rivadavia
Caleta Olivia
L.Buenos Aires
San Valentin 4058
Colonia Las Heras
L.Gfl Carrera
Deseado
C.Tres Puntas
L.Cochrane
Pta Médanosa
L.O'Higgins
L.S. Martin
Lautaro 3380
Chico
S.Julián
L.Viedma
3600 Murallón
L.Argentino
Sta Cruz
Calafate
Bahía Grande
Rio Turbio
Río Gallegos
FALKLAND ISLANDS (ISLAS MALVINAS) (U.K.)
Jason Is
C.Dolphin
West Falkland
Weddell
Stanley
East Falkland
Falkland Sd
Beauchene Is
at the same scale
Shag Rocks
South Georgia (U.K.)
C.Alexandra
Grytviken
C.Disappointment

1:15M

0 200 400 km
0 100 200

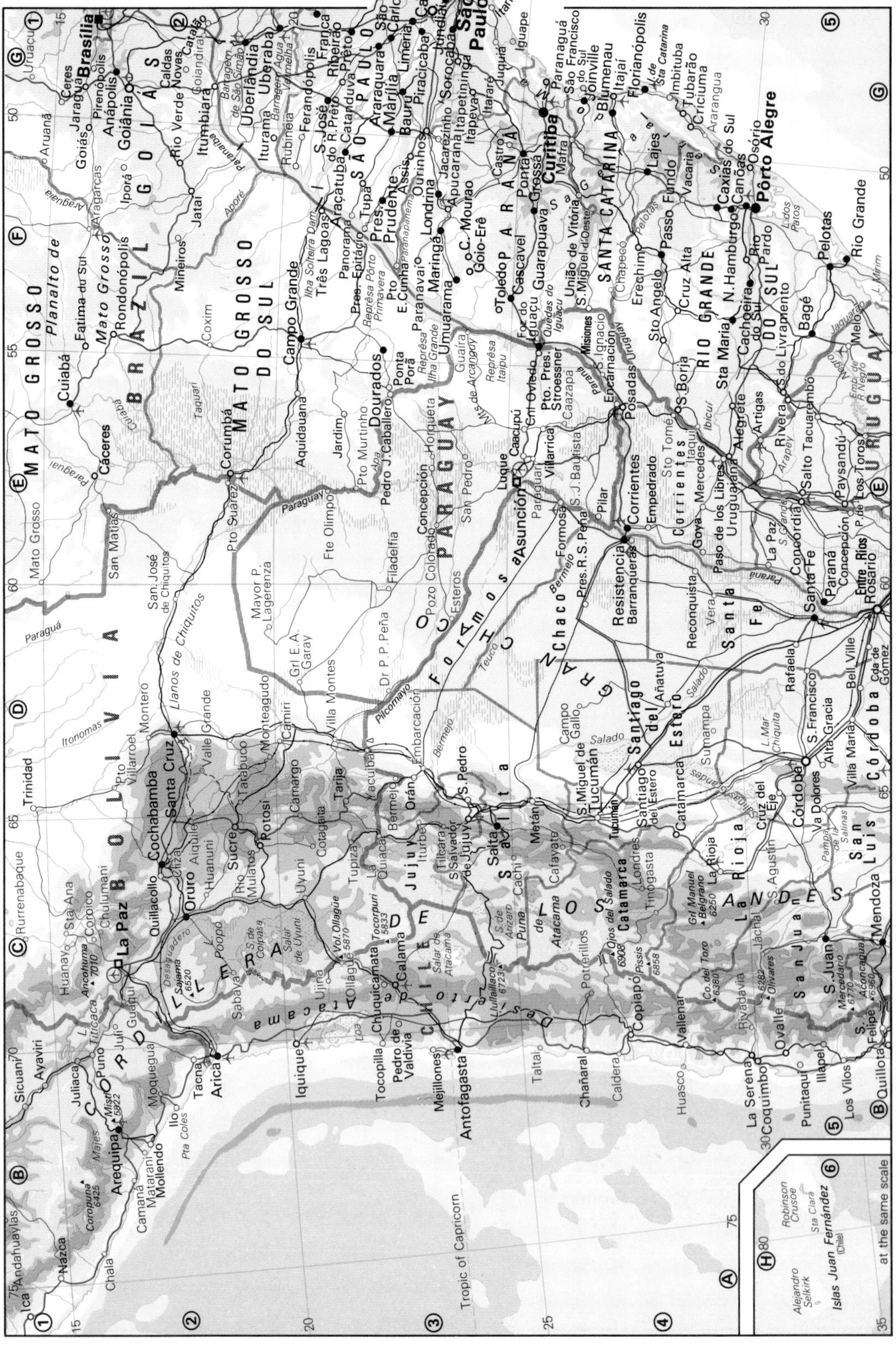
MATO GROSSO
Planalto de Mato Grosso
MATO GROSSO DO SUL
BRAZIL
GOIÁS
SÃO PAULO
PARANÁ
SANTA CATARINA
RIO GRANDE DO SUL
URUGUAY
PARAGUAY
BOLIVIA
CORDILLERA
DE LOS ANDES
GRAN CHACO
Chaco
Formosa
Santiago del Estero
Santa Fe
Corrientes
Entre Rios
Córdoba
San Luis
San Juan
La Rioja
Catamarca
Jujuy
Salta
Tucumán
Misiones
CHILE
Desierto de Atacama
Brasília
Goiânia
Anápolis
Uberlândia
Uberaba
Ribeirão Prêto
Campinas
São Paulo
Santos
Sorocaba
Curitiba
Florianópolis
Pôrto Alegre
Pelotas
Rio Grande
Londrina
Maringá
Campo Grande
Corumbá
Cuiabá
Cáceres
Asunción
Concepción
Encarnación
Posadas
Resistencia
Corrientes
Rosario
Paraná
Santa Fe
Santa Cruz
Cochabamba
Sucre
Potosí
Oruro
La Paz
Tarija
Arica
Iquique
Antofagasta
Tocopilla
Calama
Copiapó
Coquimbo
La Serena
Arequipa
Puno
Tacna
Tropic of Capricorn
Islas Juan Fernández (Chile)
Robinson Crusoe
Alejandro Selkirk
at the same scale

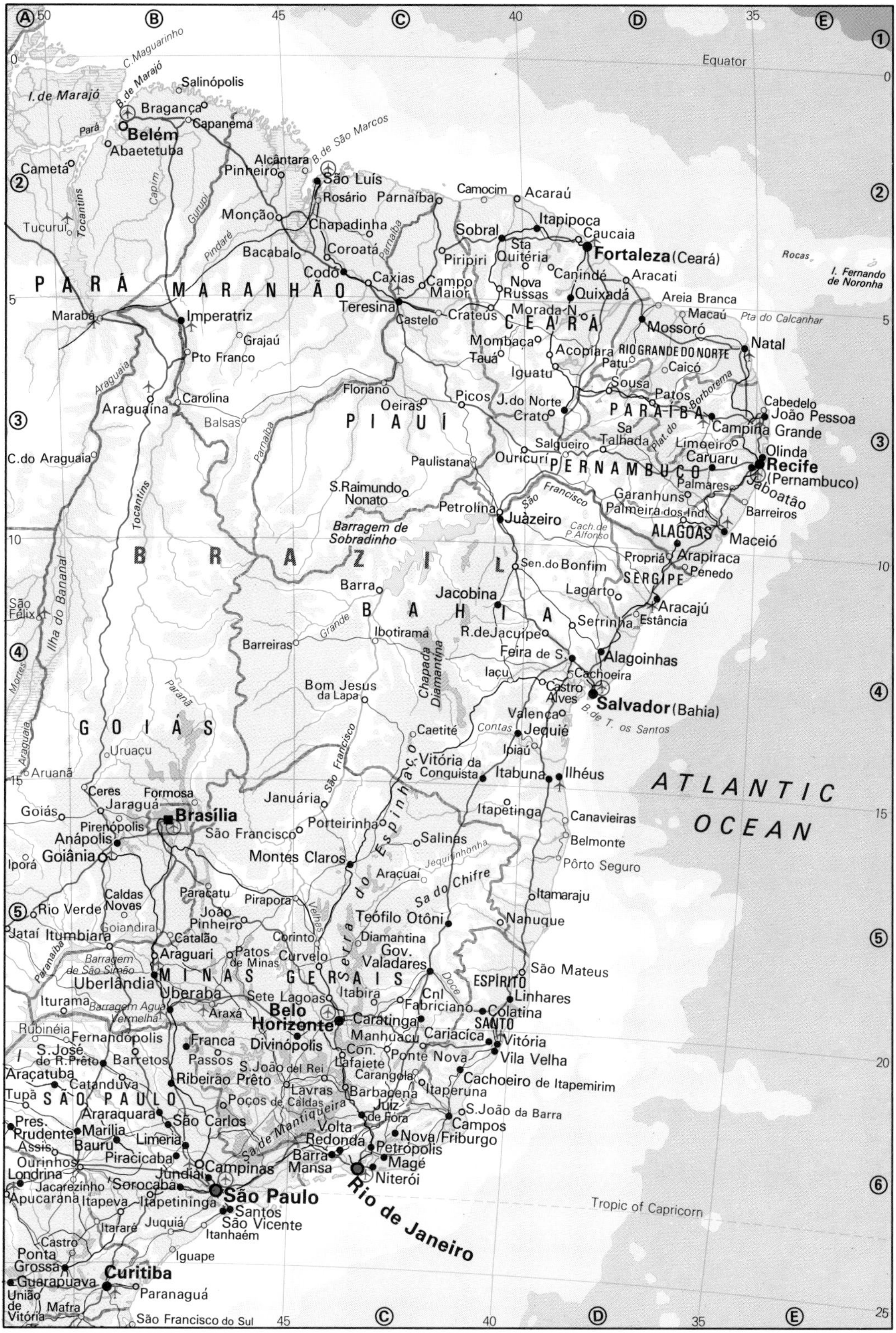
A
B
C
D
E
1
2
3
4
5
6
50
45
40
35
0
5
10
15
20
25
Equator
C. Maguarinho
I. de Marajó
B. de Marajó
Salinópolis
Bragança
Pará
Belém
Capanema
Abaetetuba
B. de São Marcos
Alcântara
Pinheiro
São Luís
Cametá
Capim
Tocantins
Gurupi
Rosário
Parnaíba
Camocim
Acaraú
Moncão
Chapadinha
Tucuruí
Pindaré
Bacabal
Coroatá
Sobral
Itapipoca
Caucaia
Fortaleza (Ceará)
Rocas
I. Fernando de Noronha
Piripiri
Sta Quitéria
Codó
Caxias
Campo Maior
Canindé
Aracati
P A R Á
M A R A N H Ã O
Nova Russas
Quixadá
Teresina
Areia Branca
Marabá
Imperatriz
Castelo
Crateús
Morada Nova
Macaú
Pta do Calcanhar
C E A R Á
Mossoró
Grajaú
Mombaça
Natal
Pto Franco
Tauá
Acopiara
RIO GRANDE DO NORTE
Patu
Caicó
Iguatu
Borborema
Araguaia
Carolina
Floriano
Sousa
Patos
Cabedelo
Picos
J. do Norte
João Pessoa
Araguaína
Oeiras
Crato
P A R A Í B A
Campina Grande
Balsas
P I A U Í
Sa Talhada
Plat. do Borborema
Salgueiro
Limoeiro
Olinda
C. do Araguaia
Paulistana
Ouricuri
Caruaru
Recife (Pernambuco)
P E R N A M B U C O
Palmares
Jaboatão
S. Raimundo Nonato
São Francisco
Garanhuns
Petrolina
Juàzeiro
Palmeira dos Índ.
Barreiros
Barragem de Sobradinho
Cach. de P. Alfonso
ALAGOAS
Maceió
B R A Z I L
Propriá
Arapiraca
Sen. do Bonfim
SERGIPE
Penedo
Barra
Jacobina
Lagarto
São Félix
Ilha do Bananal
B A H I A
Aracajú
Estância
Serrinha
Ibotirama
R. de Jacuípe
Grande
Barreiras
Feira de S.
Alagoinhas
Chapada Diamantina
Iaçu
Cachoeira
Mortes
Bom Jesus da Lapa
Castro Alves
Salvador (Bahia)
Paranã
Valença
B. de T. os Santos
G O I Á S
Caetité
Contas
Jequié
São Francisco
Ipiaú
Uruaçu
Vitória da Conquista
Itabuna
Ilhéus
Araguaia
Aruanã
A T L A N T I C
O C E A N
Ceres
Formosa
Jaraguá
Januária
Itapetinga
Goiás
Brasília
Canavieiras
Pirenópolis
São Francisco
Porteirinha
Anápolis
Salinas
Belmonte
Serra do Espinhaço
Goiânia
Montes Claros
Jequitinhonha
Iporá
Pôrto Seguro
Araçuaí
Sa do Chifre
Caldas Novas
Paracatu
Pirapora
Itamaraju
Rio Verde
João Pinheiro
Velhas
Teófilo Otôni
Goiandira
Nanuque
Jataí
Itumbiara
Catalão
Corinto
Diamantina
Paranaíba
Barragem de São Simão
Araguari
Patos de Minas
Curvelo
Gov. Valadares
São Mateus
Serra do Espinhaço
Uberlândia
M I N A S G E R A I S
Doce
ESPÍRITO SANTO
Iturama
Barragem Agua Vermelha
Uberaba
Sete Lagoas
Itabira
Cnl Fabriciano
Linhares
Araxá
Belo Horizonte
Caratinga
Colatina
Rubinéia
Fernandópolis
Manhuaçu
Cariacíca
Vitória
S. José do R. Prêto
Franca
Divinópolis
Con. Lafaiete
Ponte Nova
Vila Velha
Barretos
Passos
S. João del Rei
Araçatuba
Catanduva
Ribeirão Prêto
Carangola
Cachoeiro de Itapemirim
Lavras
Itaperuna
Tupã
S Ã O P A U L O
Poços de Caldas
Barbacena
Juiz de Fora
S. João da Barra
Araraquara
São Carlos
Sa de Mantiqueira
Campos
Pres. Prudente
Marília
Limeira
Volta Redonda
Nova Friburgo
Assis
Bauru
Piracicaba
Barra Mansa
Petrópolis
Ourinhos
Jundiaí
Campinas
Magé
Londrina
Niterói
Jacarezinho
Sorocaba
São Paulo
Rio de Janeiro
Apucarana
Itapeva
Itapetininga
Santos
Tropic of Capricorn
São Vicente
Itararé
Juquiá
Itanhaém
Castro
Ponta Grossa
Iguape
Curitiba
Guarapuava
Paranaguá
União da Vitória
Mafra
São Francisco do Sul

NICARAGUA
Bluefields
S.Carlos
I. de Perlas
I.de San Andrés (Col.)
Alajuela
Heredia
Limón
San José
Cartago
Chirripó Grande 3815
COSTA RICA
Barú 3475
David
Pto Armuelles
G.Dulce
G.de Chiriquí
I. Coiba
Pta Mariato
L.de Chiriquí
G.de los Mosquitos
Colón
Panamá
La Chorrera
PANAMA
Santiago
Chitré
Pen.de Azuero
Arch.de las Perlas
G.de Panamá
G.de Uraba
Turbo
La Palma
Guapá
Atrato
Sinú
Pta Gallinas
Pen.de Guajira
Pto Fijo
G.de Venezuela
Aruba
Curaçao (Neth.)
Bonaire
Willemstad
Is Los Roques (Ven.)
Ríohacha
Sta Marta
Ciénaga
Maicao
Sa Nevada de Sta Marta 5800
Barranquilla
Cartagena
Valledupar
Machiques
Maracaibo
Cabimas
L.de Maracaibo
Cd Ojeda
Trujillo
Valera
Coro
Riecito
Tocuyo
Pto Cabello
Maiquetía
Caracas
Valencia
Maracay
Barquisimeto
S.Juan
Acarigua
Guanare
V.de la Pascua
Mérida
Cord. de Mérida
Bolívar 5775
Barinas
S.Fernando
Apure
LLANOS
S.Jacinto
Sincelejo
El Banco
Magangué
Montería
Ocaña
Cúcuta
San Cristóbal
Pamplona
Caucasia
Cauca
Magdalena
Barrancabermeja
Bucaramanga
Arauca
Yarumal
Bello
Pto Berrio
Málaga
Itagui
Medellín
Barbosa
Sogamoso
Quibdó
C.Corrientes
Occidental
Oriental
Manizales
Tolima 5215
Tunja
Chocontá
Orocué
Meta
Pto Carreño
Orinoco
Pto Ayacucho
Vichada
Ventuari
Pereira
Cartago
Armenia
Bogotá
Ibagué
Tuluá
Buga
Girardot
Villavicencio
Buenaventura
G.de Tortugas
Palmira
Cali
Granada
Malpelo (Col.)
COLOMBIA
Guaviare
Salto Angostura
Inírida
Casiquiare
Guania
Negro
Santander
Huila 5750
Neiva
Popayán
Vol. Puracé 4700
Pto Rico
Calamar
Pitalito
Florencia
Tumaco
El Diviso
Pasto
Belén
Yari
Vaupés
Mitú
Cucuí
S.Lorenzo
Ipiales
Mocoa
Esmeraldas
Tulcán
Pto Asis
Apaporis
Içana
Ibarra
Otavalo
Cojimíes
Equator
Quito
Leguizamo
Putumayo
Lago Agrio
Jama
Coca
Napo
Salto Grande
Caquetá
Cotopaxi 5896
Tena
Manta
Chone
Ambato
C. San Lorenzo
Jipijapa
ECUADOR
Guaranda
Chimborazo 6310
Japurá
Babahoyo
Riobamba
Guayaquil
Milagro
Macas
La Libertad
Playas
I.Puná
Azogues
Cuenca
Gualaceo
Pastaza
Tigre
Içá
Solimões (Amazonas)
Iquitos
Letícia
Tabatinga
G.de Guayaquil
Tumbes
Machala
Zaruma
Loja
Santiago
Zamora
Caxias
Yavari (Javari)
Jutaí
Juruá
Marañón
Talara
Negritos
Chira
Sullana
Elvira
SELVAS
AMAZONAS
Paita
Piura
Chulucanas
Huancabamba
Catacaos
Yurimaguas
Ucayali
Tapauá
Pta Aguja
Jaén
Moyobamba
Tarapoto
Ferreñafe
Chachapoyas
Huallaga
Lambayeque
Chiclayo
Cajamarca
Cruzeiro do Sul
Chepén
Cajabamba
Pacasmayo
Huamachuco
Feijó
Otusco
Pucallpa
Purus
Bôca do Acre
PACIFIC OCEAN
Trujillo
Pomabamba
Huallanca
Huascarán 6768
Tingo María
ACRE
Sena Madureira
Chimbote
Huaráz
La Unión
Rio Branco
Casma
Huánuco
CORD. DE LOS ANDES
Abunã
Huarmey
Oxapampa
Brasiléia
Riberalta
Cobija
Porvenir
Pativilca
Barranca
Huacho
Cerro de Pasco
La Merced
Tarma
PERU
Parque Nac. de Manú
Madre de Dios
La Oroya
Mantaro
Jauja
Acobamba
Ancón
Callao
Lima
Huancayo
Pto Maldonado
Pto Heath
L.Rogaguado
Huancavelica
Quillabamba
MACHU PICCHU
Ayacucho
Apurímac
Cuzco
Beni
Chincha Alta
Abancay
Pisco
Andahuaylas
Sicuani
Pen.de Paracas
Ica
Ayaviri
Nazca
BOLIVIA
Rurrenabaque
ISLAS GALÁPAGOS (ARCHIPIÉLAGO DO COLÓN) (Equ.)
Culpepper
Wenman
Pinta
Marchena
Genovesa
Fernandina
San Salvador
Santa Cruz
Isabela
Baquerizo Moreno
San Cristóbal
Santa María
Española
at the same scale

GRENADA
St George's
I. de Margarita
Tortuga
La Asunción
Pen. de Paria
Tobago
Carúpano
Güiria
Port of Spain
TRINIDAD AND TOBAGO
Cumana
Cruz
Caripito
G. de Paria
Trinidad
San Fernando
Anaco
Maturín
Zarara
El Tigre
Tigre
Tucupita
Barrancas
Cd Bolívar
Orinoco
Cd Guayana
Upata
Mabaruma
Cd Piar
Emb. de Guri
EZUELA
Charity
Suddie
Leguan I.
La Paragua
El Dorado
Paragua
Salto del Angel
V. en Hoop
Georgetown
Bartica
New Amsterdam
Nieuw Amsterdam
Paramaribo
Marienburg
San Maigualida
La Gran Sabana
Roraima 2180
Linden
Kaieteur Falls
Nieuw Nickerie
Totness
Albina
Sinnamary
I. du Diable (Devil's I.)
Apoera
Witagron
Kourou
Cayenne
Sta Elena
GUYANA
Blommesteinmeer
Maroni
Cabo Orange
Sa Pacaraima
Ireng
Corantijn
SURINAM
FRENCH GUIANA
Julianatop 1280
Bonfim
Oiapoque
Sa Parima
Lethem
Boa Vista
Essequibo
Litani
Orinoco
RORAIMA
Caracaraí
Serra Tumucumaque
Amapá
Ilha de Maracá
AMAPÁ
Branco
Sa do Navio
Jari
Macapá
Tapurucuara
Pto Santana
Paru
C. Maguarinho
B. de Marajó
I. de Marajó
Salinópolis
Negro
Bragança
Capanema
Oriximiná
Obidos
Amazonas
Pará
Belém
Monte Alegre
Xingu
Abaetetuba
Santarem
Cametá
Manaus
Altamira
Manacapuru
Careiro
Itacoatiara
Capim
Tefé
Aveíro
Tucuruí
Tocantins
Gurupi
AZONAS
PARÁ
Tapajós
Itaituba
Parque Nacional Amazonia
Pimenta
Purus
Coari
Madeira
BRAZIL
Marabá
Imperatriz
Aripuanã
Iriri
Jacareacanga
S. Félix
Pto Franco
Araguaia
Lábrea
Humaitá
Prainha
Xingu
Carolina
Araguaína
Serra do Cachimbo
Madeira
Pôrto Velho
C. do Araguaia
Aripuanã
Teles Pires
Cachimbo
Jiparaná
Abunã
T. Roosevelt
Tocantins
Juruena
Guajará-Mirim
Rondônia
Ilha do Bananal
Mamoré
RONDÔNIA
Arinos
Sa dos Caiabis
Sa Formosa
Serra dos Parecis
São Félix
Guaporé
Itonomas
Vilhena
Pto Artur
Paranã
MATO GROSSO
Iténez
VIA
Paraguá
Mortes
Araguaia
GOIÁS
Trinidad
Mato Grosso
Uruaçu
Aruanã

Santa Fe
Entre Ríos
Córdoba
San Luis
Mendoza
San Juan
La Rioja
La Pampa
Buenos Aires
Neuquén
Buenos Aires
La Plata
Rosario
Santa Fe
Paraná
Córdoba
Río Cuarto
Mendoza
San Juan
Santiago
Valparaíso
Viña del Mar
Concepción
Talcahuano
Talca
Chillán
Rancagua
Temuco
Mar del Plata
Bahía Blanca
Santa Rosa
Neuquén
San Rafael
Concordia
Uruguay
Montevideo
OCEANO PACIFICO

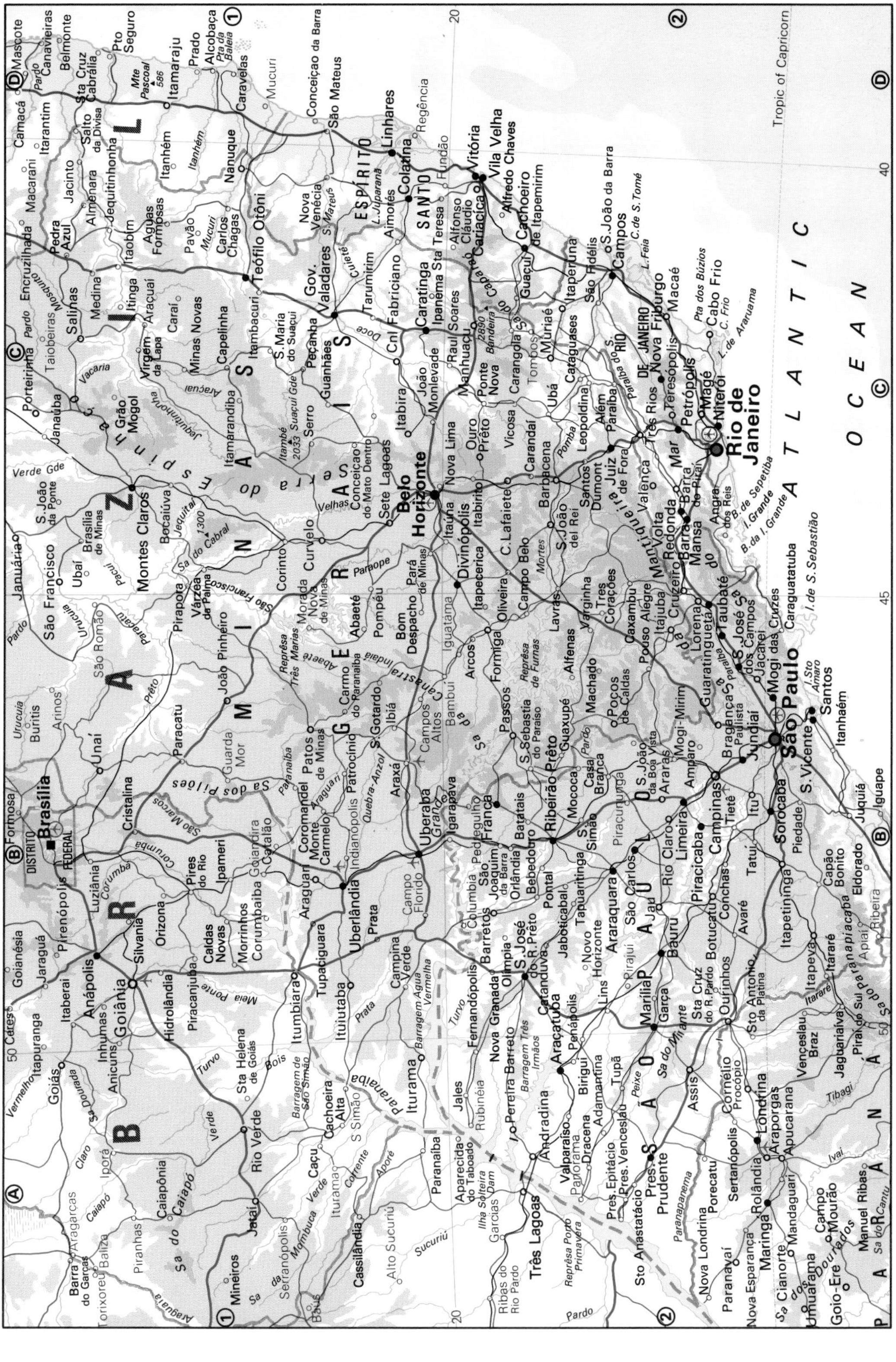
B R A Z I L
M I N A S G E R A I S
ESPÍRITO SANTO
RIO DE JANEIRO
S Ã O P A U L O
P A R A N Á
A T L A N T I C
O C E A N
Tropic of Capricorn
DISTRITO FEDERAL
Brasília
Belo Horizonte
Rio de Janeiro
São Paulo
Goiânia
Anápolis
Uberlândia
Uberaba
Ribeirão Prêto
Campinas
Santos
Vitória
Vila Velha
Niterói
Juiz de Fora
Montes Claros
Gov. Valadares
Campos
Londrina
Maringá
Bauru
Três Lagoas
Linhares
Colatina
Teófilo Otôni
Divinópolis
Sorocaba
Jundiaí
Taubaté
Petrópolis
Volta Redonda
Barra Mansa
Franca
Araraquara
S. José do R. Prêto
Presidente Prudente
Marília
Araçatuba
Ipatinga
Caratinga
Cabo Frio
Macaé
Nova Friburgo
Paranaíba
Sa do Espinhaço
Serra da Mantiqueira
Serra da Canastra
Represa de Furnas
Represa Três Marias
Paranaíba
Paraná
Grande
São Francisco
Doce
Tietê
Paranapanema
Jequitinhonha

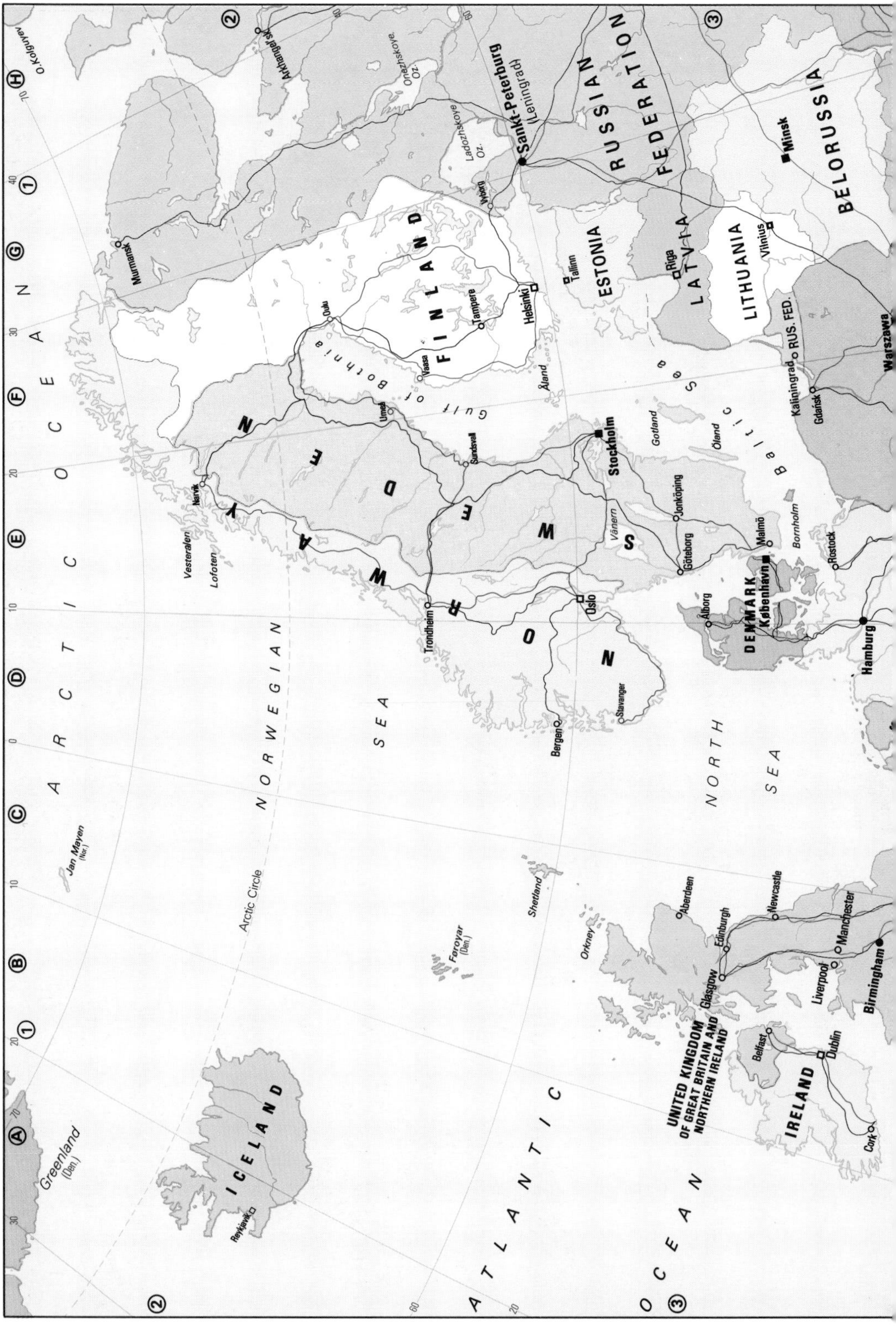
ARCTIC OCEAN
NORWEGIAN SEA
NORTH SEA
ATLANTIC OCEAN
Baltic Sea
Gulf of Bothnia
Arctic Circle
ICELAND
Reykjavík
Greenland (Den.)
Jan Mayen (Nor.)
Føroyar (Den.)
Shetland
Orkney
UNITED KINGDOM OF GREAT BRITAIN AND NORTHERN IRELAND
IRELAND
Aberdeen
Edinburgh
Glasgow
Newcastle
Manchester
Liverpool
Birmingham
Belfast
Dublin
Cork
NORWAY
SWEDEN
FINLAND
DENMARK
Vesterålen
Lofoten
Narvik
Trondheim
Bergen
Stavanger
Oslo
Vänern
Göteborg
Jönköping
Malmö
Stockholm
Sundsvall
Umeå
Vaasa
Oulu
Tampere
Helsinki
Åland
Gotland
Öland
Bornholm
Ålborg
København
Hamburg
Rostock
Gdańsk
Kaliningrad
RUS. FED.
Warszawa
ESTONIA
Tallinn
LATVIA
Riga
LITHUANIA
Vilnius
BELORUSSIA
Minsk
RUSSIAN FEDERATION
Sankt-Peterburg (Leningrad)
Vyborg
Ladozhskoye Oz.
Onezhskoye Oz.
Murmansk
Arkhangel'sk
o. Kolguyev

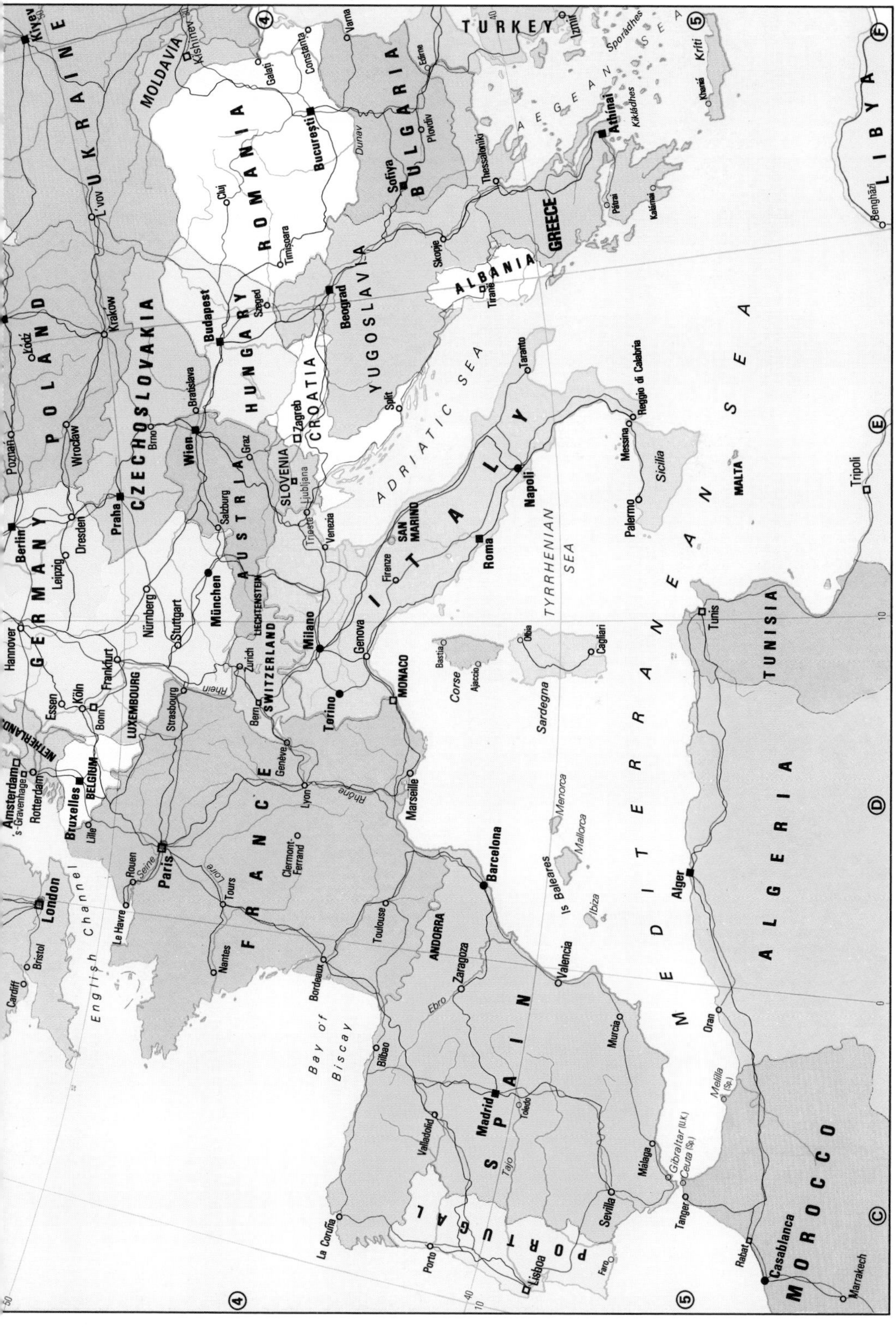
UKRAINE
Kiyev
MOLDAVIA
Kishinev
ROMANIA
Bucureşti
Cluj
Timişoara
Galaţi
Constanta
Varna
BULGARIA
Sofiya
Plovdiv
Edirne
TURKEY
Izmir
AEGEAN SEA
Sporádhes
Kikládhes
Kriti
Khaniá
Athínai
Thessaloníki
Pátrai
Kalámai
GREECE
ALBANIA
Tiranë
Skopje
YUGOSLAVIA
Beograd
Dunav
HUNGARY
Budapest
Szeged
CROATIA
Zagreb
Split
SLOVENIA
Ljubljana
POLAND
Łódź
Kraków
Wrocław
Poznań
L'vov
CZECHOSLOVAKIA
Praha
Brno
Bratislava
AUSTRIA
Wien
Graz
Salzburg
GERMANY
Berlin
Hannover
Leipzig
Dresden
Essen
Köln
Bonn
Frankfurt
Nürnberg
Stuttgart
München
LIECHTENSTEIN
SWITZERLAND
Zurich
Bern
Genève
Rhein
LUXEMBOURG
NETHERLANDS
Amsterdam
's-Gravenhage
Rotterdam
BELGIUM
Bruxelles
Lille
London
Bristol
Cardiff
English Channel
FRANCE
Paris
Rouen
Seine
Le Havre
Strasbourg
Lyon
Rhône
Clermont-Ferrand
Loire
Tours
Nantes
Bordeaux
Toulouse
Marseille
MONACO
Bay of Biscay
ANDORRA
SPAIN
Madrid
Barcelona
Zaragoza
Ebro
Valencia
Murcia
Bilbao
Valladolid
Toledo
Tajo
Sevilla
Málaga
Gibraltar (U.K.)
Ceuta (Sp.)
La Coruña
PORTUGAL
Porto
Lisboa
Faro
Is Baleares
Menorca
Mallorca
Ibiza
ITALY
Roma
Milano
Torino
Genova
Venezia
Trieste
Firenze
SAN MARINO
Napoli
Taranto
Reggio di Calabria
Messina
Palermo
Sicilia
ADRIATIC SEA
TYRRHENIAN SEA
Corse
Bastia
Ajaccio
Sardegna
Olbia
Cagliari
MEDITERRANEAN SEA
MALTA
Tunis
TUNISIA
Tripoli
LIBYA
Benghāzī
Alger
ALGERIA
Oran
Melilla (Sp.)
Tanger
Rabat
Casablanca
Marrakech
MOROCCO
40
50
10
0
C
D
E
F
4
5

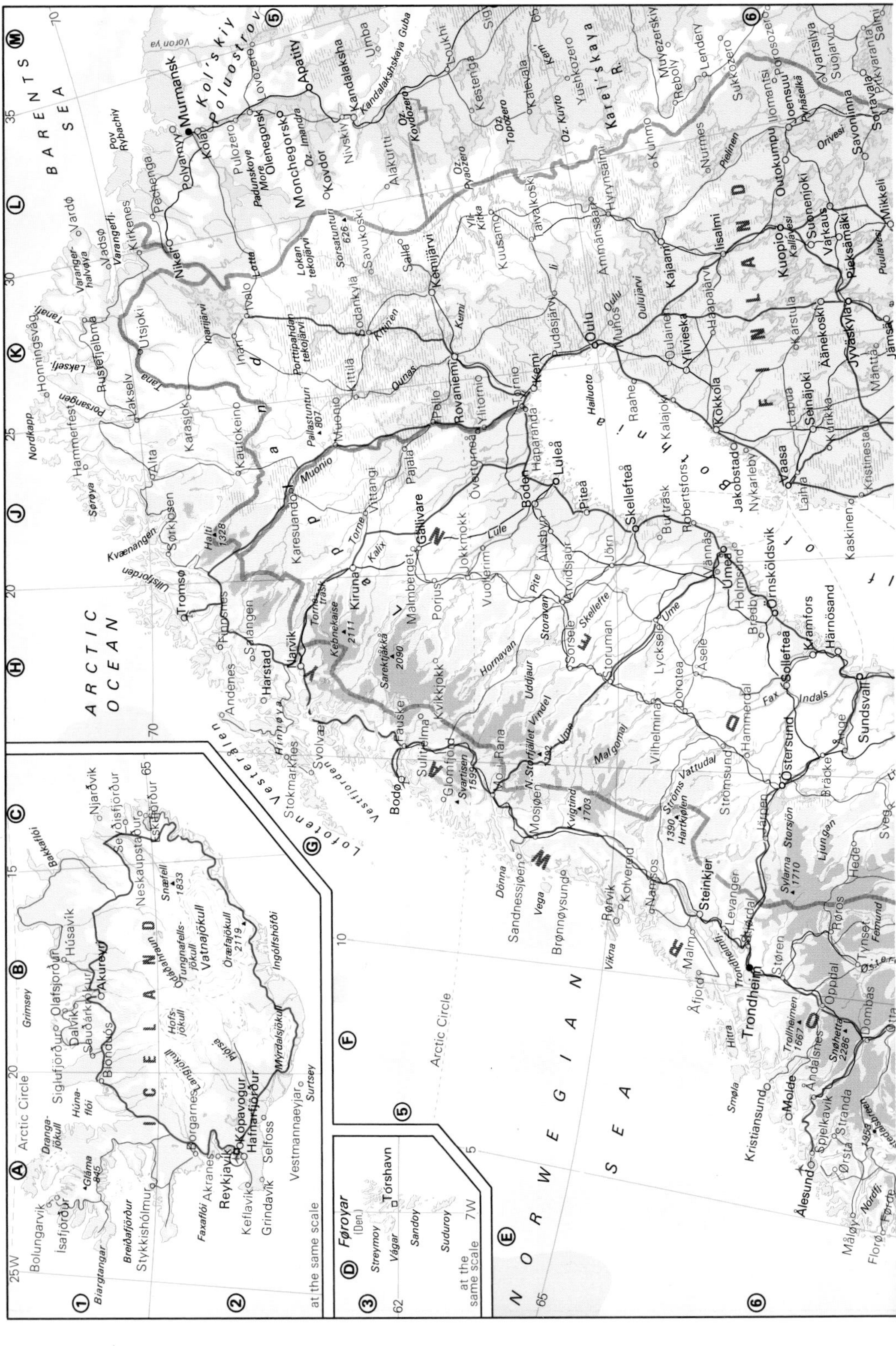
BARENTS SEA
ARCTIC OCEAN
NORWEGIAN SEA
Arctic Circle
Kol'skiy Poluostrov
Karel'skaya R.
Murmansk
Apatity
Kandalaksha
Monchegorsk
Olenegorsk
Kovdor
Polyarnyy
Kola
Pechenga
Nikel
Kirkenes
Vadsø
Vardø
Varangerfj.
Tanafj.
Laksefj.
Porsangen
Nordkapp
Honningsvåg
Hammerfest
Rustefjelbma
Lakselv
Karasjok
Kautokeino
Alta
Sørøya
Kvænangen
Ullsfjorden
Tromsø
Finnsnes
Harstad
Andenes
Narvik
Kiruna
Kebnekaise 2111
Gällivare
Malmberget
Jokkmokk
Boden
Luleå
Piteå
Skellefteå
Umeå
Örnsköldsvik
Härnösand
Sundsvall
Östersund
Storsjön
Trondheim
Steinkjer
Namsos
Mosjøen
Mo i Rana
Bodø
Svartisen 1599
Fauske
Lofoten
Vestfjorden
Vesterålen
Hinnøya
Svolvær
Stokmarknes
Molde
Kristiansund
Ålesund
Dombås
Oppdal
Røros
Snøhetta 2286
Oulu
Kemi
Tornio
Rovaniemi
Kemijärvi
Inari
Utsjoki
Ivalo
Sodankylä
Kokkola
Vaasa
Seinäjoki
Jyväskylä
Kuopio
Joensuu
Savonlinna
Mikkeli
Kajaani
Iisalmi
FINLAND
LAPLAND
Gulf of Bothnia
ICELAND
Reykjavík
Kópavogur
Hafnarfjörður
Akureyri
Húsavík
Ísafjörður
Vatnajökull
Hofsjökull
Langjökull
Mýrdalsjökull
Öræfajökull 2119
Snæfell 1833
Vestmannaeyjar
Surtsey
Grímsey
at the same scale
Føroyar (Den.)
Tórshavn
Streymoy
Vágar
Sandoy
Suðuroy
at the same scale

1:7.5M 0 100 200 300 km / 0 50 100 150 mls

1:5M 0 50 100 150 200 km / 0 50 100 mls

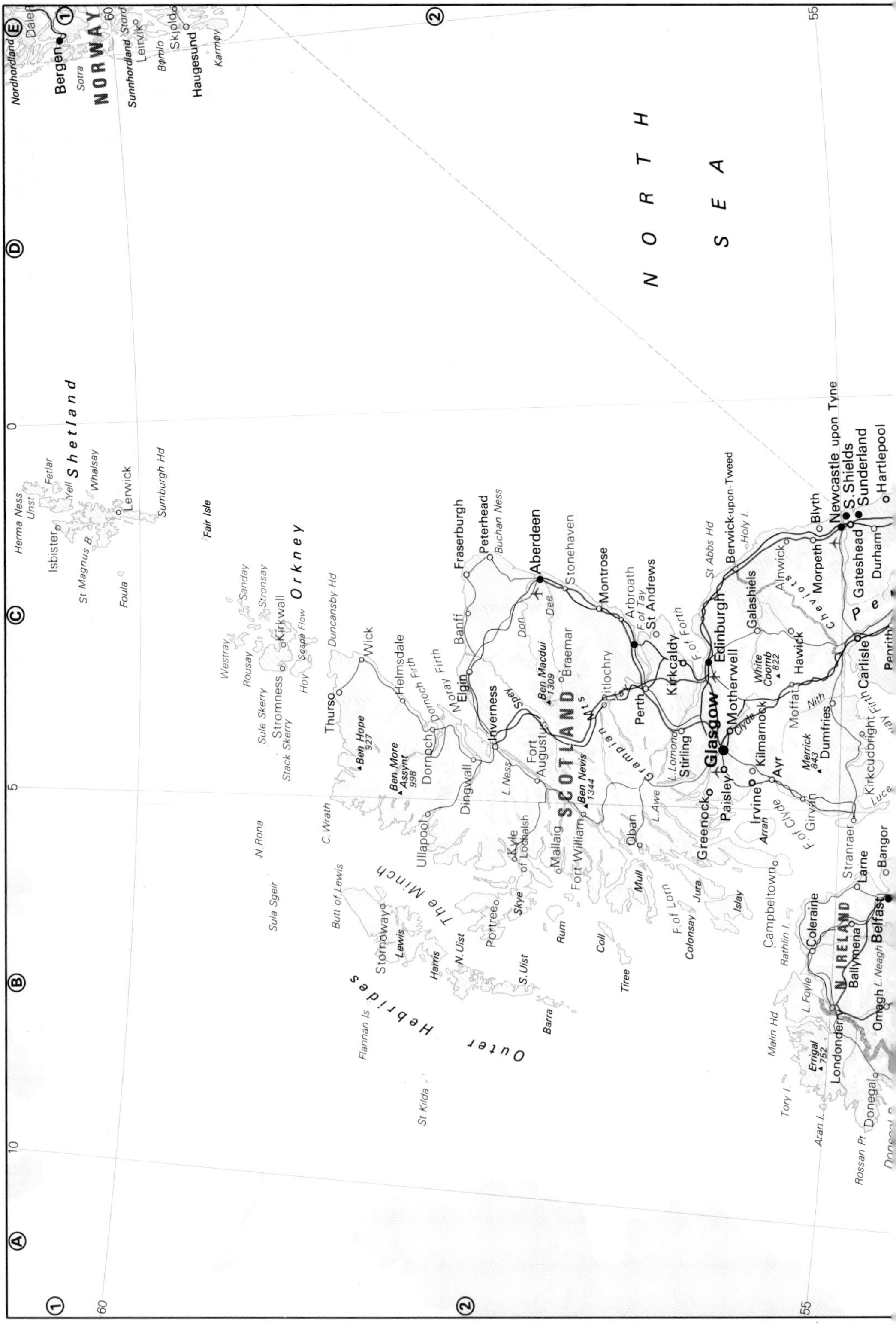
NORWAY
Bergen
Haugesund
Skjold
Leirvik
Stord
Sunnhordland
Nordhordland
Dale
Sotra
Bømlo
Karmøy
NORTH SEA
Shetland
Lerwick
Unst
Yell
Fetlar
Whalsay
Herma Ness
Isbister
St Magnus B.
Foula
Sumburgh Hd
Fair Isle
Orkney
Kirkwall
Stromness
Westray
Rousay
Sanday
Stronsay
Hoy
Scapa Flow
Sule Skerry
Stack Skerry
N. Rona
Sula Sgeir
C. Wrath
Thurso
Duncansby Hd
Wick
Ben Hope 927
Ben More Assynt 998
Helmsdale
Dornoch
Dornoch Firth
Moray Firth
Ullapool
Dingwall
Inverness
Elgin
Banff
Fraserburgh
Peterhead
Buchan Ness
Aberdeen
Stonehaven
Don
Dee
Ben Macdui 1309
Braemar
Spey
L. Ness
Fort Augustus
SCOTLAND
Grampian Mts
Ben Nevis 1344
Fort William
Mallaig
Kyle of Lochalsh
Pitlochry
Perth
Montrose
Arbroath
F. of Tay
St Andrews
Kirkcaldy
F. of Forth
Edinburgh
St Abbs Hd
Berwick-upon-Tweed
Holy I.
Galashiels
Motherwell
Glasgow
Clyde
Stirling
L. Lomond
L. Awe
Oban
Greenock
Paisley
Kilmarnock
Irvine
Ayr
F. of Clyde
Arran
Girvan
White Coomb 822
Moffat
Hawick
Nith
Dumfries
Merrick 843
Kirkcudbright
Luce
Stranraer
Cheviots
Alnwick
Morpeth
Blyth
Newcastle upon Tyne
S. Shields
Sunderland
Gateshead
Durham
Hartlepool
Carlisle
Penrith
Butt of Lewis
Flannan Is
The Minch
Stornoway
Lewis
Harris
N. Uist
S. Uist
Barra
Outer Hebrides
St Kilda
Skye
Portree
Rum
Coll
Tiree
Mull
F. of Lorn
Colonsay
Jura
Islay
Campbeltown
Rathlin I.
N. IRELAND
Coleraine
Larne
Bangor
Belfast
Ballymena
L. Neagh
Omagh
L. Foyle
Londonderry
Malin Hd
Errigal 752
Tory I.
Aran I.
Donegal
Rossan Pt

IRISH SEA
English Channel
Cardigan Bay
St George's Chan.
Bristol Chan.
The Wash
REP. OF IRELAND
WALES
ENGLAND
BELGIUM
NETHERLANDS
NORMANDIE
PICARDIE
ÎLE DE FRANCE
Dublin
Baile Atha Cliath
Dun Laoghaire
Bray
Wicklow
Arklow
Wexford
Rosslare
Drogheda
Dundalk
Newry
Armagh
Portadown
Monaghan
Cavan
Enniskillen
L. Erne
Sligo
Sligo B.
Ballina
Castlebar
Boyle
Roscommon
Longford
Mullingar
Athlone
Galway
Galway B.
Aran Is
Ennis
Kilrush
Limerick
Tipperary
Nenagh
Monasterevan
Port Laoise
Carlow
Kilkenny
Clonmel
Waterford
Dungarvan
Youghal
Cork
Killarney
Tralee
Dingle
Dingle B.
Bantry
Bantry B.
C. Clear
Carrauntoohill 1041
Old Hd of Kinsale
Shannon
Wicklow Mts
Blackwater
Barrow
Suir
L. Derg
L. Ree
L. Allen
L. Mask
L. Conn
L. Corrib
Clew B.
Achill I.
Erris Hd
Slyne Hd
Isle of Man
Douglas
Scafell Pike 977
Kendal
Barrow-in-Furness
Morecambe
Lancaster
Blackpool
Preston
Liverpool
Birkenhead
Holyhead
Anglesey
Bangor
Snowdon 1085
Pwllheli
Aberystwyth
Fishguard
Carmarthen
Pembroke
St David's Hd
Swansea
Builth Wells
Brecon
Newport
Cardiff
Bristol
Bath
Weston-super-Mare
Taunton
Barnstaple
Lundy I.
Bude
Exeter
Torquay
Dartmoor
Plymouth
Truro
Falmouth
Newquay
Penzance
Land's End
Lizard Pt
Isles of Scilly
Prawle Pt
Weymouth
Bournemouth
Salisbury
Swindon
Gloucester
Worcester
Wye
Severn
Hereford
Shrewsbury
Wolverhampton
Birmingham
Coventry
Leicester
Northampton
Milton Keynes
Oxford
Luton
Bedford
Cambridge
Peterborough
Nottingham
Derby
Stoke-on-Trent
Crewe
Chester
Warrington
Manchester
Bolton
Huddersfield
Bradford
Leeds
Harrogate
York
Sheffield
Doncaster
Lincoln
Hull
Grimsby
Humber
Spurn Hd
Scarborough
Flamborough Hd
Middlesbrough
Darlington
Yorkshire Moors
Ouse
Trent
Nene
Dee
King's Lynn
Norwich
Great Yarmouth
Lowestoft
Newmarket
Ipswich
Felixstowe
Harwich
Colchester
Chelmsford
Southend-on-Sea
Thames
London
Windsor
Reading
Guildford
Winchester
Southampton
Portsmouth
Isle of Wight
Brighton
Crawley
Maidstone
Hastings
Eastbourne
Canterbury
Dover
Folkestone
Calais
Boulogne
Dunkerque
Oostende
Brugge
Gent
Antwerpen
Mechelen
Bruxelles (Brüssel)
Zeebrugge
Vlissingen
Schelde
's-Gravenhage (Den Haag)
Rotterdam
Esbjerg
Kortrijk
Tourcoing
Roubaix
Lille
Tournai
Mons
Valenciennes
Denain
Douai
Arras
Cambrai
Béthune
St Omer
Montreuil
Abbeville
Amiens
St-Quentin
Laon
Compiègne
Soissons
Oise
Senlis
Château-Thierry
Meaux
Beauvais
Montdidier
Neufchâtel
Dieppe
Le Tréport
Fécamp
Bolbec
Le Havre
Rouen
Seine
Elbeuf
Louviers
Evreux
Eure
Mantes
Cergy-Pontoise
Paris
Versailles
Rambouillet
Étampes
Chartres
Dreux
Fontainebleau
Melun
Provins
Sézanne
Romilly-s.-S
Sens
Deauville
Lisieux
Caen
Bayeux
Orne
Argentan
Alençon
Mayenne
Domfront
Cherbourg
pte de Barfleur
Valognes
C. de la Hague
Alderney
Sark
Guernsey
Jersey
Channel Is (U.K.)
St Helier
St-Lô
Coutances
Granville
Golfe de St-Malo
Mont-St-Michel
Fougères
St-Malo
Dinan
St-Brieuc
Carhaix-Plouguer
Morlaix
Roscoff
Brest
I. d'Ouessant
FRANCE
50
5
B
C
D
3
4

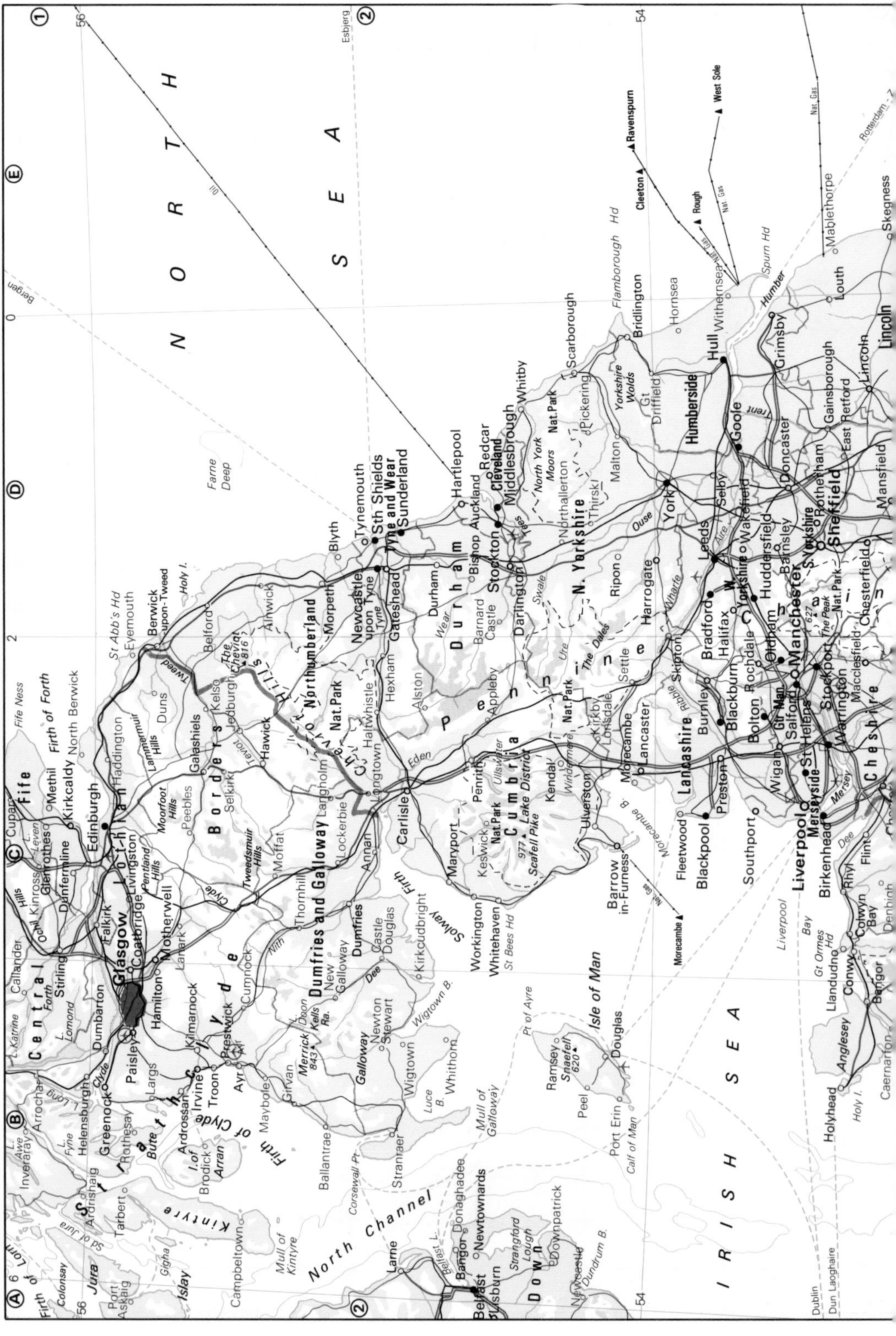
NORTH SEA
IRISH SEA
North Channel
Firth of Forth
Firth of Clyde
Solway Firth
Morecambe B.
Liverpool Bay
Farne Deep
Flamborough Hd
Spurn Hd
Humber
Isle of Man
Anglesey
Edinburgh
Glasgow
Paisley
Greenock
Stirling
Kirkcaldy
Dunfermline
Falkirk
Motherwell
Hamilton
Kilmarnock
Ayr
Troon
Irvine
Ardrossan
Largs
Dumbarton
Helensburgh
Callander
Stranraer
Girvan
Maybole
Ballantrae
Dumfries
Annan
Lockerbie
Moffat
Langholm
Hawick
Selkirk
Galashiels
Peebles
Kelso
Jedburgh
Duns
Berwick upon-Tweed
Eyemouth
Alnwick
Morpeth
Blyth
Tynemouth
Newcastle upon Tyne
Gateshead
Sth Shields
Sunderland
Hexham
Haltwhistle
Carlisle
Penrith
Keswick
Workington
Whitehaven
Maryport
Kendal
Ulverston
Barrow in-Furness
Lancaster
Morecambe
Blackpool
Preston
Fleetwood
Southport
Liverpool
Birkenhead
St Helens
Warrington
Wigan
Bolton
Manchester
Salford
Stockport
Oldham
Rochdale
Blackburn
Burnley
Skipton
Settle
Bradford
Halifax
Huddersfield
Leeds
Wakefield
Barnsley
Sheffield
Rotherham
Doncaster
Goole
Selby
York
Harrogate
Ripon
Thirsk
Northallerton
Darlington
Stockton
Middlesbrough
Hartlepool
Redcar
Whitby
Scarborough
Pickering
Malton
Bridlington
Gt Driffield
Hornsea
Hull
Withernsea
Grimsby
Louth
Mablethorpe
Skegness
Lincoln
Gainsborough
East Retford
Mansfield
Chesterfield
Macclesfield
Durham
Bishop Auckland
Barnard Castle
Appleby
Alston
Douglas
Ramsey
Peel
Port Erin
Holyhead
Llandudno
Conwy
Colwyn Bay
Rhyl
Flint
Bangor
Caernarfon
Belfast
Lisburn
Larne
Bangor
Newtownards
Donaghadee
Downpatrick
Newcastle
Campbeltown
Kintyre
Arran
Bute
Islay
Jura
Northumberland
Durham
Cumbria
N. Yorkshire
Humberside
Lancashire
Merseyside
Cheshire
Borders
Dumfries and Galloway
Central
Fife
Lothian
Strathclyde
Tyne and Wear
Cleveland
Pennines
The Cheviot 816
Scafell Pike 977
Snaefell 620
Merrick 843
Ravenspurn
West Sole
Rough
Cleeton
Morecambe
Nat. Gas
Oil
Bergen
Esbjerg
Rotterdam
Dublin
Dun Laoghaire

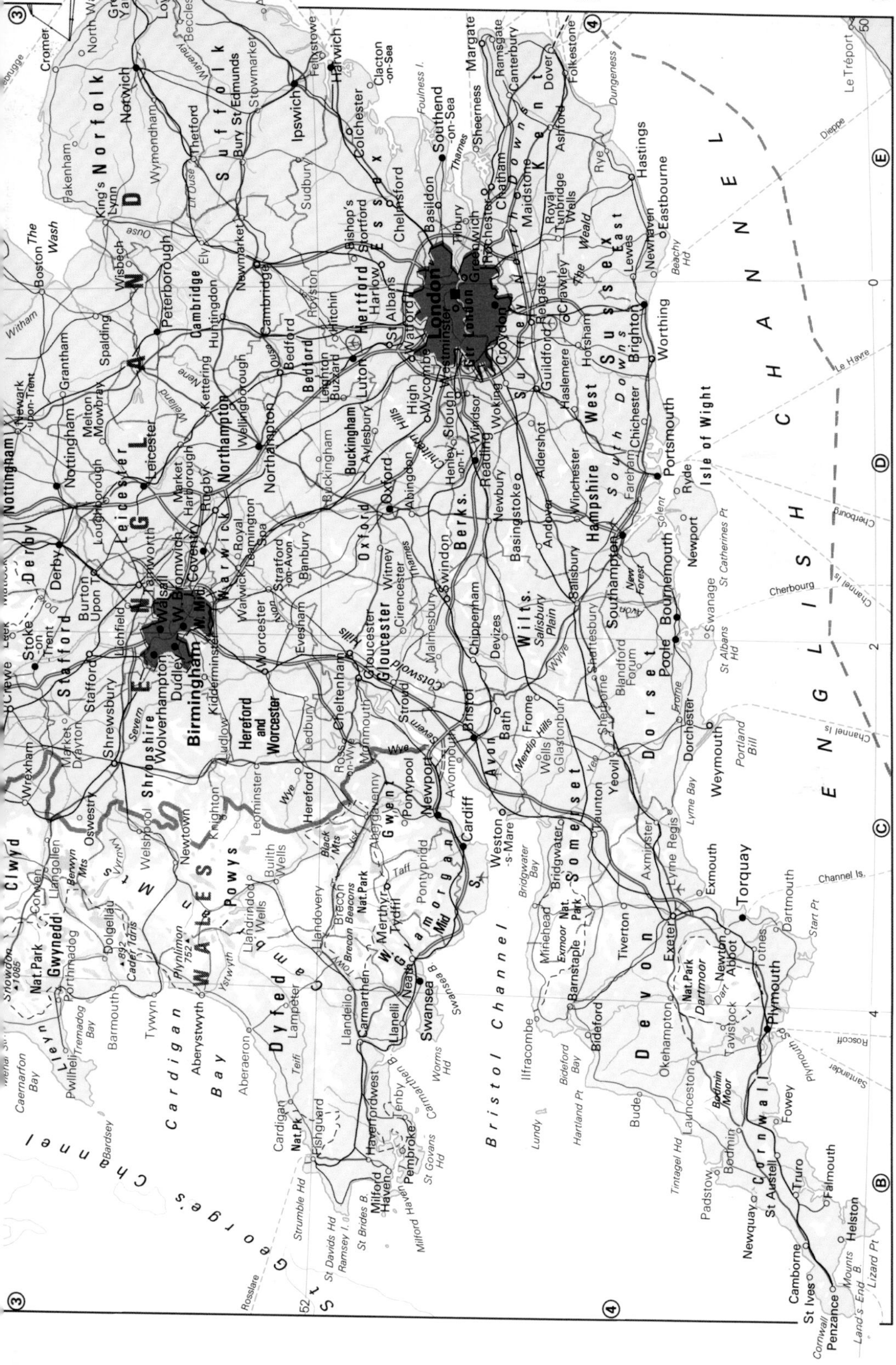
0 25 50 75 100 km
0 25 50 mls
E N G L A N D
W A L E S
E N G L I S H C H A N N E L
Bristol Channel
Cardigan Bay
St George's Channel
Norfolk
Suffolk
Essex
Kent
East Sussex
West Sussex
Surrey
Hampshire
Isle of Wight
Dorset
Devon
Cornwall
Somerset
Avon
Wilts.
Berks.
Oxford
Gloucester
Hereford and Worcester
Shropshire
Stafford
Derby
Nottingham
Leicester
Northampton
Warwick
Buckingham
Bedford
Hertford
Cambridge
Gtr London
W. Mid.
Clwyd
Gwynedd
Powys
Dyfed
Gwent
Mid Glamorgan
W. Glamorgan
S. Glamorgan
London
Birmingham
Bristol
Cardiff
Swansea
Newport
Plymouth
Exeter
Torquay
Southampton
Portsmouth
Bournemouth
Brighton
Oxford
Reading
Cambridge
Norwich
Ipswich
Peterborough
Leicester
Nottingham
Derby
Coventry
Wolverhampton
Northampton
Luton
Southend -on-Sea
Stoke -on Trent
Gloucester
Cheltenham
Worcester
Hereford
Swindon
Salisbury
Winchester
Canterbury
Dover
Folkestone
Hastings
Eastbourne
Weymouth
Penzance
Land's End
Lizard Pt
Dartmoor
Exmoor
Bodmin Moor
Salisbury Plain
New Forest
The Wash
Thames
Severn
Wye
Le Havre
Cherbourg
Dieppe
Roscoff
Le Tréport
Channel Is.

1:2.5M

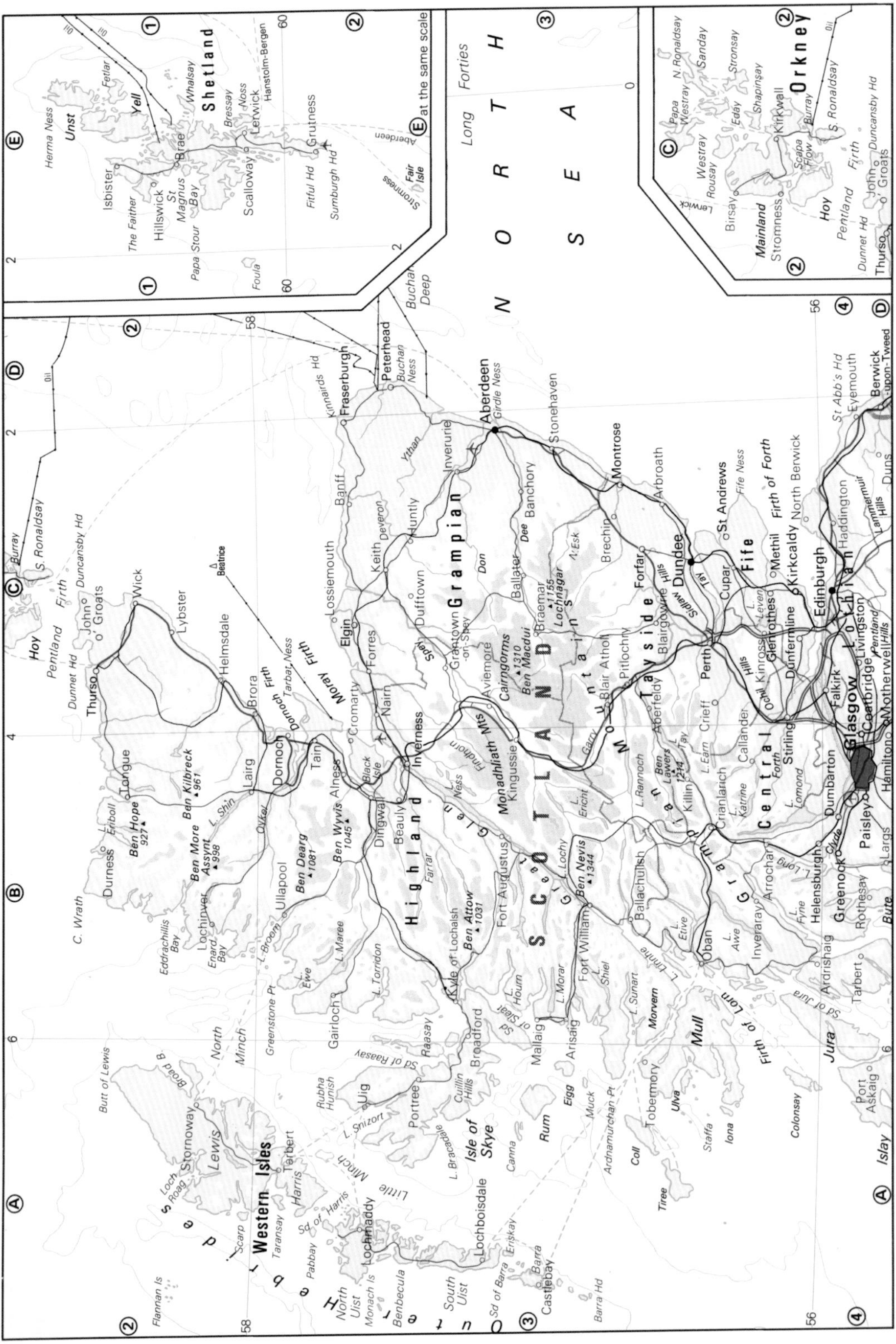

0 25 50 75 100 km
0 25 50 mls
Shetland
Unst
Yell
Fetlar
Whalsay
Herma Ness
Isbister
Hillswick
St Magnus Bay
The Faither
Papa Stour
Brae
Bressay
Noss
Lerwick
Hanstolm-Bergen
Scalloway
Foula
Fitful Hd
Sumburgh Hd
Grutness
Fair Isle
Aberdeen
Stromness
at the same scale
Orkney
Papa Westray
N. Ronaldsay
Sanday
Stronsay
Westray
Rousay
Eday
Shapinsay
Kirkwall
Burray
S. Ronaldsay
Duncansby Hd
Birsay
Mainland
Stromness
Hoy
Scapa Flow
Pentland Firth
John o' Groats
Dunnet Hd
Thurso
Lerwick
Long Forties
NORTH SEA
Buchan Deep
Peterhead
Buchan Ness
Fraserburgh
Kinnairds Hd
Aberdeen
Girdle Ness
Stonehaven
Montrose
Arbroath
Brechin
Forfar
Dundee
St Andrews
Fife Ness
Fife
Cupar
Firth of Forth
North Berwick
Haddington
Lammermuir Hills
Duns
Berwick-upon-Tweed
Eyemouth
St Abb's Hd
Edinburgh
Kirkcaldy
Methil
Glenrothes
Dunfermline
Kinross
Ochil Hills
Livingston
Pentland Hills
Lothian
Falkirk
Stirling
Glasgow
Coatbridge
Motherwell
Hamilton
Paisley
Dumbarton
Greenock
Largs
Helensburgh
Clyde
Rothesay
Bute
Inveraray
Arrochar
Ardrishaig
Tarbert
Jura
Islay
Port Askaig
Colonsay
Crianlarich
Callander
Central
L. Lomond
L. Katrine
Killin
Ben Lawers 1214
Perth
Crieff
Aberfeldy
Pitlochry
Blair Atholl
Tayside
Blairgowrie
Sidlaw Hills
Tay
Braemar
Lochnagar 1155
Ballater
Banchory
Dee
Don
Grampian
Inverurie
Ythan
Huntly
Banff
Deveron
Keith
Dufftown
Lossiemouth
Elgin
Forres
Nairn
Grantown-on-Spey
Spey
Aviemore
Cairngorms
Ben Macdui 1310
Grampian Mountains
SCOTLAND
Kingussie
Monadhliath Mts
Findhorn
Inverness
Cromarty
Moray Firth
Tarbat Ness
Beatrice
Dornoch Firth
Dornoch
Tain
Alness
Black Isle
Dingwall
Beauly
Highland
Great Glen
L. Ness
Fort Augustus
Ben Nevis 1344
Fort William
Ballachulish
L. Etive
Oban
L. Awe
Mull
Firth of Lorn
Tobermory
Morvern
L. Sunart
Ardnamurchan Pt
Coll
Tiree
Ulva
Staffa
Iona
Mallaig
Arisaig
L. Morar
L. Shiel
Eigg
Muck
Rum
Canna
Isle of Skye
Cuillin Hills
Broadford
Kyle of Lochalsh
Ben Attow 1031
Portree
Uig
Raasay
Sd of Raasay
Gairloch
L. Torridon
L. Maree
L. Ewe
Ullapool
Ben Dearg 1081
Ben Wyvis 1045
Lochinver
Ben More Assynt 998
Durness
Ben Hope 927
Ben Kilbreck 961
Tongue
Lairg
L. Shin
Brora
Helmsdale
Lybster
Wick
Duncansby Hd
C. Wrath
North Minch
Little Minch
Lewis
Stornoway
Butt of Lewis
Harris
Tarbert
Western Isles
Lochmaddy
North Uist
Benbecula
South Uist
Lochboisdale
Eriskay
Barra
Castlebay
Barra Hd
Flannan Is
Monach Is
Outer Hebrides

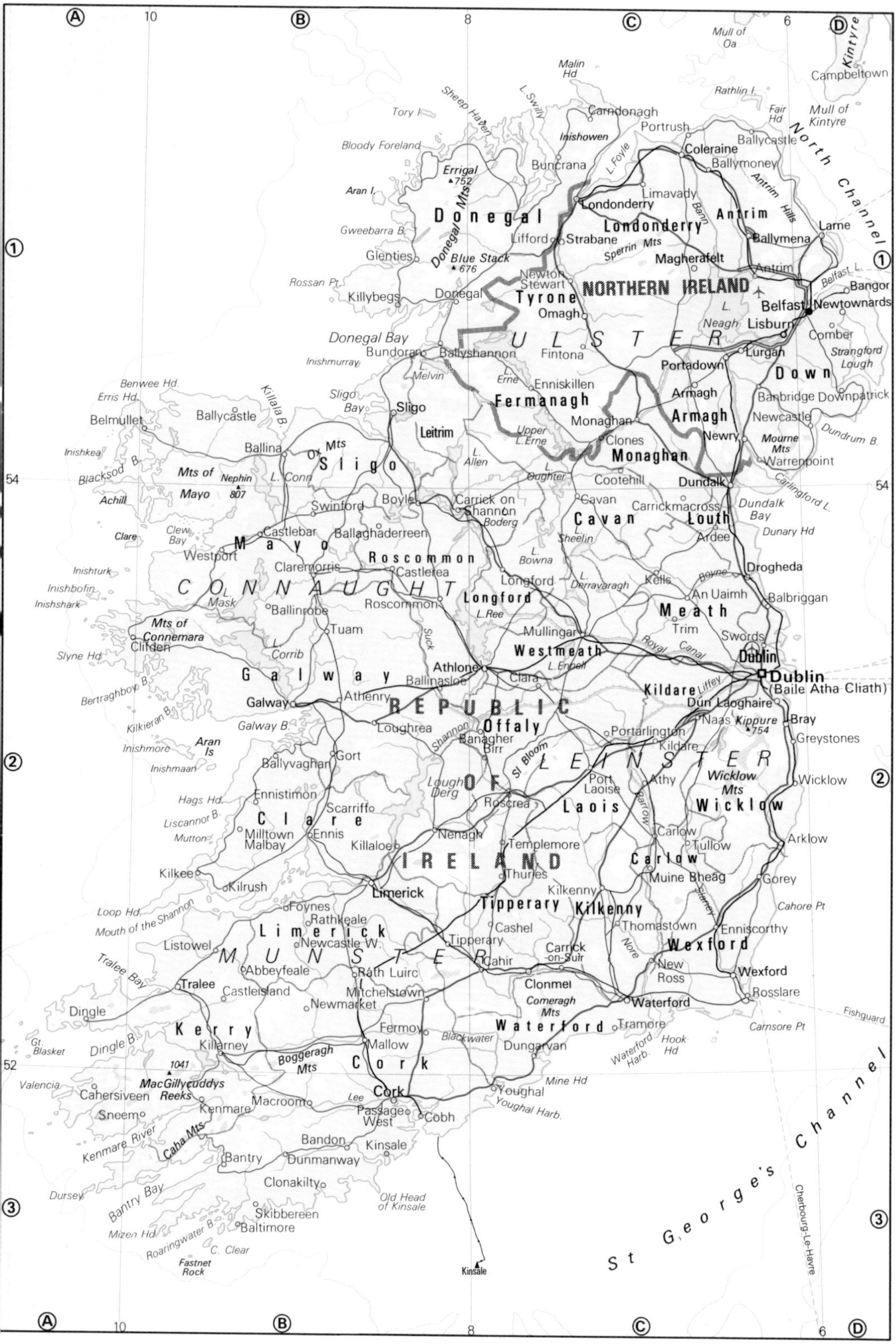
A
B
C
D
10
8
6
54
52
1
2
3
Mull of Oa
Kintyre
Campbeltown
Malin Hd
Rathlin I.
Fair Hd
Mull of Kintyre
Sheep Haven
L. Swilly
Tory I.
Carndonagh
Portrush
Bloody Foreland
Inishowen
Ballycastle
Coleraine
North Channel
Errigal 752
Buncrana
L. Foyle
Ballymoney
Aran I.
Limavady
Bann
Antrim Hills
Londonderry
Donegal
Antrim
Larne
Gweebarra B.
Lifford
Strabane
Londonderry
Ballymena
Sperrin Mts
Glenties
Donegal Mts
Magherafelt
Blue Stack 676
Antrim
Belfast L.
Rossan Pt
Newton Stewart
NORTHERN IRELAND
Bangor
Killybegs
Donegal
Tyrone
L. Neagh
Belfast
Newtownards
Omagh
Lisburn
Comber
Donegal Bay
ULSTER
Bundoran
Ballyshannon
Fintona
Lurgan
Strangford Lough
Inishmurray
L. Melvin
Portadown
Down
Benwee Hd.
L. Erne
Enniskillen
Erris Hd.
Killala B.
Sligo Bay
Armagh
Banbridge
Downpatrick
Sligo
Fermanagh
Armagh
Belmullet
Ballycastle
Leitrim
Monaghan
Newcastle
Upper L.Erne
Newry
Dundrum B.
Inishkea
Ballina
Ox Mts
Clones
Mourne Mts
Sligo
L. Allen
Monaghan
Warrenpoint
Blacksod B.
Mts of Mayo
Nephin 807
L. Conn
L. Oughter
Cootehill
Dundalk
Carlingford L.
Achill
Boyle
Carrick on Shannon
Cavan
Carrickmacross
Dundalk Bay
Swinford
L. Boderg
Cavan
Louth
Clare
Clew Bay
Castlebar
Ballaghaderreen
L. Sheelin
Ardee
Dunany Hd
Mayo
Westport
Roscommon
L. Bowna
Inishturk
Claremorris
Castlerea
L. Derravaragh
Boyne
Drogheda
Inishbofin
CONNAUGHT
Longford
Kells
An Uaimh
Inishshark
L. Mask
Roscommon
Longford
Balbriggan
Ballinrobe
L. Ree
Meath
Mts of Connemara
Tuam
Suck
Trim
Clifden
Mullingar
Swords
L. Corrib
Royal Canal
Slyne Hd
Westmeath
Dublin
Athlone
L. Ennell
Galway
Dublin
(Baile Atha Cliath)
Bertraghboy B.
Ballinasloe
Clara
Liffey
Kildare
Athenry
REPUBLIC
Dún Laoghaire
Galway
Naas
Kippure 754
Bray
Kilkieran B.
Offaly
Loughrea
Galway B.
Shannon
Portarlington
Greystones
Aran Is
Banagher
Kildare
Inishmore
Birr
Gort
Sl Bloom
LEINSTER
Inishmaan
Ballyvaghan
Port Laoise
Athy
Wicklow
Wicklow Mts
Lough Derg
OF
Ennistimon
Hags Hd.
Roscrea
Laois
Wicklow
Barrow
Liscannor B.
Scarriff
Clare
Carlow
Mutton
Milltown Malbay
Ennis
Nenagh
Templemore
Arklow
Tullow
Killaloe
IRELAND
Carlow
Kilkee
Thurles
Muine Bheag
Gorey
Slaney
Kilrush
Limerick
Kilkenny
Kilkenny
Loop Hd.
Foynes
Tipperary
Cahore Pt
Mouth of the Shannon
Rathkeale
Cashel
Limerick
Thomastown
Enniscorthy
Newcastle W.
Tipperary
Nore
Listowel
Wexford
MUNSTER
Carrick-on-Suir
Tralee Bay
Cahir
New Ross
Abbeyfeale
Ráth Luirc
Wexford
Clonmel
Tralee
Castleisland
Mitchelstown
Rosslare
Dingle
Newmarket
Comeragh Mts
Waterford
Fishguard
Fermoy
Waterford
Tramore
Carnsore Pt
Kerry
Blackwater
Hook Hd
Gt. Blasket
Dingle B.
Killarney
Mallow
Dungarvan
Waterford Harb.
Boggeragh Mts
Cork
1041
Valencia
MacGillycuddys Reeks
Mine Hd
Cahersiveen
Cork
Youghal
Lee
Macroom
Kenmare
Youghal Harb.
Sneem
Passage West
Cobh
St George's Channel
Kenmare River
Caha Mts
Bandon
Kinsale
Bantry
Dunmanway
Clonakilty
Dursey
Bantry Bay
Old Head of Kinsale
Cherbourg-Le-Havre
Skibbereen
Mizen Hd
Baltimore
Roaringwater B.
C. Clear
Fastnet Rock
Kinsale

Paris - Brussels - Ruhr

1:2.5M

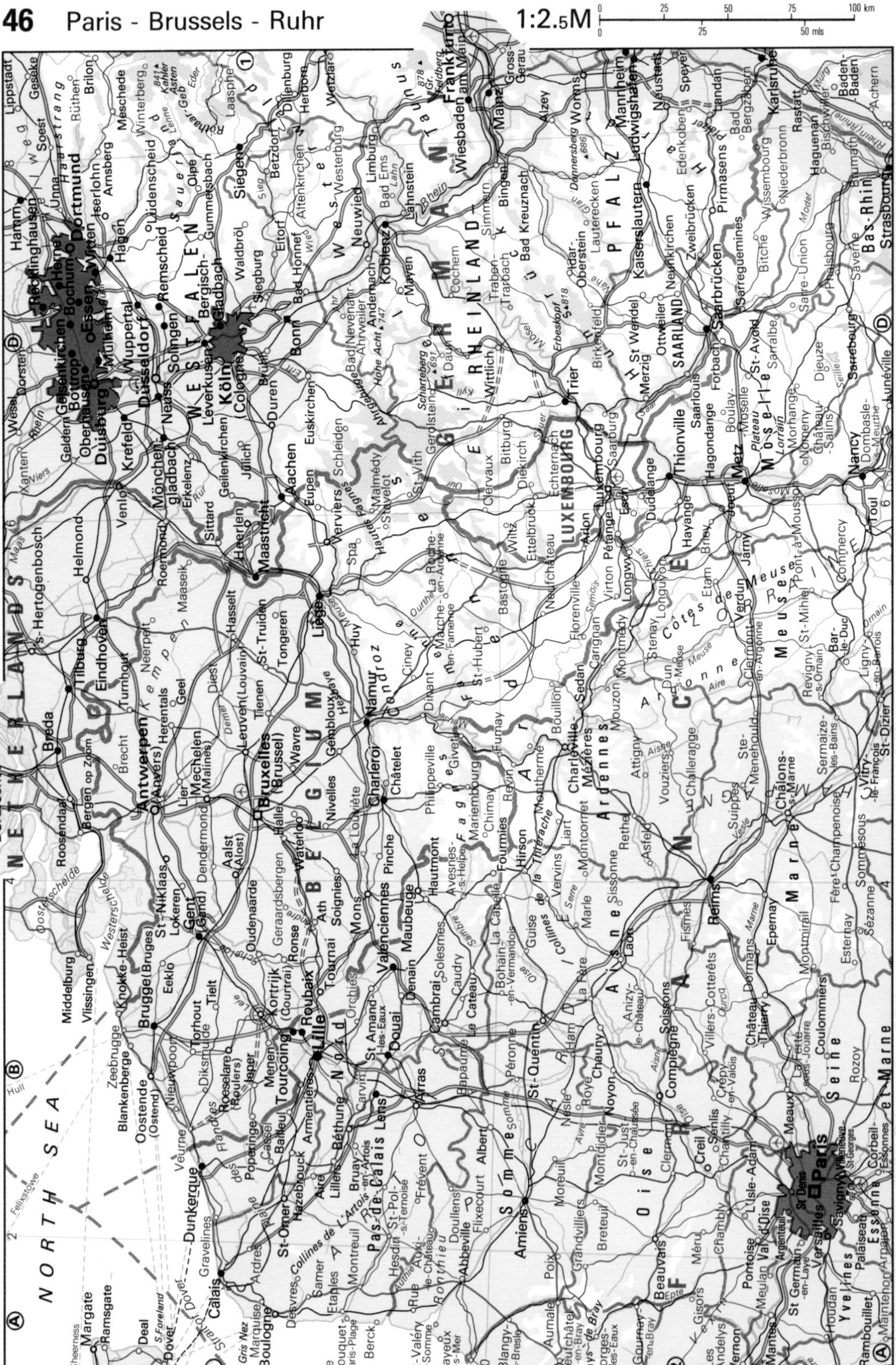

0
25
50
75
100 km
25
50 mls
NORTH SEA
NETHERLANDS
BELGIUM
LUXEMBOURG
NORDRHEIN-WESTFALEN
RHEINLAND-PFALZ
SAARLAND
Rotterdam
Antwerpen (Anvers)
Bruxelles (Brussel)
Gent (Gand)
Brugge (Bruges)
Liège
Namur
Charleroi
Lille
Roubaix
Tourcoing
Calais
Dunkerque
Boulogne
Amiens
Reims
Paris
Versailles
Metz
Nancy
Trier
Luxembourg
Köln (Cologne)
Bonn
Aachen
Düsseldorf
Duisburg
Essen
Dortmund
Koblenz
Mainz
Wiesbaden
Frankfurt am Main
Mannheim
Ludwigshafen
Kaiserslautern
Saarbrücken
Karlsruhe
Strasbourg
Maastricht
Eindhoven
Breda
Tilburg
Dover
Margate
Ramsgate
Deal
Oostende (Ostend)
Ardennes
Marne
Somme
Oise
Aisne
Seine
Meuse
Moselle
Pas-de-Calais
Nord

SWITZERLAND
AUSTRIA
FRANCE
LIECHTENSTEIN
VORALBERG
TIROL
LOMBARDIA
PIEMONTE
VENETO
TRENTINO
VALLE D'AOSTA
Bern (Berne)
Zürich
Basel (Basle)
Luzern (Lucerne)
Lausanne
Genève (Geneva)
Innsbruck
Bolzano (Bozen)
Trento
Verona
Vicenza
Padova (Padua)
Venezia (Venice)
Milano (Milan)
Torino (Turin)
Brescia
Bergamo
Novara
Piacenza
Parma
Modena
Bologna
Ferrara
Mantova (Mantua)
Cremona
Pavia
Alessandria
Asti
Aosta
Annecy
Chambéry
Besançon
Grenoble
Sion
Chur
St Gallen
Bregenz
Lago Maggiore
Lago di Garda
Bodensee (L. Constance)
L. Léman (L. of Geneva)
Mt Blanc 4810
Matterhorn 4478
Mt Rosa 4634
Jungfrau 4158
Finsteraarhorn 4274
Gran Paradiso 4061
Mt Viso 3841
Po
Adige
Rhône
Rhein
Inn
Ticino

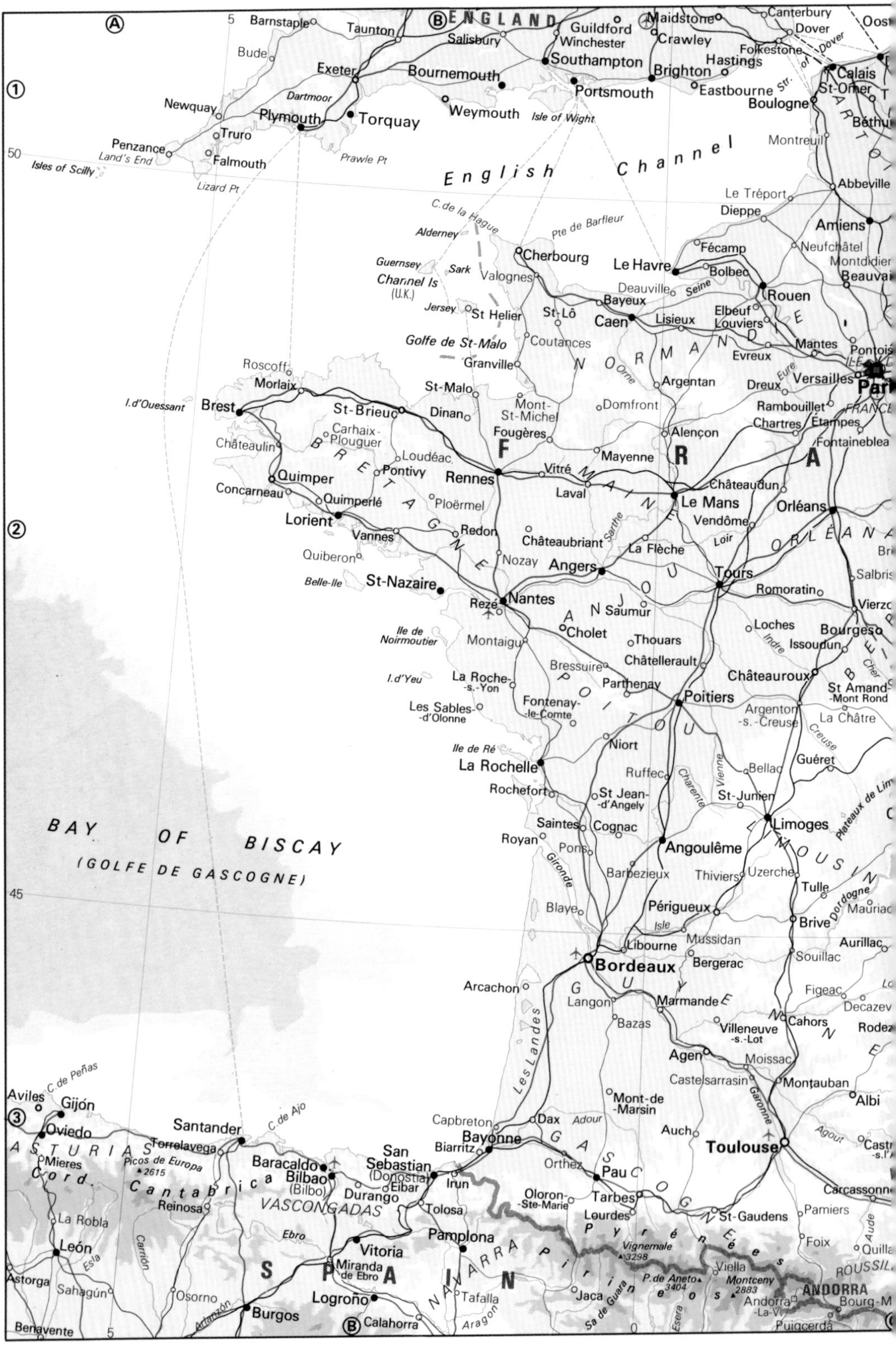
A
B
1
2
3
5
50
45
ENGLAND
Barnstaple
Taunton
Salisbury
Guildford
Winchester
Maidstone
Canterbury
Dover
Crawley
Folkestone
Bude
Southampton
Hastings
Str. of Dover
Calais
Exeter
Bournemouth
Brighton
Eastbourne
St-Omer
Dartmoor
Portsmouth
Boulogne
Newquay
Plymouth
Torquay
Weymouth
Isle of Wight
Truro
Penzance
Land's End
Falmouth
Prawle Pt
Montreuil
Isles of Scilly
Lizard Pt
English Channel
Abbeville
Le Tréport
Dieppe
Amiens
C. de la Hague
Alderney
Pte de Barfleur
Fécamp
Neufchâtel
Montdidier
Cherbourg
Le Havre
Bolbec
Beauvais
Guernsey
Sark
Valognes
Channel Is
(U.K.)
Deauville
Seine
Rouen
Bayeux
Jersey
St Helier
St-Lô
Caen
Lisieux
Elbeuf
Louviers
Golfe de St-Malo
Coutances
Mantes
Evreux
NORMANDIE
Pontoise
Granville
Roscoff
Morlaix
Argentan
Dreux
Eure
Versailles
Orne
Paris
St-Malo
I.d'Ouessant
Brest
St-Brieuc
Dinan
Mont-St-Michel
Domfront
Rambouillet
Chartres
Étampes
Carhaix-Plouguer
Fougères
Alençon
Fontainebleau
Châteaulin
Loudéac
F
Mayenne
R
A
BRETAGNE
Pontivy
Rennes
Vitré
MAINE
Châteaudun
Quimper
Laval
Le Mans
Concarneau
Quimperlé
Ploërmel
Orléans
Lorient
Vendôme
Vannes
Redon
Châteaubriant
Sarthe
La Flèche
Loir
ORLÉANAIS
Quiberon
Nozay
Angers
Salbris
Belle-Ile
St-Nazaire
Tours
Romorantin
Rezé
Nantes
ANJOU
Saumur
Vierzon
Ile de Noirmoutier
Cholet
Loches
Bourges
Montaigu
Thouars
Issoudun
Indre
Châtellerault
Cher
Bressuire
I.d'Yeu
La Roche-s.-Yon
Châteauroux
Parthenay
POITOU
St Amand-Mont Rond
Poitiers
Les Sables-d'Olonne
Fontenay-le-Comte
Argenton-s.-Creuse
La Châtre
Creuse
Ile de Ré
Niort
La Rochelle
Guéret
Ruffec
Bellac
Charente
Vienne
Rochefort
St Jean-d'Angely
St-Junien
Plateaux de Limousin
Limoges
Saintes
Cognac
Royan
LIMOUSIN
BAY OF BISCAY
(GOLFE DE GASCOGNE)
Angoulême
Pons
Gironde
Barbezieux
Thiviers
Uzerche
Tulle
Dordogne
Mauriac
Blaye
Périgueux
Brive
Isle
Mussidan
Aurillac
Libourne
Souillac
Bordeaux
Bergerac
GUYENNE
Arcachon
Figeac
Langon
Decazeville
Marmande
Cahors
Rodez
Bazas
Villeneuve-s.-Lot
Les Landes
Agen
Moissac
Castelsarrasin
Montauban
Mont-de-Marsin
Albi
C. de Peñas
Aviles
Gijón
C. de Ajo
Capbreton
Dax
Adour
Auch
Garonne
Oviedo
Santander
Bayonne
Agout
Biarritz
GASCOGNE
Toulouse
Castres
ASTURIAS
Torrelavega
Mieres
Picos de Europa
2615
Baracaldo
San Sebastian
(Donostia)
Bilbao
Orthez
Pau
Cord. Cantabrica
(Bilbo)
Eibar
Irun
Oloron-Ste-Marie
Tarbes
Carcassonne
Reinosa
Durango
VASCONGADAS
Tolosa
Lourdes
St-Gaudens
Pamiers
La Robla
Ebro
Pamplona
Pyrénées
Vignemale
3298
Aude
Foix
León
Carrión
Esla
Vitoria
NAVARRA
Pirineos
Viella
Quillan
Miranda de Ebro
P. de Aneto
3404
Montceny
2883
ROUSSILLON
Astorga
Sahagún
S P A I N
ANDORRA
Tafalla
Jaca
Osorno
Logroño
Sa de Guara
Esera
Andorra-La-Vi
Bourg-M
Arlanzón
Burgos
Aragón
Benavente
Calahorra
Puigcerdá

1:5M
0 50 100 150 200 km
0 50 100 mls
Vlissingen
Zeebrugge
Eindhoven
Antwerpen
(Anvers)
Brugge
Mechelen
Hasselt
Maastricht
Gent
Bruxelles
(Brüssel)
Leuven
St-Truiden
Kortrijk
Roubaix
Tournai
Soignies
Mons
Namur
Liège
Valenciennes
Charleroi
Arras
Denain
Maubeuge
Cambrai
Fourmies
St-Quentin
Charleville-
-Mézières
Sedan
Compiègne
Laon
Soissons
Reims
Château-
-Thierry
Epernay
Châlons
-s.-M.
Meaux
Sézanne
Provins
Romilly-s.-S
Melun
Troyes
Sens
Joigny
Montargis
Auxerre
Châtillon
Avallon
Nevers
Autun
Le Creusot
Montceau-
-l.-M.
Moulins
Digoin
Montluçon
Lapalisse
Vichy
Roanne
Riom
Thiers
Tarare
Issoire
Lempdes
Massif
Central
Le Puy
Mt Mézenc
1754
Pradelles
Aubenas
Mende
Mt Aigoual
1565
Alès
Bagnols
-s.-Cèze
Nîmes
Montpellier
Sète
Narbonne
Golfe du Lion
Perpignan
C. de Creus
BELGIUM
Ardennes
Marche
Bastogne
LUXEM
BOURG
Arlon
Luxembourg
Longwy
Thionville
Meuse
Verdun
Metz
Sarrelouis
Sarreguemines
Sarrebourg
Nancy
Toul
St-Dizier
Vitry-l.-F.
Bar-s-A.
Chaumont
Langres
Épinal
St Dié
Vosges
Colmar
Strasbourg
Mulhouse
Belfort
Montbéliard
Vesoul
Besançon
Dijon
Dôle
Beaune
Chalon-s.-S.
Lons-
-l.-S.
St
Claude
Mâcon
Bourg
Bellegarde
Villefranche
Lyon
Villeurbanne
St-Chamond
St-Étienne
Vienne
Annonay
Romans-s.-I.
Bourg
d.-P.
Valence
Montélimar
Nyons
Orange
Carpentras
Avignon
Cavaillon
Arles
Salon d.-P.
Martigues
Marseille
Aubagne
Aix-en-Provence
Toulon
Hyères
Iles d'Hyères
St Tropez
St Raphaël
Cannes
Grasse
Draguignan
Castellane
Nice
Monte Carlo
MONACO
Côte d'Azur
Digne
Sisteron
Gap
Briançon
Corps
Grenoble
Massif
du Pelvoux
Voiron
Chambéry
Aix-
-l.-B.
Annecy
Genève
Albertville
Mt Blanc
4807
LORRAINE
CHAMPAGNE
FRANCE
BOURGOGNE
NIVERNAIS
FRANCHE-COMTÉ
Jura
SAVOIE
DAUPHINÉ
PROVENCE
AUVERGNE
LANGUEDOC
PICARDIE
ALSACE
Düsseldorf
Mönchen-
gladbach
WESTFALEN
Köln
Aachen
Bonn
Bad Godesberg
Euskirchen
Siegen
Marburg
HESSEN
Giessen
Alsfeld
Fulda
Bad
Hersfeld
Eisenach
Erfurt
Jena
Gera
Zwickau
Thüringer Wald
Plauen
Hof
Coburg
Cheb
GERMANY
Andernach
Koblenz
Limburg
Frankfurt
Offenbach
Wiesbaden
Mainz
Bingen
Bitburg
Mosel
Bad-Kreuznach
Darmstadt
Aschaffenburg
Schweinfurt
Bamberg
Bayreuth
Weiden
Würzburg
Kitzingen
Erlangen
Amberg
Fürth
Nürnberg
Trier
RHEINLAND
-PFALZ
Worms
Ludwigshafen
Mannheim
Heidelberg
SAAR-
LAND
Kaiserslautern
Saarbrücken
Pirmasens
Speyer
Ansbach
Crailsheim
Heilbronn
Karlsruhe
Pforzheim
Rastatt
Stuttgart
Esslingen
Ludwigsburg
Baden-Baden
BADEN
Regensburg
Donauwörth
Ingolstadt
Parsberg
Fränkische Alb
BAYERN
Heidenheim
Tübingen
Reutlingen
Schwäbische Alb
Ulm
Augsburg
Landshut
Dachau
München
Offenburg
Schwarzwald
Freiburg
Lörrach
Basel
Biberach
WÜRTTEMBERG
Tuttlingen
Ravensburg
Landsberg
Memmingen
Kempten
Starnberg
Rosenheim
Bad Tolz
Füssen
Garmisch-P.
Kufstein
Konstanz
Friedrichshafen
Lindau
Schaffhausen
Winterthur
Zurich
St Gallen
Dornbirn
Feldkirch
LIECHTEN
STEIN
Vaduz
Bludenz
Landeck
AUSTRIA
Innsbruck
Brenner
1370
Wildspitze
3774
Brunico
Merano
Bolzano
Marmolada
3342
Olten
Zug
Schwyz
Luzern
Biel
Neuchâtel
Bern
Pontarlier
Fribourg
Thun
Interlaken
Lausanne
Vevey
Montreux
L. Léman
SWITZERLAND
Jungfrau
4158
2112
St Gotthard
Rhein
Chur
Arosa
St Moritz
Ortles
3899
Brig
Rhône
Simplon
2009
Martigny
2469
Col du Gd
St Bernard
Matterhorn
4477
Aosta
Bellinzona
Domodossola
L. Maggiore
Lugano
L. di
Como
Sondrio
Edolo
Trento
Rovereto
Bassano
Lovere
Lecco
Varese
Como
Bergamo
L. di
Garda
Vicenza
Biella
Busto
Arsizio
Monza
Brescia
Verona
Novara
Milano
(Milan)
Lodi
Cremona
Mantova
Adige
Rovigo
Gran Paradiso
4061
Ivrea
Vercelli
Pavia
Casale
Monf.
Piacenza
Po
Col du
Mt Cenis
2803
Susa
Torino
(Turin)
Asti
Alessandria
Parma
Carpi
Ferrara
Modena
Reggio
n.-E.
Bologna
Ovada
Novi Ligure
Alba
Appno Ligure
Genova
(Genoa)
Taro
Mondovi
Stura
Mte Viso
3841
Cuneo
Mt Pelat
3053
C. de Tende
1870
Var
Durance
Verdon
Savona
G. di Genova
Rapallo
Mte Cimone
2165
Carrara
La Spezia
Massa
Pistoia
Prato
Viareggio
Lucca
Firenze
(Florence)
Alassio
Imperia
San Remo
Ligurian
Sea
Pisa
Pontedera
Livorno
Siena
Cecina
Piombino
Follonica
Portoferraio
Grosseto
Elba
Pianosa
Orbetello
Giglio
Montecristo
Cap Corse
G. de
St Florent
Bastia
Calvi
Mt Cinto
2710
Ponte Lecca
CORSE
(CORSICA)
Corte
Ajaccio
C. Rosso
Cateraggio
ITALY
ALPS
1
2
3
D
E

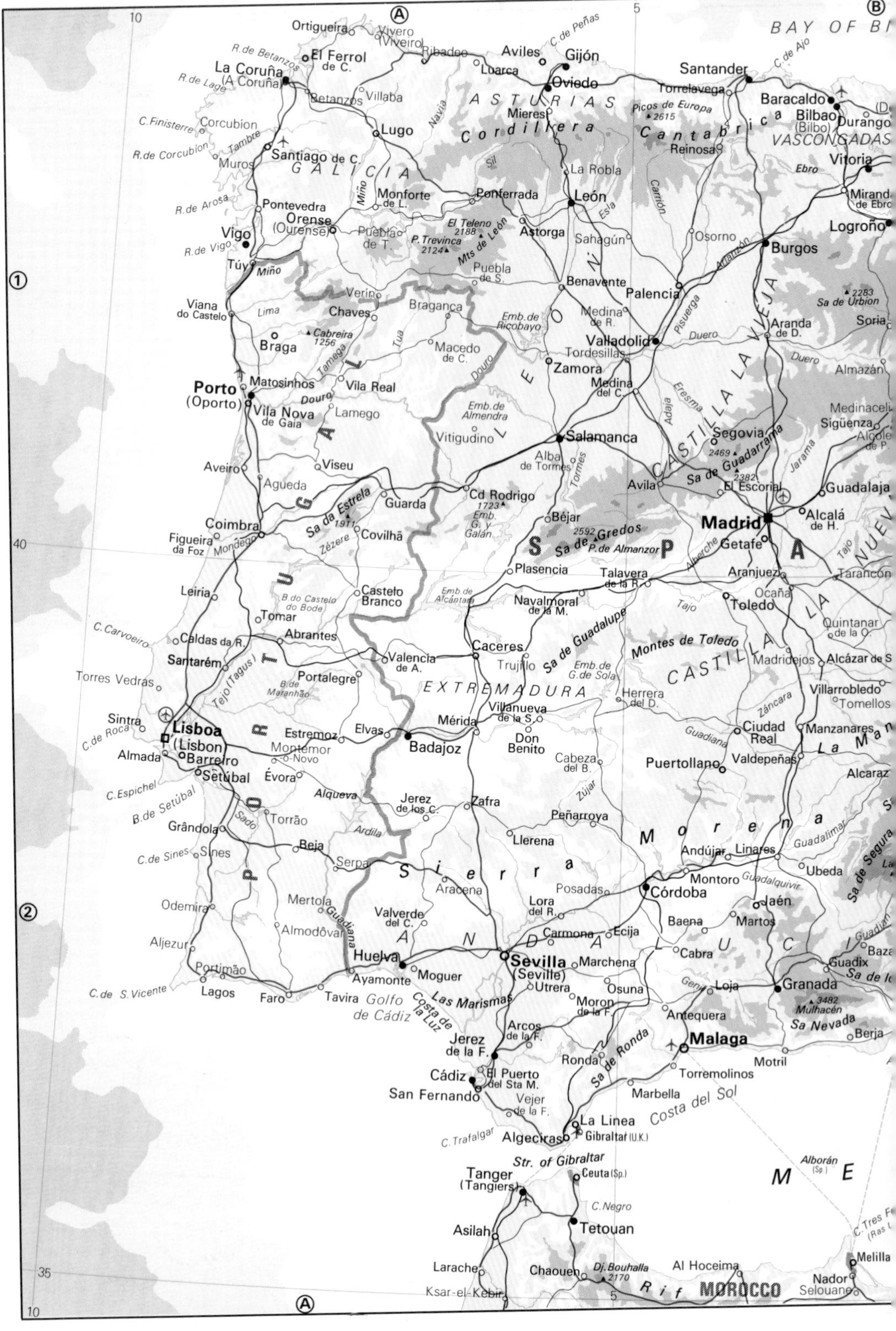

BAY OF BI
Ortigueira
Vivero (Viveiro)
Ribadeo
Aviles
C. de Peñas
Gijón
C. de Ajo
Santander
R. de Betanzos
El Ferrol de C.
La Coruña (A Coruña)
Luarca
Oviedo
Torrelavega
Baracaldo
Bilbao (Bilbao)
Durango
R. de Lage
Betanzos
Villaba
ASTURIAS
Picos de Europa 2615
Mieres
Cordillera Cantabrica
Reinosa
VASCONGADAS
C. Finisterre
Corcubíon
Lugo
R. de Corcubíon
Tambre
Santiago de C.
GALICIA
Muros
Sil
La Robla
Ebro
Vitoria
Navia
Miño
Carrión
R. de Arosa
Pontevedra
Monforte de L.
Ponferrada
León
Miranda de Ebro
Orense (Ourense)
Puebla de T.
El Teleno 2188
P. Trevinca 2124
Mts de León
Astorga
Esla
Sahagún
Osorno
Logroño
Vigo
R. de Vigo
Túy
Miño
Arlanzón
Burgos
Puebla de S.
Benavente
Palencia
Verín
Bragança
Chaves
Viana do Castelo
Lima
Emb. de Ricobayo
Medina de R.
Pisuerga
2283 Sa de Urbion
Soria
Aranda de D.
Cabreira 1256
Braga
Tamega
Tua
Macedo de C.
Valladolid
Tordesillas
Duero
Zamora
Douro
Almazán
Porto (Oporto)
Matosinhos
Vila Real
Medina del C.
Eresma
Adaja
CASTILLA LA VIEJA
Douro
Vila Nova de Gaia
Lamego
Emb. de Almendra
Medinaceli
Sigüenza
Vitigudino
Salamanca
Segovia
Alcolea de P.
2469
Sa de Guadarrama
Jarama
Alba de Tormes
Tormes
Aveiro
Viseu
2382
Avila
El Escorial
Agueda
Guadalajara
Guarda
Cd Rodrigo
Sa da Estrela 1911
1723
Emb. G. y Galán
Madrid
Alcalá de H.
Béjar
Coimbra
Covilhã
2592 Gredos
Sa de Gredos
P. de Almanzor
Figueira da Foz
Mondego
Zêzere
Getafe
Alberche
Tajo
NUEVA
SPAIN
Plasencia
Talavera de la R.
Aranjuez
Tarancón
Leiria
Castelo Branco
Emb. de Alcántara
Navalmoral de la M.
Ocaña
B. do Castelo do Bode
Tajo
Toledo
Tomar
Quintanar de la O.
C. Carvoeiro
Caldas da R.
Abrantes
Sa de Guadalupe
Caceres
Montes de Toledo
Valencia de A.
Trujillo
Madridejos
Alcázar de S
Santarém
Tejo (Tagus)
Emb. de G. de Sola
CASTILLA LA NUEVA
Torres Vedras
Portalegre
B. de Maranhão
EXTREMADURA
Herrera del D.
Villarrobledo
Tomelloso
Villanueva de la S.
Záncara
Sintra
Mérida
Ciudad Real
Manzanares
C. de Roca
Lisboa (Lisbon)
Estremoz
Elvas
Guadiana
La Mancha
Almada
Barreiro
Montemor-o-Novo
Badajoz
Don Benito
Valdepeñas
Cabeza del B.
Puertollano
PORTUGAL
Setúbal
Évora
Alcaraz
C. Espichel
B. de Setúbal
Alqueva
Jerez de los C.
Zafra
Zújar
Sado
Torrão
Peñarroya
Sierra Morena
Grândola
Ardila
Llerena
Guadalimar
C. de Sines
Sines
Beja
Andújar
Linares
Sa de Segura
Serpa
Sierra
Ubeda
Aracena
Montoro
Guadalquivir
Posadas
Córdoba
Mertola
Odemira
Lora del R.
Jaén
Valverde del C.
Guadiana
Baena
Martos
Almodôvar
Carmona
Ecija
ANDALUCIA
Aljezur
Huelva
Sevilla (Seville)
Marchena
Cabra
Baza
Guadix
Portimão
Moguer
Sa de la
Genil
Loja
Granada
C. de S. Vicente
Lagos
Faro
Tavira
Ayamonte
Golfo de Cádiz
Costa de la Luz
Las Marismas
Utrera
Osuna
Moron de la F.
3482 Mulhacén
Sa Nevada
Antequera
Arcos de la F.
Berja
Jerez de la F.
Sa de Ronda
Malaga
Ronda
Motril
Cádiz
El Puerto del Sta M.
Torremolinos
San Fernando
Marbella
Costa del Sol
Vejer de la F.
C. Trafalgar
La Linea
Algeciras
Gibraltar (U.K.)
Str. of Gibraltar
Alborán (Sp.)
Tanger (Tangiers)
Ceuta (Sp.)
ME
C. Negro
C. Tres Fo (Ras
Asilah
Tetouan
Melilla
Larache
Chaouen
Dj. Bouhalla 2170
Al Hoceima
Nador
Rif
MOROCCO
Selouane
Ksar-el-Kebir

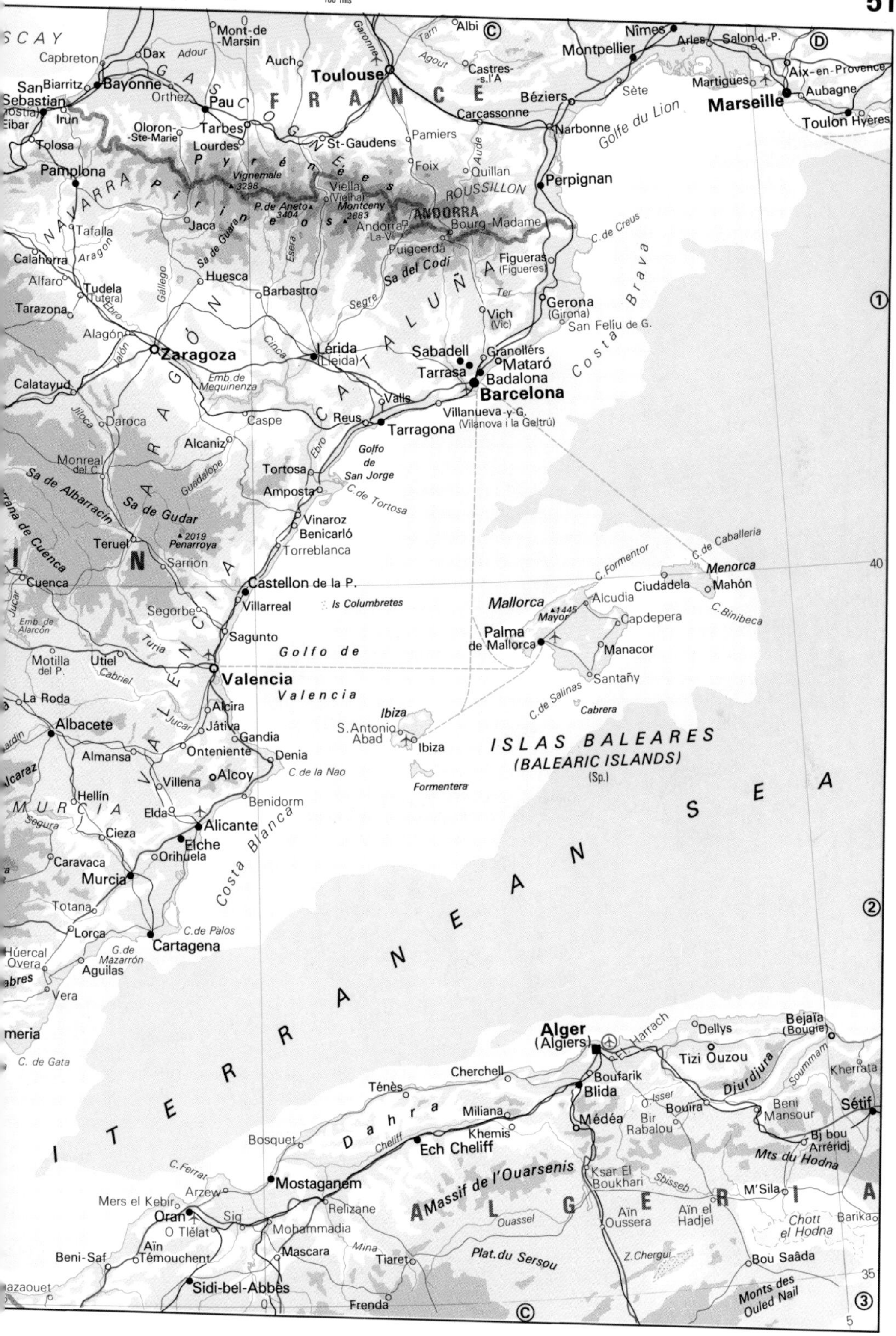
FRANCE
Toulouse
Albi
Montpellier
Nîmes
Arles
Salon-d.-P.
Aix-en-Provence
Marseille
Martigues
Aubagne
Toulon
Hyères
Béziers
Sète
Carcassonne
Narbonne
Golfe du Lion
Perpignan
ROUSSILLON
Castres-s.l'A
Auch
Mont-de-Marsin
Dax
Bayonne
Biarritz
Capbreton
San Sebastian
Irun
Eibar
Tolosa
Pau
Tarbes
Lourdes
Oloron-Ste-Marie
Orthez
St-Gaudens
Pamiers
Foix
Quillan
Pyrénées
Vignemale 3298
P.de Aneto 3404
Montceny 2883
Viella (Vielha)
ANDORRA
Andorra-La-V.
Bourg-Madame
Puigcerdá
Sa del Codi
Pamplona
NAVARRA
Tafalla
Calahorra
Alfaro
Tudela (Tutera)
Tarazona
Jaca
Sa de Guara
Huesca
Barbastro
Zaragoza
Alagón
Calatayud
ARAGÓN
CATALUÑA
Lérida (Lleida)
Figueras (Figueres)
Gerona (Girona)
San Felíu de G.
Vich (Vic)
Granollérs
Sabadell
Tarrasa
Mataró
Badalona
Barcelona
Costa Brava
C. de Creus
Valls
Reus
Tarragona
Villanueva-y-G. (Vilanova i la Geltrú)
Emb. de Mequinenza
Caspe
Alcaniz
Daroca
Monreal del C.
Tortosa
Amposta
Golfo de San Jorge
C. de Tortosa
Vinaroz
Benicarló
Torreblanca
Sa de Albarracín
Sa de Gudar
2019 Penarroya
Teruel
Sarrion
Cuenca
Castellon de la P.
Villarreal
Is Columbretes
Segorbe
Sagunto
Golfo de Valencia
Valencia
VALENCIA
Utiel
Motilla del P.
La Roda
Albacete
Alcira
Játiva
Gandia
Onteniente
Denia
C. de la Nao
Almansa
Alcoy
Villena
Benidorm
Hellín
MURCIA
Elda
Alicante
Elche
Orihuela
Costa Blanca
Cieza
Caravaca
Murcia
Totana
Lorca
Cartagena
C. de Palos
G. de Mazarrón
Aguilas
Húercal Overa
Vera
C. de Gata
Menorca
C. de Caballeria
Ciudadela
Mahón
C. Binibeca
C. Formentor
Mallorca
Alcudia
1445 Mayor
Capdepera
Palma de Mallorca
Manacor
Santañy
C. de Salinas
Cabrera
Ibiza
S. Antonio Abad
Formentera
ISLAS BALEARES (BALEARIC ISLANDS) (Sp.)
MEDITERRANEAN SEA
Alger (Algiers)
El Harrach
Dellys
Bejaïa (Bougie)
Tizi Ouzou
Djurdjura
Kherrata
Sétif
Cherchell
Boufarik
Blida
Ténès
Miliana
Médéa
Bouira
Beni Mansour
Bir Rabalou
Bj bou Arréridj
Mts du Hodna
Dahra
Ech Cheliff
Khemis
Bosquet
Massif de l'Ouarsenis
Ksar El Boukhari
M'Sila
C. Ferrat
Mostaganem
Arzew
Mers el Kebir
Oran
Sig
O Tlélat
Relizane
Mohammadia
Mascara
Aïn Témouchent
Beni-Saf
Tiaret
Plat. du Sersou
Aïn Oussera
Aïn el Hadjel
Chott el Hodna
Barika
Z. Chergui
Bou Saâda
Monts des Ouled Nail
Sidi-bel-Abbès
Frenda
ALGERIA
40
35
5
0
1
2
3
C
D

SWITZERLAND
AUSTRIA
HUNGARY
SLOVENIA
CROATIA
YUGOSLAVIA
FRANCE
GER.
ADRIATIC
Ligurian Sea
CORSE (CORSICA)
Wien
Budapest
München
Zagreb
Ljubljana
Sarajevo
Milano (Milan)
Torino (Turin)
Genova (Genoa)
Venezia (Venice)
Firenze (Florence)
Bologna
Trieste
Ancona
Pescara
Perugia
Livorno
Pisa
Bern
Zürich
Basel
Genève
Lausanne
Innsbruck
Salzburg
Graz
Klagenfurt
Bolzano
Trento
Verona
Padova
Brescia
Bergamo
Parma
Modena
Rimini
Ravenna
Split (Spalato)
Rijeka (Fiume)
Nice
Cannes
Ajaccio
Bastia
Elba
Appno Tosco-Emiliano
Appno Umbro-Marchigiano
Dolomitiche
Tevere (Tiber)
Po
Rhein
Rhône
Drava
Sava

1:5M 0 50 100 150 200 km
0 50 100 mls

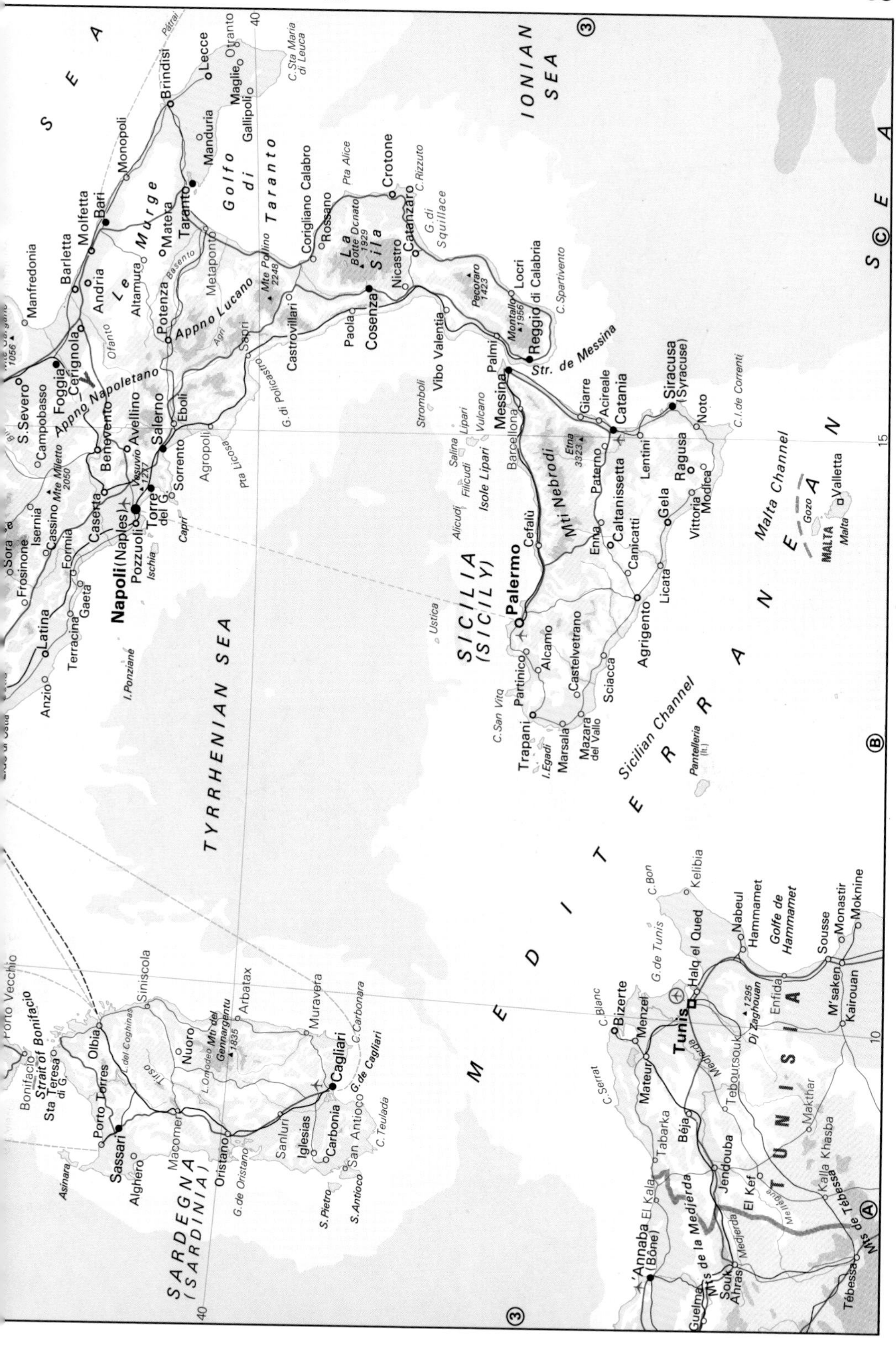

BLACK SEA
HUNGARY
ROMANIA
BULGARIA
YUGOSLAVIA
SERBIA
UKRAINE
MOLDAVIA
BOSNIA AND HERZEGOVINA
MONTENEGRO
CROATIA
KOSOVO
Vojvodina
Carpatii Meridionali (Transylvanian Alps)
Stara Planina
Ludogorie
Budapest
Bucureşti (Bucharest)
Beograd (Belgrade)
Sofiya
Odessa
Kishinev (Chişinău)
İstanbul
Üsküdar
Sarajevo
Skopje
Constanţa
Varna
Burgas
Plovdiv
Cluj-Napoca
Timişoara
Iaşi
Craiova
Braşov
Ploieşti
Galaţi
Brăila
Debrecen
Szeged
Novi Sad
Niš
Ruse
Pleven
Edirne
Karadeniz Boğazı (Bosporus)
Istranca Dağları

1:5M
0 50 100 150 200 km
0 50 100 mls
MACEDONIA
GREECE
TURKEY
AEGEAN SEA
IONIAN SEA
IÓNIOI NÍSOI
(Ionian Islands)
Sea of Marmara
Sea of Crete
Mirtoan Sea
SPORÁDHES
(DODECANESE)
Kikládhes
(Cyclades)
Kríti
Strait of Otranto
Tiranë
Durrës
Kavajë
Lushnjë
Elbasan
Fier
Berat
Ballsh
Vlorë
Gjirokastër
Sarandë
Korçë
Tomorrit 2480
Grámmos 2503
Smólikas 2633
Ohrid
Bitola
Prilep
Kavadarci
Gevgelija
Flórina
Kastoría
Edhessa
Yiannitsá
Véroia
Ptolemaïs
Kozáni
Kateríni
Ólimbos (Olympus) 2917
Kilkís
Sérrai
Dráma
Kavála
Xánthi
Komotiní
Sápai
Alexandroúpolis
Nigríta
Thessaloníki
(Salonica)
Khalkidhikí
Políyiros
K.Strimonikós
K.Singitikós
K.Toronaíos
Áthos 2033
Thermaïkós Kólpos
Thásos
Samothráki
Gökçeada
Límnos
Kástron
Bozcaada
Áyios Evstrátios
Lésvos
Mitilíni
Kallonis K.
Brindisi
Lecce
Otranto
Maglie
Gallipoli
C.Sta Maria di Leuca
Kérkira
Kérkira (Corfu)
Igoumenítsa
Ioánnina
Tzouméika 2429
Kalabáka
Tírnavos
Lárisa
Vólos
Fársala
Almirós
Kardhítsa
Dhomokós
Timfristós 2316
Óthris 1726
Lamía
Árta
Préveza
Levkás
Amfilokhía
Agrínion
Gióna 2510
Ámfissa
Levádhia
Návpaktos
Mesolóngion
Kefallinía
Argostólion
Zákinthos
Skíathos
Skópelos
Iliodhrómia
Skíros
Istiáia
Évvoia
Livanátais
Kími
Khalkís
Thívai
Akharnái
Athínai
(Athens)
Piraiévs
Mégara
Pátrai
Aíyion
Sikionía
Killíni 2376
Kórinthos
Korinthiakós K.
Amaliás
Pírgos
Trípolis
Árgos
Návplion
Megalópolis
Kiparissiakós Kólpos
Kiparissía
Filiatrá
Kalámai
Spartí
Messíni
Párnon Ó. 1935
Píloc
Yíthion
Moláoi
Neápolis
Akr. Maléa
Akr. Taínaron
Messiniakós Kólpos
Lakonikós Kólpos
Argolikós K.
Saronikós K.
Aíyna
Ídhra
Kíthira
Andikíthira
Kéa
Kíthnos
Sérifos
Sífnos
Mílos
Síros
Tínos
Ándros
Kárístos
Akr. Kafiréfs
Míkonos
Náxos
Páros
Síkinos
Íos
Thíra
Anáfi
Amorgós
Astipálaia
Khíos
Psará
Çeşme
Urla
İzmir
Bornova
Menemen
Çandarlı K.
Manisa
Turgutlu
Salihli
Alaşehir 2157
Boz Dağları
Ödemiş
Tire
Torbalı
Selçuk
Aydın
Nazilli
Buldan
Denizli
Kuşadası K.
Sámos
Ikaría
Pagondhas
Foúrnoi
Pátmos
Léros
Kálimnos
Kós
Mandalya K.
Bodrum
Kerme K.
Milas
Muğla
Marmaris
Sími
Tílos
Alimniá
Khálki
Ródhos
Lindos
Kárpathos
Kásos
Söke
Çine
Ak
Kula
Gediz
Akhisar
Kirkağaç
Soma
Sindirği
Bigadiç
Simav
Ak Dağ 2089
Balıkesir
Dursunbey
Tavşanlı
Edremit
Edremit K.
Burhaniye
Ayvalık
Bergama
Ayvacık
Ezine
Çanakkale
Eceabat
Gelibolu (Gallipoli)
Saros Körfezi
Biga
Gönen
Bandırma
Karacabey
Mustafa-Kemalpaşa
Bursa
Gemlik
Yalova
Iznik G.
Orhaneli
Kus G.
Marmara Adi
Tekirdağ
Tekir D.
Malkara
Keşan
Ipsala
Khaniá
Akr. Spátha
Kastélli
Lévka Óri 2452
Réthimnon
Ídhi Óros 2456
Iráklion
Dhíkti Óri 2148
K. Merabéllou
Akr. Sídheros
Sitía
Ierápetra
Timbákion
Akr. Líthinon

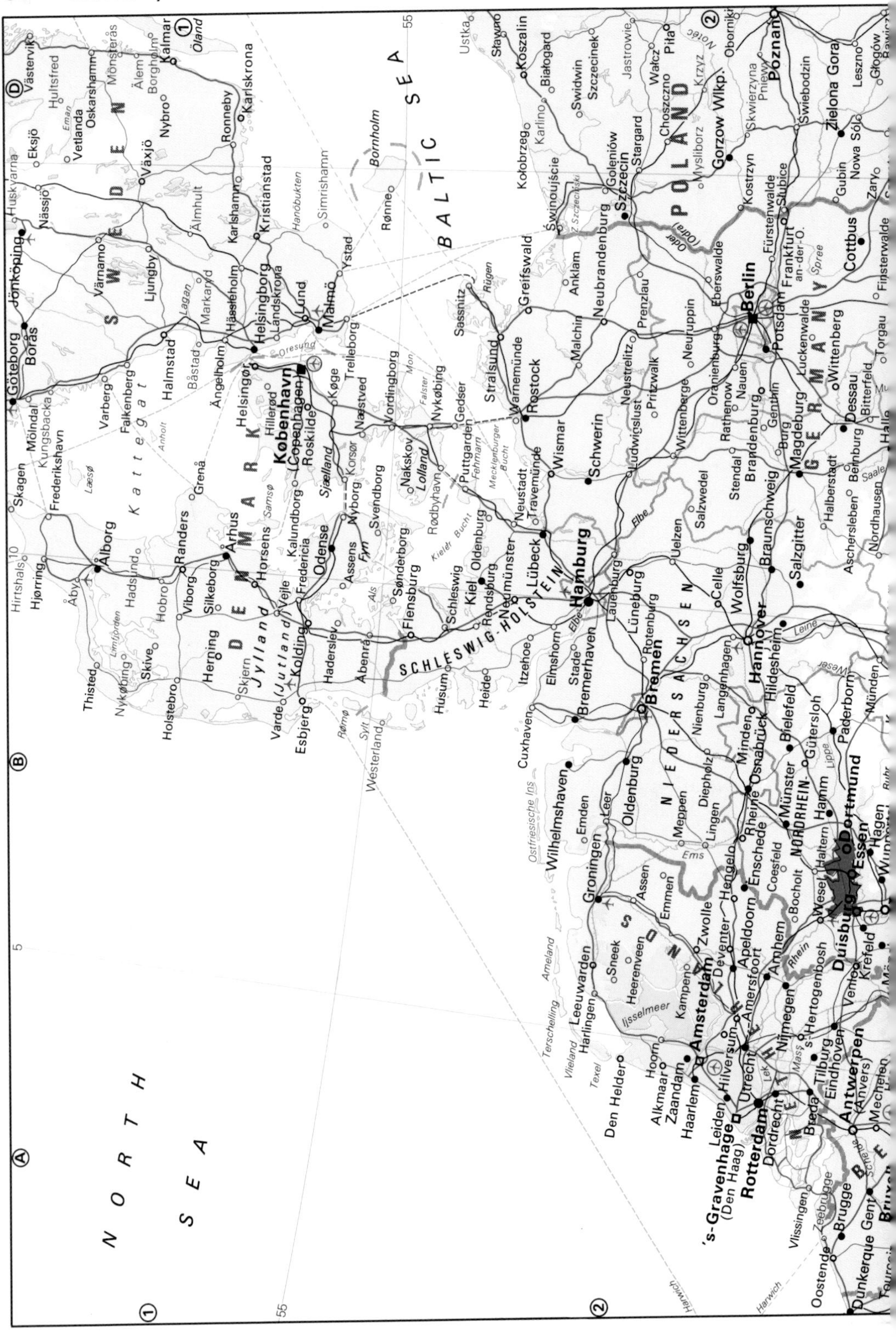
NORTH SEA
BALTIC SEA
Kattegat
SWEDEN
DENMARK
POLAND
GERMANY
NIEDERSACHSEN
NORDRHEIN-
SCHLESWIG-HOLSTEIN
Göteborg
Borås
Jönköping
Västervik
Eksjö
Vetlanda
Hultsfred
Oskarshamn
Mönsterås
Kalmar
Öland
Nässjö
Växjö
Älmhult
Nybro
Karlskrona
Ronneby
Karlshamn
Kristianstad
Hässleholm
Helsingborg
Landskrona
Lund
Malmö
Trelleborg
Ystad
Simrishamn
Hanöbukten
Bornholm
Rønne
Värnamo
Ljungby
Markaryd
Halmstad
Båstad
Ängelholm
Falkenberg
Varberg
Kungsbacka
Mölndal
Frederikshavn
Skagen
Læsø
Anholt
Grenå
Helsingør
Hillerød
København
(Copenhagen)
Roskilde
Køge
Næstved
Vordingborg
Nykøbing
Falster
Gedser
Sjælland
Korsør
Nyborg
Svendborg
Odense
Fyn
Kalundborg
Samsø
Århus
Randers
Ålborg
Hjørring
Hirtshals
Hadsund
Hobro
Viborg
Silkeborg
Horsens
Vejle
Fredericia
Kolding
Herning
Skive
Thisted
Nykøbing
Holstebro
Skjern
Jylland
(Jutland)
Varde
Esbjerg
Haderslev
Åbenrå
Sønderborg
Als
Flensburg
Schleswig
Husum
Heide
Rømø
Sylt
Westerland
Kiel
Rendsburg
Neumünster
Lübeck
Kieler Bucht
Oldenburg
Puttgarden
Fehmarn
Rødbyhavn
Nakskov
Lolland
Neustadt
Travemünde
Wismar
Rostock
Warnemünde
Stralsund
Sassnitz
Rügen
Greifswald
Anklam
Świnoujście
Szczecin
Goleniów
Stargard
Kołobrzeg
Koszalin
Białogard
Sławno
Ustka
Piła
Wałcz
Choszczno
Szczecinek
Swidwin
Gorzów Wlkp.
Myślibórz
Kostrzyn
Poznań
Zielona Góra
Świebodzin
Nowa Sól
Leszno
Głogów
Oder (Odra)
Frankfurt an-der-O.
Słubice
Fürstenwalde
Cottbus
Berlin
Potsdam
Eberswalde
Prenzlau
Neubrandenburg
Malchin
Neustrelitz
Neuruppin
Oranienburg
Nauen
Rathenow
Brandenburg
Genthin
Wittenberge
Pritzwalk
Ludwigslust
Schwerin
Hamburg
Lauenburg
Lüneburg
Uelzen
Salzwedel
Stendal
Burg
Magdeburg
Dessau
Wittenberg
Luckenwalde
Torgau
Bitterfeld
Halle
Bernburg
Halberstadt
Aschersleben
Nordhausen
Braunschweig
Wolfsburg
Salzgitter
Celle
Hannover
Hildesheim
Elbe
Weser
Leine
Itzehoe
Elmshorn
Stade
Cuxhaven
Bremerhaven
Bremen
Rotenburg
Wilhelmshaven
Oldenburg
Emden
Leer
Nienburg
Langenhagen
Minden
Bielefeld
Osnabrück
Gütersloh
Paderborn
Münden
Diepholz
Meppen
Lingen
Rheine
Münster
Hamm
Dortmund
Essen
Duisburg
Hagen
Krefeld
Wesel
Bocholt
Haltern
Coesfeld
Enschede
Hengelo
Ems
Ostfriesische Ins.
Groningen
Assen
Emmen
Zwolle
Deventer
Apeldoorn
Arnhem
Nijmegen
Venlo
Leeuwarden
Harlingen
Sneek
Heerenveen
Kampen
IJsselmeer
Ameland
Terschelling
Vlieland
Texel
Den Helder
Hoorn
Alkmaar
Zaandam
Amsterdam
Haarlem
Hilversum
Amersfoort
Utrecht
Leiden
's-Gravenhage
(Den Haag)
Rotterdam
Dordrecht
Breda
Tilburg
's-Hertogenbosch
Eindhoven
Antwerpen
(Anvers)
Mechelen
Vlissingen
Zeebrugge
Brugge
Gent
Oostende
Dunkerque
Harwich
Rhein
Lek
Maas

1:5M

0 50 100 150 200 km

0 50 100 mls

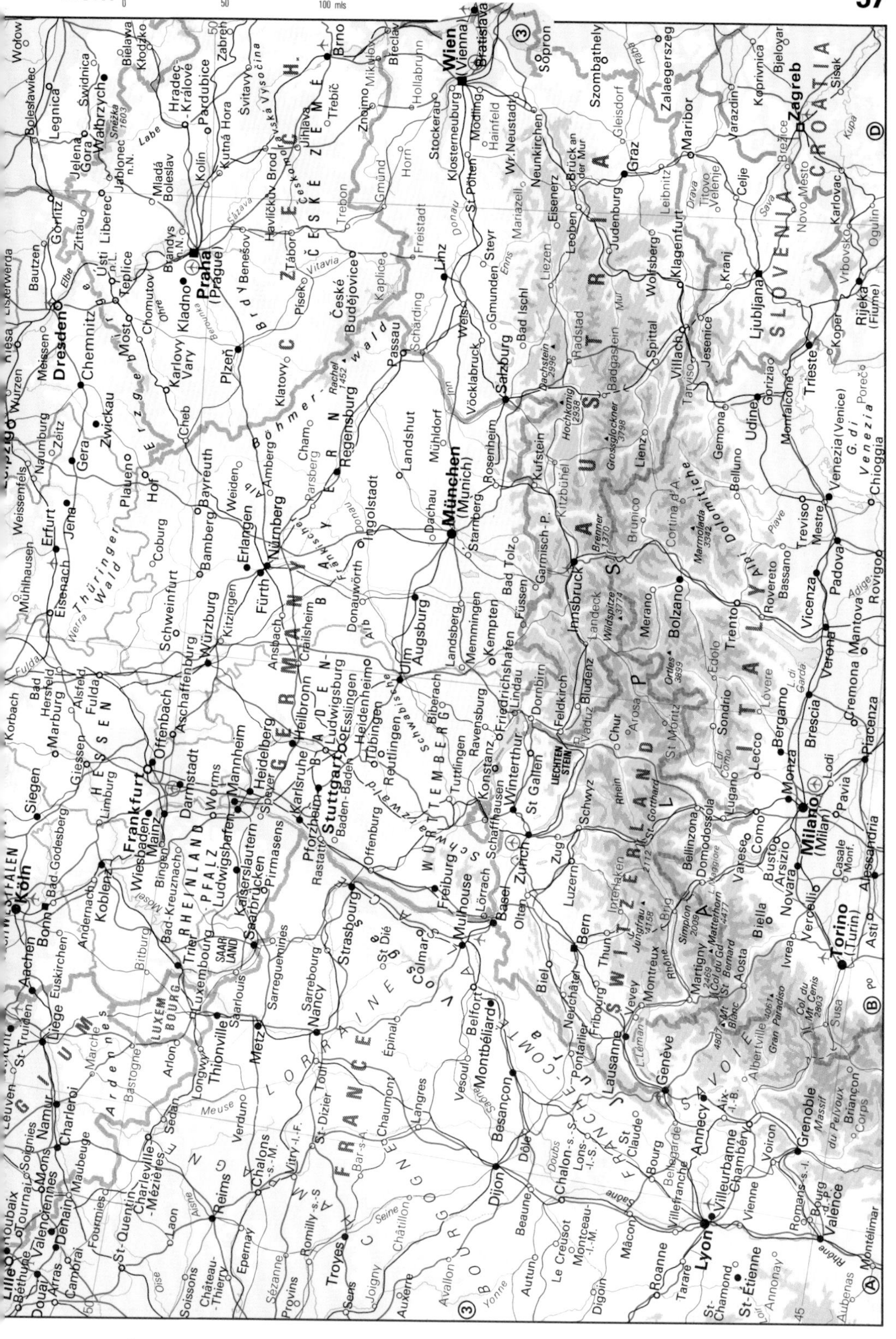

RUSSIAN FEDERATION
LATVIA
LITHUANIA
BELORUSSIA
POLAND
SWEDEN
BALTIC SEA
RUS. FED.
Gulf of Riga
Gulf of Gdańsk (Z. Gdańska)
Courland Lagoon
Gotland
Öland
Bornholm
Rügen
Hanöbukten
Riga
Vilnius
Minsk
Warszawa
Kaunas (Kovno)
Kaliningrad (Königsberg)
Gdańsk (Danzig)
Gdynia
Sopot
Elbląg
Olsztyn
Białystok
Grodno
Brest
Pinsk
Baranovichi
Daugavpils
Liepāja
Klaipėda
Ventspils
Jelgava
Jūrmala
Šiauliai
Panevėžys
Polotsk
Novopolotsk
Molodechno
Borisov
Zhodino
Slutsk
Soligorsk
Lida
Szczecin
Poznań
Bydgoszcz
Toruń
Łódź
Kalisz
Płock
Gorzow Wlkp.
Zielona Gora
Koszalin
Słupsk
Cottbus
Frankfurt an-der-O
Karlskrona
Kalmar
Växjö
Kristianstad
Jönköping
Visby
Rønne
Ystad
Sassnitz
Daugava
Neman
Nemunas
Wisła (Vistula)
Narew
Bug
Odra (Oder)
Pripyat'
Berezina
Venta
Gauja
Lielupe
Noteć
Spree
Pregolya
20
55
15
B
C
D
1
2

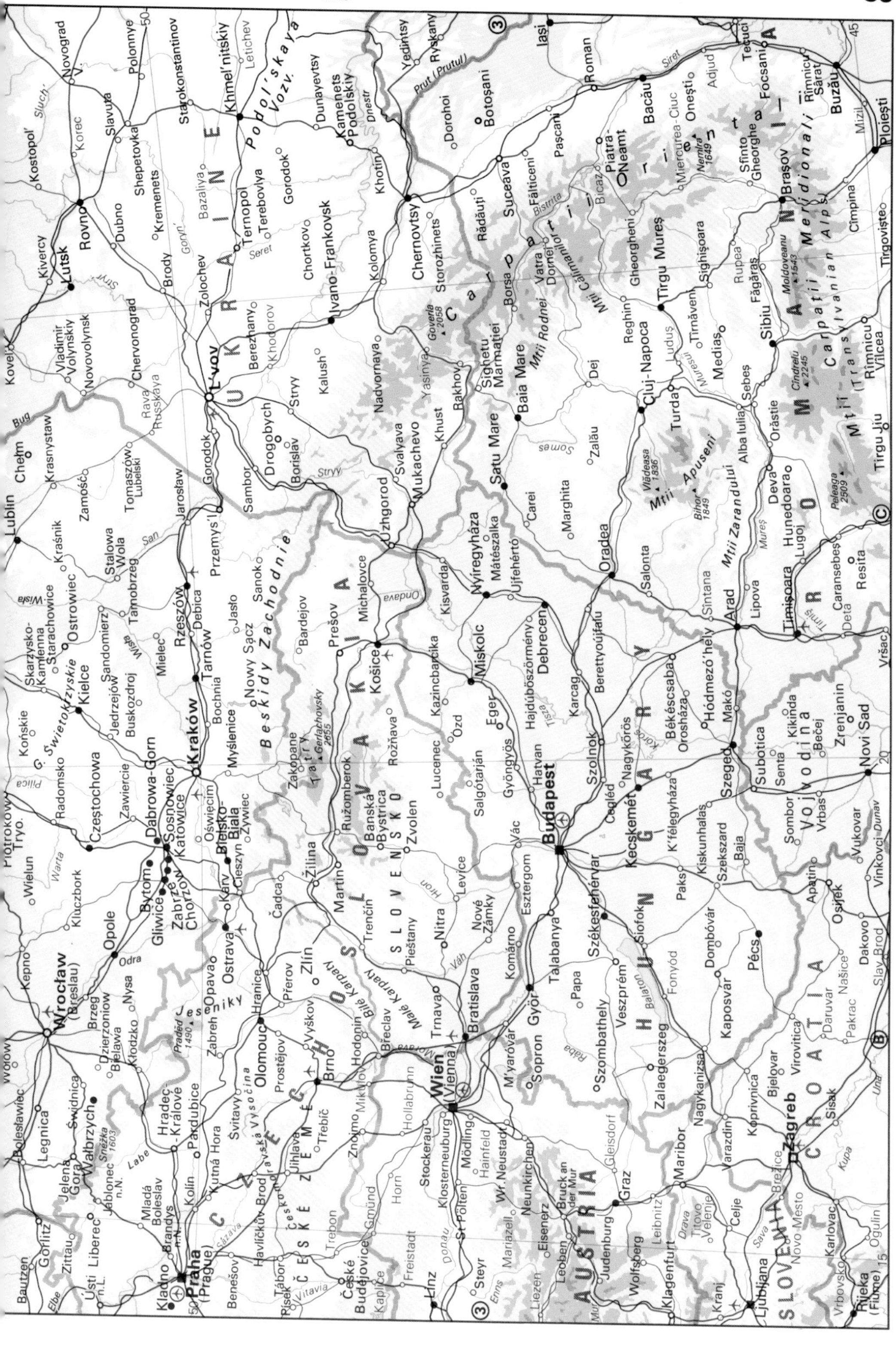
1:5M
0 50 100 150 200 km
0 50 100 mls
UKRAINE
CZECHOSLOVAKIA
ČESKÉ ZEMĚ
SLOVENSKO
HUNGARY
ROMANIA
AUSTRIA
SLOVENIA
CROATIA
Vojvodina
Beskidy Zachodnie
Podol'skaya Vozv.
Carpații Meridionali
(Transylvanian Alps)
Mtii Apuseni
Mtii Rodnei
Mtii Zarandului
Budapest
Wien (Vienna)
Praha (Prague)
Bratislava
Zagreb
Ljubljana
Kraków
Wrocław (Breslau)
L'vov
Lublin
Iași
Cluj-Napoca
Debrecen
Košice
Brno
Graz
Rijeka (Fiume)
Miskolc
Szeged
Pécs
Oradea
Arad
Timișoara
Brașov
Ploiești
Chernovtsy
Rovno
Lutsk
Katowice
Ostrava
Olomouc
Linz

Stockholm
Södertälje
Nynäshamn
Katrineholm
Nyköping
Norrköping
Linköping
Tranås
Nässjö
Västervik
Visby
Oskarshamn
Gotland
Hemse
Borgholm
Öland
Kalmar
Karlskrona
B A L T I C S E A
Hangö
Karis
Helsinki
Porvoo
Kotka
Gulf of Finland
Tallinn
Kohtla-Järve
Hiiumaa
Haapsalu
Saaremaa
Pärnu
Kuressaare
E S T O N I A
Narva
Tapa
Viljandi
Lake Peipus
Tartu
Valga
Võru
Gulf of Riga
Ventspils
Kuldiga
Liepāja
Riga
Jūrmala
Cēsis
Jelgava
L A T V I A
Jekabpils
Mazeikiai
Klaipeda
Šiauliai
Panevežys
Daugavpils
Daugava
Rēzekne
L I T H U A N I A
Kaliningrad
Sovetsk
Nemunas
RUS. FED.
Kaunas
Chernyakhovsk
Marijampole
Ukmerge
Vilnius
Alytus
Vyborg
Ladozhskoye Ozero
Sankt-Peterburg (Leningrad)
Lomonosov
Gatchina
Pushkin
Volkhov
Tosno
Kirishi
Luga
Chudovo
Novgorod
Oz. Il'men
Staraya Russa
Pskov
Ostrov
Dno
Valday
Borovichi
Olonets
Podporozh'ye
Lodeynoye Pole
Vepsovskaya Vozv.
Vytegra
Belozersk
Beloye O.
Tikhvin
Babayevo
Cherepovets
R U S S I A
Pestovo
Rybinskoye Vdkhr.
Rybinsk
Bologoye
Vyshniy-Volochek
Bezhetsk
Uglich
Valdayskaya
Ostashkov
Torzhok
Kalyazin
Kimry
Tver'
Dubna
Volga
Vozvyshennost
Opochka
Toropets
Rzhev
Klin
Dmitrov
Zagorsk
Velikiye Luki
Nevel
Nelidovo
Moskva (Moscow)
Noginsk
Lyublino
Polotsk
Gagarin
Vitebsk
Glubokoye
Lepel
Yartsevo
Vyaz'ma
Naro-Fominsk
Podolsk
Smolensk
Orsha
Smorgon'
Molodechno
Borisov
Lida
Neman
Grodno
Novogrudok
Minsk
Mogilev
Cherven'
Volkovysk
Baranovichi
B E L O R U S S I A
Slonim
Slutsk
Bobruysk
Osipovichi
Krichev
Roslavl'
Kirov
Kaluga
Aleksin
Serpukhov
Tula
Sukhinichi
Shchekino
Plavsk
Uzlovaya
Novomoskovsk
Sredne-Russkaya Vozvyshennost'
Soligorsk
Dneprovskaya
Zhlobin
Bryansk
Unecha
Klintsy
Mtsensk
Orel
Yefremov
Yelets
Lipetsk
Livny
Brest
Kobrin
Pinsk
Pripyat'
Nizmennost
Kalinkovichi
Gomel'
Novozybkov
Navlya
Desna
Dobrush
Mozyr
Khoyniki
Shchors
Shostka
Sarny
Ovruch
Chernobyl
Chernigov
Glukhov
Rylsk
Kursk
Shchigry
Seym
Kovel'
Lutsk
Korosten
Nezhin
Konotop
Bakhmach
Sumy
Sula
Oboyan'
Staryy Oskol
Semiluki
Rovno
Dubno
Novograd Volynskiy
Kiyev (Kiev)
Romny
Priluki
Vasil'kov
Borisovka
Belgorod
Brody
Shepetovka
Zhitomir
Fastov
Berdichev
Lubny
Akhtyrka
Dergachi
Valuyki
Khar'kov
Kupyansk
U K R A I N E
Khmel'nitskiy
Vinnitsa
Zhmerinka
Cherkassy
Smela
Kremenchugskoye Vdkhr.
Poltava
Kremenchug
Sev. Donets
Mogilev Podol'skiy
Gaysin
Uman'
Tal'noye
Kirovograd
Dneprodzerzhinsk
Dnepropetrovsk
Slavyansk
Kramatorsk
Lisichansk
Gorlovka
Donetsk
Makeyevka
Soroki
Balta
Pervomaysk
Krivoy Rog
Zaporozh'ye
Nikopol
Kotovsk
Voznesensk
Prichernomorskaya Nizmennost
Berezovka
Nikolayev
Kakhovskoye Vdkhr.
Melitopol'
Taganrog
Mariupol'
Novocherkassk
Yeysk
Berdyansk
Kherson
Novaya Kakhovka
Dnepr
Odessa
Belgorod Dnestrovskiy
Azovskoye More
Primorsko-Akhtarsk
Karkinitskiy Z.
Dzhankoy
Krym
Kerch'
Timashevsk
Yevpatoriya
Simferopol'
Feodosiya
Sevastopol'
Yalta
M. Sarych
Krasnodar
Krymsk
Novorossiysk
Tuapse
Kishinev (Chişinău)
Tiraspol
Bendery
Bel'tsy
Iaşi
Prut
M O L D A V I A
Dnestr
Bolgrad
Izmail
Tulcea
Sulina
Galaţi
Brăila
Slupsk
Gdańsk (Danzig)
Gdynia
Elblag
Chojnice
Wisla
Olsztyn
Suwałki
Ostróda
Ełk
Bydgoszcz
Grudziadz
Toruń
Włocławek
Białystok
Łomza
Płońsk
Ostrów Mazowiecka
Kutno
Płock
Łowicz
Warszawa (Warsaw)
P O L A N D
Łódź
Siedlce
Piotrków Trybunalski
Radom
Dęblin
Lublin
Bug
Częstochowa
Kielce
Chełm
Ostrowiec
Sosnowiec
Vladimir Volynskiy
Rzeszów
Cracow (Kraków)
Przemyśl
Jarosław
L'vov
Gerlachovsky 2663
CZECH.
Prešov
Košice
Stryy
Ternopol
Uzhgorod
Ivano-Frankovsk
Carpathians
Miskolc
Tisza
HUNGARY
Nyiregyháza
Mukachevo
Kolomyya
Debrecen
2058 Goverla
Khotin
Chernovtsy
Satu Mare
Baia Mare
Botoşani
Oradea
Suceava
2305 Pietrosu
Dej
Piatra Neamţ
Békéscsaba
Cluj
1849 Bihor
Roman
Arad
R O M A N I A
Tîrgu Mureş
Mureşul
Bacău
Timişoara
Bîrlad
Resita
Sibiu
Negolu 2544
Braşov
Mtii Carpaţii Meridionali
Rîmnicu Vîlcea
Buzău
Tîrgu Jiu
Turnu Severin
Piteşti
Ploieşti
Danube
YUGOSLAVIA
Craiova
Zaječar
Bucureşti (Bucharest)
Roşiori de Vede
Dunărea
Cernavodă
Lom
Dunav
Ruse
Silistra
Constanţa
Niš
Pleven
Veliko Turnovo
Dobrich
Shumen
Stara Planina
Pernik
Sofiya (Sofia)
Kazanlŭk
Sliven
Varna
Pazardzhik
BULGARIA
Plovdiv
Stara Zagora
Yambol
Burgas
Blagoevgrad
Khaskovo
B L A C K S E A
55
50
45
30
35
A B C D E
2 3 4 5

1:10M 0 100 200 300 400 km 0 100 200 mls

Podyuga
Konosha
Vel'sk
Velikiy Ustyug
Krasavino
Luza
Luza
Griva
Kazhim
Kama
Gayny
Solikamsk
Berezniki
Kizel
Serov
Sos'va
Nov. Lyalya
Tura
Pinyug
Brusenets
Lesnoy
Tot'ma
Kharovsk
Sokol
Sukhona
Roslyatino
Nikol'sk
Oparino
Vyatka
Kirs
Kudymkar
Kamskoye Vdkhr.
Kachkanar
Kushva
Chusovoy
Nizhniy Tagil
Turinsk
Alapayevsk
Irbit
Artemovskiy
Vologda
Gryazovets
Unzha
Murashi
Moloma
Kirov
Omutninsk
Vereshchagino
Krasnokamsk
Lys'va
Nev'yansk
Rezh
Asbest
Kamyshlov
Kostroma
Buy
Galich
Manturovo
Neya
Sharya
Khalturin
Kotel'nich
Zuyevka
Novo-Vyatsk
Glazov
Balezino
Ocher
Perm
Kungur
Kirovgrad
Shamary
Yekaterinburg
Pervoural'sk
Revda
Bogdanovich
Kamensk-Ural'skiy
Kostroma
Makaryev
Shakhun'ya
Vetluga
Nolinsk
Bogorodskoye
Igra
Udmurtskaya R.
Kama
Votkinsk
Osa
Chaykovskiy
Krasnoufimsk
Nizhniye Sergi
Sysert'
Techa
Kasli
Kyshtym
Yaroslavl'
Kineshma
Volga
Vichuga
Rostov
Ivanovo
Shuya
Uren'
Sovetsk
Yaransk
Urzhum
Kil'mez
Izhevsk
Sarapul
Chernushka
Sanchursk
Gor'kovskoye Vdkhr
Semenov
Yoshkar Ola
Malmyzh
Mozhga
Agryz
Kambarka
Nizhnekamskoye Vdkhr.
Ufa
Nyazepetrovsk
1003
G. Yurma
Chelyabinsk
Gorodets
Nizhniy Novgorod
Mariyskaya R.
Cheboksary
Arsk
Naberezhnye Chelny
Menzelinsk
Belaya
Pavlovka
Kusa
Zlatoust
Satka
Kopeysk
Miass
Korkino
Kovrov
Dzerzhinsk
Vladimir
Vyazniki
Gus' Khrustalnyy
Koz'modemyansk
Pavlovo
Zelenodol'sk
Chuvashkaya R.
Kazan
Mamadysh
Tatarskaya R.
Zainsk
Birsk
Asha
Ust' Katav
Bakal
Plast
Orekhovo Zuyevo
Murom
Arzamas
Shumerlya
Kanash
Chistopol
Al'met'yevsk
Bashkirskaya R.
Tirlyanskiy
Beloretsk
Verkhneural'sk
Kolomna
Oka
Sergach
Alatyr
Tetyushi
Kuybyshevskoye Vdkhr.
Leninogorsk
Bugul'ma
Oktyabr'skiy
Davlekanovo
Krasnousol'skiy
Magnitogorsk
Kasimov
Pervomaysk
Nurlat
Belebey
Kartaly
Ryazan'
Sasovo
Moksha
Mordovskaya R.
Saransk
Ul'yanovsk
Dimitrovgrad
Sernovodsk
Buguruslan
Abdulino
Sterlitamak
Salavat
Skopin
Novomoskovsk
Shilovo
Kovylkino
Privolzhskaya
Barysh
Tol'yatti
Meleuz
Belaya
Sibay
Ural
Baymak
Bredy
Ryazhsk
Sura
Nikol'sk
Kinel'
Samara
Jok
Kumertau
Yuzhnyy Ural
Nizhniy Lomov
Morshansk
Penza
Syzran'
Chaplygin
Kamenka
Kuznetsk
Buzuluk
Sorochinsk
Michurinsk
Vozvyshennost
Saratovskoye Vdkhr.
Bol. Irgiz
Obshchiy Syrt
Tambov
Rasskazovo
Serdobsk
Petrovsk
Khvalynsk
Vol'sk
Balakovo
Orenburg
Saraktash
Mednogorsk
Orsk
Gryazi
Rtishchevo
Pugachev
Ural
Kuvandyk
Novotroitsk
Arkadak
Volga
Sol'-Iletsk
Akbulak
Dombarovskiy
Zherdevka
Atkarsk
Voronezh
Balashov
Saratov
Yershov
Ural'sk
Aksay
Ilek
Mugodzhary
Borisoglebsk
Engel's
Aktyubinsk
Liski
Povorino
Krasnoarmeysk
Krasnyy Kut
Alga
Buturlinovka
Uryupinsk
Volgogradskoye Vdkhr.
Novo Uzensk
Kushum
Novoalekseyevka
Pavlovsk
Novoanninskiy
Chapayevo
Oktyabr'sk
Kalach
Medvedista
Pallasovka
Shubar-Kuduk
Rossosh
Mikhaylovka
Kamyshin
Bol. Uzen
Mal. Uzen
Emba
Nikolayevsk
Prikaspiyskaya Nizmennost'
Uil
Frolovo
Don
Masteksay
Inderborskiy
Perelazovskiy
Millerovo
Volzhskiy
Kalach-na-Donu
Saykhin
KAZAKHSTAN
Zharkamys
Emba
Volgograd (Stalingrad)
Akhtubinsk
Ryn Peski
Makat
Lugansk
Krasnyy Luch
Morozovsk
Tsimlyanskoye Vdkhr.
Kulakshi
Gur'yev
Balykshi
Kul'sary
Aktumsyk
Shakhty
Don
Volgodonsk
Kotel'nikovo
Kharabali
Sal
Rostov-na-Donu
Kalmykskaya R.
Volga
Sarykamys
Sal'sk
Proletarskaya
Krasnyy Yar
Astrakhan'
Yegorlyk
Yashkul'
Elista
Sor Mertvyy Kultuk
Beyneu
Tikhoretsk
Divnoye
Chernyye Zemli
Burynshik
Mumra
Kropotkin
Ipatovo
Kaspiyskiy
Ova Tyuleni
Plato Ustyurt
UZBEKISTAN
Ust' Labinsk
Stavropol'
Armavir
Kuma
M. Tyub-Karagan
Say-Utes
Budennovsk
Ft Shevchenko
Poluostrov Mangyshlak
Maykop
Labinsk
Nevinnomyssk
Cherkessk
Georgiyevsk
Kislovodsk
Pyatigorsk
Shevchenko
Novyy Uzen
Sochi
Prokhladnyy
CASPIAN SEA
Elbrus 5642
Nal'chik
Groznyy
Makhachkala
Fetisovo
Gagra
Dykh Tau 5203
Abkhazskaya R.
Alagir
Vladikavkaz
Buynaksk
F
H
J
K
2
3
4
40
45
50
55
60

1:45M

0 600 1200 1800 km
0 300 600 900 mls

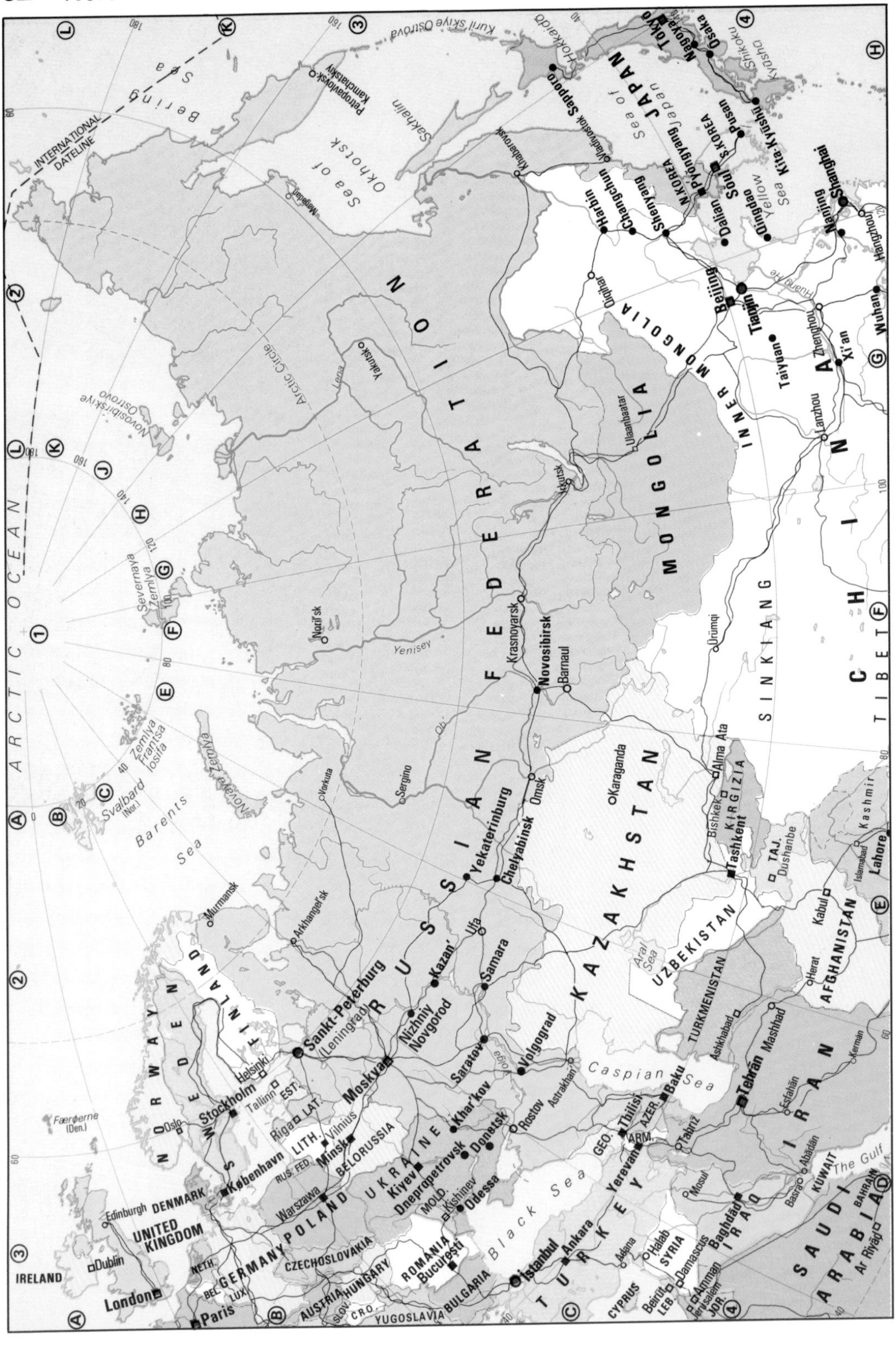

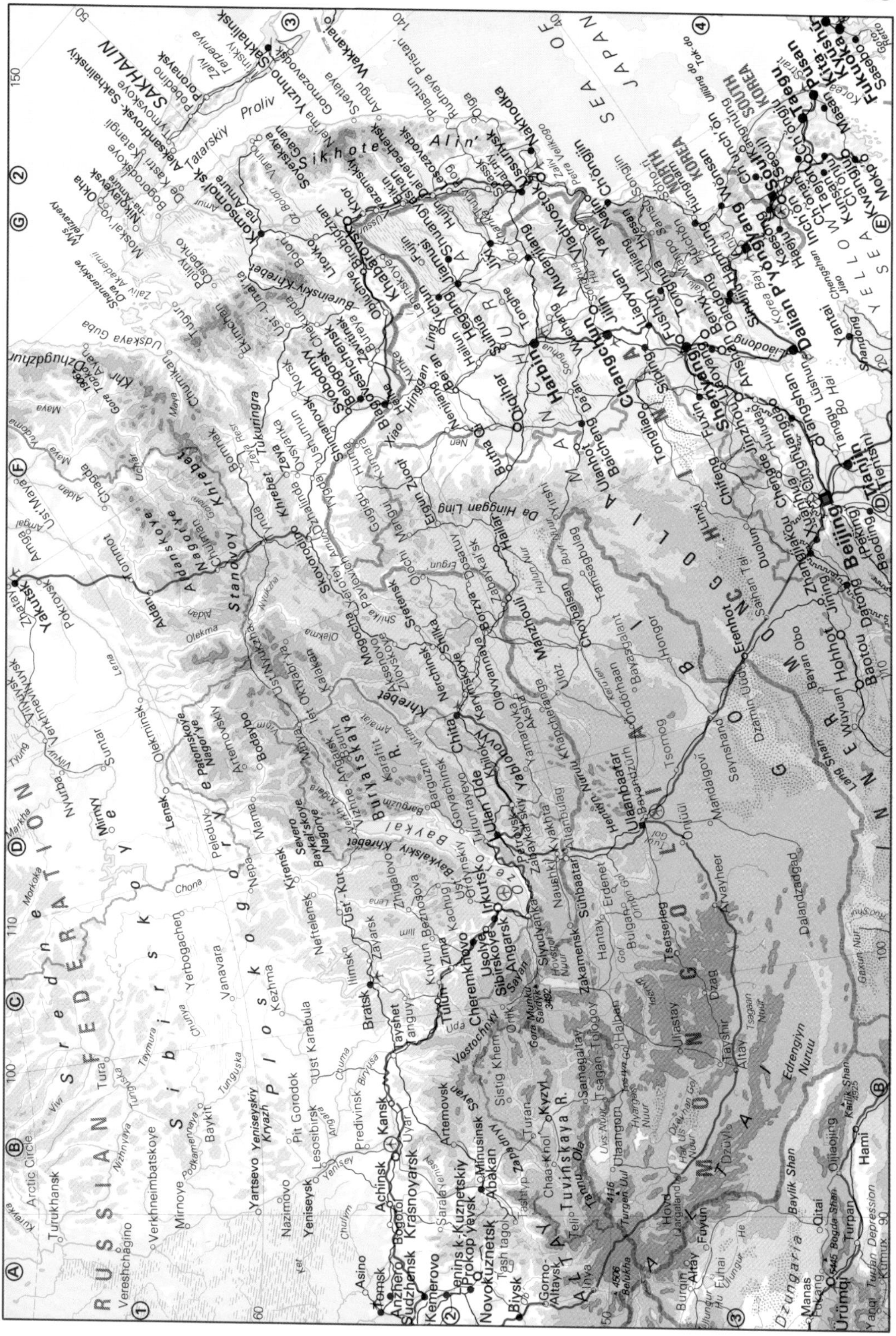
RUSSIAN FEDERATION
Srednesibirskoye Ploskogor'ye
MONGOLIA
CHINA
SEA OF JAPAN
YELLOW SEA
NORTH KOREA
SOUTH KOREA
SAKHALIN
Yakutsk
Aldan
Lensk
Mirnyy
Bratsk
Krasnoyarsk
Achinsk
Kansk
Tomsk
Kemerovo
Novokuznetsk
Abakan
Kyzyl
Irkutsk
Angarsk
Ulan Ude
Chita
Ulaanbaatar
Blagoveshchensk
Khabarovsk
Komsomol'sk-na-Amure
Vladivostok
Nakhodka
Yuzhno-Sakhalinsk
Harbin
Changchun
Jilin
Shenyang
Dalian
Beijing
Tianjin
Hohhot
Baotou
Datong
Qiqihar
Hailar
Ürümqi
Turpan
Hami
P'yŏngyang
Seoul
Taegu
Pusan
Fukuoka
Ozero Baykal
Stanovoy Khrebet
Sikhote Alin'
Da Hinggan Ling
Xiao Hinggan Ling
Yablonovyy Khrebet
Baykal'skiy Khrebet
Arctic Circle

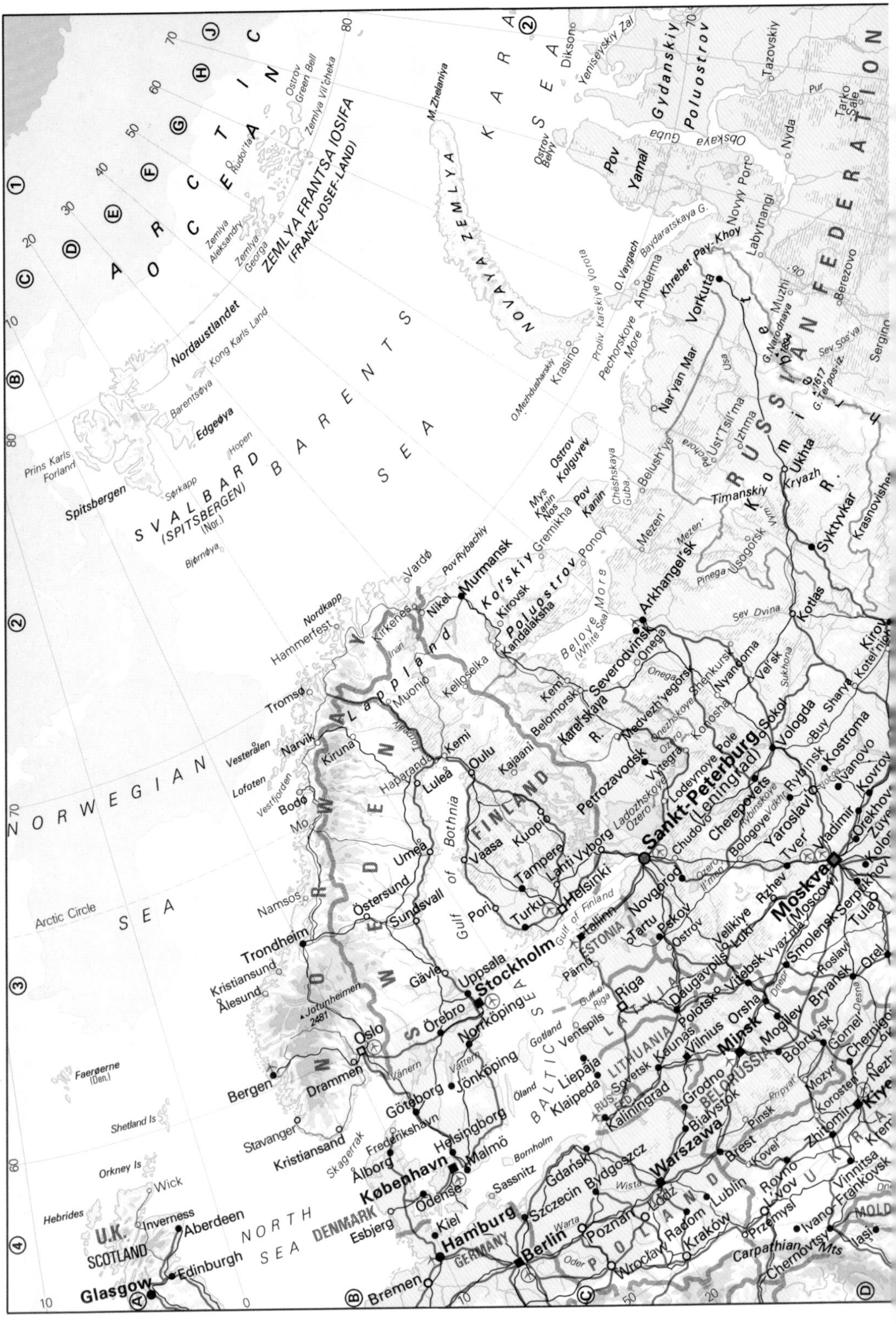
ARCTIC OCEAN
KARA SEA
BARENTS SEA
NORWEGIAN SEA
NORTH SEA
BALTIC SEA
ZEMLYA FRANTSA IOSIFA (FRANZ JOSEF LAND)
NOVAYA ZEMLYA
SVALBARD (SPITSBERGEN) (Nor.)
Spitsbergen
Nordaustlandet
Edgeøya
Bjørnøya
Gydanskiy Poluostrov
Pov Yamal
Obskaya Guba
Kol'skiy Poluostrov
Lappland
Beloye More (White Sea)
Gulf of Bothnia
Gulf of Finland
Arctic Circle
RUSSIAN FEDERATION
Komi R.
FINLAND
SWEDEN
NORWAY
ESTONIA
LATVIA
LITHUANIA
BELORUSSIA
POLAND
DENMARK
GERMANY
UKRAINE
U.K.
SCOTLAND
Faerøerne (Den.)
Shetland Is
Orkney Is
Hebrides
Vorkuta
Nar'yan Mar
Ukhta
Syktyvkar
Kotlas
Arkhangel'sk
Severodvinsk
Murmansk
Kirovsk
Kandalaksha
Vologda
Kostroma
Yaroslavl
Rybinsk
Cherepovets
Sankt-Peterburg (Leningrad)
Petrozavodsk
Novgorod
Pskov
Tver
Moskva (Moscow)
Smolensk
Vitebsk
Minsk
Orsha
Mogilev
Gomel
Bryansk
Tula
Oulu
Kemi
Vaasa
Kuopio
Tampere
Turku
Helsinki
Tallinn
Tartu
Riga
Daugavpils
Vilnius
Kaunas
Kaliningrad
Klaipeda
Liepaja
Grodno
Bialystok
Warszawa
Łódź
Lublin
Kraków
Poznań
Gdańsk
Szczecin
Bydgoszcz
Berlin
Hamburg
Bremen
Kiel
København
Odense
Malmö
Helsingborg
Göteborg
Jönköping
Norrköping
Örebro
Stockholm
Uppsala
Gävle
Sundsvall
Östersund
Umeå
Luleå
Kiruna
Narvik
Tromsø
Hammerfest
Nordkapp
Bodø
Trondheim
Kristiansund
Ålesund
Bergen
Stavanger
Kristiansand
Oslo
Drammen
Ålborg
Esbjerg
Aberdeen
Inverness
Edinburgh
Glasgow
Wick

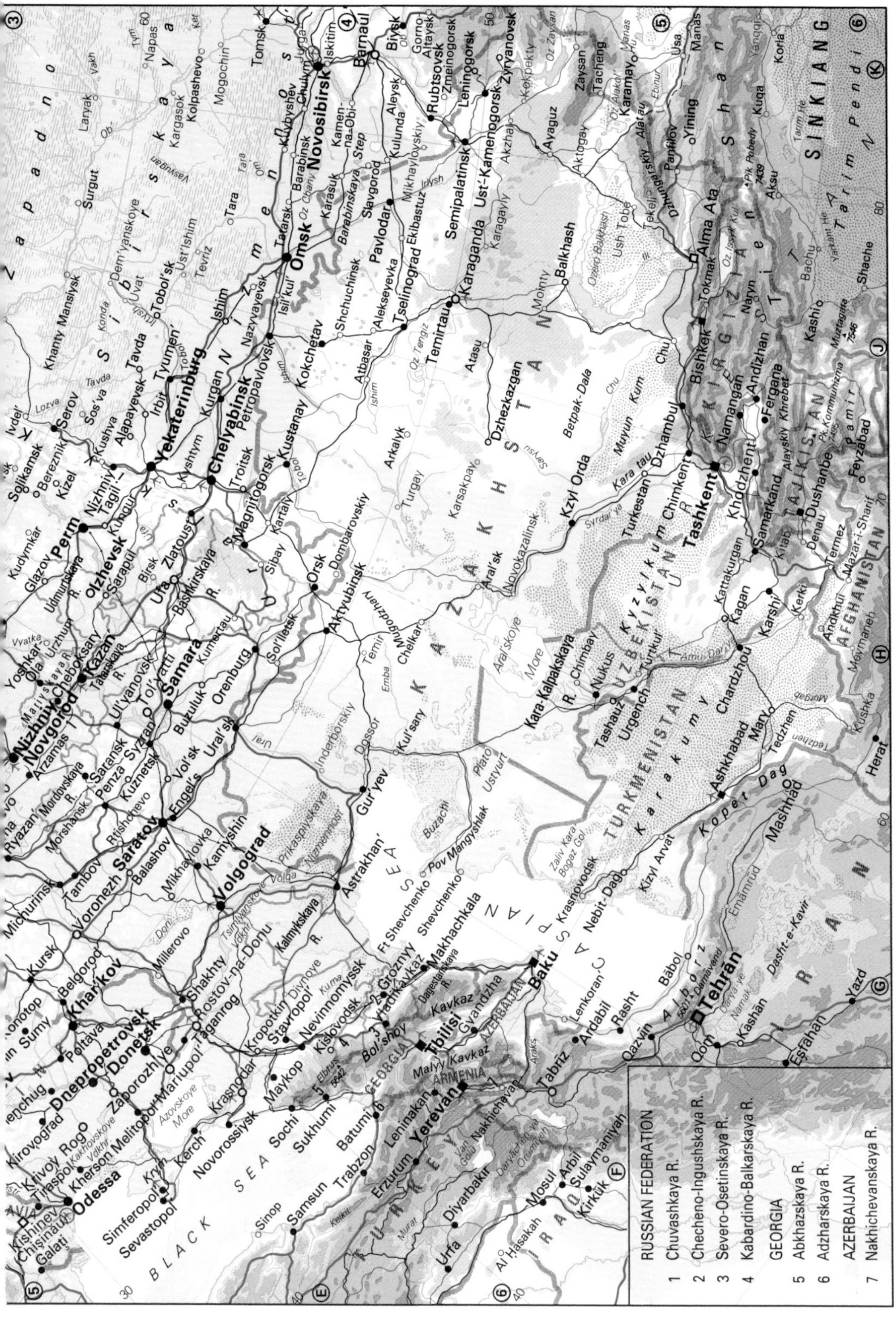
RUSSIAN FEDERATION
1 Chuvashskaya R.
2 Checheno-Ingushskaya R.
3 Severo-Osetinskaya R.
4 Kabardino-Balkarskaya R.
GEORGIA
5 Abkhazskaya R.
6 Adzharskaya R.
AZERBAIJAN
7 Nakhichevanskaya R.

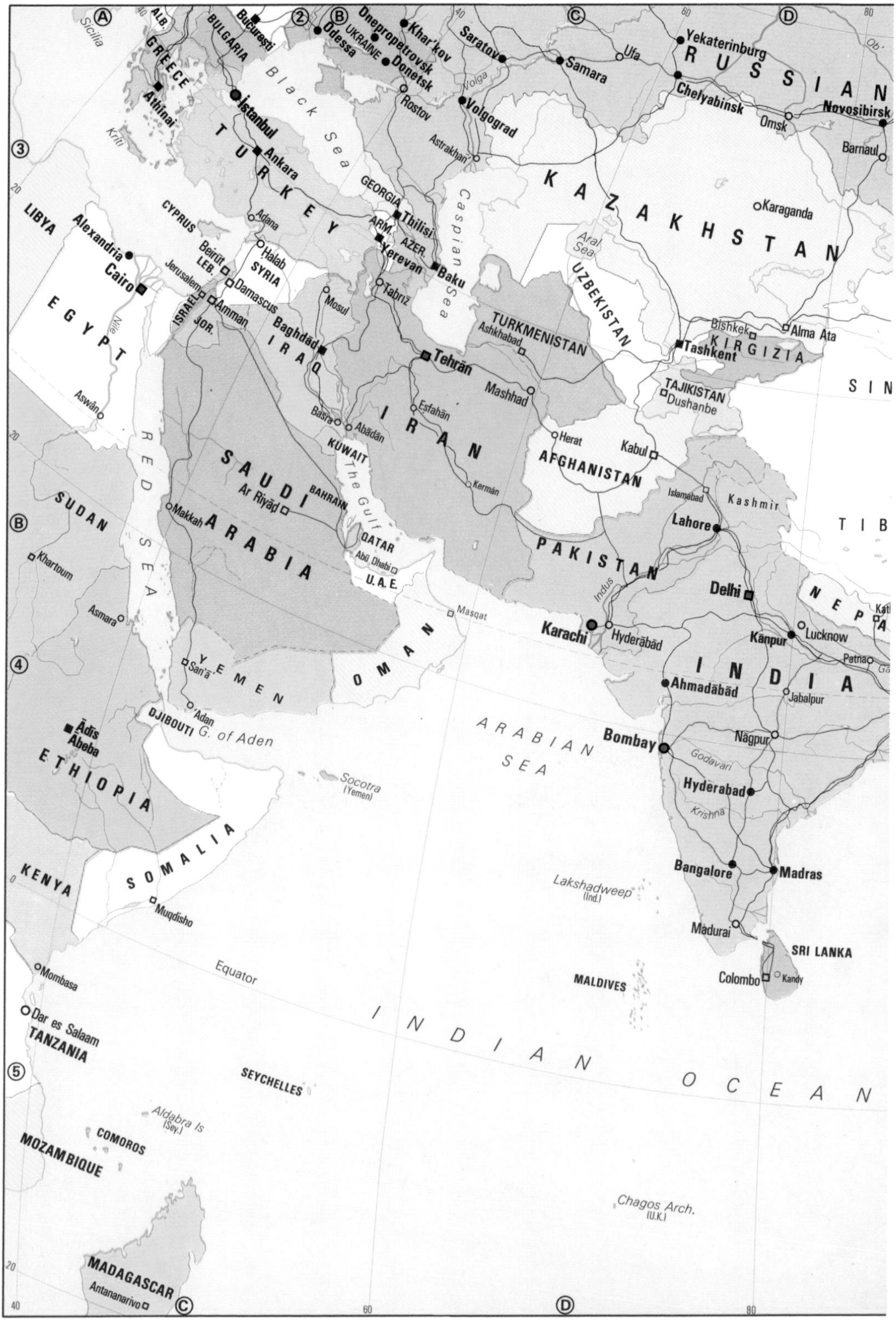

RUSSIAN
KAZAKHSTAN
TURKEY
IRAN
IRAQ
SAUDI ARABIA
EGYPT
LIBYA
SUDAN
ETHIOPIA
SOMALIA
KENYA
TANZANIA
MOZAMBIQUE
MADAGASCAR
COMOROS
SEYCHELLES
MALDIVES
SRI LANKA
INDIA
PAKISTAN
AFGHANISTAN
TURKMENISTAN
UZBEKISTAN
TAJIKISTAN
KIRGIZIA
YEMEN
OMAN
U.A.E.
QATAR
BAHRAIN
KUWAIT
JOR.
ISRAEL
LEB.
SYRIA
CYPRUS
GEORGIA
ARM.
AZER.
UKRAINE
BULGARIA
GREECE
ALB.
DJIBOUTI
NEPAL
Black Sea
Caspian Sea
Aral Sea
The Gulf
RED SEA
G. of Aden
ARABIAN SEA
INDIAN OCEAN
Equator
Socotra (Yemen)
Lakshadweep (Ind.)
Chagos Arch. (U.K.)
Aldabra Is (Sey.)
Kashmir
Sicilia
Kriti
Nile
Volga
Indus
Godavari
Krishna
Ob'
Bucureşti
Odessa
Dnepropetrovsk
Khar'kov
Donetsk
Rostov
Saratov
Samara
Ufa
Yekaterinburg
Chelyabinsk
Omsk
Novosibirsk
Barnaul
Volgograd
Astrakhan'
Karaganda
Athínai
İstanbul
Ankara
Adana
Halab
Beirut
Damascus
Jerusalem
Amman
Alexandria
Cairo
Aswân
Tbilisi
Yerevan
Baku
Tabriz
Mosul
Baghdād
Basra
Abādān
Tehrān
Esfahān
Mashhad
Kermān
Ashkhabad
Tashkent
Bishkek
Alma Ata
Dushanbe
Herat
Kabul
Islamabad
Lahore
Delhi
Karachi
Hyderābād
Kānpur
Lucknow
Patna
Ahmadābād
Jabalpur
Bombay
Nāgpur
Hyderabad
Bangalore
Madras
Madurai
Colombo
Kandy
Ar Riyād
Makkah
Abū Dhabi
Masqat
San'ā'
'Adan
Khartoum
Asmara
Ādīs Ābeba
Muqdisho
Mombasa
Dar es Salaam
Antananarivo

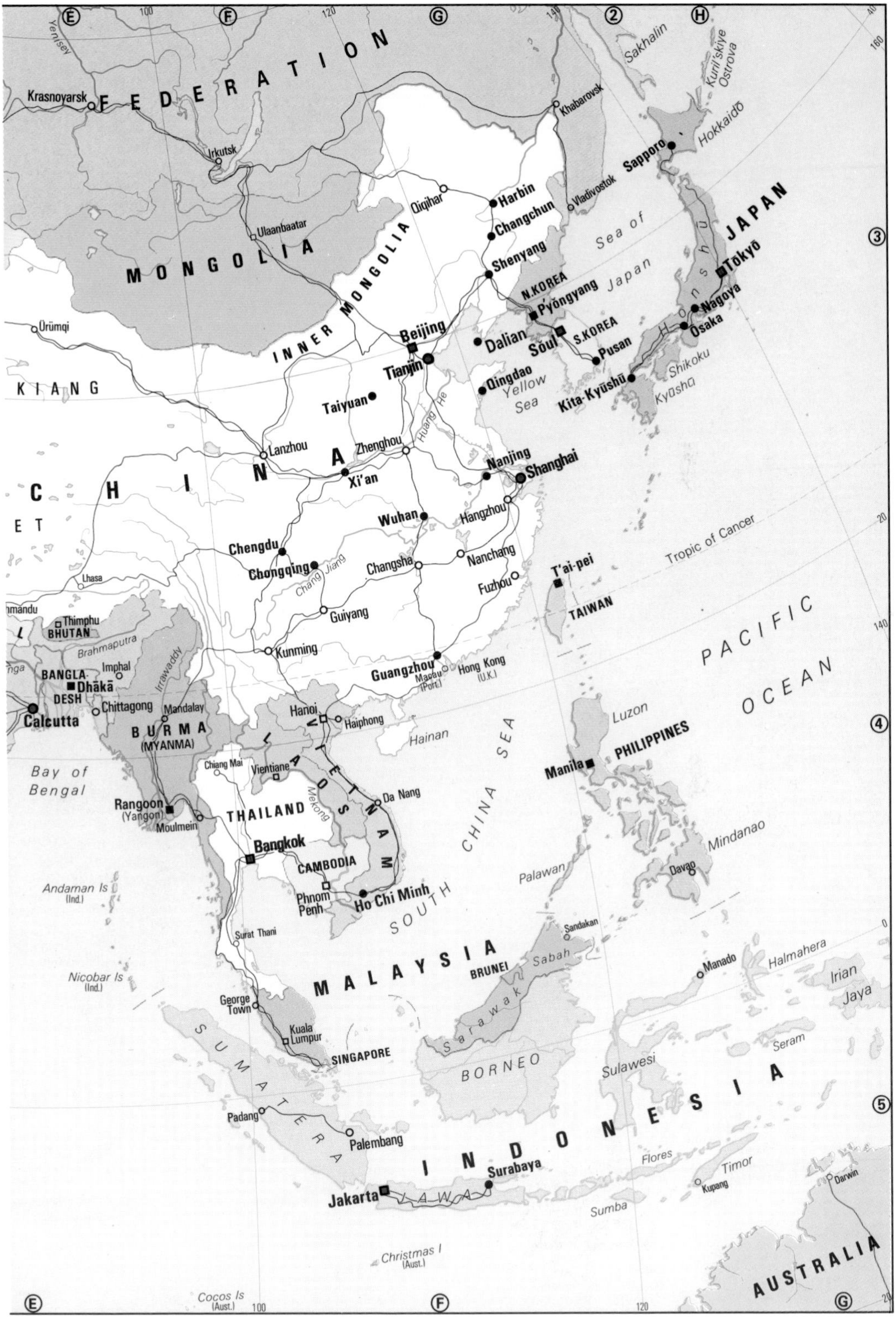
FEDERATION
Krasnoyarsk
Irkutsk
Yenisey
Khabarovsk
Sakhalin
Kuril'skiye Ostrova
Hokkaidō
Sapporo
Vladivostok
Harbin
Qiqihar
Changchun
Ulaanbaatar
MONGOLIA
INNER MONGOLIA
Shenyang
N.KOREA
P'yŏngyang
S.KOREA
Soul
Pusan
Dalian
Beijing
Tianjin
Sea of Japan
JAPAN
Honshu
Tōkyō
Nagoya
Ōsaka
Shikoku
Kyūshū
Kita-Kyūshū
Ürümqi
KIANG
Qingdao
Yellow Sea
Taiyuan
Huang He
Lanzhou
Zhenghou
Xi'an
C H I N A
Nanjing
Shanghai
Hangzhou
Wuhan
Chengdu
Chongqing
Chang Jiang
Changsha
Nanchang
Fuzhou
T'ai-pei
TAIWAN
Tropic of Cancer
Lhasa
Thimphu
BHUTAN
Brahmaputra
Imphal
Guiyang
Kunming
BANGLA-DESH
Dhākā
Chittagong
Calcutta
Irrawaddy
Mandalay
BURMA (MYANMA)
Guangzhou
Macau (Port.)
Hong Kong (U.K.)
PACIFIC OCEAN
Hanoi
Haiphong
Hainan
LAOS
VIETNAM
Luzon
PHILIPPINES
Manila
Bay of Bengal
Chiang Mai
Vientiane
Mekong
Da Nang
SOUTH CHINA SEA
Rangoon (Yangon)
Moulmein
THAILAND
Bangkok
CAMBODIA
Mindanao
Davao
Palawan
Andaman Is (Ind.)
Phnom Penh
Ho Chi Minh
Surat Thani
Sandakan
Sabah
BRUNEI
MALAYSIA
Sarawak
Manado
Halmahera
Irian Jaya
Nicobar Is (Ind.)
George Town
Kuala Lumpur
SINGAPORE
SUMATERA
BORNEO
Sulawesi
Seram
INDONESIA
Padang
Palembang
Flores
Timor
Surabaya
Kupang
Darwin
Jakarta
JAWA
Sumba
Christmas I (Aust.)
AUSTRALIA
Cocos Is (Aust.)

A
B
D
1
2
3
4
5
Mikhaylovskiy
Biysk
Tashtagol
RUS. FED.
Rubtsovsk
Gorno-Altaysk
Tashtyp
Vostochnyy Sayan
Turan
Sistig Khem
Zima
Cheremkhovo
Usolye Sibirskoye
Angarsk
Irkutsk
Ust'-Ordynskiy
Karaftit
Barguzin
Yerofey Pavlo
Aksenovo
Zilovskoye
Mogoch
Tuvinskaya R.
Kyzyl
Orlik
Goryachinsk
Buryatskaya R.
Khrebet
Chita
Leninogorsk
Teli
Chaa-Khol
G. Munku-Sardyk 3492
Slyudyanka
Ozero Baykal
Turuntayevo
Ulan Ude
Domna
Sretensk
Nerchinsk
Shilka
Ust'-Kamenogorsk
Akzhal
Belukha 4506
Inya
Tannu Ola
Turgen Uul 4116
Samagaltay
Uvs Nuur
Hövsgöl Nuur
Petrovsk-Zabaykal'skiy
Khilok
Yablonovyy
Karymskoye
Zyryanovsk
Kokpekty
Tsagan-Tologoy
Zakamensk
Naushki
Kyakhta
Yamarovka
Olovyannaya
Borzya
Ergun
RUS. FED.
Oz. Zaysan
Ulaangom
Testyn Gol
Hyargas Nuur
Sühbaatar
Altanbulag
Aksha
Dosatuy
Burqin
Halban
Hantay
Erdenet
Khapcheranga
Zaysan
Ulungur Hu
Altay
Fuyun
Hovd
Jargalant
Har Us Nuur
Ideriyn Gol
Bulgan
Orhon Gol
Hentiyn Nuruu
Zabaykal'sk
Manzhouli
Hailar
Fuhai
Uliastay
Uldz
Hulun Nur
Karamay
Manas Hu
Ulungur
MONGOLIA
Tsetserleg
Ulaanbaatar
Bayandzürh
Kerulen
Choybalsan
Tayshir
Dzag
Tuul Gol
Öndörhaan
Buyr Nuur
Dzüyl
Altay
Baytik Shan
Bayasgalant
Tamsagbulag
Usa
Manas
Dzungaria
Fukang
Qitai
Tsagaan Nuur
Arvayheer
Onjüül
Tsomog
Ürümqi
Bogda Shan 5445
Edrengiyn Nuruu
Mandalgovi
Hongor
Turpan
Qijiaojing
GOBI
Saynshand
Yanqqi
Turfan Depression
Karlik Shan 4925
Hami
Bosten Hu
Dalandzadgad
Dzamin Üüd
Erenhot
SINKIANG
Kuruktag
Xingxingxia
Gaxun Nur
INNER MONGOLIA
Linxi
Bei Shan
Lop Nur
Saihan Tal
Duolun
Chifeng
40
Shule He
Lang Shan
Bayan Obo
Dunhuang
Anxi
Ruo Shui
Wuyuan
Hohhot
Zhangjiakou
Ruoqiang
Altun Shan
Yumen
Jiayuguan
Baotou
Jining
Chengde
Jinzhou
Huludao
Ala Shan
Xuanhua
Ayakkum Hu
Sukai Hu
Qilian Shan
Datong
Beijing (Peking)
Qinhuangdao
Mangnai
Harhu
Zhangye
Ordos
Tangshan
Qaidam Pendi
Da Qaidam
Yinchuan
Ningwu
Tianjin (Tientsin)
Tanggu
Wuwei
Huang He
Yulin
Xin Xian
Baoding
Bo Hai
Qinghai Hu
Datong
Taiyuan
Cangzhou
Hah Xil Hu
Hoh Sai Hu
Golmud
Dulan
Haiyang
Suide
Fenyang
Shijiazhuang
Hoh Xil Shan
Yangquan
Dezhou
Xining
Yanchang
Xingtai
Ulan Ul Hu
Lanzhou
Yan'an
Handan
Jinan
Weifang
90
Ngoring Hu
Donggi Cona
Qingyang
Linfen
Zibo
Gyaring Hu
Changzhi
Anyang
Qingdao
Joma 6800
Bayan Har Shan
Pingliang
Tongchuan
Xinxiang
Tongtian He
Yanzhou
Zhengzhou
Jining
Linyi
Tanggula Shan
Tianshui
Baoji
Sanmenxia
Kaifeng
Lianyungang
Yushu
Wei He
Xi'an
Luoyang
Shanqiu
Xuzhou
Sog Xian
Ningjing Shan
Hua Shan
Xuchang
Qingjiang
TIBET
Pingwu
Hanzhong
Luohe
Zhoukouzhen
Hongze Hu
Nagqu
Dêgê
Dadu He
Guangyuan
Nanyang
Bengbu
Qamdo
Yalong
Ankang
Fuyang
Huainan
Gaoyou Hu
Nyainqentanglha Shan
CHINA
Mianyang
Lanzhong
Daba Shan
Xiangfan
Xinyang
Nanjing
Lhasa
Dawu
Chengdu
Sui Xian
Lu'an
Hefei
Wuxi
Namjagbarwa Feng 7756
Batang
Red Basin
Wanzian
Nyingchi
Kangding
Ya'an
Nanchong
Yichang
Wuhu
Tai Hu
Lhunze
Gongga Shan 7556
Hechuan
Enshi
Shashi
Wuhan
Anqing
Tongling
Kangto 7090
Zayü
Leshan
Fuling
Huangshi
Hangzhou
Chongqing
Dongting Hu
Jiujiang
Shaoxing
Tawang
Sadiya
Yibin
Luzhou
Youyang
Changde
Jingdezhen
Tunxi
Dibrugarh
Putao
Hengduan Shan
Mekong
Zhougdian
Xichang
Yuanling
Yiyang
Yueyang
Nanchang
Qu Xian
Brahmaputra
Jorhat
Naga Hills
Kumon Ra.
Lijiang
Zhaotong
Dalou Shan
Lengshuijiang
Changsha
Qingjiang
Yingtan
Shangrao
Zunyi
Xiangtan
Zhuzhou
Fuzhou
Chong'an
INDIA
Lushui
Dukou
Guiyang
Wu Jiang
Zhijiang
Pingxiang
Jianyang
Dali
Xuanwei
Shaoyang
Ji'an
Myitkyina
Dongchuan
Hengyang
Nanping
Ningde
Imphal
Baoshan
Anshun
Duyun
Lingling
Wuyi Shan
Sanming
Xiaguan
Qujing
Fuzhou
Katha
Luixi
Chuxiong
Kunming
Chen Xian
Changting
Putian
Chindwin
Bhamo
Dian Chi
Guilin
Ganzhou
Lincang
Hongshui
Lian Xian
Nanxiong
Quanzhou
Irrawaddy
Nanpan Jiang
Yishan
Lashio
Shaoguan
Zhangzhou
Hsin-chu
Shwebo
Bose
Liuzhou
Mei Xian
Formosa Str.
Monywa
Gejiu
Pu'er
Wenshan
Wuzhou
Qingyuan
Chao'an
Xiamen
Chang-hua
Pakokku
Sagaing
Maymyo
Babian
Xun Jiang
Mandalay
Ha Giang
Nanning
Guangzhou (Canton)
Heyuan
Shantou
Myingyan
Kengtung
Lao Cai
Yulin
Foshan
Huizhou
T'ai-nan
Meiktila
BURMA (MYANMA)
Lai Chau
Hong
Pingxiang
Kao-hsiung
Minbu
Taung-gyi
Lang Son
Jiangmen
Kowloon
Magwe
Muong Sing
Beihai
Xiangjiang
HONG KONG (U.K.)
Tung-Chiang
Arakan Yoma
Luang Namtha
Sam Neua
Hanoi
Bac Ninh
Macau (Port.)
20
Salween
M. Chiang Rai
B. Houei Sai
Leizhou Bandao
Zhanjiang
Haiphong
Pegu
Luang Prabang
Prome
LAOS
Nam Dinh
Gulf of Tongkin
Xuwen
Dongsha Qundao
Toungoo
Myanaung
Chiang Mai
Muang Nan
Thanh Hoa
Lingao
Haikou
M. Lampang
Pak Sane
Dongfang
Wuzhi Shan 1879
Henzada
Pegu
Hainan
Bassein
Rangoon (Yangon)
Tak
Ultaradit
Vientiane
Vinh
Sawankhalok
Nong Khai
Thakhek
Dong Hoi
Yulin
110
C. Bojeador
Laoag

SEA OF OKHOTSK
SAKHALIN
Skovorodino
Zeya
Ovsyanka
Tugur
Okha
Nikolayevsk-na-Amure
Bogorodskoye
Opala
Mys Lopatka
Paramushir
Dzhalinda
Tygda
Ushumun
Ekimchan
Peliny Osipenko
Katangli
Guqigu
Shimanovsk
Huma
Norsk
Ust'-Umal'ta
Oz. Chukchagirskoye
Oz Zvoron
De Kastri
Aleksandrovsk-Sakhalinskiy
Tymovskoye
Mangui
Kumara
Svobodnyy
Belogorsk
Chekunda
Bureinskiy Khrebet
Komsomol'sk na-Amure
Onekotan
Shiashkotan
Ergun Zuoqi
Blagoveshchensk
Zavitinsk
Bureya
Bolon'
Pobedino
Poronaysk
Anhui
Litovko
Oz. Bolon'
Uglegorsk
Proliv Tartarskiy
Zaliv Terpeniya
Il'inskiy
Rasshua
Nenjiang
Xunke
Obluch'ye
Vanino
Sovetskaya Gavan'
Kuril'skiye Ostrova (Kuril Islands)
Simushir
Butha Qi
Bei'an
Birobidzhan
Leninskoye
Khabarovsk
Khor
Yuzhno-Sakhalinsk
Korsakov
Mys Aniva
Urup
Qiqihar
Yichun
Hailun
Fujin
Hegang
Vyazemskiy
Bikin
Nel'ma
Gornozavodsk
Svetlaya
Suihua
Jiamusi
Shuangyashan
Dal'nerechensk
Amgu
La Perouse Strait
Wakkanai
Iturup
(Rus.Fed. admin/claimed by Japan)
Daqing
MANCHURIA
Harbin
Hulin
Lesozavodsk
Sikhote Alin
Vityaz Depth 10542
Da'an
Songhua
Jixi
Turiy Rog
Plastun
Oz. Khanka
Abashiri
Kunashir
Shikotan
Wuchang
Mudanjiang
Spassk-Dal'niy
Rudnaya Pristan'
Rumoi
Asahi Dake 2290
Nemuro
Changchun
Jilin
Ussuriysk
Olga
Asahikawa
Otaru
Sapporo
Muroran
Kushiro
HOKKAIDŌ
Tongliao
Shuangliao
Songhua Hu
Vladivostok
Nakhodka
Erimo-misaki
Siping
Liaoyuan
Zaliv Petra Velikogo
Uchiura-wan
Hakodate
Tieling
Fushun
Yanji
Najin
Linjiang
Ch'ŏngjin
Tsugaru-kaikyō
Aomori
Hirosaki
Hachinohe
Benxi
Tonghua
Hyesan
Anshan
Manpo
Samsu
Songjin
Noshiro
Akita
Morioka
Yalu
Dandong
Hüich'ŏn
Sŏho-ri
SEA OF JAPAN
NORTH KOREA
Liaodong
Hamhŭng
Hŭngnam
Sinuiju
Anju
Sakata
Ishinomaki
Korea Bay
Dalian
P'yŏngyang
Wŏnsan
Yamagata
Sendai
Lüshun
Sado
Niigata
Fukushima
Haeju
Ch'unch'ŏn
Kangnŭng
Nagaoka
Kaesŏng
Ullung do
Tok-do
HONSHŪ
Takaoka
Utsunomiya
Yantai
Inch'ŏn
Sŏul (Seoul)
SOUTH KOREA
Kanazawa
Mito
Chengshan Jiao
Chŏnan
Ch'ongju
Fukui
Tōkyō
Yokohama
Taejŏn
Oki
Tottori
Gifu
Fuji-san 3776
Kunsan
Taegu
Matsue
Kyōto
Nagoya
YELLOW SEA
Chŏnju
Kwangju
Pusan
Ōsaka
Kōbe
Sakai
Shizuoka
Mokp'o
Masan
Hiroshima
Kure
Toyohashi
Korea Strait
Tsushima
Wakayama
Miyake
Cheju haehyŏp
Shimonoseki
Kita-Kyūshū
Matsuyama
Kōchi
Kii-suidō
Hachijo
Cheju
Cheju do
Fukuoka
Sasebo
Shikoku
Nagasaki
Kumamoto
Bungo-suidō
Myojin
Nantong
Kyūshū
Miyazaki
Sumisu
Suzhou
Kagoshima
Tori
Ramapo Deep 10374
Shanghai
Ōsumi-kaikyō
Tanega
Sofu Gan
Wangpan Yang
EAST CHINA SEA
Yaku
Ningbo
Tokara Retto
Muko-jima
Chichi-jima
Amami
Amami gunto
Nishino-shima
Ogasawara Gunto (Bonin Islands) (Jap.)
Haha-jima
Wenzhou
Tokuno
RYŪKYŪ RETTO
Okinawa
Kitalo
Naha
Okinawa
gunto
Kazan Retto (Volcano Is) (Jap.)
Senkaku Gunto
Daitō Is
Iwo Jima
Fleming Deep 8651
Chi-lung
T'ai-pei
Sakishima guntō
Miyako
Ishigaki
Iriomote
Hsüeh Shan 3884
Tropic of Cancer
Hua-lien
Chia-i
TAIWAN (FORMOSA)
T'ai-tung (China Nat. Rep.)
P'ing-tung
PACIFIC OCEAN
Farallon de Pajaros
Maug Is
MARIANAS
Asuncion
Agrihan
Parece Vela
Batan Is
Luzon Strait
Pagan
Alamagan
Guguan
Babuyan Is
Northern Marianas
Sarigan
Anatahan
C.Engaño
Aparri
E
F
G
H
1
2
3
4
5
130
150
140
50
40
30
20

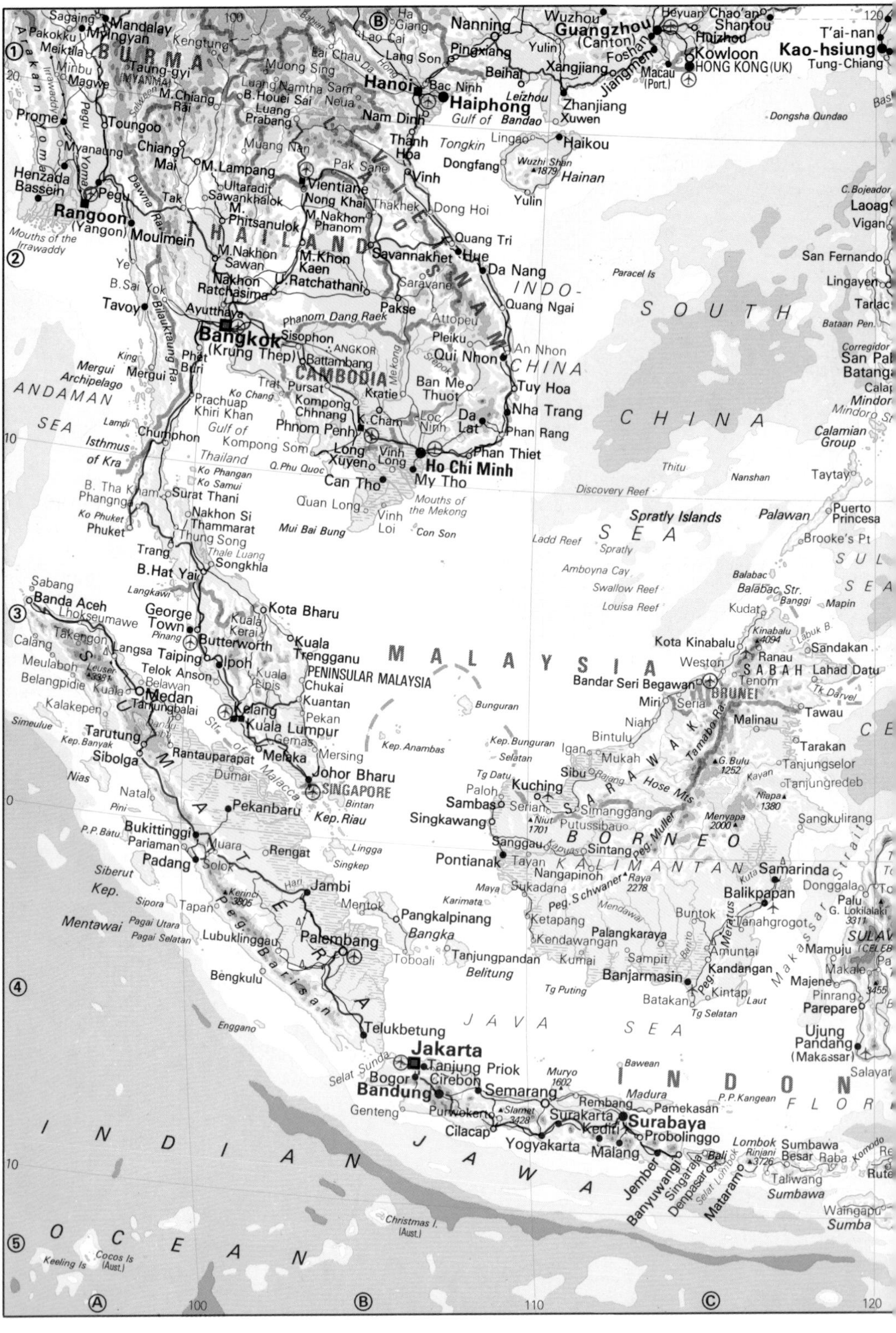

BURMA (MYANMAR)
THAILAND
LAOS
VIETNAM
CAMBODIA
MALAYSIA
PENINSULAR MALAYSIA
SINGAPORE
BRUNEI
SABAH
SARAWAK
BORNEO
KALIMANTAN
SUMATERA
JAWA
INDONESIA
Mandalay
Rangoon (Yangon)
Moulmein
Bangkok (Krung Thep)
Vientiane
Hanoi
Haiphong
Nanning
Guangzhou (Canton)
HONG KONG (UK)
Macau (Port.)
Kao-hsiung
Hainan
Haikou
Da Nang
Hue
Phnom Penh
Ho Chi Minh
Kuala Lumpur
Johor Bharu
Kuching
Kota Kinabalu
Bandar Seri Begawan
Medan
Padang
Palembang
Jambi
Pontianak
Banjarmasin
Balikpapan
Samarinda
Jakarta
Bandung
Semarang
Surabaya
Yogyakarta
Malang
Ujung Pandang (Makassar)
Gulf of Tongkin
Gulf of Thailand
Isthmus of Kra
ANDAMAN SEA
SOUTH CHINA SEA
Spratly Islands
Paracel Is
Str. of Malacca
JAVA SEA
INDIAN OCEAN
Christmas I. (Aust.)
Cocos Is (Aust.)
Keeling Is
Mouths of the Irrawaddy
Mouths of the Mekong
Palawan
Sulu Sea
Makasar Strait
Bali
Lombok
Sumbawa
Sumba

TAIWAN (FORMOSA)
T'ai-tung (China Nat. Rep.)
Batan Is
Luzon Strait
Babuyan Is
C. Engaño
Aparri
Tuguegarao
Ilagan
LUZON
Baler
Cabanatuan
Quezon City
Polillo Is
PHILIPPINES
Manila
Daet
Catanduanes
Naga
Legazpi
Boac
Romblon
Bulan
Catarman
Masbate
Masbate
Samar
Catbalogan
Panay
Roxas
Iloilo
Tacloban
Leyte
Bacolod
Cebu
Negros
Bohol
Dinagat
Siargao
Surigao
Bohol Sea
Siaton
Butuan
Manukan
Cagayan de Oro
Ozamiz
Marawi
MINDANAO
L. Lanao
Malanbang
Cotabato
Davao
Zamboanga
Basilan
Moro Gulf
Digos
Davao G.
Jolo
Jolo
General Santos
Sulu Arch
Tinaca Pt
Kepulauan Talaud
Karakelong
Tahuna
Sangine
Kepulauan Sangihe
CELEBES SEA
Manado
Buol
Kuandang
Belang
Gorontalo
Molucca Sea
Kep. Togian
Luwuk
Poso
Peleng
Kep. Banggai
Teluk Tolo
Danau Towuti
Kendari
Kolaka
Wowoni
Butung
Muna
Baubau
Kep. Tukangbesi
Morotai
Tobelo
Ternate
Halmahera
Teluk Weda
Bacan
MOLUCCAS
Taliabu
Mangole
Obi
Kep Sula
CERAM SEA
Namlea
Buru
Piru
3019
Bula
Seram
Ambon
Kep. Banda
BANDA SEA
Nila
Teun
Damar
Romang
Wetar
Alor
Lomblen
Flores
Selat Wetar
Kep. Leti
Babar
Sermata
Oekusi
Endeh
Atambua
TIMOR
Savu Sea
Sawu
Kupang
Roti
TIMOR SEA
PACIFIC OCEAN
Parece Vela
Farallon de Pajaros
Maug Is
Asuncion
Agrihan
Pagan
Alamagan
Guguan
Sarigan
Anatahan
Farallon de Medinilla
Saipan
Tinian
Rota
Northern Marianas
MARIANAS
Guam (U.S.A.)
Nero Deep 9637
Challenger Deep 11033
Mansyu Deep 9818
Ulithi
Fais
Gaferut
Yap
Faraulep
Ngulu
Sorol
Lamotrek
Fed. States of Micronesia
Woleai
Ifalik
Eauripik
Palau Islands (U.S.A)
Koror
CAROLINE ISLANDS
Sonsorol
Pulo Anna
Merir
Tobi
Helen Reef
Mapia
Equator
Ninigo Group
Waigeo
Supiori
Biak
Selat Dampier
Kwoka 3000
Manokwari
Cendrawasih
Peg. Arfak 2939
Numfoor
Yapen
Sorong
Tg d'Urville
Sarmi
Mamberamo
Jayapura
Misoöl
Teluk Cendrawasih
Dom 1340
Teluk Berau
Fakfak
Kaimana
IRIAN JAYA
Pegunungan Maoke
Angemuk 3741
Pk Jaya 5029
Pk Mandala 4702
Adi
Kokonau
Kep. Kai
Dobo
Wokam
Kep. Aru
Kobroör
Trangan
Tk Flamingo
Yamdena
Kepulauan Tanimbar
Saumlaki
Selaru
P. Kolepom
Tg Vals
Komoran
Merauke
Digul
Tanahmerah
Aitape
Schouten Is
Wewak
Karkar
PAPUA NEW GUINEA
Sepik
Ramu
Madang
Long I.
Central Ra.
Mt Hagen
Goroka
Finschhafen
Mendi
Kubor 4359
Lae
Bulolo
Wau
Salamaua
L. Murray
PAPUA
Kikori
Fly
Kerema
Albert Edward 3993
Gulf of Papua
Mt Victoria 4073
Kokoda
Daru
Port Moresby
Saibai
Mulgrave I.
Banks I.
Torres Strait
Thursday I.
Pr. of Wales I.
C. York
Somerset
Great Barrier Rf
CORAL SEA
C. Grenville
Iron Range
Weipa
Albatross B.
ARAFURA SEA
C. V. Diemen
Melville I.
Dundas Str.
Croker I.
Bathurst I.
Coburg Pen.
Wessel Is
AUSTRALIA
Gove Pen.
C. Arnhem
Nhulunbuy
Clarence Str.
Darwin
Arnhem Land

MONGOLIA
NEI MONGGOL
Yin Shan
Ningxia
Qinghai
Shaanxi
Shanxi
Hebei
Henan
Shandong
Jiangsu
Anhui
Liaoning
Jilin
BO HAI
KOREA BAY
YELLOW SEA (HUANG HAI)
Liaodong Wan
Bohai Wan
Laizhou Wan
Haizhou Wan
Mu Us Shamo
Tengger Shamo
Badain Jaran Shamo
Lüliang Shan
Taihang Shan
Qin Ling
Liupan Shan
Min Shan
Longshou Shan
Huang He
Wei He
Fen He
Han Shui
Changchun
Siping
Liaoyuan
Shenyang
Fushun
Benxi
Liaoyang
Anshan
Dandong
Yingkou
Dalian
Lüshun
Jin Xian
Fuxin
Jinzhou
Chaoyang
Beipiao
Qinhuangdao
Tangshan
Tianjin (Tientsin)
Beijing (Peking)
Zhangjiakou
Xuanhua
Chengde
Chifeng
Baoding
Cangzhou
Shijiazhuang
Xingtai
Handan
Anyang
Hebi
Xinxiang
Zhengzhou
Kaifeng
Luoyang
Pingdingshan
Xuchang
Nanyang
Jiaozuo
Sanmenxia
Taiyuan
Yangquan
Yuci
Datong
Changzhi
Linfen
Houma
Xi'an (Sian)
Xianyang
Baoji
Tongchuan
Yan'an
Yulin
Baotou
Hohhot
Jining
Erenhot
Yinchuan
Wuhai
Lanzhou
Xining
Tianshui
Hanzhong
Jinan (Tsinan)
Zibo
Weifang
Qingdao (Tsingtao)
Yantai
Weihai
Lianyungang
Xuzhou
Huaibei
Huainan
Bengbu
Qingjiang
Yangzhou
Zhenjiang
Taizhou
Nantong
Jining
Zaozhuang
Tai'an

1:10M 0 100 200 300 400 km 0 100 200 mls

Hubei
Anhui
Zhejiang
Jiangxi
Fujian
Hunan
Guizhou
Guangdong
Guangxi
Sichuan
Yunnan
TAIWAN
VIETNAM
LAOS
SOUTH CHINA SEA
GULF OF TONGKIN
FORMOSA STRAIT (TAIWAN HAIXIA)
Shanghai
Wuhan
Chongqing (Chungking)
Chengdu
Guangzhou (Canton)
Hanoi
Haiphong
Kao-hsiung
T'ai-pei
Kunming
Guiyang
Nanning
Changsha
Nanchang
Hangzhou

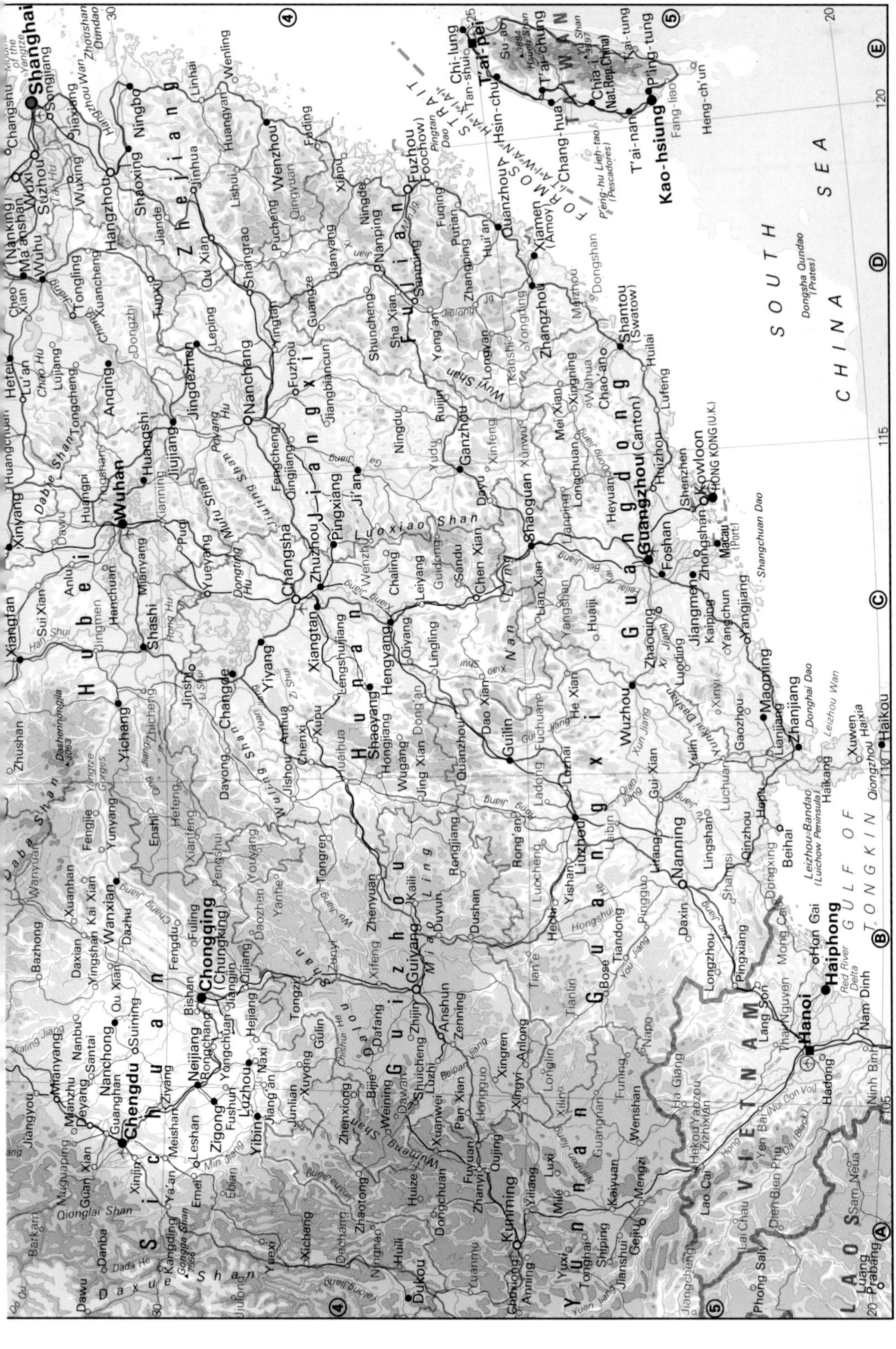

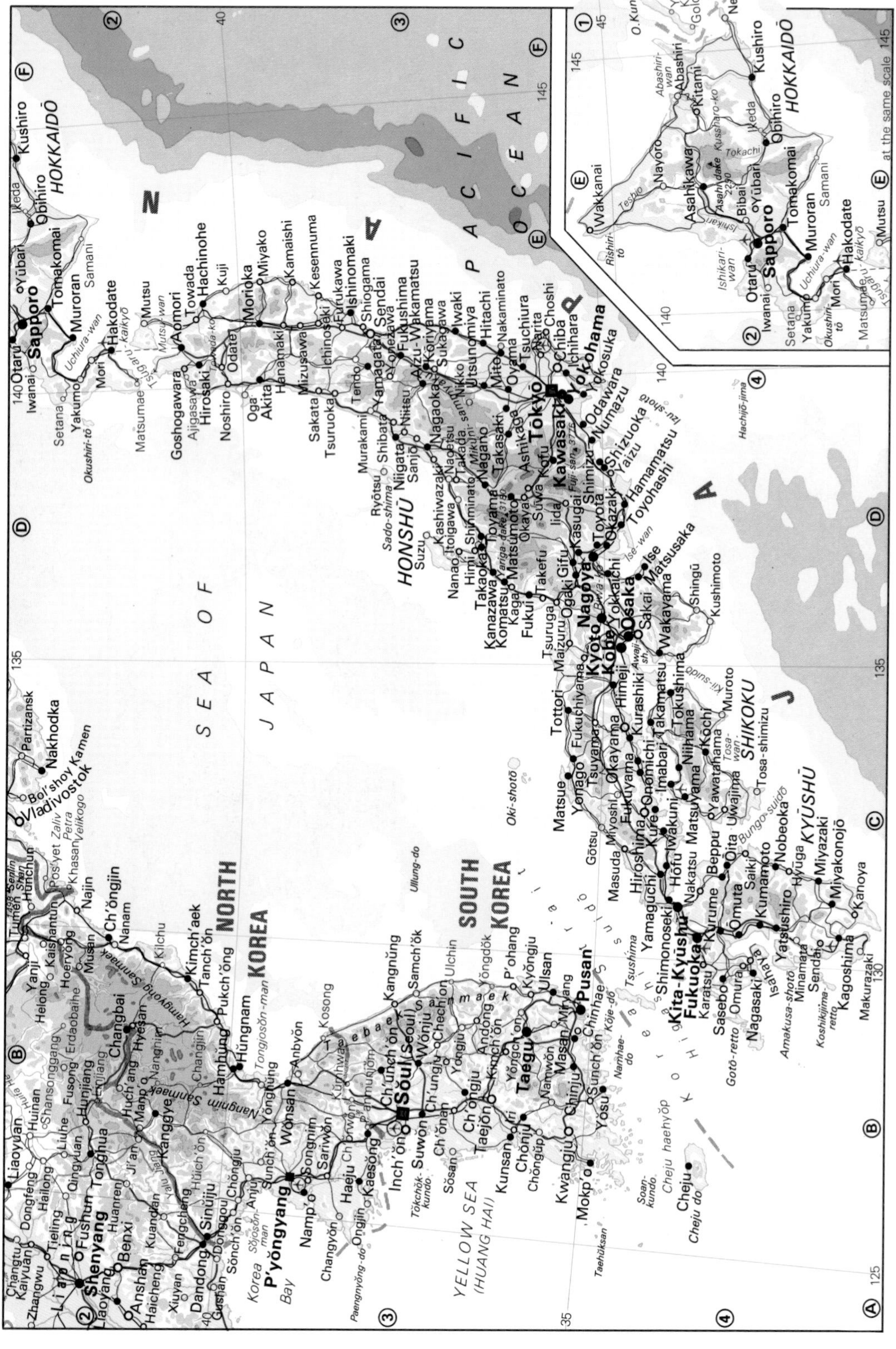
0 100 200 300 km
0 100 200 mls
SEA OF JAPAN
PACIFIC OCEAN
YELLOW SEA (HUANG HAI)
Korea Bay
Korea Strait
NORTH KOREA
SOUTH KOREA
JAPAN
HONSHŪ
SHIKOKU
KYŪSHŪ
HOKKAIDŌ
Tōkyō
Yokohama
Kawasaki
Nagoya
Kyōto
Kōbe
Ōsaka
Sapporo
Sendai
Hiroshima
Fukuoka
Kita-Kyūshū
Kagoshima
Nagasaki
Niigata
Kanazawa
Hakodate
Aomori
Akita
Morioka
Shizuoka
Hamamatsu
Okayama
Matsuyama
Kōchi
Tokushima
Takamatsu
Wakayama
Sŏul (Seoul)
P'yŏngyang
Pusan
Taegu
Inch'ŏn
Kwangju
Taejŏn
Ulsan
Hamhŭng
Wŏnsan
Kaesŏng
Sinŭiju
Ch'ŏngjin
Shenyang
Vladivostok
Nakhodka
Cheju
Cheju do
Tsushima
Oki-shotō
Sado-shima
Ullung-do
Fuji-san 3776
at the same scale

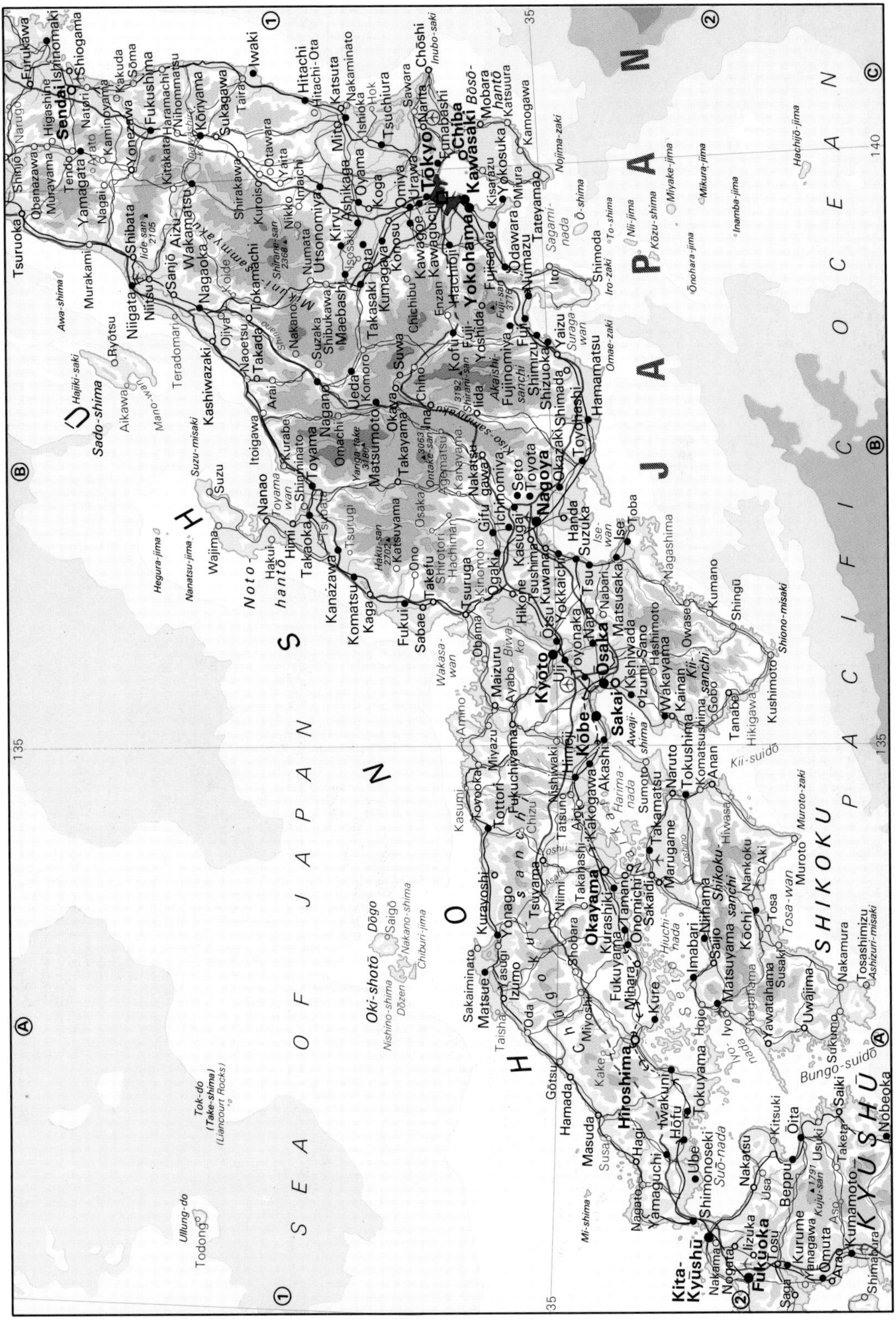
SEA OF JAPAN
HONSHU
JAPAN
PACIFIC OCEAN
SHIKOKU
KYŪSHŪ
Sado-shima
Noto-hantō
Oki-shotō
Dōgo
Tōkyō
Yokohama
Kawasaki
Chiba
Nagoya
Kyōto
Ōsaka
Kōbe
Sakai
Hiroshima
Okayama
Sendai
Niigata
Kanazawa
Toyama
Nagano
Shizuoka
Hamamatsu
Wakayama
Tokushima
Takamatsu
Matsuyama
Kōchi
Fukuoka
Kita-Kyūshū
Ōita
Kumamoto
Shimonoseki
Fukushima
Kōriyama
Iwaki
Mito
Utsunomiya
Maebashi
Kōfu
Matsumoto
Fukui
Tottori
Matsue
Gifu
Tsu
Nara
Ōtsu
Biwa-ko
Ise-wan
Suruga-wan
Sagami-nada
Harima-nada
Kii-suidō
Bungo-suidō
Tosa-wan
Hachijō-jima
Miyake-jima
Ullung-do
Tok-do (Take-shima) (Liancourt Rocks)
Fuji-san 3776
Hakusan 2702
135
140
35

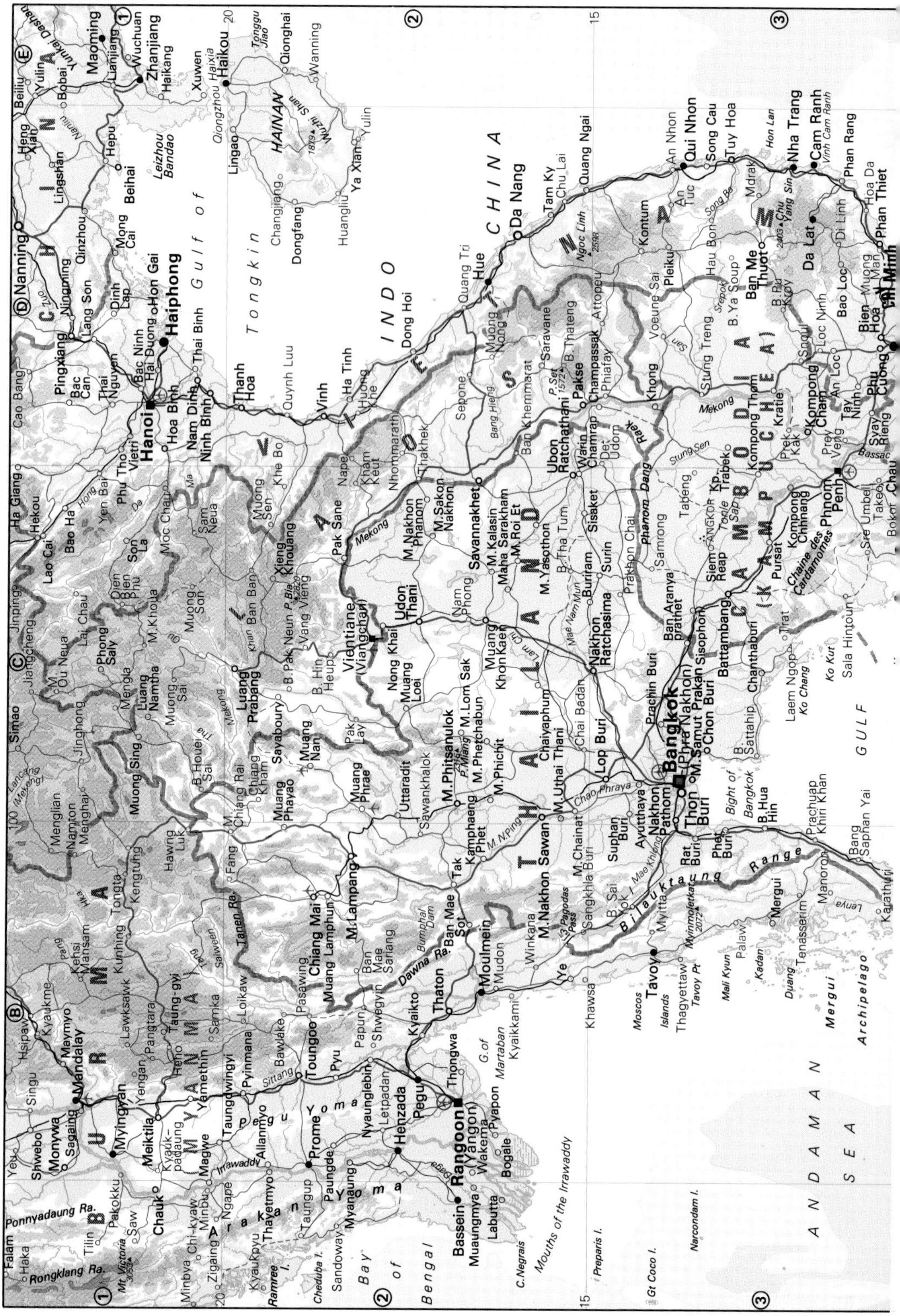
INDO CHINA
BURMA
MYANMAR
THAILAND
LAOS
VIETNAM
CAMBODIA
(KAMPUCHEA)
CHINA
HAINAN
Gulf of Tongkin
Bay of Bengal
ANDAMAN SEA
GULF
Bight of Bangkok
G. of Martaban
Mergui Archipelago
Mouths of the Irrawaddy
Arakan Yoma
Pegu Yoma
Dawna Ra.
Tanen Ra.
Bilauktaung Range
Ponnyadaung Ra.
Rongklang Ra.
Chaîne des Cardamomes
Mekong
Irrawaddy
Salween
Sittang
Chao Phraya
Hanoi
Haiphong
Nanning
Zhanjiang
Haikou
Hue
Da Nang
Vientiane (Viangchan)
Luang Prabang
Bangkok (Phra Nakhon)
Phnom Penh
Rangoon (Yangon)
Mandalay
Moulmein
Bassein
Prome
Toungoo
Pegu
Henzada
Tavoy
Mergui
Chiang Mai
Udon Thani
Nakhon Ratchasima
Ubon Ratchathani
Savannakhet
Pakse
Qui Nhon
Nha Trang
Cam Ranh
Da Lat
Ban Me Thuot
Vinh
Thanh Hoa
Battambang
Siem Reap
Kompong Cham
Ho Chi Minh
Phan Thiet
Phan Rang
Mt. Victoria 3053
Preparis I.
Gt Coco I.
Narcondam I.
Cheduba I.
Ramree I.
C.Negrais
Moscos Islands
Ko Chang
Ko Kut
1
2
3
B
C
D
E
100
15
20

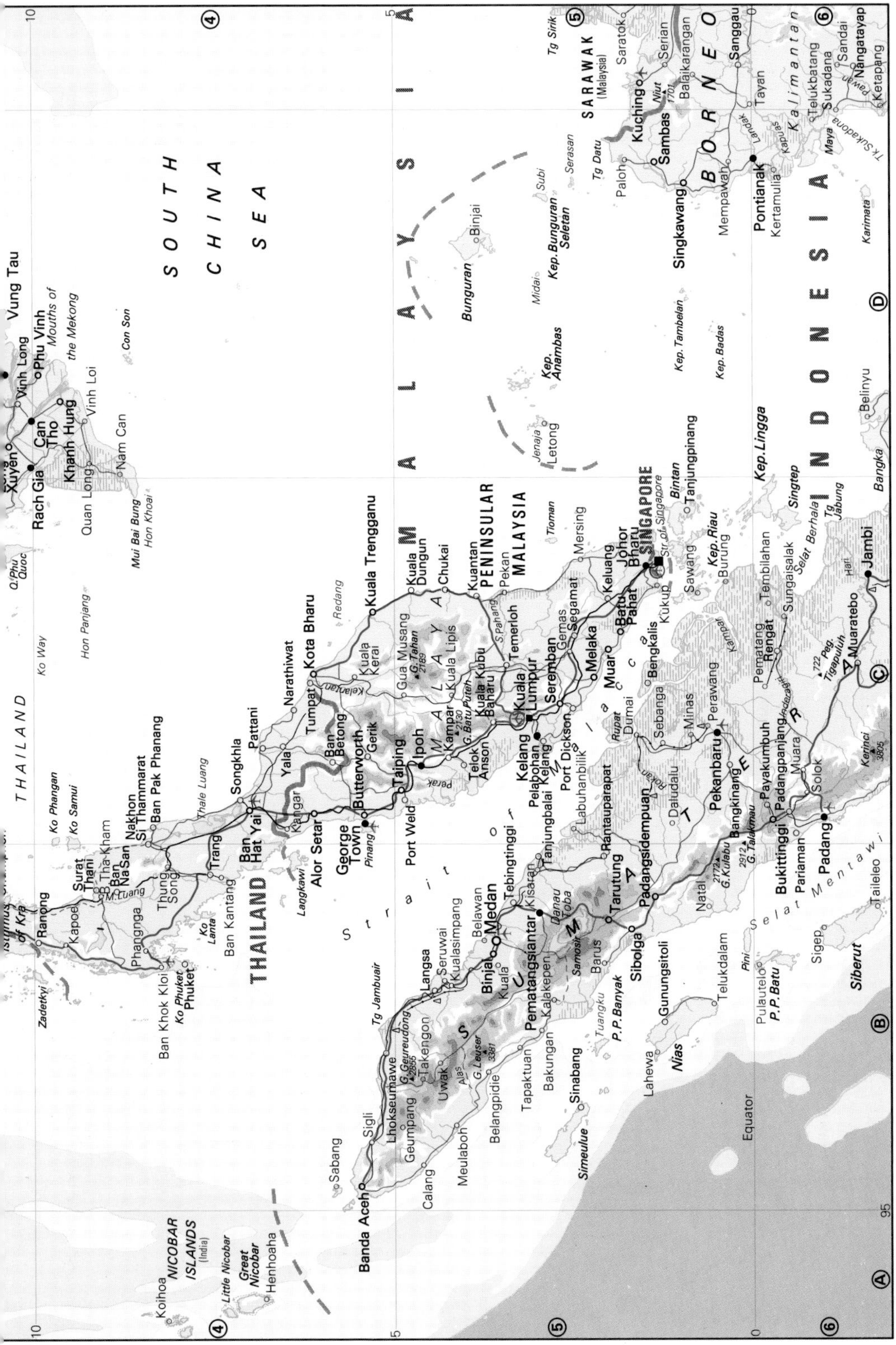
SOUTH CHINA SEA
THAILAND
MALAYSIA
PENINSULAR MALAYSIA
INDONESIA
SUMATERA
BORNEO
SARAWAK
(Malaysia)
Kalimantan
SINGAPORE
NICOBAR ISLANDS
(India)
Little Nicobar
Great Nicobar
Strait of Malacca
Selat Mentawai
Str. of Singapore
Selat Berhala
Banda Aceh
Sabang
Sigli
Lhokseumawe
Langsa
Medan
Binjai
Belawan
Tebingtinggi
Pematangsiantar
Kisaran
Tanjungbalai
Sibolga
Tarutung
Padangsidempuan
Rantauparapat
Dumai
Pekanbaru
Bukittinggi
Padang
Payakumbuh
Padangpanjang
Solok
Muaratebo
Jambi
Rengat
Pematang
Tembilahan
Bengkalis
Gunungsitoli
Nias
Siberut
Simeulue
Sinabang
P. P. Banyak
P. P. Batu
Equator
Ranong
Phuket
Ko Phuket
Surat Thani
Nakhon Si Thammarat
Songkhla
Hat Yai
Pattani
Yala
Narathiwat
Trang
Alor Setar
George Town
Pinang
Butterworth
Taiping
Ipoh
Kota Bharu
Kuala Trengganu
Kuantan
Kuala Lumpur
Kelang
Seremban
Port Dickson
Melaka
Muar
Batu Pahat
Johor Bharu
Kluang
Mersing
Tanjungpinang
Bintan
Kep. Riau
Kep. Lingga
Singkep
Bangka
Kuching
Pontianak
Singkawang
Sambas
Kep. Anambas
Kep. Bunguran Seletan
Bunguran
Vung Tau
Phu Vinh
Vinh Long
Can Tho
Rach Gia
Long Xuyen
Khanh Hung
Quan Long
Mouths of the Mekong
Con Son
Ko Samui
Ko Phangan
Langkawi
Danau Toba
G. Leuser 3381
G. Kerinci 3805
G. Tahan 2189

1:10M

0 100 200 300 400 km
0 100 200 mls

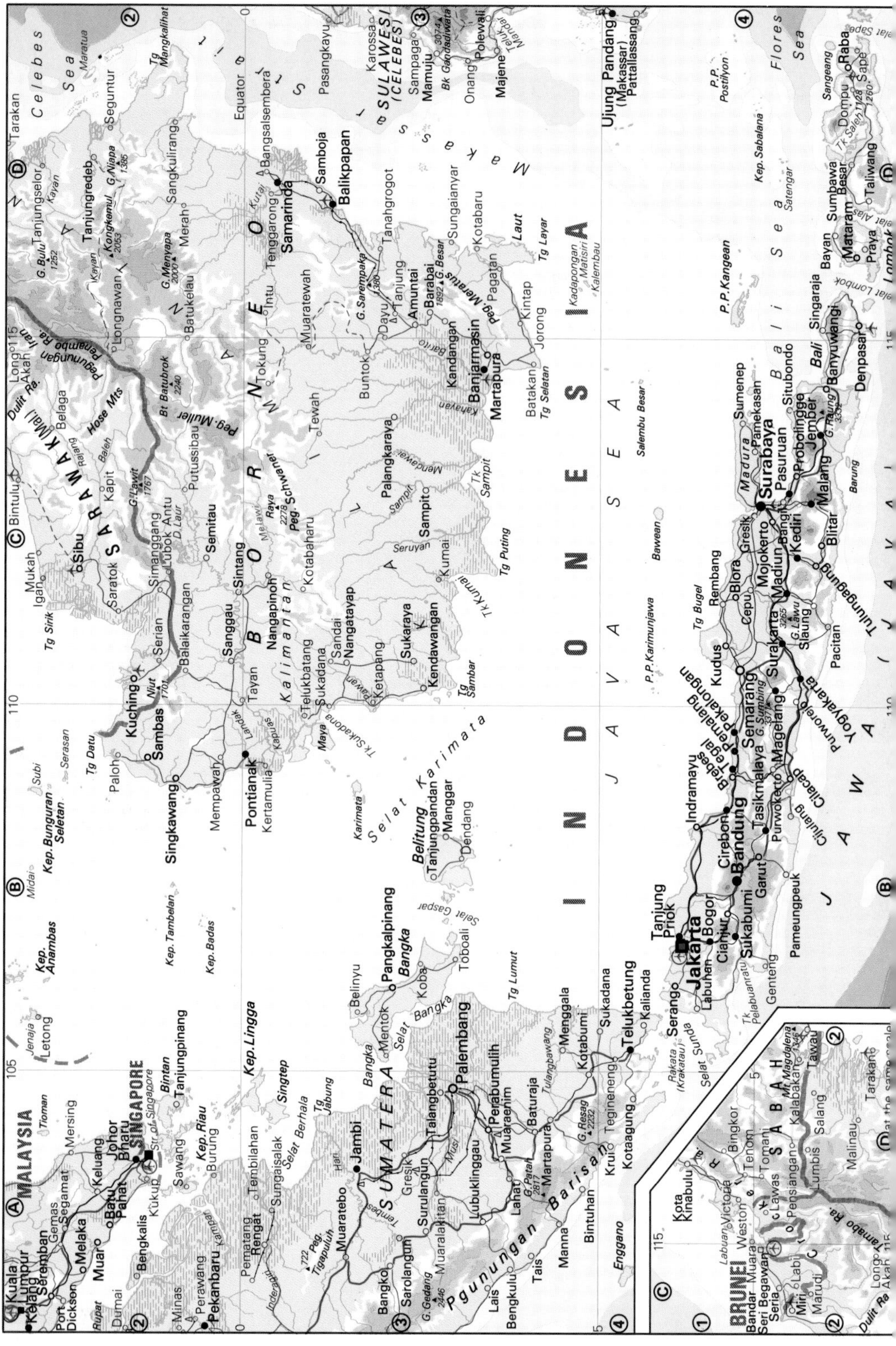

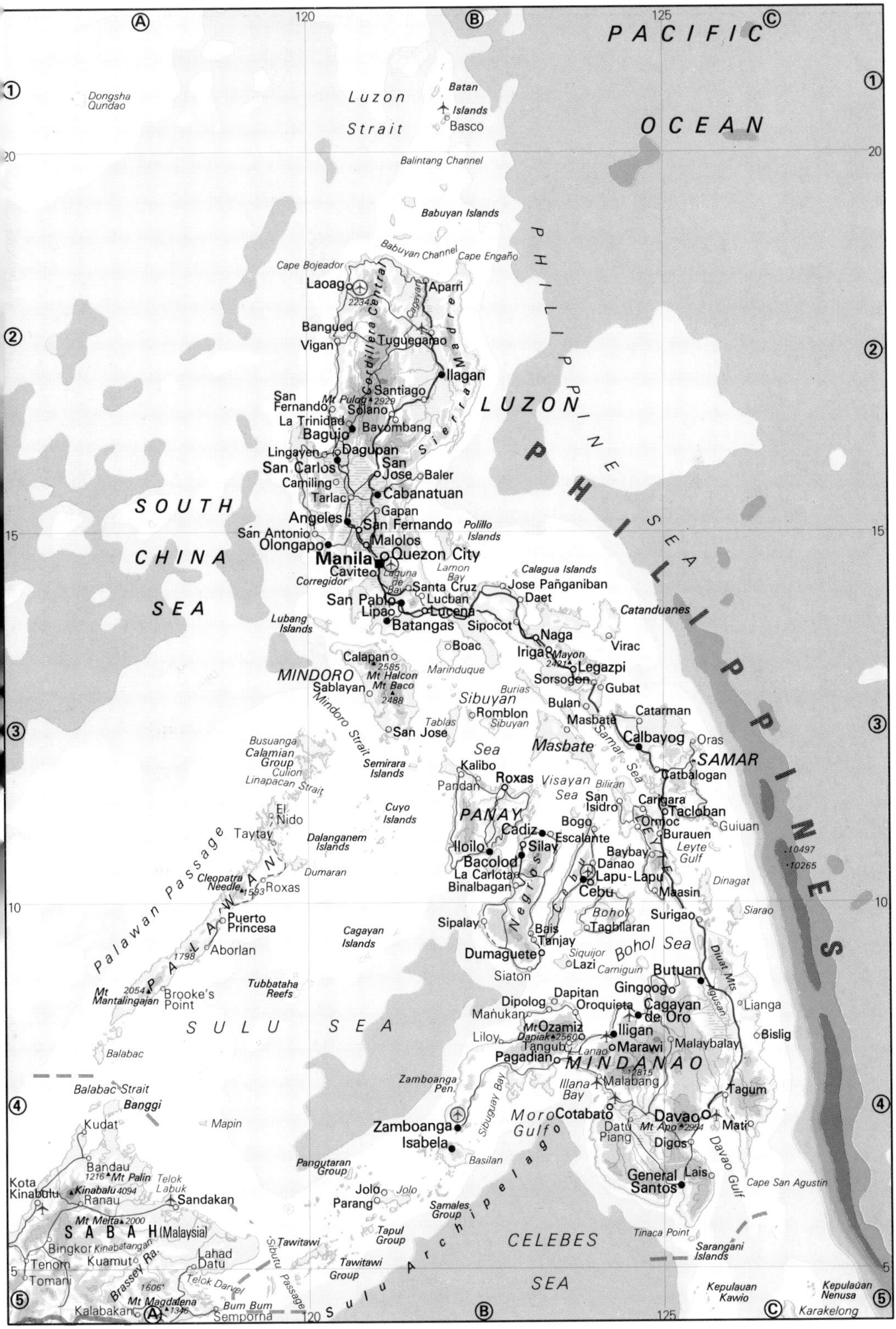
PACIFIC
OCEAN
PHILIPPINE SEA
PHILIPPINES
SOUTH
CHINA
SEA
SULU SEA
CELEBES
SEA
LUZON
MINDORO
PANAY
SAMAR
LEYTE
MINDANAO
PALAWAN
SABAH (Malaysia)
Dongsha
Qundao
Luzon
Strait
Batan
Islands
Basco
Balintang Channel
Babuyan Islands
Babuyan Channel
Cape Engaño
Cape Bojeador
Laoag
2234
Aparri
Cagayan
Cordillera Central
Sierra Madre
Bangued
Vigan
Tuguegarao
Ilagan
Santiago
San
Fernando
Mt Pulog
2929
Solano
La Trinidad
Baguio
Bayombang
Lingayen
Dagupan
San Carlos
San
Jose
Baler
Camiling
Cabanatuan
Tarlac
Gapan
Angeles
San Fernando
Polillo
Islands
San Antonio
Malolos
Olongapo
Manila
Quezon City
Cavite
Laguna
de
Bay
Lamon
Bay
Corregidor
Calagua Islands
Jose Pañganiban
Santa Cruz
Daet
San Pablo
Lucban
Lipao
Lucena
Catanduanes
Batangas
Sipocot
Lubang
Islands
Naga
Virac
Boac
Iriga
Mayon
2421
Legazpi
Calapan
2585
Mt Halcon
Marinduque
Sorsogon
Gubat
Mt Baco
2488
Sablayan
Burias
Sibuyan
Bulan
Romblon
Sibuyan
Catarman
Tablas
Masbate
Mindoro Strait
San Jose
Calbayog
Oras
Busuanga
Calamian
Group
Culion
Sea
Masbate
Samar Sea
Semirara
Islands
Linapacan Strait
Kalibo
Catbalogan
Pandan
Roxas
Visayan
Sea
Biliran
El
Nido
Cuyo
Islands
San
Isidro
Carigara
Tacloban
Bogo
Ormoc
Guiuan
Taytay
Dalanganem
Islands
Cadiz
Silay
Escalante
Burauen
Iloilo
Bacolod
Baybay
Leyte
Gulf
10497
Palawan Passage
Cleopatra
Needle
1593
Roxas
Dumaran
La Carlota
Danao
Lapu-Lapu
10265
Binalbagan
Cebu
Maasin
Dinagat
Negros
Cebu
Siargao
Puerto
Princesa
Sipalay
Bohol
Tagbilaran
Surigao
Bais
Tanjay
Cagayan
Islands
Bohol Sea
1798
Aborlan
Dumaguete
Siquijor
Lazi
Camiguin
Diuata Mts
Siaton
Butuan
Agusan
Mt
Mantalingajan
2054
Brooke's
Point
Tubbataha
Reefs
Dapitan
Gingoog
Dipolog
Oroquieta
Cagayan
de Oro
Lianga
Manukan
Mt Ozamiz
Iligan
Liloy
Dapiak 2560
Tangub
Lanao
Marawi
Malaybalay
Bislig
Balabac
Pagadian
2815
Balabac Strait
Banggi
Zamboanga
Pen.
Illana
Bay
Malabang
Tagum
Sibuguay Bay
Moro
Gulf
Cotabato
Davao
Kudat
Mapin
Zamboanga
Datu
Piang
Mt Apo 2954
Mati
Isabela
Digos
Davao Gulf
Bandau
1216 Mt Palin
Telok
Labuk
Basilan
Pangutaran
Group
General
Santos
Lais
Cape San Agustin
Kota
Kinabalu
Kinabalu 4094
Ranau
Sandakan
Jolo
Jolo
Parang
Samales
Group
Mt Melta 2000
Tapul
Group
Sulu Archipelago
Tinaca Point
Sarangani
Islands
Bingkor
Kinabatangan
Tawitawi
Tenom
Kuamut
Lahad
Datu
Sibutu Passage
Tawitawi
Group
Tomani
Brassey Ra.
1606
Telok Darvel
Kepulauan
Kawio
Kepulauan
Nenusa
Mt Magdalena
1346
Bum Bum
Kalabakan
Semporna
Karakelong
120
125
20
15
10
5
A
B
C
1
2
3
4
5

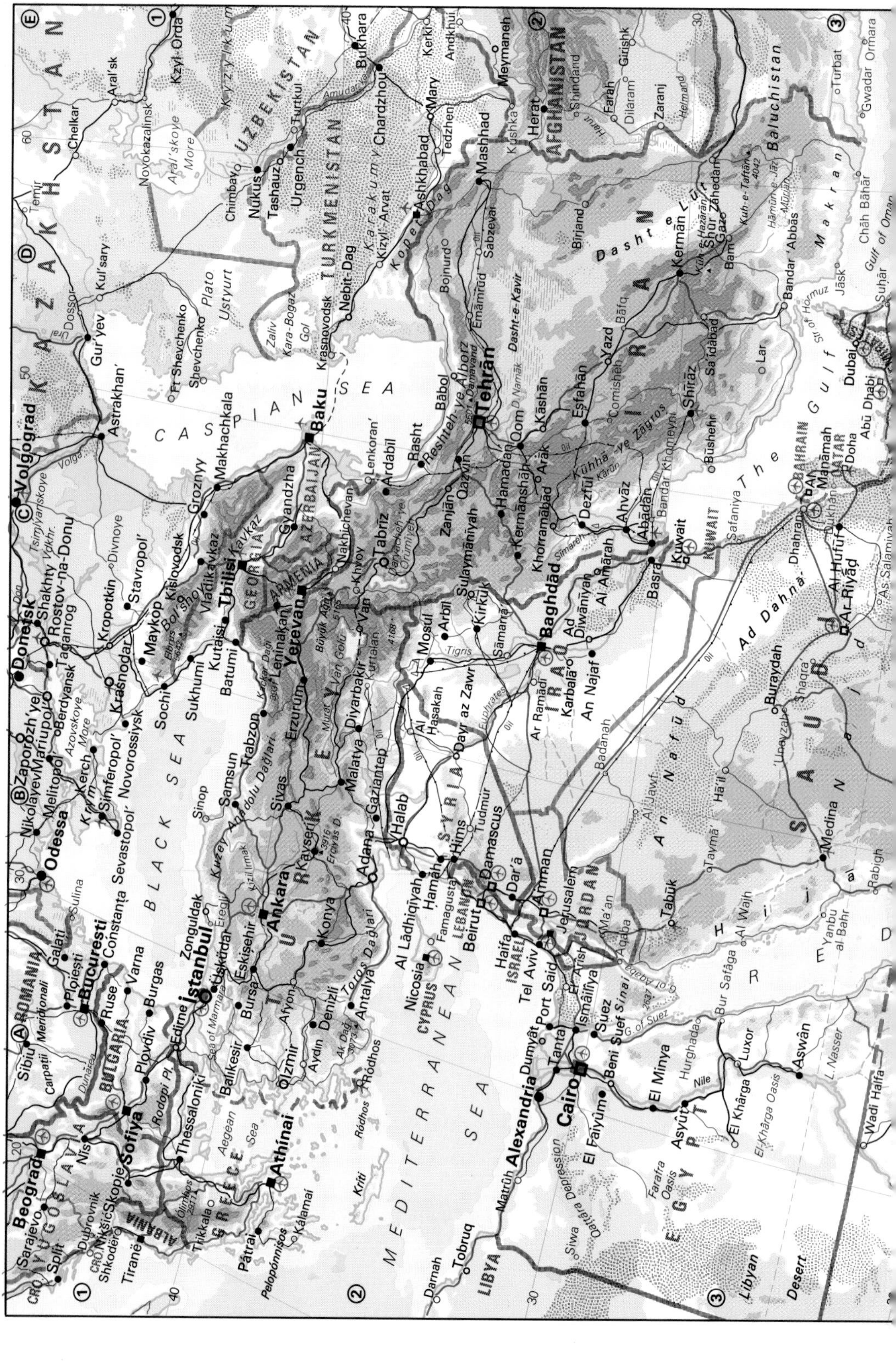
KAZAKHSTAN
UZBEKISTAN
TURKMENISTAN
AFGHANISTAN
Baluchistan
Aral'sk
Kzyl-Orda
Chelkar
Novokazalinsk
Aral'skoye More
Temir
Kul'sary
Dossor
Gur'yev
Astrakhan'
Volgograd
Plato Ustyurt
Ft Shevchenko
Shevchenko
Chimbay
Nukus
Tashauz
Urgench
Turtkul
Chardzhou
Bukhara
Mary
Tedzhen
Kerki
Andkhui
Meymaneh
Herat
Shindand
Farah
Dilaram
Zaranj
Girishk
Helmand
Kara-Bogaz Gol
Krasnovodsk
Nebit-Dag
Kizyl-Arvat
Ashkhabad
Kopet Dag
Mashhad
Kushka
Bojnurd
Sabzevar
Emamrud
Dasht-e-Kavir
Dasht-e Lut
Birjand
Zahedan
Kerman
Bam
Makran
Turbat
Gwadar
Ormara
Chah Bahar
Gulf of Oman
Jask
Bandar 'Abbas
Str. of Hormuz
CASPIAN SEA
Baku
Makhachkala
Groznyy
Tehran
Babol
Rasht
Ardabil
Lenkoran'
Qazvin
Zanjan
Tabriz
Qom
Kashan
Esfahan
Yazd
Shiraz
Sa'idabad
Lar
Bushehr
Arak
Hamadan
Kermanshah
Khorramabad
Dezful
Ahvaz
Abadan
Bandar Khomeyni
Kuhha-ye Zagros
IRAN
Donetsk
Rostov-na-Donu
Taganrog
Stavropol'
Kropotkin
Krasnodar
Maykop
Kislovodsk
Vladikavkaz
Tbilisi
Kutaisi
Batumi
Sukhumi
Sochi
Novorossiysk
GEORGIA
ARMENIA
AZERBAIJAN
Yerevan
Gyandzha
Nakhichevan
Leninakan
Khvoy
Van
Erzurum
Trabzon
Samsun
Sinop
Sivas
Malatya
Diyarbakir
Kayseri
Ankara
Konya
Adana
Gaziantep
Eskisehir
Bursa
Istanbul
Üsküdar
Zonguldak
Izmir
Aydin
Denizli
Antalya
Afyon
Balikesir
Edirne
Toros Daglari
TURKEY
BLACK SEA
Odessa
Nikolayev
Sevastopol'
Simferopol'
Kerch
Zaporozh'ye
Mariupol'
Melitopol'
Berdyansk
Azovskoye More
Constanta
Sulina
Galati
Ploiesti
Bucuresti
ROMANIA
Ruse
Varna
Burgas
Plovdiv
Sofiya
BULGARIA
Sibiu
Beograd
Nis
Sarajevo
Dubrovnik
Split
Skopje
Tirane
Shkoder
ALBANIA
Thessaloniki
Tikkala
Patrai
Kalamai
Athinai
GREECE
Aegean Sea
Rodhos
Kriti
Nicosia
CYPRUS
MEDITERRANEAN SEA
Halab
Hamah
Hims
Al Ladhiqiyah
Beirut
LEBANON
Damascus
Tudmur
Dar'a
Dayr az Zawr
Al Hasakah
SYRIA
Mosul
Arbil
Kirkuk
Sulaymaniyah
Samarra
Baghdad
Ar Ramadi
Karbala
An Najaf
Ad Diwaniyah
Al Amarah
Basra
IRAQ
Kuwait
KUWAIT
Haifa
Tel Aviv
ISRAEL
Jerusalem
Amman
JORDAN
Ma'an
Aqaba
Tabuk
Al Jawf
Ha'il
Buraydah
Medina
Rabigh
Yanbu al Bahr
Al Wajh
Tayma'
An Nafud
Ad Dahna
Ar Riyad
Al Hufuf
Dhahran
Manamah
BAHRAIN
Doha
QATAR
Abu Dhabi
Dubai
The Gulf
Tobruq
Darnah
LIBYA
Alexandria
Matruh
Port Said
Ismailiya
Suez
Tanta
Cairo
El Faiyum
Beni Suef
El Minya
Asyut
Luxor
Aswan
L. Nasser
Wadi Halfa
El Kharga
Siwa
Qattara Depression
Farafra Oasis
EGYPT
Libyan Desert
Sinai
G. of Suez
Bur Safaga
Hurghada

1:20M 0 200 400 600 800 km
0 200 400 mls

KAZAKHSTAN
UZBEKISTAN
KIRGIZIA
TAJIKISTAN
AFGHANISTAN
PAKISTAN
INDIA
NEPAL
BHUTAN
BANGLADESH
MONGOLIA
INNER MONGOLIA
SINKIANG
TIBET
QINGHAI
KASHMIR
Tashkent
Alma-Ata
Bishkek
Dushanbe
Kabul
Islamabad
Delhi
Kathmandu
Thimphu
Dhākā
Karachi
Lahore
Lhasa
Ürümqi
Lanzhou
Xining
Samarkand
Bukhara
Kandahar
Herat
Quetta
Peshawar
Rawalpindi
Amritsar
Kashi
Hotan
Aksu
Yarkant
Golmud
Kānpur
Lucknow
Agra
Jaipur
Allahābād
Vārānasi
Patna
Mandalay
Mashhad
Tarim Pendi
Takla Makan
Kunlun Shan
Tian Shan
Karakoram
Himalaya
Hindu Kush
Pamir
Gangdise Shan
Tanggula Shan
Qilian Shan
Qaidam
Dzungaria
Turfan Depression
Balochistan
Thar
Betpak-Dala
Muyun Kum
Kyzyl Kum
Mt Everest 8848
K2 (Godwin Austen) 8611
Nanga Parbat 8126
Kangchenjunga 8598
Annapurna 8078
Pik Pobedy 7439
Pik Kommunizma 7495
Muztagata 7546
Muztag 7723
Bogda 5445
Ozero Balkhash
Oz. Issyk Kul'
Lop Nor
Qinghai Hu
Indus
Ganga
Brahmaputra
Amudar'ya
Syrdar'ya
Yangtze
Mekong
Salween
Irrawaddy

1:20M

0 200 400 600 800 km
0 200 400 mls

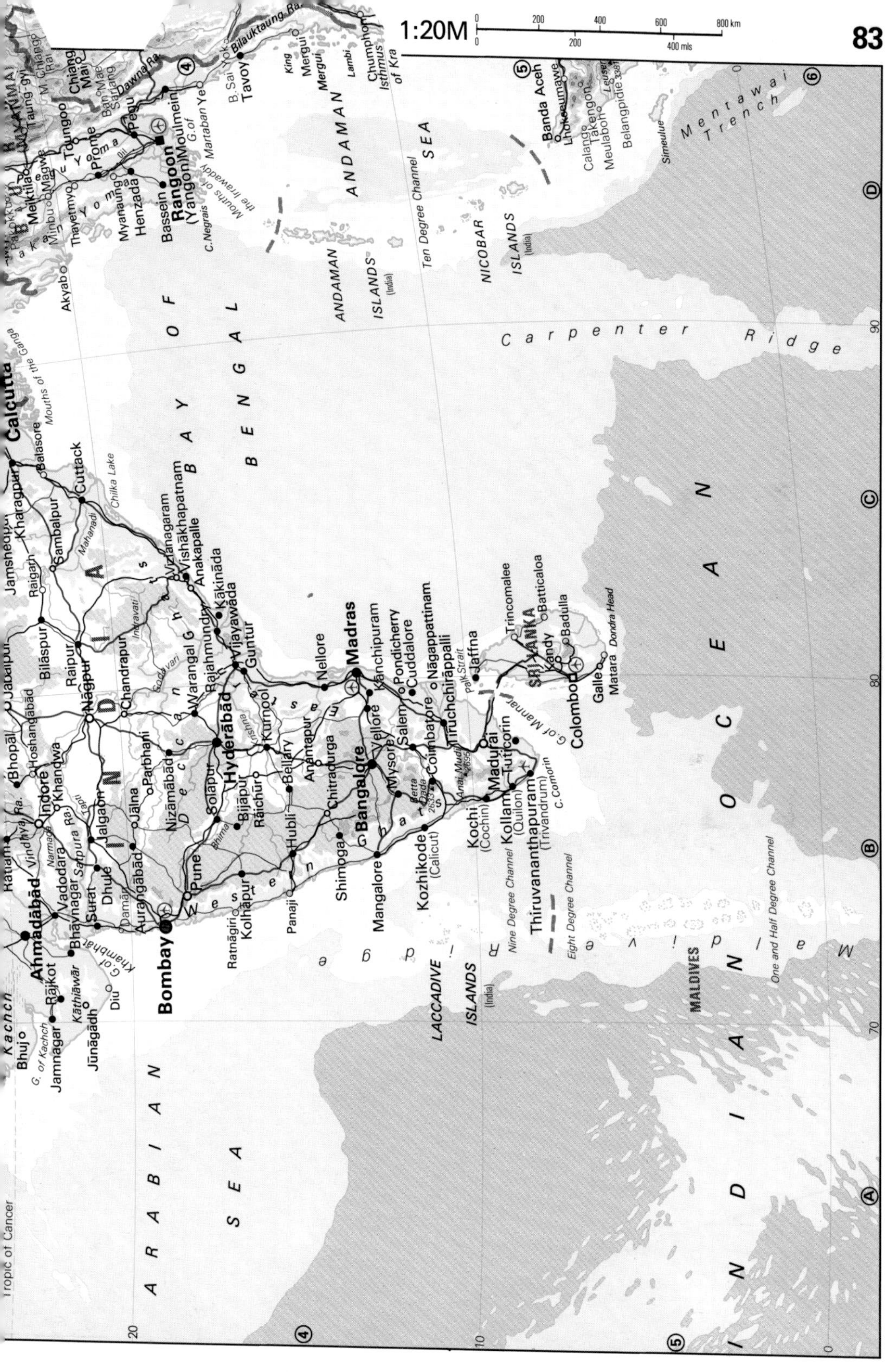

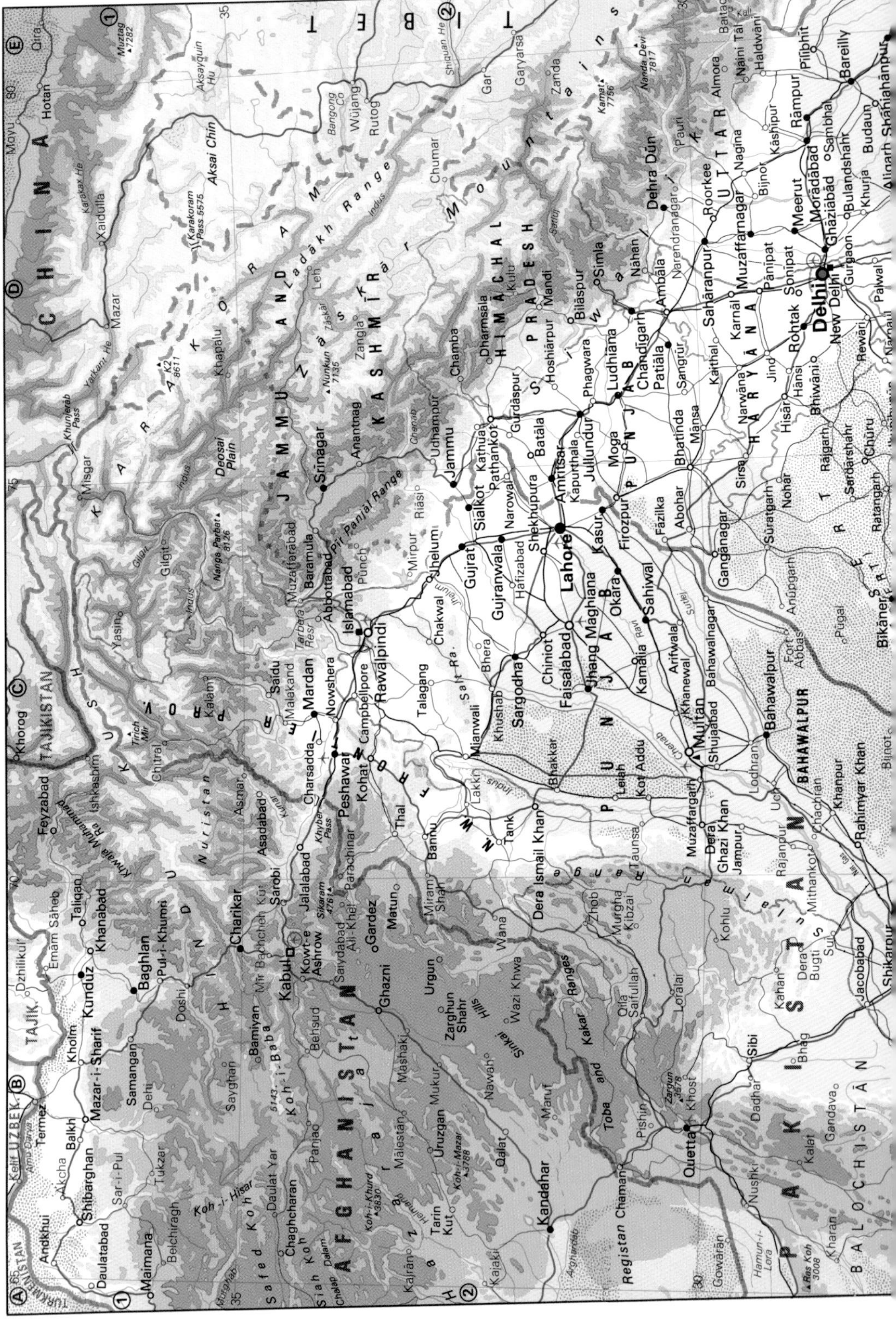
C H I N A
T I B E T
AFGHANISTAN
PAKISTAN
TAJIKISTAN
UZBEK.
TURKMENISTAN
JAMMU AND KASHMIR
HIMACHAL PRADESH
PUNJAB
HARYANA
UTTAR
RAJASTHAN
BALOCHISTAN
BAHAWALPUR
K A R A K O R A M
Ladakh Range
Pir Panjal Range
Hindu Kush
Toba and Kakar Ranges
Sulaiman Range
Salt Ra.
Nuristan
Aksai Chin
Deosai Plain
Khyber Pass
Karakoram Pass 5575
Khunjerab Pass
K2 8611
Nanga Parbat 8126
Tirich Mir
Nunkun 7135
Kamet 7756
Nanda Devi 7817
Muztag 7282
Sikaram 4761
Koh-i-Baba
Safed Koh
Koh-i-Hisar
Registan
Thar
Indus
Chenab
Jhelum
Sutlej
Ravi
Helmand
Amu Darya
Hotan
Xaidulla
Mazar
Rutog
Kabul
Kandahar
Ghazni
Jalalabad
Mazar-i-Sharif
Kunduz
Baghlan
Charikar
Faizabad
Islamabad
Rawalpindi
Peshawar
Lahore
Faisalabad
Multan
Quetta
Bahawalpur
Sargodha
Gujranwala
Sialkot
Sahiwal
Srinagar
Jammu
Leh
Gilgit
Delhi
New Delhi
Amritsar
Ludhiana
Chandigarh
Simla
Dehra Dun
Meerut
Moradabad
Bareilly
Bikaner

RĀJASTHĀN
MADHYA PRADESH
GUJARĀT
MAHĀRĀSHTRA
SIND
KHAIRPUR
ARABIAN SEA
Gulf of Khambhat
G. of Kachchh
Rann of Kachchh
Mouths of the Indus
Tropic of Cancer
Kirthar Range
Central Makran Range
Makran Coast Range
Sonmiani Bay
Aravalli Range
Vindhya Range
Sātpura Range
Mahadeo Hills
Gir Hills
Kāthiāwār
Plateau of Mālwa
Karachi
Hyderabad
Sukkur
Bombay
Ahmadābād
Kānpur
Jaipur
Āgra
Gwalior
Jhānsi
Jabalpur
Bhopāl
Indore
Ujjain
Nāgpur
Kota
Ajmer
Jodhpur
Udaipur
Vadodara
Sūrat
Rājkot
Jāmnagar
Bhāvnagar
Aurangābād
Nāsik
Pune (Poona)
Thāne
Kalyān
Jalgaon
Dhule
Akola
Amrāvati
Nānded
Ahmadnagar
Diu (Goa, Daman & Diu)
Damān (G.D. & D.)
Silvassa
Alwar
Mathura
Jaisalmer
Bārmer
Bhuj
Porbandar
Dwārka
Veräval
Jūnāgadh
Sāgar
Sāgar
Chhindwāra
Chandrapur
Bīkaner
Sīkar
Tonk
Bhīlwāra
Chittaurgarh
Ratlām
Mandsaur
Godhra
Dāhod
Bhusāwal
Burhānpur
Khandwa
Hoshangābād
Vidisha
Guna
Shivpuri
Etāwah
Firozābād
Hāthras
Datia
Orai
Kālpi
Hamīrpur
Mahoba
Damoh
Seoni
Bhandāra
Wardha
Yavatmāl
Nizāmābād
Ādilābād
Parbhani
Jālna
Bīr
Latur
Udgīr
Bodhan
Mālegaon
Nandurbār
Bharūch
Navsāri
Valsād
Mahesāna
Pātan
Pālanpur
Gāndhīnagar
Nadiād
Surendranagar
Morbi
Gondal
Amreli
Mahuva
Kundla
Pālitāna
Indus
Ganga (Ganges)
Yamuna
Chambal
Narmada
Tāpi
Godāvari
Betwa
Sindh
25
20
70
75
3
4
5
B
C
D

1:7.5M

0 100 200 300 km
0 50 100 150 mls

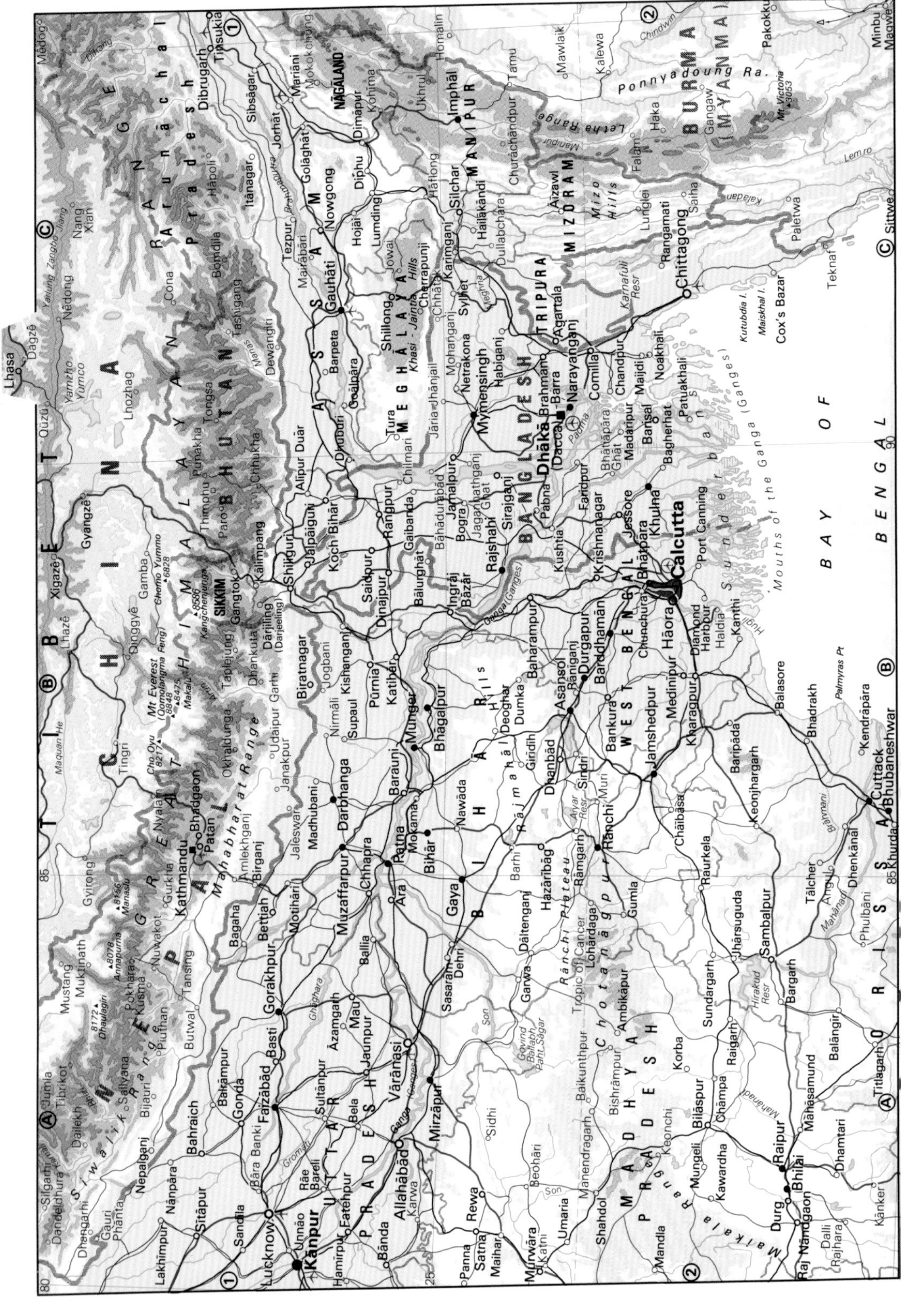

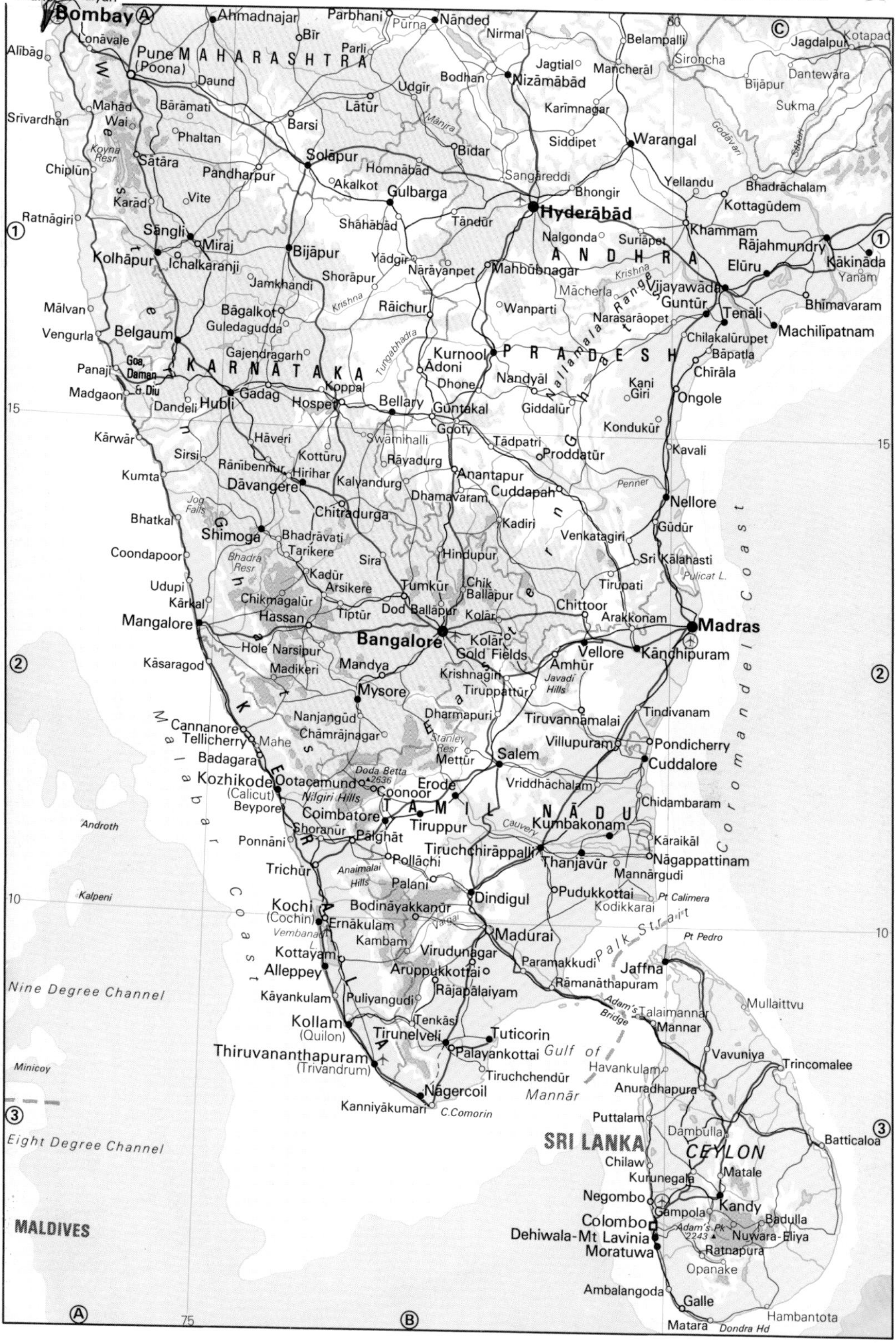
1:7.5M
0 100 200 300 km
0 50 100 150 mls
Thāne
Kalyān
Bombay
Alībāg
Lonāvale
Pune
(Poona)
MAHARASHTRA
Ahmadnajar
Bīr
Parbhani
Pūrna
Nānded
Parli
Daund
Mahād
Wai
Bārāmati
Srīvardhan
Phaltan
Barsi
Lātūr
Udgīr
Koyna Resr
Sātāra
Chiplūn
Pandharpur
Solāpur
Homnābād
Bidar
Akalkot
Gulbarga
Vite
Karād
Ratnāgiri
Sāngli
Miraj
Kolhāpur
Ichalkaranji
Bijāpur
Shāhābād
Tāndūr
Yādgir
Nārāyanpet
Jamkhandi
Shorāpur
Krishna
Rāichur
Mālvan
Bāgalkot
Guledagudda
Vengurla
Belgaum
Gajendragarh
Goa, Daman & Diu
Panaji
Madgaon
KARNATAKA
Gadag
Hubli
Dandeli
Koppal
Hospet
Tungabhadra
Bellary
Kārwār
Hāveri
Kottūru
Swāmihalli
Rāyadurg
Sirsi
Rānibennur
Hirihar
Kumta
Dāvangere
Kalyandurg
Jog Falls
Chitradurga
Bhatkal
Shimoga
Bhadrāvati
Tarikere
Coondapoor
Bhadra Resr
Kadūr
Sira
Arsikere
Udupi
Kārkal
Chikmagalūr
Tiptūr
Tumkūr
Dod Ballāpur
Mangalore
Hassan
Bangalore
Hole Narsipur
Kāsaragod
Madikeri
Mandya
Mysore
Nanjangūd
Chāmrājnagar
Cannanore
Tellicherry
Mahe
Badagara
Kozhikode
(Calicut)
Beypore
Ootacamund
Doda Betta 2636
Coonoor
Nilgiri Hills
Coimbatore
Shoranūr
Pālghāt
Ponnāni
Pollāchi
Trichūr
Anaimalai Hills
Palani
Kochi
(Cochin)
Ernākulam
Vembanad L.
Bodināyakkanūr
Kambam
Kottayam
Alleppey
Kāyankulam
Puliyangudi
Kollam
(Quilon)
Tirunelveli
Thiruvananthapuram
(Trivandrum)
Nāgercoil
Kanniyākumari
C.Comorin
Malabar Coast
Androth
Kalpeni
Nine Degree Channel
Minicoy
Eight Degree Channel
MALDIVES
Nirmal
Jagtial
Nizāmābād
Bodhan
Mancherāl
Belampalli
Sironcha
Karīmnagar
Siddipet
Warangal
Godāvari
Sangāreddi
Bhongir
Hyderābād
Nalgonda
Suriāpet
Yellandu
Bhadrāchalam
Kottagūdem
Khammam
Rājahmundry
Kākināda
Yanam
Eluru
ANDHRA
PRADESH
Mahbūbnagar
Krishna
Māncherla
Vijayawāda
Guntūr
Tenāli
Bhīmavaram
Machilīpatnam
Wanparti
Narasarāopet
Chilakalūrupet
Bāpatla
Chīrāla
Kurnool
Ādoni
Dhone
Nandyāl
Nallamala Range
Giddalūr
Kani Giri
Ongole
Guntakal
Gooty
Tādpatri
Kondukūr
Proddatūr
Kavali
Anantapur
Penner
Dhamavaram
Cuddapah
Nellore
Kadiri
Gūdūr
Venkatagiri
Sri Kālahasti
Hindupur
Pulicat L.
Chik Ballāpur
Tirupati
Chittoor
Kolār
Arakkonam
Madras
Kolār Gold Fields
Vellore
Kānchipuram
Krishnagiri
Āmhūr
Javadi Hills
Tiruppattūr
Dharmapuri
Tiruvannāmalai
Tindivanam
Stanley Resr
Mettūr
Villupuram
Pondicherry
Salem
Cuddalore
Erode
Vriddhāchalam
Chidambaram
TAMIL NADU
Tiruppur
Cauvery
Kumbakonam
Kāraikāl
Tiruchchirāppalli
Thanjāvūr
Nāgappattinam
Mannārgudi
Dindigul
Pudukkottai
Kodikkarai
Pt Calimera
Madurai
Virudunagar
Aruppukkottai
Paramakkudi
Palk Strait
Rāmanāthapuram
Rājapālaiyam
Tenkāsi
Tuticorin
Palayankottai
Tiruchchendūr
Gulf of Mannār
Coromandel Coast
Western Ghats
Eastern Ghats
Pt Pedro
Jaffna
Mullaittvu
Adam's Bridge
Talaimannar
Mannar
Vavuniya
Trincomalee
Havankulam
Anuradhapura
Puttalam
SRI LANKA
Dambulla
CEYLON
Batticaloa
Chilaw
Kurunegala
Matale
Negombo
Kandy
Gampola
Colombo
Badulla
Adam's Pk 2243
Nuwara-Eliya
Dehiwala-Mt Lavinia
Moratuwa
Ratnapura
Opanake
Ambalangoda
Galle
Matara
Dondra Hd
Hambantota
Jagdalpur
Kotapad
Dantewāra
Bijāpur
Sukma
Sabari
80
15
10
75

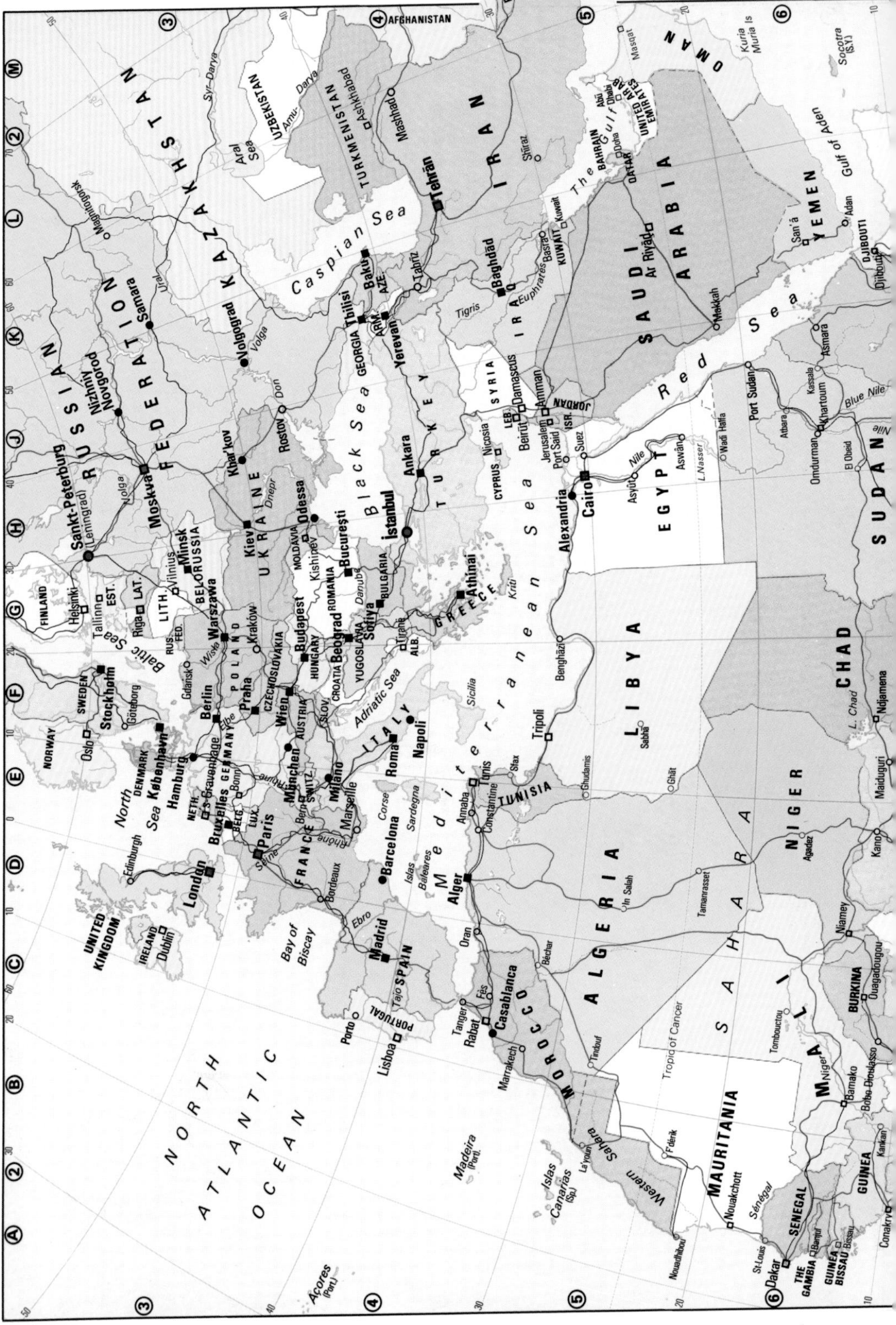
NORTH ATLANTIC OCEAN
UNITED KINGDOM
IRELAND
Dublin
London
Edinburgh
NORWAY
Oslo
SWEDEN
Stockholm
Göteborg
FINLAND
Helsinki
EST.
Tallinn
LAT.
Riga
LITH.
Vilnius
DENMARK
København
North Sea
Baltic Sea
NETH.
BELG.
Bruxelles
LUX.
Paris
FRANCE
Bordeaux
Marseille
Seine
Rhône
GERMANY
Hamburg
Berlin
Bonn
München
Elbe
Rhine
POLAND
Warszawa
Kraków
Gdańsk
Wisła
CZECHOSLOVAKIA
Praha
AUSTRIA
Wien
SWITZ.
Bern
HUNGARY
Budapest
SLOV.
CROATIA
YUGOSLAVIA
Beograd
ROMANIA
București
BULGARIA
Sofiya
ALB.
Tiranë
GREECE
Athinai
ITALY
Milano
Roma
Napoli
Adriatic Sea
Corse
Sardegna
Sicilia
SPAIN
Madrid
Barcelona
Ebro
Tajo
PORTUGAL
Lisboa
Porto
Bay of Biscay
Islas Baleares
Açores (Port.)
Madeira (Port.)
Islas Canarias (Sp.)
RUS. FED.
BELORUSSIA
Minsk
UKRAINE
Kiev
Khar'kov
Odessa
Dnepr
MOLDAVIA
Kishinev
Danube
RUSSIAN FEDERATION
Sankt-Peterburg (Leningrad)
Moskva
Nizhniy Novgorod
Samara
Volgograd
Rostov
Volga
Don
Ural
Magnitogorsk
KAZAKHSTAN
Aral Sea
Syr-Darya
Amu-Darya
UZBEKISTAN
TURKMENISTAN
Ashkhabad
AFGHANISTAN
PAK.
Caspian Sea
Black Sea
GEORGIA
Tbilisi
ARM.
Yerevan
AZE.
Baku
TURKEY
İstanbul
Ankara
CYPRUS
Nicosia
SYRIA
Damascus
LEB.
Beirut
ISR.
Jerusalem
JORDAN
Amman
IRAQ
Baghdād
Tigris
Euphrates
Basra
KUWAIT
Kuwait
IRAN
Tehrān
Tabrīz
Mashhad
Shīraz
The Gulf
BAHRAIN
QATAR
Doha
UNITED ARAB EMIRATES
Abu Dhabi
OMAN
Masqat
Kuria Muria Is
SAUDI ARABIA
Ar Riyāḑ
Makkah
YEMEN
San'ā
Adan
Gulf of Aden
Socotra (S.Y.)
DJIBOUTI
Djibouti
Red Sea
Mediterranean Sea
Kriti
Alexandria
Port Said
Suez
Cairo
EGYPT
Asyūt
Aswān
Nile
L. Nasser
Wadi Halfa
SUDAN
Port Sudan
Khartoum
Omdurman
Atbara
Kassala
Asmara
El Obeid
Blue Nile
LIBYA
Tripoli
Benghāzi
Sabhā
TUNISIA
Tunis
Sfax
Ghudamis
ALGERIA
Alger
Oran
Annaba
Constantine
Béchar
In Salah
Tamanrasset
Ghāt
Tindouf
MOROCCO
Rabat
Casablanca
Tanger
Fès
Marrakech
Western Sahara
La'youn
SAHARA
Tropic of Cancer
MAURITANIA
Nouakchott
Nouadhibou
F'dérik
MALI
Tombouctou
Bamako
Niger
NIGER
Niamey
Agadez
CHAD
Ndjamena
L. Chad
Kano
Maiduguri
BURKINA
Ouagadougou
Bobo-Dioulasso
SENEGAL
Dakar
St-Louis
Sénégal
THE GAMBIA
Banjul
GUINEA-BISSAU
Bissau
GUINEA
Conakry
Kankan

1:40M 0 400 800 1200 1600 km 0 400 800 mls

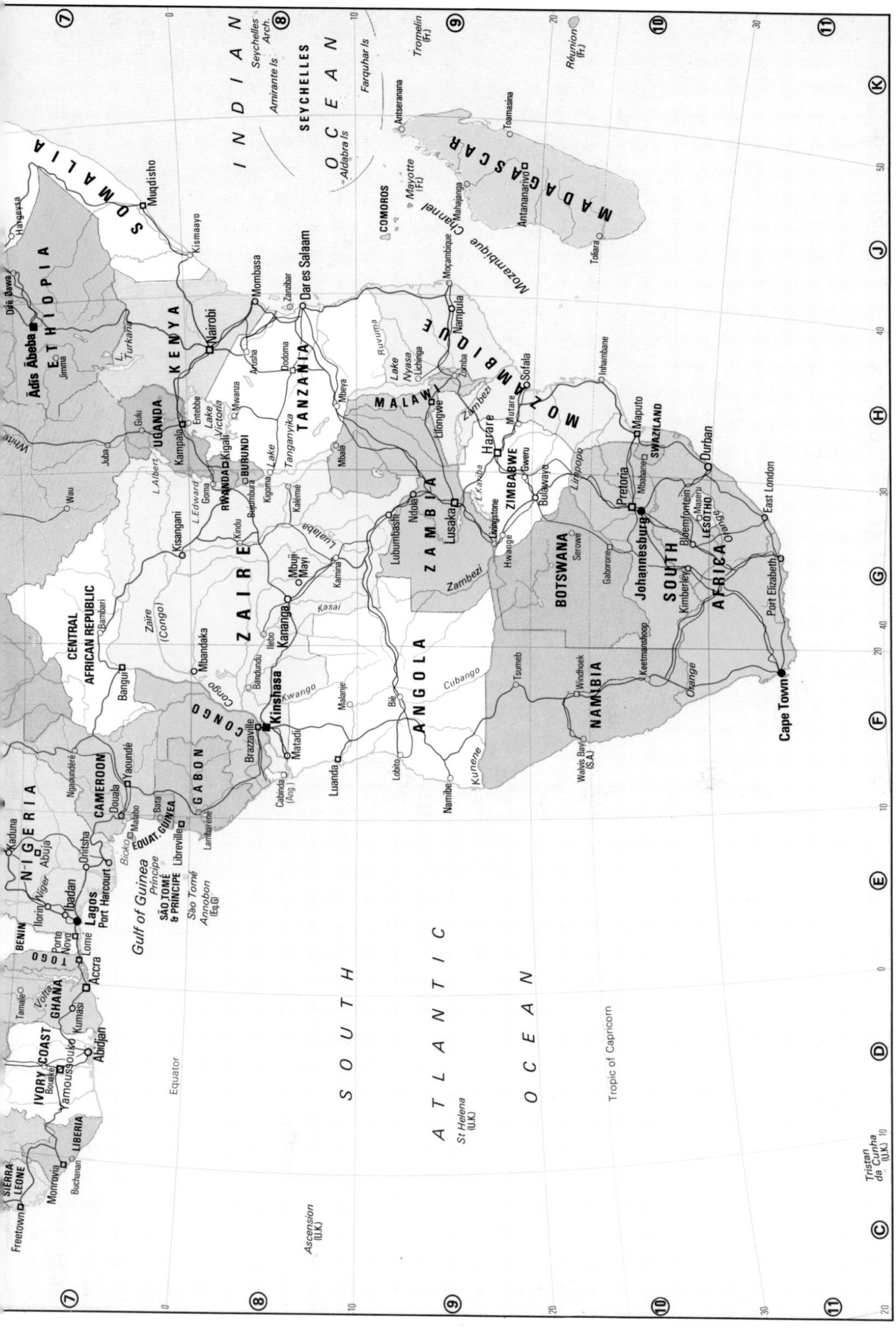

INDIAN OCEAN
SOUTH ATLANTIC OCEAN
Gulf of Guinea
Mozambique Channel
SEYCHELLES
Seychelles Arch.
Amirante Is
Farquhar Is
Aldabra Is
Tromelin (Fr.)
Réunion (Fr.)
COMOROS
Mayotte (Fr.)
MADAGASCAR
Antseranana
Toamasina
Mahajanga
Antananarivo
Toliara
SOMALIA
Muqdisho
Kismaayo
Hargeysa
ETHIOPIA
Ādīs Ābeba
Dirē Dawa
Jimma
L. Turkana
White
KENYA
Nairobi
Mombasa
UGANDA
Kampala
Entebbe
Gulu
Juba
Wau
Lake Victoria
TANZANIA
Dar es Salaam
Zanzibar
Dodoma
Arusha
Mwanza
Mbeya
Lake Tanganyika
Kigoma
RWANDA
Kigali
BURUNDI
Bujumbura
ZAIRE
Kinshasa
Kisangani
Kananga
Mbuji Mayi
Kindu
Goma
Kalémié
Mbandaka
Bandundu
Ilebo
Kamina
Lubumbashi
L. Albert
L. Edward
Zaïre (Congo)
Congo
Kasai
Lualaba
Kwango
CONGO
Brazzaville
CENTRAL AFRICAN REPUBLIC
Bangui
Bambari
CAMEROON
Yaoundé
Douala
Ngaoundéré
GABON
Libreville
Lambaréné
EQUAT. GUINEA
Bata
Malabo
Bioko
SÃO TOMÉ & PRINCIPE
Príncipe
São Tomé
Annobon (Eq.G)
NIGERIA
Lagos
Abuja
Ibadan
Kaduna
Ilorin
Onitsha
Port Harcourt
Niger
BENIN
Porto Novo
TOGO
Lomé
GHANA
Accra
Kumasi
Tamale
Volta
IVORY COAST
Abidjan
Yamoussoukro
Bouaké
LIBERIA
Monrovia
Buchanan
SIERRA LEONE
Freetown
ANGOLA
Luanda
Cabinda (Ang.)
Matadi
Malanje
Bié
Lobito
Namibe
Cubango
Kunene
ZAMBIA
Lusaka
Ndola
Livingstone
Zambezi
MALAWI
Lilongwe
Zomba
Lake Nyasa
Lichinga
Mbala
MOZAMBIQUE
Maputo
Nampula
Moçambique
Sofala
Inhambane
Ruvuma
ZIMBABWE
Harare
Bulawayo
Gweru
Mutare
Hwange
L. Kariba
Limpopo
BOTSWANA
Gaborone
Serowe
NAMIBIA
Windhoek
Tsumeb
Keetmanshoop
Walvis Bay (S.A.)
SOUTH AFRICA
Pretoria
Johannesburg
Cape Town
Durban
Port Elizabeth
East London
Bloemfontein
Kimberley
Orange
SWAZILAND
Mbabane
LESOTHO
Maseru
Ascension (U.K.)
St Helena (U.K.)
Tristan da Cunha (U.K.)
Equator
Tropic of Capricorn

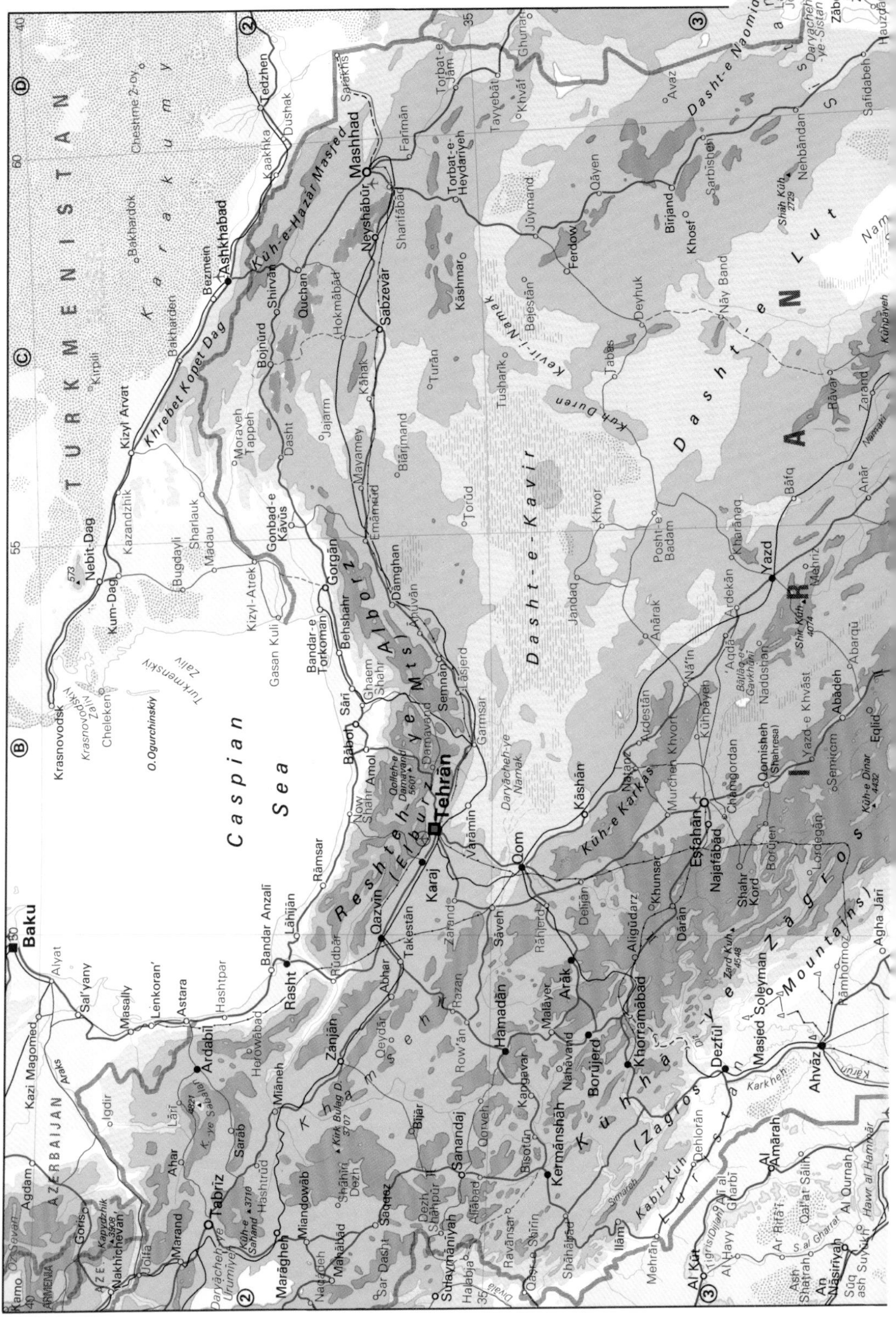
TURKMENISTAN
AZERBAIJAN
ARMENIA
IRAN
Caspian Sea
Dasht-e-Kavir
Dasht-e Lut
Dasht-e Naomid
Karakumy
Reshteh-ye Alborz (Elburz Mts)
Kūh-e Zāgros (Zagros Mountains)
Khrebet Kopet Dag
Kūh-e-Hazār Masjed
Kūh-e Karkas
Kevir-i-Namak
Kūh Duren
Khamseh
Lurestan
Kabir Kuh
Baku
Tehrān
Tabrīz
Mashhad
Esfahān
Yazd
Qom
Rasht
Ardabīl
Qazvīn
Karaj
Hamadān
Arāk
Kermānshāh
Sanandaj
Ahvāz
Dezfūl
Khorramābād
Borūjerd
Ashkhabad
Krasnovodsk
Nebit-Dag
Kum-Dag
Gorgān
Sāri
Bābol
Semnān
Dāmghan
Shāhrūd
Sabzevār
Neyshābūr
Bojnūrd
Quchan
Shirvān
Kāshān
Nā'īn
Birjand
Ferdow
Tabas
Zābol
Kirk Bulag D. 3707
Kūh-e Sahand 3710
Kūh-e Sabalān 4821
Qolleh-ye Damāvand 5601
Zard Kūh 4548
Shīr Kūh 4074
Kūh-e Dīnār 4432
Shāh Kūh 2729
Al Kūt
Al 'Amārah
An Nāşirīyah
Al Qurnah
Hawr al Hammār

1:7.5M

0 100 200 300 km

0 50 100 150 mls

The Gulf

Gulf of Oman

Strait of Hormuz

Trucial Coast

Larestan

Kuh-e Jebal Barez

K.-ye Bashakerd

Al Hajar ash Sharqi

Al Hajar al Gharbi

Al Batinah

Az Zahirah

Musandam Pen. (Oman)

KUWAIT

BAHRAIN

QATAR

U.A.E.

OMAN

MUSCAT

SAUDI ARABIA

Ad Dahna

Al Hasa

Al Jafurah

As Summan

Al Biyadh

Al Kidan

Al Liwa'

Al Humrah

Ad Dibdibah

Al Haniyah

Kuwait

Basra

Khorramshahr

Abadan

Bushehr

Shiraz

Kerman

Bam

Zahedan

Bandar 'Abbas

Qeshm

Doha

Al Manamah

Al Muharraq

Ad Dammam

Al Hufuf

Al Mubarraz

Ar Riyad (Riyadh)

Abu Dhabi

Dubai

Sharjah

Ajman

Umm al Qaiwain

Ras al Khaimah

Fujairah

Masqat (Muscat)

Matrah

Sur

Ra's al Hadd

Nazwa

Ibri

Suhar

Al Buraymi

Al 'Ayn

Chah Bahar

Jask

Tropic of Cancer

Bdy under dispute

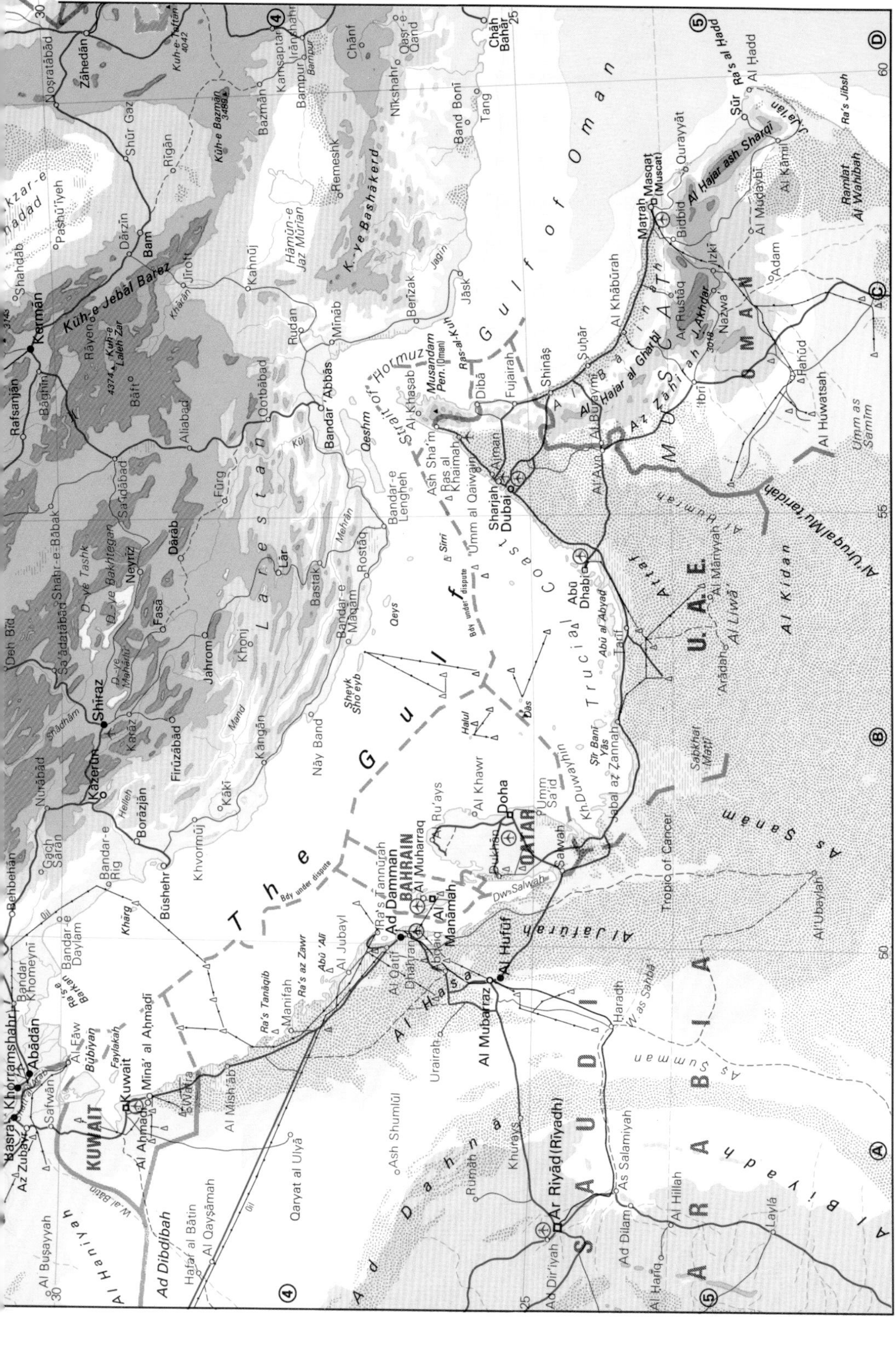

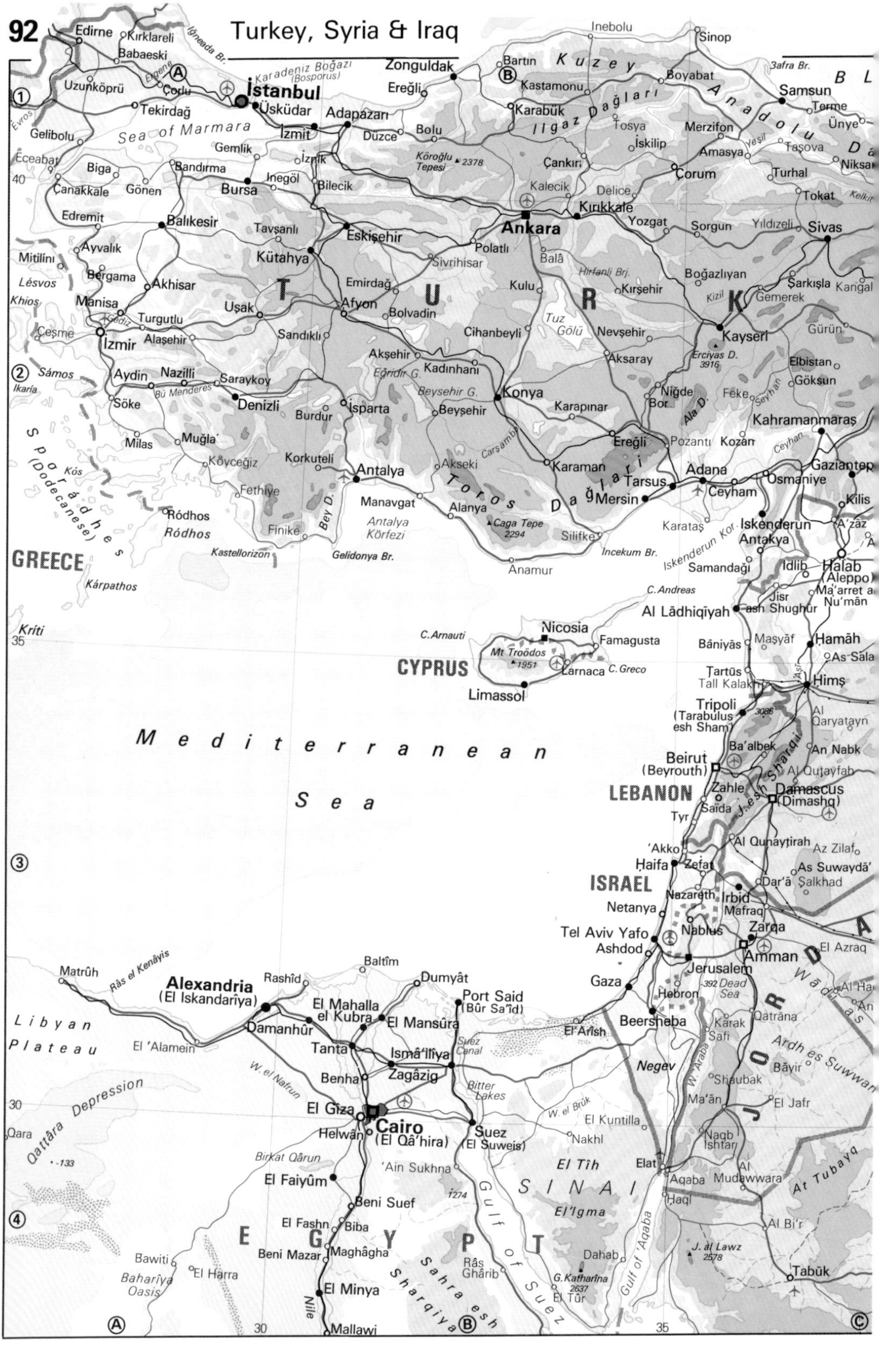
Edirne
Kırklareli
Babaeski
İğneada Br.
Ergene
Uzunköprü
Çorlu
Karadeniz Boğazı (Bosporus)
İstanbul
Üsküdar
Tekirdağ
Evros
Gelibolu
Sea of Marmara
İzmit
Adapazarı
Zonguldak
Ereğli
Bartın
Kuzey Anadolu Dağları
Inebolu
Sinop
Boyabat
Kastamonu
Karabük
Ilgaz Dağları
Tosya
İskilip
Merzifon
Samsun
Terme
Ünye
Amasya
Yeşil
Taşova
Niksar
Turhal
Tokat
Kelkit
Düzce
Bolu
Köroğlu Tepesi 2378
Çankırı
Çorum
Gemlik
İznik
Eceabat
Biga
Bandırma
Çanakkale
Gönen
Bursa
İnegöl
Bilecik
Kalecik
Delice
Kırıkkale
Yozgat
Ankara
Sorgun
Yıldızeli
Sivas
Edremit
Balıkesir
Tavşanlı
Eskişehir
Polatlı
Mitilíni
Ayvalık
Kütahya
Sivrihisar
Balâ
Lésvos
Bergama
Akhisar
Hirfanli Brj.
Boğazlıyan
Şarkışla
Kangal
Khios
Manisa
Emirdağ
Kulu
Kırşehir
Kızıl
Gemerek
Turgutlu
Uşak
Afyon
Bolvadin
Gediz
TURKEY
Tuz Gölü
Çeşme
İzmir
Alaşehir
Sandıklı
Cihanbeyli
Nevşehir
Kayseri
Gürün
Akşehir
Kadınhanı
Aksaray
Erciyas D. 3916
Elbistan
Sámos
Ikaría
Aydin
Nazilli
Saraykoy
Eğirdir G.
Beyşehir G.
Konya
Niğde
Feke
Göksun
Bü Menderes
Söke
Denizli
Burdur
İsparta
Beyşehir
Karapınar
Bor
Ala D.
Seyhan
Kahramanmaraş
Milas
Muğla
Çarşamba
Ereğli
Pozantı
Kozan
Ceyhan
Spóradhes (Dodecanese)
Kós
Köyceğiz
Korkuteli
Antalya
Akseki
Karaman
Adana
Gaziantep
Fethiye
Toros Dağları
Tarsus
Osmaniye
Manavgat
Mersin
Ceyhan
Kilis
Ródhos
Alanya
Bey D.
Caga Tepe 2294
Karataş
Iskenderun
A'zāz
Finike
Antalya Körfezi
Silifke
Antakya
GREECE
Kastellorizon
Gelidonya Br.
Incekum Br.
Iskenderun Kor.
Samandağı
Idlib
Halab (Aleppo)
Anamur
Kárpathos
C. Andreas
Jisr ash Shughūr
Ma'arret an Nu'mān
Al Lādhiqīyah
Kríti
C. Arnauti
Nicosia
Famagusta
Bāniyās
Maşyāf
Hamāh
Mt Troödos 1951
As Sala
CYPRUS
Larnaca
C. Greco
Ţarţūs
Tall Kalakh
Ḩimş
Limassol
Tripoli (Tarabulus esh Sham)
3086
Al Qaryatayn
Mediterranean Sea
Ba'albek
Jesh Sharqi
An Nabk
Beirut (Beyrouth)
Al Quţayfah
LEBANON
Zahle
Damascus (Dimashq)
Saida
Tyr
'Akko
Al Qunayţirah
Az Zilaf
Ḩaifa
Zefat
As Suwaydā'
ISRAEL
Dar'ā
Şalkhad
Nazareth
Irbid
Netanya
Mafraq
Tel Aviv Yafo
Nablus
Zarqa
Ashdod
Amman
El Azraq
Matrûh
Râs el Kenâyis
Baltîm
Jerusalem
Alexandria (El Iskandarîya)
Rashîd
Dumyât
Gaza
-392 Dead Sea
Hebron
Port Said (Bûr Sa'îd)
El Mahalla el Kubra
Libyan Plateau
El Mansûra
Beersheba
Qatrāna
Damanhûr
El 'Arîsh
Karak
Safi
El 'Alamein
Tanta
Suez Canal
Ismâ'ilîya
Negev
W. Araba
JORDAN
Bāyir
Ardh es Suwwan
W. el Nafrun
Benha
Zagâzig
Bitter Lakes
Shaubak
Qattâra Depression
El Gîza
W. el Brûk
Ma'ān
El Jafr
Cairo (El Qâ'hira)
Suez (El Suweis)
El Kuntilla
Qara
Helwân
Nakhl
Naqb Ishtar
-133
Birkat Qârun
'Ain Sukhna
El Tîh
Elat
Al Mudawwara
At Tubayq
El Faiyûm
SINAI
Aqaba
1274
Beni Suef
Haql
El Fashn
Biba
El'Igma
Al Bi'r
EGYPT
Gulf of Suez
J. al Lawz 2578
Beni Mazar
Maghâgha
Dahab
Bawiti
El Harra
Râs Ghârib
Baharîya Oasis
Sahra esh Sharqiya
G. Katharîna 2637
Gulf of 'Aqaba
Tabūk
El Minya
El Tûr
Nile
Mallawi
GREECE
30
35
40
1
2
3
4
A
B
C

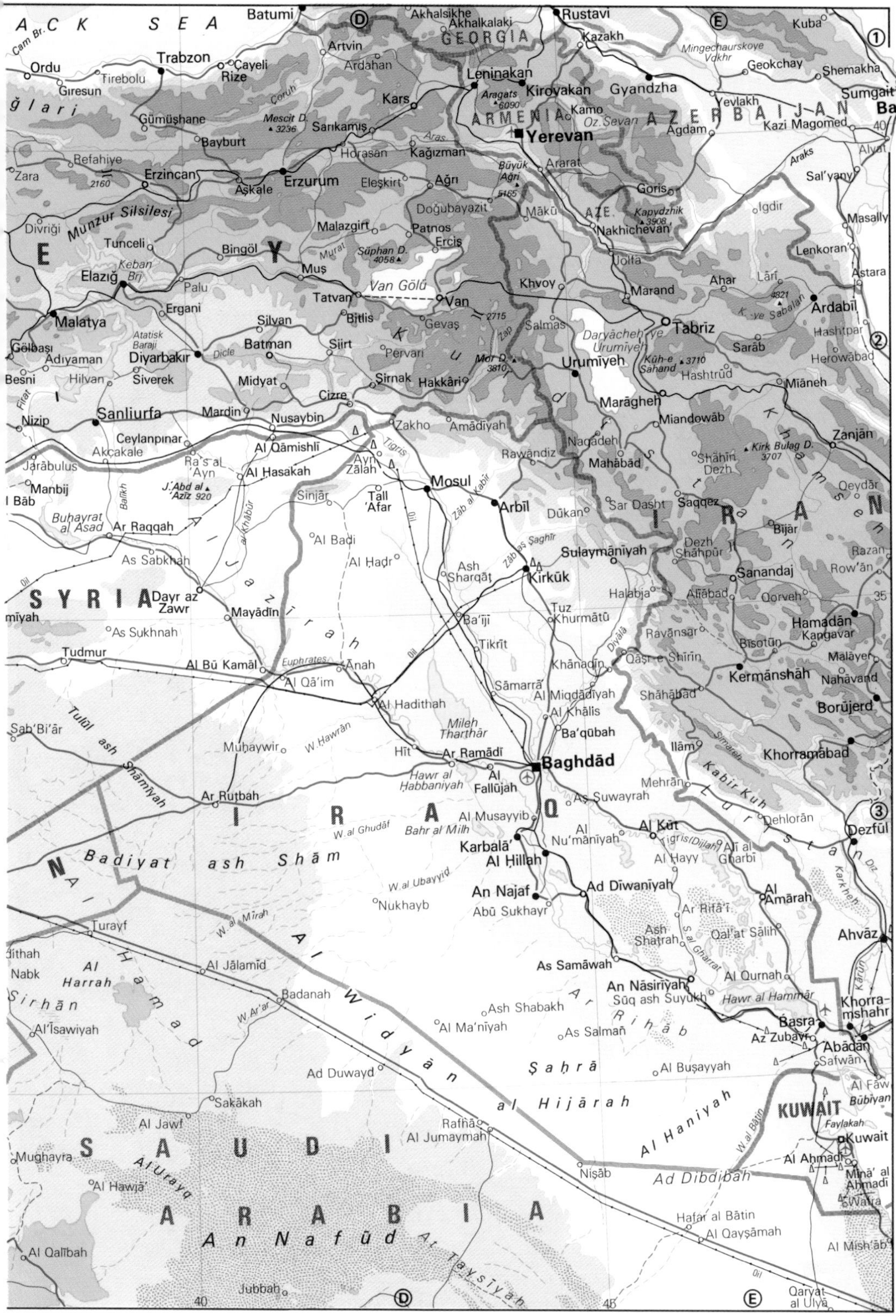
A C K S E A
Batumi
Cam Br.
Ordu
Tirebolu
Giresun
Trabzon
Çayeli
Rize
Artvin
Ardahan
Akhalsikhe
Akhalkalaki
GEORGIA
Rustavi
Kazakh
Mingechaurskoye Vdkhr
Kuba
Geokchay
Shemakha
Sumgait
Baku
ğ l a r i
Gümüşhane
Çoruh
Mescit D. 3236
Bayburt
Sarıkamış
Kars
Leninakan
Aragats 6090
Kirovakan
Gyandzha
Yevlakh
ARMENIA
Kamo
Oz. Sevan
A Z E R B A I J A N
Agdam
Kazi Magomed
Yerevan
Aras
Horasan
Kağızman
Refahiye
Zara
2160
Erzincan
Aşkale
Erzurum
Eleşkirt
Ağrı
Büyük Ağri 5165
Ararat
Araks
Alyat
Sal'yany
Goris
Munzur Silsilesi
Divriği
Doğubayazit
Mākū
AZE.
Kapydzhik 3908
Nakhichevan
Igdir
Masally
Malazgirt
Patnos
Erciş
Süphan D. 4058
Tunceli
Bingöl
Murat
Lenkoran
E
Y
Keban Brj
Elazığ
Muş
Jolfa
Astara
Palu
Tatvan
Van Gölü
Van
Khvoy
Marand
Ahar
Lārī
4821
K.-ye Sabalan
Ardabīl
Ergani
Malatya
Bitlis
Gevaş
2715
Zap
Salmās
Tabrīz
Silvan
Atatisk Baraji
K u
Daryācheh-ye Urūmīyeh
Hashtpar
Gölbaşı
Adıyaman
Diyarbakır
Dicle
Batman
Siirt
Pervari
Mor D. 3810
Urūmīyeh
Kūh-e Sahand 3710
Sarāb
Herowābād
Besni
Hilvan
Siverek
Midyat
Şirnak
Hakkâri
d
Hashtrūd
Mīāneh
Fırat
Cizre
Marāgheh
Nizip
Sanliurfa
Mardin
Nusaybin
Zakho
Amādīyah
Miandowāb
Ceylanpınar
Al Qāmishlī
Tigris
Naqadeh
Kh
Zanjān
Akçakale
Ra's al 'Ayn
Ayn Zālah
Rawāndiz
Mahābād
Shāhīn Dezh
Kirk Bulag D. 3707
Jarābulus
Al Hasakah
Mosul
Manbij
J. 'Abd al 'Azīz 920
Sinjār
Tall 'Afar
Zāb al Kabīr
Arbīl
Sar Dasht
Saqqez
Qeydār
l Bāb
Balīkh
Oil
Dūkan
I
R
A
N
Bījār
Buhayrat al Asad
Ar Raqqah
al Khābūr
Al Badi
Zāb aş Şaghīr
Sulaymānīyah
Dezh Shāhpūr
Razan
As Sabkhah
Al Hadr
Ash Sharqāt
Kirkūk
Sanandaj
Row'ān
S Y R I A
Dayr az Zawr
Al Jazīrah
Halabja
Alīābād
Qorveh
35
mīyah
Mayādīn
Tuz Khurmātū
Ba'ījī
Hamadān
Kangāvar
As Sukhnah
Ravānsar
Tikrīt
Diyālā
Bīsotūn
Tudmur
Al Bū Kamāl
Euphrates
Ānah
Khānaqīn
Qaşr-e Shīrīn
Malāyer
Kermānshāh
Nahāvand
Al Qā'im
Sāmarrā'
Al Miqdādīyah
Shāhābād
Borūjerd
Al Hadithah
Al Khālis
Tulūl ash Shāmīyah
Sab'Bi'ār
Mileh Tharthār
Ba'qūbah
W. Hawrān
Muhaywir
Hīt
Ar Ramādī
Ilām
Simareh
Khorramābād
Baghdād
Hawr al Habbaniyah
Al Fallūjah
Kabir Kuh
Mehrān
Ar Rutbah
Aş Şuwayrah
Luristan
I R A Q
Al Musayyib
3
Dehlorān
Bahr al Milh
W. al Ghudāf
Al Nu'mānīyah
Al Kūt
Dezfūl
Karbalā'
Tigris (Dijlah)
'Alī al Gharbī
Badiyat ash Shām
Al Hillah
Al Hayy
Dez
N A
W. al Ubayyid
Ad Dīwanīyah
Karkheh
An Najaf
Al 'Amārah
Nukhayb
Abū Sukhayr
Ar Rifā'ī
Turayf
W. al Mīrah
Ash Shatrah
Qal'at Sālih
Ahvāz
dīthah
Al Hamad
Shatt al Gharraf
As Samāwah
Karun
Nabk
Al Jālamīd
Al Qurnah
Al Harrah
An Nāsirīyah
Sirhān
Badanah
Sūq ash Suyūkh
Hawr al Hammār
Khorramshahr
W. Ar'ar
Ash Shabakh
Ar Rihāb
Basra
Al 'Īsawiyah
Al Ma'nīyah
As Salmān
Az Zubayr
Abādān
Al Widyān
Safwān
Ad Duwayd
Şahrā al Hijārah
Al Buşayyah
Al Fāw
Būbiyān
Sakākah
KUWAIT
Faylakah
Al Jawf
Rafhā
Al Jumaymah
Al Haniyah
W. al Bātin
Kuwait
Mughayra
S A U D I
Al Ahmadī
Al 'Urayq
Nişāb
Ad Dibdibah
Mīnā' al Ahmadī
Al Hawjā'
Az Zawr
A R A B I A
Hafar al Bātin
Al Qayşāmah
An Nafūd
At Taysīyah
Al Qalībah
Oil
Al Mish'āb
Jubbah
40
D
46
E
Qaryat al Ulya
1
2

1:2.5M

0 25 50 75 100 km
0 25 50 mls

CYPRUS
Larnaca
Limassol
LEBANON
Beirut (Beyrouth)
Tripoli (Tarābulus esh Sham)
SYRIA
Damascus (Dimashq)
ISRAEL
Haifa (Hefa)
Tel Aviv-Yafo (Jaffa)
Jerusalem (El Quds) (Yerushalayim)
JORDAN
Amman
EGYPT
MEDITERRANEAN SEA
Gaza
Gaza Strip
Beersheba (Be'er Sheva)
Nazareth
Nablus
Hebron (El Khalil)
Bethlehem (Bayt Lahm)
Jericho (Arīhā)
Dead Sea (Bahrat Lut)
L. Tiberias (Yam Kinneret) (Sea of Galilee)
Tiberias
Netanya
Ashdod
Ashqelon
Eilat
Tyr (Tyre, Sour)
Saïda (Sidon)
Zahle
Ba'albek
Hims (Homs)
Irbid
Zarqa
Dar'a
Mafraq
Karak
Negev
CEASE FIRE LINES 1974
ARMISTICE LINE
CEASE FIRE LINE

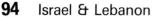

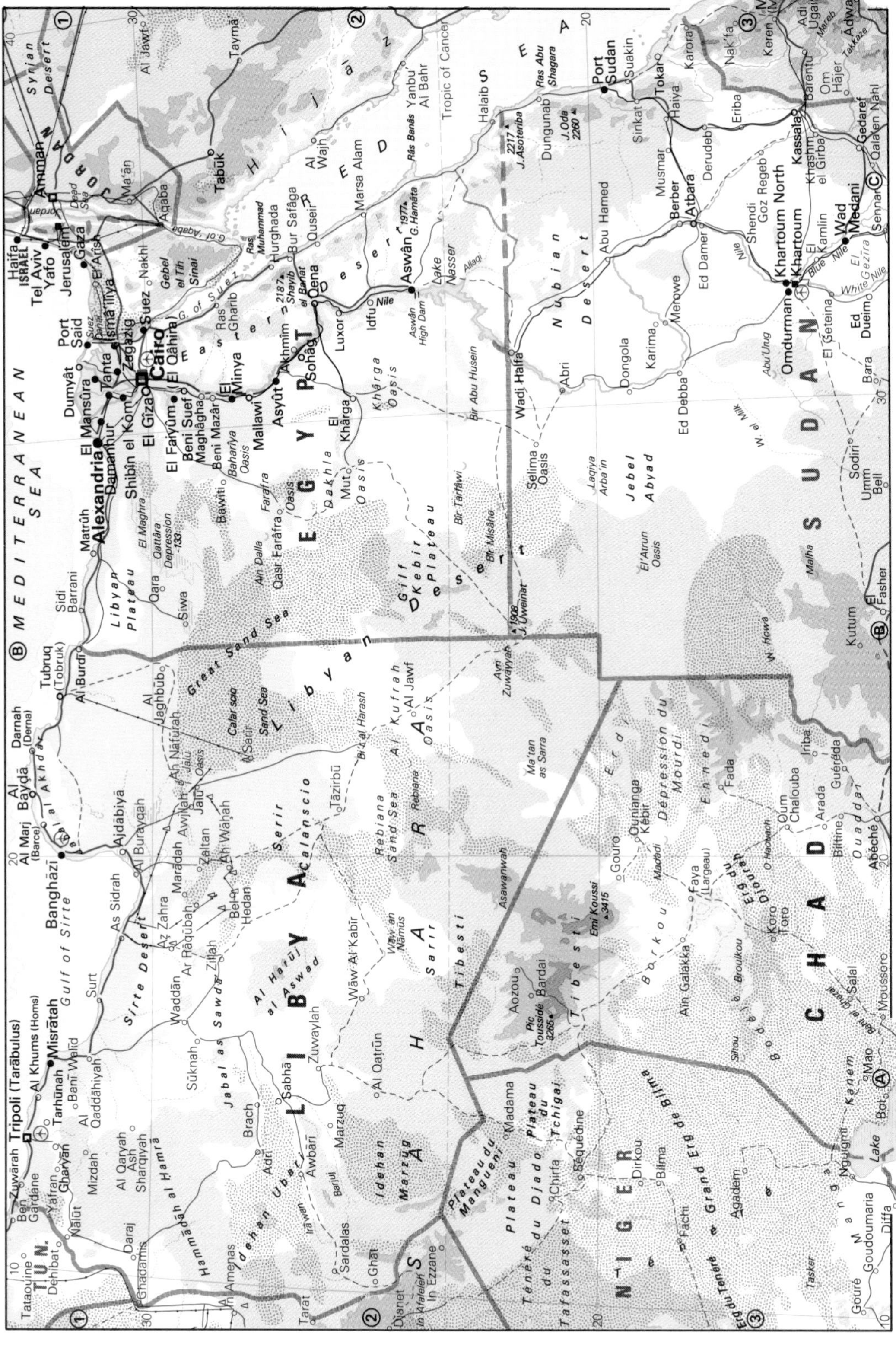
MEDITERRANEAN SEA
EGYPT
LIBYA
SUDAN
CHAD
NIGER
ISRAEL
JORDAN
TUN.
RED SEA
Libyan Desert
Eastern Desert
Nubian Desert
Great Sand Sea
Calanscio Sand Sea
Rebiana Sand Sea
Serir Calanscio
Sahara
Tibesti
Sirte Desert
Gulf of Sirte
Hijaz
Tropic of Cancer
Lake Nasser
Lake Chad
Cairo
El Qâhira
Alexandria
El Giza
Port Said
Suez
Aswân
Luxor
Asyût
El Minya
Tanta
Damanhur
El Mansûra
Dumyât
Zagazig
Ismâ'ilîya
Qena
Sohâg
El Faiyûm
Beni Suef
Matrûh
Siwa
El Khârga
Tripoli (Tarābulus)
Misrātah
Banghāzī
Tubruq (Tobruk)
Darnah (Derna)
Al Kufrah
Sabhā
Khartoum
Khartoum North
Omdurman
Port Sudan
Kassala
Wad Medani
Atbara
Wadi Halfa
Dongola
El Fasher
Abéché
Faya (Largeau)
Amman
Jerusalem
Tel Aviv Yafo
Haifa
Gaza
Tabūk
Asmera
Mits'iwa (Massawa)
Emi Koussi 3415
Pic Toussidé 3265
Gilf Kebir Plateau
Jebel Abyad
Qattâra Depression -133
Libyan Plateau
Blue Nile
White Nile
Nile
El Gezira

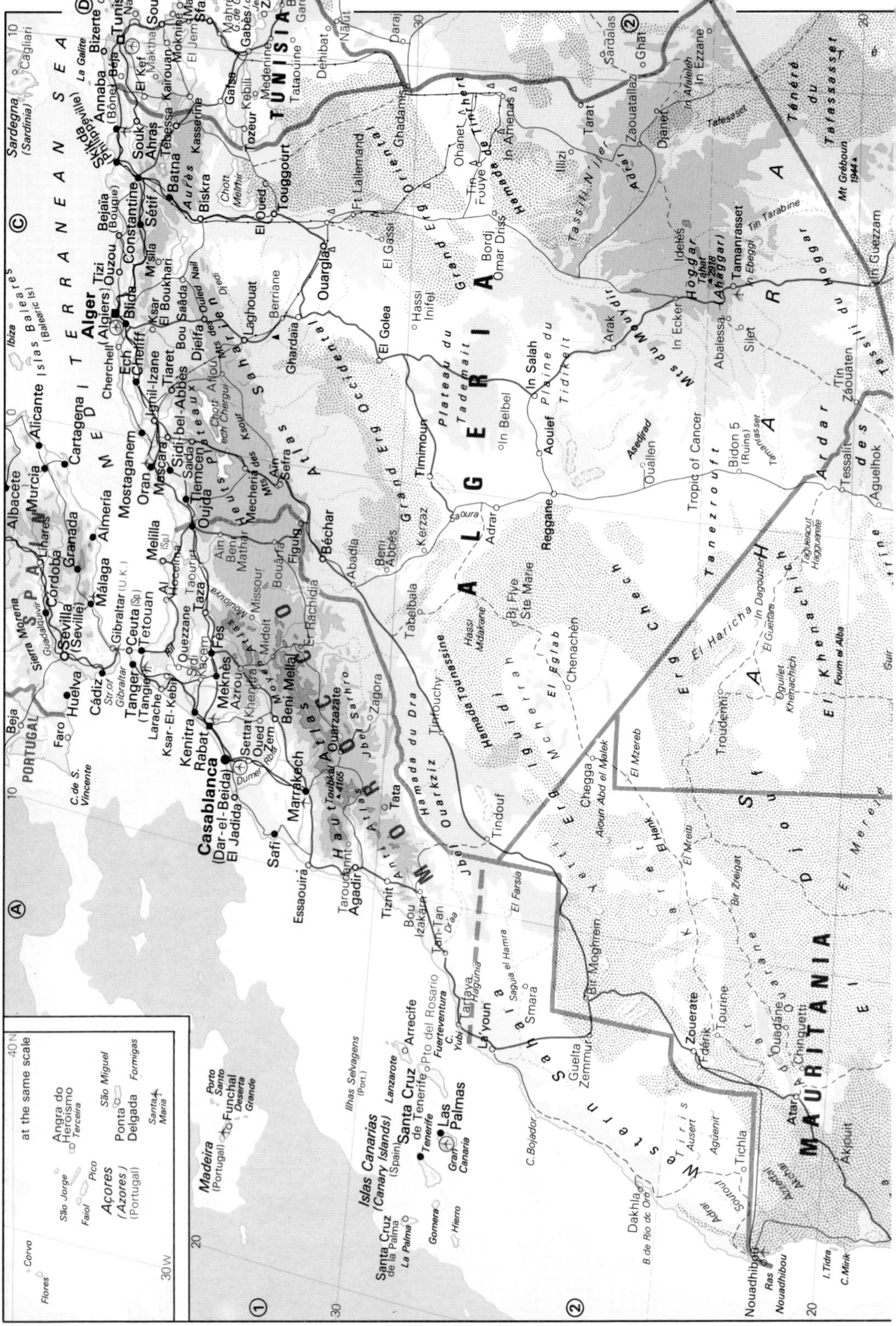
MEDITERRANEAN SEA
SPAIN
PORTUGAL
MOROCCO
ALGERIA
TUNISIA
MAURITANIA
Western Sahara
SAHARA
Sardegna (Sardinia)
Islas Baleares (Balearic Is)
Madeira (Portugal)
Islas Canarias (Canary Islands) (Spain)
Açores (Azores) (Portugal)
at the same scale
Alger (Algiers)
Tunis
Casablanca (Dar-el-Beida)
Rabat
Marrakech
Fès
Meknès
Tanger (Tangier)
Oran
Constantine
Annaba (Bône)
Sfax
Sousse
Bizerte
Sevilla (Seville)
Córdoba
Granada
Málaga
Murcia
Alicante
Cartagena
Almería
Cádiz
Huelva
Faro
Gibraltar (U.K.)
Ceuta (Sp.)
Melilla (Sp.)
Tetouan
Agadir
Essaouira
Safi
El Jadida
Ouarzazate
Béchar
Ghardaïa
Ouargla
Laghouat
Biskra
Touggourt
El Golea
Timimoun
Adrar
Reggane
In Salah
Tamanrasset
Djanet
Tindouf
Tarfaya
La'youn
Smara
Dakhla
Nouadhibou
Atar
Zouerate
Las Palmas
Santa Cruz de Tenerife
Funchal
Tropic of Cancer
Grand Erg Occidental
Grand Erg Oriental
Haut Atlas
Moyen Atlas
Anti Atlas
Hoggar (Ahaggar)
Tassili N'Ajjer
Tanezrouft
Erg Chech
El Djouf

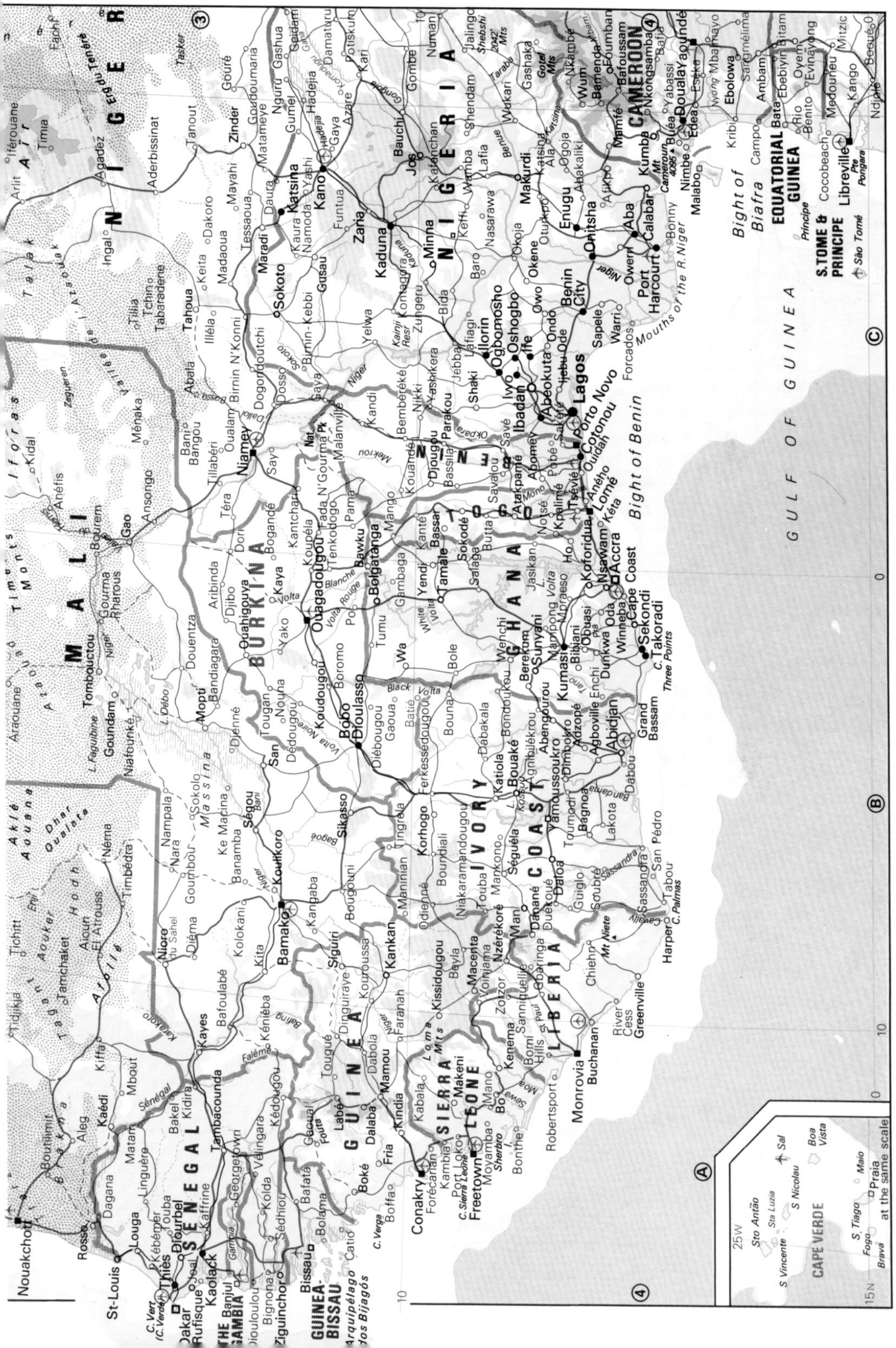
NIGER
MALI
BURKINA
NIGERIA
BENIN
TOGO
GHANA
IVORY COAST
LIBERIA
SIERRA LEONE
GUINEA
GUINEA-BISSAU
SENEGAL
THE GAMBIA
CAMEROON
EQUATORIAL GUINEA
S.TOME & PRINCIPE
CAPE VERDE
at the same scale
GULF OF GUINEA
Bight of Benin
Bight of Biafra
Mouths of the R. Niger
Aïr
Niamey
Bamako
Ouagadougou
Accra
Lomé
Porto Novo
Lagos
Abidjan
Yamoussoukro
Monrovia
Freetown
Conakry
Bissau
Banjul
Dakar
Nouakchott
Yaoundé
Douala
Malabo
Libreville
São Tomé
Praia
Kano
Kaduna
Ibadan
Kumasi
Tombouctou
Gao
Mopti
Ségou
Bobo Dioulasso
Sokoto
Zinder
Maradi
Agadez
Saint-Louis
Kaolack
Tambacounda
Kankan
Korhogo
Bouaké
Tamale
Parakou
Cotonou
Benin City
Port Harcourt
Enugu
Onitsha
Calabar
Jos
Makurdi
Mt Cameroun 4095
Mt Nimba

CHAD
NIGERIA
CAMEROON
CENTRAL AFRICAN REPUBLIC
EQUAT. GUINEA
GABON
CONGO
ZAIRE
ANGOLA
Lake Chad
Kanem
Ouaddai
Bornu
Baguirmi
Dar Rounga
Massif des Bongo
Haute Kotto
Massif de l'Adamaoua
Bight of Biafra
Zinder
Gouré
Goudoumaria
Diffa
Nguigmi
Tessaoua
Matameye
Daura
Nguru
Gashua
Geidam
Gumel
Hadejia
Kano
Gaya
Azare
Maiduguri
Damaturu
Potiskum
Kari
Biu
Mubi
Bauchi
Jos
Gombe
Kafanchan
Numan
Yola
Wamba
Shendam
Lafia
Jalingo
Wukari
Makurdi
Gashaka
Katsina Ala
Ogoja
Abakaliki
Calabar
Mao
Bol
Moussoro
Massakori
Salal
Ndjamena
(Ft Lamy)
Bokoro
Mongo
Massenya
Melfi
Bongor
Bousso
Mokolo
Maroua
Guider
Léré
Garoua
Lai
Pala
Moundou
Doba
Sarh
Dik
Maro
Kousseri
Bama
Biltine
Arada
Guéréda
Abéché
Oum Hadjer
Ati
Am Dam
Mangalmé
Goz-Beida
Adré
Abou Deïa
Am Timan
Harazé
Birao
Ndélé
Ouanda Djallé
Ouadda
Bamingui Bangoran Nat. Pk
Kutum
El Fasher
Geneina
Zalingei
Jebel Marra
3071
Nyala
Keddada
Umm
Taweisha
Ed Da'ein
El Muglad
Buram
Nyamlell
Raga
Aweil
Deim Zubeir
Djéma
Obo
Doruma
Niangara
Bambili
Isiro
Tchollire
Poli
Shebshi Mts
2042
Gotel Mts
Ngaoundéré
Goré
Baïbokoum
Batangafo
Bocaranga
Bossangoa
Bouca
Bozoum
Meiganga
Nkambé
Wum
Bamenda
Tibati
Foumban
Bafoussam
Mamfé
Kumba
Nkongsamba
Mt Cameroun 4095
Buéa
Limbe
Douala
Edea
Yabassi
Bafia
Bertoua
Garoua Boulai
Bouar
Carnot
Boyali
Berbérati
Bangui
Boda
Mbaïki
Zongo
Libenge
Nanga Eboko
Abong Mbang
Yaoundé
Eséka
Mbalmayo
Yokadouma
Nola
Malabo
Kribi
Ebolowa
Sangmélima
Campo
Ambam
Bata
Ebebiyin
Bitam
Oyem
Rio Benito
Evinayong
Cocobeach
Libreville
Kango
Medouneu
Mitzic
Port Gentil
Lambaréné
Ndjolé
Booué
Lastoursville
Koulamoutou
Mouila
Fougamou
Omboué
Iguéla
Tchibanga
Mayumba
Ndendé
Mbinda
Mossendjo
Kibangou
Sibiti
Madingou
Moanda
Masuku
Okondja
Makokou
Mekambo
Souanké
Moloundou
Ouesso
Mbendza
Makoua
Fort Rousset
Kellé
Ewo
Okoyo
Mossaka
Olombo
Gamboma
Ngo
Djambala
Zanaga
Ngabé
Mouyondzi
Mayama
Brazzaville
Kinshasa
(Léopoldville)
Luobomo
Madingo Kayes
Pte Noire
Cabinda
Boma
Matadi
Mbanza-Ngungu
Tshela
Luozi
Madimba
Impfondo
Pikounda
Liranga
Lukolela
Bolobo
Mushie
Nioki
Kutu
Bandundu
Kenge
Masi-Manimba
Kikwit
Idiofa
Gungu
Tshikapa
Mbandaka
(Coquilhatville)
Bikoro
Inongo
Kiri
Monkoto
Makanza
Basankusu
Bongandanga
Yahuma
Gemena
Bozene
Lisala
Bumba
Monveda
Akéti
Buta
Bondo
Titule
Lienart
Bangassou
Mobaye
Mobayi
Yakoma
Monga
Rafai
Zemio
Gwane
Kisangani
(Stanleyville)
Yangambi
Banalia
Bafwasende
Isangi
Yatolema
Djolu
Befale
Mompono
Boende
Bokungu
Ikela
Opala
Ubundu
Lomela
Loto
Dekese
Oshwe
Lodja
Katako-kombe
Kindu
Kibombo
Kasongo
Lusambo
Ilebo
Mweka
Luebo
Kananga
(Luluabourg)
Mbuji-Mayi
Kabinda
Mwene Ditu
Kamina
Bukama
Kolwezi
Likasi
(Jadotville)
Lubumbashi
Luanda
Caxito
Catete
Uige
Ambriz
N'zeto
Malanje
Saurimo
Dilolo
Luena
Lobito
Benguela
Huambo
(Nova Lisboa)
Sumbe
(Novo Redondo)
Chililabombwe
Chingola
Solwezi
Mwinilunga

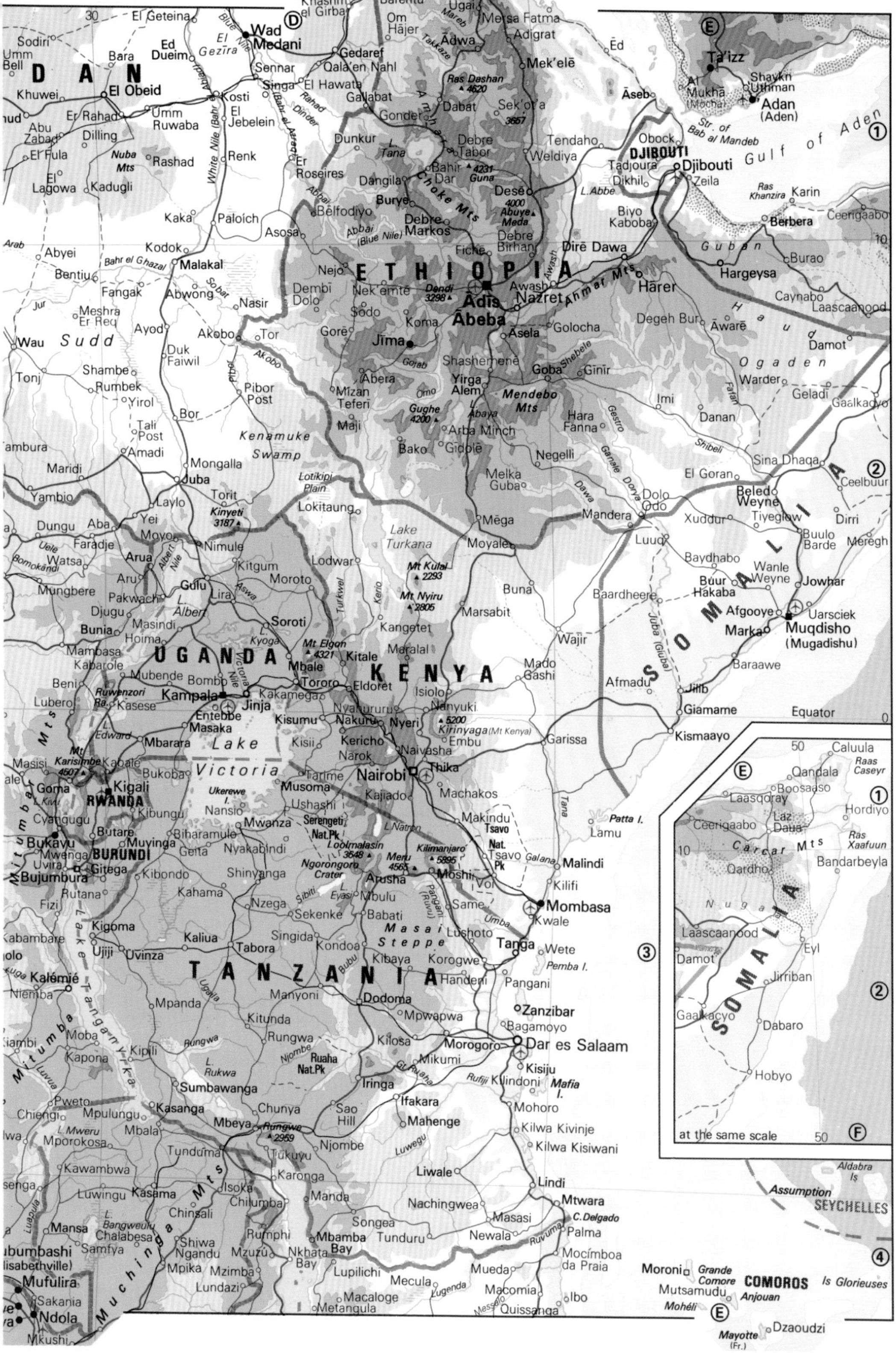
Kassala
Keren
Massawa
Asmera
Khashm el Girba
Barentu
Adi Ugai
Adwa
Mersa Fatma
Adigrat
Om Hajer
Mareb
Takkaze
Ed
El Geteina
Wad Medani
Blue Nile
El Gezira
Sodiri
Bara
Ed Dueim
Gedaref
Qala'en Nahl
Sennar
Umm Bell
DAN
El Obeid
Khuwei
Kosti
Singa
El Hawata
Gallabat
Ras Dashan 4620
Mek'elē
Ta'izz
Al Mukhā (Mocha)
Shaykh Uthman
Adan (Aden)
Āseb
Er Rahad
Umm Ruwaba
El Jebelein
Rahad
Dinder
Gonder
Dabat
Sek'ot'a 3657
Abu Zabad
Dilling
El Fula
Nuba Mts
Rashad
White Nile (Bahr el Abyad)
Renk
Er Roseires
Dunkur
L. Tana
Debre Tabor
4231 Guna
Tendaho
Weldiya
Obock
DJIBOUTI
Djibouti
Tadjoura
Dikhil
Str. of Bab al Mandeb
Gulf of Aden
1
El Lagowa
Kadugli
Bahir Dar
Dangila
Burye
Choke Mts
Desē
4000 Abuye Meda
L. Abbe
Zeila
Ras Khanzira
Karin
Kaka
Paloich
Asosa
Bēlfodiyo
Debre Markos
Abbai (Blue Nile)
Debre Birhan
Biyo Kaboba
Berbera
Ceerigaabo
Arab
Abyei
Kodok
Malakal
Fichē
Awash
Dirē Dawa
Guban
Burao
10
Bahr el Ghazal
Bentiu
Nejo
ETHIOPIA
Dembī Dolo
Nek'emtē
Dendi 3298
Ādīs Ābeba
Nazret
Ahmar Mts
Hārer
Hargeysa
Fangak
Abwong
Sobat
Nasir
Jur
Meshra Er Req
Sodo
Koma
Caynabo
Haud
Laascaanood
Ayod
Akobo
Tor
Gorē
Jīma
Āsela
Golocha
Degeh Bur
Āwarē
Wau
Sudd
Duk Faiwil
Gojab
Shashemenē
Goba
Shebele
Gīnīr
Damot
Ogaden
Shambe
Tonj
Rumbek
Akobo
Pibor
Pibor Post
Ābera
Mīzan Teferī
Omo
Yirga Alem
Mendebo Mts
Abaya
Warder
Fafan
Imī
Geladī
Galkayo
Yirol
Bor
Gughe 4200
Hara Fanna
Gestro
Danan
Tali Post
Amadi
Tambura
Maji
Bako
Arba Minch
Gidolē
Kenamuke Swamp
Shibeli
Ganale Dorya
Maridi
Mongalla
Negelli
Sina Dhaqa
2
Juba
Melka Guba
El Goran
Ceelbuur
Yambio
Laylo
Torit
Lotikipi Plain
Dawa
Beled Weyne
Kinyeti 3187
Lokitaung
Dolo Odo
Mandera
Xuddur
Tiyeglow
Dirri
Dungu
Aba
Yei
Lake Turkana
Mēga
Moyale
Luuq
Buulo Barde
Meregh
Faradje
Uele
Watsa
Bomokandi
Moyo
Arua
Albert Nile
Nimule
Kitgum
Lodwar
Mt Kulal 2293
Baydhabo
Wanle Weyne
Jowhar
Aru
Mungbere
Pakwach
Gulu
Lira
Moroto
Aswa
Turkwel
Kerio
Mt Nyiru 2805
Buna
Baardheere
Buur Hakaba
Afgooye
Djugu
L. Albert
Soroti
Marsabit
Juba (Giuba)
Uarsciek
Muqdisho (Mugadishu)
Bunia
Masindi
Hoima
L. Kyoga
Kangetet
Marka
Wajir
Mambasa
Kabarole
UGANDA
Mt Elgon 4321
Kitale
Maralal
Mado Gashi
Baraawe
SOMALIA
Beni
Mubende
Bombo
Victoria Nile
Mbale
KENYA
Afmadu
Ruwenzori Ra.
Kampala
Jinja
Tororo
Eldoret
Isiolo
Jilib
Lubero
Kasese
Entebbe
Kakamega
Kisumu
Nyahururu
Nanyuki
Giamame
Equator
0
Masaka
Nakuru
Nyeri
5200 Kirinyaga (Mt Kenya)
Kismaayo
L. Edward
Mbarara
Lake Victoria
Kisii
Kericho
Naivasha
Embu
Garissa
Masisi
Mt Karisimbe 4507
Kabale
Bukoba
Tarime
Narok
Nairobi
Thika
Goma
L. Kivu
Kigali
RWANDA
Ukerewe I.
Musoma
Kajiado
Machakos
Cyangugu
Nansio
Kibungu
Ushashi
L. Natron
Makindu
Tsavo Nat. Pk
Tana
Patta I.
Lamu
Bukavu
Butare
Biharamulo
Mwanza
Serengeti Nat. Pk
Mwenga
Muyinga
BURUNDI
Geita
Nyakabindi
Loolmalasin 3648
Meru 4565
Kilimanjaro 5895
Galana
Malindi
Uvira
Bujumbura
Gitega
Kibondo
Shinyanga
Ngorongoro Crater
Arusha
Moshi
Voi
Kilifi
Mitumba Mts
Rutana
Kahama
L. Eyasi
Mbulu
Pangani (Ruvu)
Same
Mombasa
Fizi
Nzega
Sibiti
Sekenke
Babati
Umba
Kwale
Kigoma
Masai Steppe
Lushoto
Tanga
Wete
3
Kabambare
Ujiji
Uvinza
Kaliua
Tabora
Singida
Kondoa
Bubu
Kibaya
Korogwe
Pemba I.
Kalemie
Lake Tanganyika
TANZANIA
Handeni
Pangani
Niemba
Luga
Ugalla
Manyoni
Dodoma
Mpwapwa
Zanzibar
Mpanda
Kitunda
Bagamoyo
Moba
Mitumba
Rungwa
Kilosa
Morogoro
Dar es Salaam
Kapona
Kipili
Njombe
Ruaha Nat. Pk
Mikumi
Kisiju
L. Rukwa
Gt Ruaha
Rufiji
Kilindoni
Mafia I.
Luvua
Sumbawanga
Iringa
Pweto
Mpulungu
Kasanga
Chunya
Sao Hill
Ifakara
Mohoro
Chiengi
L. Mweru
Mbala
Mbeya
Rungwe 2959
Mahenge
Kilwa Kivinje
Mporokosa
Tunduma
Tukuyu
Luwegu
Kilwa Kisiwani
Kawambwa
Karonga
Liwale
Luwingu
Kasama
Isoka
Muchinga Mts
Chilumba
Manda
Lindi
Mtwara
L. Bangweulu
Chinsali
Nachingwea
C. Delgado
Mansa
Chalabesa
Samfya
Shiwa Ngandu
Rumphi
Songea
Masasi
Luapula
Lubumbashi (Elisabethville)
Mpika
Mzuzu
Mbamba Bay
Nkhata Bay
Tunduru
Newala
Ruvuma
Palma
Mocímboa da Praia
Mzimba
Lupilichi
Mecula
Mueda
Mufulira
Lundazi
Lugenda
Macomia
Sakania
Ndola
Macaloge
Metangula
Messalo
Quissanga
Ibo
Mkushi
Moroni
Grande Comore
COMOROS
Is Glorieuses
Mutsamudu
Anjouan
Mohéli
Mayotte (Fr.)
Dzaoudzi
Aldabra Is
Assumption
SEYCHELLES
4
E
D
F
50
Caluula
Raas Caseyr
Qandala
Boosaaso
Laasqoray
Hordiyo
Ceerigaabo
Laz Daua
Ras Xaafuun
Carcar Mts
Bandarbeyla
Qardho
Nugaal
Laascaanood
Eyl
Damot
Jirriban
Gaalkacyo
Dabaro
Hobyo
at the same scale

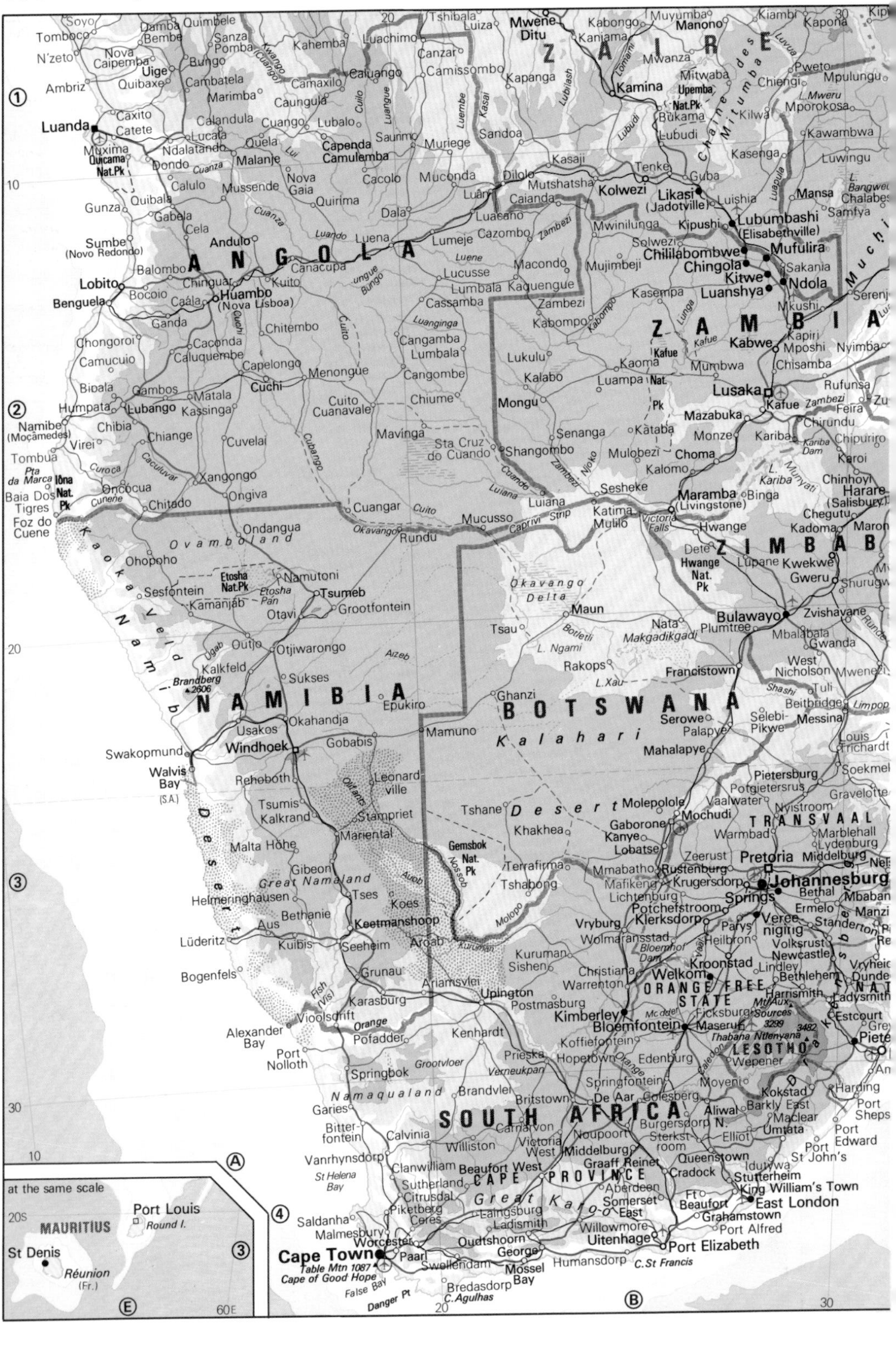

Soyo
Tomboco
N'zeto
Ambriz
Damba
Bembe
Quimbele
Sanza Pomba
Nova Caipemba
Bungo
Uige
Quibaxe
Cambatela
Kahemba
Kwango (Cuango)
Luachimo
Tshibala
Luiza
Mwene Ditu
Kabongo
Kaniama
Muyumba
Manono
Kiambi
Kapona
ZAIRE
Lomami
Mwanza
Luvua
Chaîne des Mitumba
Pweto
Mpulungu
Chiengi
Mitwaba
Kamina
Upemba Nat.Pk
Bukama
Lubudi
Kilwa
Mporokosa
L. Mweru
Kawambwa
Caxito
Catete
Luanda
Muxima
Quicama Nat.Pk
Calandula
Lucala
Ndalatando
Dondo
Cuanza
Malanje
Quela
Cuango
Lubalo
Capenda Camulemba
Saurimo
Muriege
Sandoa
Kasaji
Caluango
Camaxilo
Caungula
Marimba
Cuilo
Luangue
Luembe
Kasai
Lubilash
Kapanga
Canzar
Camissombo
Tenke
Guba
Kasenga
Luwingu
Luapula
Mansa
Chalabesa
Samfya
L. Bangweulu
10
Calulo
Mussende
Nova Gaia
Cacolo
Muconda
Dilolo
Mutshatsha
Kolwezi
Likasi (Jadotville)
Luishia
Lubumbashi (Elisabethville)
Kipushi
Quibala
Gunza
Gabela
Cela
Quirima
Dala
Luau
Caianda
Luacano
Mwinilunga
Sumbe (Novo Redondo)
Andulo
Luena
Lumeje
Cazombo
Zambezi
Solwezi
Chililabombwe
Mufulira
Chingola
Kitwe
Ndola
Luanshya
Sakania
Serenje
Muchinga
ANGOLA
Balombo
Lobito
Benguela
Bocoio
Chinguar
Kuito
Canacupa
Huambo (Nova Lisboa)
Caála
Ganda
Cuchi
Luene
Lungue Bungo
Lucusse
Macondo
Lumbala Kaquengue
Mujimbeji
Kasempa
Cassamba
Zambezi
Kabompo
Lunga
Kafue
Mkushi
ZAMBIA
Kabwe
Kapiri Mposhi
Chitembo
Cuito
Luanginga
Cangamba
Lumbala
Chongoroi
Camucuio
Caconda
Caluquembe
Capelongo
Menongue
Cangombe
Lukulu
Kaoma
Kafue Nat. Pk
Mumbwa
Chisamba
Nyimba
Bipala
Gambos
Matala
Cuchi
Kalabo
Luampa
Lusaka
Rufunsa
Mongu
Humpata
Lubango
Kassinga
Cuito Cuanavale
Chiume
Kafue
Zambezi
Feira
Namibe (Moçâmedes)
Chibia
Chiange
Cuvelai
Mavinga
Sta Cruz do Cuando
Shangombo
Senanga
Kataba
Mazabuka
Monze
Chirundu
Kariba
Kariba Dam
Chipuriro
Virei
Tombua
Cubango
Mulobezi
Choma
Karoi
Pta da Marca
Iôna Nat. Pk
Curoca
Caculuvar
Xangongo
Cuando
Njoko
Kalomo
L. Kariba
Munyati
Chinhoyi
Harare (Salisbury)
Baia Dos Tigres
Oncocua
Ongiva
Luiana
Sesheke
Maramba (Livingstone)
Binga
Foz do Cuene
Cunene
Chitado
Cuangar
Cuito
Luiana
Katima Mulilo
Caprivi Strip
Victoria Falls
Hwange
Chegutu
Kadoma
Ondangua
Mucusso
Okavango
Rundu
Dete
Lupane
Kwekwe
ZIMBABWE
Ovamboland
Kaokoveld
Ohopoho
Hwange Nat. Pk
Gweru
Shurugwi
Etosha Nat.Pk
Namutoni
Sesfontein
Etosha Pan
Tsumeb
Okavango Delta
Kamanjab
Grootfontein
Otavi
Maun
Tsau
Nata
Makgadikgadi
Plumtree
Bulawayo
Zvishavane
Botletli
L. Ngami
Mbalabala
Gwanda
20
Ugab
Outjo
Otjiwarongo
Aizeb
Rakops
Francistown
West Nicholson
Mwenezi
Kalkfeld
Sukses
L. Xau
Shashi
Tuli
Brandberg 2606
NAMIBIA
Epukiro
Ghanzi
BOTSWANA
Beitbridge
Limpopo
Serowe
Selebi-Pikwe
Messina
Palapye
Usakos
Okahandja
Namib
Gobabis
Mamuno
Kalahari
Swakopmund
Windhoek
Mahalapye
Louis Trichardt
Walvis Bay (S.A.)
Rehoboth
Leonardville
Olifants
Pietersburg
Soekmekaar
Potgietersrus
Gravelotte
Tsumis
Kalkrand
Stampriet
Tshane
Desert
Molepolole
Vaalwater
Nylstroom
Mochudi
TRANSVAAL
Mariental
Gaborone
Warmbad
Marblehall
Lydenburg
Khakhea
Kanye
Lobatse
Malta Höhe
Gemsbok Nat. Pk
Nossob
Zeerust
Pretoria
Middelburg
Nelspruit
Terrafirma
Mmabatho
Rustenburg
Gibeon
Great Namaland
Auob
Tshabong
Mafikeng
Krugersdorp
Johannesburg
Bethal
Mbabane
Tses
Lichtenburg
Springs
Ermelo
Helmeringhausen
Koes
Potchefstroom
Klerksdorp
Vereeniging
Standerton
Bethanie
Molopo
Vryburg
Parys
Heilbron
Keetmanshoop
Aus
Kuruman
Wolmaransstad
Bloemhof Dam
Vaal
Lüderitz
Kuibis
Seeheim
Aroab
Kuruman
Sishen
Kroonstad
Volksrust
Newcastle
Bogenfels
Grunau
Christiana
Welkom
Lindley
Bethlehem
Vryheid
Dundee
Warrenton
ORANGE FREE STATE
Harrismith
Ladysmith
Fish (Vis)
Ariamsvlei
Upington
Postmasburg
Mt Aux Sources 3299
Karasburg
Kimberley
Modder
Ficksburg
Estcourt
Vioolsdrift
Orange
Bloemfontein
Maseru
Thabana Ntlenyana 3482
Alexander Bay
Pofadder
Kenhardt
Koffiefontein
LESOTHO
Pietermaritzburg
Port Nolloth
Prieska
Hopetown
Edenburg
Caledon
Wepener
Springbok
Grootvloer
Verneukpan
Orange
Springfontein
Moyeni
Kokstad
Harding
Drakensberg
Brandvlei
Namaqualand
Britstown
De Aar
Colesberg
Aliwal N.
Barkly East
Port Shepstone
30
Garies
SOUTH AFRICA
Burgersdorp
Maclear
Umtata
Bitterfontein
Calvinia
Carnarvon
Noupoort
Sterkstroom
Elliot
Port Edward
Williston
Victoria West
Middelburg
Queenstown
Port St John's
Vanrhynsdorp
10
Clanwilliam
Beaufort West
Graaff Reinet
Cradock
Idutywa
Stutterheim
St Helena Bay
CAPE PROVINCE
Aberdeen
King William's Town
Sutherland
Citrusdal
Great Karoo
Somerset East
Ft Beaufort
East London
Piketberg
Ceres
Laingsburg
Grahamstown
Saldanha
Ladismith
Willowmore
Port Alfred
Malmesbury
Worcester
Oudtshoorn
Uitenhage
Port Elizabeth
Cape Town
Paarl
George
Humansdorp
C. St Francis
Table Mtn 1087
Cape of Good Hope
Swellendam
Mossel Bay
False Bay
Bredasdorp
Danger Pt
C. Agulhas
20
30
at the same scale
20S
MAURITIUS
Port Louis
Round I.
St Denis
Réunion (Fr.)
60E

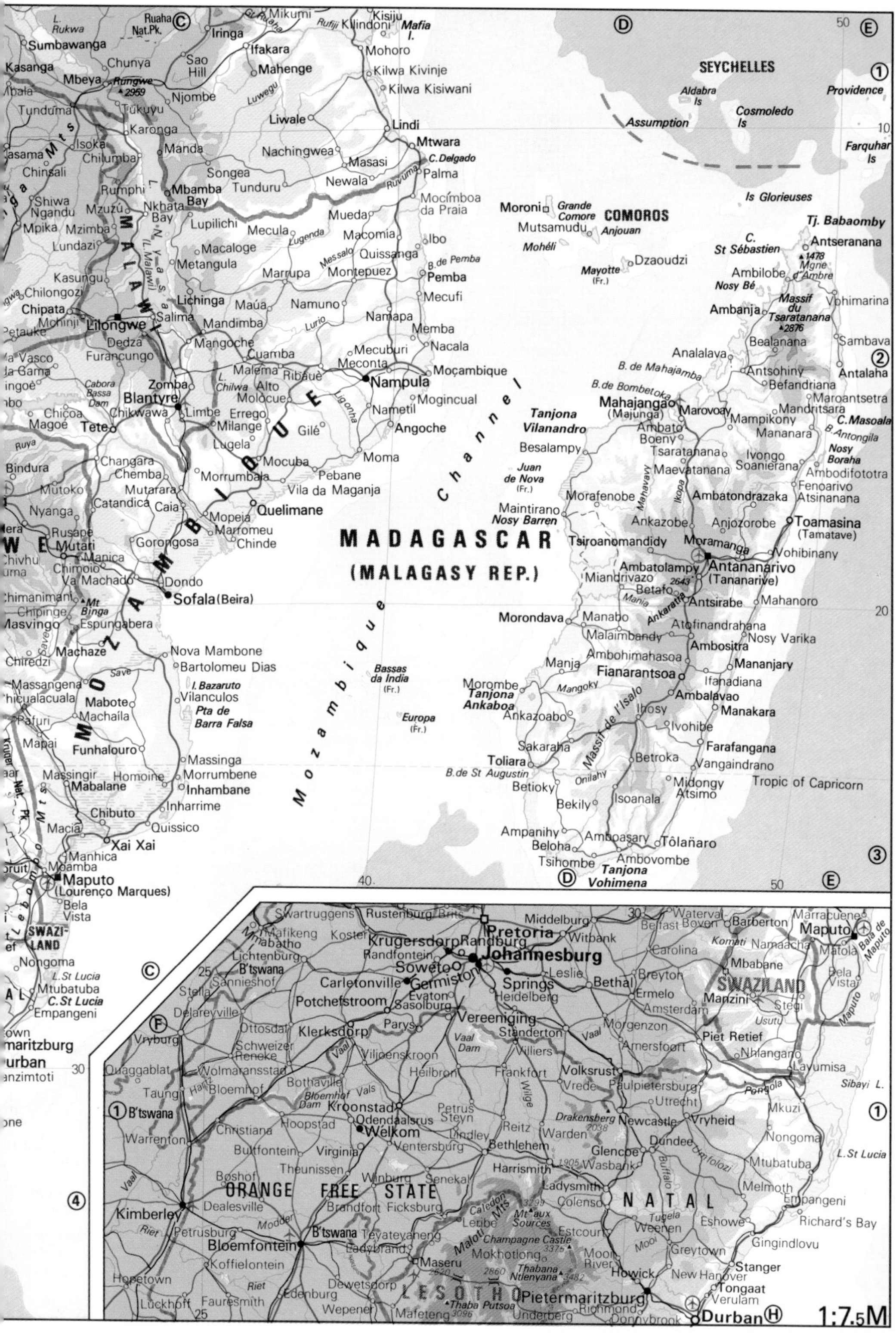
SEYCHELLES
Aldabra Is
Cosmoledo Is
Assumption
Providence
Farquhar Is
Is Glorieuses
COMOROS
Moroni
Grande Comore
Mutsamudu
Anjouan
Mohéli
Mayotte (Fr.)
Dzaoudzi
MADAGASCAR
(MALAGASY REP.)
Mozambique Channel
Tj. Babaomby
Antseranana
C. St Sébastien
1478 Mgne d'Ambre
Ambilobe
Nosy Bé
Ambanja
Massif du Tsaratanana
2876
Vohimarina
Bealanana
Sambava
Analalava
B. de Mahajamba
Antsohihy
Antalaha
Befandriana
B.de Bombetoka
Maroantsetra
Mahajangao (Majunga)
Marovoay
Mandritsara
Mampikony
C.Masoala
Ambato Boeny
Mananara
B.Antongila
Tanjona Vilanandro
Besalampy
Tsaratanana
Ivongo Soanierana
Nosy Boraha
Maevatanana
Ambodifototra
Juan de Nova (Fr.)
Fenoarivo Atsinanana
Mahavavy
Ikopa
Morafenobe
Ambatondrazaka
Maintirano
Nosy Barren
Ankazobe
Anjozorobe
Toamasina (Tamatave)
Tsiroanomandidy
Moramanga
Vohibinany
Ambatolampy
Antananarivo (Tananarive)
Miandrivazo
2643
Betafo
Mania
Ankaratra
Antsirabe
Mahanoro
Morondava
Manabo
Atofinandrahana
Malaimbandy
Ambositra
Nosy Varika
Ambohimahasoa
Manja
Fianarantsoa
Mananjary
Ifanadiana
Morombe
Tanjona Ankaboa
Mangoky
Massif de l'Isalo
Ambalavao
Ihosy
Manakara
Ankazoabo
Ivohibe
Sakaraha
Farafangana
Toliara
Betroka
Vangaindrano
B.de St Augustin
Onilahy
Midongy Atsimo
Tropic of Capricorn
Betioky
Isoanala
Bekily
Ampanihy
Amboasary
Tôlañaro
Beloha
Tsihombe
Ambovombe
Tanjona Vohimena
Bassas da India (Fr.)
Europa (Fr.)
L. Rukwa
Ruaha Nat.Pk.
Mikumi
Kisiju
Mafia I.
Rufiji
Kilindoni
Iringa
Sumbawanga
Ifakara
Mohoro
Chunya
Sao Hill
Kasanga
Mbeya
Rungwe 2959
Mahenge
Kilwa Kivinje
Kilwa Kisiwani
Njombe
Tunduma
Tukuyu
Luwegu
Karonga
Liwale
Lindi
Isoka
Manda
Mtwara
Nachingwea
Chilumba
C.Delgado
Masasi
Chinsali
Songea
Palma
Newala
Ruvuma
Rumphi
Mbamba Bay
Tunduru
Shiwa Ngandu
Mzuzu
Nkhata Bay
Mocímboa da Praia
Mpika
Mzimba
Mueda
Lundazi
Lupilichi
Mecula
Lugenda
Macomia
Ibo
MALAWI
Macaloge
Quissanga
Metangula
Messalo
B.de Pemba
Kasungu
Marrupa
Montepuez
Pemba
Chilongozi
Lichinga
Mecufi
Chipata
Maúa
Namuno
Salima
Lurio
Namapa
Lilongwe
Mandimba
Petauke
Memba
Dedza
Mangoche
Nacala
Mecuburi
Furancungo
Cuamba
Meconta
Vasco da Gama
Malema
Ribáuè
Moçambique
Cabora Bassa Dam
Zomba
L. Chilwa
Alto Molócuè
Nampula
Blantyre
Ligonha
Mogincual
Chicoa
Chikwawa
Limbe
Erregro
Nametil
Magoé
Tete
Milange
Gilé
Angoche
Lugela
Ruya
Mocuba
Moma
Bindura
Changara
Chemba
Pebane
Morrumbala
Mutoko
Mutarara
Vila da Maganja
Catandica
Caia
Nyanga
Quelimane
Mopeia
Rusape
Marromeu
Mutare
Chinde
Gorongosa
Chivhu
Manica
Chimoio
Vila Machado
Dondo
Chimanimani
Mt Binga
Sofala (Beira)
Chipinge
Masvingo
Espungabera
MOZAMBIQUE
Nova Mambone
Machaze
Bartolomeu Dias
Chiredzi
Save
I. Bazaruto
Massangena
Vilanculos
Chicualacuala
Mabote
Pta de Barra Falsa
Pafuri
Machaíla
Mapai
Funhalouro
Massinga
Massingir
Homoine
Morrumbene
Mabalane
Inhambane
Inharrime
Chibuto
Macia
Quissico
Xai Xai
Manhica
Moamba
Maputo (Lourenço Marques)
Bela Vista
SWAZILAND
Nongoma
L.St Lucia
Mtubatuba
C.St Lucia
Empangeni
Pietermaritzburg
Durban
Amanzimtoti
Lebombo Mts
Kruger Nat. Pk.
40
50
10
20
30
C
D
E
F
H
1
2
3
4
Swartruggens
Rustenburg
Brits
Pretoria
Middelburg
Waterval Boven
Barberton
Marracuene
Maputo
Baía de Maputo
Mafikeng
Mmabatho
Koster
Krugersdorp
Randburg
Witbank
Belfast
Komati
Namaacha
Matola
Lichtenburg
Randfontein
Johannesburg
Carolina
Mbabane
B'tswana
Soweto
Leslie
Bela Vista
Sannieshof
Carletonville
Germiston
Springs
Bethal
Breyton
SWAZILAND
Stella
Evaton
Heidelberg
Ermelo
Manzini
Potchefstroom
Sasolburg
Amsterdam
Stegi
Delareyville
Vereeniging
Usutu
Maputo
Ottosdal
Klerksdorp
Parys
Standerton
Morgenzon
Vryburg
Vaal Dam
Vaal
Amersfoort
Piet Retief
Schweizer Reneke
Viljoenskroon
Villiers
Nhlangano
Quaggablat
Wolmaransstad
Heilbron
Frankfort
Volksrust
Lavumisa
Bothaville
Taung
Harts
Bloemhof
Bloemhof Dam
Vals
Wilge
Vrede
Paulpietersburg
Pongola
Sibayi L.
Kroonstad
Petrus Steyn
Drakensberg 2038
Utrecht
Mkuzi
Christiana
Hoopstad
Odendaalsrus
Welkom
Reitz
Newcastle
Vryheid
Warrenton
Lindley
Warden
Nongoma
Bultfontein
Virginia
Ventersburg
Bethlehem
Glencoe
Dundee
Theunissen
Harrismith
1905
Wasbank
Buffalo
Umfolozi
Mtubatuba
L.St Lucia
Boshof
Winburg
Senekal
Ladysmith
ORANGE FREE STATE
NATAL
Melmoth
Kimberley
Dealesville
Brandfort
Ficksburg
Caledon
3299
Mt aux Sources
Colenso
Empangeni
Modder
Tugela
Riet
Petrusburg
B'tswana
Teyateyaneng
Leribe
Maloti Mts
Estcourt
Weenen
Eshowe
Richard's Bay
Bloemfontein
Ladybrand
Champagne Castle 3375
Mooi
Greytown
Gingindlovu
Koffiefontein
Maseru
Mokhotlong
Mooi River
Stanger
Hopetown
2520
2860
Thabana Ntlenyana 3482
Howick
New Hanover
Riet
Dewetsdorp
Tongaat
Verulam
Luckhoff
Fauresmith
Edenburg
LESOTHO
Pietermaritzburg
Wepener
Mafeteng
Thaba Putsoa 3096
Underberg
Richmond
Donnybrook
Durban
25
1:7.5M

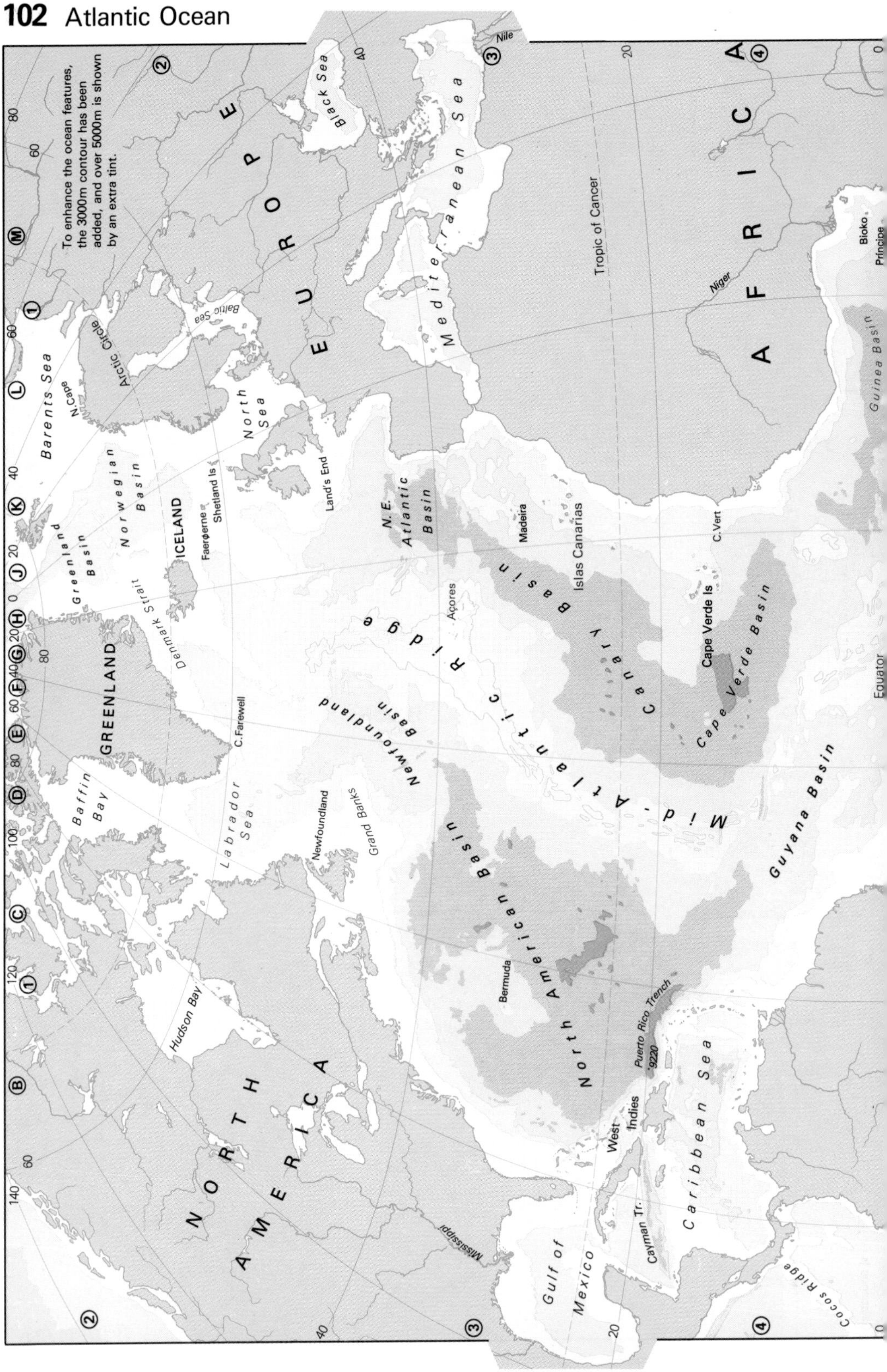

To enhance the ocean features, the 3000m contour has been added, and over 5000m is shown by an extra tint.
EUROPE
AFRICA
NORTH AMERICA
GREENLAND
ICELAND
Barents Sea
N.Cape
Arctic Circle
Baltic Sea
North Sea
Norwegian Basin
Greenland Basin
Denmark Strait
Faerøerne
Shetland Is
Land's End
Black Sea
Nile
Mediterranean Sea
Tropic of Cancer
Niger
Bioko
Príncipe
Guinea Basin
N.E. Atlantic Basin
Madeira
Islas Canarias
C.Vert
Canary Basin
Cape Verde Is
Cape Verde Basin
Açores
Mid-Atlantic Ridge
Newfoundland Basin
C.Farewell
Baffin Bay
Labrador Sea
Newfoundland
Grand Banks
Hudson Bay
Bermuda
North American Basin
Guyana Basin
Equator
Puerto Rico Trench
9220
West Indies
Caribbean Sea
Cayman Tr.
Gulf of Mexico
Mississippi
Cocos Ridge

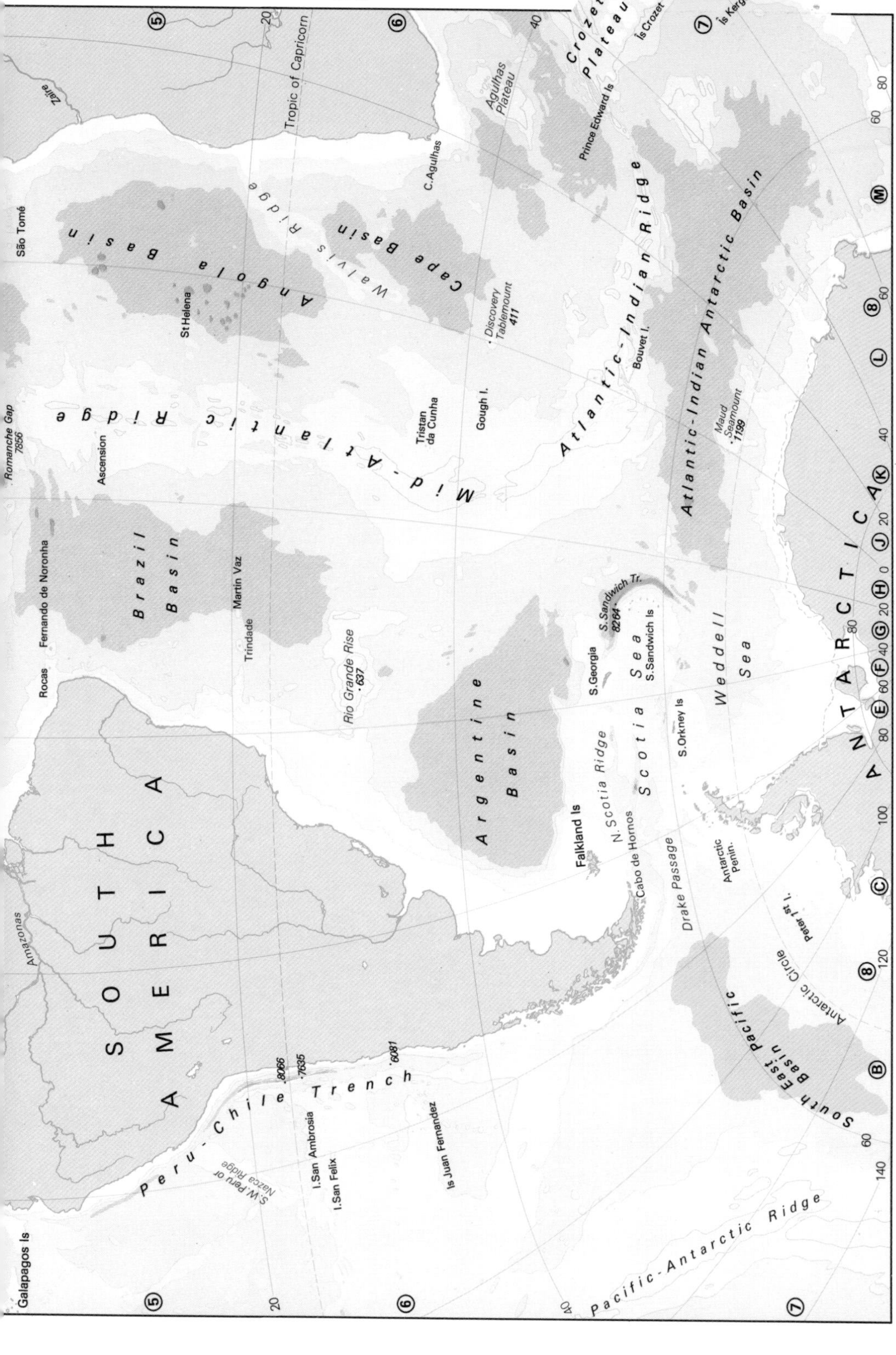
SOUTH AMERICA
ANTARCTICA
Amazonas
Zaïre
São Tomé
Romanche Gap 7856
Ascension
Rocas
Fernando de Noronha
Brazil Basin
Martin Vaz
Trindade
Rio Grande Rise 637
St Helena
Angola Basin
Walvis Ridge
Tropic of Capricorn
Mid-Atlantic Ridge
Tristan da Cunha
Gough I.
Cape Basin
C.Agulhas
Agulhas Plateau
Discovery Tablemount 411
Crozet Plateau
Is Crozet
Is Kerguelen
Prince Edward Is
Atlantic-Indian Ridge
Bouvet I.
Atlantic-Indian Antarctic Basin
Maud Seamount 1199
Argentine Basin
S.Georgia
S.Sandwich Tr.
8264
S.Sandwich Is
Scotia Sea
Weddell Sea
S.Orkney Is
N.Scotia Ridge
Falkland Is
Cabo de Hornos
Drake Passage
Antarctic Penin.
Peter 1st I.
Antarctic Circle
South East Pacific Basin
Pacific-Antarctic Ridge
Peru-Chile Trench
8066
7635
6081
I.San Ambrosia
I.San Felix
Is Juan Fernandez
S.W.Peru or Nazca Ridge
Galapagos Is

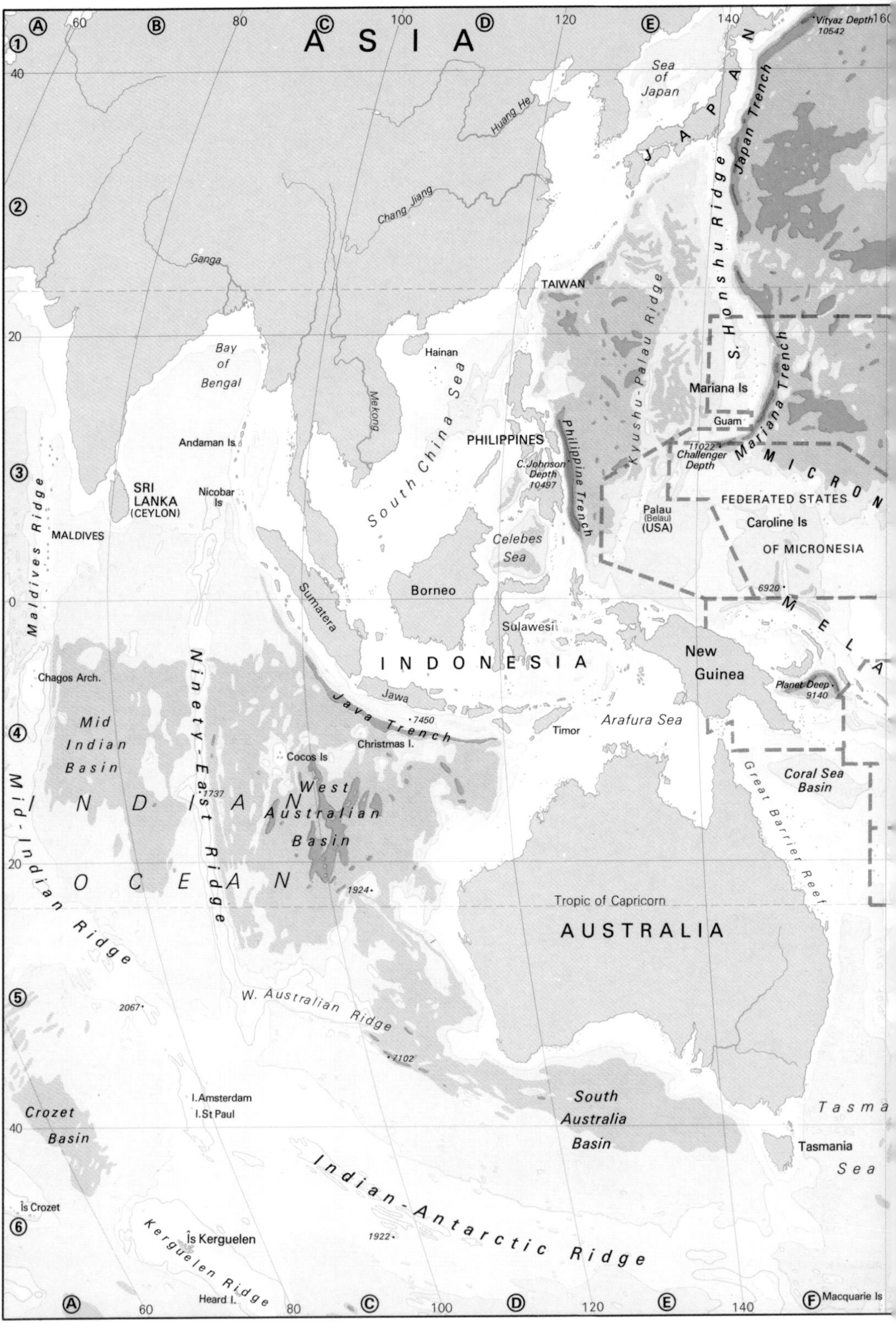
ASIA
Sea of Japan
JAPAN
Japan Trench
Vityaz Depth 10542
Huang He
Chang Jiang
Ganga
TAIWAN
Kyushu-Palau Ridge
S. Honshu Ridge
Bay of Bengal
Hainan
South China Sea
Mekong
Mariana Is
Mariana Trench
Guam
11022 Challenger Depth
Andaman Is
PHILIPPINES
Philippine Trench
C.Johnson Depth 10497
SRI LANKA (CEYLON)
Nicobar Is
MICRONESIA
FEDERATED STATES OF MICRONESIA
Caroline Is
Palau (Belau) (USA)
Maldives Ridge
MALDIVES
Celebes Sea
Borneo
Sumatera
Sulawesi
6920
MELANESIA
INDONESIA
New Guinea
Chagos Arch.
Jawa
Java Trench
7450
Planet Deep 9140
Mid Indian Basin
Ninety-East Ridge
Christmas I.
Timor
Arafura Sea
Cocos Is
Great Barrier Reef
Coral Sea Basin
West Australian Basin
1737
INDIAN OCEAN
Mid-Indian Ridge
1924
Tropic of Capricorn
AUSTRALIA
W. Australian Ridge
2067
7102
Crozet Basin
I.Amsterdam
I.St Paul
South Australia Basin
Tasman Sea
Tasmania
Indian-Antarctic Ridge
Îs Crozet
Îs Kerguelen
Kerguelen Ridge
1922
Heard I.
Macquarie Is

1:60M 0 600 1200 1800 2400 km / 0 600 1200 mls

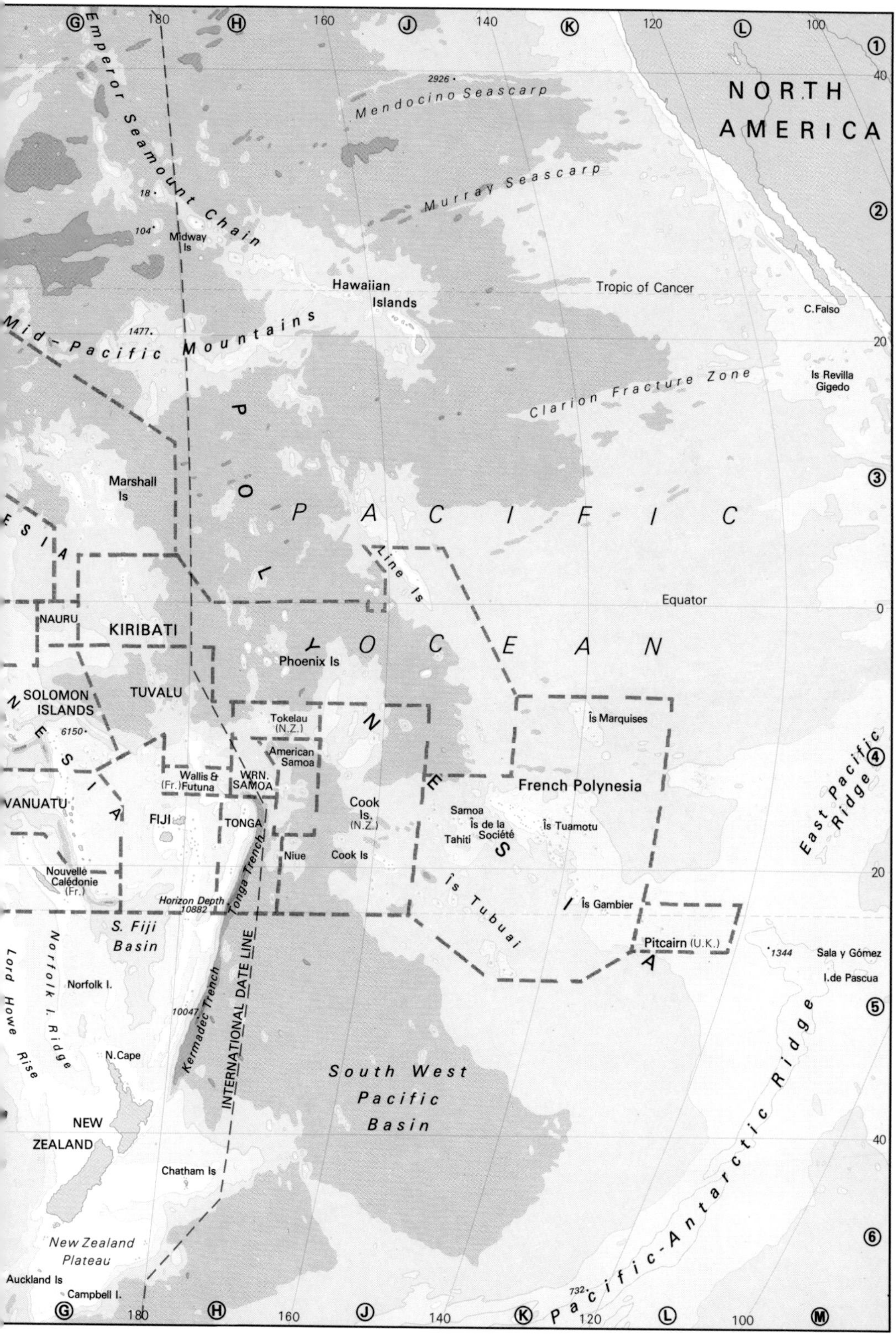

NORTH AMERICA
Emperor Seamount Chain
Mendocino Seascarp
2926
Murray Seascarp
18
104
Midway Is
Hawaiian Islands
Tropic of Cancer
C.Falso
Mid-Pacific Mountains
1477
Is Revilla Gigedo
Clarion Fracture Zone
POLYNESIA
PACIFIC OCEAN
Marshall Is
Line Is
Equator
NAURU
KIRIBATI
Phoenix Is
SOLOMON ISLANDS
TUVALU
6150
Tokelau (N.Z.)
Îs Marquises
American Samoa
Wallis & Futuna (Fr.)
WRN. SAMOA
French Polynesia
East Pacific Ridge
VANUATU
FIJI
TONGA
Cook Is. (N.Z.)
Samoa
Îs de la Société
Tahiti
Îs Tuamotu
Niue
Cook Is
Nouvelle Calédonie (Fr.)
Tonga Trench
Horizon Depth 10882
Îs Tubuai
Îs Gambier
S. Fiji Basin
Pitcairn (U.K.)
1344
Sala y Gómez
I.de Pascua
Lord Howe Rise
Norfolk I. Ridge
Norfolk I.
10047
Kermadec Trench
INTERNATIONAL DATE LINE
N.Cape
South West Pacific Basin
NEW ZEALAND
Pacific-Antarctic Ridge
Chatham Is
New Zealand Plateau
Auckland Is
Campbell I.
732

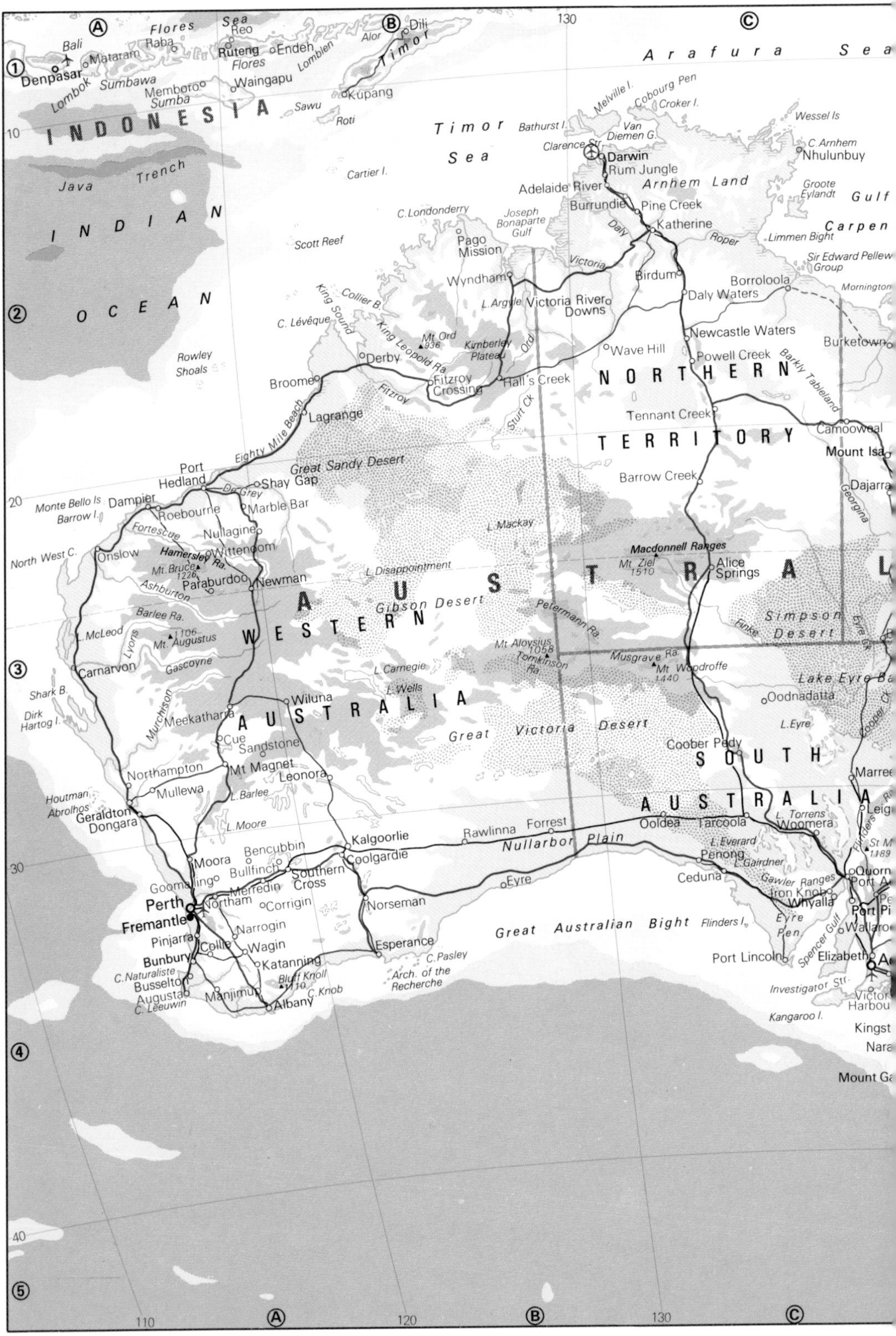

A
B
C
130
Flores Sea
Bali
Denpasar
Mataram
Lombok
Sumbawa
Raba
Reo
Ruteng
Endeh
Flores
Lomblen
Alor
Dili
Timor
Kupang
Memboro
Waingapu
Sumba
Sawu
Roti
INDONESIA
Arafura Sea
10
Timor Sea
Java Trench
INDIAN OCEAN
Cartier I.
Scott Reef
Rowley Shoals
Bathurst I.
Melville I.
Cobourg Pen
Croker I.
Van Diemen G.
Clarence Str.
Darwin
Rum Jungle
Adelaide River
Arnhem Land
Burrundie
Pine Creek
Katherine
Daly
Roper
Wessel Is
C. Arnhem
Nhulunbuy
Groote Eylandt
Gulf
Carpen
Limmen Bight
Sir Edward Pellew Group
Mornington
C. Londonderry
Joseph Bonaparte Gulf
Pago Mission
Wyndham
Victoria
Birdum
Borroloola
Daly Waters
Collier B.
King Sound
C. Lévêque
King Leopold Ra
Mt Ord 936
L. Argyle
Victoria River Downs
Kimberley Plateau
Ord
Newcastle Waters
Burketown
Wave Hill
Powell Creek
Barkly Tableland
Derby
Broome
Fitzroy Crossing
Fitzroy
Hall's Creek
NORTHERN TERRITORY
Lagrange
Sturt Ck
Tennant Creek
Camooweal
Mount Isa
Eighty Mile Beach
Port Hedland
Great Sandy Desert
Shay Gap
De Grey
Marble Bar
Barrow Creek
Dajarra
Georgina
20
Monte Bello Is
Barrow I.
Dampier
Roebourne
Fortescue
Nullagine
L. Mackay
North West C.
Onslow
Hamersley Ra.
Wittenoom
Macdonnell Ranges
Mt. Ziel 1510
Alice Springs
Mt. Bruce 1226
Paraburdoo
Newman
L. Disappointment
Ashburton
AUSTRALIA
WESTERN AUSTRALIA
Gibson Desert
Petermann Ra.
Simpson Desert
Finke
Eyre Ck
Barlee Ra.
L. McLeod
1106 Mt. Augustus
Lyons
Mt Aloysius 1058
Tomkinson Ra.
Musgrave Ra.
Mt Woodroffe 1440
Carnarvon
Gascoyne
L. Carnegie
L. Wells
Lake Eyre Ba
Shark B.
Dirk Hartog I.
Murchison
Meekatharra
Wiluna
Oodnadatta
Cooper Ck
Cue
Sandstone
Great Victoria Desert
L. Eyre
Coober Pedy
SOUTH AUSTRALIA
Northampton
Mt Magnet
Leonora
Marree
Houtman Abrolhos
Mullewa
L. Barlee
Geraldton
Dongara
L. Moore
Ooldea
Tarcoola
L. Torrens
Woomera
Leigh
Flinders Ra.
St M 1189
Rawlinna
Forrest
Nullarbor Plain
Kalgoorlie
Coolgardie
Bencubbin
Bullfinch
Moora
Southern Cross
L. Everard
Penong
L. Gairdner
Quorn
Port A
30
Goomalling
Merredin
Eyre
Ceduna
Gawler Ranges
Iron Knob
Whyalla
Perth
Northam
Corrigin
Norseman
Port Pi
Fremantle
Narrogin
Great Australian Bight
Flinders I.
Eyre Pen.
Spencer Gulf
Wallaroo
Pinjarra
Collie
Wagin
Esperance
Bunbury
Katanning
C. Pasley
Port Lincoln
Elizabeth
C. Naturaliste
Busselton
Bluff Knoll 1110
Arch. of the Recherche
Augusta
C. Leeuwin
Manjimup
Albany
C. Knob
Investigator Str.
Victor Harbou
Kangaroo I.
Kingst
Nara
Mount Ga
40
110
120

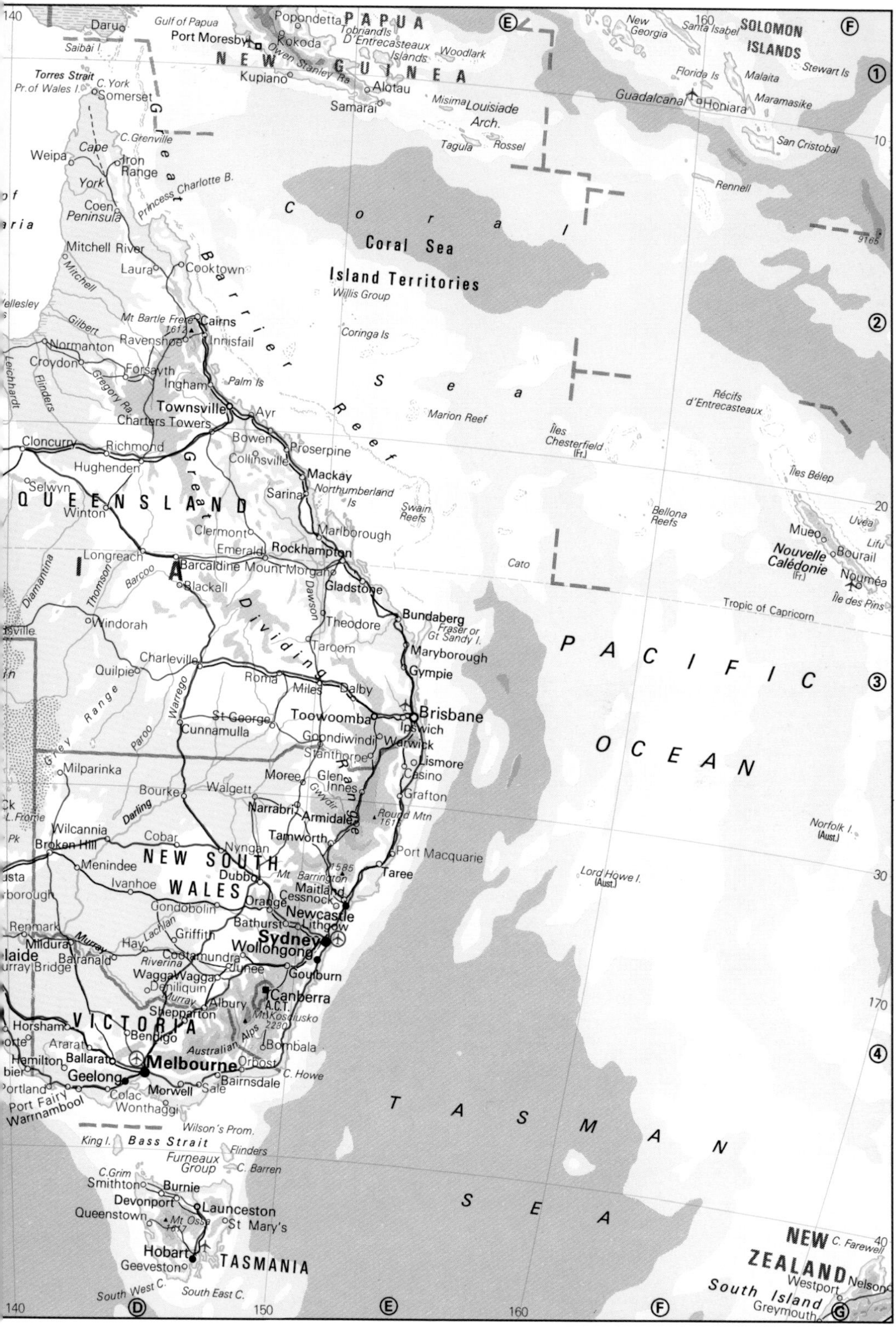
PAPUA
NEW GUINEA
Daru
Gulf of Papua
Port Moresby
Popondetta
Kokoda
Tobriand Is
D'Entrecasteaux Islands
Woodlark
Owen Stanley Ra
Kupiano
Alotau
Samarai
Misima
Louisiade Arch.
Tagula
Rossel
Saibai I.
Torres Strait
Pr. of Wales I.
C. York
Somerset
C. Grenville
Weipa
Cape York Peninsula
Iron Range
Princess Charlotte B.
Coen
Mitchell River
Mitchell
Laura
Cooktown
Great Barrier Reef
Coral Sea
Coral Sea Island Territories
Willis Group
Coringa Is
Mt Bartle Frere 1612
Cairns
Innisfail
Gilbert
Normanton
Ravenshoe
Croydon
Forsayth
Gregory Ra
Flinders
Leichhardt
Ingham
Palm Is
Townsville
Ayr
Charters Towers
Bowen
Collinsville
Proserpine
Cloncurry
Richmond
Hughenden
Mackay
Northumberland Is
Sarina
Swain Reefs
Marion Reef
Selwyn
QUEENSLAND
Winton
Great Dividing Range
Clermont
Emerald
Rockhampton
Marlborough
Longreach
Barcaldine
Mount Morgan
Barcoo
Thomson
Diamantina
Blackall
Gladstone
Dawson
Bundaberg
Fraser or Gt Sandy I.
Theodore
Taroom
Maryborough
Windorah
Charleville
Quilpie
Gympie
Roma
Miles
Dalby
Warrego
Grey Range
Paroo
St George
Cunnamulla
Toowoomba
Brisbane
Ipswich
Goondiwindi
Warwick
Stanthorpe
Lismore
Casino
Milparinka
Moree
Glen Innes
Gwydir
Grafton
Bourke
Walgett
Darling
Narrabri
Armidale
Round Mtn 1615
L. Frome
Wilcannia
Broken Hill
Cobar
Nyngan
Tamworth
Port Macquarie
Menindee
NEW SOUTH WALES
Taree
Ivanhoe
Dubbo
Mt Barrington 1585
Maitland
Cessnock
Newcastle
Condobolin
Orange
Bathurst
Lithgow
Renmark
Mildura
Murray
Lachlan
Hay
Griffith
Sydney
Wollongong
Balranald
Riverina
Cootamundra
Murray Bridge
Wagga Wagga
Junee
Goulburn
Deniliquin
Canberra
A.C.T.
Albury
Shepparton
Mt Kosciusko 2230
Horsham
VICTORIA
Australian Alps
Bendigo
Ararat
Bombala
Hamilton
Ballarat
Melbourne
Orbost
C. Howe
Geelong
Bairnsdale
Portland
Morwell
Sale
Colac
Port Fairy
Warrnambool
Wonthaggi
Wilson's Prom.
King I.
Bass Strait
Flinders
Furneaux Group
C. Barren
C. Grim
Smithton
Burnie
Devonport
Launceston
Queenstown
Mt Ossa 1617
St Mary's
Hobart
TASMANIA
Geeveston
South West C.
South East C.
TASMAN SEA
PACIFIC OCEAN
New Georgia
Santa Isabel
SOLOMON ISLANDS
Florida Is
Malaita
Stewart Is
Guadalcanal
Honiara
Maramasike
San Cristobal
Rennell
Récifs d'Entrecasteaux
Îles Chesterfield (Fr.)
Îles Bélep
Bellona Reefs
Cato
Mueo
Nouvelle Calédonie (Fr.)
Bourail
Uvea
Lifu
Nouméa
Île des Pins
Tropic of Capricorn
Norfolk I. (Aust.)
Lord Howe I. (Aust.)
NEW ZEALAND
C. Farewell
Nelson
Westport
South Island
Greymouth
140
150
160
170
10
20
30
40
9165
D
E
F
G
1
2
3
4

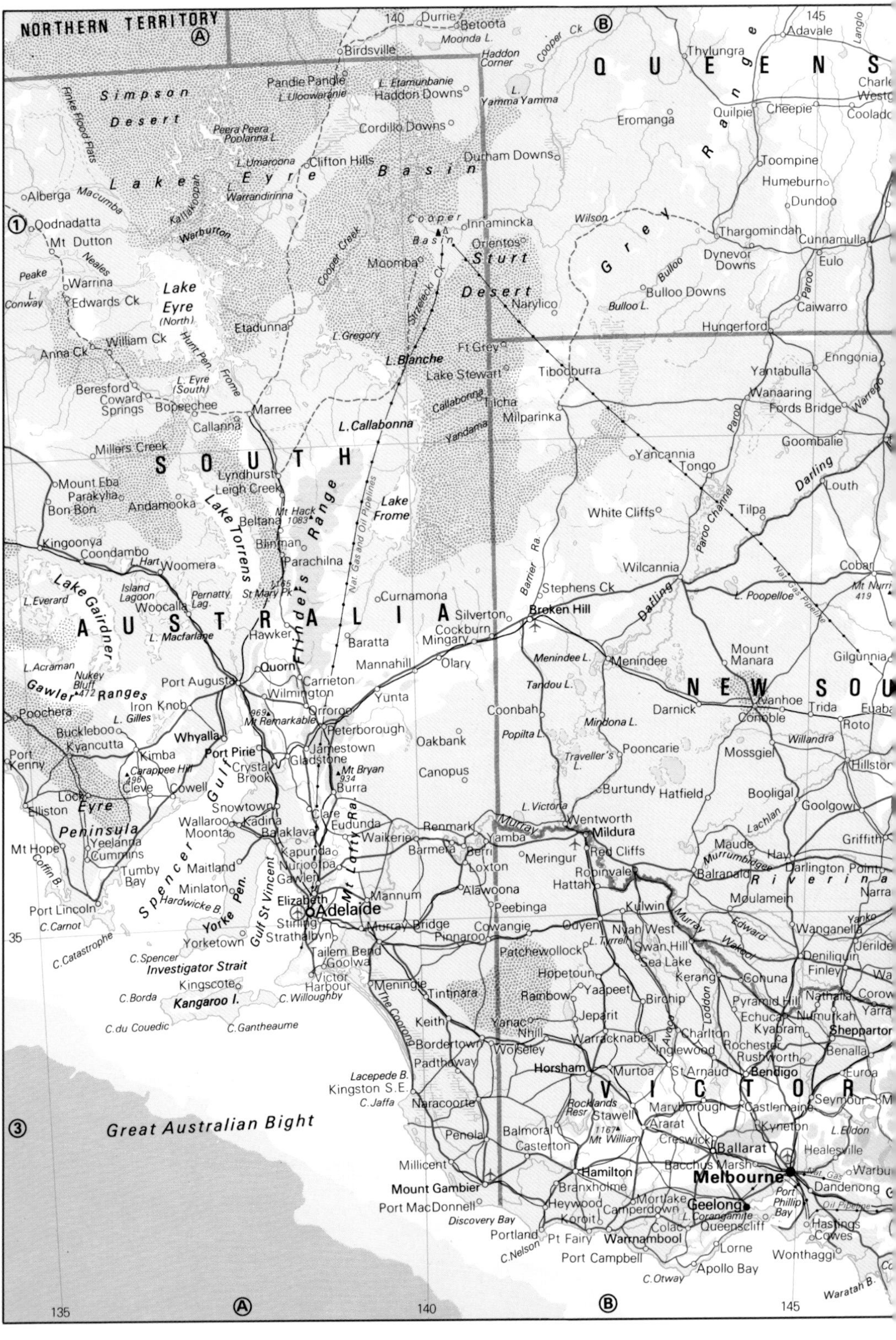

NORTHERN TERRITORY
A
140
Durrie
Betoota
Moonda L.
B
145
Adavale
Langlo
Birdsville
Haddon Corner
Cooper Ck
Thylungra
QUEENS
Pandie Pandie
L. Etamunbanie
Haddon Downs
Simpson
L. Uloowaranie
L. Yamma Yamma
Charle
Westc
Cheepie
Quilpie
Cooladd
Desert
Peera Peera Poolanna L.
Cordillo Downs
Eromanga
Finke Flood Flats
L. Umaroona
Clifton Hills
Durham Downs
Range
Toompine
Lake Eyre Basin
Humeburn
Warrandirinna
Kallakoopah
Alberga
Macumba
Dundoo
Oodnadatta
Cooper
Innamincka
Wilson
Grey
Warburton
Thargomindah
Mt Dutton
Basin
Orientos
Cunnamulla
Neales
Moomba
Sturt
Dynevor Downs
Eulo
Peake
Cooper Creek
Bulloo
Warrina
Lake Eyre (North)
Strzelecki Ck
Paroo
L. Conway
Edwards Ck
Desert
Narylico
Bulloo Downs
Bulloo L.
Caiwarro
Etadunna
Hungerford
Hunt Pen.
L. Gregory
William Ck
Frome
Ft Grey
Anna Ck
L. Blanche
Enngonia
Lake Stewart
Tibooburra
Yantabulla
L. Eyre (South)
Beresford
Coward Springs
Bopeechee
Marree
Callabonna
Tilcha
Wanaaring
Fords Bridge
Warrego
Milparinka
Callanna
L. Callabonna
Yandama
Paroo
Goombalie
Millers Creek
SOUTH
Yancannia
Tongo
Mount Eba
Lyndhurst
Darling
Parakylia
Leigh Creek
Louth
Bon Bon
Andamooka
Lake Torrens
Mt Hack 1083
Lake Frome
Tilpa
Paroo Channel
White Cliffs
Beltana
Flinders Range
Kingoonya
Blinman
Coondambo
Barrier Ra.
Wilcannia
Cobar
L. Hart
Woomera
Parachilna
Nat. Gas and Oil Pipelines
Lake Gairdner
Island Lagoon
L. 1165 St Mary Pk
Stephens Ck
Mt Nurri 419
L. Everard
Pernatty Lag.
Curnamona
Darling
L. Poopelloe
Woocalla
Nat. Gas Pipeline
AUSTRALIA
Silverton
Broken Hill
L. Macfarlane
Hawker
Cockburn
Mingary
Baratta
Mount Manara
L. Acraman
Menindee L.
Menindee
Gilgunnia
Nukey Bluff 472
Mannahill
Olary
Quorn
Gawler Ranges
Port Augusta
Carrieton
Tandou L.
NEW SOU
Wilmington
Yunta
Iron Knob
Coonbah
Darnick
Ivanhoe
Trida
Euaba
Poochera
969 Mt Remarkable
Orroroo
Cobble
L. Gilles
Mindona L.
Roto
Buckleboo
Whyalla
Peterborough
Kyancutta
Oakbank
Popilta L.
Willandra
Port Pirie
Jamestown
Pooncarie
Mossgiel
Hillston
Kimba
Port Kenny
Gladstone
Traveller's L.
Carappee Hill 496
Crystal Brook
Mt Bryan 934
Canopus
Cleve
Cowell
Burra
Burtundy
Hatfield
Booligal
Lock
Gulf
Eyre
Goolgowi
Elliston
Snowtown
Clare
L. Victoria
Peninsula
Wallaroo
Kadina
Eudunda
Renmark
Wentworth
Lachlan
Moonta
Balaklava
Murray
Mildura
Yeelanna
Mt Hope
Waikerie
Yamba
Maude
Griffith
Cummins
Spencer
Kapunda
Barmera
Berri
Red Cliffs
Hay
Coffin B.
Maitland
Nuriootpa
Mt Lofty Ra.
Meringur
Murrumbidgee
Tumby Bay
Gulf St Vincent
Loxton
Robinvale
Balranald
Darlington Point
Gawler
Riverina
Minlaton
Hattah
Narra
Elizabeth
Mannum
Alawoona
Hardwicke B.
Yorke Pen.
Moulamein
Port Lincoln
Adelaide
Peebinga
Kulwin
C. Carnot
Yanko
Stirling
Murray Bridge
Cowangie
Ouyen
Nyah West
Murray
Edward
Wanganella
35
Strathalbyn
Jerilde
C. Catastrophe
Yorketown
Pinnaroo
L. Tyrrell
Swan Hill
Wakool
Tailem Bend
Patchewollock
Deniliquin
C. Spencer
Goolwa
Sea Lake
Investigator Strait
Hopetoun
Finley
Kerang
Cohuna
Victor Harbour
Wa
Kingscote
Meningie
Tintinara
Yaapeet
Nathalia
Corow
C. Borda
Kangaroo I.
C. Willoughby
Rainbow
Birchip
Loddon
Pyramid Hill
Yarra
Echuca
Numurkah
Jeparit
The Coorong
Avoca
Kyabram
C. du Couedic
C. Gantheaume
Keith
Yanac
Charlton
Shepparton
Nhill
Warracknabeal
Rochester
Bordertown
Wolseley
Inglewood
Rushworth
Benalla
Padthaway
Horsham
Murtoa
St Arnaud
Bendigo
Lacepede B.
Euroa
Kingston S.E.
VICTOR
C. Jaffa
Naracoorte
Rocklands Resr
Stawell
Maryborough
Castlemaine
Seymour
Great Australian Bight
3
Ararat
Kyneton
L. Eildon
1167 Mt William
Penola
Balmoral
Creswick
Casterton
Ballarat
Healesville
Millicent
Bacchus Marsh
Hamilton
Melbourne
Warbu
Mount Gambier
Branxholme
Nat. Gas
Dandenong
Mortlake
Port Phillip Bay
Heywood
Geelong
Port MacDonnell
Camperdown
Oil Pipeline
Koroit
L. Corangamite
Queenscliff
Discovery Bay
Colac
Hastings
Portland
Pt Fairy
Warrnambool
Cowes
C. Nelson
Lorne
Port Campbell
Wonthaggi
Apollo Bay
C. Otway
Waratah B.
135
A
140
B
145
1

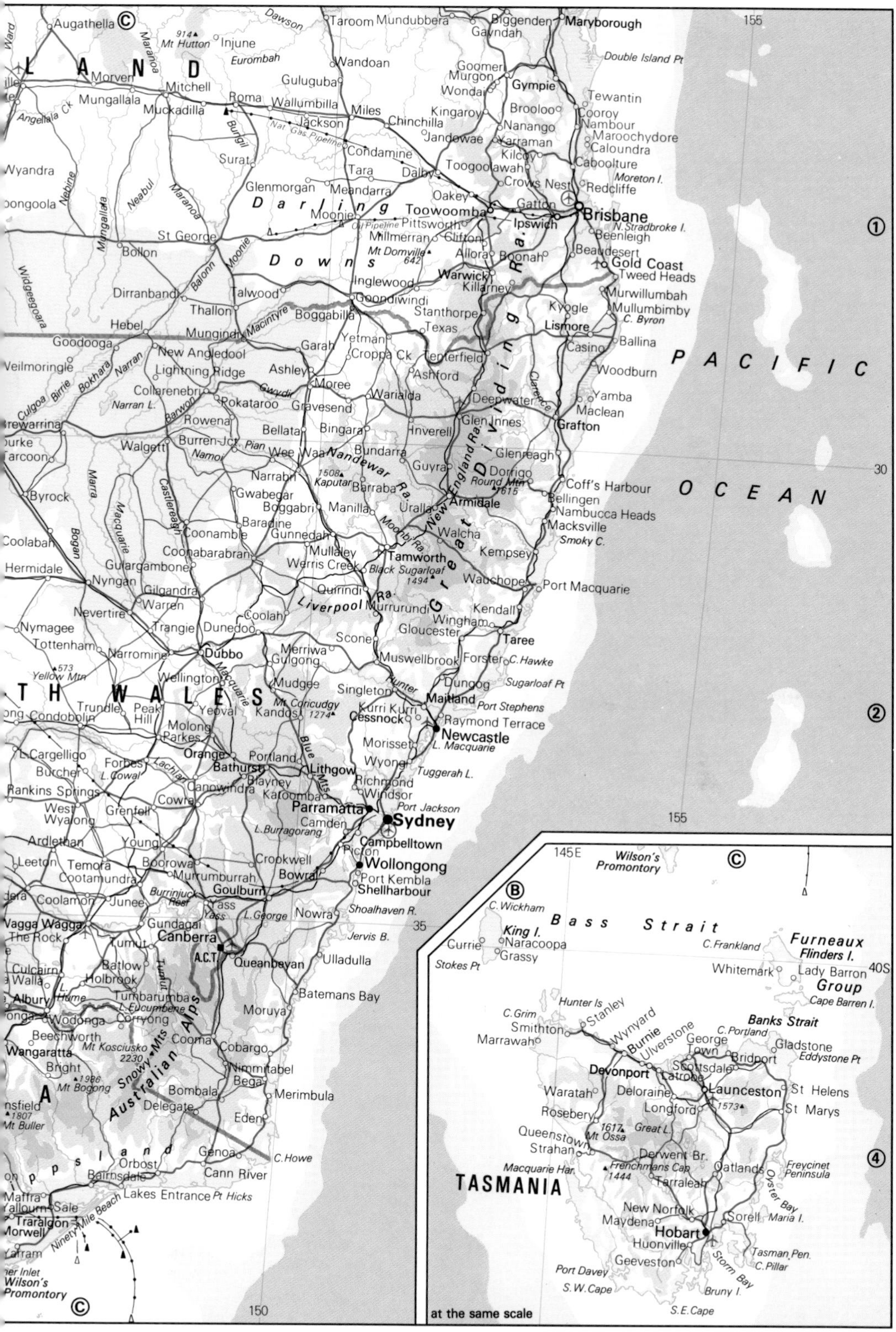
Augathella
Ward
Maranoa
Dawson
914 Mt Hutton
Injune
Eurombah
Taroom
Mundubbera
Biggenden
Maryborough
Gayndah
155
L A N D
Morven
Mitchell
Wandoan
Double Island Pt
Goomeri
Murgon
Gympie
Wondai
Guluguba
Tewantin
Mungallala
Roma
Wallumbilla
Miles
Kingaroy
Brooloo
Cooroy
Angellala Ck
Muckadilla
Bungil
Nambour
Jackson
Chinchilla
Nanango
Nat. Gas Pipeline
Maroochydore
Jandowae
Yarraman
Caloundra
Condamine
Kilcoy
Surat
Caboolture
Wyandra
Tara
Dalby
Toogoolawah
Nebine
Moreton I.
Crows Nest
Neabul
Glenmorgan
Meandarra
Oakey
Redcliffe
Maranoa
Mungallala
Darling
Toowoomba
Gatton
Brisbane
Boongoola
Moonie
Oil Pipeline
Pittsworth
Ipswich
N. Stradbroke I.
St George
Millmerran
Clifton
Beenleigh
Bollon
Moonie
Mt Domville 642
Allora
Boonah
Beaudesert
Downs
Gold Coast
Widgeegoara
Balonne
Warwick
Tweed Heads
Inglewood
Killarney
Dirranbandi
Talwood
Goondiwindi
Murwillumbah
Kyogle
Thallon
Stanthorpe
Mullumbimby
Boggabilla
C. Byron
Hebel
Macintyre
Texas
Lismore
Mungindi
Goodooga
Garah
Yetman
Casino
Ballina
Croppa Ck
Tenterfield
P A C I F I C
New Angledool
Ashley
Weilmoringle
Lightning Ridge
Ashford
Woodburn
Narran
Bokhara
Moree
Collarenebri
Yamba
Culgoa
Birrie
Gwydir
Warialda
Deepwater
Narran L.
Pokataroo
Gravesend
Maclean
Brewarrina
Clarence
Rowena
Glen Innes
Grafton
Barwon
Bingara
Bourke
Bellata
Inverell
Walgett
Burren Jct.
Pian
Bundarra
Tarcoon
Wee Waa
Glenreagh
Namoi
Nandewar
Guyra
Marra
Narrabri
Dorrigo
30
1508 Kaputar
Coff's Harbour
Round Mtn 1615
Byrock
Castlereagh
Gwabegar
Barraba
Bellingen
O C E A N
Boggabri
Manilla
Uralla
Armidale
Macquarie
Nambucca Heads
Baradine
Macksville
Gunnedah
Walcha
Coolabah
Bogan
Coonamble
Smoky C.
New England Ra.
Mullaley
Kempsey
Coonabarabran
Hermidale
Werris Creek
Tamworth
Moonbi Ra.
Gulargambone
Black Sugarloaf 1494
Dividing
Nyngan
Wauchope
Port Macquarie
Gilgandra
Quirindi
Great
Warren
Ra.
Liverpool
Nevertire
Murrurundi
Kendall
Coolah
Wingham
Nymagee
Trangie
Dunedoo
Gloucester
Scone
Taree
Tottenham
Merriwa
Narromine
Dubbo
Muswellbrook
Forster
C. Hawke
Gulgong
573 Yellow Mtn
Wellington
Hunter
Dungog
Sugarloaf Pt
Macquarie
Mudgee
Singleton
TH WALES
Trundle
Peak Hill
Maitland
Mt Coricudgy 1274
Port Stephens
Yeoval
Kandos
Kurri Kurri
Condobolin
Cessnock
Raymond Terrace
Molong
Newcastle
Parkes
Blue Mts
Morisset
L. Macquarie
L. Cargelligo
Orange
Portland
Forbes
Lachlan
Bathurst
Wyong
Burcher
Lithgow
Tuggerah L.
L. Cowal
Blayney
Richmond
Rankins Springs
Canowindra
Katoomba
Windsor
Cowra
Parramatta
Port Jackson
West Wyalong
Grenfell
Sydney
Camden
155
L. Burragorang
Ardlethan
Young
Campbelltown
Picton
Leeton
Temora
Boorowa
Crookwell
Wollongong
Cootamundra
Murrumburrah
Bowral
Port Kembla
Burrinjuck Res.
Shellharbour
Jerilderie
Coolamon
Junee
Goulburn
Yass
Shoalhaven R.
Gundagai
L. George
Nowra
Wagga Wagga
Canberra
35
The Rock
Tumut
Jervis B.
A.C.T.
Queanbeyan
Ulladulla
Culcairn
Batlow
Walla Walla
L. Hume
Holbrook
Batemans Bay
Albury
Tumbarumba
L. Eucumbene
Wodonga
Corryong
Moruya
Beechworth
Snowy Mts
Australian Alps
Cooma
Wangaratta
Mt Kosciusko 2230
Cobargo
Bright
Nimmitabel
1986 Mt Bogong
Bega
Mansfield
Bombala
Merimbula
1807 Mt Buller
Delegate
Eden
Gippsland
Genoa
C. Howe
Orbost
Cann River
Bairnsdale
Maffra
Lakes Entrance
Pt Hicks
Sale
Yallourn
Ninety Mile Beach
Traralgon
Morwell
Yarram
Corner Inlet
Wilson's Promontory
150
145E
Wilson's Promontory
C. Wickham
Bass Strait
King I.
Currie
Naracoopa
C. Frankland
Furneaux
Flinders I.
Grassy
Stokes Pt
Whitemark
Lady Barron
40S
Group
Cape Barren I.
Hunter Is
Stanley
C. Grim
Banks Strait
Wynyard
Smithton
C. Portland
Burnie
Ulverstone
George Town
Marrawah
Gladstone
Eddystone Pt
Devonport
Scottsdale
Bridport
Latrobe
Launceston
St Helens
Waratah
Deloraine
Longford
1573
St Marys
Rosebery
1617 Mt Ossa
Great L.
Queenstown
Strahan
Derwent Br.
Frenchmans Cap 1444
Oatlands
Freycinet Peninsula
Macquarie Har.
TASMANIA
Tarraleah
Oyster Bay
New Norfolk
Sorell
Maria I.
Maydena
Hobart
Huonville
Storm Bay
Tasman Pen.
Geeveston
C. Pillar
Port Davey
S.W. Cape
Bruny I.
S.E. Cape
at the same scale

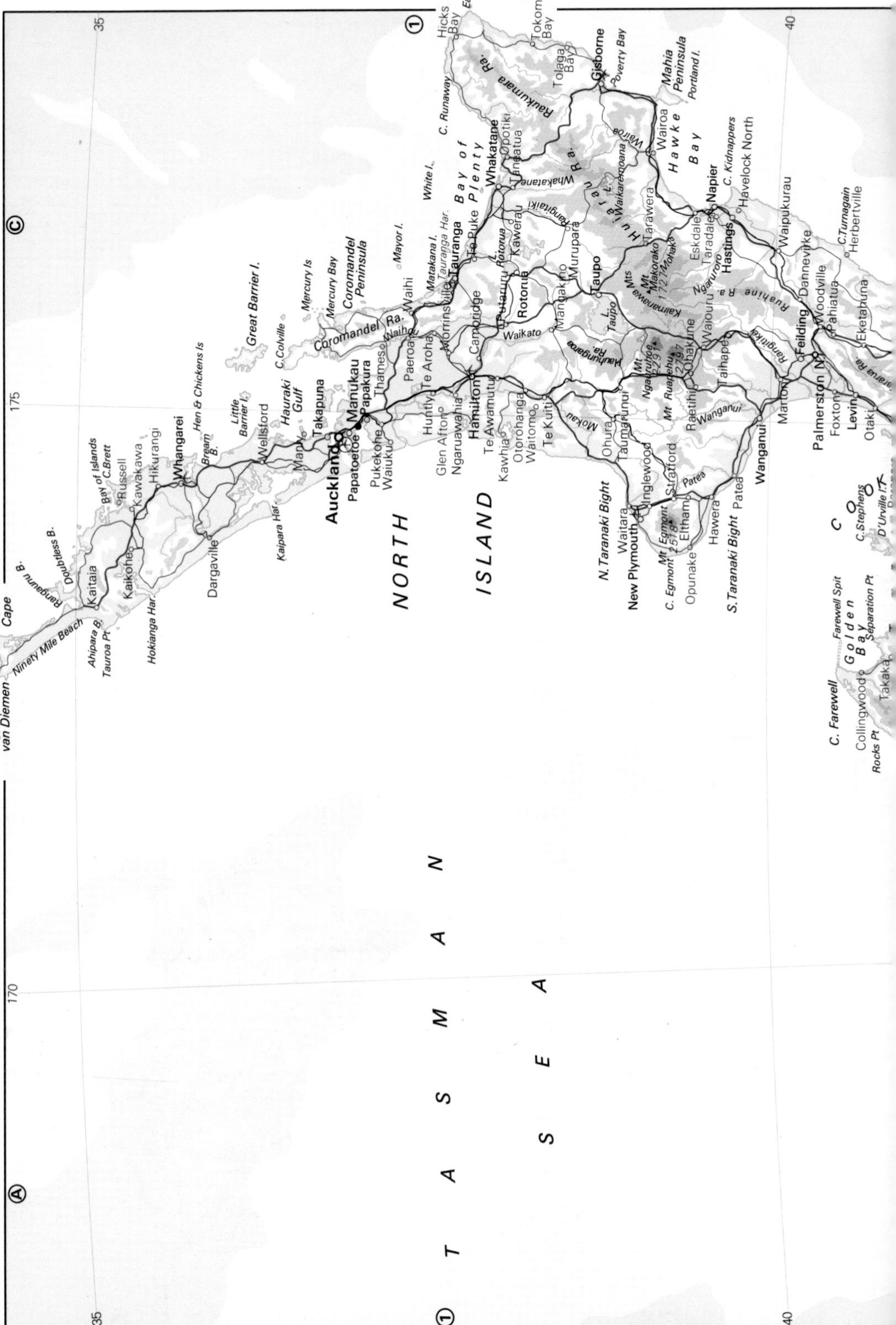

C. Maria van Diemen
North Cape
Ninety Mile Beach
Rangaunu B.
Doubtless B.
Kaitaia
Ahipara B.
Tauroa Pt
Kaikohe
Hokianga Har.
Bay of Islands
C.Brett
Russell
Kawakawa
Hikurangi
Whangarei
Bream B.
Hen & Chickens Is
Dargaville
Kaipara Har.
Wellsford
Little Barrier I.
Great Barrier I.
Hauraki Gulf
C.Colville
Takapuna
Auckland
Manukau
Papakura
Papatoetoe
Pukekohe
Waiuku
Thames
Coromandel Ra.
Coromandel Peninsula
Mercury Is
Mercury Bay
Mayor I.
Waihi
Paeroa
Te Aroha
Huntly
Ngaruawahia
Glen Afton
Hamilton
Te Awamutu
Cambridge
Morrinsville
Matakana I.
Tauranga Har.
Tauranga
Te Puke
Bay of Plenty
White I.
Whakatane
Opotiki
C. Runaway
Raukumara Ra.
Hicks Bay
East C.
Tokomaru Bay
Tolaga Bay
Gisborne
Poverty Bay
Mahia Peninsula
Portland I.
Wairoa
Hawke Bay
C. Kidnappers
Havelock North
Napier
Hastings
Taradale
Eskdale
Tarawera
Rotorua
L. Rotorua
Kawerau
Putaruru
Waikato
Mangakino
Murupara
Taupo
L. Taupo
Kaimanawa Mts
Mt. Makorako 1727
Ngaruroro
Ruahine Ra.
Hauhungaroa Ra.
Mt. Ngauruhoe 2291
Mt. Ruapehu 2797
Ohakune
Waiouru
Taihape
Raetihi
Taumarunui
Te Kuiti
Otorohanga
Waitomo
Kawhia
Mokau
Ohura
N. Taranaki Bight
Waitara
New Plymouth
Inglewood
Stratford
Mt. Egmont 2518
C. Egmont
Eltham
Opunake
Hawera
Patea
S. Taranaki Bight
Wanganui
Marton
Feilding
Palmerston N.
Foxton
Levin
Otaki
Waipukurau
Dannevirke
Woodville
Pahiatua
Eketahuna
C.Turnagain
Herbertville
NORTH ISLAND
TASMAN SEA
C O O K
C. Farewell
Farewell Spit
Golden Bay
Separation Pt
Collingwood
Takaka
Rocks Pt
C.Stephens
D'Urville I.
35
40
170
175
A
B
C
1

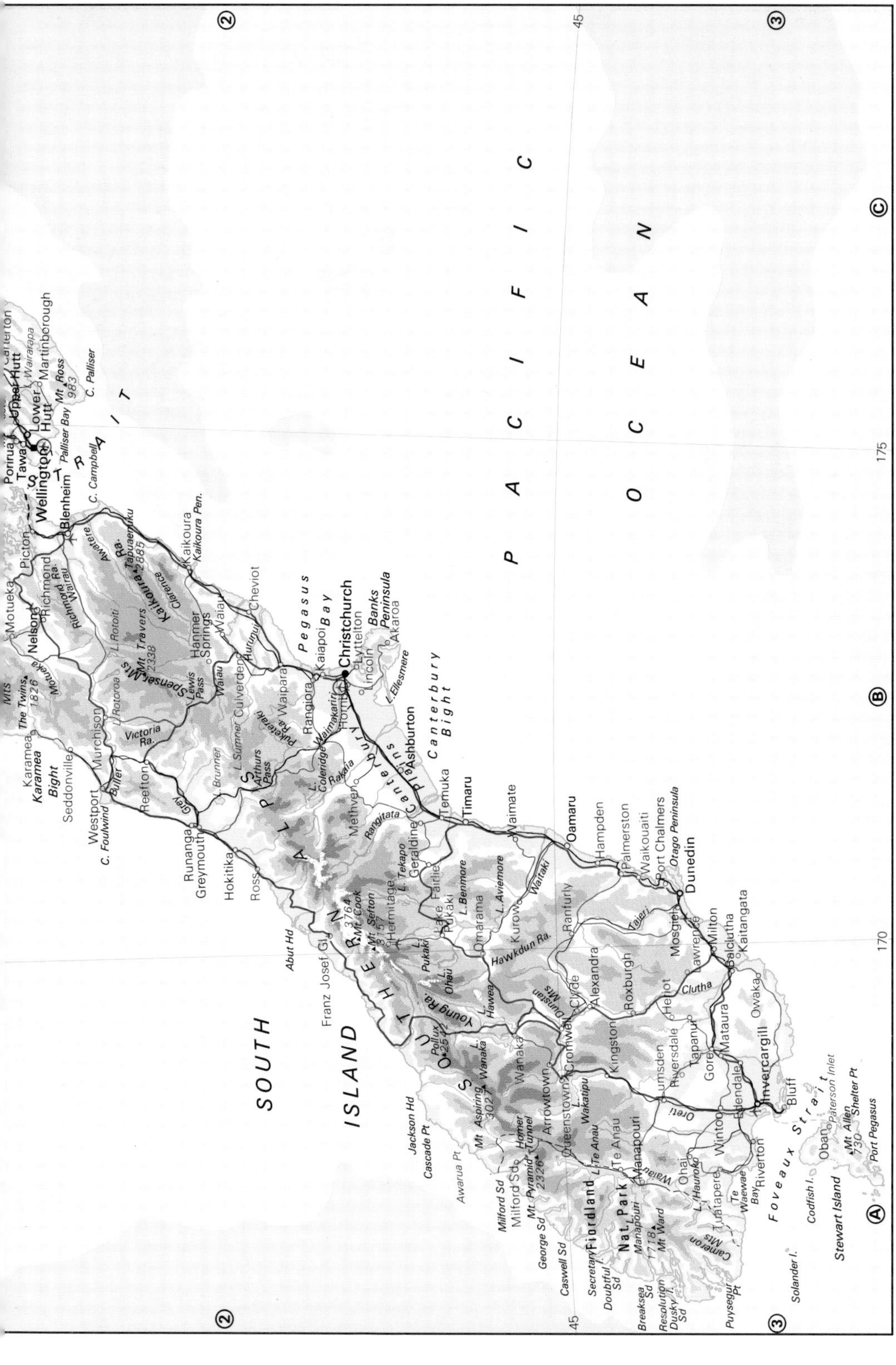
SOUTH ISLAND
PACIFIC OCEAN
Canterbury Bight
Pegasus Bay
Karamea Bight
Foveaux Strait
Wellington
Porirua
Tawa
Upper Hutt
Lower Hutt
Martinborough
Wairarapa
Palliser Bay
Mt Ross 983
C. Palliser
C. Campbell
Blenheim
Picton
Nelson
Motueka
Richmond
Richmond Ra.
Wairau
Awatere
Tapuaenuku 2885
Kaikoura Ra.
Clarence
Kaikoura
Kaikoura Pen.
Cheviot
Waiau
Hanmer Springs
Mt Travers 2338
L. Rotoiti
L. Rotoroa
Spenser Mts
Lewis Pass
Culverden
Hurunui
Waipara
The Twins 1826
Karamea
Seddonville
Murchison
Buller
Victoria Ra.
Westport
C. Foulwind
Reefton
Grey
Runanga
Greymouth
Hokitika
Ross
Brunner
L. Sumner
Arthurs Pass
Puketeraki Ra.
Rangiora
Kaiapoi
Christchurch
Lyttelton
Lincoln
Banks Peninsula
Akaroa
L. Ellesmere
Hornby
Waimakariri
L. Coleridge
Rakaia
Canterbury Plains
Ashburton
Methven
Rangitata
Geraldine
Temuka
Timaru
Waimate
Oamaru
Hampden
Palmerston
Waikouaiti
Port Chalmers
Otago Peninsula
Dunedin
Mosgiel
Taieri
Milton
Lawrence
Balclutha
Kaitangata
Clutha
Owaka
L. Tekapo
Fairlie
Hermitage
L. Benmore
L. Aviemore
Waitaki
Kurow
Ranfurly
Omarama
Hawkdun Ra.
Mt Cook 3764
Mt Sefton 3157
L. Pukaki
Pukaki
L. Ohau
Franz Josef Gl.
Abut Hd
SOUTHERN ALPS
Young Ra.
L. Hawea
Pollux 2542
L. Wanaka
Wanaka
Mt Aspiring 3027
Dunstan Mts
Clyde
Alexandra
Roxburgh
Heriot
Cromwell
Arrowtown
Queenstown
L. Wakatipu
Kingston
Lumsden
Riversdale
Tapanui
Gore
Mataura
Edendale
Invercargill
Bluff
Oreti
Winton
Riverton
Te Waewae Bay
Tuatapere
Ohai
L. Hauroko
Waiau
Manapouri
L. Manapouri
Te Anau
L. Te Anau
Homer Tunnel
Mt Pyramid 2326
Milford Sd
Milford Sd.
Jackson Hd
Cascade Pt
Awarua Pt
George Sd
Caswell Sd
Fiordland Nat. Park
Mt Ward 1718
Cameron Mts
Secretary I.
Doubtful Sd
Breaksea Sd
Resolution I.
Dusky Sd
Puysegur Pt
Solander I.
Codfish I.
Stewart Island
Oban
Paterson Inlet
Mt Allen 730
Shelter Pt
Port Pegasus
45
170
175
A
B
C
2
3

1:40M

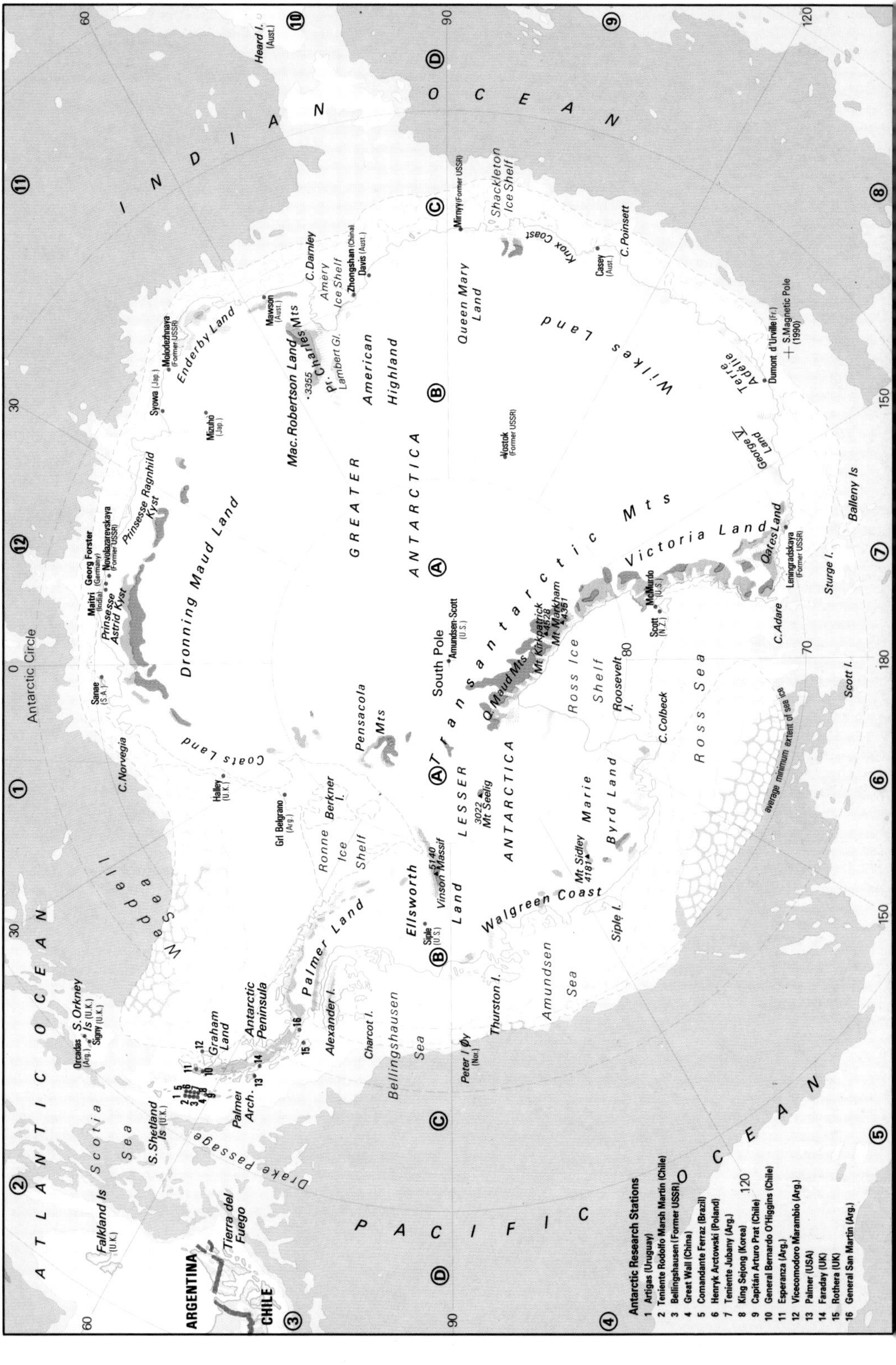
0 400 800 1200 1600 km
0 400 800 mls
INDIAN OCEAN
ATLANTIC OCEAN
PACIFIC OCEAN
Antarctic Circle
Heard I. (Aust.)
Mirnyy (Former USSR)
Shackleton Ice Shelf
Knox Coast
C. Poinsett
Casey (Aust.)
Queen Mary Land
Wilkes Land
Terre Adélie
Dumont d'Urville (Fr.)
S.Magnetic Pole (1990)
George V Land
Vostok (Former USSR)
C. Darnley
Amery Ice Shelf
Zhongshan (China)
Davis (Aust.)
Mawson (Aust.)
Mac. Robertson Land
Prince Charles Mts
3355
Lambert Gl.
American Highland
Enderby Land
Molodezhnaya (Former USSR)
Syowa (Jap.)
Mizuho (Jap.)
Prinsesse Ragnhild Kyst
Georg Forster (Germany)
Novolazarevskaya (Former USSR)
Maitri (India)
Prinsesse Astrid Kyst
Dronning Maud Land
GREATER ANTARCTICA
Sanae (S.A.)
Coats Land
C. Norvegia
Halley (U.K.)
Grl Belgrano (Arg.)
Berkner I.
Ronne Ice Shelf
Pensacola Mts
South Pole
Amundsen-Scott (U.S.)
Transantarctic Mts
Q. Maud Mts
Mt Kirkpatrick 4528
Mt Markham 4351
Victoria Land
Oates Land
Leningradskaya (Former USSR)
McMurdo (U.S.)
Scott (N.Z.)
C. Adare
Balleny Is
Sturge I.
Scott I.
Ross Ice Shelf
Roosevelt I.
C. Colbeck
Ross Sea
Marie Byrd Land
average minimum extent of sea ice
LESSER ANTARCTICA
3022 Mt Seelig
Mt Sidley 4181
5140 Vinson Massif
Ellsworth Land
Walgreen Coast
Siple I.
Siple (U.S.)
Amundsen Sea
Thurston I.
Peter I Øy (Nor.)
Bellingshausen Sea
Charcot I.
Alexander I.
Palmer Land
Antarctic Peninsula
Graham Land
Palmer Arch.
Weddell Sea
S. Orkney Is (U.K.)
Orcades (Arg.)
Signy (U.K.)
S. Shetland Is (U.K.)
Scotia Sea
Drake Passage
Falkland Is (U.K.)
Tierra del Fuego
ARGENTINA
CHILE
Antarctic Research Stations
1 Artigas (Uruguay)
2 Teniente Rodolfo Marsh Martin (Chile)
3 Bellingshausen (Former USSR)
4 Great Wall (China)
5 Comandante Ferraz (Brazil)
6 Henryk Arctowski (Poland)
7 Teniente Jubany (Arg.)
8 King Sejong (Korea)
9 Capitán Arturo Prat (Chile)
10 General Bernardo O'Higgins (Chile)
11 Esperanza (Arg.)
12 Vicecomodoro Marambio (Arg.)
13 Palmer (USA)
14 Faraday (UK)
15 Rothera (UK)
16 General San Martín (Arg.)

Index

In the index, the first number refers to the page, and the following letter and number to the section of the map in which the index entry can be found. For example, 48C2 **Paris** means that Paris can be found on page 48 where column C and row 2 meet.

Abbreviations used in the index

Afghan	Afghanistan	Germ	Germany	Phil	Philippines	Arch	Archipelago
Alb	Albania	Hung	Hungary	Pol	Poland	B	Bay
Alg	Algeria	Ind	Indonesia	Port	Portugal	C	Cape
Ant	Antarctica	Irish Rep	Ireland	Rom	Romania	Chan	Channel
Arg	Argentina	Leb	Lebanon		Russian	Gl	Glacier
Aust	Australia	Lib	Liberia	Russian Fed	Federation	I(s)	Island(s)
Bang	Bangladesh	Liech	Liechtenstein	S Arabia	Saudi Arabia	Lg	Lagoon
Belg	Belgium	Lux	Luxembourg	Scot	Scotland	L	Lake
Bol	Bolivia	Madag	Madagascar	Sen	Senegal	Mt(s)	Mountain(s)
Bulg	Bulgaria	Malay	Malaysia	S Africa	South Africa	O	Ocean
Burk	Burkina	Maur	Mauritania	S Yemen	South Yemen	P	Pass
Camb	Cambodia	Mor	Morocco	Switz	Switzerland	Pen	Peninsula
Can	Canada	Mozam	Mozambique	Tanz	Tanzania	Plat	Plateau
CAR	Central African Republic	Neth	Netherlands	Thai	Thailand	Pt	Point
Czech	Czechoslovakia	NZ	New Zealand	Turk	Turkey	Res	Reservoir
Den	Denmark	Nic	Nicaragua		United States	R	River
Dom Rep	Dominican Republic	N Ire	Northern Ireland	USA	of America	S	Sea
El Sal	El Salvador	Nig	Nigeria	Urug	Uruguay	Sd	Sound
Eng	England	Nor	Norway	Ven	Venezuela	Str	Strait
Eq Guinea	Equatorial Guinea	Pak	Pakistan	Viet	Vietnam	V	Valley
Eth	Ethiopia	PNG	Papua New Guinea	Yugos	Yugoslavia		
Fin	Finland	Paar	Paraguay	Zim	Zimbabwe		

A

57B2 **Aachen** Germany
46C1 **Aalst** Belg
38K6 **Äänekoski** Fin
47C1 **Aarau** Switz
47B1 **Aare** *R* Switz
72A3 **Aba** China
97C4 **Aba** Nig
99D2 **Aba** Zaïre
91A3 **Ābādān** Iran
90B3 **Ābādeh** Iran
96B1 **Abadla** Alg
35B1 **Abaeté** Brazil
35B1 **Abaeté** *R* Brazil
31B2 **Abaetetuba** Brazil
72D1 **Abagnar Qi** China
97C4 **Abakaliki** Nig
63B2 **Abakan** Russian Fed
97C3 **Abala** Niger
96C2 **Abalessa** Alg
32C6 **Abancay** Peru
90B3 **Abarqū** Iran
74E2 **Abashiri** Japan
74E2 **Abashiri-wan** *B* Japan
71F4 **Abau** PNG
99D2 **Abaya** *L* Eth
99D1 **Abbai** *R* Eth
99E1 **Abbe** *L* Eth
48C1 **Abbeville** France
19B4 **Abbeville** Louisiana, USA
17B1 **Abbeville** S Carolina, USA
45B2 **Abbeyfeale** Irish Rep
47C2 **Abbiategrasso** Italy
20B1 **Abbotsford** Can
84C2 **Abbottabad** Pak
61H3 **Abdulino** Russian Fed
98C1 **Abéché** Chad
39F7 **Åbenrå** Den
97C4 **Abeokuta** Nig
99D2 **Abera** Eth
43B3 **Aberaeron** Wales
15C3 **Aberdeen** Maryland, USA
100B4 **Aberdeen** S Africa
44C3 **Aberdeen** Scot
8D2 **Aberdeen** S Dakota, USA
8A2 **Aberdeen** Washington, USA
4J3 **Aberdeen L** Can
44C3 **Aberfeldy** Scot
43C4 **Abergavenny** Wales
43B3 **Aberystwyth** Wales
81C4 **Abhā** S Arabia
90A2 **Abhar** Iran
97B4 **Abidjan** Ivory Coast
18A2 **Abilene** Kansas, USA
9D3 **Abilene** Texas, USA
43D4 **Abingdon** Eng
7B4 **Abitibi** *R* Can
7C5 **Abitibi,L** Can
61F5 **Abkhazskaya** Respublika, Georgia
84C2 **Abohar** India
97C4 **Abomey** Benin
98B2 **Abong Mbang** Cam
79A4 **Aborlan** Phil
98B1 **Abou Deïa** Chad
91A4 **Abqaiq** S Arabia
50A2 **Abrantes** Port
95C2 **Abri** Sudan
106A3 **Abrolhos** *Is* Aust
8B2 **Absaroka Range** *Mts* USA
91B5 **Abū al Abyad** *I* UAE
91A4 **Abū 'Ali** *I* S Arabia
91B5 **Abū Dhabi** UAE
95C3 **Abu Hamed** Sudan
97C4 **Abuja** Nig
33D5 **Abunã** Brazil
32D6 **Abunã** *R* Bol
93D3 **Abú Sukhayr** Iraq
111B2 **Abut Head** *C* NZ
95C3 **Abu 'Urug** *Well* Sudan
99D1 **Abuye Meda** *Mt* Eth
99C1 **Abu Zabad** Sudan
99D2 **Abwong** Sudan
56B1 **Åby** Den
94B3 **Aby 'Aweigîla** *Well* Egypt
99C2 **Abyei** Sudan
24B2 **Acambaro** Mexico
24B2 **Acaponeta** Mexico
24B3 **Acapulco** Mexico
31D2 **Acaraú** Brazil
32D2 **Acarigua** Ven
24C3 **Acatlán** Mexico
23B2 **Acatzingo** Mexico
97B4 **Accra** Ghana
85D4 **Achalpur** India
29B4 **Achao** Chile
47D1 **Achensee** *L* Austria
46E2 **Achern** Germany
41A3 **Achill** *I* Irish Rep
63B2 **Achinsk** Russian Fed
53C3 **Acireale** Italy
26C2 **Acklins** *I* Caribbean S
32C6 **Acobamba** Peru
29B2 **Aconcagua** *Mt* Chile
31D3 **Acopiara** Brazil
88B4 **Açores** *Is* Atlantic O
A Coruña = La Coruña
47C2 **Acqui** Italy
108A2 **Acraman,L** Aust
Acre = 'Akko
32C5 **Acre** State, Brazil
22C3 **Acton** USA
23B1 **Actopan** Mexico
19A3 **Ada** USA
50B1 **Adaja** *R* Spain
91C5 **Adam** Oman
35A2 **Adamantina** Brazil
98B2 **Adamaoua** Region, Nig/Cam
47D1 **Adamello** *Mt* Italy
16C1 **Adams** USA
87B3 **Adam's Bridge** India/Sri Lanka
13D2 **Adams L** Can
8A2 **Adams,Mt** USA
87C3 **Adam's Peak** *Mt* Sri Lanka
81C4 **'Adan** Yemen
92C2 **Adana** Turk
60D5 **Adapazari** Turk
112B7 **Adare,C** Ant
108B1 **Adavale** Aust
47C2 **Adda** *R* Italy
91A4 **Ad Dahna'** Region, S Arabia
96A2 **Ad Dakhla** Mor
81C4 **Ad Dālī'** Yemen
91B4 **Ad Damman** S Arabia
91A4 **Ad Dibdibah** Region, S Arabia
91A5 **Ad Dilam** S Arabia
91A5 **Ad Dir'iyah** S Arabia
93D3 **Ad Dīwanīyah** Iraq
93D3 **Ad Duwayd** S Arabia
106C4 **Adelaide** Aust
4J3 **Adelaide Pen** Can
22D3 **Adelanto** USA
Aden = 'Adan
81C4 **Aden,G of** Yemen/Somalia
97C3 **Aderbissinat** Niger
94C2 **Adhra** Syria
71E4 **Adi** *I* Indon
52B1 **Adige** *R* Italy
99D1 **Adigrat** Eth
85D5 **Adilābād** India
20B2 **Adin** USA
15D2 **Adirondack Mts** USA
99D2 **Ādīs Ābeba** Eth
95C3 **Adi Ugai** Eth
93C2 **Adıyaman** Turk
54C1 **Adjud** Rom
4E4 **Admiralty I** USA
6B2 **Admiralty Inlet** *B* Can
87B1 **Ādoni** India
48B3 **Adour** *R* France
96A2 **Adrar** Region, Maur
96C2 **Adrar** *Mts* Alg
96A2 **Adrar Soutouf** Region, Mor
98C1 **Adré** Chad
95A2 **Adri** Libya
47E2 **Adria** Italy

14B2 **Adrian** Michigan, USA
52B2 **Adriatic S** S Europe
99D1 **Ādwa** Eth
97B4 **Adzopé** Ivory Coast
55B3 **Aegean** *S* Greece
80E2 **Afghanistan** Republic, Asia
99E2 **Afgooye** Somalia
97C4 **Afikpo** Nig
38G6 **Åfjord** Nor
96C1 **Aflou** Alg
99E2 **Afmadu** Somalia
97A3 **Afollé** Region, Maur
94B2 **Afula** Israel
92B2 **Afyon** Turk
95A3 **Agadem** Niger
97C3 **Agadez** Niger
96B1 **Agadir** Mor
85D4 **Agar** India
86C2 **Agartala** India
20B1 **Agassiz** Can
97B4 **Agboville** Ivory Coast
93E1 **Agdam** Azerbaijan
75B1 **Agematsu** Japan
48C3 **Agen** France
90A3 **Agha Jārī** Iran
96A2 **Aghwinit** *Well* Mor
47D2 **Agno** *R* Italy
47E1 **Agordo** Italy
48C3 **Agout** *R* France
85D3 **Āgra** India
93D2 **Ağri** Turk
53C2 **Agri** *R* Italy
53B3 **Agrigento** Italy
55B3 **Agrínion** Greece
34A3 **Agrio** *R* Chile
53B2 **Agropoli** Italy
61H2 **Agryz** Russian Fed
6E3 **Agto** Greenland
27D3 **Aguadilla** Puerto Rico
24B1 **Agua Prieta** Mexico
24B2 **Aguascalientes** Mexico
23A1 **Aguascalientes** State, Mexico
35C1 **Aguas Formosas** Brazil
50A1 **Agueda** Port
96C3 **Aguelhok** Mali
50B2 **Aguilas** Spain
23A2 **Aguililla** Mexico
100B4 **Agulhas,C** S Africa
79C4 **Agusan** *R* Phil
Ahaggar = Hoggar
93E2 **Ahar** Iran
110B1 **Ahipara B** NZ
85C4 **Ahmadābād** India
87A1 **Ahmadnagar** India
99E2 **Ahmar** *Mts* Eth
46D1 **Ahr** *R* Germany
46D1 **Ahrgebirge** Region, Germany
23A1 **Ahuacatlán** Mexico
23A1 **Ahualulco** Mexico
39G7 **Åhus** Sweden
90B2 **Āhuvān** Iran
90A3 **Ahvāz** Iran
26A4 **Aiajuela** Costa Rica
47B1 **Aigle** Switz
47B2 **Aiguille d'Arves** *Mt* France
47B2 **Aiguille de la Grand Sassière** *Mt* France
75B1 **Aikawa** Japan
17B1 **Aiken** USA
73A5 **Ailao Shan** *Upland* China
35C1 **Aimorés** Brazil
96B1 **Ain Beni Mathar** Mor
95B2 **Ain Dalla** *Well* Egypt
51C2 **Aïn el Hadjel** Alg
95A3 **Aïn Galakka** Chad
96B1 **Aïn Sefra** Alg
92B4 **'Ain Sukhna** Egypt
75A2 **Aioi** Japan
96B2 **Aioun Abd el Malek** *Well* Maur
97B3 **Aïoun El Atrouss** Maur
30C2 **Aiquile** Bol
97C3 **Aïr** *Desert Region* Niger
13E2 **Airdrie** Can
46B1 **Aire** France
42D3 **Aire** *R* Eng
46C2 **Aire** *R* France
6C3 **Airforce I** Can
47C1 **Airolo** Switz
4E3 **Aishihik** Can
12G2 **Aishihik L** Can
46B2 **Aisne** Department, France
49C2 **Aisne** *R* France
71F4 **Aitape** PNG
58D1 **Aiviekste** *R* Latvia
72B2 **Aixa Zuogi** China
49D3 **Aix-en-Provence** France
47A2 **Aix-les-Bains** France
86B2 **Aiyar Res** India
55B3 **Aíyion** Greece
55B3 **Aíyna** *I* Greece
86C2 **Āīzawl** India
100A3 **Aizeb** *R* Namibia
74E3 **Aizu-Wakamatsu** Japan
52A2 **Ajaccio** Corse
23B2 **Ajalpan** Mexico
95B1 **Ajdābiyā** Libya
74E2 **Ajigasawa** Japan
94B2 **Ajlūn** Jordan
91C4 **Ajman** UAE
85C3 **Ajmer** India
9B3 **Ajo** USA
23A2 **Ajuchitan** Mexico
55C3 **Ak** *R* Turk
75B1 **Akaishi-sanchi** *Mts* Japan
87B1 **Akalkot** India
111B2 **Akaroa** NZ
75A2 **Akashi** Japan
61J3 **Akbulak** Russian Fed
93C2 **Akçakale** Turk
96A2 **Akchar** *Watercourse* Maur
55C3 **Akdağ** *Mt* Turk
98C2 **Aketi** Zaïre
93D1 **Akhalkalaki** Georgia
93D1 **Akhalsikhe** Georgia
55B3 **Akharnái** Greece
12D3 **Akhiok** USA
92A2 **Akhisar** Turk
58D1 **Akhiste** Latvia
95C2 **Akhmîm** Egypt
61G4 **Akhtubinsk** Russian Fed
60D4 **Akhtyrka** Ukraine
75A2 **Aki** Japan
7B4 **Akimiski I** Can
74E3 **Akita** Japan
96A3 **Akjoujt** Maur
94B2 **'Akko** Israel
4E3 **Aklavik** USA
97B3 **Aklé Aouana** *Desert Region* Maur
99D2 **Akobo** Sudan
99D2 **Akobo** *R* Sudan
84B1 **Akoha** Afghan
85D4 **Akola** India
85D4 **Akot** India
6D3 **Akpatok I** Can
55B3 **Ákra Kafirévs** *C* Greece
55B3 **Ákra Maléa** *C* Greece
38A2 **Akranes** Iceland
55C3 **Ákra Sídheros** *C* Greece
55B3 **Ákra Spátha** *C* Greece
55B3 **Ákra Taínaron** *C* Greece
10B2 **Akron** USA
94A1 **Akrotiri B** Cyprus
84D1 **Aksai Chin** *Mts* China
92B2 **Aksaray** Turk
61H3 **Aksay** Kazakhstan
84D1 **Aksayquin Hu** *L* China
92B2 **Akşehir** Turk
92B2 **Akseki** Turk
63D2 **Aksenovo Zilovskoye** Russian Fed
68D1 **Aksha** Russian Fed
82C1 **Aksu** China
65J5 **Aktogay** Kazakhstan
61J4 **Aktumsyk** Kazakhstan
65G4 **Aktyubinsk** Kazakhstan
38B1 **Akureyri** Iceland
65K5 **Akzhal** Kazakhstan
11B3 **Alabama** State, USA
11B3 **Alabama** *R* USA
17A1 **Alabaster** USA
92C2 **Ala Dağlari** *Mts* Turk
61F5 **Alagir** Russian Fed
47B2 **Alagna** Italy
31D3 **Alagoas** State, Brazil
31D4 **Alagoinhas** Brazil
51B1 **Alagón** Spain
93E4 **Al Ahmadi** Kuwait
25D3 **Alajuela** Costa Rica
12B2 **Alakanuk** USA
38L5 **Alakurtti** Russian Fed
93E3 **Al Amārah** Iraq
21A2 **Alameda** USA
23B1 **Alamo** Mexico
9C3 **Alamogordo** USA
9C3 **Alamosa** USA
39H6 **Åland** *I* Fin
92B2 **Alanya** Turk
17B1 **Alapaha** *R* USA
65H4 **Alapayevsk** Russian Fed
92A2 **Alaşehir** Turk
68C3 **Ala Shan** *Mts* China
4C3 **Alaska** State, USA
4D4 **Alaska,G of** USA
12C3 **Alaska Pen** USA
4C3 **Alaska Range** *Mts* USA
52A2 **Alassio** Italy
12D1 **Alatna** *R* USA
61G3 **Alatyr** Russian Fed
108B2 **Alawoona** Aust
91C5 **Al'Ayn** UAE
82B2 **Alayskiy Khrebet** *Mts* Tajikistan
49D3 **Alba** Italy
92C2 **Al Bāb** Syria
51B2 **Albacete** Spain
50A1 **Alba de Tormes** Spain
93D2 **Al Badi** Iraq
54B1 **Alba Iulia** Rom
54A2 **Albania** Republic, Europe
106A4 **Albany** Aust
17B1 **Albany** Georgia, USA
15D2 **Albany** New York, USA
8A2 **Albany** Oregon, USA
7B4 **Albany** *R* Can
34B2 **Albardón** Arg
91C5 **Al Batinah** Region, Oman
71F5 **Albatross B** Aust
95B1 **Al Bayḍā** Libya
11C3 **Albemarle Sd** USA
50B1 **Alberche** *R* Spain
108A1 **Alberga** Aust
46B1 **Albert** France
5G4 **Alberta** Province, Can
99D2 **Albert,L** Uganda/Zaïre
10A2 **Albert Lea** USA
99D2 **Albert Nile** *R* Uganda
49D2 **Albertville** France
48C3 **Albi** France
18B1 **Albia** USA
33G2 **Albina** Suriname
14B2 **Albion** Michigan, USA
15C2 **Albion** New York, USA
92C4 **Al Bi'r** S Arabia
91A5 **Al Biyadh** Region, S Arabia
50B2 **Alborán** *I* Spain
39G7 **Ålborg** Den
93D3 **Al Bū Kamāl** Syria
47C1 **Albula** *R* Switz
9C3 **Albuquerque** USA
91C5 **Al Buraymi** Oman
95A1 **Al Burayqah** Libya
95B1 **Al Burdī** Libya
107D4 **Albury** Aust
93E3 **Al Buşayyah** Iraq
50B1 **Alcalá de Henares** Spain
53B3 **Alcamo** Italy
51B1 **Alcaniz** Spain
31C2 **Alcântara** Brazil
50B2 **Alcaraz** Spain
50B2 **Alcázar de San Juan** Spain
51B2 **Alcira** Spain
35D1 **Alcobaça** Brazil
50B1 **Alcolea de Pinar** Spain
51B2 **Alcoy** Spain
51C2 **Alcudia** Spain
89J8 **Aldabra** *Is* Indian O
63E2 **Aldan** Russian Fed
63E2 **Aldanskoye Nagor'ye** *Upland* Russian Fed
43E3 **Aldeburgh** Eng
48B2 **Alderney** *I* UK
43D4 **Aldershot** Eng
97A3 **Aleg** Maur
30E4 **Alegrete** Brazil
34C2 **Alejandro Roca** Arg
30H6 **Alejandro Selkirk** *I* Chile
63G2 **Aleksandrovsk Sakhalinskiy** Russian Fed
65J4 **Alekseyevka** Kazakhstan
60E3 **Aleksin** Russian Fed
58B1 **Ålem** Sweden
35C2 **Além Paraíba** Brazil
49C2 **Alençon** France
21C4 **Alenuihaha Chan** Hawaiian Is
Aleppo = Ḥalab
6D1 **Alert** Can
49C3 **Alès** France
52A2 **Alessandria** Italy
64B3 **Ålesund** Nor
12C3 **Aleutian Range** *Mts* USA
4E4 **Alexander Arch** USA
100A3 **Alexander Bay** S Africa
17A1 **Alexander City** USA
112C3 **Alexander I** Ant
111A3 **Alexandra** NZ
29G8 **Alexandra,C** South Georgia
6C2 **Alexandra Fjord** Can
95B1 **Alexandria** Egypt
11A3 **Alexandria** Louisiana, USA
10A2 **Alexandria** Minnesota, USA
10C3 **Alexandria** Virginia, USA
55C2 **Alexandroúpolis** Greece
13C2 **Alexis Creek** Can
94B2 **Aley** Leb
65K4 **Aleysk** Russian Fed
93D3 **Al Fallūjah** Iraq
51B1 **Alfaro** Spain
54C2 **Alfatar** Bulg
93E3 **Al Fāw** Iraq
35B2 **Alfensas** Brazil
55B3 **Alfiós** *R* Greece
47D2 **Alfonsine** Italy
35C2 **Alfonzo Cláudio** Brazil
35C2 **Alfredo Chaves** Brazil
61J4 **Alga** Kazakhstan
34B3 **Algarrobo del Águila** Arg
50A2 **Algeciras** Spain
96C1 **Alger** Alg

96B2 **Algeria** Republic, Africa
53A2 **Alghero** Sardegna
Algiers = Alger
15C1 **Algonquin Park** Can
91C5 **Al Hadd** Oman
93D3 **Al Hadīthah** Iraq
92C3 **Al Hadīthah** S Arabia
93D2 **Al Hadr** Iraq
91C5 **Al Hajar al Gharbī** *Mts* Oman
91C5 **Al Hajar ash Sharqī** *Mts* Oman
93C3 **Al Hamad** *Desert Region* Jordan/ S Arabia
93E4 **Al Haniyah** *Desert Region* Iraq
91A5 **Al Harīq** S Arabia
93C3 **Al Harrah** *Desert Region* S Arabia
95A2 **Al Harūj al Aswad** *Upland* Libya
91A4 **Al Hasa** Region, S Arabia
93D2 **Al Hasakah** Syria
93C4 **Al Hawjā'** S Arabia
93E3 **Al Hayy** Iraq
94C2 **Al Hījānah** Syria
93D3 **Al Hillah** Iraq
91A5 **Al Hillah** S Arabia
96B1 **Al Hoceima** Mor
91A4 **Al Hufūf** S Arabia
91B5 **Al Humrah** Region, UAE
91C5 **Al Huwatsah** Oman
90A2 **Alīābad** Iran
91C4 **Aliabad** Iran
55B2 **Aliákmon** *R* Greece
93E3 **Alī al Gharbī** Iraq
87A1 **Alībāg** India
51B2 **Alicante** Spain
9D4 **Alice** USA
106C3 **Alice Springs** Aust
53B3 **Alicudi** *I* Italy
84D3 **Aligarh** India
90A3 **Aligūdarz** Iran
84B2 **Ali-Khel** Afghan
55C3 **Alimniá** *I* Greece
86B1 **Alīpur Duār** India
14B2 **Aliquippa** USA
22B2 **Alisal** USA
93C3 **Al' Isawiyah** S Arabia
100B4 **Aliwal North** S Africa
95B2 **Al Jaghbūb** Libya
93D3 **Al Jālamīd** S Arabia
95B2 **Al Jawf** Libya
93C4 **Al Jawf** S Arabia
93D2 **Al Jazīrah** *Desert Region* Syria/Iraq
50A2 **Aljezur** Port
91A4 **Al Jubayl** S Arabia
91C5 **Al Kāmil** Oman
93D2 **Al Khābūr** *R* Syria
91C5 **Al Khābūrah** Oman
93D3 **Al Khālis** Iraq
91C4 **Al Khasab** Oman
91B4 **Al Khawr** Qatar
95A1 **Al Khums** Libya
91B5 **Al Kidan** Region, S Arabia
94C2 **Al Kiswah** Syria
56A2 **Alkmaar** Neth
95B2 **Al Kufrah Oasis** Libya
93E3 **Al Kūt** Iraq
92C2 **Al Lādhiqīyah** Syria
86A1 **Allahābād** India
94C2 **Al Lajāh** *Mt* Syria
12D1 **Allakaket** USA
76B2 **Allanmyo** Burma
95C2 **'Allaqi** *Watercourse* Egypt
17B1 **Allatoona L** USA
15C2 **Allegheny** *R* USA
10C3 **Allegheny Mts** USA
17B1 **Allendale** USA
111A3 **Allen,Mt** NZ
15C2 **Allentown** USA
87B3 **Alleppey** India
49C2 **Aller** *R* France
47D1 **Allgäu** *Mts* Germany
8C2 **Alliance** USA
81C3 **Al Līth** S Arabia
91B5 **Al Liwā** Region, UAE
109D1 **Allora** Aust
14B2 **Alma** Michigan, USA
82B1 **Alma Ata** Kazakhstan
50A2 **Almada** Port
Al Madinah = Medina
71F2 **Almagan** *I* Pacific O
91B4 **Al Manāmah** Bahrain
93D3 **Al Ma'nīyah** Iraq
21A1 **Almanor,L** USA
51B2 **Almansa** Spain
13B1 **Alma Peak** *Mt* Can
91B5 **Al Māriyyah** UAE
95B1 **Al Marj** Libya
50B1 **Almazán** Spain
35C1 **Almenara** Brazil
50B2 **Almeria** Spain
61H3 **Al'met'yevsk** Russian Fed
56C1 **Älmhult** Sweden
93E3 **Al Miqdādīyah** Iraq
112C3 **Almirante Brown** *Base* Ant
34A1 **Almirante Latorre** Chile
55B3 **Almirós** Greece
91A4 **Al Mish'āb** S Arabia
50A2 **Almodôvar** Port
84D3 **Almora** India
91A4 **Al Mubarraz** S Arabia
92C4 **Al Mudawwara** Jordan
91C5 **Al Mudaybi** Oman
91B4 **Al Muharraq** Bahrain
81C4 **Al Mukallā** Yemen
81C4 **Al Mukhā** Yemen
93D3 **Al Musayyib** Iraq
44B3 **Alness** Scot
93E3 **Al Nu'mānīyah** Iraq
42D2 **Alnwick** Eng
71D4 **Alor** *I* Indon
77C4 **Alor Setar** Malay
Alost = Aalst
107E2 **Alotau** PNG
106B3 **Aloysius,Mt** Aust
34C3 **Alpachiri** Arg
14B1 **Alpena** USA
47B2 **Alpes du Valais** *Mts* Switz
52B1 **Alpi Dolomitiche** *Mts* Italy
47B2 **Alpi Graie** *Mts* Italy
9C3 **Alpine** Texas, USA
47C1 **Alpi Orobie** *Mts* Italy
47B2 **Alpi Pennine** *Mts* Italy
47C1 **Alpi Retiche** *Mts* Switz
47D1 **Alpi Venoste** *Mts* Italy
52A1 **Alps** *Mts* Europe
95A1 **Al Qaddāhiyah** Libya
94C1 **Al Qadmūs** Syria
93D3 **Al Qā'im** Iraq
93C4 **Al Qalībah** S Arabia
93D2 **Al Qāmishlī** Syria
95A1 **Al Qaryah Ash Sharqiyah** Libya
92C3 **Al Qaryatayn** Syria
91A4 **Al Qātif** S Arabia
95A2 **Al Qatrūn** Libya
91A4 **Al Qaysāmah** S Arabia
94C2 **Al Quatayfah** Syria
50A2 **Alqueva** *R* Port
92C3 **Al Qunaytirah** Syria
81C4 **Al Qunfidhah** S Arabia
93E3 **Al Qurnah** Iraq
94C1 **Al Qusayr** Syria
92C3 **Al Qutayfah** Syria
56B1 **Als** *I* Den
49D2 **Alsace** Region, France
57B2 **Alsfeld** Germany
42C2 **Alston** Eng
38J5 **Alta** Nor
29D2 **Alta Gracia** Arg
27D5 **Altagracia de Orituco** Ven
68A2 **Altai** *Mts* Mongolia
17B1 **Altamaha** *R* USA
33G4 **Altamira** Brazil
23B1 **Altamira** Mexico
53C2 **Altamura** Italy
68C1 **Altanbulag** Mongolia
71F4 **Altape** PNG
24B2 **Altata** Mexico
63A3 **Altay** China
63B3 **Altay** Mongolia
63A2 **Altay** *Mts* Russian Fed
47C1 **Altdorf** Switz
46D1 **Altenkirchen** Germany
34B3 **Altiplanicie del Payún** *Plat* Arg
47B1 **Altkirch** France
101C2 **Alto Molócue** Mozam
10A3 **Alton** USA
15C2 **Altoona** USA
34B2 **Alto Pencoso** *Mts* Arg
35A1 **Alto Sucuriú** Brazil
23B2 **Altotonga** Mexico
23A2 **Altoyac de Alvarez** Mexico
82C2 **Altun Shan** *Mts* China
20B2 **Alturas** USA
9D3 **Altus** USA
91B5 **Al'Ubaylah** S Arabia
93C4 **Al Urayq** *Desert Region* S Arabia
91B5 **Al'Uruq al Mu'taridah** Region, S Arabia
9D2 **Alva** USA
23B2 **Alvarado** Mexico
19A3 **Alvarado** USA
39G6 **Älvdalen** Sweden
19A4 **Alvin** USA
38J5 **Alvsbyn** Sweden
80B3 **Al Wajh** S Arabia
85D3 **Alwar** India
93D3 **Al Widyān** *Desert Region* Iraq/S Arabia
72A2 **Alxa Yougi** China
93E2 **Alyat** Azerbaijan
39J8 **Alytus** Lithuania
46E2 **Alzey** Germany
23B2 **Amacuzac** *R* Mexico
99D2 **Amadi** Sudan
93D2 **Amādīyah** Iraq
6C3 **Amadjuak L** Can
74B4 **Amakusa-shotō** *I* Japan
39G7 **Åmål** Sweden
63D2 **Amalat** *R* Russian Fed
55B3 **Amaliás** Greece
85D4 **Amalner** India
69E4 **Amami** *I* Japan
69E4 **Amami gunto** *Arch* Japan
100C4 **Amanzimtoti** S Africa
33G3 **Amapá** Brazil
33G3 **Amapá** State, Brazil
9C3 **Amarillo** USA
60E5 **Amasya** Turk
23A1 **Amatitan** Mexico
Amazonas = Solimões
32D4 **Amazonas** State, Brazil
28C3 **Amazonas** *R* Brazil
84D2 **Ambāla** India
87C3 **Ambalangoda** Sri Lanka
101D3 **Ambalavao** Madag
98B2 **Ambam** Cam
101D2 **Ambanja** Madag
1C7 **Ambarchik** Russian Fed
32B4 **Ambato** Ecuador
101D2 **Ambato-Boeny** Madag
101D2 **Ambatolampy** Madag
101D2 **Ambatondrazaka** Madag
57C3 **Amberg** Germany
25D3 **Ambergris Cay** *I* Belize
86A2 **Ambikāpur** India
101D2 **Ambilobe** Madag
101D3 **Amboasary** Madag
101D2 **Ambodifototra** Madag
101D3 **Ambohimahasoa** Madag
71D4 **Ambon** Indon
101D3 **Ambositra** Madag
101D3 **Ambovombe** Madag
98B3 **Ambriz** Angola
98C1 **Am Dam** Chad
64H3 **Amderma** Russian Fed
24B2 **Ameca** Mexico
23B2 **Amecacameca** Mexico
34C2 **Ameghino** Arg
56B2 **Ameland** *I* Neth
16C2 **Amenia** USA
112B10 **American Highland** *Upland* Ant
105H4 **American Samoa** *Is* Pacific O
17B1 **Americus** USA
101G1 **Amersfoort** S Africa
112C10 **Amery Ice Shelf** Ant
55B3 **Amfilokhía** Greece
55B3 **Amfíssa** Greece
63F1 **Amga** Russian Fed
63F1 **Amgal** *R* Russian Fed
69F2 **Amgu** Russian Fed
69F1 **Amgun'** *R* Russian Fed
99D1 **Amhara** *Region* Eth
7D5 **Amherst** Can
16C1 **Amherst** Massachusetts, USA
87B2 **Amhūr** India
48C2 **Amiens** France
75B1 **Amino** Japan
94B1 **Amioune** Leb
89K8 **Amirante Is** Indian O
86B1 **Amlekhgan** Nepal
92C3 **Amman** Jordan
38K6 **Ämmänsaario** Fin
56B2 **Ammersfoort** Neth
90B2 **Amol** Iran
55C3 **Amorgós** *I* Greece
7C5 **Amos** Can
Amoy = Xiamen
101D3 **Ampanihy** Madag
35B2 **Amparo** Brazil
51C1 **Amposta** Spain
85D4 **Amrāvati** India
85C4 **Amreli** India
84C2 **Amritsar** India
56A2 **Amsterdam** Neth
101H1 **Amsterdam** S Africa
15D2 **Amsterdam** USA
98C1 **Am Timan** Chad
88L3 **Amu Darya** *R* Uzbekistan
6A2 **Amund Ringes I** Can
4F2 **Amundsen G** Can
112B4 **Amundsen S** Ant
80E **Amundsen-Scott** *Base* Ant
78D3 **Amuntai** Indon
63E2 **Amur** *R* Russian Fed
33E2 **Anaco** Ven
8B2 **Anaconda** USA
20B1 **Anacortes** USA
55C3 **Anáfi** *I* Greece
93D3 **'ānah** Iraq
21B3 **Anaheim** USA
87B2 **Anaimalai Hills** India
83C4 **Anakapalle** India
12E1 **Anaktuvuk P** USA

101D2 **Analalaya** Madag
92B2 **Anamur** Turk
75A2 **Anan** Japan
87B2 **Anantapur** India
84D2 **Anantnag** India
31B5 **Anápolis** Brazil
90C3 **Anār** Iran
90B3 **Anārak** Iran
71F2 **Anatahan** *I* Pacific O
30D4 **Añatuya** Arg
74B3 **Anbyŏn** N Korea
22C4 **Ancapa Is** USA
4D3 **Anchorage** USA
30C2 **Ancohuma** *Mt* Bol
32B6 **Ancón** Peru
52B2 **Ancona** Italy
16C1 **Ancram** USA
29B4 **Ancud** Chile
34A3 **Andacollo** Arg
108A1 **Andado** Aust
32C6 **Andahuaylas** Peru
38F6 **Andalsnes** Nor
50A2 **Andalucia** Region, Spain
17A1 **Andalusia** USA
83D4 **Andaman Is** Burma
83D4 **Andaman S** Burma
108A2 **Andamooka** Aust
38H5 **Andenes** Nor
47C1 **Andermatt** Switz
57B2 **Andernach** Germany
14A2 **Anderson** Indiana, USA
18B2 **Anderson** Missouri, USA
17B1 **Anderson** S Carolina, USA
4F3 **Anderson** *R* Can
87B1 **Andhra Pradesh** State, India
55B3 **Andikíthira** *I* Greece
65J5 **Andizhan** Uzbekistan
65H6 **Andkhui** Afghan
74B3 **Andong** S Korea
51C1 **Andorra** Principality, SW Europe
51C1 **Andorra-La-Vella** Andorra
43D4 **Andover** Eng
35A2 **Andradina** Brazil
12B2 **Andreafsky** USA
92B2 **Andreas,C** Cyprus
53C2 **Andria** Italy
11C4 **Andros** *I* The Bahamas
55B3 **Ándros** *I* Greece
87A2 **Androth** *I* India
50B2 **Andújar** Spain
100A2 **Andulo** Angola
97C4 **Anécho** Togo
97C3 **Anéfis** Mali
34B3 **Añelo** Arg
63C2 **Angarsk** Russian Fed
38H6 **Ånge** Sweden
24A2 **Angel de la Guarda** *I* Mexico
79B2 **Angeles** Phil
39G7 **Angelholm** Sweden
109C1 **Angellala Creek** *R* Aust
22B1 **Angels Camp** USA
71E4 **Angemuk** *Mt* Indon
48B2 **Angers** France
76C3 **Angkor** *Hist Site* Camb
41C3 **Anglesey** *I* Wales
19A4 **Angleton** USA
6G3 **Angmagssalik** Greenland
101D2 **Angoche** Mozam
29B3 **Angol** Chile
14B2 **Angola** Indiana, USA
100A2 **Angola** Republic, Africa
103H6 **Angola Basin** Atlantic O
12H3 **Angoon** USA
48C2 **Angoulême** France
96A1 **Angra do Heroismo** Açores
35C2 **Angra dos Reis** Brazil
34C3 **Anguil** Arg
27E3 **Anguilla** *I* Caribbean S
26B2 **Anguilla Cays** *Is* Caribbean S
86B2 **Angul** India
99C3 **Angumu** Zaïre
56C1 **Anholt** *I* Den
73C4 **Anhua** China
72D3 **Anhui** Province, China
12C2 **Aniak** USA
35B1 **Anicuns** Brazil
46B2 **Anizy-le-Château** France
4C3 **Anjak** USA
48B2 **Anjou** Republic, France
101D2 **Anjouan** *I* Comoros
101D2 **Anjozorobe** Madag
74B3 **Anju** N Korea
72B3 **Ankang** China
92B2 **Ankara** Turk
101D2 **Ankaratra** *Mt* Madag
101D3 **Ankazoabo** Madag
101D2 **Ankazobe** Madag
56C2 **Anklam** Germany
76D3 **An Loc** Viet
73B4 **Anlong** China
73C3 **Anlu** China
18C2 **Anna** USA
96C1 **'Annaba** Alg
92C3 **An Nabk** S Arabia
92C3 **An Nabk** Syria
108A1 **Anna Creek** Aust
80C3 **An Nafūd** *Desert* S Arabia
93D3 **An Najaf** Iraq
42C2 **Annan** Scot
15C3 **Annapolis** USA
86A1 **Annapurna** *Mt* Nepal
14B2 **Ann Arbor** USA
94C1 **An Nāsirah** Syria
93E3 **An Nāsirīyah** Iraq
47B2 **Annecy** France
47B1 **Annemasse** France
76D3 **An Nhon** Viet
73A5 **Anning** China
17A1 **Anniston** USA
89E8 **Annobon** *I* Eq Guinea
49C2 **Annonay** France
27J1 **Annotto Bay** Jamaica
73D3 **Anqing** China
72B2 **Ansai** China
57C3 **Ansbach** Germany
26C3 **Anse d'Hainault** Haiti
72E1 **Anshan** China
73B4 **Anshun** China
97C3 **Ansongo** Mali
14B3 **Ansted** USA
92C2 **Antakya** Turk
101E2 **Antalaha** Madag
92B2 **Antalya** Turk
92B2 **Antalya Körfezi** *B* Turk
101D2 **Antananarivo** Madag
112C1 **Antarctic Circle** Ant
112C3 **Antarctic Pen** Ant
50B2 **Antequera** Spain
96B2 **Anti-Atlas** *Mts* Mor
7D5 **Anticosti, Î. d'** Can
27E3 **Antigua** *I* Caribbean S
Anti Lebanon = Jebel esh Sharqi
21A2 **Antioch** USA
19A3 **Antlers** USA
30B3 **Antofagasta** Chile
45C1 **Antrim** County, N Ire
45C1 **Antrim** N Ire
45C1 **Antrim Hills** N Ire
101D2 **Antseranana** Madag
101D2 **Antsirabe** Madag
101D2 **Antsohiny** Madag
76D3 **An Tuc** Viet
46C1 **Antwerpen** Belg
45C2 **An Uaimh** Irish Rep
84C3 **Anupgarh** India
87C3 **Anuradhapura** Sri Lanka
Anvers = Antwerpen
4B3 **Anvik** USA
63B3 **Anxi** China
72C2 **Anyang** China
72A3 **A'nyêmaqên Shan** *Upland* China
47C2 **Anza** *R* Italy
13E1 **Anzac** Can
65K4 **Anzhero-Sudzhensk** Russian Fed
53B2 **Anzio** Italy
74E2 **Aomori** Japan
52A1 **Aosta** Italy
97B3 **Aoukar** *Desert Region* Maur
96C2 **Aoulef** Alg
95A2 **Aozou** Chad
30E3 **Apa** *R* Brazil/Par
11B4 **Apalachee B** USA
17B2 **Apalachicola** USA
17A2 **Apalachicola B** USA
23B2 **Apan** Mexico
64E3 **Apatity** Russian Fed
32C3 **Apaporis** *R* Colombia
35A2 **Aparecida do Taboado** Brazil
79B2 **Aparri** Phil
54A1 **Apatin** Croatia
64E3 **Apatity** Russian Fed
24B3 **Apatzingan** Mexico
56B2 **Apeldoorn** Neth
35B2 **Apiai** Brazil
33F2 **Apoera** Surinam
108B3 **Apollo Bay** Aust
79C4 **Apo,Mt** *Mt* Phil
17B2 **Apopka,L** USA
30F2 **Aporé** *R* Brazil
10A2 **Apostle Is** USA
10A2 **Apostle L** USA
23A1 **Apozol** Mexico
11B3 **Appalachian Mts** USA
52B2 **Appennino Abruzzese** *Mts* Italy
52A2 **Appennino Ligure** *Mts* Italy
53C2 **Appennino Lucano** *Mts* Italy
53B2 **Appennino Napoletano** *Mts* Italy
52B2 **Appennino Tosco-Emilliano** *Mts* Italy
52B2 **Appennino Umbro-Marchigiano** *Mts* Italy
47C1 **Appenzell** Switz
42C2 **Appleby** Eng
14A2 **Appleton** Wisconsin, USA
30F3 **Apucarana** Brazil
23B1 **Apulco** Mexico
32D2 **Apure** *R* Ven
32C6 **Apurimac** *R* Peru
92C4 **'Aqaba** Jordan
92B4 **'Aqaba,G of** Egypt/ S Arabia
90B3 **'Aqdā** Iran
30E3 **Aquidauana** Brazil
23A2 **Aquila** Mexico
86A1 **Ara** India
17A1 **Arab** USA
81D4 **Arabian** *S* Asia/ Arabian Pen
31D4 **Aracajú** Brazil
30E3 **Aracanguy, Mts de** Par
31D2 **Aracati** Brazil
30F3 **Araçatuba** Brazil
50A2 **Aracena** Spain
31C5 **Araçuai** Brazil
94B3 **Arad** Israel
60B4 **Arad** Rom
98C1 **Arada** Chad
91B5 **'Arādah** UAE
106C1 **Arafura S** Indon/Aust
30F2 **Aragarças** Brazil
51B1 **Aragón** Region, Spain
50B1 **Aragon** *R* Spain
33G6 **Araguaia** *R* Brazil
31B3 **Araguaína** Brazil
31B5 **Araguari** Brazil
35B1 **Araguari** *R* Brazil
75B1 **Arai** Japan
96C2 **Arak** Alg
90A3 **Arāk** Iran
76A2 **Arakan Yoma** *Mts* Burma
87B2 **Arakkonam** India
93E2 **Araks** *R* Azerbaijan
Aral S = Aral'skoye More
80E1 **Aral'sk** Kazakhstan
65G5 **Aral'skoye More** *S* Kazakhstan/ Uzbekistan
40B2 **Aran** *I* Irish Rep
50B1 **Aranda de Duero** Spain
23A1 **Arandas** Mexico
50B1 **Aranjuez** Spain
75A2 **Arao** Japan
97B3 **Araouane** Mali
29E2 **Arapey** *R* Urug
31D4 **Arapiraca** Brazil
35A2 **Araporgas** Brazil
30G4 **Ararangua** Brazil
31B6 **Araraquara** Brazil
35B2 **Araras** Brazil
93D2 **Ararat** Armenia
107D4 **Ararat** Aust
93D1 **Aras** *R* Turk
75C1 **Arato** Japan
32D2 **Arauca** *R* Ven
34A3 **Arauco** Chile
32C2 **Arauea** Colombia
85C4 **Arāvalli Range** *Mts* India
31B5 **Araxá** Brazil
99D2 **Arba Minch** Eth
53A3 **Arbatax** Sardegna
93D2 **Arbīl** Iraq
47A1 **Arbois** France
39H6 **Arbrå** Sweden
44C3 **Arbroath** Scot
47A1 **Arc** France
47B2 **Arc** *R* France
48B3 **Arcachon** France
17B2 **Arcadia** USA
20B2 **Arcata** USA
23A2 **Arcelia** Mexico
26B2 **Archipiélago de Camaguey** *Arch* Cuba
29B6 **Archipiélago de la Reina Adelaida** *Arch* Chile
29B4 **Archipiélago de las Chones** *Arch* Chile
32B2 **Archipiélago de las Perlas** *Arch* Panama
35B2 **Arcos** Brazil
50A2 **Arcos de la Frontera** Spain
6B2 **Arctic Bay** Can
1C1 **Arctic Circle**
4E3 **Arctic Red** Can
4E3 **Arctic Red R** Can
4D3 **Arctic Village** USA
54C2 **Arda** *R* Bulg
65F6 **Ardabīl** Iran
93D1 **Ardahan** Turk
39F6 **Ardal** Nor
96C2 **Ardar des Iforas** *Upland* Alg/Mali
45C2 **Ardee** Irish Rep
90B3 **Ardekān** Iran
46C2 **Ardennes** Department, France
57A2 **Ardennes** Region, Belg
90B3 **Ardestan** Iran
92C3 **Ardh es Suwwan** *Desert Region* Jordan
50A2 **Ardila** *R* Port
109C2 **Ardlethan** Aust
9D3 **Ardmore** USA
44A3 **Ardnamurchan** *Pt* Scot
46A1 **Ardres** France

44B3 **Ardrishaig** Scot
42B2 **Ardrossan** Scot
27D3 **Arecibo** Puerto Rico
31D2 **Areia Branca** Brazil
21A2 **Arena,Pt** USA
39F7 **Arendal** Nor
30B2 **Arequipa** Peru
52B2 **Arezzo** Italy
52B2 **Argenta** Italy
49C2 **Argentan** France
46B2 **Argenteuil** France
28C7 **Argentina** Republic, S America
103F7 **Argentine Basin** Atlantic O
48C2 **Argenton-sur-Creuse** France
54C2 **Argeş** *R* Rom
84B2 **Arghardab** *R* Afghan
55B3 **Argolikós Kólpos** *G* Greece
46C2 **Argonne** Region, France
55B3 **Árgos** Greece
55B3 **Argostólion** Greece
22B3 **Arguello,Pt** USA
106B2 **Argyle,L** Aust
56C1 **Århus** Den
100A3 **Ariamsvlei** Namibia
50B1 **Arian zón** *R* Spain
34C2 **Arias** Arg
97B3 **Aribinda** Burkina
30B2 **Arica** Chile
84C2 **Arifwala** Pak
Arihā = Jericho
27L1 **Arima** Trinidad
35B1 **Arinos** Brazil
33F6 **Arinos** *R* Brazil
23A2 **Ario de Rosales** Mexico
27L1 **Aripo,Mt** Trinidad
33E5 **Aripuana** Brazil
33E5 **Aripuanã** *R* Brazil
44B3 **Arisaig** Scot
87B2 **Ariskere** India
13B2 **Aristazabal I** Can
34B3 **Arizona** Arg
9B3 **Arizona** State, USA
39G7 **Årjäng** Sweden
61F3 **Arkadak** Russian Fed
19B3 **Arkadelphia** USA
65H4 **Arkaly** Kazakhstan
11A3 **Arkansas** State, USA
11A3 **Arkansas** *R* USA
18A2 **Arkansas City** USA
64F3 **Arkhangel'sk** Russian Fed
41B3 **Arklow** Irish Rep
47D1 **Arlberg P** Austria
49C3 **Arles** France
19A3 **Arlington** Texas, USA
15C3 **Arlington** Virginia, USA
20B1 **Arlington** Washington, USA
97C3 **Arlit** Niger
57B3 **Arlon** Belg
Armageddon = Megiddo
45C1 **Armagh** County, N Ire
45C1 **Armagh** N Ire
61F5 **Armavir** Russian Fed
23A2 **Armena** Mexico
32B3 **Armenia** Colombia
65F5 **Armenia** Republic, Europe
107E4 **Armidale** Aust
13D2 **Armstrong** Can
7C3 **Arnaud** *R* Can
92B2 **Arnauti** *C* Cyprus
56B2 **Arnhem** Neth
106C2 **Arnhem,C** Aust
106C2 **Arnhem Land** Aust
22B1 **Arnold** USA
15C1 **Arnprior** Can
46E1 **Arnsberg** Germany
100A3 **Aroab** Namibia
47C2 **Arona** Italy
12B2 **Aropuk L** USA
52A1 **Arosa** Switz
97A3 **Arquipélago dos Bijagós** *Arch* Guinea-Bissau
93D3 **Ar Ramādī** Iraq
42B2 **Arran** *I* Scot
93C2 **Ar Raqqah** Syria
95A2 **Ar Rāqūbah** Libya
49C1 **Arras** France
96A2 **Arrecife** Canary Is
34C2 **Arrecifes** Arg
23A1 **Arriaga** Mexico
93E3 **Ar Rifā't** Iraq
93E3 **Ar Rihāb** *Desert Region* Iraq
91A5 **Ar Riyāḍ** S Arabia
44B3 **Arrochar** Scot
111A2 **Arrowtown** NZ
23B1 **Arroyo Seco** Mexico
91B4 **Ar Ru'ays** Qatar
91C5 **Ar Rustaq** Oman
93D3 **Ar Rutbah** Iraq
47D2 **Arsiero** Italy
49D2 **Arsizio** Italy
61G2 **Arsk** Russian Fed
55B3 **Árta** Greece
23A2 **Arteaga** Mexico
63B2 **Artemovsk** Russian Fed
63D2 **Artemovskiy** Russian Fed
9C3 **Artesia** USA
111B2 **Arthurs P** NZ
112C2 **Artigas** *Base* Ant
29E2 **Artigas** Urug
4H3 **Artillery L** Can
48C1 **Artois** Region, France
112C2 **Arturo Prat** *Base* Ant
93D1 **Artvin** Turk
99D2 **Aru** Zaïre
33G6 **Aruanã** Brazil
27C4 **Aruba** *I* Caribbean S
86B1 **Arun** *R* Nepal
86C1 **Arunāchal Pradesh** Union Territory, India
87B3 **Aruppukkottai** India
99D3 **Arusha** Tanz
98C2 **Aruwimi** *R* Zaïre
68C2 **Arvayheer** Mongolia
47B2 **Arve** *R* France
7C5 **Arvida** Can
38H5 **Arvidsjaur** Sweden
39G7 **Arvika** Sweden
21B2 **Arvin** USA
94B1 **Arwad** *I* Syria
61F2 **Arzamas** Russian Fed
84C2 **Asadabad** Afghan
75A2 **Asahi** *R* Japan
74E2 **Asahi dake** *Mt* Japan
74E2 **Asahikawa** Japan
86B2 **Asansol** India
95A2 **Asawanwah** *Well* Libya
61K2 **Asbest** Russian Fed
15D2 **Asbury Park** USA
103H5 **Ascension** *I* Atlantic O
57B3 **Aschaffenburg** Germany
56C2 **Aschersleben** Germany
52B2 **Ascoli Piceno** Italy
47C1 **Ascona** Switz
99E1 **Aseb** Eth
96C2 **Asedjirad** *Upland* Alg
99D2 **Āsela** Eth
38H6 **Åsele** Sweden
54B2 **Asenovgrad** Bulg
46C2 **Asfeld** France
61J2 **Asha** Russian Fed
17B1 **Ashburn** USA
111B2 **Ashburton** NZ
106A3 **Ashburton** *R* Aust
92B3 **Ashdod** Israel
19B3 **Ashdown** USA
11B3 **Asheville** USA
109D1 **Ashford** Aust
43E4 **Ashford** Eng
74D3 **Ashikaga** Japan
75A2 **Ashizuri-misaki** *Pt* Japan
65G6 **Ashkhabad** Turkmenistan
10B3 **Ashland** Kentucky, USA
18A1 **Ashland** Nebraska, USA
14B2 **Ashland** Ohio, USA
8A2 **Ashland** Oregon, USA
109C1 **Ashley** Aust
16B2 **Ashokan Res** USA
94B3 **Ashqelon** Israel
93D3 **Ash Shabakh** Iraq
91C4 **Ash Sha'm** UAE
93D2 **Ash Sharqāt** Iraq
93E3 **Ash Shatrah** Iraq
81C4 **Ash Shihr** Yemen
91A4 **Ash Shumlul** S Arabia
14B2 **Ashtabula** USA
7D4 **Ashuanipi L** Can
92C3 **'Aṣī** *R* Syria
47D2 **Asiago** Italy
53A2 **Asinara** *I* Medit S
65K4 **Asino** Russian Fed
93D2 **Aşkale** Turk
39G7 **Askersund** Sweden
84C1 **Asmar** Afghan
95C3 **Asmera** Eth
75A2 **Aso** Japan
99D1 **Asosa** Eth
111A2 **Aspiring,Mt** NZ
93C2 **As Sabkhah** Syria
91A5 **As Salamiyah** S Arabia
92C2 **As Salamīyah** Syria
93D3 **As Salmān** Iraq
86C1 **Assam** State, India
93E3 **As Samāwah** Iraq
91B5 **As Ṣanām** Region, S Arabia
94C2 **As Sanamayn** Syria
56B2 **Assen** Neth
56B1 **Assens** Den
95A1 **As Sidrah** Libya
5H5 **Assiniboia** Can
5G4 **Assiniboine,Mt** Can
30F3 **Assis** Brazil
93C3 **As Sukhnah** Syria
91A5 **As Summan** Region, S Arabia
99E3 **Assumption** *I* Seychelles
92C3 **As Suwaydā'** Syria
93D3 **As Suwayrah** Iraq
93E2 **Astara** Azerbaijan
52A2 **Asti** Italy
55C3 **Astipálaia** *I* Greece
50A1 **Astorga** Spain
8A2 **Astoria** USA
61G4 **Astrakhan'** Russian Fed
50A1 **Asturias** Region, Spain
30E4 **Asunción** Par
99D2 **Aswa** *R* Uganda
80B3 **Aswân** Egypt
95C2 **Aswân High Dam** Egypt
95C2 **Asyût** Egypt
92C3 **As Zilaf** Syria
97C4 **Atakpamé** Togo
71D4 **Atambua** Indon
6E3 **Atangmik** Greenland
96A2 **Atar** Maur
65J5 **Atasu** Kazakhstan
95C3 **Atatisk Baraji** *Res* Turkmenistan
95C3 **Atbara** Sudan
65H4 **Atbasar** Kazakhstan
11A4 **Atchafalaya B** USA
10A3 **Atchison** USA
16B3 **Atco** USA
23A1 **Atenguillo** Mexico
52B2 **Atessa** Italy
46B1 **Ath** Belg
13E2 **Athabasca** Can
5G4 **Athabasca** *R* Can
5H4 **Athabasca L** Can
45B2 **Athenry** Irish Rep
Athens = Athínai
11B3 **Athens** Georgia, USA
14B3 **Athens** Ohio, USA
19A3 **Athens** Texas, USA
55B3 **Athínai** Greece
41B3 **Athlone** Irish Rep
16C1 **Athol** USA
55B2 **Áthos** *Mt* Greece
45C2 **Athy** Irish Rep
98B1 **Ati** Chad
7A5 **Atikoken** Can
61F3 **Atkarsk** Russian Fed
18B2 **Atkins** USA
23B2 **Atlacomulco** Mexico
11B3 **Atlanta** Georgia, USA
14B2 **Atlanta** Michigan, USA
18A1 **Atlantic** USA
10C3 **Atlantic City** USA
16B2 **Atlantic Highlands** USA
103H8 **Atlantic Indian Basin** Atlantic O
103H7 **Atlantic Indian Ridge** Atlantic O
96C1 **Atlas Saharien** *Mts* Alg
4E4 **Atlin** Can
4E4 **Atlin L** Can
94B2 **'Atlit** Israel
23B2 **Atlixco** Mexico
11B3 **Atmore** USA
101D3 **Atofinandrahana** Madag
12D3 **Atognak I** USA
19A3 **Atoka** USA
23A1 **Atotonilco** Mexico
23B2 **Atoyac** *R* Mexico
32B2 **Atrato** *R* Colombia
91B5 **Attaf** Region, UAE
81C3 **At Tā'if** S Arabia
94C2 **At Tall** Syria
17A1 **Attalla** USA
7B4 **Attauapiskat** Can
7B4 **Attauapiskat** *R* Can
93D3 **At Taysīyah** *Desert Region* S Arabia
14A2 **Attica** Indiana, USA
46C2 **Attigny** France
15D2 **Attleboro** Massachusetts, USA
76D3 **Attopeu** Laos
92C4 **At Tubayq** *Upland* S Arabia
34B3 **Atuel** *R* Arg
39H7 **Atvidaberg** Sweden
22B2 **Atwater** USA
49D3 **Aubagne** France
46C2 **Aube** Department, France
49C3 **Aubenas** France
17A1 **Auburn** Alabama, USA
21A2 **Auburn** California, USA
14A2 **Auburn** Indiana, USA
18A1 **Auburn** Nebraska, USA
15C2 **Auburn** New York, USA
20B1 **Auburn** Washington, USA
48C3 **Auch** France
110B1 **Auckland** NZ
105G6 **Auckland Is** NZ
48C3 **Aude** *R* France
7B4 **Auden** Can
47B1 **Audincourt** France
109C1 **Augathella** Aust
57C3 **Augsburg** Germany
106A4 **Augusta** Aust
11B3 **Augusta** Georgia, USA
18A2 **Augusta** Kansas, USA
10D2 **Augusta** Maine, USA
12D3 **Augustine I** USA
58C2 **Augustow** Pol
106A3 **Augustus,Mt** Aust

46A2 **Aumale** France
85D3 **Auraiya** India
85D5 **Aurangābād** India
96C1 **Aurès** *Mts* Alg
48C3 **Aurillac** France
8C3 **Aurora** Colorado, USA
10B2 **Aurora** Illinois, USA
14B3 **Aurora** Indiana, USA
18B2 **Aurora** Mississippi, USA
100A3 **Aus** Namibia
14B2 **Au Sable** USA
10A2 **Austin** Minnesota, USA
21B2 **Austin** Nevada, USA
9D3 **Austin** Texas, USA
107D4 **Australian Alps** *Mts* Aust
37E4 **Austria** Federal Republic, Europe
46A1 **Authie** *R* France
24B3 **Autlán** Mexico
49C2 **Autun** France
49C2 **Auvergne** Region, France
49C2 **Auxerre** France
46B1 **Auxi-le-Château** France
49C2 **Avallon** France
22C4 **Avalon** USA
7E5 **Avalon Pen** Can
35B2 **Avaré** Brazil
90D3 **Avaz** Iran
94B3 **Avedat** *Hist Site* Israel
33F4 **Aveíro** Brazil
50A1 **Aveiro** Port
29E2 **Avellaneda** Arg
53B2 **Avellino** Italy
46B1 **Avesnes-sur-Helpe** France
39H6 **Avesta** Sweden
52B2 **Avezzano** Italy
44C3 **Aviemore** Scot
111B2 **Aviemore,L** NZ
47B2 **Avigliana** Italy
49C3 **Avignon** France
50B1 **Avila** Spain
50A1 **Aviles** Spain
47D1 **Avisio** *R* Italy
108B3 **Avoca** *R* Aust
43C4 **Avon** County, Eng
43D4 **Avon** *R* Dorset, Eng
43D3 **Avon** *R* Warwick, Eng
43C4 **Avonmouth** Wales
17B2 **Avon Park** USA
46B2 **Avre** *R* France
54A2 **Avtovac** Bosnia & Herzegovina, Yugos
94C2 **A'waj** *R* Syria
74D4 **Awaji-shima** *B* Japan
99E2 **Awarē** Eth
111A2 **Awarua Pt** NZ
99E2 **Awash** Eth
99E2 **Awash** *R* Eth
75B1 **Awa-shima** *I* Japan
111B2 **Awatere** *R* NZ
95A2 **Awbārī** Libya
98C2 **Aweil** Sudan
95B2 **Awjilah** Libya
96A2 **Awserd** *Well* Mor
6A2 **Axel Heiburg I** Can
43C4 **Axminster** Eng
75B1 **Ayabe** Japan
29E3 **Ayacucho** Arg
32C6 **Ayacucho** Peru
65K5 **Ayaguz** Kazakhstan
82C2 **Ayakkum Hu** *L* China
50A2 **Ayamonte** Spain
63F2 **Ayan** Russian Fed
32C6 **Ayauiri** Peru
92A2 **Aydin** Turk
55C3 **Áyios Evstrátios** *I* Greece
43D4 **Aylesbury** Eng
13D2 **Aylmer,Mt** Can
94C2 **'Ayn al Fījah** Syria
93D2 **Ayn Zālah** Iraq
95B2 **Ayn Zuwayyah** *Well* Libya
99D2 **Ayod** Sudan
107D2 **Ayr** Aust
42B2 **Ayr** Scot
42B2 **Ayr** *R* Scot
42B2 **Ayre,Pt of** Eng
54C2 **Aytos** Bulg
76C3 **Aytthaya** Thai
23A1 **Ayutla** Mexico
55C3 **Ayvacik** Turk
55C3 **Ayvalik** Turk
86A1 **Āzamgarh** India
97B3 **Azaouad** *Desert Region* Mali
97D3 **Azare** Nig
92C2 **A'Zāz** Syria
Azbine = Aïr
65F5 **Azerbaijan** Republic, Russian Fed
32B4 **Azogues** Ecuador
Azores = Açores
98C1 **Azoum** *R* Chad
60E4 **Azovskoye More** *S* Russian Fed/Ukraine
96B1 **Azrou** Mor
34D3 **Azucena** Arg
32A2 **Azuero,Pen de** Panama
29E3 **Azúl** Arg
94C2 **Az-Zabdānī** Syria
91C5 **Az Zāhirah** *Mts* Oman
95A2 **Az Zahra** Libya
96A2 **Azzeffal** *R* Maur
93E3 **Az Zubayr** Iraq

B

94B2 **Ba'abda** Leb
92C3 **Ba'albek** Leb
94B3 **Ba'al Hazor** *Mt* Israel
99E2 **Baardheere** Somalia
54C2 **Babadag** Rom
92A1 **Babaeski** Turk
32B4 **Babahoyo** Ecuador
81C4 **Bāb al Mandab** *Str* Djibouti/Yemen
71D4 **Babar** *I* Indon
99D3 **Babati** Tanz
60E2 **Babayevo** Russian Fed
14B2 **Baberton** USA
13B1 **Babine** *R* Can
5F4 **Babine L** Can
90B2 **Bābol** Iran
79B2 **Babuyan Chan** Phil
79B2 **Babuyan Is** Phil
31C2 **Bacabal** Brazil
71D4 **Bacan** *I* Indon
60C4 **Bačau** Rom
76D1 **Bac Can** Viet
108B3 **Bacchus Marsh** Aust
82B2 **Bachu** China
4J3 **Back** *R* Can
12J2 **Backbone Ranges** *Mts* Can
76D1 **Bac Ninh** Viet
79B3 **Bacolod** Phil
79B3 **Baco,Mt** Phil
87B2 **Badagara** India
72A1 **Badain Jaran Shamo** *Desert* China
50A2 **Badajoz** Spain
51C1 **Badalona** Spain
93D3 **Badanah** S Arabia
46D2 **Bad Bergzabern** Germany
46D1 **Bad Ems** Germany
47C1 **Baden** Switz
57B3 **Baden-Baden** Germany
57B3 **Baden-Württemberg** State, Germany
57C3 **Badgastein** Austria
22C2 **Badger** USA
57B2 **Bad-Godesberg** Germany
57B2 **Bad Hersfeld** Germany
46D1 **Bad Honnef** Germany
85B4 **Badin** Pak
52B1 **Bad Ischl** Austria
93C3 **Badiyat ash Sham** *Desert Region* Jordan/Iraq
57B3 **Bad-Kreuznach** Germany
46D1 **Bad Nevenahr-Ahrweiler** Germany
47C1 **Bad Ragaz** Switz
57C3 **Bad Tolz** Germany
87C3 **Badulla** Sri Lanka
50B2 **Baena** Spain
97A3 **Bafatá** Guinea-Bissau
4H2 **Baffin** *Region* Can
6C2 **Baffin B** Greenland/Can
6C2 **Baffin I** Can
98B2 **Bafia** Cam
97A3 **Bafing** *R* Mali
97A3 **Bafoulabé** Mali
98B2 **Bafoussam** Cam
90C3 **Bāfq** Iran
60E5 **Bafra Burun** *Pt* Turk
91C4 **Bāft** Iran
98C2 **Bafwasende** Zaïre
86A1 **Bagaha** India
87B1 **Bāgalkot** India
99D3 **Bagamoyo** Tanz
29F2 **Bagé** Brazil
93D3 **Baghdād** Iraq
86B2 **Bagherhat** Bang
91C3 **Bāghīn** Iran
84B1 **Baghlan** Afghan
49C3 **Bagnols-sur-Cèze** France
97B3 **Bagoé** *R* Mali
79B2 **Baguio** Phil
86B1 **Bāhādurābād** India
11C4 **Bahamas,The** *Is* Caribbean S
86B2 **Baharampur** India
92A4 **Baharīya Oasis** Egypt
84C3 **Bahawalpur** Pak
84C3 **Bahawalpur** Province, Pak
85C3 **Bahawathagar** Pak
Bahia = Salvador
31C4 **Bahia** State, Brazil
29D3 **Bahía Blanca** Arg
29D3 **Bahía Blanca** *B* Arg
34A3 **Bahia Concepción** *B* Chile
35C2 **Bahia da Ilha Grande** *B* Brazil
24B2 **Bahia de Banderas** *B* Mexico
24C2 **Bahia de Campeche** *B* Mexico
25D3 **Bahia de la Ascension** *B* Mexico
24B3 **Bahia de Petacalco** *B* Mexico
96A2 **Bahia de Rio de Oro** *B* Mor
35C2 **Bahia de Sepetiba** *B* Brazil
29C6 **Bahía Grande** *B* Arg
9B4 **Bahia Kino** Mexico
24A2 **Bahia Magdalena** *B* Mexico
24A2 **Bahia Sebastia Vizcaino** *B* Mexico
99D1 **Bahar Dar** Eth
86A1 **Bahraich** India
80D3 **Bahrain** Sheikdom, Arabian Pen
93D3 **Bahr al Milh** *L* Iraq
98C2 **Bahr Aouk** *R* Chad/CAR
Bahrat Lut = Dead S
98C2 **Bahr el Arab** *Watercourse* Sudan
99D2 **Bahr el Ghazal** *R* Sudan
98B1 **Bahr el Ghazal** *Watercourse* Chad
101H1 **Baia de Maputo** *B* Mozam
31B2 **Baia de Marajó** *B* Brazil
101D2 **Baiá de Pemba** *B* Mozam
31C2 **Baia de São Marcos** *B* Brazil
50A2 **Baia de Setúbal** *B* Port
31D4 **Baia de Todos os Santos** *B* Brazil
100A2 **Baia dos Tigres** Angola
60B4 **Baia Mare** Rom
98B2 **Baïbokoum** Chad
69E2 **Baicheng** China
101E2 **Baie Antongila** *B* Madag
7D5 **Baie-Comeau** Can
101D2 **Baie de Bombetoka** *B* Madag
101D2 **Baie de Mahajamba** *B* Madag
101D3 **Baie de St Augustin** *B* Madag
94B2 **Baie de St Georges** *B* Leb
10D2 **Baie des Chaleurs** *B* Can
7C4 **Baie-du-Poste** Can
72B3 **Baihe** China
72C3 **Bai He** *R* China
93D3 **Ba'ījī** Iraq
86A2 **Baikunthpur** India
Baile Atha Cliath = Dublin
54B2 **Băilesti** Rom
46B1 **Bailleul** France
72A3 **Baima** China
17B1 **Bainbridge** USA
12B2 **Baird Inlet** USA
4B3 **Baird Mts** USA
72D1 **Bairin Youqi** China
72D1 **Bairin Zuoqi** China
107D4 **Bairnsdale** Aust
79B4 **Bais** Phil
54A1 **Baja** Hung
9B3 **Baja California** State, Mexico
24A1 **Baja California** *Pen* Mexico
61J2 **Bakal** Russian Fed
98C2 **Bakala** CAR
97A3 **Bakel** Sen
8C2 **Baker** Montana, USA
8B2 **Baker** Oregon, USA
6A3 **Baker Foreland** *Pt* Can
4J3 **Baker L** Can
4J3 **Baker Lake** Can
8A2 **Baker,Mt** USA
9B3 **Bakersfield** USA
90C2 **Bakharden** Turkmenistan
90C2 **Bakhardok** Turkmenistan
60D3 **Bakhmach** Ukraine
38C1 **Bakkaflói** *B* Iceland
99D2 **Bako** Eth
98C2 **Bakouma** CAR
65F5 **Baku** Azerbaijan
92B2 **Balâ** Turk
79A4 **Balabac** *I* Phil
70C3 **Balabac** *Str* Malay
78C2 **Balaikarangan** Indon
108A2 **Balaklava** Aust
61G3 **Balakovo** Russian Fed
86A2 **Balāngīr** India
61F3 **Balashov** Russian Fed
86B2 **Balasore** India
80A3 **Balât** Egypt
52C1 **Balaton** *L* Hung
45C2 **Balbriggan** Irish Rep
29E3 **Balcarce** Arg
54C2 **Balchik** Bulg
111B3 **Balclutha** NZ
18B2 **Bald Knob** USA
17B1 **Baldwin** USA
9C3 **Baldy Peak** *Mt* USA
Balearic Is = Islas Baleares
78C2 **Baleh** *R* Malay
79B2 **Baler** Phil
61H2 **Balezino** Russian Fed
106A1 **Bali** *I* Indon
92A2 **Balıkesir** Turk

93C2 **Balīkh** *R* Syria
78D3 **Balikpapan** Indon
79B2 **Balintang Chan** Phil
78C4 **Bali S** Indon
35A1 **Baliza** Brazil
84B1 **Balkh** Afghan
65J5 **Balkhash** Kazakhstan
44B3 **Ballachulish** Scot
45B2 **Ballaghaderreen** Irish Rep
42B2 **Ballantrae** Scot
4G2 **Ballantyne Str** Can
87B2 **Ballapur** India
107D4 **Ballarat** Aust
44C3 **Ballater** Scot
112C7 **Balleny Is** Ant
86A1 **Ballia** India
109D1 **Ballina** Aust
41B3 **Ballina** Irish Rep
45B2 **Ballinasloe** Irish Rep
45B2 **Ballinrobe** Irish Rep
55A2 **Ballsh** Alb
45B1 **Ballycastle** Irish Rep
45C1 **Ballycastle** N Ire
45C1 **Ballymena** N Ire
45C1 **Ballymoney** N Ire
45B1 **Ballyshannon** Irish Rep
45B2 **Ballyvaghan** Irish Rep
108B3 **Balmoral** Aust
34C2 **Balnearia** Arg
84B3 **Balochistān** Region, Pak
100A2 **Balombo** Angola
109C1 **Balonn** *R* Aust
85C3 **Balotra** India
86A1 **Balrāmpur** India
107D4 **Balranald** Aust
31B3 **Balsas** Brazil
23B2 **Balsas** Mexico
24B3 **Balsas** *R* Mexico
60C4 **Balta** Ukraine
39H7 **Baltic S** N Europe
92B3 **Baltîm** Egypt
45B3 **Baltimore** Irish Rep
10C3 **Baltimore** USA
86B1 **Bālurghāt** India
61H4 **Balykshi** Kazakhstan
91C4 **Bam** Iran
98B1 **Bama** Nig
97B3 **Bamako** Mali
98C2 **Bambari** CAR
17B1 **Bamberg** USA
57C3 **Bamberg** Germany
98C2 **Bambili** Zaïre
35B2 **Bambui** Brazil
98B2 **Bamenda** Cam
13C3 **Bamfield** Can
98B2 **Bamingui** *R* CAR
98B2 **Bamingui Bangoran** *National Park* CAR
84B2 **Bamiyan** Afghan
91D4 **Bampur** Iran
91D4 **Bampur** *R* Iran
98C2 **Banalia** Zaïre
97B3 **Banamba** Mali
76C3 **Ban Aranyaprathet** Thai
76C2 **Ban Ban** Laos
77C4 **Ban Betong** Thai
45C1 **Banbridge** N Ire
43D3 **Banbury** Eng
44C3 **Banchory** Scot
25D3 **Banco Chinchorro** *Is* Mexico
15C1 **Bancroft** Can
86A1 **Bānda** India
70A3 **Banda Aceh** Indon
97B4 **Bandama** *R* Ivory Coast
91C4 **Bandar Abbās** Iran
90A2 **Bandar Anzalī** Iran
99F2 **Bandarbeyla** Somalia
91B4 **Bandar-e Daylam** Iran
91B4 **Bandar-e Lengheh** Iran
91B4 **Bandar-e Māqām** Iran
91B4 **Bandar-e Rig** Iran
90B2 **Bandar-e Torkoman** Iran
91A3 **Bandar Khomeynī** Iran
78C2 **Bandar Seri Begawan** Brunei
71D4 **Banda S** Indon
91C4 **Band Bonī** Iran
35C2 **Bandeira** *Mt* Brazil
97B3 **Bandiagara** Mali
60C5 **Bandirma** Turk
45B3 **Bandon** Irish Rep
98B3 **Bandundu** Zaïre
78B4 **Bandung** Indon
25E2 **Banes** Cuba
13D2 **Banff** Can
44C3 **Banff** Scot
5G4 **Banff** *R* Can
13D2 **Banff Nat Pk** Can
87B2 **Bangalore** India
98C2 **Bangassou** CAR
70C3 **Banggi** *I* Malay
95B1 **Banghāzī** Libya
76D2 **Bang Hieng** *R* Laos
78B3 **Bangka** *I* Indon
78A3 **Bangko** Indon
76C3 **Bangkok** Thai
82C3 **Bangladesh** Republic, Asia
84D2 **Bangong Co** *L* China
10D2 **Bangor** Maine, USA
45D1 **Bangor** N Ire
16B2 **Bangor** Pennsylvania, USA
42B3 **Bangor** Wales
78D3 **Bangsalsembera** Indon
76B3 **Bang Saphan Yai** Thai
79B2 **Bangued** Phil
98B2 **Bangui** CAR
100C2 **Bangweulu** *L* Zambia
77C4 **Ban Hat Yai** Thai
76C2 **Ban Hin Heup** Laos
76C1 **Ban Houei Sai** Laos
76B3 **Ban Hua Hin** Thai
97B3 **Bani** *R* Mali
97C3 **Bani Bangou** Niger
95A1 **Banī Walīd** Libya
92C2 **Bāniyās** Syria
94B2 **Baniyas** Syria
52C2 **Banja Luka** Bosnia & Herzegovina, Yugos
78C3 **Banjarmasin** Indon
97A3 **Banjul** The Gambia
77B4 **Ban Kantang** Thai
76D2 **Ban Khemmarat** Laos
77B4 **Ban Khok Kloi** Thai
71F5 **Banks I** Aust
5E4 **Banks I** British Columbia, Can
4F2 **Banks I** Northwest Territories, Can
20C1 **Banks L** USA
111B2 **Banks Pen** NZ
109C4 **Banks Str** Aust
86B2 **Bankura** India
76B2 **Ban Mae Sariang** Thai
76B2 **Ban Mae Sot** Thai
76D3 **Ban Me Thuot** Viet
45C1 **Bann** *R* N Ire
77B4 **Ban Na San** Thai
84C2 **Bannu** Pak
34A3 **Baños Maule** Chile
76C2 **Ban Pak Neun** Laos
77C4 **Ban Pak Phanang** Thai
76D3 **Ban Ru Kroy** Camb
76B3 **Ban Sai Yok** Thai
76C3 **Ban Sattahip** Thai
59B3 **Banská Bystrica** Czech
85C4 **Bānswāra** India
77B4 **Ban Tha Kham** Thai
76D2 **Ban Thateng** Laos
76C2 **Ban Tha Tum** Thai
41B3 **Bantry** Irish Rep
41A3 **Bantry** *B* Irish Rep
76D3 **Ban Ya Soup** Viet
78C4 **Banyuwangi** Indon
72C3 **Baofeng** China
76C1 **Bao Ha** Viet
72B3 **Baoji** China
76D3 **Bao Loc** Viet
68B4 **Baoshan** China
72C1 **Baotou** China
87C1 **Bāpatla** India
46B1 **Bapaume** France
93D3 **Ba'Qūbah** Iraq
32J7 **Baquerizo Morena** Ecuador
54A2 **Bar** Montenegro, Yugos
99D1 **Bara** Sudan
99E2 **Baraawe** Somalia
78D3 **Barabai** Indon
86A1 **Bāra Banki** India
65J4 **Barabinsk** Russian Fed
65J4 **Barabinskaya Step** *Steppe* Kazakhstan/ Russian Fed
50B1 **Baracaldo** Spain
26C2 **Baracoa** Cuba
94C2 **Baradá** *R* Syria
109C2 **Baradine** Aust
87A1 **Bārāmati** India
84C2 **Baramula** Pak
85D3 **Bārān** India
79B3 **Barangas** Phil
4E4 **Baranof I** USA
60C3 **Baranovichi** Belorussia
108A2 **Baratta** Aust
86B1 **Barauni** India
31C6 **Barbacena** Brazil
27F4 **Barbados** *I* Caribbean S
51C1 **Barbastro** Spain
101H1 **Barberton** S Africa
48B2 **Barbezieux** France
32C2 **Barbòsa** Colombia
27E3 **Barbuda** *I* Caribbean S
107D3 **Barcaldine** Aust
Barce = Al Marj
53C3 **Barcellona** Italy
51C1 **Barcelona** Spain
33E1 **Barcelona** Ven
107D3 **Barcoo** *R* Aust
34B3 **Barda del Medio** Arg
95A2 **Bardai** Chad
29C3 **Bardas Blancas** Arg
86B2 **Barddhamān** India
59C3 **Bardejov** Czech
47C2 **Bardi** Italy
47B2 **Bardonecchia** Italy
43B3 **Bardsey** *I* Wales
84D3 **Bareilly** India
64D2 **Barentsøya** *I* Barents S
64E2 **Barents S** Russian Fed
95C3 **Barentu** Eth
86A2 **Bargarh** India
47B2 **Barge** Italy
63D2 **Barguzin** Russian Fed
63D2 **Barguzin** *R* Russian Fed
86B2 **Barhi** India
53C2 **Bari** Italy
51D2 **Barika** Alg
32C2 **Barinas** Ven
86B2 **Baripāda** India
85C4 **Bari Sādri** India
86C2 **Barisal** Bang
78C3 **Barito** *R* Indon
95A2 **Barjuj** *Watercourse* Libya
73A3 **Barkam** China
18C2 **Barkley,L** USA
13B3 **Barkley Sd** Can
100B4 **Barkly East** S Africa
106C2 **Barkly Tableland** *Mts* Aust
46C2 **Bar-le-Duc** France
106A3 **Barlee,L** Aust
106A3 **Barlee Range** *Mts* Aust
53C2 **Barletta** Italy
85C3 **Barmer** India
108B2 **Barmera** Aust
43B3 **Barmouth** Wales
42D2 **Barnard Castle** Eng
65K4 **Barnaul** Russian Fed
16B3 **Barnegat** USA
16B3 **Barnegat B** USA
6C2 **Barnes Icecap** Can
17B1 **Barnesville** Georgia, USA
14B3 **Barnesville** Ohio, USA
42D3 **Barnsley** Eng
43B4 **Barnstaple** Eng
97C4 **Baro** Nig
86C1 **Barpeta** India
32D1 **Barquisimeto** Ven
31C4 **Barra** Brazil
44A3 **Barra** *I* Scot
109D2 **Barraba** Aust
23A2 **Barra de Navidad** Mexico
35C2 **Barra de Piraí** Brazil
35A1 **Barragem de São Simão** *Res* Brazil
35A1 **Barra do Garças** Brazil
35B1 **Barragem Agua Vermelha** *Res* Brazil
50A2 **Barragem do Castelo do Bode** *Res* Port
50A2 **Barragem do Maranhão** *Res* Port
35A2 **Barragem Três Irmãos** *Res* Brazil
44A3 **Barra Head** *Pt* Scot
31C6 **Barra Mansa** Brazil
32B6 **Barranca** Peru
32C2 **Barrancabermeja** Colombia
33E2 **Barrancas** Ven
30E4 **Barranqueras** Arg
32C1 **Barranquilla** Colombia
44A3 **Barra,Sound of** *Chan* Scot
16C1 **Barre** USA
34B2 **Barreal** Arg
31C4 **Barreiras** Brazil
50A2 **Barreiro** Port
31D3 **Barreiros** Brazil
107D5 **Barren,C** Aust
12D3 **Barren Is** USA
31B6 **Barretos** Brazil
13E2 **Barrhead** Can
14C2 **Barrie** Can
13C2 **Barrière** Can
108B2 **Barrier Range** *Mts* Aust
107E4 **Barrington,Mt** Aust
27N2 **Barrouaillie** St Vincent
4C2 **Barrow** USA
45C2 **Barrow** *R* Irish Rep
106C3 **Barrow Creek** Aust
106A3 **Barrow I** Aust
42C2 **Barrow-in-Furness** Eng
4C2 **Barrow,Pt** USA
6A2 **Barrow Str** Can
15C1 **Barry's Bay** Can
87B1 **Barsi** India
9B3 **Barstow** USA
49C2 **Bar-sur-Aube** France
33F2 **Bartica** Guyana
92B1 **Bartın** Turk
107D2 **Bartle Frere,Mt** Aust
9D3 **Bartlesville** USA
101C3 **Bartolomeu Dias** Mozam
58C2 **Bartoszyce** Pol
78C4 **Barung** *I* Indon
85D4 **Barwāh** India
85C4 **Barwāni** India
109C1 **Barwon** *R* Aust
61G3 **Barysh** Russian Fed
98B2 **Basankusu** Zaïre
34D2 **Basavilbas** Arg
79B1 **Basco** Phil
52A1 **Basel** Switz
53C2 **Basento** *R* Italy
13E2 **Bashaw** Can
79B1 **Bashi Chan** Phil
61H3 **Bashkirskaya Respublika** Russian Fed
79B4 **Basilan** *I* Phil
43E4 **Basildon** Eng
43D4 **Basingstoke** Eng

8B2 **Basin Region** USA
93E3 **Basra** Iraq
46D2 **Bas-Rhin** Department, France
76D3 **Bassac** *R* Camb
13E2 **Bassano** Can
52B1 **Bassano** Italy
47D2 **Bassano del Grappa** Italy
97C4 **Bassari** Togo
101C3 **Bassas da India** *I* Mozam Chan
76A2 **Bassein** Burma
27E3 **Basse Terre** Guadeloupe
97C4 **Bassila** Benin
22C2 **Bass Lake** USA
107D4 **Bass Str** Aust
39G7 **Båstad** Sweden
91B4 **Bastak** Iran
86A1 **Basti** India
52A2 **Bastia** Corse
57B3 **Bastogne** Belg
19B3 **Bastrop** Louisiana, USA
19A3 **Bastrop** Texas, USA
98A2 **Bata** Eq Guinea
78C3 **Batakan** Indon
84D2 **Batala** India
68B3 **Batang** China
98B2 **Batangafo** CAR
79B1 **Batan Is** Phil
35B2 **Batatais** Brazil
15C2 **Batavia** USA
109D3 **Batemans Bay** Aust
17B1 **Batesburg** USA
18B2 **Batesville** Arkansas, USA
19C3 **Batesville** Mississippi, USA
43C4 **Bath** Eng
15C2 **Bath** New York, USA
98B1 **Batha** *R* Chad
107D4 **Bathurst** Aust
7D5 **Bathurst** Can
4F2 **Bathurst,C** Can
106C2 **Bathurst I** Aust
4H2 **Bathurst I** Can
4H3 **Bathurst Inlet** *B* Can
97B3 **Batié** Burkina
90B3 **Bātlāq-e-Gavkhūnī** *Salt Flat* Iran
109C3 **Batlow** Aust
93D2 **Batman** Turk
96C1 **Batna** Alg
11A3 **Baton Rouge** USA
94B1 **Batroun** Leb
76C3 **Battambang** Camb
87C3 **Batticaloa** Sri Lanka
13F2 **Battle** *R* Can
10B2 **Battle Creek** USA
7E4 **Battle Harbour** Can
20C2 **Battle Mountain** USA
78D2 **Batukelau** Indon
65F5 **Batumi** Georgia
77C5 **Batu Pahat** Malay
78A3 **Baturaja** Indon
94B2 **Bat Yam** Israel
71D4 **Baubau** Indon
97C3 **Bauchi** Nig
47B2 **Bauges** *Mts* France
7E4 **Bauld,C** Can
47B1 **Baumes-les-Dames** France
63D2 **Baunt** Russian Fed
31B6 **Bauru** Brazil
35A1 **Baus** Brazil
57C2 **Bautzen** Germany
78C4 **Baween** *I* Indon
95B2 **Bawîti** Egypt
97B3 **Bawku** Ghana
76B2 **Bawlake** Burma
108A2 **Bawlen** Aust
17B1 **Baxley** USA
25E2 **Bayamo** Cuba
78D4 **Bayan** Indon
68C2 **Bayandzürh** Mongolia
68B3 **Bayan Har Shan** *Mts* China
72A1 **Bayan Mod** China
72B1 **Bayan Obo** China
47A2 **Bayard** *P* France
12J3 **Bayard,Mt** Can
63D3 **Bayasgalant** Mongolia
79B3 **Baybay** Phil
93D1 **Bayburt** Turk
10B2 **Bay City** Michigan, USA
19A4 **Bay City** Texas, USA
92B2 **Bay Dağlari** Turk
64H3 **Baydaratskaya Guba** *B* Russian Fed
99E2 **Baydhabo** Somalia
48B2 **Bayeux** France
47D1 **Bayerische Alpen** *Mts* Germany
57C3 **Bayern** State, Germany
92C3 **Bāyir** Jordan
63C2 **Baykalskiy Khrebet** *Mts* Russian Fed
63B1 **Baykit** Russian Fed
63B3 **Baylik Shan** *Mts* China/Mongolia
61J3 **Baymak** Russian Fed
79B2 **Bayombang** Phil
48B3 **Bayonne** France
57C3 **Bayreuth** Germany
19C3 **Bay St Louis** USA
15D2 **Bay Shore** USA
15C1 **Bays,L of** Can
68A2 **Baytik Shan** *Mts* China
Bayt Lahm = Bethlehem
19B4 **Baytown** USA
50B2 **Baza** Spain
59D3 **Bazaliya** Ukraine
48B3 **Bazas** France
73B3 **Bazhong** China
91D4 **Bazmān** Iran
94C1 **Bcharre** Leb
16B3 **Beach Haven** USA
43E4 **Beachy Head** Eng
16C2 **Beacon** USA
101D2 **Bealanana** Madag
18B1 **Beardstown** USA
Bear I = Bjørnøya
22B1 **Bear Valley** USA
8D2 **Beatrice** USA
44C2 **Beatrice** *Oilfield* N Sea
13C1 **Beatton** *R* Can
5F4 **Beatton River** Can
29E6 **Beauchene Is** Falkland Is
109D1 **Beaudesert** Aust
1B5 **Beaufort S** Can
100B4 **Beaufort West** S Africa
15D1 **Beauharnois** Can
44B3 **Beauly** Scot
21B3 **Beaumont** California, USA
11A3 **Beaumont** Texas, USA
49C2 **Beaune** France
48C2 **Beauvais** France
13F1 **Beauval** Can
12E1 **Beaver** Alaska, USA
13F2 **Beaver** *R* Saskatchewan, Can
4D3 **Beaver Creek** Can
12E1 **Beaver Creek** USA
18C2 **Beaver Dam** Kentucky, USA
13E2 **Beaverhill L** Can
14A1 **Beaver I** USA
18B2 **Beaver L** USA
13D1 **Beaverlodge** Can
85C3 **Beawar** India
34B2 **Beazley** Arg
35B2 **Bebedouro** Brazil
43E3 **Beccles** Eng
54B1 **Bečej** Serbia, Yugos
96B1 **Béchar** Alg
12C3 **Becharof L** USA
11B3 **Beckley** USA
43D3 **Bedford** County, Eng
43D3 **Bedford** Eng
14A3 **Bedford** Indiana, USA
27M2 **Bedford Pt** Grenada
4D2 **Beechey** Pt USA
109C3 **Beechworth** Aust
109D1 **Beenleigh** Aust
92B3 **Beersheba** Israel
Beèr Sheva = Beersheba
94B3 **Beér Sheva** *R* Israel
9D4 **Beeville** USA
98C2 **Befale** Zaïre
101D2 **Befandriana** Madag
109C3 **Bega** Aust
91B3 **Behbehān** Iran
12H3 **Behm Canal** *Sd* USA
90B2 **Behshahr** Iran
84B2 **Behsud** Afghan
69E2 **Bei'an** China
73B5 **Beihai** China
72D2 **Beijing** China
76E1 **Beiliu** China
73B4 **Beipan Jiang** *R* China
72E1 **Beipiao** China
Beira = Sofala
92C3 **Beirut** Leb
68B2 **Bei Shan** *Mts* China
94B2 **Beit ed Dīne** Leb
94B3 **Beit Jala** Israel
50A2 **Beja** Port
96C1 **Beja** Tunisia
96C1 **Bejaïa** Alg
50A1 **Béjar** Spain
90C3 **Bejestān** Iran
59C3 **Békéscsaba** Hung
101D3 **Bekily** Madag
86A1 **Bela** India
85B3 **Bela** Pak
78C2 **Belaga** Malay
16A3 **Bel Air** USA
87B1 **Belamoalli** India
71D3 **Belang** Indon
70A3 **Belangpidie** Indon
Belau = Palau Is.
101C3 **Bela Vista** Mozam
70A3 **Belawan** Indon
61J2 **Belaya** *R* Ukraine
6A2 **Belcher Chan** Can
7C4 **Belcher Is** Can
84B1 **Belchiragh** Afghan
61H3 **Belebey** Russian Fed
99E2 **Beled Weyne** Somalia
31B2 **Belém** Brazil
32B3 **Belén** Colombia
34D2 **Belén** Urug
9C3 **Belen** USA
45D1 **Belfast** N Ire
101H1 **Belfast** S Africa
45D1 **Belfast Lough** *Estuary* N Ire
99D1 **Bēlfodiyo** Eth
42D2 **Belford** Eng
49D2 **Belfort** France
87A1 **Belgaum** India
56A2 **Belgium** Kingdom, N W Europe
60E3 **Belgorod** Russian Fed
60D4 **Belgorod Dnestrovskiy** Ukraine
Belgrade = Beograd
95A2 **Bel Hedan** Libya
78B3 **Belinyu** Indon
78B3 **Belitung** *I* Indon
25D3 **Belize** Belize
25D3 **Belize** Republic, Cent America
48C2 **Bellac** France
5F4 **Bella Coola** Can
47C2 **Bellagio** Italy
19A4 **Bellaire** USA
47C1 **Bellano** Italy
87B1 **Bellary** India
109C1 **Bellata** Aust
47B2 **Belledonne** *Mts* France
8C2 **Belle Fourche** USA
49D2 **Bellegarde** France
17B2 **Belle Glade** USA
7E4 **Belle I** Can
48B2 **Belle-Ile** *I* France
7E4 **Belle Isle,Str of** Can
7C5 **Belleville** Can
18A2 **Belleville** Kansas, USA
20B1 **Bellevue** Washington, USA
109D2 **Bellingen** Aust
8A2 **Bellingham** USA
112C2 **Bellingshausen** *Base* Ant
112C3 **Bellingshausen S** Ant
52A1 **Bellinzona** Switz
32B2 **Bello** Colombia
107E3 **Bellona Reefs** Nouvelle Calédonie
22B1 **Bellota** USA
15D2 **Bellows Falls** USA
6B3 **Bell Pen** Can
52B1 **Belluno** Italy
29D2 **Bell Ville** Arg
31D5 **Belmonte** Brazil
25D3 **Belmopan** Belize
45B1 **Belmullet** Irish Rep
69E1 **Belogorsk** Russian Fed
101D3 **Beloha** Madag
31C5 **Belo Horizonte** Brazil
10B2 **Beloit** Wisconsin, USA
64E3 **Belomorsk** Russian Fed
61J3 **Beloretsk** Russian Fed
60C3 **Belorussia** Republic, Europe
101D2 **Belo-Tsiribihina** Madag
64E3 **Beloye More** *S* Russian Fed
60E1 **Beloye Ozero** *L* Russian Fed
60E1 **Belozersk** Russian Fed
14B3 **Belpre** USA
108A2 **Beltana** Aust
19A3 **Belton** USA
59D3 **Bel'tsy** Moldavia
16B2 **Belvidere** New Jersey, USA
98B3 **Bembe** Angola
97C3 **Bembéréke** Benin
10A2 **Bemidji** USA
39G6 **Bena** Nor
98C3 **Bena Dibele** Zaïre
108C3 **Benalla** Aust
44B3 **Ben Attow** *Mt* Scot
50A1 **Benavente** Spain
44A3 **Benbecula** *I* Scot
106A4 **Bencubbin** Aust
8A2 **Bend** USA
44B3 **Ben Dearg** *Mt* Scot
60C4 **Bendery** Moldavia
107D4 **Bendigo** Aust
57C3 **Benešov** Czech
53B2 **Benevento** Italy
83C4 **Bengal,B of** Asia
96D1 **Ben Gardane** Tunisia
72D3 **Bengbu** China
78A2 **Bengkalis** Indon
78A3 **Bengkulu** Indon
100A2 **Benguela** Angola
92B3 **Benha** Egypt
44B2 **Ben Hope** *Mt* Scot
99C2 **Beni** Zaïre
32D6 **Béni** *R* Bol
96B1 **Beni Abbes** Alg
51C1 **Benicarló** Spain
7A5 **Benidji** USA
51B2 **Benidorm** Spain
51C2 **Beni Mansour** Alg
95C2 **Beni Mazar** Egypt
96B1 **Beni Mellal** Mor
97C4 **Benin** Republic, Africa
97C4 **Benin City** Nig
95C2 **Beni Suef** Egypt
44B2 **Ben Kilbreck** *Mt* Scot
44B3 **Ben Lawers** *Mt* UK
109C4 **Ben Lomond** *Mt* Aust
44C3 **Ben Macdui** *Mt* Scot

44B2 **Ben More Assynt** *Mt* Scot
111B2 **Benmore,L** NZ
44B3 **Ben Nevis** *Mt* Scot
15D2 **Bennington** USA
94B2 **Bennt Jbail** Leb
98B2 **Bénoué** *R* Cam
9B3 **Benson** Arizona, USA
99C2 **Bentiu** Sudan
19B3 **Benton** Arkansas, USA
18C2 **Benton** Kentucky, USA
14A2 **Benton Harbor** USA
97C4 **Benue** *R* Nig
45B1 **Benwee Hd** *C* Irish Rep
44B3 **Ben Wyvis** *Mt* Scot
72E1 **Benxi** China
54B2 **Beograd** Serbia, Yugos
86A2 **Beohāri** India
74C4 **Beppu** Japan
55A2 **Berat** Alb
95C3 **Berber** Sudan
99E1 **Berbera** Somalia
98B2 **Berbérati** CAR
46A1 **Berck** France
60C4 **Berdichev** Ukraine
60E4 **Berdyansk** Ukraine
97B4 **Berekum** Ghana
22B2 **Berenda** USA
5J4 **Berens** *R* Can
5J4 **Berens River** Can
108A1 **Beresford** Aust
59C3 **Berettyoújfalu** Hung
58D2 **Bereza** Belorussia
59C3 **Berezhany** Ukraine
65G4 **Berezniki** Russian Fed
60D4 **Berezovka** Ukraine
64H3 **Berezovo** Russian Fed
92A2 **Bergama** Turk
52A1 **Bergamo** Italy
39F6 **Bergen** Nor
46C1 **Bergen op Zoom** Neth
48C3 **Bergerac** France
46D1 **Bergisch-Gladbach** Germany
12F2 **Bering Gl** USA
1C6 **Bering Str** USA/ Russian Fed
91C4 **Berīzak** Iran
50B2 **Berja** Spain
8A3 **Berkeley** USA
112B2 **Berkner I** Ant
54B2 **Berkovitsa** Bulg
43D4 **Berkshire** County, Eng
16C1 **Berkshire Hills** USA
13D2 **Berland** *R* Can
56C2 **Berlin** Germany
56C2 **Berlin** State, Germany
15D2 **Berlin** New Hampshire, USA
30D3 **Bermejo** Bol
30D4 **Bermejo** *R* Arg
3M5 **Bermuda** *I* Atlantic O
52A1 **Bern** Switz
16B2 **Bernardsville** USA
34C3 **Bernasconi** Arg
56C2 **Bernburg** Germany
47B1 **Berner Oberland** *Mts* Switz
6B2 **Bernier B** Can
57C3 **Berounka** *R* Czech
108B2 **Berri** Aust
96C1 **Berriane** Alg
48C2 **Berry** Region, France
22A1 **Berryessa,L** USA
11C4 **Berry Is** The Bahamas
98B2 **Bertoua** Cam
45B2 **Bertraghboy B** Irish Rep
15C2 **Berwick** USA
42C2 **Berwick-upon-Tweed** Eng
43C3 **Berwyn** *Mts* Wales
101D2 **Besalampy** Madag
49D2 **Besançon** France
59C3 **Beskidy Zachodnie** *Mts* Pol
93C2 **Besni** Turk
94B3 **Besor** *R* Israel
11B3 **Bessemer** USA
101D2 **Betafo** Madag
50A1 **Betanzos** Spain
94B3 **Bet Guvrin** Israel
101G1 **Bethal** S Africa
100A3 **Bethanie** Namibia
18B1 **Bethany** Missouri, USA
18A2 **Bethany** Oklahoma, USA
4B3 **Bethel** Alaska, USA
16C2 **Bethel** Connecticut, USA
14B2 **Bethel Park** USA
15C3 **Bethesda** USA
94B3 **Bethlehem** Israel
101G1 **Bethlehem** S Africa
15C2 **Bethlehem** USA
48C1 **Bethune** France
101D3 **Betioky** Madag
108B1 **Betoota** Aust
98B2 **Betou** Congo
82A1 **Betpak Dala** *Steppe* Kazakhstan
101D3 **Betroka** Madag
7D5 **Betsiamites** Can
86A1 **Bettiah** India
12D1 **Bettles** USA
47C2 **Bèttola** Italy
85D4 **Bētul** India
85D3 **Betwa** *R* India
46D1 **Betzdorf** Germany
12C3 **Beverley,L** USA
16D1 **Beverly** USA
21B3 **Beverly Hills** USA
97B4 **Beyla** Guinea
87B2 **Beypore** India
Beyrouth = Beirut
92B2 **Beyşehir** Turk
92B2 **Beysehir Gölü** *L* Turk
94B2 **Beyt Shean** Israel
47C1 **Bezau** Austria
60E2 **Bezhetsk** Russian Fed
49C3 **Béziers** France
90C2 **Bezmein** Turkmenistan
63C2 **Beznosova** Russian Fed
86B1 **Bhadgaon** Nepal
87C1 **Bhadrāchalam** India
86B2 **Bhadrakh** India
87B2 **Bhadra Res** India
87B2 **Bhadrāvati** India
84B3 **Bhag** Pak
86B1 **Bhāgalpur** India
84C2 **Bhakkar** Pak
82D3 **Bhamo** Burma
85D4 **Bhandāra** India
85D3 **Bharatpur** India
85C4 **Bharūch** India
86B2 **Bhātiāpāra Ghat** Bang
84C2 **Bhatinda** India
87A2 **Bhatkal** India
86B2 **Bhātpāra** India
85C4 **Bhāvnagar** India
84C2 **Bhera** Pak
86A1 **Bheri** *R* Nepal
86A2 **Bhilai** India
85C3 **Bhīlwāra** India
87C1 **Bhīmavaram** India
85D3 **Bhind** India
84D3 **Bhiwāni** India
87B1 **Bhongir** India
85D4 **Bhopāl** India
86B2 **Bhubaneshwar** India
85B4 **Bhuj** India
85D4 **Bhusāwal** India
82C3 **Bhutan** Kingdom, Asia
71E4 **Biak** *I* Indon
58C2 **Biala Podlaska** Pol
58B2 **Bialograd** Pol
58C2 **Bialystok** Pol
38A1 **Biargtangar** *C* Iceland
90C2 **Bīarjmand** Iran
48B3 **Biarritz** France
47C1 **Biasca** Switz
92B4 **Biba** Egypt
74E2 **Bibai** Japan
100A2 **Bibala** Angola
57B3 **Biberach** Germany
97B4 **Bibiani** Ghana
54C1 **Bicaz** Rom
97C4 **Bida** Nig
87B1 **Bīdar** India
91C5 **Bidbid** Oman
43B4 **Bideford** Eng
43B4 **Bideford B** Eng
96C2 **Bidon 5** Alg
58C2 **Biebrza** Pol
52A1 **Biel** Switz
59B2 **Bielawa** Pol
56B2 **Bielefeld** Germany
47B1 **Bieler See** *L* Switz
52A1 **Biella** Italy
58C2 **Bielsk Podlaski** Pol
76D3 **Bien Hoa** Viet
53B2 **Biferno** *R* Italy
92A1 **Biga** Turk
55C3 **Bigadiç** Turk
19C3 **Big Black** *R* USA
18A1 **Big Blue** *R* USA
17B2 **Big Cypress Swamp** USA
4D3 **Big Delta** USA
49D2 **Bigent** Germany
13F2 **Biggar** Can
5H4 **Biggar Kindersley** Can
109D1 **Biggenden** Aust
12G3 **Bigger,Mt** Can
8C2 **Bighorn** *R* USA
76C3 **Bight of Bangkok** *B* Thai
97C4 **Bight of Benin** *B* W Africa
97C4 **Bight of Biafra** *B* Cam
6C3 **Big I** Can
47C1 **Bignasco** Switz
97A3 **Bignona** Sen
21B2 **Big Pine** USA
17B2 **Big Pine Key** USA
22C3 **Big Pine Mt** USA
14A2 **Big Rapids** USA
5H4 **Big River** Can
9C3 **Big Spring** USA
7A4 **Big Trout L** Can
7B4 **Big Trout Lake** Can
52C2 **Bihać** Bosnia & Herzegovina, Yugos
86B1 **Bihār** India
86B2 **Bihar** State, India
99D3 **Biharamulo** Tanz
60B4 **Bihor** *Mt* Rom
87B1 **Bijāpur** India
87C1 **Bījāpur** India
90A2 **Bījār** Iran
86A1 **Bijauri** Nepal
54A2 **Bijeljina** Bosnia & Herzegovina, Yugos
73B4 **Bijie** China
84D3 **Bijnor** India
84C3 **Bijnot** Pak
84C3 **Bikāner** India
94B2 **Bikfaya** Leb
69F2 **Bikin** Russian Fed
98B3 **Bikoro** Zaïre
85C3 **Bilara** India
84D2 **Bilaspur** India
86A2 **Bilāspur** India
76B3 **Bilauktaung Range** *Mts* Thai
50B1 **Bilbao** Spain
Bilbo = Bilbao
59B3 **Bílé** *R* Czech
54A2 **Bileça** Bosnia & Herzegovina, Yugos
92B1 **Bilecik** Turk
98C2 **Bili** *R* Zaïre
79B3 **Biliran** *I* Phil
8C2 **Billings** USA
95A3 **Bilma** Niger
11B3 **Biloxi** USA
98C1 **Biltine** Chad
85D4 **Bina-Etawa** India
79B3 **Binalbagan** Phil
101C2 **Bindura** Zim
100B2 **Binga** Zim
101C2 **Binga** *Mt* Zim
109D1 **Bingara** Aust
57B3 **Bingen** Germany
10C2 **Binghamton** USA
78D1 **Bingkor** Malay
93D2 **Bingöl** Turk
72D3 **Binhai** China
78A2 **Bintan** *I* Indon
78A3 **Bintuhan** Indon
78C2 **Bintulu** Malay
29B3 **Bió Bió** *R* Chile
102J4 **Bioko** *I* Atlantic O
87B1 **Bīr** India
95B2 **Bīr Abu Husein** *Well* Egypt
95B2 **Bi'r al Harash** *Well* Libya
98C1 **Birao** CAR
86B1 **Biratnagar** Nepal
12E1 **Birch Creek** USA
108B3 **Birchip** Aust
5G4 **Birch Mts** Can
7A4 **Bird** Can
106C3 **Birdsville** Aust
106C2 **Birdum** Aust
86A1 **Birganj** Nepal
94A3 **Bîr Gifgâfa** *Well* Egypt
94A3 **Bîr Hasana** *Well* Egypt
35A2 **Birigui** Brazil
90C3 **Birjand** Iran
92B4 **Birkat Qarun** *L* Egypt
46D2 **Birkenfeld** Germany
42C3 **Birkenhead** Eng
60C4 **Bîrlad** Rom
94A3 **Bir Lahfân** *Well* Egypt
43C3 **Birmingham** Eng
11B3 **Birmingham** USA
95B2 **Bîr Misâha** *Well* Egypt
96A2 **Bir Moghrein** Maur
97C3 **Birnin Kebbi** Nig
97C3 **Birni N'Konni** Nig
69F2 **Birobidzhan** Russian Fed
45C2 **Birr** Irish Rep
51C2 **Bir Rabalou** Alg
109C1 **Birrie** *R* Aust
44C2 **Birsay** Scot
61J2 **Birsk** Russian Fed
95B2 **Bîr Tarfâwi** *Well* Egypt
63B2 **Biryusa** Russian Fed
39J7 **Biržai** Lithuania
96B2 **Bir Zreigat** *Well* Maur
48A2 **Biscay,B of** France/ Spain
17B2 **Biscayne B** USA
46D2 **Bischwiller** France
73B4 **Bishan** China
82B1 **Bishkek** Kirgizia
8B3 **Bishop** USA
42D2 **Bishop Auckland** Eng
43E4 **Bishop's Stortford** Eng
86A2 **Bishrāmpur** India
96C1 **Biskra** Alg
79C4 **Bislig** Phil
8C2 **Bismarck** USA
90A3 **Bīsotūn** Iran
97A3 **Bissau** Guinea-Bissau
10A1 **Bissett** Can
5G4 **Bistcho L** Can
54C1 **Bistrita** *R* Rom
98B2 **Bitam** Gabon
57B3 **Bitburg** Germany
46D2 **Bitche** France
93D2 **Bitlis** Turk
55B2 **Bitola** Macedonia, Yugos
56C2 **Bitterfeld** Germany
100A4 **Bitterfontein** S Africa
92B3 **Bitter Lakes** Egypt
8B2 **Bitteroot Range** *Mts* USA
74D3 **Biwa-ko** *L* Japan

99E1 Biyo Kaboba Eth
65K4 Biysk Russian Fed
96C1 Bizerte Tunisia
51C2 Bj bou Arréridj Alg
52C1 Bjelovar Croatia
96B2 Bj Flye Ste Marie Alg
64C2 Bjørnøya I Barents S
12F1 Black R USA
18B2 Black R USA
107D3 Blackall Aust
42C3 Blackburn Eng
4D3 Blackburn,Mt USA
13E2 Black Diamond Can
5H5 Black Hills USA
44B3 Black Isle Pen Scot
27R3 Blackman's Barbados
43C4 Black Mts Wales
43C3 Blackpool Eng
27H1 Black River Jamaica
8B2 Black Rock Desert USA
65E5 Black S Asia/Europe
45A1 Blacksod B Irish Rep
109D2 Black Sugarloaf Mt Aust
97B3 Black Volta R Ghana
41B3 Blackwater R Irish Rep
18A2 Blackwell USA
54B2 Blagoevgrad Bulg
63E2 Blagoveshchensk Russian Fed
20B1 Blaine USA
44C3 Blair Atholl Scot
44C3 Blairgowrie Scot
17B1 Blakely USA
108A1 Blanche,L Aust
34A2 Blanco R Arg
34B1 Blanco R Arg
8A2 Blanco,C USA
7E4 Blanc Sablon Can
43C4 Blandford Forum Eng
46A2 Blangy-sur-Bresle France
46B1 Blankenberge Belg
101C2 Blantyre Malawi
48B2 Blaye France
109C2 Blayney Aust
111B2 Blenheim NZ
96C1 Blida Alg
14B1 Blind River Can
108A2 Blinman Aust
78C4 Blitar Indon
15D2 Block I USA
16D2 Block Island Sd USA
101G1 Bloemfontein S Africa
101G1 Bloemhof S Africa
101G1 Bloemhof Dam Res S Africa
33F3 Blommesteinmeer L Surinam
38A1 Blonduós Iceland
45B1 Bloody Foreland C Irish Rep
14A3 Bloomfield Indiana, USA
18B1 Bloomfield Iowa, USA
10B2 Bloomington Illinois, USA
14A3 Bloomington Indiana, USA
16A2 Bloomsburg USA
78C4 Blora Indon
6H3 Blosseville Kyst Mts Greenland
57B3 Bludenz Austria
11B3 Bluefield USA
32A1 Bluefields Nic
26B3 Blue Mountain Peak Mt Jamaica
16A2 Blue Mt USA
109D2 Blue Mts Aust
27J1 Blue Mts Jamaica
8A2 Blue Mts USA
Blue Nile = Bahr el Azraq
99D1 Blue Nile R Sudan
4G3 Bluenose L Can
11B3 Blue Ridge Mts USA
13D2 Blue River Can
45B1 Blue Stack Mt Irish Rep
111A3 Bluff NZ
106A4 Bluff Knoll Mt Aust
30G4 Blumenau Brazil
49D2 Blundez Austria
20B2 Bly USA
12E3 Blying Sd USA
42D2 Blyth Eng
9B3 Blythe USA
11B3 Blytheville USA
97A4 Bo Sierra Leone
79B3 Boac Phil
72D2 Boading China
14B2 Boardman USA
63C3 Boatou China
33E3 Boa Vista Brazil
97A4 Boa Vista I Cape Verde
76E1 Bobai China
47C2 Bóbbio Italy
97B3 Bobo Dioulasso Burkina
60C3 Bobruysk Belorussia
17B2 Boca Chica Key I USA
32D5 Bõca do Acre Brazil
35C1 Bocaiúva Brazil
98B2 Bocaranga CAR
17B2 Boca Raton USA
59C3 Bochnia Pol
56B2 Bocholt Germany
46D1 Bochum Germany
100A2 Bocoio Angola
98B2 Boda CAR
63D2 Bodaybo Russian Fed
21A2 Bodega Head Pt USA
95A3 Bodélé Region Chad
38J5 Boden Sweden
47C1 Bodensee L Switz/Germany
87B1 Bodhan India
87B2 Bodināyakkanūr India
43B4 Bodmin Eng
43B4 Bodmin Moor Upland Eng
38G5 Bodø Nor
55C3 Bodrum Turk
98C3 Boende Zaïre
97A3 Boffa Guinea
76B2 Bogale Burma
19C3 Bogalusa USA
109C2 Bogan R Aust
97B3 Bogandé Burkina
6H3 Bogarnes Iceland
92C2 Boğazlıyan Turk
61K2 Bogdanovich Russian Fed
68A2 Bogda Shan Mt China
100A3 Bogenfels Namibia
109D1 Boggabilla Aust
109C2 Boggabri Aust
45B2 Boggeragh Mts Irish Rep
79B3 Bogo Phil
109C3 Bogong,Mt Aust
78B4 Bogor Indon
61H2 Bogorodskoye Russian Fed
32C3 Bogotá Colombia
63A2 Bogotol Russian Fed
86B2 Bogra Bang
72D2 Bo Hai B China
46B2 Bohain-en-Vermandois France
72D2 Bohai Wan B China
57C3 Böhmer-Wald Upland Germany
79B4 Bohol I Phil
79B4 Bohol S Phil
35A1 Bois R Brazil
14B1 Bois Blanc I USA
8B2 Boise USA
96A2 Bojador,C Mor
79B2 Bojeador,C Phil
90C2 Bojnūrd Iran
97A3 Boké Guinea
109C1 Bokhara R Aust
39F7 Boknafjord Inlet Nor
98B3 Boko Congo
76C3 Bokor Camb
98C3 Bokungu Zaïre
98B1 Bol Chad
23A1 Bolaānos Mexico
97A3 Bolama Guinea-Bissau
23A1 Bolanos R Mexico
48C2 Bolbec France
97B4 Bole Ghana
59B2 Boleslawiec Pol
97B3 Bolgatanga Ghana
60C4 Bolgrad Ukraine
34C3 Bolívar Arg
18B2 Bolivar Missouri, USA
18C2 Bolivar Tennessee, USA
30C2 Bolivia Republic, S America
38H6 Bollnas Sweden
109C1 Bollon Aust
32C2 Bollvar Mt Ven
52B2 Bologna Italy
60D2 Bologoye Russian Fed
69F2 Bolon' Russian Fed
61G3 Bol'shoy Irgiz R Russian Fed
74C2 Bol'shoy Kamen Russian Fed
65F5 Bol'shoy Kavkaz Mts Georgia
61G4 Bol'shoy Uzen R Kazakhstan
9C4 Bolson de Mapimi Desert Mexico
43C3 Bolton Eng
92B1 Bolu Turk
38A1 Bolungarvik Iceland
92B2 Bolvadin Turk
52B1 Bolzano Italy
98B3 Boma Zaïre
107D4 Bombala Aust
87A1 Bombay India
99D2 Bombo Uganda
35B1 Bom Despacho Brazil
86C1 Bomdila India
97A4 Bomi Hills Lib
31C4 Bom Jesus da Lapa Brazil
63E2 Bomnak Russian Fed
99C2 Bomokandi R Zaïre
98C2 Bomu R CAR/Zaïre
27D4 Bonaire I Caribbean S
12F2 Bona,Mt USA
25D3 Bonanza Nic
7E5 Bonavista Can
108A2 Bon Bon Aust
98C2 Bondo Zaïre
97B4 Bondoukou Ivory Coast
Bône = 'Annaba
33E3 Bonfim Guyana
98C2 Bongandanga Zaïre
98B1 Bongor Chad
19A3 Bonham USA
53A2 Bonifacio Corse
52A2 Bonifacio,Str of Chan Medit S
Bonin Is = Ogasawara Gunto
17B2 Bonita Springs USA
57B2 Bonn Germany
20C1 Bonners Ferry USA
12H1 Bonnet Plume R Can
13E2 Bonnyville Can
97A4 Bonthe Sierra Leone
99E1 Booaaso Somalia
108B2 Booligal Aust
109D1 Boonah Aust
15C2 Boonville USA
109C2 Boorowa Aust
6A2 Boothia,G of Can
6A2 Boothia Pen Can
98B3 Booué Gabon
108A1 Bopeechee Aust
99D2 Bor Sudan
92B2 Bor Turk
54B2 Bor Serbia, Yugos
8B2 Borah Peak Mt USA
39G7 Borås Sweden
91B4 Borāzjān Iran
108A3 Borda,C Aust
48B3 Bordeaux France
4G2 Borden I Can
6B2 Borden Pen Can
16B2 Bordentown USA
42C2 Borders Region, Scot
108B3 Bordertown Aust
96C2 Bordi Omar Dris Alg
8D1 Borens River Can
38A2 Borgarnes Iceland
9C3 Borger USA
39H7 Borgholm Sweden
47C2 Borgosia Italy
47D1 Borgo Valsugana Italy
59C3 Borislav Ukraine
61F3 Borisoglebsk Russian Fed
60C3 Borisov Belorussia
60E3 Borisovka Russian Fed
95A3 Borkou Region Chad
39H6 Borlänge Sweden
47C2 Bormida Italy
47D1 Bormio Italy
67F5 Borneo I Malay/Indon
39H7 Bornholm I Den
55C3 Bornova Turk
98C2 Boro R Sudan
97B3 Boromo Burkina
60D2 Borovichi Russian Fed
106C2 Borroloola Aust
54B1 Borsa Rom
90A3 Borūjed Iran
90B3 Borūjen Iran
58B2 Bory Tucholskie Region, Pol
63D2 Borzya Russian Fed
73B5 Bose China
101G1 Boshof S Africa
54A2 Bosna R Bosnia & Herzegovina, Yugos
37E4 Bosnia & Herzegovina Republic, Yugos
75C1 Bōsō-hantō B Japan
Bosporus = Karadeniz Boğazi
51C2 Bosquet Alg
98B2 Bossangoa CAR
98B2 Bossèmbélé CAR
19B3 Bossier City USA
65K5 Bosten Hu L China
43D3 Boston Eng
10C2 Boston USA
11A3 Boston Mts USA
85C4 Botād India
54B2 Botevgrad Bulg
101G1 Bothaville S Africa
64C3 Bothnia,G of Sweden/Fin
100B3 Botletli R Botswana
60C4 Botosani Rom
100B3 Botswana Republic, Africa
53C3 Botte Donato Mt Italy
46D1 Bottrop Germany
35B2 Botucatu Brazil
7E5 Botwood Can
89D7 Bouaké Ivory Coast
98B2 Bouar CAR
96B1 Bouârfa Mor
98B2 Bouca CAR
51C2 Boufarik Alg
Bougie = Bejaïa
97B3 Bougouni Mali
46C2 Bouillon France
96B2 Bou Izakarn Mor
46D2 Boulay-Moselle France

8C2 **Boulder** Colorado, USA
9B3 **Boulder City** USA
22A2 **Boulder Creek** USA
48C1 **Boulogne** France
98B2 **Boumba** *R* CAR
97B4 **Bouna** Ivory Coast
8B3 **Boundary Peak** *Mt* USA
97B4 **Boundiali** Ivory Coast
107F3 **Bourail** Nouvelle Calédonie
97B3 **Bourem** Mali
49D2 **Bourg** France
49D2 **Bourg de Péage** France
48C2 **Bourges** France
48C3 **Bourg-Madame** France
49C2 **Bourgogne** Region, France
47B2 **Bourg-St-Maurice** France
108C2 **Bourke** Aust
43D4 **Bournemouth** Eng
96C1 **Bou Saâda** Alg
98B1 **Bousso** Chad
97A3 **Boutilmit** Maur
103J7 **Bouvet I** Atlantic O
34D2 **Bovril** Arg
13E2 **Bow** *R* Can
107D2 **Bowen** Aust
19A3 **Bowie** Texas, USA
13E2 **Bow Island** Can
11B3 **Bowling Green** Kentucky, USA
18B2 **Bowling Green** Missouri, USA
14B2 **Bowling Green** Ohio, USA
15C3 **Bowling Green** Virginia, USA
15C2 **Bowmanville** Can
109D2 **Bowral** Aust
13C2 **Bowron** *R* Can
72D3 **Bo Xian** China
72D2 **Boxing** China
92B1 **Boyabat** Turk
98B2 **Boyali** CAR
5J4 **Boyd** Can
16B2 **Boyertown** USA
13E2 **Boyle** Can
41B3 **Boyle** Irish Rep
45C2 **Boyne** *R* Irish Rep
17B2 **Boynoton Beach** USA
98C2 **Boyoma Falls** Zaïre
55C3 **Bozca Ada** *I* Turk
55C3 **Boz Dağlari** *Mts* Turk
8B2 **Bozeman** USA
Bozen = Bolzano
98B2 **Bozene** Zaïre
98B2 **Bozoum** CAR
47B2 **Bra** Italy
52C2 **Brač** *I* Croatia
15C1 **Bracebridge** Can
95A2 **Brach** Libya
38H6 **Bräcke** Sweden
17B2 **Bradenton** USA
42D3 **Bradford** Eng
44E1 **Brae** Scot
44C3 **Braemar** Scot
50A1 **Braga** Port
34C3 **Bragado** Arg
50A1 **Bragana** Port
31B2 **Bragança** Brazil
35B2 **Bragança Paulista** Brazil
86C2 **Brahman-Baria** Bang
86B2 **Brāhmani** *R* India
86C1 **Brahmaputra** *R* India
7E5 **Braie Verte** Can
60C4 **Brăila** Rom
10A2 **Brainerd** USA
97A3 **Brakna** Region, Maur
5F4 **Bralorne** Can
14C2 **Brampton** Can
33E3 **Branco** *R* Brazil
100A3 **Brandberg** *Mt* Namibia
56C2 **Brandenburg** Germany
56C2 **Brandenburg** State, Germany
101G1 **Brandfort** S Africa
8D2 **Brandon** Can
100B4 **Brandvlei** S Africa
57C2 **Brandys nad Lebem** Czech
58B2 **Braniewo** Pol
10B2 **Brantford** Can
108B3 **Branxholme** Aust
7D5 **Bras D'Or L** Can
35C1 **Brasíla de Minas** Brazil
32D6 **Brasiléia** Brazil
31B5 **Brasilia** Brazil
54C1 **Brasov** Rom
78D1 **Brassay Range** *Mts* Malay
59B3 **Bratislava** Czech
63C2 **Bratsk** Russian Fed
15D2 **Brattleboro** USA
56C2 **Braunschweig** Germany
97A4 **Brava** *I* Cape Verde
9B3 **Brawley** USA
45C2 **Bray** Irish Rep
6C3 **Bray I** Can
13D2 **Brazeau** *R* Can
13D2 **Brazeau,Mt** Can
28D4 **Brazil** Republic, S America
103G5 **Brazil Basin** Atlantic O
9D3 **Brazos** *R* USA
98B3 **Brazzaville** Congo
57C3 **Brdy** *Upland* Czech
111A3 **Breaksea Sd** NZ
110B1 **Bream B** NZ
78B4 **Brebes** Indon
44C3 **Brechin** Scot
46C1 **Brecht** Belg
59B3 **Břeclav** Czech
43C4 **Brecon** Wales
43C4 **Brecon Beacons** *Mts* Wales
43B3 **Brecon Beacons Nat Pk** Wales
56A2 **Breda** Neth
100B4 **Bredasdorp** S Africa
38H6 **Bredbyn** Sweden
61J3 **Bredy** Russian Fed
15C2 **Breezewood** USA
47C1 **Bregenz** Austria
47C1 **Bregenzer Ache** *R* Austria
38A1 **Breiðafjörður** *B* Iceland
47C2 **Brembo** *R* Italy
17A1 **Bremen** USA
56B2 **Bremen** Germany
56B2 **Bremerhaven** Germany
20B1 **Bremerton** USA
19A3 **Brenham** USA
57C3 **Brenner** *P* Austria/Italy
47D2 **Breno** Italy
47D2 **Brenta** *R* Italy
22B2 **Brentwood** USA
52B1 **Brescia** Italy
Breslau = Wrocław
47D1 **Bressanone** Italy
44E1 **Bressay** *I* Scot
48B2 **Bressuire** France
58C2 **Brest** Belorussia
48B2 **Brest** France
48B2 **Bretagne** Region, France
46B2 **Breteuil** France
16B2 **Breton Woods** USA
110B1 **Brett,C** NZ
109C1 **Brewarrina** Aust
16C2 **Brewster** New York, USA
20C1 **Brewster** Washington, USA
101G1 **Breyten** S Africa
52C1 **Brežice** Slovenia
98C2 **Bria** CAR
49D3 **Briancon** France
49C2 **Briare** France
21B2 **Bridgeport** California, USA
15D2 **Bridgeport** Connecticut, USA
19A3 **Bridgeport** Texas, USA
22C1 **Bridgeport Res** USA
16B3 **Bridgeton** USA
27F4 **Bridgetown** Barbados
7D5 **Bridgewater** Can
16D2 **Bridgewater** USA
43C4 **Bridgwater** Eng
43C4 **Bridgwater B** Eng
42D2 **Bridlington** Eng
109C4 **Bridport** Aust
47B1 **Brienzer See** *L* Switz
46C2 **Briey** France
52A1 **Brig** Switz
8B2 **Brigham City** USA
109C3 **Bright** Aust
43D4 **Brighton** Eng
46E1 **Brilon** Germany
55A2 **Brindisi** Italy
19B3 **Brinkley** USA
107E3 **Brisbane** Aust
15D2 **Bristol** Connecticut, USA
43C4 **Bristol** Eng
15D2 **Bristol** Pennsylvania, USA
16D2 **Bristol** Rhode Island, USA
11B3 **Bristol** Tennessee, USA
12B3 **Bristol B** USA
43B4 **Bristol Chan** Eng/Wales
4D3 **British** *Mts* USA
5F4 **British Columbia** Province, Can
6B1 **British Empire Range** *Mts* Can
101G1 **Brits** S Africa
100B4 **Britstown** S Africa
48C2 **Brive** France
59B3 **Brno** Czech
17B1 **Broad** *R* USA
7C4 **Broadback** *R* Can
44A2 **Broad Bay** *Inlet* Scot
44B3 **Broadford** Scot
5H4 **Brochet** Can
4G2 **Brock I** Can
15C2 **Brockport** USA
16D1 **Brockton** USA
15C2 **Brockville** Can
6B2 **Brodeur Pen** Can
42B2 **Brodick** Scot
58B2 **Brodnica** Pol
60C3 **Brody** Ukraine
19B3 **Broken Bow** Oklahoma, USA
19B3 **Broken Bow L** USA
107D4 **Broken Hill** Aust
47C2 **Broni** Italy
38G5 **Brønnøysund** Nor
16C2 **Bronx** Borough, New York, USA
79A4 **Brooke's Point** Phil
18B2 **Brookfield** Missouri, USA
11A3 **Brookhaven** USA
20B2 **Brookings** Oregon, USA
8D2 **Brookings** South Dakota, USA
16D1 **Brookline** USA
16C2 **Brooklyn** Borough, New York, USA
5G4 **Brooks** Can
12C3 **Brooks,L** USA
12A1 **Brooks Mt** USA
4C3 **Brooks Range** *Mts* USA
17B2 **Brooksville** USA
109D1 **Brooloo** Aust
106B2 **Broome** Aust
44C2 **Brora** Scot
20B2 **Brothers** USA
95A3 **Broulkou** Chad
13E3 **Browning** USA
9D4 **Brownsville** USA
9D3 **Brownwood** USA
46B1 **Bruay-en-Artois** France
106A3 **Bruce,Mt** Aust
14B1 **Bruce Pen** Can
59B3 **Brück an der Mur** Austria
Bruges = Brugge
46B1 **Brugge** Belg
46D1 **Brühl** Germany
78C2 **Brunei** Sultanate, S E Asia
52B1 **Brunico** Italy
111B2 **Brunner,L** NZ
11B3 **Brunswick** Georgia, USA
18B2 **Brunswick** Mississippi, USA
29B6 **Brunswick,Pen de** Chile
109C4 **Bruny I** Aust
61F1 **Brusenets** Russian Fed
26A3 **Brus Laguna** Honduras
Brüssel = Bruxelles
56A2 **Bruxelles** Belg
9D3 **Bryan** USA
108A2 **Bryan,Mt** Aust
60D3 **Bryansk** Russian Fed
19B3 **Bryant** USA
59B2 **Brzeg** Pol
93E4 **Būbīyan** *I* Kuwait/Iraq
99D3 **Bubu** *R* Tanz
32C2 **Bucaramanga** Colombia
44D3 **Buchan** *Oilfield* N Sea
97A4 **Buchanan** Lib
44D3 **Buchan Deep** N Sea
6C2 **Buchan G** Can
40C2 **Buchan Ness** *Pen* Scot
7E5 **Buchans** Can
34C2 **Buchardo** Arg
Bucharest = București
47C1 **Buchs** Switz
43D3 **Buckingham** Eng
12B1 **Buckland** USA
12B1 **Buckland** *R* USA
108A2 **Buckleboo** Aust
98B3 **Buco Zau** Congo
54C2 **București** Rom
59B3 **Budapest** Hung
84D3 **Budaun** India
43B4 **Bude** Eng
19B3 **Bude** USA
61F5 **Budennovsk** Russian Fed
54A2 **Budva** Montenegro, Yugos
98A2 **Buéa** Cam
22B3 **Buellton** USA
34B2 **Buena Esperanza** Arg
32B3 **Buenaventura** Colombia
23A2 **Buenavista** Mexico
29E2 **Buenos Aires** Arg
29D3 **Buenos Aires** State, Arg
18B2 **Buffalo** Mississipi, USA
10C2 **Buffalo** New York, USA
8C2 **Buffalo** South Dakota, USA
19A3 **Buffalo** Texas, USA
8C2 **Buffalo** Wyoming, USA
101H1 **Buffalo** *R* S Africa
13E2 **Buffalo L** Alberta, Can
5G3 **Buffalo L** Northwest Territories, Can
5H4 **Buffalo Narrows** Can
17B1 **Buford** USA
54C2 **Buftea** Rom
59C2 **Bug** *R* Pol/Ukraine
32B3 **Buga** Colombia

90B2 **Bugdayli** Turkmenistan
61H3 **Bugulma** Russian Fed
61H3 **Buguruslan** Russian Fed
93C2 **Buhayrat al Asad** *Res* Syria
41C3 **Builth Wells** Wales
34A2 **Buin** Chile
99C3 **Bujumbura** Burundi
98C3 **Bukama** Zaïre
99C3 **Bukavu** Zaïre
80E2 **Bukhara** Uzbekistan
78C2 **Bukit Batubrok** *Mt* Indon
70B4 **Bukittinggi** Indon
99D3 **Bukoba** Tanz
78D3 **Buku Gandadiwata** *Mt* Indon
71E4 **Bula** Indon
79B3 **Bulan** Phil
84D3 **Bulandshahr** India
100B3 **Bulawayo** Zim
55C3 **Buldan** Turk
85D4 **Buldāna** India
68C2 **Bulgan** Mongolia
54B2 **Bulgaria** Republic, Europe
47B1 **Bulle** Switz
111B2 **Buller** *R* NZ
109C3 **Buller,Mt** Aust
106A4 **Bullfinch** Aust
108B1 **Bulloo** *R* Aust
108B1 **Bulloo Downs** Aust
108B1 **Bulloo L** Aust
18B2 **Bull Shoals Res** USA
34A3 **Bulnes** Chile
71F4 **Bulolo** PNG
101G1 **Bultfontein** S Africa
98C2 **Bumba** Zaïre
76B2 **Bumphal Dam** Thai
99D2 **Buna** Kenya
106A4 **Bunbury** Aust
45C1 **Buncrana** Irish Rep
107E3 **Bundaberg** Aust
109D2 **Bundarra** Aust
85D3 **Būndi** India
45B1 **Bundoran** Irish Rep
109C1 **Bungil** *R* Aust
98B3 **Bungo** Angola
75A2 **Bungo-suidō** *Str* Japan
70B3 **Bunguran** *I* Ind
99D2 **Bunia** Zaïre
18B2 **Bunker** USA
19B3 **Bunkie** USA
17B2 **Bunnell** USA
78C3 **Buntok** Indon
71D3 **Buol** Indon
94C2 **Burāq** Syria
98C1 **Buram** Sudan
99E2 **Burao** Somalia
79B3 **Burauen** Phil
80C3 **Buraydah** S Arabia
21B3 **Burbank** USA
109C2 **Burcher** Aust
92B2 **Burdur** Turk
63F3 **Bureinskiy Khrebet** *Mts* Russian Fed
56C2 **Burg** Germany
54C2 **Burgas** Bulg
17C1 **Burgaw** USA
47B1 **Burgdorf** Switz
100B4 **Burgersdorp** S Africa
50B1 **Burgos** Spain
58B1 **Burgsvik** Sweden
55C3 **Burhaniye** Turk
85D4 **Burhānpur** India
79B3 **Burias** *I* Phil
76C2 **Buriram** Thai
35B1 **Buritis** Brazil
13B2 **Burke Chan** Can
106C2 **Burketown** Aust
97B3 **Burkina** Republic, Africa
15C1 **Burks Falls** Can
8B2 **Burley** USA
10A2 **Burlington** Iowa, USA
16B2 **Burlington** New Jersey, USA
10C2 **Burlington** Vermont, USA
20B1 **Burlington** Washington, USA
83D3 **Burma** Republic, Asia
20B2 **Burney** USA
16A2 **Burnham** USA
107D5 **Burnie** Aust
42C3 **Burnley** Eng
20C2 **Burns** USA
5F4 **Burns Lake** Can
82C1 **Burqin** China
108A2 **Burra** Aust
109D2 **Burragorang,L** Aust
44C2 **Burray** *I* Scot
109C2 **Burren Junction** Aust
109C2 **Burrinjuck Res** Aust
60C5 **Bursa** Turk
80B3 **Bur Safâga** Egypt
Bûr Sa'îd = Port Said
14B2 **Burton** USA
43D3 **Burton upon Trent** Eng
38J6 **Burtrask** Sweden
108B2 **Burtundy** Aust
71D4 **Buru** Indon
99C3 **Burundi** Republic, Africa
78A2 **Burung** Indon
63D2 **Buryatskaya Respublika,** Russian Fed
99D1 **Burye** Eth
61H4 **Burynshik** Kazakhstan
43E3 **Bury St Edmunds** Eng
91B4 **Būshehr** Iran
98B3 **Busira** *R* Zaïre
58C2 **Buskozdroj** Pol
94C2 **Busrā ash Shām** Syria
106A4 **Busselton** Aust
49D2 **Busto** Italy
52A1 **Busto Arsizio** Italy
79A3 **Busuanga** *I* Phil
98C2 **Buta** Zaïre
34B3 **Buta Ranquil** Arg
99C3 **Butare** Rwanda
42B2 **Bute** *I* Scot
69E2 **Butha Qi** China
14C2 **Butler** USA
8B2 **Butte** USA
77C4 **Butterworth** Malay
40B2 **Butt of Lewis** *C* Scot
6D3 **Button Is** Can
79C4 **Butuan** Phil
71D4 **Butung** *I* Indon
61F3 **Buturlinovka** Russian Fed
86A1 **Butwal** Nepal
99E2 **Buulo Barde** Somalia
99E2 **Buur Hakaba** Somalia
61F2 **Buy** Russian Fed
72B1 **Buyant Ovvo** Mongolia
61G5 **Buynaksk** Russian Fed
63D3 **Buyr Nuur** *L* Mongolia
93D2 **Büyük Ağri** *Mt* Turk
92A2 **Büyük Menderes** *R* Turk
54C1 **Buzău** Rom
54C1 **Buzau** *R* Rom
61H3 **Buzuluk** Russian Fed
16D2 **Buzzards B** USA
54C2 **Byala** Bulg
54B2 **Byala Slatina** Bulg
4H2 **Byam Martin** *Chan* Can
4H2 **Byam Martin I** Can
Byblos = Jubail
94B1 **Byblos** Hist Site, Leb
58B2 **Bydgoszcz** Pol
39F7 **Bygland** Nor
6C2 **Bylot I** Can
109C2 **Byrock** Aust
22B2 **Byron** USA
109D1 **Byron,C** Aust
59B2 **Bytom** Pol

C

30E4 **Caacupé** Par
100A2 **Caála** Angola
13B2 **Caamano Sd** Can
30E4 **Caazapá** Par
79B2 **Cabanatuan** Phil
31E3 **Cabedelo** Brazil
50A2 **Cabeza del Buey** Spain
34C3 **Cabildo** Arg
34A2 **Cabildo** Chile
32C1 **Cabimas** Ven
98B3 **Cabinda** Angola
98B3 **Cabinda** Province, Angola
27C3 **Cabo Beata** Dom Rep
51C2 **Cabo Binibeca** *C* Spain
53A3 **Cabo Carbonara** *C* Sardegna
34A3 **Cabo Carranza** *C* Chile
50A2 **Cabo Carvoeiro** *C* Port
9B3 **Cabo Colnett** *C* Mexico
32B2 **Cabo Corrientes** *C* Colombia
24B2 **Cabo Corrientes** *C* Mexico
26B3 **Cabo Cruz** *C* Cuba
50B1 **Cabo de Ajo** *C* Spain
51C1 **Cabo de Caballeria** *C* Spain
51C1 **Cabo de Creus** *C* Spain
50B2 **Cabo de Gata** *C* Spain
29C7 **Cabo de Hornos** *C* Chile
51C2 **Cabo de la Nao** *C* Spain
50A1 **Cabo de Peñas** *C* Spain
50A2 **Cabo de Roca** *C* Port
51C2 **Cabo de Salinas** *C* Spain
35C2 **Cabo de São Tomé** *C* Brazil
50A2 **Cabo de São Vicente** *C* Port
50A2 **Cabo de Sines** *C* Port
51C1 **Cabo de Tortosa** *C* Spain
29C4 **Cabo Dos Bahias** *C* Arg
50A2 **Cabo Espichel** *C* Port
9B4 **Cabo Falso** *C* Mexico
51B2 **Cabo Ferrat** *C* Alg
50A1 **Cabo Finisterre** *C* Spain
51C1 **Cabo Formentor** *C* Spain
35C2 **Cabo Frio** Brazil
35C2 **Cabo Frio** *C* Brazil
26A4 **Cabo Gracias à Dios** Honduras
31B2 **Cabo Maguarinho** *C* Brazil
50A2 **Cabo Negro** *C* Mor
109D1 **Caboolture** Aust
33G3 **Cabo Orange** *C* Brazil
21B3 **Cabo Punta Banda** *C* Mexico
101C2 **Cabora Bassa Dam** Mozam
24A1 **Caborca** Mexico
24C2 **Cabo Rojo** *C* Mexico
23B1 **Cabos** Mexico
29C6 **Cabo San Diego** *C* Arg
32A4 **Cabo San Lorenzo** *C* Ecuador
53A3 **Cabo Teulada** *C* Sardegna
50A2 **Cabo Trafalgar** *C* Spain
50B2 **Cabo Tres Forcas** *C* Mor
29C5 **Cabo Tres Puntas** *C* Arg
7D5 **Cabot Str** Can
50B2 **Cabra** Spain
50A1 **Cabreira** *Mt* Port
51C2 **Cabrera** *I* Spain
34A3 **Cabrero** Chile
51B2 **Cabriel** *R* Spain
23B2 **Cacahuamilpa** Mexico
54B2 **Čačak** Serbia, Yugos
23B2 **C A Carillo** Mexico
30E2 **Cáceres** Brazil
50A2 **Caceres** Spain
18B2 **Cache** *R* USA
13C2 **Cache Creek** Can
30C4 **Cachi** Arg
33G5 **Cachimbo** Brazil
31D4 **Cachoeira** Brazil
35A1 **Cachoeira Alta** Brazil
31D3 **Cachoeira de Paulo Alfonso** *Waterfall* Brazil
29F2 **Cachoeira do Sul** Brazil
31C6 **Cachoeiro de Itapemirim** Brazil
22C3 **Cachuma,L** USA
100A2 **Cacolo** Angola
100A2 **Caconda** Angola
35A1 **Caçu** Brazil
100A2 **Çaculuvar** *R* Angola
59B3 **Čadca** Czech
43C3 **Cader Idris** *Mts* Wales
10B2 **Cadillac** USA
79B3 **Cadiz** Phil
50A2 **Cadiz** Spain
48B2 **Caen** France
42B3 **Caernarfon** Wales
43B3 **Caernarfon B** Wales
94B2 **Caesarea** *Hist Site* Israel
31C4 **Caetité** Brazil
30C4 **Cafayate** Arg
92B2 **Caga Tepe** Turk
79B2 **Cagayan** *R* Phil
79B4 **Cagayan de Oro** Phil
79B4 **Cagayan Is** Phil
53A3 **Cagliari** Sardegna
27D3 **Caguas** Puerto Rico
45B3 **Caha Mts** Irish Rep
45A3 **Cahersiveen** Irish Rep
45C2 **Cahir** Irish Rep
45C2 **Cahone Pt** Irish Rep
48C3 **Cahors** France
101C2 **Caia** Mozam
100B2 **Caianda** Angola
35A1 **Caiapó** *R* Brazil
35A1 **Caiapônia** Brazil
31D3 **Caicó** Brazil
26C2 **Caicos Is** Caribbean S
11C4 **Caicos Pass** The Bahamas
12C2 **Cairn Mt** USA
44C3 **Cairngorms** *Mts* Scot
107D2 **Cairns** Aust
92B3 **Cairo** Egypt
11B3 **Cairo** USA
108B1 **Caiwarro** Aust
32B5 **Cajabamba** Peru
32B5 **Cajamarca** Peru
27D5 **Calabozo** Ven
54B2 **Calafat** Rom
29B6 **Calafate** Arg
79B3 **Calagua Is** Phil
51B1 **Calahorra** Spain
48C1 **Calais** France
30C3 **Calama** Chile
32C3 **Calamar** Colombia
79A3 **Calamian Group** *Is* Phil
98B3 **Calandula** Angola
70A3 **Calang** Indon
95B2 **Calanscio Sand Sea** Libya
79B3 **Calapan** Phil
54C2 **Calarasi** Rom
51B1 **Calatayud** Spain
22B2 **Calaveras Res** USA
79B3 **Calbayog** Phil
19B4 **Calcasieu L** USA
86B2 **Calcutta** India
50A2 **Caldas da Rainha** Port
31B5 **Caldas Novas** Brazil
30B4 **Caldera** Chile

8B2 **Caldwell** USA
29C5 **Caleta Olivia** Arg
9B3 **Calexico** USA
5G4 **Calgary** Can
17B1 **Calhoun** USA
17B1 **Calhoun Falls** USA
32B3 **Cali** Colombia
8B3 **Caliente** Nevada, USA
8A3 **California** State, USA
22C3 **California Aqueduct** USA
87B2 **Calimera,Pt** India
34B2 **Calingasta** Arg
22A1 **Calistoga** USA
108B1 **Callabonna** *R* Aust
108A1 **Callabonna,L** Aust
15C1 **Callander** Can
44B3 **Callander** Scot
108A1 **Callanna** Aust
32B6 **Callao** Peru
13E1 **Calling L** Can
23B1 **Calnali** Mexico
17B2 **Caloosahatchee** *R* USA
109D1 **Caloundra** Aust
23B2 **Calpulalpan** Mexico
53B3 **Caltanissetta** Italy
98B3 **Caluango** Angola
100A2 **Calulo** Angola
100A2 **Caluquembe** Angola
99F1 **Caluula** Somalia
13B2 **Calvert I** Can
52A2 **Calvi** Corse
23A1 **Calvillo** Mexico
100A4 **Calvinia** S Africa
25E2 **Camagüey** Cuba
25E2 **Camagüey,Arch de** *Is* Cuba
30B2 **Camaná** Peru
30C3 **Camargo** Bol
22C3 **Camarillo** USA
29C4 **Camarones** Arg
20B1 **Camas** USA
98B3 **Camaxilo** Angola
98B3 **Cambatela** Angola
76C3 **Cambodia** Republic, S E Asia
43B4 **Camborne** Eng
49C1 **Cambrai** France
43C3 **Cambrian Mts** Wales
14B2 **Cambridge** Can
43D3 **Cambridge** County, Eng
43E3 **Cambridge** Eng
27H1 **Cambridge** Jamaica
15C3 **Cambridge** Maryland, USA
15D2 **Cambridge** Massachussets, USA
110C1 **Cambridge** NZ
14B2 **Cambridge** Ohio, USA
4H3 **Cambridge Bay** Can
60E5 **Cam Burun** *Pt* Turk
11A3 **Camden** Arkansas, USA
109D2 **Camden** Aust
15D3 **Camden** New Jersey, USA
17B1 **Camden** South Carolina, USA
18B2 **Cameron** Missouri, USA
19A3 **Cameron** Texas, USA
4H2 **Cameron I** Can
111A3 **Cameron Mts** NZ
98A2 **Cameroon** Federal Republic, Africa
98A2 **Cameroun** *Mt* Cam
31B2 **Cametá** Brazil
79B4 **Camiguin** *I* Phil
79B2 **Camiling** Phil
17B1 **Camilla** USA
22B1 **Camino** USA
30D3 **Camiri** Bol
31C2 **Camocim** Brazil
98C3 **Camissombo** Angola
106C2 **Camooweal** Aust
34D2 **Campana** Arg
29A5 **Campana** *I* Chile
13B2 **Campania I** Can
111B2 **Campbell,C** NZ
13B2 **Campbell I** Can
105G6 **Campbell I** NZ
4E3 **Campbell,Mt** Can
84C2 **Campbellpore** Pak
5F5 **Campbell River** Can
7D5 **Campbellton** Can
109D2 **Campbelltown** Aust
42B2 **Campbeltown** Scot
25C3 **Campeche** Mexico
108B3 **Camperdown** Aust
31D3 **Campina Grande** Brazil
31B6 **Campinas** Brazil
35B1 **Campina Verde** Brazil
98A2 **Campo** Cam
53B2 **Campobasso** Italy
35B2 **Campo Belo** Brazil
35B1 **Campo Florido** Brazil
30D4 **Campo Gallo** Arg
30F3 **Campo Grande** Brazil
31C2 **Campo Maior** Brazil
30F3 **Campo Mourão** Brazil
35C2 **Campos** Brazil
35B1 **Campos Altos** Brazil
47D1 **Campo Tures** Italy
76D3 **Cam Ranh** Viet
5G4 **Camrose** Can
100A2 **Camucuio** Angola
27K1 **Canaan** Tobago
16C1 **Canaan** USA
100A2 **Canacupa** Angola
2F3 **Canada** Dominion, N America
29D2 **Cañada de Gomez** Arg
9C3 **Canadian** *R* USA
60C5 **Canakkale** Turk
34B3 **Canalejas** Arg
13D2 **Canal Flats** Can
24A1 **Cananea** Mexico
102G3 **Canary Basin** Atlantic O
Canary Is = Islas Canarias
23A2 **Canas** Mexico
24B2 **Canatlán** Mexico
11B4 **Canaveral,C** USA
31D5 **Canavieiras** Brazil
107D4 **Canberra** Aust
20B2 **Canby** California, USA
55C3 **Çandarli Körfezi** *B* Turk
16C2 **Candlewood,L** USA
29E2 **Canelones** Urug
18A2 **Caney** USA
100A2 **Cangamba** Angola
100B2 **Cangombe** Angola
72D2 **Cangzhou** China
7D4 **Caniapiscau** *R* Can
7D4 **Caniapiscau,L** Can
53B3 **Canicatti** Italy
31D2 **Canindé** Brazil
92B1 **Çankırı** Turk
13D2 **Canmore** Can
44A3 **Canna** *I* Scot
87B2 **Cannanore** India
49D3 **Cannes** France
109C3 **Cann River** Aust
30F4 **Canõas** Brazil
13F1 **Canoe L** Can
9C3 **Canon City** USA
108B2 **Canopus** Aust
5H4 **Canora** Can
109C2 **Canowindra** Aust
45C2 **Cansore Pt** Irish Rep
43E4 **Canterbury** Eng
111B2 **Canterbury Bight** *B* NZ
111B2 **Canterbury Plains** NZ
77D4 **Can Tho** Viet
Canton = Guangzhou
19C3 **Canton** Mississippi, USA
18B1 **Canton** Missouri, USA
10B2 **Canton** Ohio, USA
12E2 **Cantwell** USA
20C2 **Canyon City** USA
12J2 **Canyon Range** *Mts* Can
20B2 **Canyonville** USA
98C3 **Canzar** Angola
76D1 **Cao Bang** Viet
31B2 **Capanema** Brazil
35B2 **Capão Bonito** Brazil
48B3 **Capbreton** France
24B2 **Cap Corrientes** *C* Mexico
52A2 **Cap Corse** *C* Corse
48B2 **Cap de la Hague** *C* France
15D1 **Cap-de-la-Madeleine** Can
6C3 **Cap de Nouvelle-France** *C* Can
51C2 **Capdepera** Spain
23A2 **Cap de Tancitiario** *C* Mexico
109C4 **Cape Barren I** Aust
103J6 **Cape Basin** Atlantic O
7E5 **Cape Breton I** Can
97B4 **Cape Coast** Ghana
15D2 **Cape Cod B** USA
6C3 **Cape Dorset** Can
17C1 **Cape Fear** *R* USA
18C2 **Cape Girardeau** USA
6B3 **Cape Henrietta Maria** Can
Cape Horn = Cabo de Hornos
104E3 **Cape Johnston Depth** Pacific O
35C1 **Capelinha** Brazil
4B3 **Cape Lisburne** USA
100A2 **Capelongo** Angola
15D3 **Cape May** USA
5F5 **Cape Mendocino** USA
98B3 **Capenda Camulemba** Angola
4F2 **Cape Perry** Can
100B4 **Cape Province** S Africa
7A4 **Cape Tatnam** Can
100A4 **Cape Town** S Africa
102G4 **Cape Verde** *Is* Atlantic O
102G4 **Cape Verde Basin** Atlantic O
12F3 **Cape Yakataga** USA
107D2 **Cape York Pen** Aust
46A1 **Cap Gris Nez** *C* France
26C3 **Cap-Haitien** Haiti
31B2 **Capim** *R* Brazil
112C2 **Capitán Arturo Prat** *Base* Ant
27P2 **Cap Moule à Chique** *C* St Lucia
53C3 **Capo Isola de Correnti** *C* Italy
53C3 **Capo Rizzuto** *C* Italy
55A3 **Capo Santa Maria di Leuca** *C* Italy
53B3 **Capo San Vito** Italy
53C3 **Capo Spartivento** *C* Italy
27P2 **Cap Pt** St Lucia
53B2 **Capri** *I* Italy
100B2 **Caprivi Strip** Region, Namibia
52A2 **Cap Rosso** *C* Corse
102H4 **Cap Vert** *C* Sen
32C4 **Caquetá** *R* Colombia
54B2 **Caracal** Rom
33E3 **Caracaraí** Brazil
32D1 **Caracas** Ven
35B2 **Caraguatatuba** Brazil
29B3 **Carahue** Chile
35C1 **Caraí** Brazil
35C2 **Carandaí** Brazil
31C6 **Carangola** Brazil
54B1 **Caransebeş** Rom
108A2 **Carappee Hill** *Mt* Aust
26A3 **Caratasca** Honduras
35C1 **Caratinga** Brazil
51B2 **Caravaca** Spain
35D1 **Caravelas** Brazil
18C2 **Carbondale** Illinois, USA
53A3 **Carbonia** Sardegna
7E5 **Carborear** Can
5G4 **Carcaion** Can
99E1 **Carcar Mts** Somalia
48C3 **Carcassonne** France
4E3 **Carcross** Can
23B2 **Cardel** Mexico
25D2 **Cardenas** Cuba
23B1 **Cárdenas** Mexico
43C4 **Cardiff** Wales
43B3 **Cardigan** Wales
43B3 **Cardigan B** Wales
13E2 **Cardston** Can
54B1 **Carei** Rom
33F4 **Careiro** Brazil
34A2 **Carén** Chile
14B2 **Carey** USA
48B2 **Carhaix-Plouguer** France
29D3 **Carhué** Arg
31C6 **Cariacica** Brazil
5J4 **Caribou** Can
5G4 **Caribou Mts** Alberta, Can
5F4 **Caribou Mts** British Columbia, Can
79B3 **Carigara** Phil
46C2 **Carignan** France
33E1 **Caripito** Ven
15C1 **Carleton Place** Can
101G1 **Carletonville** S Africa
18C2 **Carlinville** USA
42C2 **Carlisle** Eng
15C2 **Carlisle** USA
34C3 **Carlos** Arg
35C1 **Carlos Chagas** Brazil
45C2 **Carlow** County, Irish Rep
45C2 **Carlow** Irish Rep
21B3 **Carlsbad** California, USA
9C3 **Carlsbad** New Mexico, USA
5H5 **Carlyle** Can
12G2 **Carmacks** Can
47B2 **Carmagnola** Italy
43B4 **Carmarthen** Wales
43B4 **Carmarthen B** Wales
22B2 **Carmel** California, USA
16C2 **Carmel** New York, USA
94B2 **Carmel,Mt** Israel
34D2 **Carmelo** Urug
22B2 **Carmel Valley** USA
9B4 **Carmen** *I* Mexico
29D4 **Carmen de Patagones** Arg
18C2 **Carmi** USA
21A2 **Carmichael** USA
35B1 **Carmo do Paranaiba** Brazil
50A2 **Carmona** Spain
106A3 **Carnarvon** Aust
100B4 **Carnarvon** S Africa
35D1 **Carncacá** Brazil
45C1 **Carndonagh** Irish Rep
106B3 **Carnegi,L** Aust
98B2 **Carnot** CAR
108A2 **Carnot,C** Aust
17B2 **Carol City** USA
31B3 **Carolina** Brazil
101H1 **Carolina** S Africa
17C1 **Carolina Beach** USA
104F3 **Caroline Is** Pacific O
60B4 **Carpathians** *Mts* E Europe
59D3 **Carpatii Orientali** *Mts* Rom
106C2 **Carpentaria,G of** Aust
83C5 **Carpenter Ridge** Indian O
49D3 **Carpentras** France
52B2 **Carpi** Italy
22C3 **Carpinteria** USA
17B2 **Carrabelle** USA
52B2 **Carrara** Italy
41B3 **Carrauntoohill** *Mt* Irish Rep
45C2 **Carrickmacross** Irish Rep
45B2 **Carrick on Shannon** Irish Rep
45C2 **Carrick-on-Suir** Irish Rep
108A2 **Carrieton** Aust

8D2 **Carrington** USA
50B1 **Carrión** *R* Spain
10A2 **Carroll** USA
17A1 **Carrollton** Georgia, USA
14A3 **Carrollton** Kentucky, USA
18B2 **Carrollton** Missouri, USA
18C2 **Carruthersville** USA
60E5 **Carsamba** Turk
92B2 **Carsamba** *R* Turk
8B3 **Carson City** USA
14B2 **Carsonville** USA
26B4 **Cartagena** Colombia
51B2 **Cartagena** Spain
32B3 **Cartago** Colombia
25D4 **Cartago** Costa Rica
111C2 **Carterton** NZ
18B2 **Carthage** Missouri, USA
15C2 **Carthage** New York, USA
19B3 **Carthage** Texas, USA
106B2 **Cartier I** Timor S
7E4 **Cartwright** Can
31D3 **Caruaru** Brazil
33E1 **Carúpano** Ven
46B1 **Carvin** France
34A2 **Casablanca** Chile
96B1 **Casablanca** Mor
35B2 **Casa Branca** Brazil
9B3 **Casa Grande** USA
52A1 **Casale Monferrato** Italy
47D2 **Casalmaggiore** Italy
34C3 **Casares** Arg
13C3 **Cascade Mts** Can/USA
111A2 **Cascade Pt** NZ
8A2 **Cascade Range** *Mts* USA
30F3 **Cascavel** Brazil
53B2 **Caserta** Italy
112C9 **Casey** *Base* Ant
45C2 **Cashel** Irish Rep
34C2 **Casilda** Arg
107E3 **Casino** Aust
32B5 **Casma** Peru
51B1 **Caspe** Spain
8C2 **Casper** USA
65G6 **Caspian S** Asia/Europe
14C3 **Cass** USA
100B2 **Cassamba** Angola
46B1 **Cassel** France
12J3 **Cassiar** Can
4E3 **Cassiar Mts** Can
35A1 **Cassilândia** Brazil
53B2 **Cassino** Italy
22C3 **Castaic** USA
34B2 **Castaño** *R* Arg
47D2 **Castelfranco** Italy
49D3 **Castellane** France
34D3 **Castelli** Arg
51B2 **Castellon de la Plana** Spain
31C3 **Castelo** Brazil
50A2 **Castelo Branco** Port
48C3 **Castelsarrasin** France
53B3 **Castelvetrano** Italy
108B3 **Casterton** Aust
50B2 **Castilla La Nueva** Region, Spain
50B1 **Castilla La Vieja** Region, Spain
41B3 **Castlebar** Irish Rep
44A3 **Castlebay** Scot
42C2 **Castle Douglas** Scot
20C1 **Castlegar** Can
45B2 **Castleisland** Irish Rep
108B3 **Castlemain** Aust
45B2 **Castlerea** Irish Rep
109C2 **Castlereagh** Aust
48C3 **Castres-sur-l'Agout** France
27E4 **Castries** St Lucia
29B4 **Castro** Arg
30F3 **Castro** Brazil
31D4 **Castro Alves** Brazil
53C3 **Castrovillari** Italy
22B2 **Castroville** USA
111A2 **Caswell Sd** NZ
25E2 **Cat** *I* The Bahamas
79B3 **Catabalogan** Phil
32A5 **Catacaos** Peru
35C2 **Cataguases** Brazil
19B3 **Catahoula L** USA
35B1 **Catalão** Brazil
51C1 **Cataluña** Region, Spain
30C4 **Catamarca** Arg
30C4 **Catamarca** State, Arg
101C2 **Catandica** Mozam
79B3 **Catanduanes** *I* Phil
31B6 **Catanduva** Brazil
53C3 **Catania** Italy
53C3 **Catanzaro** Italy
79B3 **Catarman** Phil
108A2 **Catastrophe,C** Aust
26C5 **Catatumbo** *R* Ven
16A2 **Catawissa** USA
23B2 **Catemaco** Mexico
49D3 **Cater** Corse
52A2 **Cateraggio** Corse
98B3 **Catete** Angola
97A3 **Catio** Guinea-Bissau
7A4 **Cat Lake** Can
13D3 **Catlegar** Can
107E3 **Cato** *I* Aust
25D2 **Catoche,C** Mexico
16A3 **Catoctin Mt** USA
15C3 **Catonsville** USA
34C3 **Catrilo** Arg
15D2 **Catskill** USA
15D2 **Catskill Mts** USA
32C2 **Cauca** *R* Colombia
31D2 **Caucaia** Brazil
32B2 **Caucasia** Colombia
Caucasus = Bol'shoy Kavkaz
46B1 **Caudry** France
98B3 **Caungula** Angola
29B3 **Cauquenes** Chile
87B2 **Cauvery** *R* India
49D3 **Cavaillon** France
47D1 **Cavalese** italy
97B4 **Cavally** *R* Lib
45C2 **Cavan** County, Irish Rep
45C2 **Cavan** Irish Rep
79B3 **Cavite** Phil
31C2 **Caxias** Brazil
32C4 **Caxias** Brazil
30F4 **Caxias do Sul** Brazil
98B3 **Caxito** Angola
17B1 **Cayce** USA
93D1 **Çayeli** Turk
33G3 **Cayenne** French Guiana
46A1 **Cayeux-sur-Mer** France
25E3 **Cayman Brac** *I* Caribbean S
26A3 **Cayman Is** Caribbean S
26A3 **Cayman Trench** Caribbean S
99E2 **Caynabo** Somalia
25E2 **Cayo Romana** *I* Cuba
25D3 **Cayos Miskitos** *Is* Nic
26A2 **Cay Sal** *I* Caribbean S
100B2 **Cazombo** Angola
Ceará = Fortaleza
31C3 **Ceara** State, Brazil
79B3 **Cebu** Phil
79B3 **Cebu** *I* Phil
16B3 **Cecilton** USA
52B2 **Cecina** Italy
8B3 **Cedar City** USA
19A3 **Cedar Creek Res** USA
5J4 **Cedar L** Can
10A2 **Cedar Rapids** USA
17A1 **Cedartown** USA
24A2 **Cedros** *I* Mexico
106C4 **Ceduna** Aust
99E2 **Ceelbuur** Somalia
99E1 **Ceerigaabo** Somalia
53B3 **Cefalù** Italy
59B3 **Cegléd** Hung
100A2 **Cela** Angola
24B2 **Celaya** Mexico
Celebes = Sulawesi
70C3 **Celebes S** S E Asia
14B2 **Celina** USA
52C1 **Celje** Slovenia
56C2 **Celle** Germany
71E4 **Cendrawasih** *Pen* Indon
47C2 **Ceno** *R* Italy
19B3 **Center** USA
16C2 **Center Moriches** USA
17A1 **Center Point** USA
47D2 **Cento** Italy
44B3 **Central** Region, Scot
98B2 **Central African Republic** Africa
16D2 **Central Falls** USA
18C2 **Centralia** Illinois, USA
8A2 **Centralia** Washington, USA
20B2 **Central Point** USA
71F4 **Central Range** *Mts* PNG
16A3 **Centreville** Maryland, USA
78C4 **Cepu** Indon
Ceram = Seram
71D4 **Ceram Sea** Indon
34C3 **Cereales** Arg
31B5 **Ceres** Brazil
100A4 **Ceres** S Africa
22B2 **Ceres** USA
48C2 **Cergy-Pontoise** France
53C2 **Cerignola** Italy
60C5 **Cernavodă** Rom
9C4 **Cerralvo** *I* Mexico
23A1 **Cerritos** Mexico
34B2 **Cerro Aconcagua** *Mt* Arg
23B1 **Cerro Azul** Mexico
34A3 **Cerro Campanario** *Mt* Chile
34C2 **Cerro Champaqui** *Mt* Arg
23A2 **Cerro Cuachaia** *Mt* Mexico
23B1 **Cerro de Astillero** Mexico
34B2 **Cerro de Olivares** *Mt* Arg
32B6 **Cerro de Pasco** Peru
27D3 **Cerro de Punta** *Mt* Puerto Rico
23A2 **Cerro El Cantado** *Mt* Mexico
34B3 **Cerro El Nevado** *Mt* Arg
23A2 **Cerro Grande** *Mts* Mexico
34A2 **Cerro Juncal** *Mt* Arg/Chile
23A1 **Cerro la Ardilla** *Mts* Mexico
34B1 **Cerro las Tortolas** *Mt* Chile
23A2 **Cerro Laurel** *Mt* Mexico
34A2 **Cerro Mercedario** *Mt* Arg
34A3 **Cerro Mora** *Mt* Chile
27C4 **Cerron** *Mt* Ven
34B3 **Cerro Payún** *Mt* Arg
23B2 **Cerro Penón del Rosario** *Mt* Mexico
34B2 **Cerro Sosneado** *Mt* Arg
23A2 **Cerro Teotepec** *Mt* Mexico
34B2 **Cerro Tupungato** *Mt* Arg
23B2 **Cerro Yucuyacau** *Mt* Mexico
47C2 **Cervo** *R* Italy
52B2 **Cesena** Italy
60B2 **Cēsis** Latvia
57C3 **České Budějovice** Czech
57C3 **České Zemé** Region, Czech
59B3 **Českomoravská Vysočina** *U* Czech
55C3 **Çeşme** Turk
107E4 **Cessnock** Aust
52C2 **Cetina** *R* Croatia
96B1 **Ceuta** N W Africa
92C2 **Ceyham** Turk
92C2 **Ceyhan** *R* Turk
93C2 **Ceylanpınar** Turk
Ceylon = Sri Lanka
63B2 **Chaa-Khol** Russian Fed
48C2 **Chaâteaudun** France
47B1 **Chablais** Region, France
34C2 **Chacabuco** Arg
32B5 **Chachapoyas** Peru
34B3 **Chacharramendi** Arg
84C3 **Chachran** Pak
30D4 **Chaco** State, Arg
98B1 **Chad** Republic, Africa
98B1 **Chad** *L* C Africa
34B3 **Chadileuvu** *R* Arg
8C2 **Chadron** USA
18C2 **Chaffee** USA
85A3 **Chagai** Pak
63F2 **Chagda** Russian Fed
84B2 **Chaghcharan** Afghan
104B4 **Chagos Arch** Indian O
27L1 **Chaguanas** Trinidad
91D4 **Chāh Bahār** Iran
76C2 **Chai Badan** Thai
76C3 **Chaine des Cardamomes** *Mts* Camb
98C4 **Chaine des Mitumba** *Mts* Zaïre
76C2 **Chaiyaphum** Thai
34D2 **Chajari** Arg
84C2 **Chakwal** Pak
30B2 **Chala** Peru
100C2 **Chalabesa** Zambia
84A2 **Chalap Dalam** *Mts* Afghan
73C4 **Chaling** China
85C4 **Chālisgaon** India
12F1 **Chalkyitsik** USA
46C2 **Challerange** France
46C2 **Châlons sur Marne** France
49C2 **Chalon sur Saône** France
57C3 **Cham** Germany
84B2 **Chaman** Pak
84D2 **Chamba** India
85D3 **Chambal** *R* India
15C3 **Chambersburg** USA
49D2 **Chambéry** France
46B2 **Chambly** France
85A3 **Chambor Kalat** Pak
90B3 **Chamgordan** Iran
34B2 **Chamical** Arg
47B2 **Chamonix** France
86A2 **Champa** India
49C2 **Champagne** Region, France
101G1 **Champagne Castle** *Mt* Lesotho
47A1 **Champagnole** France
10B2 **Champaign** USA
76D3 **Champassak** Laos
10C2 **Champlain,L** USA
87B2 **Chāmrājnagar** India
30B4 **Chañaral** Chile
34A3 **Chanco** Chile
4D3 **Chandalar** USA
4D3 **Chandalar** *R* USA
84D2 **Chandīgarh** India
86C2 **Chandpur** Bang
85D5 **Chandrapur** India
91D4 **Chānf** Iran
101C2 **Changara** Mozam
74B2 **Changbai** China
69E2 **Changchun** China
73C4 **Changde** China
68E4 **Chang-hua** Taiwan
76D2 **Changjiang** China
73D3 **Chang Jiang** *R* China
74B2 **Changjin** N Korea
73C4 **Changsha** China
72E3 **Changshu** China
74A2 **Changtu** China
72B2 **Changwu** China
74B3 **Changyŏn** N Korea
72C2 **Changzhi** China
73E3 **Changzhou** China
48B2 **Channel Is** Europe
9B3 **Channel Is** USA

7E5 **Channel Port-aux-Basques** Can
76C3 **Chanthaburi** Thai
46B2 **Chantilly** France
18A2 **Chanute** USA
73D5 **Chaoàn** China
73D5 **Chao'an** China
73D3 **Chao Hu** *L* China
76C3 **Chao Phraya** *R* Thai
72E1 **Chaoyang** China
31C4 **Chapada Diamantina** *Mts* Brazil
31C2 **Chapadinha** Brazil
23A1 **Chapala** Mexico
23A1 **Chapala,Lac de** *L* Mexico
61H3 **Chapayevo** Kazakhstan
30F4 **Chapecó** Brazil
27H1 **Chapeltown** Jamaica
7B5 **Chapleau** Can
61E3 **Chaplygin** Russian Fed
112C3 **Charcot I** Ant
80E2 **Chardzhou** Turkmenistan
48C2 **Charente** *R* France
98B1 **Chari** *R* Chad
98B1 **Chari Baguirmi** Region, Chad
84B1 **Charikar** Afghan
18B1 **Chariton** *R* USA
33F2 **Charity** Guyana
85D3 **Charkhāri** India
46C1 **Charleroi** Belg
18C2 **Charleston** Illinois, USA
18C2 **Charleston** Missouri, USA
11C3 **Charleston** S Carolina, USA
10B3 **Charleston** W Virginia, USA
98C3 **Charlesville** Zaïre
107D3 **Charleville** Aust
49C2 **Charleville-Mézières** France
14A1 **Charlevoix** USA
14B2 **Charlotte** Michigan, USA
11B3 **Charlotte** N Carolina, USA
17B2 **Charlotte Harbor** *B* USA
10C3 **Charlottesville** USA
7D5 **Charlottetown** Can
27K1 **Charlotteville** Tobago
108B3 **Charlton** Aust
10C1 **Charlton I** Can
84C2 **Charsadda** Pak
107D3 **Charters Towers** Aust
48C2 **Chartres** France
29E3 **Chascomús** Arg
13D2 **Chase** Can
48B2 **Châteaubriant** France
48C2 **Châteaudun** France
48B2 **Châteaulin** France
48C2 **Châteauroux** France
46D2 **Chäteau-Salins** France
49C2 **Cháteau-Thierry** France
46C1 **Châtelet** Belg
48C2 **Châtellerault** France
43E4 **Chatham** Eng
7D5 **Chatham** New Brunswick, Can
16C1 **Chatham** New York, USA
14B2 **Chatham** Ontario, Can
13A2 **Chatham Sd** Can
12H3 **Chatham Str** USA
49C2 **Châtillon** France
47B2 **Châtillon** Italy
16B3 **Chatsworth** USA
17B1 **Chattahoochee** USA
17A1 **Chattahoochee** *R* USA
11B3 **Chattanooga** USA
76A1 **Chauk** Burma
49D2 **Chaumont** France
46B2 **Chauny** France
77D3 **Chau Phu** Viet
50A1 **Chaves** Port
61H2 **Chaykovskiy** Russian Fed
50B2 **Chazaouet** Alg
34C2 **Chazón** Arg
32C2 **Chcontá** Colombia
57C2 **Cheb** Czech
65F4 **Cheboksary** Russian Fed
10B2 **Cheboygan** USA
74B3 **Chech'on** S Korea
85C3 **Chechro** Pak
18A2 **Checotah** USA
76A2 **Cheduba** *I* Burma
108B1 **Cheepie** Aust
96B2 **Chegga** Maur
100C2 **Chegutu** Zim
20B1 **Chehalis** USA
74B4 **Cheju** S Korea
74B4 **Cheju do** *I* S Korea
74B4 **Cheju-haehyŏp** *Str* S Korea
63F2 **Chekunda** Russian Fed
20B1 **Chelan,L** USA
90B2 **Cheleken** Turkmenistan
34B3 **Chelforo** Arg
80D1 **Chelkar** Kazakhstan
59C2 **Chelm** Pol
58B2 **Chelmno** Pol
43E4 **Chelmsford** Eng
43C4 **Cheltenham** Eng
65H4 **Chelyabinsk** Russian Fed
101C2 **Chemba** Mozam
57C2 **Chemnitz** Germany
84D2 **Chenab** *R* India/Pak
96B2 **Chenachane** Alg
20C1 **Cheney** USA
18A2 **Cheney Res** USA
72D1 **Chengda** China
73A3 **Chengdu** China
72E2 **Chengshan Jiao** *Pt* China
73C4 **Chenxi** China
73C4 **Chen Xian** China
73D3 **Cheo Xian** China
32B5 **Chepén** Peru
34B2 **Chepes** Arg
48C2 **Cher** *R* France
23A2 **Cheran** Mexico
17C1 **Cheraw** USA
48B2 **Cherbourg** France
96C1 **Cherchell** Alg
63C2 **Cheremkhovo** Russian Fed
60E2 **Cherepovets** Russian Fed
60D4 **Cherkassy** Ukraine
61F5 **Cherkessk** Russian Fed
60D3 **Chernigov** Ukraine
60D2 **Chernobyl** Ukraine
60C4 **Chernovtsy** Ukraine
61J2 **Chernushka** Russian Fed
60B3 **Chernyakhovsk** Russian Fed
61G4 **Chernyye Zemli** Region, Russian Fed
18A2 **Cherokees,L o'the** USA
34A3 **Cherquenco** Chile
86C1 **Cherrapunji** India
60C3 **Cherven'** Belorussia
59C2 **Chervonograd** Ukraine
10C3 **Chesapeake** *B* USA
42C3 **Cheshire** County, Eng
16C1 **Cheshire** USA
64F3 **Chëshskaya Guba** *B* Russian Fed
21A1 **Chester** California, USA
42C3 **Chester** Eng
18C2 **Chester** Illinois, USA
16C1 **Chester** Massachusets, USA
15C3 **Chester** Pennsylvania, USA
17B1 **Chester** S Carolina, USA
16A3 **Chester** *R* USA
42D3 **Chesterfield** Eng
6A3 **Chesterfield Inlet** Can
16A3 **Chestertown** USA
25D3 **Chetumal** Mexico
13C1 **Chetwynd** Can
12A2 **Chevak** USA
111B2 **Cheviot** NZ
40C2 **Cheviots** *Hills* Eng/Scot
13D3 **Chewelah** USA
8C2 **Cheyenne** USA
86A1 **Chhapra** India
86C1 **Chhātak** Bang
85D4 **Chhatarpur** India
85D4 **Chhindwāra** India
86B1 **Chhuka** Bhutan
73E5 **Chia'i** Taiwan
100A2 **Chiange** Angola
76C2 **Chiang Kham** Thai
76B2 **Chiang Mai** Thai
47C1 **Chiavenna** Italy
74E3 **Chiba** Japan
86B2 **Chībāsa** India
100A2 **Chibia** Angola
7C4 **Chibougamou** Can
75A1 **Chiburi-jima** *I* Japan
101C3 **Chibuto** Mozam
10B2 **Chicago** USA
14A2 **Chicago Heights** USA
12G3 **Chichagof I** USA
43D4 **Chichester** Eng
75B1 **Chichibu** Japan
69G4 **Chichi-jima** *I* Japan
11B3 **Chickamauga L** USA
19C3 **Chickasawhay** *R* USA
9D3 **Chickasha** USA
12F2 **Chicken** USA
32A5 **Chiclayo** Peru
8A3 **Chico** USA
29C4 **Chico** *R* Arg
101C2 **Chicoa** Mozam
15D2 **Chicopee** USA
7C5 **Chicoutimi** Can
101C3 **Chicualacuala** Mozam
87B2 **Chidambaram** India
6D3 **Chidley,C** Can
17B2 **Chiefland** USA
99C3 **Chiengi** Zambia
47B2 **Chieri** Italy
46C2 **Chiers** *R* France
47C1 **Chiesa** Italy
47D2 **Chiese** *R* Italy
52B2 **Chieti** Italy
72D1 **Chifeng** China
12C3 **Chiginigak,Mt** USA
4C3 **Chigmit Mts** USA
23B2 **Chignahuapán** Mexico
12C3 **Chignik** USA
24B2 **Chihuahua** Mexico
87B2 **Chik Ballāpur** India
87B2 **Chikmagalūr** India
12C2 **Chikuminuk L** USA
101C2 **Chikwawa** Malawi
76A1 **Chi-kyaw** Burma
87C1 **Chilakalūrupet** India
23B2 **Chilapa** Mexico
87B3 **Chilaw** Sri Lanka
28B6 **Chile** Republic
34B2 **Chilecito** Mendoza, Arg
100B2 **Chililabombwe** Zambia
86B2 **Chilka** *L* India
13C2 **Chilko** *R* Can
5F4 **Chilko L** Can
13C2 **Chilkotin** *R* Can
34A3 **Chillán** Chile
34D3 **Chillar** Arg
18B2 **Chillicothe** Missouri, USA
14B3 **Chillicothe** Ohio, USA
13C3 **Chilliwack** Can
86B1 **Chilmari** India
101C2 **Chilongozi** Zambia
20B2 **Chiloquin** USA
24C3 **Chilpancingo** Mexico
43D4 **Chiltern Hills** *Upland* Eng
14A2 **Chilton** USA
101C2 **Chilumba** Malawi
69E4 **Chi-lung** Taiwan
101C2 **Chilwa** *L* Malawi
100C2 **Chimanimani** Zim
46C1 **Chimay** Belg
65G5 **Chimbay** Uzbekistan
32B4 **Chimborazo** *Mt* Ecuador
32B5 **Chimbote** Peru
65H5 **Chimkent** Kazakhstan
101C2 **Chimoio** Mozam
67E3 **China** Republic, Asia
China National Republic = Taiwan
25D3 **Chinandega** Nic
32B6 **Chincha Alta** Peru
109D1 **Chinchilla** Aust
101C2 **Chinde** Mozam
86C2 **Chindwin** *R* Burma
100B2 **Chingola** Zambia
100A2 **Chinguar** Angola
96A2 **Chinguetti** Maur
74B3 **Chinhae** S Korea
100C2 **Chinhoyi** Zim
12D3 **Chiniak,C** USA
84C2 **Chiniot** Pak
74B3 **Chinju** S Korea
98C2 **Chinko** *R* CAR
75B1 **Chino** Japan
101C2 **Chinsali** Zambia
52B1 **Chioggia** Italy
101C2 **Chipata** Zambia
101C3 **Chipinge** Zim
87A1 **Chiplūn** India
43C4 **Chippenham** Eng
10A2 **Chippewa Falls** USA
32A4 **Chira** *R* Peru
87C1 **Chīrāla** India
101C3 **Chiredzi** Zim
95A2 **Chirfa** Niger
32A2 **Chiriqui** *Mt* Panama
54C2 **Chirpan** Bulg
32A2 **Chirrípo Grande** *Mt* Costa Rica
100B2 **Chirundu** Zim
100B2 **Chisamba** Zambia
7C4 **Chisasibi** Can
73B4 **Chishui He** *R* China
Chişinău = Kishinev
47B2 **Chisone** *R* Italy
61H2 **Chistopol** Russian Fed
68D1 **Chita** Russian Fed
100A2 **Chitado** Angola
100A2 **Chitembo** Angola
12F2 **Chitina** USA
12F2 **Chitina** *R* USA
87B2 **Chitradurga** India
84C1 **Chitral** Pak
32A2 **Chitré** Panama
86C2 **Chittagong** Bang
85C4 **Chittaurgarh** India
87B2 **Chittoor** India
100B2 **Chiume** Angola
47D1 **Chiusa** Italy
47B2 **Chivasso** Italy
100C2 **Chivhu** Zim
29D2 **Chivilcoy** Arg
100C2 **Chivu** Zim
75A1 **Chizu** Japan
29C3 **Choele Choel** Arg
34C3 **Choique** Arg
24B2 **Choix** Mexico
58B2 **Chojnice** Pol
99D1 **Choke** *Mts* Eth
48B2 **Cholet** France
23B2 **Cholula** Mexico
100B2 **Choma** Zambia
86B1 **Chomo Yummo** *Mt* China/India
57C2 **Chomutov** Czech
63C1 **Chona** *R* Russian Fed
74B3 **Ch'ŏnan** S Korea
76C3 **Chon Buri** Thai
32A4 **Chone** Ecuador
74B2 **Ch'ŏngjin** N Korea
74B3 **Chongju** N Korea

74B3 **Ch'ŏngju** S Korea
100A2 **Chongoroi** Angola
73B4 **Chongqing** China
74B3 **Chŏngŭp** S Korea
74B3 **Chŏnju** S Korea
86B1 **Chooyu** *Mt* China/Nepal
59D3 **Chortkov** Ukraine
74B3 **Ch'ŏrwŏn** N Korea
59B2 **Chorzow** Pol
74E3 **Choshi** Japan
34A3 **Chos-Malal** Arg
58B2 **Choszczno** Pol
86A2 **Chotanāgpur** Region, India
96C1 **Chott Melrhir** Alg
22B2 **Chowchilla** USA
63D3 **Choybalsan** Mongolia
6A3 **Chrantrey Inlet** *B* Can
111B2 **Christchurch** NZ
101G1 **Christiana** S Africa
6D2 **Christian,C** Can
12H3 **Christian Sd** USA
6E3 **Christianshab** Greenland
104D4 **Christmas I** Indian O
65J5 **Chu** Kazakhstan
65J5 **Chu** *R* Kazakhstan
29C4 **Chubut** State, Arg
29C4 **Chubut** *R* Arg
60D2 **Chudovo** Russian Fed
Chudskoye Ozero = Peipus, Lake
4D3 **Chugach Mts** USA
12E2 **Chugiak** USA
75A1 **Chūgoku-sanchi** *Mts* Japan
29F2 **Chuí** Brazil
29B3 **Chuillán** Chile
77C5 **Chukai** Malay
76D2 **Chu Lai** Viet
21B3 **Chula Vista** USA
12E2 **Chulitna** USA
63E2 **Chulman** Russian Fed
32A5 **Chulucanas** Peru
30C2 **Chulumani** Bol
65K4 **Chulym** Russian Fed
63A2 **Chulym** *R* Russian Fed
63B2 **Chuma** *R* Russian Fed
84D2 **Chumar** India
63F2 **Chumikan** Russian Fed
77B3 **Chumphon** Thai
74B3 **Ch'unch'ŏn** S Korea
86B2 **Chunchura** India
74B3 **Ch'ungju** S Korea
Chungking = Chongqing
99D3 **Chunya** Tanz
63C1 **Chunya** *R* Russian Fed
27L1 **Chupara Pt** Trinidad
30C3 **Chuquicamata** Chile
52A1 **Chur** Switz
86C2 **Churāchāndpur** India
7A4 **Churchill** Can
7D4 **Churchill** *R* Labrador, Can
7A4 **Churchill** *R* Manitoba, Can
7A4 **Churchill,C** Can
7D4 **Churchill Falls** Can
5H4 **Churchill L** Can
84C3 **Chūru** India
23A2 **Churumuco** Mexico
61J2 **Chusovoy** Russian Fed
61G2 **Chuvashkaya Respublika,** Russian Fed
68B4 **Chuxiong** China
76D3 **Chu Yang Sin** *Mt* Viet
78B4 **Cianjur** Indon
47D2 **Ciano d'Enza** Italy
35A2 **Cianorte** Brazil
58C2 **Ciechanow** Pol
25E2 **Ciego de Avila** Cuba
32C1 **Ciénaga** Colombia
25D2 **Cienfuegos** Cuba
59B3 **Cieszyn** Pol
51B2 **Cieza** Spain
92B2 **Cihanbeyli** Turk
23A2 **Cihuatlán** Mexico
78B4 **Cijulang** Indon
78B4 **Cilacap** Indon
54C1 **Cîmpina** Rom
51C1 **Çinca** *R* Spain
52C2 **Činčer** *Mt* Bosnia & Herzegovina, Yugos
10B3 **Cincinnati** USA
54B1 **Cindrelu** *Mt* Rom
55C3 **Cine** *R* Turk
46C1 **Ciney** Belg
34B3 **Cipolletti** Arg
4D3 **Circle** Alaska, USA
14B3 **Circleville** USA
78B4 **Cirebon** Indon
43D4 **Cirencester** Eng
47D2 **Citadella** Italy
24C3 **Citlaltepetl** *Mt* Mexico
100A4 **Citrusdal** S Africa
52B2 **Citta del Vaticano** Italy
52B2 **Città di Castello** Italy
24B2 **Ciudad Acuña** Mexico
23A2 **Ciudad Altamirano** Mexico
33E2 **Ciudad Bolivar** Ven
24B2 **Ciudad Camargo** Mexico
25C3 **Ciudad del Carmen** Mexico
23B1 **Ciudad del Maiz** Mexico
51C1 **Ciudadela** Spain
33E2 **Ciudad Guayana** Ven
24B3 **Ciudad Guzman** Mexico
23A2 **Ciudad Hidalgo** Mexico
24B1 **Ciudad Juárez** Mexico
9C4 **Ciudad Lerdo** Mexico
24C2 **Ciudad Madero** Mexico
23B2 **Ciudad Mendoza** Mexico
24B2 **Ciudad Obregon** Mexico
27C4 **Ciudad Ojeda** Ven
33E2 **Ciudad Piar** Ven
50B2 **Ciudad Real** Spain
50A1 **Ciudad Rodrigo** Spain
24C2 **Ciudad Valles** Mexico
24C2 **Ciudad Victoria** Mexico
52B2 **Civitavecchia** Italy
93D2 **Cizre** Turk
43E4 **Clacton-on-Sea** Eng
5G4 **Claire,L** Can
14C2 **Clairton** USA
47A1 **Clairvaux** France
17A1 **Clanton** USA
100A4 **Clanwilliam** S Africa
45C2 **Clara** Irish Rep
34D3 **Claraz** Arg
45B2 **Clare** County, Irish Rep
14B2 **Clare** USA
45A2 **Clare** *I* Irish Rep
15D2 **Claremont** USA
18A2 **Claremore** USA
45B2 **Claremorris** Irish Rep
109D1 **Clarence** *R* Aust
111B2 **Clarence** *R* NZ
106C2 **Clarence Str** Aust
12H3 **Clarence Str** USA
19B3 **Clarendon** USA
7E5 **Clarenville** Can
5G4 **Claresholm** Can
18A1 **Clarinda** USA
15C2 **Clarion** Pennsylvania, USA
24A3 **Clarión** *I* Mexico
15C2 **Clarion** *R* USA
105J3 **Clarion Fracture Zone** Pacific O
11B3 **Clark Hill Res** USA
14B2 **Clark,Pt** Can
14B3 **Clarksburg** USA
11A3 **Clarksdale** USA
12C3 **Clarks Point** USA
20C1 **Clarkston** USA
18B2 **Clarksville** Arkansas, USA
35A1 **Claro** *R* Brazil
29D3 **Claromecó** Arg
18A2 **Clay Center** USA
44D2 **Claymore** *Oilfield* N Sea
13B3 **Clayoquot Sd** Can
9C3 **Clayton** New Mexico, USA
15C2 **Clayton** New York, USA
41B3 **Clear** *C* Irish Rep
12E3 **Cleare,C** USA
13D1 **Clear Hills** *Mts* Can
21A2 **Clear L** USA
20B2 **Clear Lake Res** USA
13D2 **Clearwater** Can
11B4 **Clearwater** USA
13E1 **Clearwater** *R* Can
13C2 **Clearwater L** Can
9D3 **Cleburne** USA
42E2 **Cleeton** *Oilfield* North Sea
22B1 **Clements** USA
79A3 **Cleopatra Needle** *Mt* Phil
107D3 **Clermont** Aust
46B2 **Clermont** France
46C2 **Clermont-en-Argonne** France
49C2 **Clermont-Ferrand** France
46D1 **Clervaux** Germany
47D1 **Cles** Italy
108A2 **Cleve** Aust
42D2 **Cleveland** County, Eng
19B3 **Cleveland** Mississippi, USA
10B2 **Cleveland** Ohio, USA
11B3 **Cleveland** Tennessee, USA
19A3 **Cleveland** Texas, USA
41B3 **Clew** *B* Irish Rep
45A2 **Clifden** Irish Rep
109D1 **Clifton** Aust
16B2 **Clifton** New Jersey, USA
108A1 **Clifton Hills** Aust
13F3 **Climax** Can
18B2 **Clinton** Arkansas, USA
5F4 **Clinton** Can
16C2 **Clinton** Connecticut, USA
16D1 **Clinton** Massachusetts, USA
19B3 **Clinton** Mississippi, USA
18B2 **Clinton** Missouri, USA
16B2 **Clinton** New Jersey, USA
4H3 **Clinton-Colden L** Can
24B3 **Clipperton I** Pacific O
30C2 **Cliza** Bol
45B3 **Clonakilty** Irish Rep
107D3 **Cloncurry** Aust
45C1 **Clones** Irish Rep
45C2 **Clonmel** Irish Rep
10A2 **Cloquet** USA
12C2 **Cloudy Mt** USA
22C2 **Clovis** California, USA
9C3 **Clovis** New Mexico, USA
60B4 **Cluj** Rom
54B1 **Cluj-Napoca** Rom
47B1 **Cluses** France
47C2 **Clusone** Italy
111A3 **Clutha** *R* NZ
43C3 **Clwyd** County, Wales
6D2 **Clyde** Can
111A3 **Clyde** NZ
42B2 **Clyde** *R* Scot
23A2 **Coahuayana** Mexico
23A2 **Coalcomán** Mexico
13E2 **Coaldale** Can
21B2 **Coaldale** USA
21A2 **Coalinga** USA
33E5 **Coari** *R* Brazil
17A1 **Coastal Plain** USA
4E4 **Coast Mts** Can
8A2 **Coast Ranges** *Mts* USA
42B2 **Coatbridge** Scot
23B2 **Coatepec** Mexico
16B3 **Coatesville** USA
15D1 **Coaticook** Can
6B3 **Coats I** Can
112B1 **Coats Land** Region, Ant
25C3 **Coatzacoalcos** Mexico
7C5 **Cobalt** Can
25C3 **Cobán** Guatemala
107D4 **Cobar** Aust
109C3 **Cobargo** Aust
45B3 **Cobh** Irish Rep
32D6 **Cobija** Bol
16B1 **Cobleskill** USA
51B2 **Cobo de Palos** *C* Spain
7C5 **Cobourg** Can
106C2 **Cobourg Pen** Aust
57C2 **Coburg** Germany
32B4 **Coca** Ecuador
17B2 **Coca** USA
30C2 **Cochabamba** Bol
46D1 **Cochem** Germany
Cochin = Kochi
13E2 **Cochrane** Alberta, Can
7B5 **Cochrane** Ontario, Can
108B2 **Cockburn** Aust
16A3 **Cockeysville** USA
27H1 **Cockpit Country,The** Jamaica
25D3 **Coco** *R* Honduras/Nic
98A2 **Cocobeach** Gabon
27L1 **Cocos B** Trinidad
104C4 **Cocos Is** Indian O
23A1 **Cocula** Mexico
10C2 **Cod,C** USA
111A3 **Codfish I** NZ
7D4 **Cod I** Can
47E2 **Codigoro** Italy
31C2 **Codó** Brazil
47C2 **Codogno** Italy
8C2 **Cody** USA
56B2 **Coesfeld** Germany
8B2 **Coeur d'Alene** USA
9D3 **Coffeyville** USA
108A2 **Coffin B** Aust
109D2 **Coff's Harbour** Aust
23B2 **Cofre de Perote** *Mt* Mexico
48B2 **Cognac** France
15D2 **Cohoes** USA
108B3 **Cohuna** Aust
29B5 **Coihaique** Chile
87B2 **Coimbatore** India
50A1 **Coimbra** Port
32A3 **Cojimies** Ecuador
107D4 **Colac** Aust
31C5 **Colatina** Brazil
112B6 **Colbeck,C** Ant
43E4 **Colchester** Eng
16C2 **Colchester** USA
47B1 **Col de la Faucille** France
13E2 **Cold L** Can
52A1 **Col du Grand St Bernard** *P* Italy/Switz
47B2 **Col du Lautaret** *P* France
52A1 **Col du Mont Cenis** *P* France/Italy
14B2 **Coldwater** USA
12F1 **Coleen** *R* USA
14B2 **Coleman** Michigan, USA
101G1 **Colenso** S Africa
45C1 **Coleraine** N Ire
111B2 **Coleridge,L** NZ
100B4 **Colesberg** S Africa
22C1 **Coleville** USA

21A2 **Colfax** California, USA
19B3 **Colfax** Louisiana, USA
20C1 **Colfax** Washington, USA
24B3 **Colima** Mexico
23A2 **Colima** State, Mexico
34A2 **Colina** Chile
44A3 **Coll** *I* Scot
109C1 **Collarenebri** Aust
52A2 **Colle de Tende** *P* France/Italy
12E2 **College** USA
17B1 **College Park** Georgia, USA
16A3 **College Park** Washington, USA
19A3 **College Station** USA
106A4 **Collie** Aust
106B2 **Collier B** Aust
46A1 **Collines de L'Artois** *Mts* France
46B2 **Collines De Thiérache** France
14B2 **Collingwood** Can
110B2 **Collingwood** NZ
19C3 **Collins** Mississippi, USA
4H2 **Collinson Pen** Can
107D3 **Collinsville** Aust
18C2 **Collinsville** Illinois, USA
18A2 **Collinsville** Oklahoma, USA
34A3 **Collipulli** Chile
49D2 **Colmar** France
Cologne = Köln
35B2 **Colômbia** Brazil
32B3 **Colombia** Republic, S America
15C3 **Colombia** USA
87B3 **Colombo** Sri Lanka
25D2 **Colon** Cuba
32B2 **Colón** Panama
29E2 **Colonia** Urug
34D2 **Colonia del Sacramento** Urug
34B3 **Colonia 25 de Mayo** Arg
29C5 **Colonia Las Heras** Arg
44A3 **Colonsay** *I* Scot
23A1 **Colontlán** Mexico
27E5 **Coloradito** Ven
8C3 **Colorado** State, USA
9B3 **Colorado** *R* Arizona, USA
29D3 **Colorado** *R* Buenos Aires, Arg
9D3 **Colorado** *R* Texas, USA
9B3 **Colorado Plat** USA
8C3 **Colorado Springs** USA
22D3 **Colton** USA
16A3 **Columbia** Maryland, USA
19C3 **Columbia** Mississippi, USA
10A3 **Columbia** Missouri, USA
15C2 **Columbia** Pennsylvania, USA
11B3 **Columbia** S Carolina, USA
11B3 **Columbia** Tennessee, USA
13D2 **Columbia** *R* Can
8A2 **Columbia** *R* USA
5G4 **Columbia,Mt** Can
20C1 **Columbia Plat** USA
11B3 **Columbus** Georgia, USA
14A3 **Columbus** Indiana, USA
11B3 **Columbus** Mississippi, USA
8D2 **Columbus** Nebraska, USA
10B2 **Columbus** Ohio, USA
19A4 **Columbus** Texas, USA
20C1 **Colville** USA
4C3 **Colville** *R* USA
110C1 **Colville,C** NZ
4F3 **Colville L** Can
42C3 **Colwyn Bay** Wales
47E2 **Comacchio** Italy
22B1 **Comanche Res** USA
112C2 **Comandante Ferraz** *Base* Ant
25D3 **Comayagua** Honduras
34A2 **Combarbalá** Chile
45C2 **Comeragh** *Mts* Irish Rep
86C2 **Comilla** Bang
25C3 **Comitán** Mexico
46C2 **Commercy** France
6B3 **Committees B** Can
52A1 **Como** Italy
29C5 **Comodoro Rivadavia** Arg
23A1 **Comonfort** Mexico
87B3 **Comorin,C** India
101D2 **Comoros** *Is* Indian O
49C2 **Compiègne** France
23A1 **Compostela** Mexico
34B2 **Comte Salas** Arg
86C1 **Cona** China
97A4 **Conakry** Guinea
34B2 **Concarán** Arg
48B2 **Concarneau** France
35D1 **Conceiçao da Barra** Brazil
31B3 **Conceição do Araguaia** Brazil
35C1 **Conceiçao do Mato Dentro** Brazil
29B3 **Concepción** Chile
30E3 **Concepción** Par
29E2 **Concepción** *R* Arg
24B2 **Concepcion del Oro** Mexico
34D2 **Concepcion del Uruguay** Arg
9A3 **Conception,Pt** USA
35B2 **Conchas** Brazil
9C4 **Conchos** *R* Mexico
21A2 **Concord** California, USA
10C2 **Concord** New Hampshire, USA
29E2 **Concordia** Arg
8D3 **Concordia** USA
20B1 **Concrete** USA
109D1 **Condamine** Aust
107D4 **Condobolin** Aust
20B1 **Condon** USA
46C1 **Condroz** *Mts* Belg
17A1 **Conecuh** *R* USA
47E2 **Conegliano** Italy
89F8 **Congo** Republic, Africa
89F8 **Congo** *R* Congo
Congo,R = Zaïre
14B1 **Coniston** Can
45B2 **Connaught** Region, Irish Rep
14B2 **Conneaut** USA
10C2 **Connecticut** State, USA
15D2 **Connecticut** *R* USA
15C2 **Connellsville** USA
45B2 **Connemara,Mts of** Irish Rep
14A3 **Connersville** USA
108B2 **Conoble** Aust
19A3 **Conroe** USA
35C2 **Conselheiro Lafaiete** Brazil
77D4 **Con Son** *Is* Viet
Constance,L = Bodensee
60C5 **Constanta** Rom
96C1 **Constantine** Alg
12C3 **Constantine,C** USA
29B3 **Constitución** Chile
13F3 **Consul** Can
47E2 **Contarina** Italy
31C4 **Contas** *R* Brazil
23B2 **Contreras** Mexico
4H3 **Contuoyto L** Can
11A3 **Conway** Arkansas, USA
15D2 **Conway** New Hampshire, USA
17C1 **Conway** South Carolina, USA
108A1 **Conway,L** Aust
42C3 **Conwy** Wales
106C3 **Coober Pedy** Aust
110B2 **Cook** *Str* NZ
13B2 **Cook,C** Can
4C3 **Cook Inlet** *B* USA
105H4 **Cook Is** Pacific O
111B2 **Cook,Mt** NZ
107D2 **Cooktown** Aust
109C2 **Coolabah** Aust
108C1 **Cooladdi** Aust
109C2 **Coolah** Aust
109C2 **Coolamon** Aust
106B4 **Coolgardie** Aust
109C3 **Cooma** Aust
109C2 **Coonabarabran** Aust
109C2 **Coonambie** Aust
108B2 **Coonbah** Aust
108A2 **Coondambo** Aust
87A2 **Coondapoor** India
108C1 **Coongoola** Aust
87B2 **Coonoor** India
108B1 **Cooper Basin** Aust
106C3 **Cooper Creek** Aust
108B1 **Cooper Creek** *R* Aust
108A3 **Coorong,The** Aust
109D1 **Cooroy** Aust
20B2 **Coos B** USA
20B2 **Coos Bay** USA
107D4 **Cootamundra** Aust
45C1 **Cootehill** Irish Rep
23B2 **Copala** Mexico
23B2 **Copalillo** Mexico
Copenhagen = København
30B4 **Copiapó** Chile
47D2 **Copparo** Italy
12F2 **Copper** *R* USA
4D3 **Copper Centre** USA
14B1 **Copper Cliff** Can
4G3 **Coppermine** Can
4G3 **Coppermine** *R* Can
Coquilhatville = Mbandaka
30B4 **Coquimbo** Chile
54B2 **Corabia** Rom
17B2 **Coral Gables** USA
6B3 **Coral Harbour** Can
107D2 **Coral S** Aust/PNG
104F4 **Coral Sea Basin** Pacific O
107E2 **Coral Sea Island Territories** Aust
108B3 **Corangamite,L** Aust
33F3 **Corantijn** *R* Surinam/Guyana
46B2 **Corbeil-Essonnes** France
50A1 **Corcubíon** Spain
11B3 **Cordele** USA
50A1 **Cordillera Cantabrica** *Mts* Spain
26C3 **Cordillera Central** *Mts* Dom Rep
79B2 **Cordillera Central** *Mts* Phil
34B2 **Cordillera de Ansita** *Mts* Arg
32B5 **Cordillera de los Andes** *Mts* Peru
30C4 **Cordillera del Toro** *Mt* Arg
32C2 **Cordillera de Mérida** Ven
34A3 **Cordillera de Viento** *Mts* Arg
25D3 **Cordillera Isabelia** *Mts* Nic
32B3 **Cordillera Occidental** *Mts* Colombia
32B3 **Cordillera Oriental** *Mts* Colombia
108B1 **Cordillo Downs** Aust
29D2 **Córdoba** Arg
24C3 **Córdoba** Mexico
50B2 **Córdoba** Spain
29D2 **Córdoba** State, Arg
4D3 **Cordova** USA
Corfu = Kérkira
109D2 **Coricudgy,Mt** Aust
53C3 **Corigliano Calabro** Italy
11B3 **Corinth** Mississippi, USA
31C5 **Corinto** Brazil
45B2 **Cork** County, Irish Rep
41B3 **Cork** Irish Rep
92A1 **Çorlu** Turk
31C5 **Cornel Fabriciano** Brazil
35A2 **Cornelio Procópio** Brazil
7E5 **Corner Brook** Can
109C3 **Corner Inlet** *B* Aust
15C2 **Corning** USA
7C5 **Cornwall** Can
43B4 **Cornwall** County, Eng
43B4 **Cornwall,C** Eng
4H2 **Cornwall I** Can
6A2 **Cornwallis I** Can
32D1 **Coro** Ven
31C2 **Coroatá** Brazil
30C2 **Coroico** Bol
35B1 **Coromandel** Brazil
87C2 **Coromandel Coast** India
110C1 **Coromandel Pen** NZ
110C1 **Coromandel Range** *Mts* NZ
22D4 **Corona** California, USA
13E2 **Coronation** Can
4G3 **Coronation G** Can
34C2 **Coronda** Arg
29B3 **Coronel** Chile
34D3 **Coronel Brandsen** Arg
34C3 **Coronel Dorrego** Arg
35C1 **Coronel Fabriciano** Brazil
30E4 **Coronel Oviedo** Par
29D3 **Coronel Pringles** Arg
34C3 **Coronel Suárez** Arg
34D3 **Coronel Vidal** Arg
30B2 **Coropuna** *Mt* Peru
109C3 **Corowa** Aust
49D3 **Corps** France
9D4 **Corpus Christi** USA
9D4 **Corpus Christi,L** USA
79B3 **Corregidor** *I* Phil
35A1 **Corrente** *R* Mato Grosso, Brazil
30E4 **Corrientes** Arg
30E4 **Corrientes** State, Arg
19B3 **Corrigan** USA
106A4 **Corrigin** Aust
107E2 **Corringe Is** Aust
109C3 **Corryong** Aust
52A2 **Corse** *I* Medit S
42B2 **Corsewall** *Pt* Scot
Corsica = Corse
9D3 **Corsicana** USA
52A2 **Corte** Corse
9C3 **Cortez** USA
52B1 **Cortina d'Ampezzo** Italy
15C2 **Cortland** USA
23A2 **Coruca de Catalan** Mexico
93D1 **Çoruh** *R* Turk
60E5 **Çorum** Turk
30E2 **Corumbá** Brazil
35B1 **Corumba** *R* Brazil
35B1 **Corumbaiba** Brazil
20B2 **Corvallis** USA
96A1 **Corvo** *I* Açores
43C3 **Corwen** Wales
23B2 **Coscomatopec** Mexico
53C3 **Cosenza** Italy
101D1 **Cosmoledo** *Is* Seychelles
34C2 **Cosquín** Arg
51B2 **Costa Blanca** Region, Spain
51C1 **Costa Brava** Region, Spain
50B2 **Costa de la Luz** Region, Spain
50B2 **Costa del Sol** Region, Spain
22D4 **Costa Mesa** USA
25D3 **Costa Rica** Republic, Cent America

79B4 **Cotabato** Phil
30C3 **Cotagaita** Bol
49D3 **Côte d'Azur** Region, France
46C2 **Côtes de Meuse** *Mts* France
97C4 **Cotonou** Benin
32B4 **Cotopaxi** *Mt* Ecuador
43C4 **Cotswold Hills** *Upland* Eng
20B2 **Cottage Grove** USA
56C2 **Cottbus** Germany
108A3 **Couedic,C du** Aust
20C1 **Couer d'Alene L** USA
46B2 **Coulommiers** France
15C1 **Coulonge** *R* Can
22B2 **Coulterville** USA
4B3 **Council** USA
8D2 **Council Bluffs** USA
58C1 **Courland Lagoon** *Lg* Lithuania/Russian Fed
47B2 **Courmayeur** Italy
13B3 **Courtenay** Can
Courtrai = Kortrijk
48B2 **Coutances** France
43D3 **Coventry** Eng
50A1 **Covilhã** Spain
17B1 **Covington** Georgia, USA
19B3 **Covington** Louisiana, USA
109C2 **Cowal,L** Aust
108B3 **Cowangie** Aust
15D1 **Cowansville** Can
108A1 **Coward Springs** Aust
108A2 **Cowell** Aust
108C3 **Cowes** Aust
20B1 **Cowichan L** Can
20B1 **Cowiltz** *R* USA
109C2 **Cowra** Aust
30F2 **Coxim** Brazil
16C1 **Coxsackie** USA
86C2 **Cox's Bazar** Bang
22B2 **Coyote** USA
23A2 **Coyuca de Benitez** Mexico
59B2 **Cracow** Pol
100B4 **Cradock** S Africa
8C2 **Craig** USA
57C3 **Crailsheim** Germany
54B2 **Craiova** Rom
15D2 **Cranberry L** USA
5G5 **Cranbrook** Can
20C2 **Crane** Oregon, USA
16D2 **Cranston** USA
20B2 **Crater L** USA
20B2 **Crater Lake Nat Pk** USA
31C3 **Crateus** Brazil
31D3 **Crato** Brazil
14A2 **Crawfordsville** USA
17B1 **Crawfordville** USA
43D4 **Crawley** Eng
5H4 **Cree L** Can
46B2 **Creil** France
47C2 **Crema** Italy
52B1 **Cremona** Italy
46B2 **Crépy-en-Valois** France
52B2 **Cres** *I* Yugos
20B2 **Crescent City** USA
34C2 **Crespo** Arg
13D3 **Creston** Can
18B1 **Creston** USA
17A1 **Crestview** USA
108B3 **Creswick** Aust
47A1 **Crêt de la Neige** *Mt* France
Crete = Kríti
18A1 **Crete** USA
55B3 **Crete,S of** Greece
48C2 **Creuse** *R* France
43C3 **Crewe** Eng
44B3 **Crianlarich** Scot
30G4 **Criciuma** Brazil
44C3 **Crieff** Scot
12G3 **Crillon,Mt** USA
35B1 **Cristalina** Brazil
52C1 **Croatia** Republic, Europe
78D1 **Crocker Range** *Mts* Malay
19A3 **Crockett** USA
106C2 **Croker I** Aust
44C3 **Cromarty** Scot
43E3 **Cromer** Eng
111A3 **Cromwell** NZ
11C4 **Crooked** *I* The Bahamas
13C2 **Crooked** *R* Can
8D2 **Crookston** USA
109C2 **Crookwell** Aust
109D1 **Croppa Creek** Aust
11A3 **Crossett** USA
12G3 **Cross Sd** USA
53C3 **Crotone** Italy
19B3 **Crowley** USA
27K1 **Crown Pt** Tobago
109D1 **Crows Nest** Aust
107D2 **Croydon** Aust
43D4 **Croydon** Eng
104B5 **Crozet Basin** Indian O
4F2 **Crozier Chan** Can
30F4 **Cruz Alta** Brazil
25E3 **Cruz,C** Cuba
29D2 **Cruz del Eje** Arg
35C2 **Cruzeiro** Brazil
32C5 **Cruzeiro do Sul** Brazil
13C1 **Crysdale,Mt** Can
108A2 **Crystal Brook** Aust
18B2 **Crystal City** Missouri, USA
14A1 **Crystal Falls** USA
101C2 **Cuamba** Mozam
100B2 **Cuando** *R* Angola
100A2 **Cuangar** Angola
Cuango,R = Kwango,R
34C2 **Cuarto** *R* Arg
24B2 **Cuauhtémoc** Mexico
23B2 **Cuautla** Mexico
25D2 **Cuba** Republic, Caribbean S
100A2 **Cubango** *R* Angola
100A2 **Cuchi** Angola
100A2 **Cuchi** *R* Angola
34C3 **Cuchillo Có** Arg
32D3 **Cucui** Brazil
32C2 **Cúcuta** Colombia
87B2 **Cuddalore** India
87B2 **Cuddapah** India
106A3 **Cue** Aust
32B4 **Cuenca** Ecuador
51B1 **Cuenca** Spain
24C3 **Cuernavaca** Mexico
19A4 **Cuero** USA
30E2 **Cuiabá** Brazil
30E2 **Cuiabá** *R* Brazil
23B2 **Cuicatlan** Mexico
35C1 **Cuieté** *R* Brazil
44A3 **Cuillin Hills** *Mts* Scot
98B3 **Cuilo** *R* Angola
100A2 **Cuito** *R* Angola
100A2 **Cuito Cunavale** Angola
23A2 **Cuitzeo** Mexico
77D3 **Cu Lao Hon** *I* Viet
109C3 **Culcairn** Aust
109C1 **Culgoa** *R* Aust
24B2 **Culiacán** Mexico
79A3 **Culion** *I* Phil
17A1 **Cullman** USA
47A2 **Culoz** France
15C3 **Culpeper** USA
32J7 **Culpepper** *I* Ecuador
17B2 **Culter Ridge** USA
111B2 **Culverden** NZ
33E1 **Cumaná** Ven
10C3 **Cumberland** Maryland, USA
11B3 **Cumberland** *R* USA
6D3 **Cumberland Pen** Can
6D3 **Cumbernauld Sd** Can
42C2 **Cumbria** Eng
21A2 **Cummings** USA
108A2 **Cummins** Aust
42B2 **Cumnock** Scot
34A3 **Cunco** Chile
100A2 **Cunene** *R* Angola/ Namibia
52A2 **Cuneo** Italy
107D3 **Cunnamulla** Aust
44C3 **Çupar** Scot
54B2 **Ćuprija** Serbia, Yugos
27D4 **Curaçao** *I* Caribbean S
34A3 **Curacautin** Chile
34B3 **Curaco** *R* Arg
34A3 **Curanilahue** Chile
34A3 **Curepto** Chile
29B2 **Curicó** Chile
30G4 **Curitiba** Brazil
108A2 **Curnamona** Aust
100A2 **Curoca** *R* Angola
31C5 **Curvelo** Brazil
18A2 **Cushing** USA
13D2 **Cutbank** *R* Can
17B1 **Cuthbert** USA
34B3 **Cutral-Có** Arg
86B2 **Cuttack** India
100A2 **Cuvelai** Angola
56B2 **Cuxhaven** Germany
14B2 **Cuyahoga Falls** USA
79B3 **Cuyo Is** Phil
32C6 **Cuzco** Peru
99C3 **Cyangugu** Zaïre
Cyclades = Kikládhes
13F3 **Cypress Hills** *Mts* Can
92B3 **Cyprus** Republic, Medit S
6D3 **Cyrus Field B** Can
59B3 **Czechoslovakia** Republic, Europe
59B2 **Częstochowa** Pol

D

76C1 **Da** *R* Viet
69E2 **Da'an** China
94C3 **Dab'a** Jordan
27C4 **Dabajuro** Ven
99E2 **Dabaro** Somalia
73B3 **Daba Shan** *Mts* China
99D1 **Dabat** Eth
85C4 **Dabhoi** India
73C3 **Dabie Shan** *Mts* China
97A3 **Dabola** Guinea
97B4 **Dabou** Ivory Coast
59B2 **Dabrowa Gorn** Pol
57C3 **Dachau** Germany
52B1 **Dachstein** *Mt* Austria
73A3 **Dada He** *R* China
17B2 **Dade City** USA
84B3 **Dadhar** Pak
85B3 **Dadu** Pak
68C3 **Dadu He** *R* China
79B3 **Daet** Phil
73B4 **Dafang** China
76B2 **Daga** *R* Burma
99E2 **Dagabur** Eth
97A3 **Dagana** Sen
65F5 **Dagestanskay Respublika,** Russian Fed
79B2 **Dagupan** Phil
92B4 **Dahab** Egypt
63E3 **Da Hinggan Ling** *Mts* China
17B1 **Dahlonega** USA
85C4 **Dāhod** India
51C2 **Dahra** Region, Alg
86A1 **Dailekh** Nepal
34C3 **Daireaux** Arg
69F4 **Daitō** *Is* Pacific O
106C3 **Dajarra** Aust
97A3 **Dakar** Sen
95B2 **Dakhla Oasis** Egypt
97C3 **Dakoro** Niger
54B2 **Dakovica** Serbia, Yugos
54A1 **Dakovo** Croatia
100B2 **Dala** Angola
97A3 **Dalaba** Guinea
72D1 **Dalai Nur** *L* China
68C2 **Dalandzadgad** Mongolia
79B3 **Dalanganem Is** Phil
76D3 **Da Lat** Viet
72A1 **Dalay** Mongolia
107E3 **Dalby** Aust
39F7 **Dalen** Nor
42C2 **Dales,The** *Upland* Eng
17A1 **Daleville** USA
9C3 **Dalhart** USA
4E2 **Dalhousie,C** Can
72E2 **Dalian** China
9D3 **Dallas** USA
20B1 **Dalles,The** USA
5E4 **Dall I** USA
86A2 **Dalli Rajhara** India
97C3 **Dallol** *R* Niger
97C3 **Dallol Bosso** *R* Niger
52C2 **Dalmatia** *Region* Bosnia & Herzegovina, Yugos
69F2 **Dal'nerechensk** Russian Fed
97B4 **Daloa** Ivory Coast
73B4 **Dalou Shan** *Mts* China
86A2 **Dāltenganj** India
17B1 **Dalton** Georgia, USA
16C1 **Dalton** Massachusetts, USA
106C2 **Daly** *R* Aust
21A2 **Daly City** USA
106C2 **Daly Waters** Aust
79B4 **Damaguete** Phil
85C4 **Damān** India
92B3 **Damanhûr** Egypt
71D4 **Damar** *I* Indon
98B2 **Damara** CAR
92C3 **Damascus** Syria
16A3 **Damascus** USA
97D3 **Damaturu** Nig
90B2 **Damavand** Iran
98B3 **Damba** Angola
87C3 **Dambulla** Sri Lanka
90B2 **Damghan** Iran
85D4 **Damoh** India
99E2 **Damot** Eth
94B2 **Damour** Leb
106A3 **Dampier** Aust
94B3 **Danā** Jordan
22C2 **Dana,Mt** USA
97B4 **Danané** Lib
76D2 **Da Nang** Viet
79B3 **Danao** Phil
70A3 **Danau Tobu** *L* Indon
71D4 **Danau Tuwuti** *L* Indon
73A3 **Danbu** China
15D2 **Danbury** USA
86A1 **Dandeldhura** Nepal
87A1 **Dandeli** India
108C3 **Dandenong** Aust
74A2 **Dandong** China
100A4 **Danger Pt** S Africa
99D1 **Dangila** Eth
6D1 **Danguard Jenson Land** *Region* Can
7E4 **Daniels Harbour** Can
6G3 **Dannebrogs Øy** *I* Greenland
110C2 **Dannevirke** NZ
87C1 **Dantewāra** India
Danube = Donau
10B2 **Danville** Illinois, USA
11B3 **Danville** Kentucky, USA
16A2 **Danville** Pennsylvania, USA
11C3 **Danville** Virginia, USA
Danzig = Gdańsk
73C4 **Dao Xian** China
73B4 **Daozhen** China
79B4 **Dapiak,Mt** Phil
79B4 **Dapitan** Phil
68B3 **Da Qaidam** China
69E2 **Daqing** China
94C2 **Dar'a** Syria
91B4 **Dārāb** Iran
95A1 **Daraj** Libya
90B3 **Dārān** Iran
92C3 **Dar'ā Salkhad** Syria
86B1 **Darbhanga** India
22C1 **Dardanelle** USA
18B2 **Dardanelle,L** USA
Dar-el-Beida = Casablanca
99D3 **Dar es Salaam** Tanz
110B1 **Dargaville** NZ
17B1 **Darien** USA
Darjeeling = Dārjiling
86B1 **Dārjiling** India
107D4 **Darling** *R* Aust
109C1 **Darling Downs** Aust
6C1 **Darling Pen** Can

108B2 **Darlington** Aust
42D2 **Darlington** Eng
17C1 **Darlington** USA
57B3 **Darmstadt** Germany
95B1 **Darnah** Libya
108B2 **Darnick** Aust
4F3 **Darnley B** Can
112C10 **Darnley,C** Ant
51B1 **Daroca** Spain
98C2 **Dar Rounga** Region, CAR
43C4 **Dart** *R* Eng
41C3 **Dartmoor** *Moorland* Eng
43C4 **Dartmoor Nat Pk** Eng
7D5 **Dartmouth** Can
43C4 **Dartmouth** Eng
107D1 **Daru** PNG
52C1 **Daruvar** Croatia
106C2 **Darwin** Aust
91B4 **Daryacheh-ye Bakhtegan** *L* Iran
91B4 **Daryacheh-ye Mahārlū** *L* Iran
90B3 **Daryācheh-ye Namak** *Salt Flat* Iran
90D3 **Daryacheh-ye-Sistan** *Salt L* Iran/Afghan
91B4 **Daryacheh-ye Tashk** *L* Iran
80C2 **Daryācheh-ye Orūmīyeh** *L* Iran
91C4 **Dārzīn** Iran
91B4 **Das** *I* UAE
73C3 **Dashennonglia** *Mt* China
90C2 **Dasht** Iran
90B3 **Dasht-e-Kavir** *Salt Desert* Iran
90C3 **Dasht-e Lut** *Salt Desert* Iran
90D3 **Dasht-e Naomid** *Desert Region* Iran
85D3 **Datia** India
72A2 **Datong** China
72C1 **Datong** China
72A2 **Datong He** *R* China
79B4 **Datu Piang** Phil
39K7 **Daugava** *R* Latvia
60C2 **Daugavpils** Latvia
6D1 **Dauguard Jensen Land** Greenland
84A1 **Daulatabad** Afghan
85D3 **Daulpur** India
46D1 **Daun** Germany
87A1 **Daund** India
5H4 **Dauphin** Can
16A2 **Dauphin** USA
49D2 **Dauphiné** Region, France
97C3 **Daura** Nig
85D3 **Dausa** India
87B2 **Dāvangere** India
79C4 **Davao** Phil
79C4 **Davao G** Phil
22A2 **Davenport** California, USA
10A2 **Davenport** Iowa, USA
32A2 **David** Panama
4D3 **Davidson Mts** USA
21A2 **Davis** USA
112C10 **Davis** *Base* Ant
7D4 **Davis Inlet** Can
6E3 **Davis Str** Greenland/Can
61J3 **Davlekanovo** Russian Fed
47C1 **Davos** Switz
99E2 **Dawa** *R* Eth
73A4 **Dawan** China
84B2 **Dawat Yar** Afghan
91B4 **Dawḩat Salwah** *B* Qatar/S Arabia
76B2 **Dawna Range** *Mts* Burma
4E3 **Dawson** Can
17B1 **Dawson** Georgia, USA
107D3 **Dawson** *R* Aust
5F4 **Dawson Creek** Can
13D2 **Dawson,Mt** Can
12G2 **Dawson Range** *Mts* Can
73A3 **Dawu** China
73C3 **Dawu** China
48B3 **Dax** France
73B3 **Daxian** China
73B5 **Daxin** China
73A3 **Daxue Shan** *Mts* China
73C4 **Dayong** China
94C2 **Dayr'Ali** Syria
94C1 **Dayr'Atīyah** Syria
93D2 **Dayr az Zawr** Syria
10B3 **Dayton** Ohio, USA
19B4 **Dayton** Texas, USA
20C1 **Dayton** Washington, USA
11B4 **Daytona Beach** USA
73C4 **Dayu** China
78D3 **Dayu** Indon
72D2 **Da Yunhe** *R* China
20C2 **Dayville** USA
73B3 **Dazhu** China
100B4 **De Aar** S Africa
26C2 **Deadman's Cay** The Bahamas
92C3 **Dead S** Israel/Jordan
46A1 **Deal** Eng
101G1 **Dealesville** S Africa
13B2 **Dean** *R* Can
13B2 **Dean Chan** Can
34C2 **Deán Funes** Arg
14B2 **Dearborn** USA
4F3 **Dease Arm** *B* Can
4E4 **Dease Lake** Can
9B3 **Death V** USA
48C2 **Deauville** France
97B4 **Debakala** Ivory Coast
12B2 **Debauch Mt** USA
27L1 **Débé** Trinidad
59C2 **Debica** Pol
58C2 **Deblin** Pol
97B3 **Débo,L** Mali
59C3 **Debrecen** Hung
99D2 **Debre Birhan** Eth
99D1 **Debre Markos** Eth
99D1 **Debre Tabor** Eth
11B3 **Decatur** Alabama, USA
17B1 **Decatur** Georgia, USA
10B3 **Decatur** Illinois, USA
14B2 **Decatur** Indiana, USA
48C3 **Decazeville** France
73A4 **Dechang** China
97B3 **Dédougou** Burkina
101C2 **Dedza** Malawi
42B2 **Dee** *R* Dumfries and Galloway, Scot
42C3 **Dee** *R* Eng/Wales
44C3 **Dee** *R* Grampian, Scot
15C1 **Deep River** Can
16C2 **Deep River** USA
109D1 **Deepwater** Aust
7E5 **Deer Lake** Can
8B2 **Deer Lodge** USA
34D3 **Defferrari** Arg
17A1 **De Funiak Springs** USA
68B3 **Dêgê** China
99E1 **Degeh Bur** Eth
106A3 **De Grey** *R* Aust
91B3 **Deh Bīd** Iran
84B1 **Dehi** Afghan
96D1 **Dehibat** Tunisia
87B3 **Dehiwala-Mt Lavinia** Sri Lanka
90A3 **Dehlorān** Iran
84D2 **Dehra Dūn** India
86A2 **Dehri** India
98C2 **Deim Zubeir** Sudan
94B2 **Deir Abu Sa'id** Jordan
94C1 **Deir el Ahmar** Leb
60B4 **Dej** Rom
19B3 **De Kalb** Texas, USA
63G2 **De Kastri** Russian Fed
98C3 **Dekese** Zaïre
98B2 **Dekoa** CAR
106B1 **Dekusi** Indon
9B3 **Delano** USA
10C3 **Delaware** State, USA
14B2 **Delaware** USA
15C2 **Delaware** *R* USA
10C3 **Delaware B** USA
109C3 **Delegate** Aust
47B1 **Delemont** Switz
101D2 **Delgado** *C* Mozam
84D3 **Delhi** India
15D2 **Delhi** New York, USA
92B1 **Delice** Turk
24B2 **Delicias** Mexico
90B3 **Delījān** Iran
47B1 **Delle** France
22D4 **Del Mar** USA
39F8 **Delmenhorst** Germany
4B3 **De Long** *Mts* USA
109C4 **Deloraine** Aust
5H5 **Deloraine** Can
17B2 **Delray Beach** USA
9C4 **Del Rio** USA
8B3 **Delta** USA
12E2 **Delta** *R* USA
12E2 **Delta Junction** USA
99D2 **Dembī Dolo** Eth
46C1 **Demer** *R* Belg
9C3 **Deming** USA
54C2 **Demirköy** Turk
49C1 **Denain** France
82A2 **Denau** Uzbekistan
42C3 **Denbigh** Wales
12B2 **Denbigh,C** USA
78B3 **Dendang** Indon
46C1 **Dendermond** Belg
99D2 **Dendi** *Mt* Eth
46B1 **Dèndre** *R* Belg
72B1 **Dengkou** China
72C3 **Deng Xian** China
Den Haag = 's-Gravenhage
27H1 **Denham,Mt** Jamaica
56A2 **Den Helder** Neth
51C2 **Denia** Spain
107D4 **Deniliquin** Aust
20C2 **Denio** USA
9D3 **Denison** Texas, USA
12D3 **Denison,Mt** USA
92A2 **Denizli** Turk
39F7 **Denmark** Kingdom, Europe
1C1 **Denmark Str** Greenland/Iceland
27P2 **Dennery** St Lucia
78D4 **Denpasar** Indon
16B3 **Denton** Maryland, USA
9D3 **Denton** Texas, USA
107E1 **D'Entrecasteaux Is** PNG
47B1 **Dents du Midi** *Mt* Switz
8C3 **Denver** USA
98B2 **Déo** *R* Cam
86B2 **Deoghar** India
85C5 **Deolāli** India
84D1 **Deosai Plain** India
95B3 **Dépression du Mourdi** Chad
19B3 **De Queen** USA
84C3 **Dera** Pak
84B3 **Dera Bugti** Pak
84C2 **Dera Ismail Khan** Pak
106B2 **Derby** Aust
16C2 **Derby** Connecticut, USA
43D3 **Derby** County, Eng
43D3 **Derby** Eng
18A2 **Derby** Kansas, USA
60E3 **Dergachi** Ukraine
19B3 **De Ridder** USA
Derna = Darnah
95C3 **Derudeb** Sudan
109C4 **Derwent Bridge** Aust
34B2 **Desaguadero** Arg
34B2 **Desaguadero** *R* Arg
30C2 **Désaguadero** *R* Bol
21B3 **Descanso** Mexico
20B2 **Deschutes** *R* USA
99D1 **Desē** Eth
29C5 **Deseado** Arg
29C5 **Deseado** *R* Arg
47D2 **Desenzano** Italy
96A1 **Deserta Grande** *I* Medeira
30C4 **Desierto de Atacama** *Desert* Chile
18B2 **Desloge** USA
10A2 **Des Moines** Iowa, USA
60D3 **Desna** *R* Russian Fed
29B6 **Desolación** *I* Chile
14A2 **Des Plaines** USA
56C2 **Dessau** Germany
12G2 **Destruction Bay** Can
46A1 **Desvres** France
54B1 **Deta** Rom
100B2 **Dete** Zim
10B2 **Detroit** USA
76D3 **Det Udom** Thai
54B1 **Deva** Rom
56B2 **Deventer** Neth
44C3 **Deveron** *R* Scot
85C3 **Devikot** India
22C2 **Devil Postpile Nat Mon** USA
22C1 **Devils Gate** *P* USA
Devil's Island = Isla du Diable
8D2 **Devils Lake** USA
12H3 **Devils Paw** *Mt* Can
43D4 **Devizes** Eng
85D3 **Devli** India
55B2 **Devoll** *R* Alb
43B4 **Devon** County, Eng
6A2 **Devon I** Can
107D5 **Devonport** Aust
86C1 **Dewangiri** Bhutan
85D4 **Dewās** India
101G1 **Dewetsdorp** S Africa
11B3 **Dewey Res** USA
19B3 **De Witt** USA
18C2 **Dexter** Missouri, USA
73A3 **Deyang** China
90C3 **Deyhuk** Iran
90A3 **Dezfūl** Iran
72D2 **Dezhou** China
90A2 **Dezh Shāhpūr** Iran
91B4 **Dhahran** S Arabia
86C2 **Dhākā** Bang
87B2 **Dhamavaram** India
86A2 **Dhamtari** India
86B2 **Dhanbād** India
86A1 **Dhangarhi** Nepal
86B1 **Dhankuta** Nepal
85D4 **Dhār** India
87B2 **Dharmapuri** India
84D2 **Dharmsāla** India
97B3 **Dhar Oualata** *Desert Region* Maur
86A1 **Dhaulagiri** *Mt* Nepal
86B2 **Dhenkānāi** India
94B3 **Dhibah** Jordan
55C3 **Dhikti Ori** *Mt* Greece
55C3 **Dhodhekánisos** *Is* Greece
55B3 **Dhomokós** Greece
87B1 **Dhone** India
85C4 **Dhoraji** India
85C4 **Dhrāngadhra** India
86B1 **Dhuburi** India
85C4 **Dhule** India
22B2 **Diablo,Mt** USA
21A2 **Diablo Range** *Mts* USA
34C2 **Diamante** Arg
34B2 **Diamante** *R* Arg
31C5 **Diamantina** Brazil
107D3 **Diamantina** *R* Aust
86B2 **Diamond Harbours** India
22B1 **Diamond Springs** USA
91C4 **Dibā** UAE
98C3 **Dibaya** Zaïre
86C1 **Dibrugarh** India
8C2 **Dickinson** USA
15C2 **Dickson City** USA
93D2 **Dicle** *R* Turk
13E2 **Didsbury** Can
85C3 **Dīdwāna** India
97B3 **Diebougou** Burkina
46D2 **Diekirch** Lux
97B3 **Diéma** Mali
76C1 **Dien Bien Phu** Viet
56B2 **Diepholz** Germany
48C2 **Dieppe** France
46C1 **Diest** Belg
46D2 **Dieuze** France
7D5 **Digby** Can

49D3 **Digne** France
49C2 **Digoin** France
79C4 **Digos** Phil
71E4 **Digul** *R* Indon
86C1 **Dihang** *R* India
Dijlah = Tigris
49C2 **Dijon** France
98B2 **Dik** Chad
99E1 **Dikhil** Djibouti
46B1 **Diksmuide** Belg
18I0 **Dikson** Russian Fed
82A2 **Dilaram** Afghan
106B1 **Dili** Indon
76D3 **Di Linh** Viet
46E1 **Dillenburg** Germany
99C1 **Dilling** Sudan
12C3 **Dillingham** USA
8B2 **Dillon** USA
16A2 **Dillsburg** USA
100B2 **Dilolo** Zaïre
Dimashq = Damascus
98C3 **Dimbelenge** Zaïre
97B4 **Dimbokro** Ivory Coast
54C2 **Dimitrovgrad** Bulg
61G3 **Dimitrovgrad** Russian Fed
94B3 **Dimona** Israel
86C1 **Dimāpur** India
79C3 **Dinagat** *I* Phil
86B1 **Dinajpur** India
48B2 **Dinan** France
46C1 **Dinant** Belg
92B2 **Dinar** Turk
99D1 **Dinder** *R* Sudan
87B2 **Dindigul** India
72B2 **Dingbian** China
86B1 **Dinggyê** China
41A3 **Dingle** Irish Rep
41A3 **Dingle** *B* Irish Rep
97A3 **Dinguiraye** Guinea
44B3 **Dingwall** Scot
72A2 **Dingxi** China
72D2 **Ding Xian** China
76D1 **Dinh Lap** Viet
22C2 **Dinuba** USA
97A3 **Diouloulou** Sen
86C1 **Diphu** India
99E2 **Dirē Dawa** Eth
106A3 **Dirk Hartog** *I* Aust
95A3 **Dirkou** Niger
109C1 **Dirranbandi** Aust
99E2 **Dirri** Somalia
29G8 **Disappointment,C** South Georgia
20B1 **Disappointment,C** USA
106B3 **Disappointment,L** Aust
108B3 **Discovery B** Aust
103J7 **Discovery Tablemount** Atlantic O
47C1 **Disentis Muster** Switz
6E3 **Disko** Greenland
6E3 **Disko Bugt** *B* Greenland
6E3 **Diskorjord** Greenland
58D1 **Disna** *R* Belorussia
35B1 **Distrito Federal** Federal District, Brazil
85C4 **Diu** India
79C4 **Diuat Mts** Phil
31C6 **Divinópolis** Brazil
61F4 **Divnoye** Russian Fed
93C2 **Divriği** Turk
22B1 **Dixon** California, USA
5E4 **Dixon Entrance** *Sd* Can/USA
13D1 **Dixonville** Can
93E3 **Diyālā** *R* Iraq
65F6 **Diyarbakir** Turk
90A3 **Diz** *R* Iran
98B2 **Dja** *R* Cam
96C1 **Djadi** *R* Alg
95A2 **Djado,Plat du** Niger
98B3 **Djambala** Congo
96C2 **Djanet** Alg
50A2 **Djebel Bouhalla** *Mt* Mor
96C1 **Djelfa** Alg
98C2 **Djéma** CAR
97B3 **Djenné** Mali
97B3 **Djibo** Burkina
99E1 **Djibouti** Djibouti
99E1 **Djibouti** Republic, E Africa
98C2 **Djolu** Zaïre
97C4 **Djougou** Benin
99D2 **Djugu** Zaïre
38C2 **Djúpivogur** Iceland
51C2 **Djurdjura** *Mts* Alg
60E2 **Dmitrov** Russian Fed
60D4 **Dnepr** *R* Ukraine
60D4 **Dneprodzerzhinsk** Ukraine
60E4 **Dnepropetrovsk** Ukraine
60C3 **Dneprovskaya Nizmennost'** Region, Belorussia
60B4 **Dnestr** *R* Ukraine
60D2 **Dno** Russian Fed
98B2 **Doba** Chad
58C1 **Dobele** Latvia
34C3 **Doblas** Arg
71E4 **Dobo** Indon
54A2 **Doboj** Bosnia & Herzegovina, Yugos
54B2 **Dobreta-Turnu-Severin** Rom
54C2 **Dobrich** Bulg
60D3 **Dobrush** Belorussia
31C5 **Doce** *R* Brazil
30D3 **Doctor R P Peña** Arg
87B2 **Dod** India
87B2 **Doda Betta** *Mt* India
Dodecanese = Sporádhes
9C3 **Dodge City** USA
99D3 **Dodoma** Tanz
75A1 **Dōgo** *I* Japan
97C3 **Dogondoutchi** Niger
93D2 **Doğubayazit** Turk
91B4 **Doha** Qatar
7C5 **Dolbeau** Can
49D2 **Dôle** France
43C3 **Dolgellau** Wales
47D1 **Dolomitche** *Mts* Italy
99E2 **Dolo Odo** Eth
29E3 **Dolores** Arg
34D2 **Dolores** Urug
23A1 **Dolores Hidalgo** Mexico
4G3 **Dolphin and Union Str** Can
29E6 **Dolphin,C** Falkland Is
71E4 **Dom** *Mt* Indon
65G4 **Dombarovskiy** Russian Fed
38F6 **Dombas** Nor
46D2 **Dombasle-sur-Meurthe** France
54A1 **Dombóvár** Hung
48B2 **Domfront** France
27E3 **Dominica** *I* Caribbean S
27C3 **Dominican Republic** Caribbean S
6C3 **Dominion,C** Can
7E4 **Domino** Can
68D1 **Domna** Russian Fed
52A1 **Domodossola** Italy
78D4 **Dompu** Indon
29B3 **Domuyo** *Mt* Arg
109D1 **Domville,Mt** Aust
44C3 **Don** *R* Scot
61F4 **Don** *R* Russian Fed
45C1 **Donaghadee** N Ire
57C3 **Donau** *R* Germany
57C3 **Donauwörth** Germany
50A2 **Don Benito** Spain
42D3 **Doncaster** Eng
98B3 **Dondo** Angola
101C2 **Dondo** Mozam
87C3 **Dondra Head** *C* Sri Lanka
45B1 **Donegal** County, Irish Rep
40B3 **Donegal** Irish Rep
40B3 **Donegal** *B* Irish Rep
45B1 **Donegal** *Mts* Irish Rep
60E4 **Donetsk** Ukraine
73C4 **Dong'an** China
106A3 **Dongara** Aust
73A4 **Dongchuan** China
76D2 **Dongfang** China
74B2 **Dongfeng** China
70C4 **Donggala** Indon
68B3 **Donggi Cona** *L* China
74A3 **Donggou** China
73C5 **Donghai Dao** *I* China
72A1 **Dong He** *R* China
76D2 **Dong Hoi** Viet
73C5 **Dong Jiang** *R* China
95C3 **Dongola** Sudan
73D5 **Dongshan** China
68D4 **Dongsha Qundao** *I* China
72C2 **Dongsheng** China
72E3 **Dongtai** China
73C4 **Dongting Hu** *L* China
73B5 **Dongxing** China
73D3 **Dongzhi** China
18B2 **Doniphan** USA
52C2 **Donji Vakuf** Bosnia & Herzegovina, Yugos
38G5 **Dönna** *I* Nor
21A2 **Donner** *P* USA
46D2 **Donnersberg** *Mt* Germany
101G1 **Donnybrook** S Africa
Donostia = San Sebastian
22B2 **Don Pedro Res** USA
12D1 **Doonerak,Mt** USA
79B4 **Dopolong** Phil
73A3 **Do Qu** *R* China
47B2 **Dora Baltea** *R* Italy
49D2 **Dorbirn** Austria
43C4 **Dorchester** Eng
6C3 **Dorchester,C** Can
48C2 **Dordogne** *R* France
56A2 **Dordrecht** Neth
13F2 **Dore** *L* Can
13F2 **Dore Lake** Can
97B3 **Dori** Burkina
46B2 **Dormans** France
57B3 **Dornbirn** Austria
44B3 **Dornoch** Scot
44B3 **Dornoch Firth** *Estuary* Scot
38H6 **Dorotea** Sweden
109D2 **Dorrigo** Aust
20B2 **Dorris** USA
43C4 **Dorset** County, Eng
46D1 **Dorsten** Germany
56B2 **Dortmund** Germany
98C2 **Doruma** Zaïre
63D2 **Dosatuy** Russian Fed
84B1 **Doshi** Afghan
22B2 **Dos Palos** USA
97C3 **Dosso** Niger
65G5 **Dossor** Kazakhstan
11B3 **Dothan** USA
49C1 **Douai** France
98A2 **Douala** Cam
109D1 **Double Island Pt** Aust
49D2 **Doubs** *R* France
111A3 **Doubtful Sd** NZ
97B3 **Douentza** Mali
9C3 **Douglas** Arizona, USA
42B2 **Douglas** Eng
17B1 **Douglas** Georgia, USA
8C2 **Douglas** Wyoming, USA
12A1 **Douglas,C** USA
13B2 **Douglas Chan** Can
12D3 **Douglas,Mt** USA
46B1 **Doullens** France
45C1 **Doun** County, N Ire
30F3 **Dourados** Brazil
50A1 **Douro** *R* Port
15C3 **Dover** Delaware, USA
43E4 **Dover** Eng
15D2 **Dover** New Hampshire, USA
16B2 **Dover** New Jersey, USA
14B2 **Dover** Ohio, USA
43D3 **Dover** *R* Eng
41D3 **Dover,Str of** UK/France
16B3 **Downington** USA
42B2 **Downpatrick** N Ire
13C2 **Downton,Mt** Can
16B2 **Doylestown** USA
75A1 **Dōzen** *I* Japan
96A2 **Dr'aa** *R* Mor
35A2 **Dracena** Brazil
16D1 **Dracut** USA
49D3 **Draguignan** France
101C3 **Drakensberg** *Mts* S Africa
101G1 **Drakensberg** *Mt* S Africa
103E7 **Drake Pass** Pacific/Atlantic O
55B2 **Dráma** Greece
39G7 **Drammen** Nor
38A1 **Drangajökull** Iceland
52C1 **Drava** *R* Slovenia
13D2 **Drayton Valley** Can
49C2 **Dreaux** France
57C2 **Dresden** Germany
48C2 **Dreux** France
20C2 **Drewsey** USA
54B2 **Drin** *R* Alb
54A2 **Drina** *R* Bosnia & Herzegovina/Serbia
58D1 **Drissa** *R* Belorussia
45C2 **Drogheda** Irish Rep
59C3 **Drogobych** Ukraine
112B12 **Dronning Maud Land** Region, Ant
30D3 **Dr P.P. Pená** Par
5G4 **Drumheller** Can
14B1 **Drummond I** USA
15D1 **Drummondville** Can
58C2 **Druskininksi** Lithuania
12G3 **Dry B** USA
7A5 **Dryden** Can
27H1 **Dry Harbour Mts** Jamaica
76B3 **Duang** *I* Burma
91C4 **Dubai** UAE
5H3 **Dubawnt** *R* Can
4H3 **Dubawnt L** Can
107D4 **Dubbo** Aust
45C2 **Dublin** County, Irish Rep
45C2 **Dublin** Irish Rep
17B1 **Dublin** USA
60E2 **Dubna** Russian Fed
60C3 **Dubno** Ukraine
15C2 **Du Bois** USA
13B2 **Dubose,Mt** Can
58D2 **Dubrovica** Ukraine
54A2 **Dubrovnik** Croatia
10A2 **Dubuque** USA
46D2 **Dudelange** Lux
1C10 **Dudinka** Russian Fed
43C3 **Dudley** Eng
97B4 **Duekoué** Ivory Coast
50B1 **Duero** *R* Spain
44C3 **Dufftown** Scot
52B2 **Dugi Otok** *I* Croatia
56B2 **Duisburg** Germany
93E3 **Dūkan** Iraq
99D2 **Duk Faiwil** Sudan
91B4 **Dukhān** Qatar
73A4 **Dukou** China
68B3 **Dulan** China
34C2 **Dulce** *R* Arg
78C2 **Dulit Range** *Mts* Malay
86C2 **Dullabchara** India
10A2 **Duluth** USA
94C2 **Dūmā** Syria
78A2 **Dumai** Indon
79A3 **Dumaran** *I* Phil
9C3 **Dumas** USA
94C2 **Dumayr** Syria
42B2 **Dumbarton** Scot
42C2 **Dumfries** Scot
42B2 **Dumfries and Galloway** Region, Scot
86B2 **Dumka** India
15C1 **Dumoine,L** Can
112C8 **Dumont d'Urville** *Base* Ant
95C1 **Dumyat** Egypt
54C2 **Dunărea** *R* Rom
45C2 **Dunary Head** *Pt* Irish Rep

54B2 **Dunav** *R* Bulg
59D3 **Dunayevtsy** Ukraine
13C3 **Duncan** Can
16A2 **Duncannon** USA
44C2 **Duncansby Head** *Pt* Scot
45C1 **Dundalk** Irish Rep
16A3 **Dundalk** USA
45C2 **Dundalk B** Irish Rep
6D2 **Dundas** Greenland
4G2 **Dundas Pen** Can
71E5 **Dundas Str** Aust
101H1 **Dundee** S Africa
44C3 **Dundee** Scot
108B1 **Dundoo** Aust
42B2 **Dundrum** *B* N Ire
111B3 **Dunedin** NZ
17B2 **Dunedin** USA
109C2 **Dunedoo** Aust
44C3 **Dunfermline** Scot
85C4 **Dungarpur** India
45C2 **Dungarvan** Irish Rep
43E4 **Dungeness** Eng
109D2 **Dungog** Aust
99C2 **Dungu** Zaïre
95C2 **Dungunab** Sudan
68B2 **Dunhuang** China
46B1 **Dunkerque** France
10C2 **Dunkirk** USA
99D1 **Dunkur** Eth
97B4 **Dunkwa** Ghana
41B3 **Dun Laoghaire** Irish Rep
45B3 **Dunmanway** Irish Rep
26B1 **Dunmore Town** The Bahamas
44C2 **Dunnet Head** *Pt* Scot
42C2 **Duns** Scot
20B2 **Dunsmuir** USA
111A2 **Dunstan Mts** NZ
46C2 **Dun-sur-Meuse** France
72D1 **Duolun** China
18C2 **Du Quoin** USA
94B3 **Dura** Israel
49D3 **Durance** *R* France
24B2 **Durango** Mexico
50B1 **Durango** Spain
9C3 **Durango** USA
29E2 **Durano** Urug
9D3 **Durant** USA
94C1 **Duraykīsh** Syria
101H1 **Durban** S Africa
46D1 **Duren** Germany
86A2 **Durg** India
86B2 **Durgapur** India
42D2 **Durham** County, Eng
42D2 **Durham** Eng
11C3 **Durham** N Carolina, USA
16D1 **Durham** New Hampshire, USA
108B1 **Durham Downs** Aust
54A2 **Durmitor** *Mt* Montenegro, Yugos
44B2 **Durness** Scot
55A2 **Durrës** Alb
108B1 **Durrie** Aust
45A3 **Dursey** *I* Irish Rep
55C3 **Dursunbey** Turk
110B2 **D'Urville I** NZ
90D2 **Dushak** Turkmenistan
73B4 **Dushan** China
82A2 **Dushanbe** Tajikistan
111A3 **Dusky Sd** NZ
56B2 **Düsseldorf** Germany
73B4 **Duyun** China
92B1 **Düzce** Turk
60C2 **Dvina** *R* Latvia
85B4 **Dwārka** India
6D3 **Dyer,C** Can
11B3 **Dyersburg** USA
43B3 **Dyfed** County, Wales
61F5 **Dykh Tau** *Mt* Russian Fed
108B1 **Dynevor Downs** Aust
68B2 **Dzag** Mongolia
63C3 **Dzamin Uüd** Mongolia
101D2 **Dzaoudzi** Mayotte
68C2 **Dzarnïn Uüd** Mongolia
68B2 **Dzavhan Gol** *R* Mongolia
80E1 **Dzehezkazgan** Kazakhstan
61F2 **Dzerzhinsk** Russian Fed
63E2 **Dzhalinda** Russian Fed
65J5 **Dzhambul** Kazakhstan
60D4 **Dzhankoy** Ukraine
65H4 **Dzhezkazgan** Kazakhstan
84B1 **Dzhilikul'** Tajikistan
65J5 **Dzhungarskiy Alatau** *Mts* Kazakhstan
59B2 **Dzierzoniow** Pol
63B3 **Dzüyl** Mongolia
82C1 **Dzungaria** Basin, China

E

7B4 **Eabamet L** Can
12F2 **Eagle** Alaska, USA
20B2 **Eagle L** California, USA
19A3 **Eagle Mountain L** USA
9C4 **Eagle Pass** USA
4E3 **Eagle Plain** Can
12E2 **Eagle River** USA
21B2 **Earlimart** USA
17B1 **Easley** USA
15C2 **East Aurora** USA
43E4 **Eastbourne** Eng
14A2 **East Chicago** USA
69E3 **East China Sea** China/Japan
83B4 **Eastern Ghats** *Mts* India
29E6 **East Falkland** *I* Falkland Is
12E1 **East Fork** *R* USA
21B2 **Eastgate** USA
16C1 **Easthampton** USA
16C2 **East Hampton** USA
14A2 **East Lake** USA
14B2 **East Liverpool** USA
100B4 **East London** S Africa
7C4 **Eastmain** Can
7C4 **Eastmain** *R* Can
17B1 **Eastman** USA
15C3 **Easton** Maryland, USA
15C2 **Easton** Pennsylvania, USA
16B2 **East Orange** USA
105L4 **East Pacific Ridge** Pacific O
17B1 **East Point** USA
42D3 **East Retford** Eng
11A3 **East St Louis** USA
1B7 **East Siberian S** Russian Fed
43E4 **East Sussex** County, Eng
17B1 **Eatonton** USA
10A2 **Eau Claire** USA
71F3 **Eauripik** *I* Pacific O
23B1 **Ebano** Mexico
98B2 **Ebebiyin** Eq Guinea
56C2 **Eberswalde** Germany
73A4 **Ebian** China
65K5 **Ebinur** *L* China
53C2 **Eboli** Italy
98B2 **Ebolowa** Cam
51B1 **Ebro** *R* Spain
92A1 **Eceabat** Turk
96C1 **Ech Cheliff** Alg
72D2 **Eching** China
20C1 **Echo** USA
4G3 **Echo Bay** Can
46D2 **Echternach** Lux
108B3 **Echuca** Aust
50A2 **Ecija** Spain
6B2 **Eclipse Sd** Can
32B4 **Ecuador** Republic, S America
99E1 **Ed** Eth
44C2 **Eday** *I* Scot
98C1 **Ed Da'ein** Sudan
95C3 **Ed Damer** Sudan
95C3 **Ed Debba** Sudan
44B2 **Eddrachillis** *B* Scot
99D1 **Ed Dueim** Sudan
109C4 **Eddystone Pt** Aust
98A2 **Edea** Cam
109C3 **Eden** Aust
42C2 **Eden** *R* Eng
101G1 **Edenburg** S Africa
111A3 **Edendale** NZ
46E2 **Edenkoben** Germany
46E1 **Eder** *R* Germany
6D3 **Edgell I** Can
64D2 **Edgeøya** *I* Barents S
16A3 **Edgewood** USA
94B3 **Edh Dhahiriya** Israel
55B2 **Edhessa** Greece
44C3 **Edinburgh** Scot
60C5 **Edirne** Turk
17B1 **Edisto** *R* USA
13D2 **Edith Cavell,Mt** Can
20B1 **Edmonds** USA
5G4 **Edmonton** Can
7D5 **Edmundston** Can
19A4 **Edna** USA
12H3 **Edna Bay** USA
52B1 **Edolo** Italy
94B3 **Edom** Region, Jordan
92A2 **Edremit** Turk
55C3 **Edremit Körfezi** *B* Turk
68B2 **Edrengiyn Nuruu** *Mts* Mongolia
5G4 **Edson** Can
34C3 **Eduardo Castex** Arg
12J2 **Eduni,Mt** Can
108B3 **Edward** *R* Aust
99C3 **Edward,L** Uganda/ Zaïre
108A1 **Edwards Creek** Aust
9C3 **Edwards Plat** USA
18C2 **Edwardsville** USA
12H3 **Edziza,Mt** Can
12B2 **Eek** USA
46B1 **Eeklo** Belg
10B3 **Effingham** USA
6E3 **Egedesminde** Greenland
12C3 **Egegik** USA
59C3 **Eger** Hung
39F7 **Egersund** Nor
16B3 **Egg Harbor City** USA
4G2 **Eglinton I** Can
110B1 **Egmont,C** NZ
110B1 **Egmont,Mt** NZ
92B2 **Eğridir Gölü** *L* Turk
95B2 **Egypt** Republic, Africa
50B1 **Eibar** Spain
49C2 **Eibeuf** France
46D1 **Eifel** Region, Germany
44A3 **Eigg** *I* Scot
83B5 **Eight Degree Chan** Indian O
106B2 **Eighty Mile Beach** Aust
108C3 **Eildon,L** Aust
56B2 **Eindhoven** Neth
47C1 **Einsiedeln** Switz
94B3 **Ein Yahav** Israel
57C2 **Eisenach** Germany
57C3 **Eisenerz** Austria
46D1 **Eitorf** Germany
72A1 **Ejin qi** China
23B2 **Ejutla** Mexico
110C2 **Eketahuna** NZ
65J4 **Ekibastuz** Kazakhstan
63F2 **Ekimchan** Russian Fed
92B3 **Ek Mahalla el Kubra** Egypt
39H7 **Eksjo** Sweden
10B1 **Ekwen** *R* Can
92A3 **El'Alamein** Egypt
92B3 **El'Arîsh** Egypt
92B4 **Elat** Israel
95B3 **El'Atrun Oasis** Sudan
93C2 **Elazig** Turk
92C3 **El Azraq** Jordan
52B2 **Elba** *I* Italy
95C2 **El Balyana** Egypt
32C2 **El Banco** Colombia
55B2 **Elbasan** Alb
27D5 **El Baúl** Ven
57C2 **Elbe** *R* Germany
94C1 **El Bega'a** *R* Leb
14A2 **Elberta** USA
8C3 **Elbert,Mt** USA
17B1 **Elberton** USA
92C2 **Elbistan** Turk
58B2 **Elblag** Pol
29B4 **El Bolson** Arg
61F5 **Elbrus** *Mt* Russian Fed
Elburz Mts = Reshteh-ye Alborz
21B3 **El Cajon** USA
19A4 **El Campo** USA
51B2 **Elche** Spain
51B2 **Elda** Spain
32B3 **El Diviso** Colombia
96B2 **El Djouf** *Desert Region* Maur
18B2 **Eldon** USA
11A3 **El Dorado** Arkansas, USA
35B2 **Eldorado** Brazil
9D3 **El Dorado** Kansas, USA
24B2 **El Dorado** Mexico
33E2 **El Dorado** Ven
99D2 **Eldoret** Kenya
22C1 **Eleanor,L** USA
96B2 **El Eglab** Region, Alg
50B1 **El Escorial** Spain
93D2 **Eleşkirt** Turk
11C4 **Eleuthera** *I* The Bahamas
92B4 **El Faiyûm** Egypt
96B2 **El Farsia** *Well* Mor
98C1 **El Fasher** Sudan
92B4 **El Fashn** Egypt
50A1 **El Ferrol del Caudillo** Spain
99C1 **El Fula** Sudan
96C1 **El Gassi** Alg
99D1 **El Geteina** Sudan
99D1 **El Gezīra** Region, Sudan
94B3 **El Ghor** *V* Israel/ Jordan
10B2 **Elgin** Illinois, USA
44C3 **Elgin** Scot
92B3 **El Giza** Egypt
96C1 **El Golea** Alg
99D2 **Elgon,Mt** Uganda/ Kenya
99E2 **El Goran** Eth
23A2 **El Grullo** Mexico
96B2 **El Guettara** *Well* Mali
96B2 **El Haricha** *Desert Region* Mali
92A4 **El Harra** Egypt
51C2 **El Harrach** Alg
99D1 **El Hawata** Sudan
23B1 **El Higo** Mexico
34A3 **El Huecu** Arg
92B4 **El'Igma** *Desert Region* Egypt
12B2 **Elim** USA
4H2 **Elira,C** Can
Elisabethville = Lubumbashi
39K6 **Elisenvaara** Fin
El Iskandarîya = Alexandria
61F4 **Elista** Russian Fed
106C4 **Elizabeth** Aust
15D2 **Elizabeth** USA
11C3 **Elizabeth City** USA
17C1 **Elizabethtown** N Carolina, USA
16A2 **Elizabethtown** Pennsylvania, USA
96B1 **El Jadida** Mor
92C3 **El Jafr** Jordan
99D1 **El Jebelein** Sudan
96D1 **El Jem** Tunisia
58C2 **Elk** Pol
16B3 **Elk** *R* Maryland, USA
14B3 **Elk** *R* W Virginia, USA
95C3 **El Kamlin** Sudan
22B1 **Elk Grove** USA
El Khalil = Hebron
80B3 **El Khârga** Egypt

80B3 **El-Khârga Oasis** Egypt
14A2 **Elkhart** USA
96B2 **El Khenachich** *Desert Region* Mali
54C2 **Elkhovo** Bulg
14C3 **Elkins** USA
8B2 **Elko** USA
16B3 **Elkton** USA
92B3 **El Kuntilla** Egypt
99C1 **El Lagowa** Sudan
4H2 **Ellef Ringnes I** Can
8A2 **Ellensburg** USA
16B2 **Ellenville** USA
6B2 **Ellesmere I** Can
111B2 **Ellesmere,L** NZ
16A3 **Ellicott City** USA
100B4 **Elliot** S Africa
7B5 **Elliot Lake** Can
94B3 **El Lisan** *Pen* Jordan
112B3 **Ellsworth Land** *Region* Ant
95B1 **El Maghra** *L* Egypt
92B3 **El Mansûra** Egypt
16B3 **Elmer** USA
96B3 **El Merelé** *Desert Region* Maur
34B2 **El Milagro** Arg
94B1 **El Mīna** Leb
92B4 **El Minya** Egypt
22B1 **Elmira** California, USA
10C2 **Elmira** New York, USA
96B2 **El Mreitl** *Well* Maur
56B2 **Elmshorn** Germany
98C1 **El Muglad** Sudan
96B2 **El Mzereb** *Well* Mali
79A3 **El Nido** Phil
99D1 **El Obeid** Sudan
23A2 **El Oro** Mexico
96C1 **El Oued** Alg
9C3 **El Paso** USA
21A2 **El Porta** USA
22C2 **El Portal** USA
50A2 **El Puerto del Sta Maria** Spain
El Qâhira = Cairo
El Quds = Jerusalem
94B3 **El Quseima** Egypt
9D3 **El Reno** USA
4E3 **Elsa** Can
25D3 **El Salvador** Republic, Cent America
22D4 **Elsinore L** USA
34B3 **El Sosneade** Arg
57C2 **Elsterwerde** Germany
El Suweis = Suez
50A1 **El Teleno** *Mt* Spain
110B1 **Eltham** NZ
33E2 **El Tigre** Ven
92B4 **El Tîh** *Desert Region* Egypt
34C2 **El Tio** Arg
20C1 **Eltopia** USA
92B4 **El Tûr** Egypt
87C1 **Elūru** India
50A2 **Elvas** Port
32C5 **Elvira** Brazil
34A2 **El Volcán** Chile
14A2 **Elwood** USA
43E3 **Ely** Eng
10A2 **Ely** Minnesota, USA
8B3 **Ely** Nevada, USA
14B2 **Elyria** USA
90B2 **Emāmrūd** Iran
84B1 **Emām Sāheb** Afghan
58B1 **Eman** *R* Sweden
61J4 **Emba** Kazakhstan
61J4 **Emba** *R* Kazakhstan
29C3 **Embalse Cerros Colorados** *L* Arg
51B2 **Embalse de Alarcón** *Res* Spain
50A2 **Embalse de Alcántarà** *Res* Spain
50A1 **Embalse de Almendra** *Res* Spain
50A2 **Embalse de Garcia de Sola** *Res* Spain
33E2 **Embalse de Guri** *L* Ven
51B1 **Embalse de Mequinenza** *Res* Spain
50A1 **Embalse de Ricobayo** *Res* Spain
29E2 **Embalse de Rio Negro** *Res* Urug
29C3 **Embalse El Chocón** *L* Arg
29C4 **Embalse Florentine Ameghino** *L* Arg
50A1 **Embalse Gabriel y Galan** *Res* Spain
30D3 **Embarcación** Arg
5G4 **Embarras Portage** Can
47B2 **Embrun** France
99D3 **Embu** Kenya
56B2 **Emden** Germany
73A4 **Emei** China
107D3 **Emerald** Aust
7D4 **Emeri** Can
5J5 **Emerson** Can
21B1 **Emigrant P** USA
95A3 **Emi Koussi** *Mt* Chad
34B3 **Emilo Mitre** Arg
92B2 **Emirdağ** Turk
16B2 **Emmaus** USA
56B2 **Emmen** Neth
20C2 **Emmett** USA
16A3 **Emmitsburg** USA
12B2 **Emmonak** USA
9C4 **Emory Peak** *Mt* USA
24A2 **Empalme** Mexico
101H1 **Empangeni** S Africa
30E4 **Empedrado** Arg
105G1 **Emperor Seamount Chain** Pacific O
18A2 **Emporia** Kansas, USA
56B2 **Ems** *R* Germany
44B2 **Enard** *B* Scot
23A1 **Encarnacion** Mexico
30E4 **Encarnación** Par
97B4 **Enchi** Ghana
22D4 **Encinitas** USA
35C1 **Encruzilhada** Brazil
106B1 **Endeh** Indon
13D2 **Enderby** Can
112C11 **Enderby Land** Region, Ant
15C2 **Endicott** USA
12D1 **Endicott Mts** USA
47D1 **Engadin** *Mts* Switz
79B2 **Engaño,C** Phil
94B3 **En Gedi** Israel
47C1 **Engelberg** Switz
61G3 **Engel's** Russian Fed
78A4 **Enggano** *I* Indon
41C3 **England** Country, UK
7E4 **Englee** Can
41C3 **English Channel** Eng/France
97B3 **Enji** *Well* Maur
39H7 **Enkoping** Sweden
53B3 **Enna** Italy
99C1 **En Nahud** Sudan
95B3 **Ennedi** *Region* Chad
109C1 **Enngonia** Aust
41B3 **Ennis** Irish Rep
19A3 **Ennis** Texas, USA
45C2 **Enniscorthy** Irish Rep
45C1 **Enniskillen** N Ire
45B2 **Ennistimon** Irish Rep
94B2 **Enn Nâqoûra** Leb
57C3 **Enns** *R* Austria
39F8 **Enschede** Neth
24A1 **Ensenada** Mexico
73B3 **Enshi** China
99D2 **Entebbe** Uganda
17A1 **Enterprise** Alabama, USA
20C1 **Enterprise** Oregon, USA
97C4 **Enugu** Nig
75B1 **Enzan** Japan
49C2 **Epernay** France
16A2 **Ephrata** Pennsylvania, USA
20C1 **Ephrata** Washington, USA
49D2 **Epinal** France
46A2 **Epte** *R* France
100A3 **Epukiro** Namibia
34C3 **Epu pel** Arg
90B3 **Eqlid** Iran
89D7 **Equator**
98A2 **Equatorial Guinea** Republic, Africa
47C2 **Erba** Italy
46D2 **Erbeskopf** *Mt* Germany
34A3 **Ercilla** Chile
93D2 **Erciş** Turk
92C2 **Erciyas Daglari** *Mt* Turk
74B2 **Erdaobaihe** China
72C1 **Erdene** Mongolia
68C2 **Erdenet** Mongolia
95B3 **Erdi** *Region* Chad
30F4 **Erechim** Brazil
92B1 **Ereğlī** Turk
92B2 **Ereğli** Turk
68D2 **Erenhot** China
50B1 **Eresma** *R* Spain
46D1 **Erft** *R* Germany
57C2 **Erfurt** Germany
93C2 **Ergani** Turk
96B2 **Erg Chech** *Desert Region* Alg
95A3 **Erg du Djourab** *Desert* Chad
97D3 **Erg Du Ténéré** *Desert Region* Niger
92A1 **Ergene** *R* Turk
96B2 **Erg Iguidi** *Region* Alg
58D1 **Ergli** Latvia
98B1 **Erguig** *R* Chad
68D1 **Ergun'** *R* China/Russian Fed
63E2 **Ergun Zuoqi** China
95C3 **Eriba** Sudan
10C2 **Erie** USA
10B2 **Erie,L** Can/USA
42B2 **Erin Port** Eng
44A3 **Eriskay** *I* Scot
46D1 **Erkelenz** Germany
57C3 **Erlangen** Germany
19B3 **Erling,L** USA
101G1 **Ermelo** S Africa
87B3 **Ernākulam** India
87B2 **Erode** India
108B1 **Eromanga** Aust
96B1 **Er Rachidia** Mor
99D1 **Er Rahad** Sudan
101C2 **Errego** Mozam
40B2 **Errigal** *Mt* Irish Rep
41A3 **Erris Head** *Pt* Irish Rep
99D1 **Er Roseires** Sudan
94B2 **Er Rummān** Jordan
57C2 **Erzgebirge** *Upland* Germany
93C2 **Erzincan** Turk
65F6 **Erzurum** Turk
48C3 **Esara** *R* Spain
56B1 **Esbjerg** Den
9C4 **Escalón** Mexico
10B2 **Escanaba** USA
25C3 **Escárcega** Mexico
46C2 **Esch** Lux
21B3 **Escondido** USA
24B2 **Escuinapa** Mexico
25C3 **Escuintla** Guatemala
98B2 **Eséka** Cam
51C1 **Esera** *R* Spain
90B3 **Eşfahān** Iran
101H1 **Eshowe** S Africa
110C1 **Eskdale** NZ
38C1 **Eskifjörður** Iceland
39H7 **Eskilstuna** Sweden
4E3 **Eskimo L** Can
7A3 **Eskimo Point** Can
92B2 **Eskisehir** Turk
50A1 **Esla** *R* Spain
29A5 **Esmeralda** *I* Chile
32B3 **Esmeraldas** Ecuador
26B2 **Esmerelda** Cuba
49C3 **Espalion** France
14B1 **Espanola** Can
32J7 **Española** *I* Ecuador
106B4 **Esperance** Aust
34C2 **Esperanza** Arg
112C2 **Esperanza** *Base* Ant
35C1 **Espírito Santo** State, Brazil
101C3 **Espungabera** Mozam
29B4 **Esquel** Arg
20B1 **Esquimalt** Can
34D2 **Esquina** Arg
94C2 **Es Samra** Jordan
96B1 **Essaourira** Mor
96A2 **Es Semara** Mor
56B2 **Essen** Germany
33F3 **Essequibo** *R* Guyana
43E4 **Essex** County, Eng
14B2 **Essexville** USA
57B3 **Esslingen** Germany
46B2 **Essonne** France
31D4 **Estância** Brazil
101G1 **Estcourt** S Africa
47D2 **Este** Italy
46B2 **Esternay** France
30D3 **Esteros** Par
5H5 **Estevan** Can
17B1 **Estill** USA
60B2 **Estonia** Republic, Europe
29B6 **Estrecho de Magallanes** *Str* Chile
50A2 **Estremoz** Port
59B3 **Esztergom** Hung
108A1 **Etadunna** Aust
46C2 **Etam** France
48C2 **Etampes** France
108A1 **Etamunbanie,L** Aust
46A1 **Etaples** France
85D3 **Etāwah** India
99D2 **Ethiopia** Republic, Africa
23B2 **Etla** Mexico
53B3 **Etna** *Mt* Italy
12H3 **Etolin I** USA
12A2 **Etolin Str** USA
6C2 **Eton** Can
100A2 **Etosha Nat Pk** Namibia
100A2 **Etosha Pan** *Salt L* Namibia
17B1 **Etowah** *R* USA
46D2 **Ettelbruck** Lux
109C2 **Euabalong** Aust
14B2 **Euclid** USA
109C3 **Eucumbene,L** Aust
108A2 **Eudunda** Aust
19A2 **Eufala L** USA
17A1 **Eufaula** USA
8A2 **Eugene** USA
108C1 **Eulo** Aust
19B3 **Eunice** Louisiana, USA
46D1 **Eupen** Germany
93D3 **Euphrates** *R* Iraq
19C3 **Eupora** USA
48C2 **Eure** *R* France
20B2 **Eureka** California, USA
6B1 **Eureka** Can
8B3 **Eureka** Nevada, USA
6B2 **Eureka** *Sd* Can
108C3 **Euroa** Aust
109C1 **Eurombah** *R* Aust
101D3 **Europa** *I* Mozam Chan
57B2 **Euskirchen** Germany
13B2 **Eutsuk L** Can
13D2 **Evansburg** Can
6B1 **Evans,C** Can
7C4 **Evans,L** Can
6B3 **Evans Str** Can
14A2 **Evanston** Illinois, USA
8B2 **Evanston** Wyoming, USA
11B3 **Evansville** Indiana, USA
101G1 **Evaton** S Africa
106C4 **Everard,L** Aust
82C3 **Everest,Mt** China/Nepal
8A2 **Everett** Washington, USA
16C1 **Everett,Mt** USA
11B4 **Everglades,The** *Swamp* USA
43D3 **Evesham** Eng
98B2 **Evinayong** Eq Guinea
39F7 **Evje** Nor
47B1 **Evolène** Switz
50A2 **Evora** Port
48C2 **Evreux** France

55B3 **Évvoia** *I* Greece
98B3 **Ewo** Congo
22C1 **Excelisor Mt** USA
18B2 **Excelsior Springs** USA
21B2 **Exeter** California, USA
43C4 **Exeter** Eng
15D2 **Exeter** New Hampshire, USA
43C4 **Exmoor Nat Pk** Eng
43C4 **Exmouth** Eng
50A2 **Extremadura** Region, Spain
25E2 **Exuma Sd** The Bahamas
99D3 **Eyasi** *L* Tanz
42C2 **Eyemouth** Scot
99E2 **Eyl** Somalia
106B4 **Eyre** Aust
106C3 **Eyre Creek** *R* Aust
106C3 **Eyre,L** Aust
106C4 **Eyre Pen** Aust
79B3 **Eyte** *I* Phil
23A1 **Ezatlan** Mexico
55C3 **Ezine** Turk

F

4G3 **Faber L** Can
39G7 **Fåborg** Den
52B2 **Fabriano** Italy
95A3 **Fachi** Niger
95B3 **Fada** Chad
97C3 **Fada N'Gourma** Burkina
52B2 **Faenza** Italy
6E3 **Faeringehavn** Greenland
98B2 **Fafa** *R* CAR
99E2 **Fafan** *R* Eth
54B1 **Făgăras** Rom
46C1 **Fagnes** Region, Belg
97B3 **Faguibine,L** *L* Mali
91C5 **Fahud** Oman
96A1 **Faiol** *I* Açores
4D3 **Fairbanks** USA
14B3 **Fairborn** USA
8D2 **Fairbury** USA
16A3 **Fairfax** USA
21A2 **Fairfield** California, USA
16C2 **Fairfield** Connecticut, USA
14B3 **Fairfield** Ohio, USA
45C1 **Fair Head** *Pt* N Ire
40C2 **Fair Isle** *I* Scot
111B2 **Fairlie** NZ
14B3 **Fairmont** W Virginia, USA
13D1 **Fairview** Can
4E4 **Fairweather,Mt** USA
71F3 **Fais** *I* Pacific O
84C2 **Faisalabad** Pak
8C2 **Faith** USA
44E1 **Faither,The** *Pen* Scot
86A1 **Faizābād** India
43E3 **Fakenham** Eng
39G7 **Faköping** Sweden
86C2 **Falam** Burma
24C2 **Falcon Res** Mexico/USA
97A3 **Falémé** *R* Mali/Sen
39G7 **Falkenberg** Sweden
42C2 **Falkirk** Scot
29D6 **Falkland Is** Dependency, S Atlantic
29E6 **Falkland Sd** Falkland Is
22D4 **Fallbrook** USA
8B3 **Fallon** USA
15D2 **Fall River** USA
18A1 **Falls City** USA
43B4 **Falmouth** Eng
27H1 **Falmouth** Jamaica
16D2 **Falmouth** Massachusetts, USA
100A4 **False B** S Africa
24A2 **Falso,C** Mexico
56C2 **Falster** *I* Den
54C1 **Fălticeni** Rom
39H6 **Falun** Sweden
92B2 **Famagusta** Cyprus
46C1 **Famenne** Region, Belg
76B2 **Fang** Thai
99D2 **Fangak** Sudan
73E5 **Fang liao** Taiwan
52B2 **Fano** Italy
112C3 **Faraday** *Base* Ant
99C2 **Faradje** Zaïre
101D3 **Farafangana** Madag
95B2 **Farafra Oasis** Egypt
80E2 **Farah** Afghan
71F2 **Farallon de Medinilla** *I* Pacific O
97A3 **Faranah** Guinea
71F3 **Faraulep** *I* Pacific O
43D4 **Fareham** Eng
Farewell,C = Kap Farvel
107G5 **Farewell,C** NZ
110B2 **Farewell Spit** *Pt* NZ
8D2 **Fargo** USA
94B2 **Fari'a** *R* Israel
10A2 **Faribault** USA
86B2 **Faridpur** Bang
90C2 **Farīmān** Iran
18B2 **Farmington** Missouri, USA
9C3 **Farmington** New Mexico, USA
22B2 **Farmington Res** USA
42D2 **Farne Deep** N Sea
13D2 **Farnham,Mt** Can
12H2 **Faro** Can
50A2 **Faro** Port
39H7 **Fåro** *I* Sweden
89K9 **Farquhar** *Is* Indian O
44B3 **Farrar** *R* Scot
14B2 **Farrell** USA
55B3 **Fársala** Greece
91B4 **Fasā** Iran
45B3 **Fastnet Rock** Irish Rep
60C3 **Fastov** Ukraine
86A1 **Fatehpur** India
13D1 **Father** Can
30F2 **Fatima du Sul** Brazil
101G1 **Fauresmith** S Africa
47B2 **Faverges** France
7B4 **Fawn** *R* Can
38H6 **Fax** *R* Sweden
38A2 **Faxaflói** *B* Iceland
95A3 **Faya** Chad
11A3 **Fayetteville** Arkansas, USA
11C3 **Fayetteville** N Carolina, USA
93E4 **Faylakah** *I* Kuwait
84C2 **Fāzilka** India
96A2 **Fdérik** Maur
11C3 **Fear,C** USA
21A2 **Feather Middle Fork** *R* USA
48C2 **Fécamp** France
34D2 **Federación** Arg
34D2 **Federal** Arg
71F3 **Federated States of Micronesia** *Is* Pacific O
56C2 **Fehmarn** *I* Germany
32C5 **Feijó** Brazil
73C5 **Feilai Xai Bei Jiang** *R* China
110C2 **Feilding** NZ
100C2 **Feira** Zambia
31D4 **Feira de Santan** Brazil
92C2 **Feke** Turk
57B3 **Feldkirch** Austria
34D2 **Feliciano** *R* Arg
41D3 **Felixstowe** Eng
47D1 **Feltre** Italy
38G6 **Femund** *L* Nor
74A2 **Fengcheng** China
73B4 **Fengdu** China
72D1 **Fenging** China
73B3 **Fengjie** China
72B3 **Feng Xian** China
72C1 **Fengzhen** China
72C2 **Fen He** *R* China
101D2 **Fenoarivo Atsinanana** Madag
60E5 **Feodosiya** Ukraine
90C3 **Ferdow** Iran
46B2 **Fère-Champenoise** France
82B2 **Fergana** Uzbekistan
45C1 **Fermanagh** County, N Ire
45B2 **Fermoy** Irish Rep
47D1 **Fern** *Mt* Austria
32J7 **Fernandina** *I* Ecuador
17B1 **Fernandina Beach** USA
103G5 **Fernando de Noronha** *I* Atlantic O
35A2 **Fernandópolis** Brazil
20B1 **Ferndale** USA
21B2 **Fernley** USA
52B2 **Ferrara** Italy
32B5 **Ferreñafe** Peru
19B3 **Ferriday** USA
96B1 **Fès** Mor
18B2 **Festus** USA
54C2 **Feteşti** Rom
92A2 **Fethiye** Turk
61H5 **Fetisovo** Kazakhstan
44E1 **Fetlar** *I* Scot
84C1 **Feyzabad** Afghan
101D3 **Fianarantsoa** Madag
99D2 **Fichē** Eth
101G1 **Ficksburg** S Africa
47D2 **Fidenza** Italy
55A2 **Fier** Alb
47D1 **Fiera Di Primeiro** Italy
44C3 **Fife** Region, Scot
44C3 **Fife Ness** *Pen* Scot
48C3 **Figeac** France
50A1 **Figueira da Foz** Port
51C1 **Figueras** Spain
Figueres = Figueras
96B1 **Figuig** Mor
105G4 **Fiji** *Is* Pacific O
30D3 **Filadelfia** Par
54B2 **Filiaşi** Rom
55B3 **Filiatrá** Greece
53B3 **Filicudi** *I* Italy
21B3 **Fillmore** California, USA
44B3 **Findhorn** *R* Scot
10B2 **Findlay** USA
13D2 **Findlay,Mt** Can
15C2 **Finger Lakes** USA
101C2 **Fingoè** Mozam
92B2 **Finike** Turk
106C3 **Finke** *R* Aust
108A1 **Finke Flood Flats** Aust
64D3 **Finland** Republic, N Europe
39J7 **Finland,G of** N Europe
5F4 **Finlay** *R* Can
5F4 **Finlay Forks** Can
108C3 **Finley** Aust
38H5 **Finnsnes** Nor
71F4 **Finschhafen** PNG
47C1 **Finsteraarhorn** *Mt* Switz
56C2 **Finsterwalde** Germany
45C1 **Fintona** N Ire
111A3 **Fiordland Nat Pk** NZ
94B2 **Fīq** Syria
93C2 **Firat** *R* Turk
22B2 **Firebaugh** USA
52B2 **Firenze** Italy
34C2 **Firmat** Arg
85D3 **Firozābād** India
84C2 **Firozpur** India
39H7 **Firspång** Sweden
42B2 **Firth of Clyde** *Estuary* Scot
44C3 **Firth of Forth** *Estuary* Scot
44A3 **Firth of Lorn** *Estuary* Scot
40C2 **Firth of Tay** *Estuary* Scot
91B4 **Firūzābād** Iran
100A3 **Fish** *R* Namibia
22C2 **Fish Camp** USA
16C2 **Fishers I** USA
6B3 **Fisher Str** Can
43B4 **Fishguard** Wales
6E3 **Fiskenaesset** Greenland
46B2 **Fismes** France
15D2 **Fitchburg** USA
44E2 **Fitful Head** *Pt* Scot
17B1 **Fitzgerald** USA
106B2 **Fitzroy** *R* Aust
106B2 **Fitzroy Crossing** Aust
14B1 **Fitzwilliam I** Can
Fiume = Rijeka
99C3 **Fizi** Zaïre
9B3 **Flagstaff** USA
42D2 **Flamborough Head** *C* Eng
8C2 **Flaming Gorge Res** USA
44A2 **Flannan Isles** *Is* Scot
12J2 **Flat** *R* Can
13E3 **Flathead** *R* USA
8B2 **Flathead L** USA
18B2 **Flat River** USA
8A2 **Flattery,C** USA
42C3 **Fleetwood** Eng
39F7 **Flekkefjord** Nor
69G4 **Fleming Deep** Pacific O
16B2 **Flemington** USA
56B2 **Flensburg** Germany
47B1 **Fleurier** Switz
106C4 **Flinders** *I* Aust
107D4 **Flinders** *I* Aust
107D2 **Flinders** *R* Aust
106C4 **Flinders Range** *Mts* Aust
5H4 **Flin Flon** Can
10B2 **Flint** USA
42C3 **Flint** Wales
11B3 **Flint** *R* USA
46B1 **Flixecourt** France
17A1 **Florala** USA
Florence = Firenze
11B3 **Florence** Alabama, USA
18A2 **Florence** Kansas, USA
20B2 **Florence** Oregon, USA
11C3 **Florence** S Carolina, USA
32B3 **Florencia** Colombia
46C2 **Florenville** Belg
25D3 **Flores** Guatemala
96A1 **Flores** *I* Açores
106B1 **Flores** *I* Indon
34D3 **Flores** *R* Arg
70C4 **Flores S** Indon
31C3 **Floriano** Brazil
30G4 **Florianópolis** Brazil
25D2 **Florida** State, USA
29E2 **Florida** Urug
17B2 **Florida B** USA
17B2 **Florida City** USA
107E1 **Florida Is** Solomon Is
11B4 **Florida Keys** *Is* USA
11B4 **Florida,Strs of** USA
55B2 **Flórina** Greece
38F6 **Florø** Nor
47D1 **Fluchthorn** *Mt* Austria
54C1 **Focsani** Rom
53C2 **Foggia** Italy
97A4 **Fogo** *I* Cape Verde
48C3 **Foix** France
6C3 **Foley I** Can
52B2 **Foligno** Italy
43E4 **Folkestone** Eng
17B1 **Folkston** USA
52B2 **Follonica** Italy
22B1 **Folsom** USA
22B1 **Folsom L** *L* USA
5H4 **Fond-du-Lac** Can
10B2 **Fond du Lac** USA
48C2 **Fontainebleau** France
18B2 **Fontenac** USA
48B2 **Fontenay-le-Comte** France
52C1 **Fonyód** Hung
Foochow = Fuzhou
12D2 **Foraker,Mt** USA
46D2 **Forbach** France
109C2 **Forbes** Aust
97C4 **Forcados** Nig
38F6 **Forde** Nor
108C1 **Fords Bridge** Aust
19B3 **Fordyce** USA

97A4 **Forécariah** Guinea
6G3 **Forel,Mt** Greenland
14B2 **Forest** Can
17B1 **Forest Park** USA
22A1 **Forestville** USA
44C3 **Forfar** Scot
46A2 **Forges-les-Eaux** France
20B1 **Forks** USA
52B2 **Forlì** Italy
51C2 **Formentera** *I* Spain
53B2 **Formia** Italy
96A1 **Formigas** *I* Açores
Formosa = Taiwan
30E4 **Formosa** Arg
31B5 **Formosa** Brazil
30D3 **Formosa** State, Arg
73D5 **Formosa Str** Taiwan/China
47D2 **Fornovo di Taro** Italy
38D3 **Føroyar** *Is* N Atlantic O
44C3 **Forres** Scot
106B4 **Forrest** Aust
11A3 **Forrest City** USA
107D2 **Forsayth** Aust
39J6 **Forssa** Fin
109D2 **Forster** Aust
18B2 **Forsyth** Missouri, USA
84C3 **Fort Abbas** Pak
7B4 **Fort Albany** Can
31D2 **Fortaleza** Brazil
44B3 **Fort Augustus** Scot
100B4 **Fort Beaufort** S Africa
21A2 **Fort Bragg** USA
8C2 **Fort Collins** USA
15C1 **Fort Coulogne** Can
27E4 **Fort de France** Martinique
17A1 **Fort Deposit** USA
10A2 **Fort Dodge** USA
106A3 **Fortescue** *R* Aust
7A5 **Fort Frances** Can
4F3 **Fort Franklin** Can
4F3 **Fort Good Hope** Can
108B1 **Fort Grey** Aust
44B3 **Forth** *R* Scot
7B4 **Fort Hope** Can
34B3 **Fortin Uno** Arg
4F3 **Fort Laird** Can
96C1 **Fort Lallemand** Alg
Fort Lamy = Ndjamena
11B4 **Fort Lauderdale** USA
4F3 **Fort Liard** Can
5G4 **Fort Mackay** Can
5G5 **Fort Macleod** Can
5G4 **Fort McMurray** Can
4E3 **Fort McPherson** Can
18B2 **Fort Madison** USA
8C2 **Fort Morgan** USA
11B4 **Fort Myers** USA
5F4 **Fort Nelson** Can
4F3 **Fort Norman** Can
17A1 **Fort Payne** USA
8C2 **Fort Peck Res** USA
11B4 **Fort Pierce** USA
4G3 **Fort Providence** Can
5G3 **Fort Resolution** Can
98B3 **Fort Rousset** Congo
5F4 **Fort St James** Can
13C1 **Fort St John** Can
13E2 **Fort Saskatchewan** Can
18B2 **Fort Scott** USA
4E3 **Fort Selkirk** Can
7B4 **Fort Severn** Can
61H5 **Fort Shevchenko** Kazakhstan
4F3 **Fort Simpson** Can
5G3 **Fort Smith** Can
4G3 **Fort Smith** Region, Can
11A3 **Fort Smith** USA
9C3 **Fort Stockton** USA
20B2 **Fortuna** California, USA
5G4 **Fort Vermillion** Can
17A1 **Fort Walton Beach** USA
10B2 **Fort Wayne** USA
44B3 **Fort William** Scot
9D3 **Fort Worth** USA
12F2 **Fortymile** *R* USA
12E1 **Fort Yukon** USA
73C5 **Foshan** China
47B2 **Fossano** Italy
12G3 **Foster,Mt** USA
98B3 **Fougamou** Gabon
48B2 **Fougères** France
44D1 **Foula** *I* Scot
43E4 **Foulness I** Eng
111B2 **Foulwind,C** NZ
98B2 **Foumban** Cam
49C1 **Fourmies** France
55C3 **Foúrnoi** *I* Greece
97A3 **Fouta Djallon** *Mts* Guinea
111B3 **Foveaux** *Str* NZ
43B4 **Fowey** Eng
13D2 **Fox Creek** Can
6B3 **Foxe Basin** *G* Can
6B3 **Foxe Chan** Can
6C3 **Foxe Pen** Can
110C2 **Foxton** NZ
13F2 **Fox Valley** Can
45B2 **Foynes** Irish Rep
100A2 **Foz do Cuene** Angola
30F4 **Foz do Iquaçu** Brazil
16A2 **Frackville** USA
34B2 **Fraga** Arg
16D1 **Framingham** USA
31B6 **Franca** Brazil
49C2 **France** Republic, Europe
10A2 **Frances** Can
12J2 **Frances** *R* Can
49D2 **Franche Comté** Region, France
100B3 **Francistown** Botswana
13B2 **Francois L** Can
14A2 **Frankfort** Indiana, USA
11B3 **Frankfort** Kentucky, USA
101G1 **Frankfort** S Africa
57B2 **Frankfurt** Germany
46E1 **Frankfurt am Main** Germany
56C2 **Frankfurt-an-der-Oder** Germany
57C3 **Fränkischer Alb** *Upland* Germany
14A3 **Franklin** Indiana, USA
19B4 **Franklin** Louisiana, USA
16D1 **Franklin** Massachusetts, USA
16B2 **Franklin** New Jersey, USA
14C2 **Franklin** Pennsylvania, USA
4F2 **Franklin B** Can
20C1 **Franklin D Roosevelt** *L* USA
4F3 **Franklin Mts** Can
4J2 **Franklin Str** Can
111B2 **Franz Josef Glacier** NZ
Franz-Joseph-Land = Zemlya Frantsa Iosifa
5F5 **Fraser** *R* Can
44C3 **Fraserburgh** Scot
107E3 **Fraser I** Aust
13B2 **Fraser L** Can
47B1 **Frasne** France
47C1 **Frauenfield** Switz
34D2 **Fray Bentos** Urug
40C2 **Frazerburgh** Scot
16B3 **Frederica** USA
56B1 **Fredericia** Den
15C3 **Frederick** Maryland, USA
15C3 **Fredericksburg** Virginia, USA
12H3 **Frederick Sd** USA
18B2 **Fredericktown** USA
7D5 **Fredericton** Can
6E3 **Frederikshab** Greenland
39G7 **Frederikshavn** Den
15C2 **Fredonia** USA
39G7 **Fredrikstad** Nor
16B2 **Freehold** USA
26B1 **Freeport** The Bahamas
19A4 **Freeport** Texas, USA
97A4 **Freetown** Sierra Leone
57B3 **Freiburg** Germany
57C3 **Freistadt** Austria
106A4 **Fremantle** Aust
22B2 **Fremont** California, USA
18A1 **Fremont** Nebraska, USA
14B2 **Fremont** Ohio, USA
33G3 **French Guiana** Dependency, S America
109C4 **Frenchmans Cap** *Mt* Aust
105J4 **French Polynesia** *Is* Pacific O
24B2 **Fresnillo** Mexico
8B3 **Fresno** USA
22C2 **Fresno** *R* USA
47A1 **Fretigney** France
46B1 **Frévent** France
109C4 **Freycinet Pen** Aust
97A3 **Fria** Guinea
22C2 **Friant** USA
22C2 **Friant Dam** USA
52A1 **Fribourg** Switz
57B3 **Friedrichshafen** Germany
6D3 **Frobisher B** Can
6D3 **Frobisher Bay** Can
5H4 **Frobisher L** Can
61F3 **Frolovo** Russian Fed
43C4 **Frome** Eng
108A1 **Frome** *R* Aust
43C4 **Frome** *R* Eng
106C4 **Frome,L** Aust
25C3 **Frontera** Mexico
15C3 **Front Royal** USA
53B2 **Frosinone** Italy
73C5 **Fuchuan** China
73E4 **Fuding** China
24B2 **Fuerte** *R* Mexico
30E3 **Fuerte Olimpo** Par
96A2 **Fuerteventura** *I* Canary Is
72C2 **Fugu** China
68A2 **Fuhai** China
91C4 **Fujairah** UAE
75B1 **Fuji** Japan
73D4 **Fujian** Province, China
69F2 **Fujin** China
75B1 **Fujinomiya** Japan
74D3 **Fuji-san** *Mt* Japan
75B1 **Fujisawa** Japan
75B1 **Fuji-Yoshida** Japan
63A3 **Fukang** China
74C3 **Fukuchiyima** Japan
74D3 **Fukui** Japan
74C4 **Fukuoka** Japan
74E3 **Fukushima** Japan
74C4 **Fukuyama** Japan
57B2 **Fulda** Germany
57B2 **Fulda** *R* Germany
73B4 **Fuling** China
27L1 **Fullarton** Trinidad
22D4 **Fullerton** USA
18C2 **Fulton** Kentucky, USA
15C2 **Fulton** New York, USA
46C1 **Fumay** France
75C1 **Funabashi** Japan
96A1 **Funchal** Medeira
35C1 **Fundão** Brazil
7D5 **Fundy,B of** Can
101C3 **Funhalouro** Mozam
72D3 **Funing** China
73B5 **Funing** China
97C3 **Funtua** Nig
73D4 **Fuqing** China
101C2 **Furancungo** Mozam
91C4 **Fürg** Iran
47C1 **Furka** *P* Switz
107D5 **Furneaux Group** *Is* Aust
56C2 **Fürstenwalde** Germany
57C3 **Fürth** Germany
74D3 **Furukawa** Japan
6B3 **Fury and Hecla St** Can
74A2 **Fushun** Liaoning, China
73A4 **Fushun** Sichuan, China
74B2 **Fusong** China
57C3 **Füssen** Germany
72E2 **Fu Xian** China
72E1 **Fuxin** China
72D3 **Fuyang** China
72E1 **Fuyuan** Liaoning, China
73A4 **Fuyuan** Yunnan, China
68A2 **Fuyun** China
73D4 **Fuzhou** China
56C1 **Fyn** *I* Den

G

99E2 **Gaalkacyo** Somalia
21B2 **Gabbs** USA
100A2 **Gabela** Angola
96D1 **Gabe's** Tunisia
22B2 **Gabilan Range** *Mts* USA
98B3 **Gabon** Republic, Africa
100B3 **Gaborone** Botswana
54C2 **Gabrovo** Bulg
91B3 **Gach Sārān** Iran
17A1 **Gadsden** Alabama, USA
10A1 **Gads L** Can
53B2 **Gaeta** Italy
71F3 **Gaferut** *I* Pacific O
96C1 **Gafsa** Tunisia
60D2 **Gagarin** Russian Fed
97B4 **Gagnoa** Ivory Coast
7D4 **Gagnon** Can
61F5 **Gagra** Georgia
86B1 **Gaibanda** India
29C4 **Gaimán** Arg
17B2 **Gainesville** Florida, USA
17B1 **Gainesville** Georgia, USA
19A3 **Gainesville** Texas, USA
42D3 **Gainsborough** Eng
108A2 **Gairdner,L** Aust
44B3 **Gairloch** Scot
16A3 **Gaithersburg** USA
87B1 **Gajendragarh** India
73D4 **Ga Jiang** *R* China
99D3 **Galana** *R* Kenya
103D5 **Galapagos Is** Pacific O
42C2 **Galashiels** Scot
54C1 **Galaţi** Rom
4C3 **Galena** Alaska, USA
18B2 **Galena** Kansas, USA
27L1 **Galeota Pt** Trinidad
27L1 **Galera Pt** Trinidad
10A2 **Galesburg** USA
15C2 **Galeton** USA
61F2 **Galich** Russian Fed
50A1 **Galicia** Region, Spain
Galilee,S of = Tiberias,L
27J1 **Galina Pt** Jamaica
99D1 **Gallabat** Sudan
47C2 **Gallarate** Italy
87C3 **Galle** Sri Lanka
51B1 **Gállego** *R* Spain
Gallipoli = Gelibolu
55A2 **Gallipoli** Italy
38J5 **Gällivare** Sweden
42B2 **Galloway** District
42B2 **Galloway,Mull of** *C* Scot
8C3 **Gallup** USA
22B1 **Galt** USA
96A2 **Galtat Zemmour** Mor
25C2 **Galveston** USA
11A4 **Galveston B** USA
34C2 **Galvez** Arg
49D3 **Galvi** Corse
45B2 **Galway** County, Irish Rep
41B3 **Galway** Irish Rep
41B3 **Galway** *B* Irish Rep
86B1 **Gamba** China
97B3 **Gambaga** Ghana

4A3 **Gambell** USA
97A3 **Gambia** *R* The Gambia/Sen
97A3 **Gambia,The** Republic, Africa
98B3 **Gamboma** Congo
100A2 **Gambos** Angola
87C3 **Gampola** Sri Lanka
99E2 **Ganale Dorya** *R* Eth
15C2 **Gananoque** Can
Gand = Gent
100A2 **Ganda** Angola
98C3 **Gandajika** Zaïre
84B3 **Gandava** Pak
7E5 **Gander** Can
85C4 **Gāndhīdhām** India
85C4 **Gāndhīnagar** India
85D4 **Gāndhi Sāgar** *L* India
51B2 **Gandia** Spain
86B2 **Ganga** *R* India
85C3 **Ganganar** India
86C2 **Gangaw** Burma
72A2 **Gangca** China
82C2 **Gangdise Shan** *Mts* China
Ganges = Ganga
86B1 **Gangtok** India
72B3 **Gangu** China
8C2 **Gannett Peak** *Mt* USA
72B2 **Ganquan** China
108A3 **Gantheaume** *C* Aust
39K8 **Gantsevichi** Belorussia
73D4 **Ganzhou** China
97C3 **Gao** Mali
72A2 **Gaolan** China
72C2 **Gaoping** China
97B3 **Gaoua** Burkina
97A3 **Gaoual** Guinea
72D3 **Gaoyou Hu** *L* China
73C5 **Gaozhou** China
49D3 **Gap** France
79B2 **Gapan** Phil
84D2 **Gar** China
109C1 **Garah** Aust
31D3 **Garanhuns** Brazil
21A1 **Garberville** USA
35B2 **Garça** Brazil
35A2 **Garcias** Brazil
47D2 **Garda** Italy
9C3 **Garden City** USA
14A1 **Garden Pen** USA
34D3 **Gardey** Arg
84B2 **Gardez** Afghan
16C2 **Gardiners I** USA
16D1 **Gardner** USA
47D2 **Gardone** Italy
47D2 **Gargano** Italy
85D4 **Garhākota** India
61K2 **Gari** Russian Fed
100A4 **Garies** S Africa
99D3 **Garissa** Kenya
19A3 **Garland** USA
57C3 **Garmisch-Partenkirchen** Germany
90B2 **Garmsar** Iran
18A2 **Garnett** USA
8B2 **Garnett Peak** *Mt* USA
48C3 **Garonne** *R* France
44B3 **Garry** *R* Scot
78B4 **Garut** Indon
86A2 **Garwa** India
14A2 **Gary** USA
82C2 **Garyarsa** China
4H3 **Gary L** Can
19A3 **Garza-Little Elm** *Res* USA
90B2 **Gasan Kuli** Turkmenistan
48B3 **Gascogne** Region, France
18B2 **Gasconade** *R* USA
106A3 **Gascoyne** *R* Aust
98B2 **Gashaka** Nig
97D3 **Gashua** Nig
10D2 **Gaspé** Can
10D2 **Gaspé,C. de** Can
94A1 **Gata,C** Cyprus
60C2 **Gatchina** Russian Fed
42D2 **Gateshead** Eng
19A3 **Gatesville** USA
15C1 **Gatineau** Can
15C1 **Gatineau** *R* Can
109D1 **Gatton** Aust
86C1 **Gauháti** India
58C1 **Gauja** *R* Latvia
86A1 **Gauri Phanta** India
22B3 **Gaviota** USA
39H6 **Gävle** Sweden
108A2 **Gawler Ranges** *Mts* Aust
72A1 **Gaxun Nur** *L* China
86A2 **Gaya** India
97C3 **Gaya** Niger
14B1 **Gaylord** USA
109D1 **Gayndah** Aust
61H1 **Gayny** Russian Fed
60C4 **Gaysin** Ukraine
92B3 **Gaza** Israel
92C2 **Gaziantep** Turk
97B4 **Gbaringa** Lib
58B2 **Gdańsk** Pol
58B2 **Gdańsk,G of** Pol
39K7 **Gdov** Russian Fed
58B2 **Gdynia** Pol
94A3 **Gebel Halâl** *Mt* Egypt
95C2 **Gebel Hamata** *Mt* Egypt
92B4 **Gebel Katherina** *Mt* Egypt
94A3 **Gebel Libni** *Mt* Egypt
94A3 **Gebel Maghâra** *Mt* Egypt
99D1 **Gedaref** Sudan
55C3 **Gediz** *R* Turk
56C2 **Gedser** Den
46C1 **Geel** Belg
108B3 **Geelong** Aust
109C4 **Geeveston** Aust
97D3 **Geidam** Nig
46D1 **Geilenkirchen** Germany
99D3 **Geita** Tanz
73A5 **Gejiu** China
53B3 **Gela** Italy
99E2 **Geladī** Eth
46D1 **Geldern** Germany
55C2 **Gelibolu** Turk
92B2 **Gelidonya Burun** Turk
46D1 **Gelsenkirchen** Germany
39F8 **Gelting** Germany
77C5 **Gemas** Malay
46C1 **Gembloux** Belg
98B2 **Gemena** Zaïre
92C2 **Gemerek** Turk
92A1 **Gemlik** Turk
52B1 **Gemona** Italy
100B3 **Gemsbok** *Nat Pk* Botswana
98C1 **Geneina** Sudan
34C3 **General Acha** Arg
34C3 **General Alvear** Buenos Aires, Arg
34B2 **General Alvear** Mendoza, Arg
34C2 **General Arenales** Arg
34D3 **General Belgrano** Arg
112B2 **General Belgrano** *Base* Ant
112C2 **General Bernardo O'Higgins** *Base* Ant
34D3 **General Conesa** Buenos Aires, Arg
30D3 **General Eugenio A Garay** Par
34D3 **General Guido** Arg
34C3 **General La Madrid** Arg
34C2 **General Levalle** Arg
30C4 **General Manuel Belgrano** *Mt* Arg
34D3 **General Paz** Buenos Aires, Arg
34C3 **General Pico** Arg
34C2 **General Pinto** Arg
34D3 **General Pirán** Arg
29C3 **General Roca** Arg
112C3 **General San Martin** *Base* Ant
79C4 **General Santos** Phil
34C3 **General Viamonte** Arg
34C3 **General Villegas** Arg
15C2 **Genesee** *R* USA
15C2 **Geneseo** USA
Geneva = Genève
18A1 **Geneva** Nebraska, USA
15C2 **Geneva** New York, USA
Geneva,L of = LacLéman
52A1 **Genève** Switz
50B2 **Genil** *R* Spain
Genoa = Genova
109C3 **Genoa** Aust
52A2 **Genova** Italy
32J7 **Genovesa** *I* Ecuador
46B1 **Gent** Belg
78B4 **Genteng** Indon
56C2 **Genthin** Germany
93E1 **Geokchay** Azerbaijan
100B4 **George** S Africa
7D4 **George** *R* Can
109C2 **George,L** Aust
17B2 **George,L** Florida, USA
15D2 **George,L** New York, USA
111A2 **George Sd** NZ
109C4 **George Town** Aust
15C3 **Georgetown** Delaware, USA
33F2 **Georgetown** Guyana
14B3 **Georgetown** Kentucky, USA
77C4 **George Town** Malay
27N2 **Georgetown** St Vincent
17C1 **Georgetown** S Carolina, USA
19A3 **Georgetown** Texas, USA
97A3 **Georgetown** The Gambia
112C8 **George V Land** Region, Ant
65F5 **Georgia** Republic, Europe
112C12 **Georg Forster** *Base* Ant
17B1 **Georgia** State, USA
14B1 **Georgian B** Can
13C3 **Georgia,Str of** Can
106C3 **Georgina** *R* Aust
61F5 **Georgiyevsk** Russian Fed
57C2 **Gera** Germany
46B1 **Geraardsbergen** Belg
111B2 **Geraldine** NZ
106A3 **Geraldton** Aust
10B2 **Geraldton** Can
94B3 **Gerar** *R* Israel
4C3 **Gerdine,Mt** USA
12E2 **Gerdova Peak** *Mt* USA
77C4 **Gerik** Malay
60B4 **Gerlachovsky** *Mt* Pol
13C1 **Germanson Lodge** Can
56C2 **Germany** Republic, Europe
101G1 **Germiston** S Africa
46D1 **Gerolstein** Germany
51C1 **Gerona** Spain
46E1 **Geseke** Germany
99E2 **Gestro** *R* Eth
50B1 **Getafe** Spain
16A3 **Gettysburg** Pennsylvania, USA
93D2 **Gevaş** Turk
55B2 **Gevgelija** Macedonia, Yugos
47B1 **Gex** France
94C2 **Ghabāghib** Syria
96C1 **Ghadamis** Libya
90B2 **Ghaem Shahr** Iran
86A1 **Ghāghara** *R* India
97B4 **Ghana** Republic, Africa
100B3 **Ghanzi** Botswana
96C1 **Ghardaïa** Alg
95A1 **Gharyan** Libya
95A2 **Ghāt** Libya
84D3 **Ghāziābād** India
84C3 **Ghazi Khan** Pak
84B2 **Ghazni** Afghan
54C1 **Gheorgheni** Rom
88E4 **Ghudamis** Alg
90D3 **Ghurian** Afghan
95B2 **Gialo** Libya
99E2 **Giamame** Somalia
53C3 **Giarre** Italy
100A3 **Gibeon** Namibia
50A2 **Gibraltar** Colony, SW Europe
50A2 **Gibraltar,Str of** Spain/Africa
106B3 **Gibson Desert** Aust
20B1 **Gibsons** Can
87B1 **Giddalūr** India
99D2 **Gīdolē** Eth
57B2 **Giessen** Germany
17B2 **Gifford** USA
74D3 **Gifu** Japan
42B2 **Gigha** *I* Scot
52B2 **Giglio** *I* Italy
50A1 **Gijón** Spain
107D2 **Gilbert** *R* Aust
13C2 **Gilbert,Mt** Can
101C2 **Gilé** Mozam
94B2 **Gilead** Region, Jordan
95B2 **Gilf Kebir Plat** Egypt
109C2 **Gilgandra** Aust
84C1 **Gilgit** Pak
84C1 **Gilgit** *R* Pak
108C2 **Gilgunnia** Aust
7A4 **Gillam** Can
108A2 **Gilles** *L* Aust
13B2 **Gill I** Can
14A1 **Gills Rock** USA
14A2 **Gilman** USA
22B2 **Gilroy** USA
8D1 **Gimli** Can
101H1 **Gingindlovu** S Africa
79C4 **Gingoog** Phil
99E2 **Gīnīr** Eth
55B3 **Gióna** *Mt* Greece
109C3 **Gippsland** *Mts* Aust
14B2 **Girard** USA
32C3 **Girardot** Colombia
44C3 **Girdle Ness** *Pen* Scot
93C1 **Giresun** Turk
85C4 **Gir Hills** India
98B2 **Giri** *R* Zaïre
86B2 **Girīdīh** India
Girona = Gerona
48B2 **Gironde** *R* France
42B2 **Girvan** Scot
111C2 **Gisborne** NZ
46A2 **Gisors** France
99C3 **Gitega** Burundi
Giuba,R = Juba,R
54C2 **Giurgiu** Rom
46C1 **Givet** Belg
58C2 **Gizycko** Pol
55B2 **Gjirokastër** Alb
4J3 **Gjoatlaven** Can
39G6 **Gjøvik** Nor
7D5 **Glace Bay** Can
12G3 **Glacier Bay Nat Mon** USA
13E3 **Glacier Nat Pk** USA/Can
20B1 **Glacier Peak** *Mt* USA
6B2 **Glacier Str** Can
107E3 **Gladstone** Queensland, Aust
108A2 **Gladstone** S Aust, Aust
109C4 **Gladstone** Tasmania, Aust
14A1 **Gladstone** USA
38A1 **Glama** *Mt* Iceland
39G6 **Glåma** *R* Nor
46D2 **Glan** *R* Germany
47C1 **Glarner** *Mts* Switz
47C1 **Glarus** Switz
18A2 **Glasco** USA
8C2 **Glasgow** Montana, USA
42B2 **Glasgow** Scot
16B3 **Glassboro** USA
43C4 **Glastonbury** Eng
61H2 **Glazov** Russian Fed
59B3 **Gleisdorf** Austria
110C1 **Glen Afton** NZ

16A3 **Glen Burnie** USA
101H1 **Glencoe** S Africa
9B3 **Glendale** Arizona, USA
22C3 **Glendale** California, USA
12E2 **Glenhallen** USA
109D1 **Glen Innes** Aust
109C1 **Glenmorgan** Aust
109D2 **Glenreagh** Aust
16A3 **Glen Rock** USA
19A3 **Glen Rose** USA
44C3 **Glenrothes** UK
15D2 **Glens Falls** USA
45B1 **Glenties** Irish Rep
19B3 **Glenwood** Arkansas, USA
8C3 **Glenwood Springs** USA
39F6 **Glittertind** *Mt* Nor
59B2 **Gliwice** Pol
9B3 **Globe** USA
58B2 **Głogów** Pol
38G5 **Glomfjord** Nor
109D2 **Gloucester** Aust
43C4 **Gloucester** Eng
16D1 **Gloucester** USA
58D1 **Glubokoye** Belorussia
60D3 **Glukhov** Russian Fed
59B3 **Gmünd** Austria
57C3 **Gmunden** Austria
58B2 **Gniezno** Pol
100A3 **Goabeg** Namibia
87A1 **Goa, Daman and Diu** Union Territory, India
86C1 **Goālpāra** India
99D2 **Goba** Eth
100A3 **Gobabis** Namibia
34C2 **Gobernador Crespo** Arg
34B3 **Gobernador Duval** Arg
72B1 **Gobi** *Desert* China/Mongolia
75B2 **Gobo** Japan
87B1 **Godag** India
87C1 **Godāvari** *R* India
14B2 **Goderich** Can
6E3 **Godhavn** Greenland
85C4 **Godhra** India
34B2 **Godoy Cruz** Arg
7A4 **Gods L** Can
6E3 **Godthab** Greenland
Godwin Austen = K2
35B1 **Goiandira** Brazil
35B1 **Goianésia** Brazil
35B1 **Goiânia** Brazil
35A1 **Goiás** Brazil
31B4 **Goiás** State, Brazil
35A2 **Goio-Erê** Brazil
99D2 **Gojab** *R* Eth
55C2 **Gökçeada** *I* Turk
55C3 **Gökova Körfezi** *B* Turk
92C2 **Göksun** Turk
63C3 **Gol** *R* Mongolia
86C1 **Golāghāt** India
93C2 **Gölbaşi** Turk
20C2 **Golconda** USA
20B2 **Gold Beach** USA
109D1 **Gold Coast** Aust
13D2 **Golden** Can
110B2 **Golden B** NZ
20B1 **Goldendale** USA
22A2 **Golden Gate** *Chan* USA
19B4 **Golden Meadow** USA
21B2 **Goldfield** USA
13B3 **Gold River** Can
56C2 **Goleniów** Pol
22C3 **Goleta** USA
52A2 **Golfe d'Ajaccio** *G* Corse
96D1 **Golfe de Gabes** *G* Tunisia
Golfe de Gascogne = Biscay,Bay of
52A2 **Golfe de St Florent** *G* Corse
48B2 **Golfe de St-Malo** *B* France
49C3 **Golfe du Lion** *G* France
29B4 **Golfo Corcovado** *G* Chile
50B2 **Golfo de Almeira** *G* Spain
29B4 **Golfo de Ancud** *G* Chile
25D2 **Golfo de Batabano** *G* Cuba
50A2 **Golfo de Cadiz** *G* Spain
53A3 **Golfo de Cagliari** *G* Sardegna
24A1 **Golfo de California** *G* Mexico
25D4 **Golfo de Chiriqui** *G* Panama
25D3 **Golfo de Fonseca** Honduras
26B2 **Golfo de Guacanayabo** *G* Cuba
32A4 **Golfo de Guayaquil** *G* Ecuador
26B5 **Golfo del Darien** *G* Colombia/Panama
32A2 **Golfo de los Mosquitos** *G* Panama
25D3 **Golfo del Papagaya** *G* Nic
51B2 **Golfo de Mazarrón** *G* Spain
25D4 **Golfo de Nicoya** *G* Costa Rica
53A3 **Golfo de Oristano** *G* Sardegna
25E4 **Golfo de Panamá** *G* Panama
25D3 **Golfo de Papagayo** *G* Costa Rica
27E4 **Golfo de Paria** *G* Ven
29B5 **Golfo de Penas** *G* Chile
49D3 **Golfo de St Florent** Corse
51C1 **Golfo de San Jorge** *G* Spain
24C3 **Golfo de Tehuantepec** *G* Mexico
32B3 **Golfo de Torugas** *G* Colombia
32B2 **Golfo de Uraba** *G* Colombia
51C2 **Golfo de Valencia** *G* Spain
27C4 **Golfo de Venezuela** *G* Ven
52A2 **Golfo di Genova** *G* Italy
53C3 **Golfo di Policastro** *G* Italy
53C3 **Golfo di Squillace** *G* Italy
53C2 **Golfo di Taranto** *G* Italy
52B1 **Golfo di Venezia** *G* Italy
25D4 **Golfo Dulce** *G* Costa Rica
29C5 **Golfo San Jorge** *G* Arg
29D4 **Golfo San Matías** *G* Arg
68B3 **Golmud** China
99E2 **Golocha** Eth
12B2 **Golovin B** USA
74F2 **Golovnino** Russian Fed
99C3 **Goma** Zaïre
97D3 **Gombe** Nig
60D3 **Gomel** Belorussia
96A2 **Gomera** *I* Canary Is
24B2 **Gómez Palacio** Mexico
63E2 **Gonam** *R* Russian Fed
90C2 **Gonbad-e Kāvūs** Iran
86A1 **Gonda** India
85C4 **Gondal** India
99D1 **Gonder** Eth
92A1 **Gönen** Turk
55C3 **Gonen** *R* Turk
73A4 **Gongga Shan** *Mt* China
72A2 **Gonghe** China
97D3 **Gongola** *R* Nig
22B2 **Gonzales** California, USA
19A4 **Gonzales** Texas, USA
34C3 **Gonzalez Chaves** Arg
13C2 **Good Hope Mt** Can
8C2 **Goodland** USA
12B3 **Goodnews Bay** USA
109C1 **Goodooga** *R* Aust
42D3 **Goole** Eng
108C2 **Goolgowi** Aust
108A3 **Goolwa** Aust
106A4 **Goomalling** Aust
108C2 **Goombalie** Aust
109D1 **Goomer** Aust
109D1 **Goomeri** Aust
109D1 **Goondiwindi** Aust
7E4 **Goose Bay** Can
17C1 **Goose Creek** USA
20B2 **Goose L** USA
87B1 **Gooty** India
63C2 **Gora Munku Sardyk** *Mt* Mongolia/Russian Fed
64H3 **Gora Narodnaya** *Mt* Russian Fed
64G3 **Gora Tel'pos-iz** Russian Fed
54A2 **Goražde** Bosnia & Herzegovina, Yugos
4D3 **Gordon** USA
13E1 **Gordon L** Can
15C3 **Gordonsville** USA
98B2 **Goré** Chad
99D2 **Gorē** Eth
111A3 **Gore** NZ
63F2 **Gore Topko** *Mt* Russian Fed
45C2 **Gorey** Irish Rep
90B2 **Gorgān** Iran
93E2 **Goris** Armenia
52B1 **Gorizia** Italy
61F2 **Gor'kovskoye Vodokhranilishche** *Res* Russian Fed
57C2 **Gorlitz** Germany
60E4 **Gorlovka** Ukraine
22C3 **Gorman** USA
54C2 **Gorna Orjahovica** Bulg
68A1 **Gorno-Altaysk** Russian Fed
69G2 **Gornozavodsk** Russian Fed
61F2 **Gorodets** Russian Fed
59C3 **Gorodok** Ukraine
59D3 **Gorodok** Ukraine
71F4 **Goroka** PNG
86A1 **Gorokhpur** India
101C2 **Gorongosa** Mozam
71D3 **Gorontalo** Indon
61K2 **Goro Yurma** *Mt* Russian Fed
45B2 **Gort** Irish Rep
63C2 **Goryachinsk** Russian Fed
59D3 **Goryn'** *R* Ukraine
59C2 **Góry Świetokrzyskie** *Upland* Pol
64G3 **Gory Tel'pos-iz'** *Mt* Russian Fed
39H8 **Gorzow Wielkopolski** Pol
74E2 **Goshogawara** Japan
52C2 **Gospić** Croatia
54B2 **Gostivar** Macedonia, Yugos
58B2 **Gostynin** Pol
39G7 **Göteborg** Sweden
98B2 **Gotel** *Mts* Nig
39H7 **Gotland** *I* Sweden
74B4 **Gotō-retto** *I* Japan
39H7 **Gotska Sandön** *I* Sweden
74C3 **Gōtsu** Japan
98B1 **Goudoumaria** Niger
103H7 **Gough I** Atlantic O
109C2 **Goulburn** Aust
97B3 **Goumbou** Mali
97B3 **Goundam** Mali
98B1 **Gouré** Niger
97B3 **Gourma Rharous** Mali
46A2 **Gournay-en-Bray** France
95A3 **Gouro** Chad
71E5 **Gove Pen** Aust
60B4 **Goverla** *Mt* Ukraine
35C1 **Governador Valadares** Brazil
86A2 **Govind Ballabh Paht Sāgar** *L* India
15C2 **Gowanda** USA
84B3 **Gowārān** Afghan
30E4 **Goya** Arg
98C1 **Goz-Beïda** Chad
53B3 **Gozo** *I* Medit S
95C3 **Goz Regeb** Sudan
100B4 **Graaff-Reinet** S Africa
15C1 **Gracefield** Can
109D1 **Grafton** Aust
8D2 **Grafton** N Dakota, USA
14B3 **Grafton** W Virginia, USA
5E4 **Graham** *I* Can
13C1 **Graham** *R* Can
13E1 **Graham L** Can
100B4 **Grahamstown** S Africa
31B3 **Grajaú** Brazil
58C2 **Grajewo** Pol
55B2 **Grámmos** *Mt* Greece/Alb
44C3 **Grampian** Region, Scot
44B3 **Grampian** *Mts* Scot
32C3 **Granada** Colombia
25D3 **Granada** Nic
50B2 **Granada** Spain
15D1 **Granby** Can
96A2 **Gran Canaria** *I* Canary Is
30D4 **Gran Chaco** *Region* Arg
14A2 **Grand** *R* Michigan, USA
18B1 **Grand** *R* Missouri, USA
27Q2 **Grand B** Dominica
11C4 **Grand Bahama** *I* The Bahamas
7E5 **Grand Bank** Can
102F2 **Grand Banks** Atlantic O
97B4 **Grand Bassam** Ivory Coast
9B3 **Grand Canyon** USA
26A3 **Grand Cayman** *I* Caribbean S
13E2 **Grand Centre** Can
20C1 **Grand Coulee** USA
34B3 **Grande** *R* Arg
31C4 **Grande** *R* Bahia, Brazil
35B1 **Grande** *R* Minas Gerais/São Paulo, Brazil
13D2 **Grande Cache** Can
47A2 **Grande Chartreuse** Region, France
101D2 **Grande Comore** *I* Comoros
13D1 **Grande Prairie** Can
19A3 **Grande Prairie** USA
95A3 **Grand Erg de Bilma** *Desert* Niger
96B2 **Grand erg Occidental** *Mts* Alg
96C2 **Grand erg Oriental** *Mts* Alg
7C4 **Grande Rivière de la Baleine** *R* Can
20C1 **Grande Ronde** *R* USA
7D5 **Grand Falls** New Brunswick, Can
7E5 **Grand Falls** Newfoundland, Can
20C1 **Grand Forks** Can
8D2 **Grand Forks** USA
16B1 **Grand Gorge** USA

14A2 **Grand Haven** USA
19C3 **Grand Isle** USA
19B4 **Grand L** USA
15D1 **Grand Mère** Can
50A2 **Grãndola** Port
5J4 **Grand Rapids** Can
14A2 **Grand Rapids** Michigan, USA
10A2 **Grand Rapids** Minnesota, USA
47B2 **Grand St Bernard** *P* Italy/Switz
8B2 **Grand Teton** *Mt* USA
8B2 **Grand Teton Nat Pk** USA
46A2 **Grandvilliers** France
25D1 **Grangeburg** USA
51C1 **Granollérs** Spain
52A1 **Gran Paradiso** *Mt* Italy
47D1 **Gran Pilastro** *Mt* Austria/Italy
43D3 **Grantham** Eng
21B2 **Grant,Mt** USA
44C3 **Grantown-on-Spey** Scot
9C3 **Grants** USA
20B2 **Grants Pass** USA
48B2 **Granville** France
5H4 **Granville L** Can
35C1 **Grão Mogol** Brazil
49D3 **Grasse** France
21A2 **Grass Valley** USA
5H5 **Gravelbourg** Can
46B1 **Gravelines** France
100C3 **Gravelotte** S Africa
15C2 **Gravenhurst** Can
109D1 **Gravesend** Aust
12H3 **Gravina I** USA
12B2 **Grayling** USA
20B1 **Grays Harbor** *B* USA
14B3 **Grayson** USA
18C2 **Grayville** USA
59B3 **Graz** Austria
27H1 **Great** *R* Jamaica
11C4 **Great Abaco** *I* The Bahamas
106B4 **Great Australian Bight** *G* Aust
16B3 **Great B** New Jersey, USA
25E2 **Great Bahama Bank** The Bahamas
110C1 **Great Barrier I** NZ
107D2 **Great Barrier Reef** *Is* Aust
16C1 **Great Barrington** USA
4F3 **Great Bear L** Can
9D2 **Great Bend** USA
107D3 **Great Dividing Range** *Mts* Aust
42D2 **Great Driffield** Eng
16B3 **Great Egg Harbor** *B* USA
112B10 **Greater Antarctic** Region, Ant
26B2 **Greater Antilles** *Is* Caribbean S
43D4 **Greater London** Metropolitan County, Eng
43C3 **Greater Manchester** County, Eng
25E2 **Great Exuma** *I* The Bahamas
8B2 **Great Falls** USA
44B3 **Great Glen** *V* Scot
86B1 **Great Himalayan Range** *Mts* Asia
11C4 **Great Inagua** *I* The Bahamas
100B4 **Great Karroo** *Mts* S Africa
109C4 **Great L** Aust
100A3 **Great Namaland** Region, Namibia
42C3 **Great Ormes Head** *C* Wales
11C4 **Great Ragged** *I* The Bahamas
99D3 **Great Ruaha** *R* Tanz
15D2 **Great Sacandaga L** USA
8B2 **Great Salt L** USA
95B2 **Great Sand Sea** Libya/Egypt
106B3 **Great Sandy Desert** Aust
8A2 **Great Sandy Desert** USA
Great Sandy I = Fraser I
4G3 **Great Slave L** Can
16C2 **Great South B** USA
106B3 **Great Victoria Desert** Aust
112C2 **Great Wall** *Base* Ant
72B2 **Great Wall** China
43E3 **Great Yarmouth** Eng
94B1 **Greco,C** Cyprus
55B3 **Greece** Republic, Europe
15C2 **Greece** USA
8C2 **Greeley** USA
6B1 **Greely Fjord** Can
14A1 **Green B** USA
14A2 **Green Bay** USA
14A3 **Greencastle** Indiana, USA
16C1 **Greenfield** Massachusetts, USA
14A2 **Greenfield** Wisconsin, USA
13F2 **Green Lake** Can
6F2 **Greenland** Dependency, N Atlantic O
102H1 **Greenland Basin** Greenland S
1B1 **Greenland S** Greenland
42B2 **Greenock** Scot
16C2 **Greenport** USA
16B3 **Greensboro** Maryland, USA
11C3 **Greensboro** N Carolina, USA
15C2 **Greensburg** Pennsylvania, USA
44B3 **Greenstone** *Pt* Scot
18C2 **Greenup** USA
17A1 **Greenville** Alabama, USA
97B4 **Greenville** Lib
19B3 **Greenville** Mississippi, USA
16D1 **Greenville** N Hampshire, USA
14B2 **Greenville** Ohio, USA
17B1 **Greenville** S Carolina, USA
19A3 **Greenville** Texas, USA
43E4 **Greenwich** Eng
16C2 **Greenwich** USA
16B3 **Greenwood** Delaware, USA
19B3 **Greenwood** Mississippi, USA
17B1 **Greenwood** S Carolina, USA
18B2 **Greers Ferry L** USA
108A1 **Gregory,L** Aust
107D2 **Gregory Range** *Mts* Aust
56C2 **Greifswald** Germany
64F3 **Gremikha** Russian Fed
56C1 **Grenå** Den
19C3 **Grenada** USA
27E4 **Grenada** *I* Caribbean S
27E4 **Grenadines,The** *Is* Caribbean S
109C2 **Grenfell** Aust
49D2 **Grenoble** France
27M2 **Grenville** Grenada
107D2 **Grenville,C** Aust
20B1 **Gresham** USA
78C4 **Gresik** Jawa, Indon
78A3 **Gresik** Sumatera, Indon
19B4 **Gretna** USA
111B2 **Grey** *R* NZ
12G2 **Grey Hunter Pk** *Mt* Can
7E4 **Grey Is** Can
16C1 **Greylock,Mt** USA
111B2 **Greymouth** NZ
107D3 **Grey Range** *Mts* Aust
45C2 **Greystones** Irish Rep
101H1 **Greytown** S Africa
101F1 **Griekwastad** S Africa
17B1 **Griffin** USA
108C2 **Griffith** Aust
107D5 **Grim,C** Aust
15C2 **Grimsby** Can
42D3 **Grimsby** Eng
38B1 **Grimsey** *I* Iceland
13D1 **Grimshaw** Can
39F7 **Grimstad** Nor
47C1 **Grindelwald** Switz
6A2 **Grinnell Pen** Can
6B2 **Grise Fjord** Can
61H1 **Griva** Russian Fed
39J7 **Grobina** Latvia
58C2 **Grodno** Belorussia
86A1 **Gromati** *R* India
56B2 **Groningen** Neth
106C2 **Groote Eylandt** *I* Aust
100A2 **Grootfontein** Namibia
100B3 **Grootvloer** *Salt L* S Africa
27P2 **Gros Islet** St Lucia
46E1 **Grosser Feldberg** *Mt* Germany
52B2 **Grosseto** Italy
46E2 **Gross-Gerau** Germany
57C3 **Grossglockner** *Mt* Austria
47E1 **Gross Venediger** *Mt* Austria
12C3 **Grosvenor,L** USA
22B2 **Groveland** USA
21A2 **Grover City** USA
15D2 **Groveton** USA
61G5 **Groznyy** Russian Fed
58B2 **Grudziadz** Pol
100A3 **Grünau** Namibia
44E2 **Grutness** Scot
61F3 **Gryazi** Russian Fed
61E2 **Gryazovets** Russian Fed
29G8 **Grytviken** South Georgia
45A2 **Gt Blasket** *I* Irish Rep
35C2 **Guaçuí** Brazil
23A1 **Guadalajara** Mexico
50B1 **Guadalajara** Spain
107E1 **Guadalcanal** *I* Solomon Is
50B2 **Guadalimar** *R* Spain
51B1 **Guadalope** *R* Spain
50B2 **Guadalqivir** *R* Spain
24B2 **Guadalupe** Mexico
3G6 **Guadalupe** *I* Mexico
27E3 **Guadeloupe** *I* Caribbean S
50B2 **Guadian** *R* Spain
50A2 **Guadiana** *R* Port
50B2 **Guadix** Spain
32D6 **Guajará Mirim** Brazil
32C1 **Guajira,Pen de** Colombia
32B4 **Gualaceo** Ecuador
34D2 **Gualeguay** Arg
34D2 **Gualeguaychú** Arg
71F2 **Guam** *I* Pacific O
34C3 **Guamini** Arg
77C5 **Gua Musang** Malay
23A1 **Guanajuato** Mexico
23A1 **Guanajuato** State, Mexico
32D2 **Guanare** Ven
25D2 **Guane** Cuba
73C5 **Guangdong** Province, China
73A3 **Guanghan** China
72C3 **Guanghua** China
73A4 **Guangmao Shan** *Mt* China
73B5 **Guangnan** China
72B3 **Guangyuan** China
73D4 **Guangze** China
67F3 **Guangzhou** China
35C1 **Guanhães** Brazil
32D3 **Guania** *R* Colombia
27E5 **Guanipa** *R* Ven
26B2 **Guantánamo** Cuba
72D1 **Guanting Shuiku** *Res* China
73B5 **Guanxi** Province, China
73A3 **Guan Xian** China
32B2 **Guapa** Colombia
33E6 **Guaporé** *R* Brazil/Bol
30C2 **Guaquí** Bol
32B4 **Guaranda** Ecuador
30F4 **Guarapuava** Brazil
35B2 **Guaratinguetá** Brazil
50A1 **Guarda** Port
35B1 **Guarda Mor** Brazil
9C4 **Guasave** Mexico
47D2 **Guastalla** Italy
25C3 **Guatemala** Guatemala
25C3 **Guatemala** Republic, Cent America
34C3 **Guatraché** Arg
32C3 **Guavrare** *R* Colombia
35B2 **Guaxupé** Brazil
27L1 **Guayaguayare** Trinidad
32A4 **Guayaquil** Ecuador
24A2 **Guaymas** Mexico
34D2 **Guayquiraro** *R* Arg
100B2 **Guba** Zaïre
99E2 **Guban** *Region* Somalia
79B3 **Gubat** Phil
56C2 **Gubin** Pol
87B2 **Gūdūr** India
14B2 **Guelpho** Can
26A2 **Guenabacoa** Cuba
98C1 **Guéréda** Chad
48C2 **Guéret** France
48B2 **Guernsey** *I* UK
23A2 **Guerrero** State, Mexico
99D2 **Gughe** *Mt* Eth
63E2 **Gugigu** China
71F2 **Guguan** *I* Pacific O
109C2 **Guiargambone** Aust
73C4 **Guidong** China
97B4 **Guiglo** Ivory Coast
73C5 **Gui Jiang** *R* China
43D4 **Guildford** Eng
73C4 **Guilin** China
47B2 **Guillestre** France
72A2 **Guinan** China
97A3 **Guinea** Republic, Africa
102H4 **Guinea Basin** Atlantic O
97A3 **Guinea-Bissau** Republic, Africa
97C4 **Guinea,G of** W Africa
26A2 **Güines** Cuba
97B3 **Guir** *Well* Mali
84C2 **Guiranwala** Pak
33E1 **Güiria** Ven
46B2 **Guise** France
79C3 **Guiuan** Phil
73B5 **Gui Xian** China
73B4 **Guiyang** China
73B4 **Guizhou** Province, China
85C4 **Gujarāt** State, India
84C2 **Gujrat** Pak
87B1 **Gulbarga** India
58D1 **Gulbene** Latvia
87B1 **Guledagudda** India
80D3 **Gulf,The** S W Asia
109C2 **Gulgong** Aust
73B4 **Gulin** China
12E2 **Gulkana** USA
12E2 **Gulkana** *R* USA
13E2 **Gull L** Can
13F2 **Gull Lake** Can
55C3 **Güllük Körfezi** *B* Turk
99D2 **Gulu** Uganda
109C1 **Guluguba** Aust
97C3 **Gumel** Nig
46D1 **Gummersbach** Germany

86A2 **Gumpla** India
93C1 **Gümüşhane** Turk
85D4 **Guna** India
99D1 **Guna** *Mt* Eth
109C3 **Gundagai** Aust
98B3 **Gungu** Zaïre
6H3 **Gunnbjørn Fjeld** *Mt* Greenland
109D2 **Gunnedah** Aust
87B1 **Guntakal** India
17A1 **Guntersville** USA
17A1 **Guntersville L** USA
87C1 **Guntūr** India
77C5 **Gunung Batu Putch** *Mt* Malay
78D3 **Gunung Besar** *Mt* Indon
78D2 **Gunung Bulu** *Mt* Indon
78A3 **Gunung Gedang** *Mt* Indon
78C2 **Gunung Lawit** *Mt* Malay
78C4 **Gunung Lawu** *Mt* Indon
78D2 **Gunung Menyapa** *Mt* Indon
78D2 **Gunung Niapa** *Mt* Indon
78A3 **Gunung Patah** *Mt* Indon
78C4 **Gunung Raung** *Mt* Indon
78A3 **Gunung Resag** *Mt* Indon
78D3 **Gunung Sarempaka** *Mt* Indon
78C4 **Gunung Sumbing** *Mt* Indon
77C5 **Gunung Tahan** *Mt* Malay
78A2 **Gunung Talakmau** *Mt* Indon
100A2 **Gunza** Angola
72D3 **Guoyang** China
84D2 **Gurdāspur** India
84D3 **Gurgaon** India
86A1 **Gurkha** Nepal
92C2 **Gürün** Turk
31B2 **Gurupi** *R* Brazil
100C2 **Guruve** Zim
72A1 **Gurvan Sayhan Uul** *Upland* Mongolia
61H4 **Gur'yev** Kazakhstan
97C3 **Gusau** Nig
58C2 **Gusev** Russian Fed
74A3 **Gushan** China
61F2 **Gus'khrustalnyy** Russian Fed
12G3 **Gustavus** USA
22B2 **Gustine** USA
11B3 **Guston** USA
56B2 **Gütersloh** Germany
18C2 **Guthrie** Kentucky, USA
18A2 **Guthrie** Oklahoma, USA
23B1 **Gutiérrez Zamora** Mexico
33F3 **Guyana** Republic, S America
102F4 **Guyana Basin** Atlantic O
72C1 **Guyang** China
48B3 **Guyenne** Region, France
9C3 **Guymon** USA
109D2 **Guyra** Aust
72B2 **Guyuan** China
109C2 **Gwabegar** Aust
85D3 **Gwalior** India
100B3 **Gwanda** Zim
98C2 **Gwane** Zaïre
82A3 **Gwardar** Pak
45B1 **Gweebarra B** Irish Rep
89G9 **Gwelo** Zim
43C4 **Gwent** County, Wales
100B2 **Gweru** Zim
109C1 **Gwydir** *R* Aust
43C3 **Gwynedd** Wales
65F5 **Gyandzha** Azerbaijan
86B1 **Gyangzê** China
68B3 **Gyaring Hu** *L* China
64J2 **Gydanskiy Poluostrov** *Pen* Russian Fed
86B1 **Gyirong** China
6F3 **Gyldenløues** Greenland
109D1 **Gympie** Aust
59B3 **Gyöngyös** Hung
59B3 **Györ** Hung

H

38K6 **Haapajärvi** Fin
60B2 **Haapsalu** Estonia
56A2 **Haarlem** Neth
46D1 **Haarstrang** Region, Germany
25D2 **Habana** Cuba
86C2 **Habiganj** Bang
74D4 **Hachijō-jima** *I* Japan
75B1 **Hachiman** Japan
74E2 **Hachinohe** Japan
75B1 **Hachioji** Japan
16B2 **Hackettstown** USA
108A2 **Hack,Mt** *Mt* Aust
42C2 **Haddington** Scot
108B1 **Haddon Corner** Aust
108B1 **Haddon Downs** Aust
97D3 **Hadejia** Nig
97C3 **Hadejia** *R* Nig
94B2 **Hadera** Israel
56B1 **Haderslev** Den
81D4 **Hadiboh** Socotra
4H2 **Hadley B** Can
73B5 **Hadong** Vietnam
81C4 **Haḑramawt** Region, Yemen
56C1 **Hadsund** Den
74B3 **Haeju** N Korea
91A4 **Hafar al Bātin** S Arabia
6D2 **Haffners Bjerg** *Mt* Greenland
84C2 **Hafizabad** Pak
86C1 **Hāflong** India
38A2 **Hafnafjörður** Iceland
12B3 **Hagemeister** *I* USA
56B2 **Hagen** Germany
15C3 **Hagerstown** USA
75A2 **Hagi** Japan
73A5 **Ha Giang** Vietnam
46D2 **Hagondange** France
45B2 **Hags Hd** *C* Irish Rep
46D2 **Haguenan** France
96A2 **Hagunia** *Well* Mor
69G4 **Haha-jima** *I* Japan
68B3 **Hah Xil Hu** *L* China
74A2 **Haicheng** China
76D1 **Hai Duong** Viet
94B2 **Haifa** Israel
94B2 **Haifa,B of** Israel
72D2 **Hai He** *R* China
73C5 **Haikang** China
76E1 **Haikou** China
80C3 **Ha'il** S Arabia
86C2 **Hailākāndi** India
63D3 **Hailar** China
74B2 **Hailong** China
69E2 **Hailun** China
38J5 **Hailuoto** *I* Fin
76D2 **Hainan** *I* China
12G3 **Haines** USA
12G2 **Haines Junction** Can
59B3 **Hainfeld** Austria
73B5 **Haiphong** Vietnam
26C3 **Haiti** Republic, Caribbean S
95C3 **Haiya** Sudan
72A2 **Haiyan** China
72B2 **Haiyuan** China
72D3 **Haizhou Wan** *B* China
59C3 **Hajdúböszörmény** Hung
75B1 **Hajiki-saki** *Pt* Japan
86C2 **Haka** Burma
21C4 **Hakalau** Hawaiian Is
93D2 **Hakkâri** Turk
74E2 **Hakodate** Japan
75B1 **Hakui** Japan
75B1 **Haku-san** *Mt* Japan
92C2 **Ḩalab** Syria
93E3 **Halabja** Iraq
95C2 **Halaib** Sudan
94C1 **Halba** Leb
68B2 **Halban** Mongolia
56C2 **Halberstadt** Germany
79B3 **Halcon,Mt** Phil
39G7 **Halden** Nor
86B2 **Haldia** India
84D3 **Haldwāni** India
13C1 **Halfway** *R* Can
7D5 **Halifax** Can
42D3 **Halifax** Eng
6D1 **Hall Basin** *Sd* Can
6B3 **Hall Beach** Can
46C1 **Halle** Belg
56C2 **Halle** Germany
112B1 **Halley** *Base* Ant
39F6 **Hallingdal** *R* Nor
6D3 **Hall Pen** Can
106B2 **Hall's Creek** Aust
71D3 **Halmahera** *I* Indon
39G7 **Halmstad** Sweden
56B2 **Haltern** Germany
38J5 **Halti** *Mt* Nor
42C2 **Haltwhistle** Eng
91B4 **Halul** *I* Qatar
94B3 **Haluza** *Hist Site* Israel
75A2 **Hamada** Japan
96C2 **Hamada de Tinrhert** *Desert Region* Alg
96B2 **Hamada du Dra** *Upland* Alg
90A3 **Hamadān** Iran
96B2 **Hamada Tounassine** Region, Alg
92C2 **Ḩamāh** Syria
75B2 **Hamamatsu** Japan
39G6 **Hamar** Nor
87C3 **Hambantota** Sri Lanka
19B3 **Hamburg** Arkansas, USA
18A1 **Hamburg** Iowa, USA
16B2 **Hamburg** Pennsylvania, USA
56B2 **Hamburg** Germany
16C2 **Hamden** USA
39J6 **Hämeeninna** Fin
106A3 **Hamersley Range** *Mts* Aust
74B2 **Hamgyong Sanmaek** *Mts* N Korea
74B2 **Hamhŭng** N Korea
68B2 **Hami** China
94B1 **Hamīdīyah** Syria
108B3 **Hamilton** Aust
14C2 **Hamilton** Can
110C1 **Hamilton** NZ
14B3 **Hamilton** Ohio, USA
42B2 **Hamilton** Scot
22B2 **Hamilton,Mt** USA
38K6 **Hamina** Fin
86A1 **Hamirpur** India
56B2 **Hamm** Germany
95A2 **Hammādāh al Hamra** *Upland* Libya
38H6 **Hämmerdal** Sweden
38J4 **Hammerfest** Nor
14A2 **Hammond** Illinois, USA
19B3 **Hammond** Louisiana, USA
16B3 **Hammonton** USA
111B3 **Hampden** NZ
43D4 **Hampshire** County, Eng
19B3 **Hampton** Arkansas, USA
91C4 **Hāmūn-e Jaz Mūrīan** *L* Iran
84B3 **Hamun-i-Lora** *Salt L* Pak
21C4 **Hana** Hawaiian Is
21C4 **Hanalei** Hawaiian Is
74E3 **Hanamaki** Japan
72C2 **Hancheng** China
73C3 **Hanchuan** China
15C3 **Hancock** Maryland, USA
10B2 **Hancock** Michigan, USA
75B2 **Handa** Japan
72C2 **Handan** China
99D3 **Handeni** Tanz
72B2 **Hanggin Qi** China
39J7 **Hangö** Fin
73E3 **Hangzhou** China
73E3 **Hangzhou Wan** *B* China
111B2 **Hanmer Springs** NZ
13E2 **Hanna** Can
18B2 **Hannibal** USA
56B2 **Hannover** Germany
39G7 **Hanöbukten** *B* Sweden
76D1 **Hanoi** Viet
16A3 **Hanover** USA
29B6 **Hanover** *I* Chile
72B3 **Han Shui** China
73C3 **Han Shui** *R* China
85D3 **Hānsi** India
68C2 **Hantay** Mongolia
72B3 **Hanzhong** China
86B2 **Hāora** India
38J5 **Haparanda** Sweden
86C1 **Hāpoli** India
92C4 **Haql** S Arabia
91A5 **Haradh** S Arabia
99E2 **Hara Fanna** Eth
75C1 **Haramachi** Japan
101C2 **Harare** Zim
98C1 **Harazé** Chad
14B2 **Harbor Beach** USA
85D4 **Harda** India
39F6 **Hardangerfjord** *Inlet* Nor
46D2 **Hardt** Region, Germany
108A2 **Hardwicke B** Aust
18B2 **Hardy** USA
99E2 **Harēr** Eth
99E2 **Hargeysa** Somalia
94B3 **Har Hakippa** *Mt* Israel
68B3 **Harhu** *L* China
78A3 **Hari** *R* Indon
75A2 **Harima-nada** *B* Japan
56B2 **Harlingen** Neth
9D4 **Harlingen** USA
43E4 **Harlow** Eng
94B2 **Har Meron** *Mt* Israel
20C2 **Harney Basin** USA
20C2 **Harney L** USA
38H6 **Härnösand** Sweden
63B3 **Har Nuur** *L* Mongolia
97B4 **Harper** Lib
12F2 **Harper,Mt** USA
15C3 **Harpers Ferry** USA
94B3 **Har Ramon** *Mt* Israel
7C4 **Harricanaw** *R* Can
16B3 **Harrington** USA
7E4 **Harrington Harbour** Can
44A3 **Harris** *District* Scot
18C2 **Harrisburg** Illinois, USA
16A2 **Harrisburg** Pennsylvania, USA
101G1 **Harrismith** S Africa
18B2 **Harrison** USA
15C3 **Harrisonburg** USA
7E4 **Harrison,C** Can
13C3 **Harrison L** Can
18B2 **Harrisonville** USA
44A3 **Harris,Sound of** *Chan* Scot
14B2 **Harrisville** USA
42D3 **Harrogate** Eng
94B3 **Har Saggi** *Mt* Israel
38H5 **Harstad** Nor
12G2 **Hart** *R* Can
39F6 **Hårteigen** *Mt* Nor
16C2 **Hartford** Connecticut, USA
14A2 **Hartford** Michigan, USA
38G6 **Hartkjølen** *Mt* Nor
108A2 **Hart,L** Aust
43B4 **Hartland Pt** Eng
42D2 **Hartlepool** Eng
19A3 **Hartshorne** USA
17B1 **Hartwell Res** USA
101F1 **Hartz** *R* S Africa
68B2 **Har Us Nuur** *L* Mongolia
43E4 **Harwich** Eng
84D3 **Haryāna** State, India
94B3 **Hāsā** Jordan

94B2 **Hāsbaiya** Leb
43D4 **Haselmere** Eng
75B2 **Hashimoto** Japan
90A2 **Hashtpar** Iran
90A2 **Hashtrūd** Iran
87B2 **Hassan** India
56B2 **Hasselt** Belg
96C2 **Hassi Inifel** Alg
96B2 **Hassi Mdakane** *Well* Alg
96C1 **Hassi Messaoud** Alg
108C3 **Hastings** Aust
43E4 **Hastings** Eng
8D2 **Hastings** Nebraska, USA
110C1 **Hastings** NZ
108B2 **Hatfield** Aust
12B1 **Hatham Inlet** USA
85D3 **Hāthras** India
76D2 **Ha Tinh** Viet
108B2 **Hattah** Aust
11C3 **Hatteras,C** USA
19C3 **Hattiesburg** USA
59B3 **Hatvan** Hung
76D3 **Hau Bon** Viet
99E2 **Haud** Region, Eth
39F7 **Haugesund** Nor
110C1 **Hauhungaroa Range** *Mts* NZ
13F1 **Haultain** *R* Can
110B1 **Hauraki G** NZ
111A3 **Hauroko,L** NZ
47C1 **Hausstock** *Mt* Switz
96B1 **Haut Atlas** *Mts* Mor
98C2 **Haute Kotto** Region, CAR
46C1 **Hautes Fagnes** *Mts* Belg
46B1 **Hautmont** Belg
96B1 **Hauts Plateaux** *Mts* Alg
90D3 **Hauzdar** Iran
18B1 **Havana** USA
Havana = Habana
87B3 **Havankulam** Sri Lanka
110C1 **Havelock North** NZ
43B4 **Haverfordwest** Wales
16D1 **Haverhill** USA
87B2 **Hāveri** India
16C2 **Haverstraw** USA
59B3 **Havlíčkův Brod** Czech
8C2 **Havre** USA
16A3 **Havre de Grace** USA
7D4 **Havre-St-Pierre** Can
54C2 **Havsa** Turk
21C4 **Hawaii** *I* Hawaiian Is
21C4 **Hawaii Volcanoes Nat Pk** Hawaiian Is
111A2 **Hawea,L** NZ
110B1 **Hawera** NZ
42C2 **Hawick** Scot
111A2 **Hawkdun Range** *Mts* NZ
110C1 **Hawke B** NZ
109D2 **Hawke,C** Aust
108A2 **Hawker** Aust
76B1 **Hawng Luk** Burma
93D3 **Hawr al Habbaniyah** *L* Iraq
93E3 **Hawr al Hammár** *L* Iraq
21B2 **Hawthorne** USA
108B2 **Hay** Aust
5G3 **Hay** *R* Can
46D2 **Hayange** France
4B3 **Haycock** USA
7A4 **Hayes** *R* Can
6D2 **Hayes Halvø** *Region* Greenland
12E2 **Hayes,Mt** USA
5G3 **Hay River** Can
18A2 **Haysville** USA
22A2 **Hayward** California, USA
86B2 **Hazārībāg** India
46B1 **Hazebrouck** France
19B3 **Hazelhurst** USA
4G2 **Hazel Str** Can
5F4 **Hazelton** Can
13B1 **Hazelton Mts** Can
6C1 **Hazen L** Can
94B3 **Hazeva** Israel
16B2 **Hazleton** USA
22A1 **Healdsburg** USA
108C3 **Healesville** Aust
12E2 **Healy** USA
104B6 **Heard I** Indian O
19A3 **Hearne** USA
10B2 **Hearst** Can
72D2 **Hebei** Province, China
109C1 **Hebel** Aust
72C2 **Hebi** China
72C2 **Hebian** China
7D4 **Hebron** Can
94B3 **Hebron** Israel
18A1 **Hebron** Nebraska, USA
5E4 **Hecate** *Str* Can
12H3 **Heceta I** USA
73B5 **Hechi** China
4G2 **Hecla and Griper B** Can
111C2 **Hector,Mt** NZ
38G6 **Hede** Sweden
39H6 **Hedemora** Sweden
20C1 **He Devil Mt** USA
56B2 **Heerenveen** Neth
46C1 **Heerlen** Neth
Hefa = Haifa
73D3 **Hefei** China
73B4 **Hefeng** China
69F2 **Hegang** China
75B1 **Hegura-jima** *I* Japan
94B3 **Heidan** *R* Jordan
56B2 **Heide** Germany
101G1 **Heidelberg** Transvaal, S Africa
57B3 **Heidelberg** Germany
63E2 **Heihe** China
101G1 **Heilbron** S Africa
57B3 **Heilbronn** Germany
56C2 **Heiligenstadt** Germany
38K6 **Heinola** Fin
73B4 **Hejiang** China
6J3 **Hekla** *Mt* Iceland
76C1 **Hekou** Viet
73A5 **Hekou Yaozou Zizhixian** China
72B2 **Helan** China
72B2 **Helan Shan** *Mt* China
19B3 **Helena** Arkansas, USA
8B2 **Helena** Montana, USA
22D3 **Helendale** USA
71E3 **Helen Reef** *I* Pacific O
44B3 **Helensburgh** Scot
91B4 **Helleh** *R* Iran
51B2 **Hellin** Spain
20C1 **Hells Canyon** *R* USA
46D1 **Hellweg** Region, Germany
22B2 **Helm** USA
80E2 **Helmand** *R* Afghan
100A3 **Helmeringhausen** Namibia
46C1 **Helmond** Neth
44C2 **Helmsdale** Scot
74B2 **Helong** China
39G7 **Helsingborg** Sweden
Helsingfors = Helsinki
56C1 **Helsingør** Den
38J6 **Helsinki** Fin
43B4 **Helston** Eng
92B4 **Helwân** Egypt
19A3 **Hempstead** USA
39H7 **Hemse** Sweden
72A3 **Henan** China
72C3 **Henan** Province, China
110B1 **Hen and Chicken Is** NZ
14A3 **Henderson** Kentucky, USA
9B3 **Henderson** Nevada, USA
19B3 **Henderson** Texas, USA
73E5 **Heng-ch'un** Taiwan
68B4 **Hengduan Shan** *Mts* China
56B2 **Hengelo** Neth
72B2 **Hengshan** China
72D2 **Hengshui** China
76D1 **Heng Xian** China
73C4 **Hengyang** China
77A4 **Henhoaha** Nicobar Is
43D4 **Henley-on-Thames** Eng
16B3 **Henlopen,C** USA
7B4 **Henrietta Maria,C** Can
18A2 **Henryetta** USA
112C2 **Henryk Arctowski** *Base* Ant
6D3 **Henry Kater Pen** Can
68C2 **Hentiyn Nuruu** *Mts* Mongolia
76B2 **Henzada** Burma
73B5 **Hepu** China
80E2 **Herat** Afghan
5H4 **Herbert** Can
110C2 **Herbertville** NZ
46E1 **Herborn** Germany
26A4 **Heredia** Costa Rica
43C3 **Hereford** Eng
43C3 **Hereford & Worcester** County, Eng
46C1 **Herentals** Belg
47B1 **Héricourt** France
18A2 **Herington** USA
111A3 **Heriot** NZ
47C1 **Herisau** Switz
15D2 **Herkimer** USA
44E1 **Herma Ness** *Pen* Scot
109C2 **Hermidale** Aust
111B2 **Hermitage** NZ
Hermon,Mt = Jebel ash Shaykh
24A2 **Hermosillo** Mexico
16A2 **Herndon** Pennsylvania, USA
22C2 **Herndon** California, USA
46D1 **Herne** Germany
56B1 **Herning** Den
90A2 **Herowābad** Iran
50A2 **Herrera del Duque** Spain
16A2 **Hershey** USA
43D4 **Hertford** County, Eng
94B2 **Herzliyya** Israel
46C1 **Hesbaye** Region, Belg
46B1 **Hesdin** France
72B2 **Heshui** China
22D3 **Hesperia** USA
12H2 **Hess** *R* Can
57B2 **Hessen** State, Germany
22C2 **Hetch Hetchy Res** USA
42C2 **Hexham** Eng
73C5 **He Xian** China
73C5 **Heyuan** China
108B3 **Heywood** Aust
72D2 **Heze** China
17B2 **Hialeah** USA
10A2 **Hibbing** USA
110C1 **Hicks Bay** NZ
109C3 **Hicks,Pt** Aust
23B1 **Hidalgo** State, Mexico
24B2 **Hidalgo del Parral** Mexico
35B1 **Hidrolândia** Brazil
96A2 **Hierro** *I* Canary Is
75C1 **Higashine** Japan
74B4 **Higashi-suidō** *Str* Japan
20B2 **High Desert** USA
19B4 **High Island** USA
44B3 **Highland** Region, Scot
22D3 **Highland** USA
22C1 **Highland Peak** *Mt* USA
16B2 **Highlands Falls** USA
11B3 **High Point** USA
13D1 **High Prairie** Can
5G4 **High River** Can
17B2 **High Springs** USA
16B2 **Hightstown** USA
43D4 **High Wycombe** Eng
39J7 **Hiiumaa** *I* Estonia
80B3 **Hijāz** Region, S Arabia
75B2 **Hikigawa** Japan
75B1 **Hikone** Japan
110B1 **Hikurangi** NZ
9C4 **Hildago** Mexico
9C4 **Hildago del Parral** Mexico
56B2 **Hildesheim** Germany
27R3 **Hillaby,Mt** Barbados
56C1 **Hillerød** Den
14B3 **Hillsboro** Ohio, USA
20B1 **Hillsboro** Oregon, USA
19A3 **Hillsboro** Texas, USA
108C2 **Hillston** Aust
44E1 **Hillswick** Scot
21C4 **Hilo** Hawaiian Is
93C2 **Hilvan** Turk
56B2 **Hilversum** Neth
84D2 **Himachal Pradesh** State, India
82B3 **Himalaya** *Mts* Asia
85C4 **Himatnagar** India
74C4 **Himeji** Japan
74D3 **Himi** Japan
92C3 **Himş** Syria
12E2 **Hinchinbrook Entrance** USA
12E2 **Hinchinbrook I** USA
85D3 **Hindaun** India
84B1 **Hindu Kush** *Mts* Afghan
87B2 **Hindupur** India
13D1 **Hines Creek** Can
85D4 **Hinganghāt** India
69E2 **Hinggan Ling** *Upland* China
85B3 **Hingol** *R* Pak
85D5 **Hingoli** India
38H5 **Hinnøya** *I* Nor
16C1 **Hinsdale** USA
13D2 **Hinton** Can
34B2 **Hipolito Itrogoyen** Arg
86A2 **Hirakud Res** India
92B2 **Hirfanli Baraji** *Res* Turk
87B2 **Hirihar** India
74E2 **Hirosaki** Japan
74C4 **Hiroshima** Japan
46C2 **Hirson** France
54C2 **Hîrşova** Rom
56B1 **Hirtshals** Den
84D3 **Hisār** India
26C3 **Hispaniola** *I* Caribbean S
94C1 **Hisyah** Syria
93D3 **Hīt** Iraq
74E3 **Hitachi** Japan
75C1 **Hitachi-Ota** Japan
43D4 **Hitchin** Eng
38F6 **Hitra** *I* Nor
75A2 **Hiuchi-nada** *B* Japan
75A2 **Hiwasa** Japan
56B1 **Hjørring** Den
76B1 **Hka** *R* Burma
97C4 **Ho** Ghana
76D1 **Hoa Binh** Viet
76D3 **Hoa Da** Viet
109C4 **Hobart** Aust
9C3 **Hobbs** USA
56B1 **Hobro** Den
13C2 **Hobson L** Can
99E2 **Hobyo** Somalia
76D3 **Ho Chi Minh** Viet
57C3 **Hochkonig** *Mt* Austria
54B1 **Hódmezó'hely** Hung
59B3 **Hodonin** Czech
74B2 **Hoeryong** N Korea
57C2 **Hof** Germany
38B2 **Hofsjökull** *Mts* Iceland
74C4 **Hōfu** Japan
96C2 **Hoggar** *Upland* Alg
46D1 **Hohe Acht** *Mt* Germany
72C1 **Hohhot** China
6J3 **Höhn** Iceland
68B3 **Hoh Sai Hu** *L* China
82C2 **Hoh Xil Shan** *Mts* China

99D2 **Hoima** Uganda
86C1 **Hojāi** India
75A2 **Hojo** Japan
110B1 **Hokianga Harbour** *B* NZ
111B2 **Hokitika** NZ
74E2 **Hokkaidō** Japan
90C2 **Hokmābād** Iran
109C3 **Holbrook** Aust
9B3 **Holbrook** USA
19A2 **Holdenville** USA
87B2 **Hole Narsipur** India
27R3 **Holetown** Barbados
26B2 **Holguín** Cuba
111B2 **Holitika** NZ
12C2 **Holitna** *R* USA
59B3 **Hollabrunn** Austria
14A2 **Holland** USA
22B2 **Hollister** USA
19C3 **Holly Springs** USA
22C3 **Hollywood** California, USA
17B2 **Hollywood** Florida, USA
4G2 **Holman Island** Can
38J6 **Holmsund** Sweden
94B2 **Holon** Israel
56B1 **Holstebro** Den
6E3 **Holsteinborg** Greenland
14B2 **Holt** USA
18A2 **Holton** USA
12C2 **Holy Cross** USA
42B3 **Holyhead** Wales
42D2 **Holy I** Eng
43B3 **Holy I** Wales
16C1 **Holyoke** Massachusetts, USA
86C2 **Homalin** Burma
6D3 **Home B** Can
12D3 **Homer** Alaska, USA
19B3 **Homer** Louisiana, USA
111A2 **Homer Tunnel** NZ
17B1 **Homerville** USA
17B2 **Homestead** USA
17A1 **Homewood** USA
87B1 **Homnābād** India
101C3 **Homoine** Mozam
25D3 **Hondo** *R* Mexico
25D3 **Honduras** Republic, Cent America
25D3 **Honduras,G of** Honduras
39G6 **Hønefoss** Nor
15C2 **Honesdale** USA
21A1 **Honey L** USA
76C1 **Hong** *R* Viet
76D1 **Hon Gai** Viet
73A4 **Hongguo** China
73C4 **Hong Hu** *L* China
72B2 **Honghui** China
73C4 **Hongjiang** China
73C5 **Hong Kong** Colony, S E Asia
68D2 **Hongor** Mongolia
73B5 **Hongshui He** *R* China
72A3 **Hongyuan** China
72D3 **Hongze Hu** *L* China
107E1 **Honiara** Solomon Is
77C4 **Hon Khoai** *I* Camb
76D3 **Hon Lan** *I* Viet
38K4 **Honnigsvåg** Nor
21C4 **Honolulu** Hawaiian Is
77C4 **Hon Panjang** *I* Viet
74D3 **Honshu** *I* Japan
20B1 **Hood,Mt** USA
20B1 **Hood River** USA
45C2 **Hook Head** *C* Irish Rep
12G3 **Hoonah** USA
12A2 **Hooper Bay** USA
101G1 **Hoopstad** S Africa
56A2 **Hoorn** Neth
9B3 **Hoover Dam** USA
12E2 **Hope** Alaska, USA
19B3 **Hope** Arkansas, USA
13C3 **Hope** Can
7D4 **Hopedale** Can
64D2 **Hopen** *I* Barents S
6D3 **Hopes Advance,C** Can
108B3 **Hopetoun** Aust
100B3 **Hopetown** S Africa
18C2 **Hopkinsville** USA
20B1 **Hoquiam** USA
93D1 **Horasan** Turk
99F1 **Hordiyo** Somalia
47C1 **Horgen** Switz
105H5 **Horizon Depth** Pacific O
91C4 **Hormuz,Str of** Oman/Iran
59B3 **Horn** Austria
6H3 **Horn** *C* Iceland
38H5 **Hornavan** *L* Sweden
19B3 **Hornbeck** USA
20B2 **Hornbrook** USA
111B2 **Hornby** NZ
7B5 **Hornepayne** Can
4F3 **Horn Mts** Can
42D3 **Hornsea** Eng
72B1 **Horn Uul** *Mt* Mongolia
30E3 **Horqueta** Par
15C2 **Horseheads** USA
56C1 **Horsens** Den
20B1 **Horseshoe Bay** Can
108B3 **Horsham** Aust
43D4 **Horsham** Eng
39G7 **Horten** Nor
4F3 **Horton** *R* Can
78C2 **Hose Mts** Malay
85D4 **Hoshangābād** India
84D2 **Hoshiārpur** India
87B1 **Hospet** India
29C7 **Hoste** *I* Chile
82B2 **Hotan** China
19B3 **Hot Springs** Arkansas, USA
8C2 **Hot Springs** S. Dakota, USA
4G3 **Hottah** Can
46A2 **Houdan** France
72C2 **Houma** China
19B4 **Houma** USA
16C2 **Housatonic** *R* USA
13B2 **Houston** Can
19C3 **Houston** Mississippi, USA
19A4 **Houston** Texas, USA
106A3 **Houtman** *Is* Aust
68B2 **Hovd** Mongolia
68C1 **Hövsgol Nuur** *L* Mongolia
14A2 **Howard City** USA
12C1 **Howard P** USA
109C3 **Howe,C** Aust
101H1 **Howick** S Africa
44C2 **Hoy** *I* Scot
39F6 **Høyanger** Nor
59B2 **Hradeç-Králové** Czech
59B3 **Hranice** Czech
59B3 **Hron** *R* Czech
73E5 **Hsin-chu** Taiwan
73E5 **Hsüeh Shan** *Mt* Taiwan
72B2 **Huachi** China
32B6 **Huacho** Peru
72C1 **Huade** China
72D3 **Huaibei** China
72D3 **Huaibin** China
72D3 **Huai He** *R* China
73C4 **Huaihua** China
73C5 **Huaiji** China
72D3 **Huainan** China
69E4 **Hua-lien** Taiwan
32B5 **Huallaga** *R* Peru
32B5 **Huallanca** Peru
32B5 **Huamachuco** Peru
100A2 **Huambo** Angola
30C2 **Huanay** Bol
32B5 **Huancabamba** Peru
32B6 **Huancavelica** Peru
32B6 **Huancayo** Peru
73D3 **Huangchuan** China
Huang Hai = Yellow S
72D2 **Huang He** *R* China
72B2 **Huangling** China
76D2 **Huangliu** China
73C3 **Huangpi** China
73D3 **Huangshi** China
34C3 **Huanguelén** Arg
73E4 **Huangyan** China
74B2 **Huanren** China
32B5 **Huānuco** Peru
30C2 **Huanuni** Bol
72B2 **Huan Xian** China
32B5 **Huaráz** Peru
32B6 **Huarmey** Peru
32B5 **Huascarán** *Mt* Peru
30B4 **Huasco** Chile
23B2 **Huatusco** Mexico
23B1 **Huauchinango** Mexico
23B2 **Huautla** Mexico
72C2 **Hua Xian** China
24B2 **Huayapan** *R* Mexico
73C3 **Hubei** Province, China
87B1 **Hubli** India
34C3 **Hucal** Arg
74B2 **Huch'ang** N Korea
42D3 **Huddersfield** Eng
39H6 **Hudiksvall** Sweden
17B2 **Hudson** Florida, USA
14B2 **Hudson** Michigan, USA
16C1 **Hudson** New York, USA
16C1 **Hudson** *R* USA
7B4 **Hudson B** Can
5H4 **Hudson Bay** Can
13C1 **Hudson's Hope** Can
6C3 **Hudson Str** Can
76D2 **Hue** Viet
23B1 **Huejutla** Mexico
50A2 **Huelva** Spain
23A2 **Hueramo** Mexico
51B2 **Húercal Overa** Spain
51B1 **Huesca** Spain
23B2 **Huexotla** *Hist Site* Mexico
107D3 **Hughenden** Aust
12D1 **Hughes** USA
86B2 **Hugli** *R* India
19A3 **Hugo** USA
73D4 **Hui'an** China
110C1 **Huiarau Range** *Mts* NZ
74B2 **Huich'ŏn** N Korea
74B2 **Huifa He** *R* China
32B3 **Huila** *Mt* Colombia
73D5 **Huilai** China
73A4 **Huili** China
74B2 **Huinan** China
34C2 **Huinca Renancó** Arg
25C3 **Huixtla** Mexico
73A4 **Huize** China
73C5 **Huizhou** China
23B2 **Hujuápan de Léon** Mexico
69F2 **Hulin** China
15C1 **Hull** Can
42D3 **Hull** Eng
58B1 **Hultsfred** Sweden
63D3 **Hulun Nur** *L* China
69E1 **Huma** China
33E5 **Humaita** Brazil
100B4 **Humansdorp** S Africa
42D3 **Humber** *R* Eng
42D3 **Humberside** County, Eng
5H4 **Humboldt** Can
20C2 **Humboldt** *R* USA
20B2 **Humboldt B** USA
6D2 **Humboldt Gletscher** *Gl* Greenland
21B2 **Humboldt L** USA
108C1 **Humeburn** Aust
109C3 **Hume,L** Aust
100A2 **Humpata** Angola
22C2 **Humphreys** USA
38A1 **Húnaflóri** *B* Iceland
73C4 **Hunan** Province, China
74C2 **Hunchun** China
13C2 **Hundred Mile House** Can
54B1 **Hunedoara** Rom
59B3 **Hungary** Republic, Europe
108B1 **Hungerford** Aust
74B3 **Hŭngnam** N Korea
74B2 **Hunjiang** China
46D2 **Hunsrück** Mts, Germany
109D2 **Hunter** *R* Aust
13B2 **Hunter I** Can
109C4 **Hunter Is** Aust
12D2 **Hunter,Mt** USA
14A3 **Huntingburg** USA
43D3 **Huntingdon** Eng
14A2 **Huntingdon** Indiana, USA
14B3 **Huntington** W Virginia, USA
22C4 **Huntington Beach** USA
22C2 **Huntington L** USA
110C1 **Huntly** NZ
44C3 **Huntly** Scot
12J2 **Hunt,Mt** Can
108A1 **Hunt Pen** Aust
17A1 **Huntsville** Alabama, USA
15C1 **Huntsville** Can
19A3 **Huntsville** Texas, USA
76D2 **Huong Khe** Viet
71F4 **Huon Peninsula** *Pen* PNG
109C4 **Huonville** Anst
14B1 **Hurd,C** Can
80B3 **Hurghada** Egypt
8D2 **Huron** S. Dakota, USA
14B1 **Huron,L** Can/USA
34A2 **Hurtado** Chile
111B2 **Hurunui** *R* NZ
38B1 **Husavik** Iceland
54C1 **Huşi** Rom
39G7 **Huskvarna** Sweden
12C1 **Huslia** USA
94B2 **Husn** Jordan
56B2 **Husum** Germany
109C1 **Hutton,Mt** Aust
72D2 **Hutuo He** *R* China
46C1 **Huy** Belg
72A2 **Huzhu** China
52C2 **Hvar** *I* Croatia
100B2 **Hwange** Zim
100B2 **Hwange Nat Pk** Zim
15D2 **Hyannis** USA
68B2 **Hyaryas Nuur** *L* Mongolia
5E4 **Hydaburg** Can
16C2 **Hyde Park** USA
87B1 **Hyderābād** India
85B3 **Hyderabad** Pak
49D3 **Hyères** France
12J2 **Hyland** *R* Can
8B2 **Hyndman Peak** *Mt* USA
38K6 **Hyrynsalmi** Fin
13D1 **Hythe** Can
74C4 **Hyūga** Japan
39J6 **Hyvikää** Fin

I

31C4 **Iaçu** Brazil
54C2 **Ialomiţa** *R* Rom
54C1 **Iaşi** Rom
97C4 **Ibadan** Nig
32B3 **Ibagué** Colombia
54B2 **Ibar** *R* Montenegro/Serbia, Yugos
32B3 **Ibarra** Ecuador
35B1 **Ibiá** Brazil
30E4 **Ibicui** *R* Brazil
34D2 **Ibicuy** Arg
51C2 **Ibiza** Spain
51C2 **Ibiza** *I* Spain
101D2 **Ibo** Mozam
31C4 **Ibotirama** Brazil
91C5 **'Ibrī** Oman
32B6 **Ica** Peru
32D4 **Içá** *R* Brazil
32D3 **Icana** Brazil
38A1 **Iceland** Republic, N Atlantic O
13C2 **Ice Mt** Can
87A1 **Ichalkaranji** India
74E3 **Ichihara** Japan
75B1 **Ichinomiya** Japan
74E3 **Ichinoseki** Japan
12F3 **Icy B** USA
4B2 **Icy C** USA
19B3 **Idabell** USA
8B2 **Idaho Falls** USA
20B2 **Idanha** USA
46D2 **Idar Oberstein** Germany

95A2 **Idehan Marzūg** *Desert* Libya
95A2 **Idehan Ubari** *Desert* Libya
96C2 **Idelés** Alg
68B2 **Iderlym Gol** *R* Mongolia
95C2 **Idfu** Egypt
55B3 **Ídhi Óros** *Mt* Greece
55B3 **Ídhra** *I* Greece
98B3 **Idiofa** Zaïre
12C2 **Iditarod** *R* USA
92C2 **Idlib** Syria
39K7 **Idritsa** Russian Fed
100B4 **Idutywa** S Africa
55C3 **Ierápetra** Greece
46B1 **Ieper** Belg
63D2 **Iet Oktyobr'ya** Russian Fed
99D3 **Ifakara** Tanz
71F3 **Ifalik** *I* Pacific O
101D3 **Ifanadiana** Madag
97C4 **Ife** Nig
97C3 **Iférouane** Niger
78C2 **Igan** Malay
35B2 **Igaranava** Brazil
93E2 **Igdir** Iran
39H6 **Iggesund** Sweden
34B2 **Iglesia** Arg
53A3 **Iglesias** Sardegna
6B3 **Igloolik** Can
10A2 **Ignace** Can
55B3 **Igoumenítsa** Greece
61H2 **Igra** Russian Fed
23B2 **Iguala** Mexico
35B2 **Iguape** Brazil
35B2 **Iguatama** Brazil
31D3 **Iguatu** Brazil
98A3 **Iguéla** Gabon
101D3 **Ihosy** Madag
74D3 **Iida** Japan
75B1 **Iide-san** *Mt* Japan
38K6 **Iisalmi** Fin
75A2 **Iizuka** Japan
97C4 **Ijebu Ode** Nig
56B2 **Ijsselmeer** *S* Neth
55C3 **Ikaría** *I* Greece
74E2 **Ikeda** Japan
98C3 **Ikela** Zaïre
54B2 **Ikhtiman** Bulg
12D3 **Ikolik,C** USA
101D2 **Ikopa** *R* Madag
79B2 **Ilagan** Phil
90A3 **Ilām** Iran
47C1 **Ilanz** Switz
13F1 **Île à la Crosse** Can
13F1 **Île à la Crosse,L** Can
89G8 **Ilebo** Zaïre
96D1 **Île de Jerba** *I* Tunisia
48B2 **Ile de Noirmoutier** *I* France
48B2 **Île de Ré** *I* France
107F3 **Île des Pins** *I* Nouvelle Calédonie
48A2 **Ile d'Ouessant** *I* France
48B2 **Ile d'Yeu** *I* France
61J3 **Ilek** *R* Russian Fed
107F2 **Îles Bélèp** Nouvelle Calédonie
107E2 **Îles Chesterfield** Nouvelle Calédonie
49D3 **Iles d'Hyères** *Is* France
43B4 **Ilfracombe** Eng
92B1 **Ilgaz Dağları** *Mts* Turk
101C3 **Ilha Bazaruto** *I* Mozam
33G3 **Ilha De Maracá** *I* Brazil
33G4 **Ilha de Marajó** *I* Brazil
35B2 **Ilha de São Sebastião** *I* Brazil
33G6 **Ilha do Bananal** *Region* Brazil
35C2 **Ilha Grande** *I* Brazil
35B2 **Ilha Santo Amaro** *I* Brazil
96A1 **Ilhas Selvegens** *I* Atlantic O
35A2 **Ilha Solteira Dam** Brazil
31D4 **Ilhéus** Brazil
12C3 **Iliamna L** USA
12D2 **Iliamna V** USA
79B4 **Iligan** Phil
63C2 **Ilim** *R* Russian Fed
63C2 **Ilimsk** Russian Fed
63G3 **Il'inskiy** Russian Fed
55B3 **Iliodhrómia** *I* Greece
79B4 **Illana B** Phil
34A2 **Illapel** Chile
34A2 **Illapel** *R* Chile
97C3 **Illéla** Niger
47D1 **Iller** *R* Germany
4C4 **Illiamna L** USA
10A2 **Illinois** State, USA
18B2 **Illinois** *R* USA
96C2 **Illizi** Alg
30B2 **Ilo** Peru
79B3 **Iloilo** Phil
38L6 **Ilomantsi** Fin
97C4 **Ilorin** Nig
75A2 **Imabari** Japan
75B1 **Imalchi** Japan
60C1 **Imatra** Fin
30G4 **Imbituba** Brazil
99E2 **Imi** Eth
20C2 **Imlay** USA
47D1 **Immenstadt** Germany
52B2 **Imola** Italy
31B3 **Imperatriz** Brazil
52A2 **Imperia** Italy
98B2 **Impfondo** Congo
86C2 **Imphāl** India
47D1 **Imst** Austria
12B1 **Imuruk L** USA
75B1 **Ina** Japan
96C2 **In Afahleleh** *Well* Alg
75B2 **Inamba-jima** *I* Japan
96C2 **In Amenas** Alg
38K5 **Inari** Fin
38K5 **Inarijärvi** *L* Fin
75C1 **Inawashiro-ko** *L* Japan
96C2 **In Belbel** Alg
60E5 **Ince Burun** *Pt* Turk
92B2 **Incekum Burun** *Pt* Turk
74B3 **Inch'ŏn** S Korea
96B2 **In Dagouber** *Well* Mali
35B1 **Indaia** *R* Brazil
38H6 **Indals** *R* Sweden
21B2 **Independence** California, USA
18A2 **Independence** Kansas, USA
18B2 **Independence** Missouri, USA
78A3 **Inderagiri** *R* Indon
61H4 **Inderborskly** Kazakhstan
83B3 **India** Federal Republic, Asia
14A2 **Indiana** State, USA
15C2 **Indiana** USA
104C6 **Indian-Antarctic Ridge** Indian O
14A3 **Indianapolis** USA
Indian Desert = Thar Desert
7E4 **Indian Harbour** Can
104B4 **Indian O**
18B1 **Indianola** Iowa, USA
19B3 **Indianola** Mississippi, USA
35B1 **Indianópolis** Brazil
76D2 **Indo China** Region, S E Asia
70C4 **Indonesia** Republic, S E Asia
85D4 **Indore** India
78B4 **Indramayu** Indon
48C2 **Indre** *R* France
85B3 **Indus** *R* Pak
60D5 **Inebdu** Turk
96C2 **In Ebeggi** *Well* Alg
96C2 **In Ecker** Alg
92A1 **Inegöl** Turk
96D2 **In Ezzane** Alg
97C3 **Ingal** Niger
14B2 **Ingersoll** Can
107D2 **Ingham** Aust
6D2 **Inglefield Land** *Region* Can
110B1 **Inglewood** NZ
109D1 **Inglewood** Queensland, Aust
22C4 **Inglewood** USA
108B3 **Inglewood** Victoria, Aust
38B2 **Ingólfshöfði** *I* Iceland
57C3 **Ingolstadt** Germany
86B2 **Ingrāj Bāzār** India
96C3 **In-Guezzam** *Well* Alg
101C3 **Inhambane** Mozam
101C3 **Inharrime** Mozam
35B1 **Inhumas** Brazil
32D3 **Inirida** *R* Colombia
45A2 **Inishbofin** *I* Irish Rep
45A1 **Inishkea** *I* Irish Rep
45B2 **Inishmaan** *I* Irish Rep
45B2 **Inishmore** *I* Irish Rep
45B1 **Inishmurray** *I* Irish Rep
45C1 **Inishowen** District, Irish Rep
45A2 **Inishshark** *I* Irish Rep
45A2 **Inishturk** *I* Irish Rep
109C1 **Injune** Aust
12H3 **Inklin** Can
12H3 **Inklin** *R* Can
12C1 **Inland L** USA
47D1 **Inn** *R* Austria
108B1 **Innamincka** Aust
68C2 **Inner Mongolia** Autonomous Region, China
107D2 **Innisfail** Aust
12C2 **Innoko** *R* USA
57C3 **Innsbruck** Austria
98B3 **Inongo** Zaïre
58B2 **Inowrocław** Pol
96C2 **In Salah** Alg
47B1 **Interlaken** Switz
24C3 **Intexpec** Mexico
47C2 **Intra** Italy
78D3 **Intu** Indon
75C1 **Inubo-saki** *C* Japan
7C4 **Inukjuak** Can
4E3 **Inuvik** Can
4F3 **Inuvik** *Region* Can
44B3 **Inveraray** Scot
111A3 **Invercargill** NZ
109D1 **Inverell** Aust
13D2 **Invermere** Can
44B3 **Inverness** Scot
44C3 **Inverurie** Scot
108A3 **Investigator Str** Aust
68A1 **Inya** Russian Fed
21B2 **Inyokern** USA
98B3 **Inzia** *R* Zaïre
55B3 **Ioánnina** Greece
18A2 **Iola** USA
44A3 **Iona** *I* Scot
100A2 **Iôna Nat Pk** Angola
20C1 **Ione** USA
Ionian Is = Ioníoi Nísoi
55A3 **Ionian S** Italy/Greece
55B3 **Ioníoi Nísoi** *Is* Greece
55C3 **Íos** *I* Greece
10A2 **Iowa** *R* USA
10A2 **Iowa City** USA
35B1 **Ipameri** Brazil
35C1 **Ipanema** Brazil
61F4 **Ipatovo** Russian Fed
32B3 **Ipiales** Colombia
77C5 **Ipoh** Malay
30F2 **Iporá** Brazil
55C2 **Ipsala** Turk
109D1 **Ipswich** Aust
43E3 **Ipswich** Eng
16D1 **Ipswich** USA
30B3 **Iquique** Chile
32C4 **Iquitos** Peru
55C3 **Iráklion** Greece
80D2 **Iran** Republic, S W Asia
91D4 **Irānshahr** Iran
23A1 **Irapuato** Mexico
93D3 **Iraq** Republic, S W Asia
95A2 **Irā Wan** *Watercourse* Libya
94B2 **Irbid** Jordan
61K2 **Irbit** Russian Fed
36C3 **Ireland** Republic, NW Europe
33F3 **Ireng** *R* Guyana
74B3 **Iri** S Korea
71E4 **Irian Jaya** Province, Indon
95B3 **Iriba** Chad
79B3 **Iriga** Phil
99D3 **Iringa** Tanz
69E4 **Iriomote** *I* Japan
33G5 **Iriri** *R* Brazil
42B3 **Irish S** Eng/Irish Rep
12D1 **Irkillik** *R* USA
63C2 **Irkutsk** Russian Fed
65J4 **Irlysh** *R* Kazakhstan
108A2 **Iron Knob** Aust
14A1 **Iron Mountain** USA
107D2 **Iron Range** Aust
14A1 **Iron River** USA
14B3 **Irontown** USA
10A2 **Ironwood** USA
10B2 **Iroquois Falls** Can
75B2 **Iro-zaki** *C* Japan
76A2 **Irrawaddy,Mouths of the** Burma
65H4 **Irtysh** *R* Russian Fed
51B1 **Irun** Spain
42B2 **Irvine** Scot
19A3 **Irving** USA
79B4 **Isabela** Phil
32J7 **Isabela** *I* Ecuador
4H2 **Isachsen** Can
4H2 **Isachsen,C** Can
6H3 **Ísafjörður** Iceland
74C4 **Isahaya** Japan
98C2 **Isangi** Zaïre
47D1 **Isar** *R* Germany
47D1 **Isarco** *R* Italy
44E1 **Isbister** Scot
47D1 **Ischgl** Austria
53B2 **Ischia** *I* Italy
75B2 **Ise** Japan
47D2 **Iseo** Italy
46D1 **Iserlohn** Germany
53B2 **Isernia** Italy
75B2 **Ise-wan** *B* Japan
69E4 **Ishigaki** *I* Japan
74E2 **Ishikari** *R* Japan
74E2 **Ishikari-wan** *B* Japan
65H4 **Ishim** Russian Fed
65H4 **Ishim** *R* Kazakhstan
74E3 **Ishinomaki** Japan
75C1 **Ishioka** Japan
84C1 **Ishkashim** Afghan
14A1 **Ishpeming** USA
65J4 **Isil'kul** Russian Fed
99D2 **Isiolo** Kenya
98C2 **Isiro** Zaïre
92C2 **Iskenderun** Turk
92C2 **Iskenferun Körfezi** *B* Turk
92B1 **İskilip** Turk
65K4 **Iskitim** Russian Fed
54B2 **Iskur** *R* Bulg
12H3 **Iskut** *R* Can/USA
23B2 **Isla** Mexico
34C3 **Isla Bermejo** *I* Arg
27E4 **Isla Blanquilla** Ven
32A2 **Isla Coiba** *I* Panama
9B4 **Isla de Cedros** *I* Mexico
29B4 **Isla de Chiloé** *I* Chile
25D2 **Isla de Cozumel** *I* Mexico
26C3 **Isla de la Gonâve** Cuba
26A2 **Isla de la Juventud** *I* Cuba
34D2 **Isla de las Lechiguanas** *I* Arg
3K8 **Isla del Coco** *I* Costa Rica
25D3 **Isla del Maiz** *I* Caribbean S
23B1 **Isla de Lobos** *I* Mexico

29D6 **Isla de los Estados** *I* Arg
28E2 **Isla de Marajó** *I* Brazil
105L5 **Isla de Pascua** *I* Pacific O
26A4 **Isla de Providencia** *I* Caribbean S
26A4 **Isla de San Andres** *I* Caribbean S
30G4 **Isla de Santa Catarina** *I* Brazil
33G2 **Isla du Diable** *I* French Guiana
31E2 **Isla Fernando de Noronha** *I* Brazil
29C6 **Isla Grande de Tierra del Fuego** *I* Arg/Chile
27D4 **Isla la Tortuga** *I* Ven
84C2 **Islamabad** Pak
24A2 **Isla Magdalena** *I* Mexico
27E4 **Isla Margarita** Ven
34A3 **Isla Mocha** Chile
17B2 **Islamorada** USA
10A1 **Island L** Can
108A2 **Island Lg** Aust
110B1 **Islands,B of** NZ
32A4 **Isla Puná** *I* Ecuador
103D6 **Isla San Ambrosia** *I* Pacific O
103D6 **Isla San Felix** *I* Pacific O
24A2 **Isla Santa Margarita** *I* Mexico
34A3 **Isla Santa Maria** *I* Chile
51C2 **Islas Baleares** *Is* Spain
96A2 **Islas Canarias** *Is* Atlantic O
51C2 **Islas Columbretes** *Is* Spain
25D3 **Islas de la Bahia** *Is* Honduras
26A4 **Islas del Maíz** *Is* Caribbean S
33E1 **Islas de Margarita** *Is* Ven
29C7 **Islas Diego Ramírez** *Is* Chile
32J7 **Islas Galapagos** *Is* Pacific O
30H6 **Islas Juan Fernández** Chile
32D1 **Islas los Roques** *Is* Ven
Islas Malvinas = Falkland Is
105L3 **Islas Revilla Gigedo** *Is* Pacific O
29C7 **Islas Wollaston** *Is* Chile
97A3 **Isla Tidra** *I* Maur
29B5 **Isla Wellington** *I* Chile
48C2 **Isle** *R* France
104B5 **Isle Amsterdam** *I* Indian O
43D4 **Isle of Wight** *I* Eng
10B2 **Isle Royale** *I* USA
104B5 **Isle St Paul** *I* Indian O
104A6 **Îsles Crozet** *I* Indian O
105J4 **Îsles de la Société** Pacific O
105K5 **Îsles Gambier** *Is* Pacific O
101D2 **Isles Glorieuses** *Is* Madag
104B6 **Îsles Kerguelen** *Is* Indian O
105K4 **Îsles Marquises** *Is* Pacific O
105J4 **Îsles Tuamotu** *Is* Pacific O
105J5 **Îsles Tubai** *Is* Pacific O
22B1 **Isleton** USA
92B3 **Ismâ'ilîya** Egypt
101D3 **Isoanala** Madag
101C2 **Isoka** Zambia
53B3 **Isola Egadi** *I* Italy
52B2 **Isola Ponziane** *I* Italy
53B3 **Isole Lipari** *Is* Italy
52C2 **Isoles Tremiti** *Is* Italy
75B1 **Isosaki** Japan
92B2 **Isparta** Turk
94B2 **Israel** Republic, S W Asia
51C2 **Isser** *R* Alg
48C2 **Issoire** France
49C2 **Issoudun** France
92A1 **İstanbul** Turk
55B3 **Istiáia** Greece
25C3 **Istmo de Tehuantepec** *Isthmus* Mexico
17B2 **Istokpoga,L** USA
52B1 **Istra** *Pen* Croatia
35B1 **Itaberai** Brazil
35C1 **Itabira** Brazil
35C2 **Itabirito** Brazil
31D4 **Itabuna** Brazil
33F4 **Itacoatiara** Brazil
32B2 **Itagui** Colombia
33F4 **Itaituba** Brazil
30G4 **Itajaí** Brazil
35B2 **Itajuba** Brazil
52B2 **Italy** Repubic, Europe
35D1 **Itamaraju** Brazil
35C1 **Itamarandiba** Brazil
35C1 **Itambacuri** Brazil
35C1 **Itambé** *Mt* Brazil
86C1 **Itānagar** India
35B2 **Itanhaém** Brazil
35C1 **Itanhém** Brazil
35C1 **Itanhém** *R* Brazil
35C1 **Itaobím** Brazil
35B2 **Itapecerica** Brazil
35C2 **Itaperuna** Brazil
31C5 **Itapetinga** Brazil
35B2 **Itapetininga** Brazil
35B2 **Itapeva** Brazil
31D2 **Itapipoca** Brazil
35B1 **Itapuranga** Brazil
30E4 **Itaqui** Brazil
35C1 **Itarantim** Brazil
35B2 **Itararé** Brazil
35B2 **Itararé** *R* Brazil
35C2 **Itaúna** Brazil
33E6 **Iténez** *R* Brazil/Bol
15C2 **Ithaca** USA
98C2 **Itimbiri** *R* Zaïre
35C1 **Itinga** Brazil
6E3 **Itivdleg** Greenland
75B2 **Ito** Japan
74D3 **Itoigawa** Japan
33E6 **Itonomas** *R* Bol
35B2 **Itu** Brazil
35B1 **Itumbiara** Brazil
35A1 **Iturama** Brazil
30C3 **Iturbe** Arg
35B1 **Iturutaba** Brazil
56B2 **Itzehoe** Germany
58D2 **Ivacevichi** Belorussia
35A2 **Ivai** *R* Brazil
38K5 **Ivalo** Fin
54A2 **Ivangrad** Montenegro, Yugos
108B2 **Ivanhoe** Aust
59C3 **Ivano-Frankovsk** Ukraine
61F2 **Ivanovo** Russian Fed
65H3 **Ivdel'** Russian Fed
98B2 **Ivindo** *R* Gabon
101D3 **Ivohibe** Madag
101D2 **Ivongo Soanierana** Madag
97B4 **Ivory Coast** Republic, Africa
52A1 **Ivrea** Italy
6C3 **Ivujivik** Can
74E3 **Iwaki** Japan
74C4 **Iwakuni** Japan
74E2 **Iwanai** Japan
97C4 **Iwo** Nig
69G4 **Iwo Jima** *I* Japan
23B1 **Ixmiquilpa** Mexico
23A2 **Ixtapa** Mexico
23A1 **Ixtlán** Mexico
75A2 **Iyo** Japan
75A2 **Iyo-nada** *B* Japan
65G4 **Izhevsk** Russian Fed
64G3 **Izhma** Russian Fed
91C5 **Izkī** Oman
60C4 **Izmail** Ukraine
92A2 **İzmir** Turk
55C3 **İzmir Körfezi** *B* Turk
92A1 **İzmit** Turk
92A1 **İznik** Turk
55C2 **Iznik Golü** *L* Turk
94C2 **Izra'** Syria
23B2 **Izúcar de Matamoros** Mexico
75B2 **Izumi-sano** Japan
75A1 **Izumo** Japan
74D4 **Izu-shotō** *Is* Japan

J

95B1 **Jabal al Akhdar** *Mts* Libya
94C2 **Jabal al 'Arab** Syria
95A2 **Jabal as Sawdā** *Mts* Libya
91B5 **Jabal az Zannah** UAE
94C1 **Jabal Halīmah** *Mt* Leb/Syria
83B3 **Jabalpur** India
59B2 **Jablonec nad Nisou** Czech
31D3 **Jaboatão** Brazil
35B2 **Jaboticabal** Brazil
51B1 **Jaca** Spain
23B1 **Jacala** Mexico
33F5 **Jacareacanga** Brazil
35B2 **Jacarei** Brazil
30F3 **Jacarezinho** Brazil
29C2 **Jáchal** Arg
35C1 **Jacinto** Brazil
13F2 **Jackfish L** Can
109C1 **Jackson** Aust
22B1 **Jackson** California, USA
14B2 **Jackson** Michigan, USA
19B3 **Jackson** Mississippi, USA
18C2 **Jackson** Missouri, USA
14B3 **Jackson** Ohio, USA
11B3 **Jackson** Tennessee, USA
111B2 **Jackson,C** NZ
111A2 **Jackson Head** *Pt* NZ
19B3 **Jacksonville** Arkansas, USA
17B1 **Jacksonville** Florida, USA
18B2 **Jacksonville** Illinois, USA
17C1 **Jacksonville** N Carolina, USA
19A3 **Jacksonville** Texas, USA
17B1 **Jacksonville Beach** USA
26C3 **Jacmel** Haiti
84B3 **Jacobabad** Pak
31C4 **Jacobina** Brazil
23A2 **Jacona** Mexico
Jadotville = Likasi
32B5 **Jaén** Peru
50B2 **Jaén** Spain
Jaffa = Tel Aviv Yafo
108A3 **Jaffa,C** Aust
87B3 **Jaffna** Sri Lanka
86B2 **Jagannathganj Ghat** Bang
87C1 **Jagdalpur** India
91C4 **Jagin** *R* Iran
87B1 **Jagtial** India
29F2 **Jaguarão** *R* Brazil
35B2 **Jaguarialva** Brazil
91B4 **Jahrom** Iran
85D5 **Jāina** India
72A2 **Jainca** China
85D3 **Jaipur** India
85C3 **Jaisalmer** India
90C2 **Jajarm** Iran
52C2 **Jajce** Bosnia & Herzegovina, Yugos
78B4 **Jakarta** Indon
6E3 **Jakobshavn** Greenland
38J6 **Jakobstad** Fin
23B2 **Jalaca** Mexico
84B2 **Jalai-Kut** Afghan
23B2 **Jalapa** Mexico
35A2 **Jales** Brazil
86B1 **Jaleswar** Nepal
85D4 **Jalgaon** India
97D4 **Jalingo** Nig
51B1 **Jalón** *R* Spain
85C3 **Jālor** India
23A1 **Jalostotitlan** Mexico
86B1 **Jalpāiguri** India
23B1 **Jalpan** Mexico
95B2 **Jālū Oasis** Libya
32A4 **Jama** Ecuador
26B3 **Jamaica** *I* Caribbean S
26B3 **Jamaica Chan** Caribbean S
86B2 **Jamalpur** Bang
78A3 **Jambi** Indon
85C4 **Jambussar** India
7B4 **James B** Can
5J5 **Jameston** USA
108A2 **Jamestown** Aust
8D2 **Jamestown** N. Dakota, USA
15C2 **Jamestown** New York, USA
16D2 **Jamestown** Rhode Island, USA
23B2 **Jamiltepec** Mexico
87B1 **Jamkhandi** India
84C2 **Jammu** India
84D2 **Jammu and Kashmir** State, India
85B4 **Jamnagar** India
84C3 **Jampur** Pak
38K6 **Jämsä** Fin
86B2 **Jamshedpur** India
86B1 **Janakpur** Nepal
35C1 **Janaúba** Brazil
90B3 **Jandaq** Iran
109D1 **Jandowae** Aust
1B1 **Jan Mayen** *I* Norwegian S
35C1 **Januária** Brazil
85D4 **Jaora** India
51 **Japan** Empire, E Asia
74C3 **Japan,S of** S E Asia
104F2 **Japan Trench** Pacific O
32D4 **Japurá** *R* Brazil
93C2 **Jarābulus** Syria
35B1 **Jaraguá** Brazil
50B1 **Jarama** *R* Spain
94B2 **Jarash** Jordan
30E3 **Jardim** Brazil
51B2 **Jardin** *R* Spain
26B2 **Jardines de la Reina** *Is* Cuba
Jargalant = Hovd
33G3 **Jari** *R* Brazil
86C1 **Jaria Jhānjail** Bang
46C2 **Jarny** France
58B2 **Jarocin** Pol
59C2 **Jaroslaw** Pol
38G6 **Järpen** Sweden
72B2 **Jartai** China
85C4 **Jasdan** India
97C4 **Jasikan** Ghana
91C4 **Jāsk** Iran
59C3 **Jaslo** Pol
29D6 **Jason Is** Falkland Is
18B2 **Jasper** Arkansas, USA
13D2 **Jasper** Can
17B1 **Jasper** Florida, USA
14A3 **Jasper** Indiana, USA
19B3 **Jasper** Texas, USA
13D2 **Jasper Nat Pk** Can
58B2 **Jastrowie** Pol
35A1 **Jatai** Brazil
51B2 **Játiva** Spain
35B2 **Jau** Brazil
32B6 **Jauja** Peru
86A1 **Jaunpur** India
Java = Jawa
87B2 **Javadi Hills** India
Javari = Yavari
70B4 **Java S** Indon
106A2 **Java Trench** Indon
78B4 **Jawa** *I* Indon
71F4 **Jayapura** Indon
94C2 **Jayrūd** Syria
96B2 **Jbel Ouarkziz** *Mts* Mor
96B1 **Jbel Sarhro** *Mt* Mor
19B4 **Jeanerette** USA
97C4 **Jebba** Nig

93D2 **Jebel 'Abd al 'Azīz** *Mt* Syria
95B3 **Jebel Abyad** Sudan
91C5 **Jebel Akhdar** *Mt* Oman
92C4 **Jebel al Lawz** *Mt* S Arabia
94B2 **Jebel ash Shaykh** *Mt* Syria
95C2 **Jebel Asoteriba** *Mt* Sudan
94B3 **Jebel Ed Dabab** *Mt* Jordan
94B3 **Jebel el Ata'ita** *Mt* Jordan
92C3 **Jebel esh Sharqi** *Mts* Leb/Syria
94C3 **Jebel Ithrīyat** *Mt* Jordan
91C5 **Jebel Ja'lan** *Mt* Oman
94B2 **Jebel Liban** *Mts* Leb
94C2 **Jebel Ma'lūlā** *Mt* Syria
98C1 **Jebel Marra** *Mt* Sudan
94C3 **Jebel Mudeisisat** *Mt* Jordan
95C2 **Jebel Oda** *Mt* Sudan
94B3 **Jebel Qasr ed Deir** *Mt* Jordan
94B2 **Jebel Um ed Daraj** *Mt* Jordan
95B2 **Jebel Uweinat** *Mt* Sudan
42C2 **Jedburgh** Scot
Jedda = Jiddah
59C2 **Jedrzejów** Pol
19B3 **Jefferson** Texas, USA
11A3 **Jefferson City** USA
8B3 **Jefferson,Mt** USA
14A3 **Jeffersonville** USA
60C2 **Jekabpils** Latvia
59B2 **Jelena Gora** Pol
60B2 **Jelgava** Latvia
78C4 **Jember** Indon
57C2 **Jena** Germany
78B2 **Jenaja** *I* Indon
47D1 **Jenbach** Austria
94B2 **Jenin** Israel
19B3 **Jennings** USA
59B2 **Jeseníky** *Upland* Czech
6F3 **Jensen Nunatakker** *Mt* Greenland
6B3 **Jens Munk** *I* Can
108B3 **Jeparit** Aust
31D4 **Jequié** Brazil
35C1 **Jequital** *R* Brazil
35C1 **Jequitinhonha** Brazil
31C5 **Jequitinhonha** *R* Brazil
50A2 **Jerez de la Frontera** Spain
50A2 **Jerez de los Caballeros** Spain
94B3 **Jericho** Israel
108C3 **Jerilderie** Aust
48B2 **Jersey** *I* UK
10C2 **Jersey City** USA
15C2 **Jersey Shore** USA
18B2 **Jerseyville** USA
92C3 **Jerusalem** Israel
109D3 **Jervis B** Aust
13C2 **Jervis Inlet** *Sd* Can
52B1 **Jesenice** Slovenia
86B2 **Jessore** Bang
11B3 **Jesup** USA
34C2 **Jesus Maria** Arg
16D2 **Jewett City** USA
54A2 **Jezerce** *Mt* Alb
58C2 **Jezioro Mamry** *L* Pol
58C2 **Jezioro Śniardwy** *L* Pol
94B2 **Jezzine** Leb
85C4 **Jhābua** India
85D4 **Jhālāwār** India
84C2 **Jhang Maghiana** Pak
85D3 **Jhānsi** India
86A2 **Jhārsuguda** India
84C2 **Jhelum** Pak
84C2 **Jhelum** *R* Pak
11C3 **J H Kerr L** USA
84D3 **Jhunjhunūn** India
69F2 **Jiamusi** China
73C4 **Ji'an** Jiangxi, China
74B2 **Ji'an** Jilin, China
73D4 **Jiande** China
73B4 **Jiang'an** China
73D4 **Jiangbiancun** China
73A5 **Jiangcheng** China
73B3 **Jiang Jiang** *R* China
73C5 **Jiangmen** China
72D3 **Jiangsu** Province, China
73C4 **Jiangxi** Province, China
73A3 **Jiangyou** China
72D1 **Jianping** China
73A5 **Jianshui** China
73D4 **Jian Xi** *R* China
73D4 **Jianyang** China
72E2 **Jiaonan** China
72E2 **Jiao Xian** China
72E2 **Jiaozhou Wan** *B* China
72C2 **Jiaozuo** China
73E3 **Jiaxiang** China
68B3 **Jiayuguan** China
81B3 **Jiddah** S Arabia
72D3 **Jieshou** China
72C2 **Jiexiu** China
72A3 **Jigzhi** China
59B3 **Jihlava** Czech
99E2 **Jilib** Somalia
69E2 **Jilin** China
51B1 **Jiloca** *R* Spain
99D2 **Jima** Eth
9C4 **Jiménez** Coahuila, Mexico
72D2 **Jinan** China
84D3 **Jind** India
72B2 **Jingbian** China
73D4 **Jingdezhen** China
76C1 **Jinghong** China
73C3 **Jingmen** China
72B2 **Jingning** China
73B4 **Jing Xiang** China
73D4 **Jinhua** China
72C1 **Jining** Nei Monggol, China
72D2 **Jining** Shandong, China
99D2 **Jinja** Uganda
76C1 **Jinping** China
73A4 **Jinsha Jiang** *R* China
73C4 **Jinshi** China
72E1 **Jinxi** China
72E2 **Jin Xian** China
72E1 **Jinzhou** China
33E5 **Jiparaná** *R* Brazil
32A4 **Jipijapa** Ecuador
23A2 **Jiquilpan** Mexico
91C4 **Jiroft** Iran
99E2 **Jirriban** Somalia
73B4 **Jishou** China
92C2 **Jisr ash Shughūr** Syria
54B2 **Jiu** *R* Rom
73D4 **Jiujiang** China
73A4 **Jiulong** China
73D4 **Jiulong Jiang** *R* China
69F2 **Jixi** China
94B3 **Jiza** Jordan
81C4 **Jīzan** S Arabia
97A3 **Joal** Sen
35C1 **João Monlevade** Brazil
31E3 **João Pessoa** Brazil
35B1 **João Pirheiro** Brazil
34B2 **Jocoli** Arg
85C3 **Jodhpur** India
38K6 **Joensuu** Fin
46C2 **Joeuf** France
13D2 **Joffre,Mt** Can
86B1 **Jogbani** India
87A2 **Jog Falls** India
101G1 **Johannesburg** S Africa
21B2 **Johannesburg** USA
6C2 **Johan Pen** Can
12D1 **John** *R* USA
20C2 **John Day** USA
20B1 **John Day** *R* USA
44C2 **John O'Groats** Scot
18A2 **John Redmond Res** USA
11B3 **Johnson City** Tennessee, USA
17B1 **Johnston** USA
27N2 **Johnston Pt** St Vincent
15C2 **Johnstown** Pennsylvania, USA
77C5 **Johor Bharu** Malay
49C2 **Joigny** France
30G4 **Joinville** Brazil
61H3 **Jok** *R* Russian Fed
38H5 **Jokkmokk** Sweden
93E2 **Jolfa** Iran
10B2 **Joliet** USA
7C5 **Joliette** Can
79B4 **Jolo** Phil
79B4 **Jolo** *I* Phil
82D2 **Joma** *Mt* China
58C1 **Jonava** Lithuania
72A3 **Jonê** China
11A3 **Jonesboro** Arkansas, USA
19B3 **Jonesboro** Louisiana, USA
6B2 **Jones Sd** Can
58C1 **Joniškis** Lithuania
39G7 **Jönköping** Sweden
11A3 **Joplin** USA
92C3 **Jordan** Kingdom, S W Asia
94B2 **Jordan** *R* Israel
20C2 **Jordan Valley** USA
86C1 **Jorhāt** India
38J5 **Jörn** Sweden
78C3 **Jorong** Indon
39F7 **Jørpeland** Nor
79B3 **Jose Pañganiban** Phil
106B2 **Joseph Bonaparte G** Aust
64B3 **Jotunheimen** *Mt* Nor
94B2 **Jouai'ya** Leb
94B2 **Jounié** Leb
86C1 **Jowal** India
99E2 **Jowhar** Somalia
12H2 **Joy,Mt** Can
5F5 **Juan de Fuca,Str of** Can/USA
101D2 **Juan de Nova** *I* Mozam Chan
34D3 **Juárez** Arg
31C3 **Juàzeiro** Brazil
31D3 **Juazeiro do Norte** Brazil
99D2 **Juba** Sudan
99E2 **Juba** *R* Somalia
94B1 **Jubail** Leb
93D3 **Jubbah** S Arabia
96A2 **Juby,C** Mor
51B2 **Jucar** *R* Spain
23B2 **Juchatengo** Mexico
23A1 **Juchipila** *R* Mexico
23A1 **Juchitlan** Mexico
57C3 **Judenburg** Austria
30B2 **Juilaca** Peru
73C4 **Juiling Shan** *Hills* China
31C6 **Juiz de Fora** Brazil
30C3 **Jujuy** State, Arg
30C2 **Juli** Peru
33F3 **Julianatop** *Mt* Surinam
6F3 **Julianehab** Greenland
46D1 **Jülich** Germany
84D2 **Jullundur** India
86A1 **Jumla** Nepal
94B3 **Jum Suwwāna** *Mt* Jordan
85C4 **Jūnāgadh** India
72D2 **Junan** China
9D3 **Junction City** USA
31B6 **Jundiaí** Brazil
4E4 **Juneau** USA
107D4 **Junee** Aust
22C2 **June Lake** USA
52A1 **Jungfrau** *Mt* Switz
16A2 **Juniata** *R* USA
29D2 **Junín** Arg
73A4 **Junlian** China
31B6 **Juquiá** Brazil
99C2 **Jur** *R* Sudan
42B2 **Jura** *I* Scot
49D2 **Jura** *Mts* France
44B3 **Jura,Sound of** *Chan* Scot
94B3 **Jurf ed Darāwīsh** Jordan
65K4 **Jurga** Russian Fed
60B2 **Jūrmala** Latvia
32D4 **Juruá** *R* Brazil
33F6 **Juruena** *R* Brazil
94C1 **Jūsīyah** Syria
34B2 **Justo Daract** Arg
32D4 **Jutai** *R* Brazil
25D3 **Juticalpa** Honduras
Jutland = Jylland
90C3 **Jūymand** Iran
56B1 **Jylland** *Pen* Den
38K6 **Jyväskyla** Fin

K

82B2 **K2** *Mt* China/India
90C2 **Kaakhka** Turkmenistan
101H1 **Kaapmuiden** S Africa
71D4 **Kabaena** *I* Indon
97A4 **Kabala** Sierra Leone
99D3 **Kabale** Rwanda
98C3 **Kabalo** Zaïre
98C3 **Kabambare** Zaïre
99D2 **Kabarole** Uganda
98C3 **Kabinda** Zaïre
90A3 **Kabir Kuh** *Mts* Iran
100B2 **Kabompo** Zambia
100B2 **Kabompo** *R* Zambia
98C3 **Kabongo** Zaïre
84B2 **Kabul** Afghan
85B4 **Kachchh,G of** India
61J2 **Kachkanar** Russian Fed
63C2 **Kachug** Russian Fed
76B3 **Kadan** Burma
78D3 **Kadapongan** *I* Indon
85C4 **Kadi** India
108A2 **Kadina** Aust
92B2 **Kadinhanı** Turk
87B2 **Kadiri** India
60E4 **Kadiyevka** Ukraine
100B2 **Kadoma** Zim
99C1 **Kadugli** Sudan
97C3 **Kaduna** Nig
97C3 **Kaduna** *R* Nig
87B2 **Kadūr** India
97A3 **Kaédi** Maur
21C4 **Kaena Pt** Hawaiian Is
74B3 **Kaesŏng** N Korea
97C4 **Kafanchan** Nig
97A3 **Kaffrine** Sen
94C1 **Kafrūn Bashūr** Syria
100B2 **Kafue** Zambia
100B2 **Kafue** *R* Zambia
100B2 **Kafue Nat Pk** Zambia
74D3 **Kaga** Japan
65H6 **Kagan** Kazakhstan
93D1 **Kağizman** Turk
74C4 **Kagoshima** Japan
90C2 **Kāhak** Iran
99D3 **Kahama** Tanz
84B3 **Kahan** Pak
78C3 **Kahayan** *R* Indon
98B3 **Kahemba** Zaïre
46E1 **Kahler Asten** *Mt* Germany
91C4 **Kahnūj** Iran
18B1 **Kahoka** USA
21C4 **Kahoolawe** *I* Hawaiian Is
92C2 **Kahramanmaraş** Turk
21C4 **Kahuku Pt** Hawaiian Is
111B2 **Kaiapoi** NZ
33F2 **Kaieteur Fall** Guyana
72C3 **Kaifeng** China
110B1 **Kaikohe** NZ
111B2 **Kaikoura** NZ
111B2 **Kaikoura Pen** NZ
111B2 **Kaikoura Range** *Mts* NZ
73B4 **Kaili** China
21C4 **Kailua** Hawaiian Is
71E4 **Kaimana** Indon
75B2 **Kainan** Japan
97C3 **Kainji Res** Nig

110B1 **Kaipara Harbour** *B* NZ
73C5 **Kaiping** China
96D1 **Kairouan** Tunisia
22C2 **Kaiser Peak** *Mt* USA
57B3 **Kaiserslautern** Germany
74B2 **Kaishantun** China
58D2 **Kaisiadorys** Lithuania
110B1 **Kaitaia** NZ
111A3 **Kaitangata** NZ
84D3 **Kaithal** India
21C4 **Kaiwi Chan** Hawaiian Is
73B3 **Kai Xian** China
73A5 **Kaiyuan** Liaoning, China
74A2 **Kaiyuan** Yunnan, China
12C2 **Kaiyuh Mts** USA
38K6 **Kajaani** Fin
84B2 **Kajaki** Afghan
99D3 **Kajiado** Kenya
84B2 **Kajrān** Afghan
99D1 **Kaka** Sudan
99D2 **Kakamega** Kenya
75A2 **Kake** Japan
12H3 **Kake** USA
12D3 **Kakhonak** USA
65E5 **Kakhovskoye Vodokhranilishche** *Res* Ukraine
91B4 **Kākī** Iran
87C1 **Kākināda** India
75A2 **Kakogawa** Japan
4D2 **Kaktovik** USA
75C1 **Kakuda** Japan
55B3 **Kalabáka** Greece
78D1 **Kalabakan** Malay
100B2 **Kalabo** Zambia
61F3 **Kalach** Russian Fed
61F4 **Kalach-na-Donu** Russian Fed
86C2 **Kaladan** *R* Burma
21C4 **Ka Lae** *C* Hawaiian Is
100B3 **Kalahari Desert** Botswana
38J6 **Kalajoki** Fin
63D2 **Kalakan** Russian Fed
70A3 **Kalakepen** Indon
84C1 **Kalam** Pak
55B3 **Kalámai** Greece
10B2 **Kalamazoo** USA
84B3 **Kalat** Pak
92B1 **Kalecik** Turk
78D3 **Kalembau** *I* Indon
99C3 **Kalémié** Zaïre
38L5 **Kalevala** Russian Fed
86C2 **Kalewa** Burma
12D2 **Kalgin I** USA
106B4 **Kalgoorlie** Aust
78B4 **Kalianda** Indon
79B3 **Kalibo** Phil
98C3 **Kalima** Zaïre
78C3 **Kalimantan** Province, Indon
55C3 **Kálimnos** *I* Greece
86B1 **Kālimpang** India
60B3 **Kaliningrad** Russian Fed
60C3 **Kalinkovichi** Belorussia
8B2 **Kalispell** USA
58B2 **Kalisz** Pol
99D3 **Kaliua** Tanz
38J5 **Kalix** *R* Sweden
100A3 **Kalkfeld** Namibia
100A3 **Kalkrand** Namibia
108A1 **Kallakoopah** *R* Aust
38K6 **Kallávesi** *L* Fin
55C3 **Kallonis Kólpos** *B* Greece
39H7 **Kalmar** Sweden
61G4 **Kalmykskaya Respublika,** Russian Fed
100B2 **Kalomo** Zambia
18B1 **Kalona** USA
13B2 **Kalone Peak** *Mt* Can
87A2 **Kalpeni** *I* India
85D3 **Kālpi** India
53A3 **Kalsat Khasba** Tunisia
12B2 **Kalskag** USA
12C2 **Kaltag** USA
60E3 **Kaluga** Russian Fed
39G7 **Kalundborg** Den
59C3 **Kalush** Ukraine
87B2 **Kalyandurg** India
60E2 **Kalyazin** Russian Fed
61H1 **Kama** *R* Russian Fed
74E3 **Kamaishi** Japan
84C2 **Kamalia** Pak
110C1 **Kamanawa Mts** NZ
100A2 **Kamanjab** Namibia
84D2 **Kamat** *Mt* India
87B3 **Kamban** India
61H2 **Kambarka** Russian Fed
97A4 **Kambia** Sierra Leone
59D3 **Kamenets Podolskiy** Ukraine
61F3 **Kamenka** Russian Fed
65K4 **Kamen-na-Obi** Russian Fed
61K2 **Kamensk-Ural'skiy** Russian Fed
5H3 **Kamilukuak L** Can
98C3 **Kamina** Zaïre
7A3 **Kaminak L** Can
75C1 **Kaminoyama** Japan
5F4 **Kamloops** Can
93E1 **Kamo** Armenia
75C1 **Kamogawa** Japan
99D2 **Kampala** Uganda
77C5 **Kampar** Malay
78A2 **Kampar** *R* Indon
56B2 **Kampen** Neth
76B2 **Kamphaeng Phet** Thai
77C3 **Kampot** Camb
Kampuchea = Cambodia
91D4 **Kamsaptar** Iran
61J2 **Kamskoye Vodokhranilishche** *Res* Russian Fed
85D4 **Kāmthi** India
61G3 **Kamyshin** Russian Fed
61K2 **Kamyshlov** Russian Fed
7C4 **Kanaaupscow** *R* Can
98C3 **Kananga** Zaïre
61G2 **Kanash** Russian Fed
75B1 **Kanayama** Japan
74D3 **Kanazawa** Japan
4C3 **Kanbisha** USA
87B2 **Kānchipuram** India
84B2 **Kandahar** Afghan
64E3 **Kandalaksha** Russian Fed
38L5 **Kandalakshskaya Guba** *B* Russian Fed
97C3 **Kandi** Benin
109C2 **Kandos** Aust
87C3 **Kandy** Sri Lanka
15C2 **Kane** USA
6C1 **Kane Basin** *B* Can
98B1 **Kanem** *Desert Region* Chad
97B3 **Kangaba** Mali
92C2 **Kangal** Turk
6E3 **Kangâmiut** Greenland
91B4 **Kangān** Iran
77C4 **Kangar** Malay
106C4 **Kangaroo I** Aust
6E3 **Kangâtsiaq** Greenland
90A3 **Kangavar** Iran
72C1 **Kangbao** China
82C3 **Kangchenjunga** *Mt* Nepal
73A4 **Kangding** China
6G3 **Kangerdlugssuaq** *B* Greenland
6G3 **Kangerdlugssvatsaiq** *B* Greenland
99D2 **Kangetet** Kenya
74B2 **Kanggye** N Korea
7D4 **Kangiqsualujjuaq** Can
6C3 **Kangiqsujuaq** Can
7C3 **Kangirsuk** Can
74B3 **Kangnŭng** S Korea
98B2 **Kango** Gabon
68B4 **Kangto** *Mt* China
72B3 **Kang Xian** China
77D4 **Kanh Hung** Viet
98C3 **Kaniama** Zaïre
87B1 **Kani Giri** India
39J6 **Kankaanpää** Fin
14A2 **Kankakee** USA
14A2 **Kankakee** *R* USA
97B3 **Kankan** Guinea
86A2 **Kānker** India
87B3 **Kanniyākuman** India
97C3 **Kano** Nig
74C4 **Kanoya** Japan
86A1 **Kānpur** India
9D3 **Kansas** State, USA
18A2 **Kansas** *R* USA
10A3 **Kansas City** USA
73D5 **Kanshi** China
63B2 **Kansk** Russian Fed
97C3 **Kantchari** Burkina
86B2 **Kanthi** India
12D2 **Kantishna** USA
12D2 **Kantishna** *R* USA
100B3 **Kanye** Botswana
68D4 **Kao-hsiung** Taiwan
100A2 **Kaoka Veld** *Plain* Namibia
97A3 **Kaolack** Sen
100B2 **Kaoma** Zambia
21C4 **Kapaau** Hawaiian Is
98C3 **Kapanga** Zaïre
6F3 **Kap Cort Adelaer** *C* Greenland
6H3 **Kap Dalton** *C* Greenland
39H7 **Kapellskär** Sweden
6F3 **Kap Farvel** *C* Greenland
6G3 **Kap Gustav Holm** *C* Greenland
100B2 **Kapiri** Zambia
78C2 **Kapit** Malay
19B3 **Kaplan** USA
57C3 **Kaplice** Czech
77B4 **Kapoe** Thai
99C3 **Kapona** Zaïre
52C1 **Kaposvár** Hung
6C2 **Kap Parry** *C* Can
6H3 **Kap Ravn** *C* Greenland
78B3 **Kapuas** *R* Indon
108A2 **Kapunda** Aust
84D2 **Kapurthala** India
7B5 **Kapuskasing** Can
109D2 **Kaputar** *Mt* Aust
93E2 **Kapydzhik** *Mt* Armenia
6D2 **Kap York** *C* Greenland
92B1 **Karabük** Turk
55C2 **Karacabey** Turk
85B4 **Karachi** Pak
87A1 **Karād** India
60E5 **Kara Daglari** *Mt* Turk
54C5 **Karadeniz Boğazi** *Sd* Turk
68D1 **Karaftit** Russian Fed
65J5 **Karaganda** Kazakhstan
65J5 **Karagayly** Kazakhstan
87B2 **Kāraikāl** India
90B2 **Karaj** Iran
92C3 **Karak** Jordan
65G5 **Kara Kalpakskaya Respublika,** Uzbekistan
84D1 **Karakax He** *R* China
71D3 **Karakelong** *I* Indon
84D1 **Karakoram** *Mts* India
84D1 **Karakoram** *P* India/China
97A3 **Karakoro** *R* Maur/Sen
65G6 **Karakumy** *Desert* Russian Fed
94B3 **Karama** Jordan
92B2 **Karaman** Turk
65K5 **Karamay** China
111B2 **Karamea** NZ
111B2 **Karamea Bight** *B* NZ
85D4 **Kāranja** India
92B2 **Karapınar** Turk
64H2 **Kara S** Russian Fed
100A3 **Karasburg** Namibia
38K5 **Karasjok** Nor
65J4 **Karasuk** Russian Fed
92C2 **Karataş** Turk
65H5 **Kara Tau** *Mts* Kazakhstan
76B3 **Karathuri** Burma
74B4 **Karatsu** Japan
91B4 **Karāz** Iran
93D3 **Karbalā'** Iraq
59C3 **Karcag** Hung
55B3 **Kardhítsa** Greece
64E3 **Karel'skaya Respublika,** Russian Fed
38J5 **Karesvando** Sweden
96B2 **Karet** *Desert Region* Maur
65K4 **Kargasok** Russian Fed
97D3 **Kari** Nig
100B2 **Kariba** Zim
100B2 **Kariba** *L* Zim/Zambia
100B2 **Kariba Dam** Zim/Zambia
95C3 **Karima** Sudan
78B3 **Karimata** *I* Indon
86C2 **Karimganj** Bang
87B1 **Karīmnagar** India
99E1 **Karin** Somalia
39J6 **Karis** Fin
99C3 **Karishimbe** *Mt* Zaïre
55B3 **Káristos** Greece
87A2 **Kārkal** India
71F4 **Karkar** *I* PNG
90A3 **Karkheh** *R* Iran
60D4 **Karkinitskiy Zaliv** *B* Ukraine
63B3 **Karlik Shan** *Mt* China
58B2 **Karlino** Pol
52C2 **Karlobag** Croatia
52C1 **Karlovac** Croatia
54B2 **Karlovo** Bulg
57C2 **Karlovy Vary** Czech
39G7 **Karlshamn** Sweden
39G7 **Karlskoga** Sweden
39H7 **Karlskrona** Sweden
57B3 **Karlsruhe** Germany
39G7 **Karlstad** Sweden
12D3 **Karluk** USA
86C2 **Karnafuli Res** Bang
84D3 **Karnal** India
87A1 **Karnataka** State, India
54C2 **Karnobat** Bulg
100B2 **Karoi** Zim
99D3 **Karonga** Malawi
95C3 **Karora** Sudan
78D3 **Karossa** Indon
55C3 **Kárpathos** *I* Greece
6E2 **Karrats Fjord** Greenland
93D1 **Kars** Turk
65H4 **Karsakpay** Kazakhstan
58D1 **Kārsava** Latvia
80E2 **Karshi** Uzbekistan
38J6 **Karstula** Fin
94B1 **Kartaba** Leb
54C2 **Kartal** Turk
61K3 **Kartaly** Russian Fed
90A3 **Kārūn** *R* Iran
86A1 **Karwa** India
87A2 **Kārwār** India
68D1 **Karymskoye** Russian Fed
98B3 **Kasai** *R* Zaïre
100B2 **Kasaji** Zaïre
101C2 **Kasama** Zambia
99D3 **Kasanga** Tanz
87A2 **Kāsaragod** India
5H3 **Kasba L** Can
100B2 **Kasempa** Zambia
100B2 **Kasenga** Zaïre
99D2 **Kasese** Uganda
90B3 **Kāshān** Iran
12C2 **Kashegelok** USA
82B2 **Kashi** China
84D3 **Kāshipur** India
74D3 **Kashiwazaki** Japan
90C2 **Kashmar** Iran
66D3 **Kashmir** State, India
61F3 **Kasimov** Russian Fed

18C2 **Kaskaskia** *R* USA
38J6 **Kaskinen** Fin
61K2 **Kasli** Russian Fed
5G5 **Kaslo** Can
98C3 **Kasonga** Zaïre
98B3 **Kasongo-Lunda** Zaïre
55C3 **Kásos** *I* Greece
61G4 **Kaspiyskiy** Russian Fed
95C3 **Kassala** Sudan
56B2 **Kassel** Germany
96C1 **Kasserine** Tunisia
100A2 **Kassinga** Angola
92B1 **Kastamonou** Turk
55B3 **Kastélli** Greece
92A2 **Kastellorizon** *I* Greece
55B2 **Kastoría** Greece
55C3 **Kástron** Greece
74D3 **Kasugai** Japan
75A1 **Kasumi** Japan
101C2 **Kasungu** Malawi
84C2 **Kasur** Pak
100B2 **Kataba** Zambia
98C3 **Katako-kombe** Zaïre
4D3 **Katalla** USA
63G2 **Katangli** Russian Fed
106A4 **Katanning** Aust
55B2 **Kateríni** Greece
5E4 **Kates Needle** *Mt* Can/USA
82D3 **Katha** Burma
106C2 **Katherine** Aust
85C4 **Kāthiāwār** *Pen* India
86B1 **Kathmandu** Nepal
84D2 **Kathua** India
86B1 **Katihār** India
100B2 **Katima Mulilo** Namibia
4C4 **Katmai,Mt** USA
12D3 **Katmai Nat Mon** USA
86A2 **Katni** India
109D2 **Katoomba** Aust
59B2 **Katowice** Pol
39H7 **Katrineholm** Sweden
97C3 **Katsina** Nig
97C4 **Katsina Ala** Nig
75C1 **Katsuta** Japan
75C1 **Katsuura** Japan
75B1 **Katsuy** Japan
65H6 **Kattakurgan** Uzbekistan
39G7 **Kattegat** *Str* Den/Sweden
21C4 **Kauai** *I* Hawaiian Is
21C4 **Kauai Chan** Hawaiian Is
21C4 **Kaulakahi Chan** Hawaiian Is
21C4 **Kaunakaki** Hawaiian Is
60B3 **Kaunas** Lithuania
97C3 **Kaura Namoda** Nig
38J5 **Kautokeino** Nor
55B2 **Kavadarci** Macedonia, Yugos
55A2 **Kavajë** Alb
87B2 **Kavali** India
55B2 **Kavålla** Greece
85B4 **Kāvda** India
75B1 **Kawagoe** Japan
75B1 **Kawaguchi** Japan
110B1 **Kawakawa** NZ
99C3 **Kawambwa** Zambia
86A2 **Kawardha** India
15C2 **Kawartha Lakes** Can
74D3 **Kawasaki** Japan
110C1 **Kawerau** NZ
110B1 **Kawhia** NZ
97B3 **Kaya** Burkina
12F3 **Kayak I** USA
78D2 **Kayan** *R* Indon
87B3 **Kāyankulam** India
97A3 **Kayes** Mali
92C2 **Kayseri** Turk
1B8 **Kazach'ye** Russian Fed
93E1 **Kazakh** Azerbaijan
65G5 **Kazakhstan** Republic, Asia
61G2 **Kazan'** Russian Fed
54C2 **Kazanlŭk** Bulg
69G4 **Kazan Retto** *Is* Japan
91B4 **Kāzerūn** Iran
61H1 **Kazhim** Russian Fed
93E1 **Kazi Magomed** Azerbaijan
59C3 **Kazincbarcika** Hung
55B3 **Kéa** *I* Greece
21C4 **Kealaikahiki Chan** Hawaiian Is
8D2 **Kearney** USA
93C2 **Keban Baraji** *Res* Turk
97A3 **Kébémer** Sen
96C1 **Kebili** Tunisia
94C1 **Kebīr** *R* Leb/Syria
38H5 **Kebrekaise** *Mt* Sweden
59B3 **Kecskemét** Hung
58C1 **Kedainiai** Lithuania
97A3 **Kédougou** Sen
12J2 **Keele** *R* Can
12H2 **Keele Pk** *Mt* Can
21B2 **Keeler** USA
15D2 **Keene** New Hampshire, USA
100A3 **Keetmanshoop** Namibia
18C1 **Keewanee** USA
6A3 **Keewatin** *Region* Can
55B3 **Kefallinía** *I* Greece
94B2 **Kefar Sava** Israel
97C4 **Keffi** Nig
38A2 **Keflavik** Iceland
5G4 **Keg River** Can
76B1 **Kehsi Mansam** Burma
108B3 **Keith** Aust
44C3 **Keith** Scot
4F3 **Keith Arm** *B* Can
6D3 **Kekertuk** Can
85D3 **Kekri** India
77C5 **Kelang** Malay
77C4 **Kelantan** *R* Malay
84B1 **Kelif** Turkmenistan
92C1 **Kelkit** *R* Turk
98B3 **Kellé** Congo
4F2 **Kellet,C** Can
20C1 **Kellogg** USA
64D3 **Kelloselka** Fin
45C2 **Kells** Irish Rep
42B2 **Kells Range** *Hills* Scot
58C1 **Kelme** Lithuania
5G5 **Kelowna** Can
5F4 **Kelsey Bay** Can
42C2 **Kelso** Scot
20B1 **Kelso** USA
64E3 **Kem'** Russian Fed
38L6 **Kem'** *R* Russian Fed
97B3 **Ke Macina** Mali
13B2 **Kemano** Can
65K4 **Kemerovo** Russian Fed
38J5 **Kemi** Fin
38K5 **Kemi** *R* Fin
38K5 **Kemijärvi** Fin
46C1 **Kempen** Region, Belg
26B2 **Kemps Bay** The Bahamas
109D2 **Kempsey** Aust
57C3 **Kempten** Germany
12D2 **Kenai** USA
12D3 **Kenai Mts** USA
12D2 **Kenai Pen** USA
99D2 **Kenamuke Swamp** Sudan
42C2 **Kendal** Eng
109D2 **Kendall** Aust
71D4 **Kendari** Indon
78C3 **Kendawangan** Indon
86B2 **Kendrāpāra** India
20C1 **Kendrick** USA
97A4 **Kenema** Sierra Leone
98B3 **Kenge** Zaïre
76B1 **Kengtung** Burma
100B3 **Kenhardt** S Africa
97A3 **Kéniéba** Mali
96B1 **Kenitra** Mor
45B3 **Kenmare** Irish Rep
45B3 **Kenmare** *R* Irish Rep
19B4 **Kenner** USA
18C2 **Kennett** USA
16B3 **Kennett Square** USA
20C1 **Kennewick** USA
5F4 **Kenny Dam** Can
7A5 **Kenora** Can
10B2 **Kenosha** USA
43E4 **Kent** County, Eng
20B1 **Kent** Washington, USA
14A2 **Kentland** USA
14B2 **Kenton** USA
4H3 **Kent Pen** Can
11B3 **Kentucky** State, USA
11B3 **Kentucky L** USA
19B3 **Kentwood** Louisiana, USA
14A2 **Kentwood** Michigan, USA
99D2 **Kenya** Republic, Africa
Kenya,Mt = Kirinyaga
18B1 **Keokuk** USA
86A2 **Keonchi** India
86B2 **Keonjhargarh** India
71E4 **Kepaluan Tanimbar** *Arch* Indon
6H3 **Keplavik** Iceland
59B2 **Kepno** Pol
78B2 **Kepulauan Anambas** *Arch* Indon
71E4 **Kepulauan Aru** *Arch* Indon
78B2 **Kepulauan Badas** *Is* Indon
71E4 **Kepulauan Banda** *Arch* Indon
71D4 **Kepulauan Banggai** *I* Indon
78B2 **Kepulauan Bunguran Seletan** *Arch* Indon
71E4 **Kepulauan Kai** *Arch* Indon
71D4 **Kepulauan Leti** *I* Indon
78A3 **Kepulauan Lingga** *Is* Indon
70A4 **Kepulauan Mentawi** *Arch* Indon
78A2 **Kepulauan Riau** *Arch* Indon
78D4 **Kepulauan Sabalana** *Arch* Indon
71D3 **Kepulauan Sangihe** *Arch* Indon
71D4 **Kepulauan Sula** *I* Indon
71D3 **Kepulauan Talaud** *Arch* Indon
78B2 **Kepulauan Tambelan** *Is* Indon
71E4 **Kepulauan Tanimbar** *I* Indon
71D4 **Kepulauan Togian** *I* Indon
71D4 **Kepulauan Tukambesi** *Is* Indon
87B2 **Kerala** State, India
108B3 **Kerang** Aust
39K6 **Kerava** Fin
60E4 **Kerch'** Ukraine
71F4 **Kerema** PNG
20C1 **Keremeps** Can
95C3 **Keren** Eth
104B6 **Kerguelen Ridge** Indian O
99D3 **Kericho** Kenya
70B4 **Kerinci** *Mt* Indon
99D2 **Kerio** *R* Kenya
80E2 **Kerki** Turkmenistan
55A3 **Kérkira** Greece
55A3 **Kérkira** *I* Greece
91C3 **Kerman** Iran
22B2 **Kerman** USA
90A3 **Kermānshāh** Iran
21B2 **Kern** *R* USA
13F2 **Kerrobert** Can
45B2 **Kerry** County, Irish Rep
17B1 **Kershaw** USA
78B3 **Kertamulia** Indon
63D3 **Kerulen** *R* Mongolia
96B2 **Kerzaz** Alg
55C2 **Keşan** Turk
74E3 **Kesennuma** Japan
38L5 **Kesten'ga** Russian Fed
42C2 **Keswick** Eng
65K4 **Ket** *R* Russian Fed
97C4 **Kéta** Ghana
78C3 **Ketapang** Indon
5E4 **Ketchikan** USA
97C3 **Ketia** Niger
85B4 **Keti Bandar** Pak
58C2 **Ketrzyn** Pol
43D3 **Kettering** Eng
14B3 **Kettering** USA
20C1 **Kettle** *R* Can
20C1 **Kettle River Range** *Mts* USA
7C3 **Kettlestone B** Can
90C3 **Kevir-i Namak** *Salt Flat* Iran
14A2 **Kewaunee** USA
14B1 **Key Harbour** Can
17B2 **Key Largo** USA
11B4 **Key West** USA
63C2 **Kezhma** Russian Fed
54A1 **K'félegháza** Hung
12B2 **Kgun L** USA
94C2 **Khabab** Syria
62H3 **Khabarovsk** Russian Fed
85B3 **Khairpur** Pak
85B3 **Khairpur** Region, Pak
100B3 **Khakhea** Botswana
55C3 **Khálki** *I* Greece
55B2 **Khalkidhíki** *Pen* Greece
55B3 **Khalkís** Greece
61G2 **Khalturin** Russian Fed
85C4 **Khambhāt,G of** India
85D4 **Khāmgaon** India
76C2 **Kham Keut** Laos
87C1 **Khammam** India
90A2 **Khamseh** *Mts* Iran
76C2 **Khan** *R* Laos
84B1 **Khanabad** Afghan
93E3 **Khānaqīn** Iraq
85D4 **Khandwa** India
84C2 **Khanewal** Pak
94C3 **Khan ez Zabib** Jordan
77D4 **Khanh Hung** Viet
55B3 **Khaniá** Greece
84C3 **Khanpur** Pak
65H3 **Khanty-Mansiysk** Russian Fed
94B3 **Khan Yunis** Egypt
84D1 **Khapalu** India
68C2 **Khapcheranga** Russian Fed
61G4 **Kharabali** Russian Fed
86B2 **Kharagpur** India
91C4 **Khārān** Iran
84B3 **Kharan** Pak
90B3 **Kharānaq** Iran
91B4 **Khārg** *Is* Iran
95C2 **Khârga Oasis** Egypt
85D4 **Khargon** India
60E4 **Khar'kov** Ukraine
54C2 **Kharmanli** Bulg
61F2 **Kharovsk** Russian Fed
95C3 **Khartoum** Sudan
95C3 **Khartoum North** Sudan
74C2 **Khasan** Russian Fed
95C3 **Khashm el Girba** Sudan
86C1 **Khasi-Jaīntīa Hills** India
54C2 **Khaskovo** Bulg
1B9 **Khatanga** Russian Fed
76B3 **Khawsa** Burma
76C2 **Khe Bo** Viet
85C4 **Khed Brahma** India
51C2 **Khemis** Alg
96B1 **Khenifra** Mor
51D2 **Kherrata** Alg
60D4 **Kherson** Ukraine
63D2 **Khilok** Russian Fed
55C3 **Khíos** Greece
55C3 **Khíos** *I* Greece
60C4 **Khmel'nitskiy** Ukraine

59C3 **Khodorov** Ukraine
82A1 **Khodzhent** Tajikistan
84B1 **Kholm** Afghan
76D3 **Khong** Laos
91B4 **Khonj** Iran
69F2 **Khor** Russian Fed
91A3 **Khoramshahr** Iran
91B5 **Khōr Duwayhin** *B* UAE
84C1 **Khorog** Tajikistan
90A3 **Khorramābad** Iran
90C3 **Khosf** Iran
84B2 **Khost** Pak
60C4 **Khotin** Ukraine
12C2 **Khotol** *Mt* USA
60C3 **Khoyniku** Belorussia
63F2 **Khrebet Dzhugdzhur** *Mts* Russian Fed
90C2 **Khrebet Kopet Dag** *Mts* Turkmenistan
64H3 **Khrebet Pay-khoy** *Mts* Russian Fed
82C1 **Khrebet Tarbagatay** *Mts* Kazakhstan
63E2 **Khrebet Tukuringra** *Mts* Russian Fed
86B2 **Khulna** Bang
84D1 **Khunjerab** *P* China/India
90B3 **Khunsar** Iran
91A4 **Khurays** S Arabia
86B2 **Khurda** India
84D3 **Khurja** India
84C2 **Khushab** Pak
94B2 **Khushnīyah** Syria
59C3 **Khust** Ukraine
99C1 **Khuwei** Sudan
85B3 **Khuzdar** Pak
90D3 **Khvāf** Iran
61G3 **Khvalynsk** Russian Fed
90C3 **Khvor** Iran
91B4 **Khvormūj** Iran
93D2 **Khvoy** Iran
84C1 **Khwaja Muhammad** *Mts* Afghan
84C2 **Khyber P** Afghan/Pak
99C3 **Kiambi** Zaïre
19A3 **Kiamichi** *R* USA
12B1 **Kiana** USA
98B3 **Kibangou** Congo
99D3 **Kibaya** Tanz
98C3 **Kibombo** Zaïre
99D3 **Kibondo** Tanz
99D3 **Kibungu** Rwanda
55B2 **Kičevo** Macedonia, Yugos
5G4 **Kicking Horse P** Can
97C3 **Kidal** Mali
43C3 **Kidderminster** Eng
97A3 **Kidira** Sen
110C1 **Kidnappers,C** NZ
56C2 **Kiel** Germany
59C2 **Kielce** Pol
56C2 **Kieler Bucht** *B* Germany
Kiev = Kiyev
80E2 **Kifab** Uzbekistan
97A3 **Kiffa** Maur
89H8 **Kigali** Rwanda
12A2 **Kigluaik Mts** USA
99C3 **Kigoma** Tanz
75B2 **Kii-sanchi** *Mts* Japan
74C4 **Kii-suido** *B* Japan
54B1 **Kikinda** Serbia, Yugos
55B3 **Kikládhes** *Is* Greece
71F4 **Kikori** PNG
98B3 **Kikwit** Zaïre
21C4 **Kilauea Crater** *Mt* Hawaiian Is
4C3 **Kilbuck Mts** USA
74B2 **Kilchu** N Korea
109D1 **Kilcoy** Aust
45C2 **Kildare** County, Irish Rep
45C2 **Kildare** Irish Rep
19B3 **Kilgore** USA
99D3 **Kilifi** Kenya
99D3 **Kilimanjaro** *Mt* Tanz
99D3 **Kilindoni** Tanz
92C2 **Kilis** Turk
45B2 **Kilkee** Irish Rep
45C2 **Kilkenny** County, Irish Rep
45C2 **Kilkenny** Irish Rep
45B2 **Kilkieran B** Irish Rep
55B2 **Kilkís** Greece
45B1 **Killala B** Irish Rep
45B2 **Killaloe** Irish Rep
109D1 **Killarney** Aust
41B3 **Killarney** Irish Rep
19A3 **Killeen** USA
12D1 **Killik** *R* USA
44B3 **Killin** Scot
55B3 **Killíni** *Mt* Greece
45B1 **Killybegs** Irish Rep
42B2 **Kilmarnock** Scot
61H2 **Kil'mez** Russian Fed
99D3 **Kilosa** Tanz
41B3 **Kilrush** Irish Rep
99C3 **Kilwa** Zaïre
99D3 **Kilwa Kisiwani** Tanz
99D3 **Kilwa Kivinje** Tanz
108A2 **Kimba** Aust
12F2 **Kimball,Mt** USA
13D3 **Kimberley** Can
101F1 **Kimberley** S Africa
106B2 **Kimberley Plat** Aust
74B2 **Kimch'aek** N Korea
74B3 **Kimch'ŏn** S Korea
55B3 **Kími** Greece
60E2 **Kimry** Russian Fed
70C3 **Kinabalu** *Mt* Malay
78D1 **Kinabatangan** *R* Malay
14B2 **Kincardine** Can
13B1 **Kincolith** Can
19B3 **Kinder** USA
13F2 **Kindersley** Can
97A3 **Kindia** Guinea
98C3 **Kindu** Zaïre
61H3 **Kinel'** Russian Fed
61F2 **Kineshma** Russian Fed
109D1 **Kingaroy** Aust
21A2 **King City** USA
5F4 **Kingcome Inlet** Can
7C4 **King George Is** Can
107D4 **King I** Aust
13B2 **King I** Can
106B2 **King Leopold Range** *Mts* Aust
9B3 **Kingman** USA
98C3 **Kingombe** Zaïre
108A2 **Kingoonya** Aust
22C2 **Kingsburg** USA
21B2 **Kings Canyon Nat Pk** USA
108A3 **Kingscote** Aust
106B2 **King Sd** Aust
112C2 **King Sejong** *Base* Ant
14A1 **Kingsford** USA
17B1 **Kingsland** USA
43E3 **King's Lynn** Eng
16C2 **Kings Park** USA
8B2 **Kings Peak** *Mt* USA
107C4 **Kingston** Aust
7C5 **Kingston** Can
25E3 **Kingston** Jamaica
15D2 **Kingston** New York, USA
111A3 **Kingston** NZ
27E4 **Kingstown** St Vincent
9D4 **Kingsville** USA
44B3 **Kingussie** Scot
4J3 **King William I** Can
100B4 **King William's Town** S Africa
98B3 **Kinkala** Congo
39G7 **Kinna** Sweden
44D3 **Kinnairds Head** *Pt* Scot
75B1 **Kinomoto** Japan
44C3 **Kinross** Scot
45B3 **Kinsale** Irish Rep
98B3 **Kinshasa** Zaïre
78D3 **Kintap** Indon
42B2 **Kintyre** *Pen* Scot
13D1 **Kinuso** Can
99D2 **Kinyeti** *Mt* Sudan
55B3 **Kiparissía** Greece
55B3 **Kiparissiakós Kólpos** *G* Greece
15C1 **Kipawa,L** Can
99D3 **Kipili** Tanz
12B3 **Kipnuk** USA
45C2 **Kippure** *Mt* Irish Rep
100B2 **Kipushi** Zaïre
63C2 **Kirensk** Russian Fed
65J5 **Kirgizia** Republic, Asia
82B1 **Kirgizskiy Khrebet** *Mts* Kirgizia
98B3 **Kiri** Zaïre
105G4 **Kiribati** *Is* Pacific O
92B2 **Kırıkkale** Turk
99D3 **Kirinyaga** *Mt* Kenya
60D2 **Kirishi** Russian Fed
85B3 **Kirithar Range** *Mts* Pak
55C3 **Kirkağaç** Turk
90A2 **Kirk Bulāg Dāgh** *Mt* Iran
42C2 **Kirkby** Eng
44C3 **Kirkcaldy** Scot
42B2 **Kirkcudbright** Scot
38K5 **Kirkenes** Nor
7B5 **Kirkland Lake** Can
112A **Kirkpatrick,Mt** Ant
10A2 **Kirksville** USA
93D2 **Kirkūk** Iraq
44C2 **Kirkwall** Scot
18B2 **Kirkwood** USA
60D3 **Kirov** Russian Fed
61G2 **Kirov** Russian Fed
93D1 **Kirovakan** Armenia
61J2 **Kirovgrad** Russian Fed
60D4 **Kirovograd** Ukraine
61H2 **Kirs** Russian Fed
92B2 **Kirşehir** Turk
56C2 **Kiruna** Sweden
75B1 **Kiryū** Japan
98C2 **Kisangani** Zaïre
75B1 **Kisarazu** Japan
86B1 **Kishanganj** India
85C3 **Kishangarh** India
60C4 **Kishinev** Moldavia
75B2 **Kishiwada** Japan
99D3 **Kisii** Kenya
99D3 **Kisiju** Tanz
59B3 **Kiskunhalas** Hung
65F5 **Kislovodsk** Russian Fed
99E3 **Kismaayo** Somalia
75B1 **Kiso-sammyaku** *Mts* Japan
97A4 **Kissidougou** Guinea
17B2 **Kissimmee,L** USA
99D3 **Kisumu** Kenya
59C3 **Kisvárda** Hung
97B3 **Kita** Mali
65H6 **Kitab** Uzbekistan
75C1 **Kitakata** Japan
74C4 **Kita-Kyūshū** Japan
99D2 **Kitale** Kenya
69G4 **Kitalo** *I* Japan
74E2 **Kitami** Japan
7B5 **Kitchener** Can
99D2 **Kitgum** Uganda
55B3 **Kíthira** *I* Greece
55B3 **Kíthnos** *I* Greece
94A1 **Kiti,C** Cyprus
4H3 **Kitikmeot** *Region* Can
5F4 **Kitimat** Can
38K5 **Kitnen** *R* Fin
75A2 **Kitsuki** Japan
15C2 **Kittanning** USA
38J5 **Kittilä** Fin
99D3 **Kitunda** Tanz
13B1 **Kitwanga** Can
100B2 **Kitwe** Zambia
57C3 **Kitzbühel** Austria
47E1 **Kitzbühler Alpen** *Mts* Austria
57C3 **Kitzingen** Germany
98C3 **Kiumbi** Zaïre
12B1 **Kivalina** USA
59D2 **Kivercy** Ukraine
99C3 **Kivu,L** Zaïre/Rwanda
4B3 **Kiwalik** USA
60D3 **Kiyev** Ukraine
61J2 **Kizel** Russian Fed
92C2 **Kizil** *R* Turk
80D2 **Kizyl-Arvat** Turkmenistan
90B2 **Kizyl-Atrek** Turkmenistan
57C2 **Kladno** Czech
57C3 **Klagenfurt** Austria
60B2 **Klaipēda** Lithuania
8A2 **Klamath** USA
20B2 **Klamath** *R* USA
8A2 **Klamath Falls** USA
20B2 **Klamath Mts** USA
57C3 **Klatovy** Czech
12H3 **Klawak** USA
94B1 **Kleiat** Leb
101G1 **Klerksdorp** S Africa
60E2 **Klin** Russian Fed
58B1 **Klintehamn** Sweden
60D3 **Klintsy** Russian Fed
52C2 **Ključ** Bosnia & Herzegovina, Yugos
59B2 **Kłodzko** Pol
12G2 **Klondike** *R* Can/USA
4D3 **Klondike Plat** Can/USA
59B3 **Klosterneuburg** Austria
12G2 **Kluane** *R* Can
12G2 **Kluane L** Can
12G2 **Kluane Nat Pk** Can
59B2 **Kluczbork** Pol
12G3 **Klukwan** USA
12E2 **Klutina L** USA
12E2 **Knight I** USA
43C3 **Knighton** Wales
52C2 **Knin** Croatia
106A4 **Knob,C** Aust
46B1 **Knokke-Heist** Belg
112C9 **Knox Coast** Ant
11B3 **Knoxville** Tennessee, USA
6H3 **Knud Ramsussens Land** *Region* Greenland
78B3 **Koba** Indon
6F3 **Kobbermirebugt** Greenland
74D4 **Kobe** Japan
56C1 **København** Den
57B2 **Koblenz** Germany
60B3 **Kobrin** Russian Fed
71E4 **Kobroör** *I* Indon
12C1 **Kobuk** *R* USA
54B2 **Kočani** Macedonia, Yugos
76C3 **Ko Chang** *I* Thai
86B1 **Koch Bihār** India
47D1 **Kochel** Germany
6C3 **Koch I** Can
87B3 **Kochi** India
74C4 **Kōchi** Japan
12D3 **Kodiak** USA
12D3 **Kodiak I** USA
87B2 **Kodikkarai** India
99D2 **Kodok** Sudan
100A3 **Koes** Namibia
101G1 **Koffiefontein** S Africa
97B4 **Koforidua** Ghana
74D3 **Kōfu** Japan
75B1 **Koga** Japan
39G7 **Køge** Den
84C2 **Kohat** Pak
84B2 **Koh-i-Baba** *Mts* Afghan
84B1 **Koh-i-Hisar** *Mts* Afghan
84B2 **Koh-i-Khurd** *Mt* Afghan
86C1 **Kohīma** India
84B1 **Koh-i-Mazar** *Mt* Afghan
84B3 **Kohlu** Pak
60C2 **Kohtla Järve** Estonia
75B1 **Koide** Japan
12F2 **Koidern** Can
77A4 **Koihoa** *Is* Nicobar Is
74B4 **Kōje-do** *I* S Korea
65H4 **Kokchetav** Kazakhstan
39J6 **Kokemaki** *L* Fin
38J6 **Kokkola** Fin
107D1 **Kokoda** PNG
14A2 **Kokomo** USA
71E4 **Kokonau** Indon
65K5 **Kokpekty** Kazakhstan
7D4 **Koksoak** *R* Can

100B4 **Kokstad** S Africa
76C3 **Ko Kut** *I* Thai
38L5 **Kola** Russian Fed
71D4 **Kolaka** Indon
77B4 **Ko Lanta** *I* Thai
87B3 **Kollam** India
87B2 **Kolār** India
87B2 **Kolār Gold Fields** India
97A3 **Kolda** Sen
39F7 **Kolding** Den
87A1 **Kolhāpur** India
12C3 **Koliganek** USA
59B2 **Kolín** Czech
57B2 **Köln** Germany
58B2 **Kolo** Pol
58B2 **Kolobrzeg** Pol
97B3 **Kolokani** Mali
60E2 **Kolomna** Russian Fed
60C4 **Kolomyya** Ukraine
65K4 **Kolpashevo** Russian Fed
55C3 **Kólpos Merabéllou** *B* Greece
55B2 **Kólpos Singitikós** *G* Greece
55B2 **Kólpos Strimonikós** *G* Greece
55B2 **Kólpos Toronaíos** *G* Greece
38L5 **Kol'skiy Poluostrov** *Pen* Russian Fed
38G6 **Kolvereid** Nor
100B2 **Kolwezi** Zaïre
1C7 **Kolyma** *R* Russian Fed
54B2 **Kom** *Mt* Bulg/Serbia, Yugos
99D2 **Koma** Eth
97D3 **Komaduga Gana** *R* Nig
59B3 **Komárno** Czech
101H1 **Komati** *R* S Africa
74D3 **Komatsu** Japan
75A2 **Komatsushima** Japan
64G3 **Komi Respublika,** Russian Fed
70C4 **Komodo** *I* Indon
71E4 **Komoran** *I* Indon
75B1 **Komoro** Japan
55C2 **Komotiní** Greece
76D3 **Kompong Cham** Camb
76C3 **Kompong Chhnang** *Mts* Camb
77C3 **Kompong Som** Camb
76C3 **Kompong Thom** Camb
76D3 **Kompong Trabek** Camb
63F2 **Komsomol'sk na Amure** Russian Fed
65H4 **Konda** *R* Russian Fed
99D3 **Kondoa** Tanz
87B1 **Kondukūr** India
6G3 **Kong Christian IX Land** *Region* Greenland
6F3 **Kong Frederik VI Kyst** *Mts* Greenland
64C2 **Kong Karls Land** *Is* Barents S
78D2 **Kongkemul** *Mt* Indon
98C3 **Kongolo** Zaïre
39F7 **Kongsberg** Den
39G6 **Kongsvinger** Nor
Königsberg = Kaliningrad
58B2 **Konin** Pol
54A2 **Konjic** Bosnia & Herzegovina, Yugos
61F1 **Konosha** Russian Fed
75B1 **Konosu** Japan
60D3 **Konotop** Ukraine
59C2 **Końskie** Pol
49D2 **Konstanz** Germany
97C3 **Kontagora** Nig
76D3 **Kontum** Viet
92B2 **Konya** Turk
13D3 **Kootenay** *R* Can
85C5 **Kopargaon** India
6J3 **Kópasker** Iceland
38A2 **Kópavogur** Iceland
52B1 **Koper** Slovenia
80D2 **Kopet Dag** *Mts* Iran/Turkmenistan
61K2 **Kopeysk** Russian Fed
77C4 **Ko Phangan** *I* Thai
77B4 **Ko Phuket** *I* Thai
39H7 **Köping** Sweden
87B1 **Koppal** India
52C1 **Koprivnica** Croatia
85B4 **Korangi** Pak
87C1 **Koraput** India
86A2 **Korba** India
57B2 **Korbach** Germany
4B3 **Korbuk** *R* USA
55B2 **Korçë** Alb
52C2 **Korčula** *I* Croatia
72E2 **Korea B** China/Korea
74B4 **Korea Str** S Korea/Japan
59D2 **Korec** Ukraine
92B1 **Körğlu Tepesi** *Mt* Turk
97B4 **Korhogo** Ivory Coast
85B4 **Kori Creek** India
55B3 **Korinthiakós Kólpos** *G* Greece
55B3 **Kórinthos** Greece
74E3 **Kōriyama** Japan
61K3 **Korkino** Russian Fed
92B2 **Korkuteli** Turk
82C1 **Korla** China
52C2 **Kornat** *I* Croatia
60D5 **Köroğlu Tepesi** *Mt* Turk
99D3 **Korogwe** Tanz
108B3 **Koroit** Aust
71E3 **Koror** Palau Is, Pacific O
59C3 **Körös** *R* Hung
60C3 **Korosten** Ukraine
95A3 **Koro Toro** Chad
12B3 **Korovin** *I* USA
69G2 **Korsakov** Russian Fed
39G7 **Korsør** Den
46B1 **Kortrijk** Belg
55C3 **Kós** *I* Greece
77C4 **Ko Samui** *I* Thai
58B2 **Koscierzyna** Pol
107D4 **Kosciusko** *Mt* Aust
12H3 **Kosciusko I** USA
74B4 **Koshikijima-retto** *I* Japan
59C3 **Košice** Czech
74B3 **Kosong** N Korea
54B2 **Kosovo** Aut Republic, Serbia, Yugos
97B4 **Kossou** *L* Ivory Coast
101G1 **Koster** S Africa
99D1 **Kosti** Sudan
59D2 **Kostopol'** Ukraine
61F2 **Kostroma** Russian Fed
56C2 **Kostrzyn** Pol
39H8 **Koszalin** Pol
85D3 **Kota** India
78A4 **Kotaagung** Indon
78C3 **Kotabaharu** Indon
78D3 **Kotabaru** Indon
77C4 **Kota Bharu** Malay
78A3 **Kotabum** Indon
84C2 **Kot Addu** Pak
78D1 **Kota Kinabulu** Malay
87C1 **Kotapad** India
61G2 **Kotel'nich** Russian Fed
61F4 **Kotel'nikovo** Russian Fed
39K6 **Kotka** Fin
64F3 **Kotlas** Russian Fed
12B2 **Kotlik** USA
54A2 **Kotor** Montenegro, Yugos
60C4 **Kotovsk** Ukraine
85B3 **Kotri** Pak
87C1 **Kottagūdem** India
87B3 **Kottayam** India
98C2 **Kotto** *R* CAR
87B2 **Kottūru** India
12B1 **Kotzebue** USA
4B3 **Kotzebue Sd** USA
97C3 **Kouande** Benin
98C2 **Kouango** CAR
97B3 **Koudougou** Burkina
98B3 **Koulamoutou** Gabon
97B3 **Koulikoro** Mali
97B3 **Koupéla** Burkina
33G2 **Kourou** French Guiana
97B3 **Kouroussa** Guinea
98B1 **Kousséri** Cam
39K6 **Kouvola** Fin
38L5 **Kovdor** Russian Fed
60B3 **Kovel'** Ukraine
Kovno = Kaunas
61F2 **Kovrov** Russian Fed
61F3 **Kovylkino** Russian Fed
60E1 **Kovzha** *R* Russian Fed
77C4 **Ko Way** *I* Thai
73C5 **Kowloon** Hong Kong
84B2 **Kowt-e-Ashrow** Afghan
92A2 **Köycegğiz** Turk
38L5 **Koydor** Russian Fed
87A1 **Koyna Res** India
12B2 **Koyuk** USA
12B1 **Koyuk** *R* USA
12C2 **Koyukuk** USA
12C1 **Koyukuk** *R* USA
92C2 **Kozan** Turk
55B2 **Kozańi** Greece
87B2 **Kozhikode** India
61G2 **Koz'modemyansk** Russian Fed
75B2 **Kōzu-shima** *I* Japan
39F7 **Kragerø** Nor
54B2 **Kragujevac** Serbia, Yugos
77B3 **Kra,Isthmus of** Burma/Malay
Krakatau = Rakata
94C1 **Krak des Chevaliers** *Hist Site* Syria
Kraków = Cracow
54B2 **Kraljevo** Serbia, Yugos
60E4 **Kramatorsk** Ukraine
38H6 **Kramfors** Sweden
52B1 **Kranj** Slovenia
61G1 **Krasavino** Russian Fed
64G2 **Krasino** Russian Fed
59C2 **Kraśnik** Pol
61G3 **Krasnoarmeysk** Russian Fed
60E5 **Krasnodar** Russian Fed
61J2 **Krasnokamsk** Russian Fed
61K2 **Krasnotur'insk** Russian Fed
61J2 **Krasnoufimsk** Russian Fed
61J3 **Krasnousol'-skiy** Russian Fed
65G3 **Krasnovishersk** Russian Fed
65G5 **Krasnovodsk** Turkmenistan
63B2 **Krasnoyarsk** Russian Fed
59C2 **Krasnystaw** Pol
61G3 **Krasnyy Kut** Russian Fed
60E4 **Krasnyy Luch** Ukraine
61G4 **Krasnyy Yar** Russian Fed
76D3 **Kratie** Camb
6E2 **Kraulshavn** Greenland
56B2 **Krefeld** Germany
60D4 **Kremenchug** Ukraine
60D4 **Kremenchugskoye Vodokhranilische** *Res* Ukraine
59D2 **Kremenets** Ukraine
98A2 **Kribi** Cam
60D3 **Krichev** Belorussia
47E1 **Krimml** Austria
87B1 **Krishna** *R* India
87B2 **Krishnagiri** India
86B2 **Krishnangar** India
39F7 **Kristiansand** Nor
39G7 **Kristianstad** Sweden
64B3 **Kristiansund** Nor
39G7 **Kristinehamn** Sweden
38J6 **Kristiinankaupunki** Fin
55B3 **Kríti** *I* Greece
60D4 **Krivoy Rog** Ukraine
52B1 **Krk** *I* Croatia
6G3 **Kronpris Frederik Bjerge** *Mts* Greenland
39K7 **Kronshtadt** Russian Fed
101G1 **Kroonstad** S Africa
65F5 **Kropotkin** Russian Fed
101G1 **Krugersdorp** S Africa
78A4 **Krui** Indon
55A2 **Kruje** Alb
58D2 **Krupki** Belorussia
12B1 **Krusenstern,C** USA
54B2 **Kruševac** Serbia, Yugos
39K7 **Krustpils** Latvia
12G3 **Kruzof I** USA
65E5 **Krym** *Pen* Ukraine
60E5 **Krymsk** Russian Fed
58B2 **Krzyz** Pol
96C1 **Ksar El Boukhari** Alg
96B1 **Ksar el Kebir** Mor
70A3 **Kuala** Indon
77C5 **Kuala Dungun** Malay
77C4 **Kuala Kerai** Malay
77C5 **Kuala Kubu Baharu** Malay
77C5 **Kuala Lipis** Malay
77C5 **Kuala Lumpur** Malay
77C4 **Kuala Trengganu** Malay
78D1 **Kuamut** Malay
74A2 **Kuandian** China
77C5 **Kuantan** Malay
93E1 **Kuba** Azerbaijan
71F4 **Kubar** PNG
78C2 **Kuching** Malay
70C3 **Kudat** Malay
78C4 **Kudus** Indon
61H2 **Kudymkar** Russian Fed
57C3 **Kufstein** Austria
90C3 **Kuh Duren** *Upland* Iran
91C4 **Kūh e Bazmān** *Mt* Iran
90B3 **Kūh-e Dinar** *Mt* Iran
90C2 **Kūh-e-Hazār Masjed** *Mts* Iran
91C4 **Kūh-e Jebāl Barez** *Mts* Iran
90B3 **Kūh-e Karkas** *Mts* Iran
91C4 **Kuh-e Laleh Zar** *Mt* Iran
90A2 **Kūh-e Sahand** *Mt* Iran
91D4 **Kuh e Taftān** *Mt* Iran
90A2 **Kūhhaye Sabalan** *Mts* Iran
90A3 **Kūhhā-ye Zāgros** *Mts* Iran
38K6 **Kuhmo** Fin
90B3 **Kūhpāyeh** Iran
90C3 **Kūhpāyeh** *Mt* Iran
91C4 **Kūh ye Bashākerd** *Mts* Iran
90A2 **Kūh ye Sabalan** *Mt* Iran
100A3 **Kuibis** Namibia
4B4 **Kuigillingok** USA
100A2 **Kuito** Angola
12H3 **Kuiu I** USA
74E2 **Kuji** Japan
75A2 **Kuju-san** *Mt* Japan
12C3 **Kukaklek L** USA
54B2 **Kukës** Alb
77C5 **Kukup** Malay
91C4 **Kūl** *R* Iran
55C3 **Kula** Turk
61J4 **Kulakshi** Kazakhstan
99D2 **Kulal,Mt** Kenya

55B2 **Kulata** Bulg
60B2 **Kuldīga** Latvia
61H4 **Kul'sary** Kazakhstan
84D2 **Kulu** India
92B2 **Kulu** Turk
65J4 **Kulunda** Russian Fed
108B2 **Kulwin** Aust
61G5 **Kuma** *R* Russian Fed
75B1 **Kumagaya** Japan
78C3 **Kumai** Indon
74C4 **Kumamoto** Japan
75B2 **Kumano** Japan
54B2 **Kumanovo** Macedonia, Yugos
63E2 **Kumara** China
97B4 **Kumasi** Ghana
98A2 **Kumba** Cam
87B2 **Kumbakonam** India
61J3 **Kumertau** Russian Fed
74B3 **Kŭmhwa** S Korea
39H7 **Kumla** Sweden
87A2 **Kumta** India
82C1 **Kümüx** China
84C2 **Kunar** *R* Afghan
39K7 **Kunda** Estonia
85C4 **Kundla** India
84B1 **Kunduz** Afghan
89F9 **Kunene** *R* Angola
39G7 **Kungsbacka** Sweden
61J2 **Kungur** Russian Fed
76B1 **Kunhing** Burma
82B2 **Kunlun Shan** *Mts* China
73A4 **Kunming** China
74B3 **Kunsan** S Korea
38K6 **Kuopio** Fin
52C1 **Kupa** *R* Croatia/Bosnia & Herzegovina, Yugos
106B2 **Kupang** Indon
107D2 **Kupiano** PNG
12H3 **Kupreanof I** USA
60E4 **Kupyansk** Ukraine
82C1 **Kuqa** China
75B1 **Kurabe** Japan
74C4 **Kurashiki** Japan
75A1 **Kurayoshi** Japan
54C2 **Kŭrdzhali** Bulg
74C4 **Kure** Japan
60B2 **Kuressaare** Estonia
63A1 **Kureyka** *R* Russian Fed
65H4 **Kurgan** Russian Fed
88K6 **Kuria Muria Is** Oman
38J6 **Kurikka** Fin
Kuril Is = Kuril'skoye Osrova
69H2 **Kuril'skiye Ostrova** Russian Fed
87B1 **Kurnool** India
75C1 **Kuroiso** Japan
111B2 **Kurow** NZ
109D2 **Kurri Kurri** Aust
60E3 **Kursk** Russian Fed
Kurskiy Zaliv = Courland Lagoon
68A2 **Kuruktag** *R* China
100B3 **Kuruman** S Africa
74C4 **Kurume** Japan
87C3 **Kurunegala** Sri Lanka
65K5 **Kurunktag** *R* China
61J2 **Kusa** Russian Fed
55C3 **Kuşadasi Körfezi** *B* Turk
55C2 **Kus Golü** *L* Turk
74D4 **Kushimoto** Japan
74E2 **Kushiro** Japan
86B2 **Kushtia** Bang
61H3 **Kushum** *R* Kazakhstan
80E2 **Kushra** Afgan
65G4 **Kushva** Russian Fed
12B2 **Kuskokwim** *R* USA
12B3 **Kuskokwim B** USA
12C2 **Kuskokwim Mts** USA
86A1 **Kusma** Nepal
74E2 **Kussharo-ko** *L* Japan
65H4 **Kustanay** Kazakhstan
92A2 **Kütahya** Turk
78D3 **Kutai** *R* Indon
59B3 **Kutná Hora** Czech
58B2 **Kutno** Pol
98B3 **Kutu** Zaïre
86C2 **Kutubdia I** Bang
98C1 **Kutum** Sudan
7D4 **Kuujjuaq** Can
7C4 **Kuujjuarapik** Can
38K5 **Kuusamo** Fin
61J3 **Kuvandyk** Russian Fed
93E4 **Kuwait** Kuwait
80C3 **Kuwait** Sheikdom, S W Asia
75B1 **Kuwana** Japan
65J4 **Kuybyshev** Russian Fed
61G3 **Kuybyshevskoye Vodokhranilishche** *Res* Russian Fed
63C2 **Kuytun** Russian Fed
60E5 **Kuzey Anadolu Daglari** *Mts* Turk
61G3 **Kuznetsk** Russian Fed
38J4 **Kvaenangen** *Sd* Nor
12C3 **Kvichak** USA
12C3 **Kvichak** *R* USA
12C3 **Kvichak B** USA
38G5 **Kvigtind** *Mt* Nor
38H5 **Kvikkjokk** Sweden
99D3 **Kwale** Kenya
74B3 **Kwangju** S Korea
98B3 **Kwango** *R* Zaïre
100B2 **Kwekwe** Zim
12B2 **Kwethluk** USA
12B2 **Kwethluk** *R* USA
58B2 **Kwidzyn** Pol
71E4 **Kwoka** *Mt* Indon
108C3 **Kyabram** Aust
76B2 **Kyaikkami** Burma
76B2 **Kyaikto** Burma
68C1 **Kyakhta** Russian Fed
108A2 **Kyancutta** Aust
76B1 **Kyaukme** Burma
76B1 **Kyauk-padaung** Burma
76A2 **Kyaukpyu** Burma
40B2 **Kyle of Lochalsh** Scot
46D1 **Kyll** *R* Germany
108B3 **Kyneton** Aust
99D2 **Kyoga** *L* Uganda
109D1 **Kyogle** Aust
74B3 **Kyŏngju** S Korea
74D3 **Kyoto** Japan
65H4 **Kyshtym** Russian Fed
74C4 **Kyūshū** *I* Japan
104E3 **Kyushu-Palau Ridge** Pacific O
54B2 **Kyustendil** Bulg
68B1 **Kyzyl** Russian Fed
65H5 **Kyzylkum** *Desert* Uzbekistan
65H5 **Kzyl Orda** Kazakhstan

L

99E2 **Laascaanood** Somalia
46E1 **Laasphe** Germany
99E1 **Laasqoray** Somalia
33E1 **La Asunción** Ven
96A2 **Laâyoune** Mor
23A1 **La Barca** Mexico
97A3 **Labé** Guinea
59B2 **Labe** *R* Czech
15D1 **Labelle** Can
17B2 **La Belle** USA
12G2 **Laberge,L** Can
78D1 **Labi** Brunei
13E2 **la Biche,L** Can
61F5 **Labinsk** Russian Fed
94C1 **Laboué** Leb
34C2 **Laboulaye** Arg
7D4 **Labrador** *Region* Can
7D4 **Labrador City** Can
7E4 **Labrador S** Greenland/Can
33E5 **Lábrea** Brazil
78D1 **Labuan** *I* Malay
78B4 **Labuhan** Indon
76A2 **Labutta** Burma
65H3 **Labytnangi** Russian Fed
7C4 **Lac á L'eau Claire** Can
46B2 **La Capelle** France
34C2 **La Carlota** Arg
79B3 **La Carlota** Phil
12J1 **Lac Belot** *L* Can
7C4 **Lac Bienville** *L* Can
83B4 **Laccadive Is** India
47B2 **Lac d'Annecy** *L* France
4G3 **Lac de Gras** *L* Can
47B1 **Lac de Joux** *L* Switz
47B1 **Lac de Neuchâtel** *L* Switz
23A2 **Lac de Patzcuaro** *L* Mexico
23A2 **Lac de Sayula** *L* Mexico
4F3 **Lac des Bois** *L* Can
47A2 **Lac du Bourget** *L* France
25D3 **La Ceiba** Honduras
108A3 **Lacepede B** Aust
48C2 **La Châtre** France
47B1 **La-Chaux-de-Fonds** Switz
94B3 **Lachish** *Hist Site* Israel
107D4 **Lachlan** *R* Aust
32B2 **La Chorrera** Panama
15D1 **Lachute** Can
7D4 **Lac Joseph** *L* Can
15C2 **Lackawanna** USA
5G4 **Lac la Biche** Can
4G3 **Lac la Martre** *L* Can
5H4 **Lac la Ronge** *L* Can
52A1 **Lac Léman** *L* Switz/France
10C1 **Lac Manouane** *L* Can
15D1 **Lac Megantic** Can
7C4 **Lac Mistassini** *L* Can
13E2 **Lacombe** Can
15D2 **Laconia** USA
50A1 **La Coruña** Spain
10A2 **La Crosse** USA
9C3 **La Cruces** USA
7A4 **Lac Seul** *L* Can
18B2 **La Cygne** USA
84D2 **Ladākh Range** India
85C3 **Lādnūn** India
73B5 **Ladong** China
60D1 **Ladozhskoye Ozero** *L* Ukraine
6B2 **Lady Ann Str** Can
109C4 **Lady Barron** Aust
101G1 **Ladybrand** S Africa
13C3 **Ladysmith** Can
101G1 **Ladysmith** S Africa
71F4 **Lae** PNG
76C3 **Laem Ngop** Thai
56C1 **Laesø** *I* Den
10B2 **Lafayette** Indiana, USA
11A3 **Lafayette** Louisiana, USA
46B2 **La Fère** France
46B2 **La-Ferté-sous-Jouarre** France
97C4 **Lafia** Nig
97C4 **Lafiagi** Nig
48B2 **La Flèche** France
96C1 **La Galite** *I* Tunisia
56C1 **Lagan** *R* Sweden
31D4 **Lagarto** Brazil
96C1 **Laghouat** Alg
35C2 **Lagoa de Araruama** Brazil
29F2 **Lagoa dos Patos** *Lg* Brazil
35C2 **Lagoa Feia** Brazil
32B4 **Lago Agrio** Ecuador
35C1 **Lagoa Juparanã** *L* Brazil
29D2 **Lagoa mar Chiguita** *L* Arg
29F2 **Lagoa Mirim** *L* Brazil/Urug
29B6 **Lago Argentino** *L* Arg
29B5 **Lago Buenos Aries** *L* Arg
29B5 **Lago Cochrane** *L* Arg/Chile
29C5 **Lago Colhué Huapi** *L* Arg
24B2 **Lago de Chapala** *L* Mexico
32A2 **Lago de Chiriqui** *L* Panama
23A2 **Lago de Cuitzeo** *L* Mexico
29B3 **Lago de la Laja** *L* Chile
53A2 **Lago del Coghinas** *L* Sardegna
32C2 **Lago de Maracaibo** *L* Ven
25D3 **Lago de Nicaragua** *L* Nic
32A1 **Lago de Perlas** *L* Nic
52B2 **Lago di Bolsena** *L* Italy
52B2 **Lago di Bracciano** *L* Italy
52A1 **Lago di Como** *L* Italy
47D2 **Lago d'Idro** *L* Italy
52B1 **Lago di Garda** *L* Italy
47C2 **Lago di Lecco** *L* Italy
47C2 **Lago di Lugano** *L* Italy
47D2 **Lago d'Iseo** *L* Italy
47C2 **Lago d'Orta** *L* Italy
29B5 **Lago General Carrera** *L* Chile
52A1 **Lago Maggiore** *L* Italy
29C5 **Lago Musters** *L* Arg
48B3 **Lagon** France
29B4 **Lago Nahuel Haupi** *L* Arg
29B5 **Lago O'Higgins** *L* Chile
53A2 **Lago Omodeo** *L* Sardegna
30C2 **Lago Poopó** *L* Bol
29B4 **Lago Ranco** *L* Chile
32D6 **Lago Rogaguado** *L* Bol
97C4 **Lagos** Nig
50A2 **Lagos** Port
29B5 **Lago San Martin** *L* Arg/Chile
24B2 **Lagos de Moreno** Mexico
30C2 **Lago Titicaca** Bol/Peru
29B5 **Lago Viedma** *L* Arg
8B2 **La Grande** USA
106B2 **Lagrange** Aust
11B3 **La Grange** Georgia, USA
14A3 **La Grange** Kentucky, USA
19A4 **La Grange** Texas, USA
33E2 **La Gran Sabana** *Mts* Ven
47B2 **La Grave** France
48B3 **Lagronño** Spain
34A3 **Laguna Aluminé** *L* Arg
21B3 **Laguna Beach** USA
34C3 **Laguna Colorada Grande** *L* Arg
79B3 **Laguna de Bay** *Lg* Phil
25D3 **Laguna de Caratasca** *Lg* Honduras
25D4 **Laguna de Chiriqui** *L* Panama
25D3 **Laguna de Managua** *L* Nic
25D3 **Laguna de Nicaragua** *L* Nic
26A4 **Laguna de Perlas** *Lg* Nic
23B1 **Laguna de Pueblo Viejo** *L* Mexico
24C2 **Laguna de Tamiahua** *Lg* Mexico
25C3 **Laguna de Términos** *Lg* Mexico
23A1 **Laguna de Yuriria** *L* Mexico
23B1 **Laguna le Altamira** Mexico

24C2 **Laguna Madre** *Lg* Mexico
34C2 **Laguna Mar Chiquita** *L* Arg
29B4 **Laguna Nahuel Huapi** *L* Arg
34C2 **Laguna Paiva** Arg
29B4 **Laguna Ranco** Chile
9C4 **Laguna Seca** Mexico
23B1 **Laguna Tortugas** *L* Mexico
70C3 **Lahad Datu** Malay
78A3 **Lahat** Indon
38J6 **Lahia** Fin
90B2 **Lāhījān** Iran
46D1 **Lahn** *R* Germany
46D1 **Lahnstein** Germany
84C2 **Lahore** Pak
39K6 **Lahti** Fin
23A2 **La Huerta** Mexico
98B2 **Lai** Chad
73B5 **Laibin** China
76C1 **Lai Chau** Viet
100B4 **Laingsburg** S Africa
44B2 **Lairg** Scot
78A3 **Lais** Indon
79C4 **Lais** Phil
72E2 **Laiyang** China
72D2 **Laizhou Wan** *B* China
34A3 **Laja** *R* Chile
30F4 **Lajes** Brazil
22D4 **La Jolla** USA
9C3 **La Junta** USA
109C2 **Lake Cargelligo** Aust
11A3 **Lake Charles** USA
17B1 **Lake City** Florida, USA
17C1 **Lake City** S Carolina, USA
42C2 **Lake District** Region, Eng
22D4 **Lake Elsinore** USA
106C3 **Lake Eyre Basin** Aust
15C2 **Lakefield** Can
6D3 **Lake Harbour** Can
22C3 **Lake Hughes** USA
16B2 **Lakehurst** USA
19A4 **Lake Jackson** USA
13E2 **Lake la Biche** Can
17B2 **Lakeland** USA
7A5 **Lake of the Woods** Can
20B1 **Lake Oswego** USA
21A2 **Lakeport** USA
19B3 **Lake Providence** USA
111B2 **Lake Pukaki** NZ
109C3 **Lakes Entrance** Aust
22C2 **Lakeshore** USA
108B1 **Lake Stewart** Aust
15C1 **Lake Traverse** Can
8A2 **Lakeview** USA
20B1 **Lakeview Mt** Can
19B3 **Lake Village** USA
17B2 **Lake Wales** USA
22C4 **Lakewood** California, USA
16B2 **Lakewood** New Jersey, USA
14B2 **Lakewood** Ohio, USA
17B2 **Lake Worth** USA
86A1 **Lakhīmpur** India
85B4 **Lakhpat** India
84C2 **Lakki** Pak
55B3 **Lakonikós Kólpos** *G* Greece
97B4 **Lakota** Ivory Coast
38K4 **Laksefjord** *Inlet* Nor
38K4 **Lakselv** Nor
34C2 **La Laguna** Arg
32A4 **La Libertad** Ecuador
34A2 **La Ligua** Chile
50A2 **La Linea** Spain
85D4 **Lalitpur** India
5H4 **La Loche** Can
13F1 **la Loche,L** Can
46C1 **La Louviète** Belg
26A4 **La Luz** Nic
7C5 **La Malbaie** Can
23B2 **La Malinche** *Mt* Mexico
50B2 **La Mancha** Region, Spain
9C3 **Lamar** Colorado, USA
18B2 **Lamar** Missouri, USA
19A4 **La Marque** USA
98B3 **Lambaréné** Gabon
32A5 **Lambayeque** Peru
112B10 **Lambert Gl** Ant
16B2 **Lambertville** USA
4F2 **Lamblon,C** Can
47C2 **Lambro** *R* Italy
76C2 **Lam Chi** *R* Thai
50A1 **Lamego** Port
47B2 **La Meije** *Mt* France
32B6 **La Merced** Peru
21B3 **La Mesa** USA
55B3 **Lamía** Greece
42C2 **Lammermuir Hills** Scot
39G7 **Lammhult** Sweden
79B3 **Lamon B** Phil
18B1 **Lamoni** USA
71F3 **Lamotrek** *I* Pacific O
43B3 **Lampeter** Wales
99E3 **Lamu** Kenya
47D1 **Lana** Italy
21C4 **Lanai** *I* Hawaiian Is
21C4 **Lanai City** Hawaiian Is
42C2 **Lanark** Scot
76B3 **Lanbi** *I* Burma
76C1 **Lancang** *R* China
42C3 **Lancashire** County, Eng
21B3 **Lancaster** California, USA
42C2 **Lancaster** Eng
18B1 **Lancaster** Mississippi, USA
15D2 **Lancaster** New Hampshire, USA
14B3 **Lancaster** Ohio, USA
10C3 **Lancaster** Pennsylvania, USA
17B1 **Lancaster** S Carolina, USA
6B2 **Lancaster Sd** Can
78B3 **Landak** *R* Indon
46E2 **Landan** Germany
57C3 **Landeck** Austria
8C2 **Lander** USA
34C2 **Landeta** Arg
57C3 **Landsberg** Germany
4F2 **Lands End** *C* Can
43B4 **Land's End** *Pt* Eng
57C3 **Landshut** Germany
39G7 **Làndskrona** Sweden
17A1 **Lanett** USA
56B2 **Langenhagen** Germany
47B1 **Langenthal** Switz
42C2 **Langholm** Scot
38A2 **Langjökull** *Mts* Iceland
77B4 **Langkawi** *I* Malay
13C3 **Langley** Can
108C1 **Langlo** *R* Aust
47B1 **Langnau** Switz
49D2 **Langres** France
70A3 **langsa** Indon
68C2 **Lang Shan** *Mts* China
76D1 **Lang Son** Viet
48C3 **Languedoc** Region, France
29B3 **Lanin** *Mt* Arg
79B4 **Lanoa,L** *L* Phil
16B2 **Lansdale** USA
7B4 **Lansdowne House** Can
16B2 **Lansford** USA
10B2 **Lansing** USA
47B2 **Lanslebourg** France
96A2 **Lanzarote** *I* Canary Is
72A2 **Lanzhou** China
47B2 **Lanzo Torinese** Italy
79B2 **Laoag** Phil
76C1 **Lao Cai** Viet
72D1 **Laoha He** *R* China
45C2 **Laois** County, Irish Rep
46B2 **Laon** France
32B6 **La Oroya** Peru
76C2 **Laos** Republic, S E Asia
49C2 **Lapalisse** France
32B2 **La Palma** Panama
96A2 **La Palma** *I* Canary Is
34B3 **La Pampa** State, Arg
33E2 **La Paragua** Ven
29E2 **La Paz** Arg
34B2 **La Paz** Arg
30C2 **La Paz** Bol
24A2 **La Paz** Mexico
69G2 **La Perouse Str** Japan/Russian Fed
23A1 **La Piedad** Mexico
20B2 **La Pine** USA
19B3 **Laplace** USA
23A2 **la Placita** Mexico
29E2 **La Plata** Arg
13F1 **La Plonge,L** Can
14A2 **La Porte** USA
39K6 **Lappeenranta** Fin
38H5 **Lappland** *Region* Sweden/Fin
34C3 **Laprida** Arg
1B8 **Laptev S** Russian Fed
38J6 **Lapua** Fin
79B3 **Lapu-Lapu** Phil
9B4 **La Purisma** Mexico
95B2 **Laqiya Arba'in** *Well* Sudan
30C3 **La Quiaca** Arg
52B2 **L'Aquila** Italy
91B4 **Lār** Iran
96B1 **Larache** Mor
8C2 **Laramie** USA
8C2 **Laramie Range** *Mts* USA
50B2 **Larca** Spain
9D4 **Laredo** USA
91B4 **Larestan** Region, Iran
Largeau = Faya
47B2 **L'Argentière** France
17B2 **Largo** USA
42B2 **Largs** Scot
90A2 **Lārī** Iran
30C4 **La Rioja** Arg
30C4 **La Rioja** State, Arg
55B3 **Lárisa** Greece
85B3 **Larkana** Pak
92B3 **Larnaca** Cyprus
94A1 **Larnaca B** Cyprus
45D1 **Larne** N Ire
50A1 **La Robla** Spain
46C1 **La Roche-en-Ardenne** Belg
48B2 **La Rochelle** France
47B1 **La Roche-sur-Foron** France
48B2 **La Roche-sur-Yon** France
51B2 **La Roda** Spain
27D3 **La Romana** Dom Rep
5H4 **La Ronge** Can
5H4 **La Ronge,L** Can
39F7 **Larvik** Nor
65J3 **Laryak** Russian Fed
50B2 **La Sagra** *Mt* Spain
15D1 **La Salle** Can
18C1 **La Salle** USA
7C5 **La Sarre** Can
34C1 **Las Avispas** Arg
34A2 **Las Cabras** Chile
5G4 **Lascombe** Can
9C3 **Las Cruces** USA
26C3 **La Selle** *Mt* Haiti
72B2 **Lasengmia** China
30B4 **La Serena** Chile
29E3 **Las Flores** Arg
76B1 **Lashio** Burma
53C3 **La Sila** *Mts* Italy
90B2 **Lāsjerd** Iran
34A3 **Las Lajas** Chile
50A2 **Las Marismas** *Marshland* Spain
96A2 **Las Palmas de Gran Canaria** Canary Is
52A2 **La Spezia** Italy
29C4 **Las Plumas** Arg
34C2 **Las Rosas** Arg
20B2 **Lassen Peak** *Mt* USA
20B2 **Lassen Volcanic Nat Pk** USA
23B2 **las Tinai** Mexico
98B3 **Lastoursville** Gabon
52C2 **Lastovo** *I* Croatia
24B2 **Las Tres Marias** *Is* Mexico
34C2 **Las Varillas** Arg
9C3 **Las Vegas** USA
Latakia = Al Lādhiqīyah
53B2 **Latina** Italy
34B2 **La Toma** Arg
32D1 **La Tortuga** *I* Ven
79B2 **La Trinidad** Phil
109C4 **Latrobe** Aust
94B3 **Latrun** Israel
7C5 **La Tuque** Can
87B1 **Lātūr** India
60B2 **Latvia** Republic, Europe
107D5 **Launceston** Aust
43B4 **Launceston** Eng
29B4 **La Unión** Chile
25D3 **La Union** El Salvador
23A2 **La Union** Mexico
32B5 **La Unión** Peru
107D2 **Laura** Aust
15C3 **Laurel** Delaware, USA
16A3 **Laurel** Maryland, USA
11B3 **Laurel** Mississippi, USA
17B1 **Laurens** USA
17C1 **Laurinburg** USA
52A1 **Lausanne** Switz
78D3 **Laut** *I* Indon
29B5 **Lautaro** *Mt* Chile
46D2 **Lauterecken** Germany
15D1 **Laval** Can
48B2 **Laval** France
22B2 **Laveaga Peak** *Mt* USA
47C2 **Laveno** Italy
31B6 **Lavras** Brazil
4A3 **Lavrentiya** Russian Fed
101H1 **Lavumisa** Swaziland
78D1 **Lawas** Malay
76B1 **Lawksawk** Burma
18A2 **Lawrence** Kansas, USA
15D2 **Lawrence** Massachusetts, USA
111A3 **Lawrence** NZ
14A3 **Lawrenceville** Illinois, USA
9D3 **Lawton** USA
91A5 **Layla** S Arabia
99D2 **Laylo** Sudan
23A2 **Lázaro Cárdenas** Mexico
99E1 **Laz Daua** Somalia
79B4 **Lazi** Phil
8C2 **Lead** USA
13F2 **Leader** Can
18A2 **Leavenworth** USA
58B2 **Leba** Pol
18B2 **Lebanon** Missouri, USA
20B2 **Lebanon** Oregon, USA
15C2 **Lebanon** Pennsylvania, USA
92C3 **Lebanon** Republic, S W Asia
101C3 **Lebombo** *Mts* Mozam/S Africa/ Swaziland
58B2 **Lebork** Pol
47A2 **Le Bourg-d'Oisans** France
47B1 **Le Brassus** Switz
29B3 **Lebu** Chile
47B1 **Le Buet** *Mt* France
46B1 **Le Cateau** France
55A2 **Lecce** Italy
52A1 **Lecco** Italy
47D1 **Lech** *R* Austria
47D1 **Lechtaler Alpen** *Mts* Austria
49C2 **Le Creusot** France
43C3 **Ledbury** Eng
13E2 **Leduc** Can
16C1 **Lee** USA
45B3 **Lee** *R* Irish Rep

41C3 **Leeds** Eng
43C3 **Leek** Eng
56B2 **Leer** Germany
17B2 **Leesburg** Florida, USA
16A3 **Leesburg** Virginia, USA
19B3 **Leesville** USA
109C2 **Leeton** Aust
56B2 **Leeuwarden** Neth
106A4 **Leeuwin,C** Aust
22C2 **Lee Vining** USA
27E3 **Leeward Is** Caribbean S
94A1 **Lefkara** Cyprus
79B3 **Legazpi** Phil
47D2 **Legnago** Italy
59B2 **Legnica** Pol
33F2 **Leguan Inlet** Guyana
32C4 **Leguizamo** Colombia
84D2 **Leh** India
48C2 **Le Havre** France
16B2 **Lehigh** *R* USA
16B2 **Lehighton** USA
84C2 **Leiah** Pak
59B3 **Leibnitz** Austria
43D3 **Leicester** County, Eng
43D3 **Leicester** Eng
107C2 **Leichhardt** *R* Aust
56A2 **Leiden** Neth
46B1 **Leie** *R* Belg
106C4 **Leigh Creek** Aust
43D4 **Leighton Buzzard** Eng
56B2 **Leine** *R* Germany
45C2 **Leinster** Region, Irish Rep
57C2 **Leipzig** Germany
50A2 **Leiria** Port
39F7 **Leirvik** Nor
45B1 **Leitrim** County, Irish Rep
73C4 **Leiyang** China
73B5 **Leizhou Bandao** *Pen* China
73C5 **Leizhou Wan** *B* China
56A2 **Lek** *R* Neth
96C1 **Le Kef** Tunisia
19B3 **Leland** USA
54A2 **Lelija** *Mt* Bosnia & Herzegovina, Yugos
47B1 **Le Locle** France
48C2 **Le Mans** France
6D3 **Lemicux Is** Can
8C2 **Lemmon** USA
21B2 **Lemoore** USA
49C2 **Lempdes** France
86C2 **Lemro** *R* Burma
52C2 **Le Murge** Region, Italy
63C2 **Lena** *R* Russian Fed
38L6 **Lendery** Russian Fed
73C4 **Lengshujiang** China
65F5 **Leninakan** Armenia
Leningrad = Sankt-Peterburg
112B7 **Leningradskaya** *Base* Ant
61H3 **Leninogorsk** Tatarskaya Respublika, Russian Fed
68A1 **Leninogorsk** Kazakhstan
65K4 **Leninsk-Kuznetskiy** Russian Fed
69F2 **Leninskoye** Russian Fed
65F6 **Lenkoran'** Azerbaijan
46E1 **Lenne** *R* Germany
16C1 **Lenox** USA
46B1 **Lens** France
63D1 **Lensk** Russian Fed
53B3 **Lentini** Italy
76B3 **Lenya** *R* Burma
52B1 **Leoben** Austria
43C3 **Leominster** Eng
16D1 **Leominster** USA
24B2 **Leon** Mexico
25D3 **León** Nic
50A1 **Leon** Region, Spain
50A1 **León** Spain
100A3 **Leonardville** Namibia
106B3 **Leonora** Aust
35C2 **Leopoldina** Brazil
Léopoldville = Kinshasa
60C3 **Lepel** Belorussia
73D4 **Leping** China
49C2 **Le Puy** France
98B2 **Léré** Chad
101G1 **Leribe** Lesotho
47C2 **Lerici** Italy
51C1 **Lérida** Spain
23A1 **Lerma** *R* Mexico
47D1 **Lermoos** Austria
55C3 **Léros** *I* Greece
44E1 **Lerwick** Scot
46A2 **Les Andelys** France
26C3 **Les Cayes** Haiti
47B2 **Les Ecrins** *Mt* France
73A4 **Leshan** China
54B2 **Leskovac** Serbia, Yugos
48B3 **Les Landes** Region, France
101G1 **Leslie** S Africa
61H2 **Lesnoy** Russian Fed
63B2 **Lesosibirsk** Russian Fed
101G1 **Lesotho** Kingdom, S Africa
69F2 **Lesozavodsk** Russian Fed
48B2 **Les Sables-d'Olonne** France
112A **Lesser Antarctica** Region, Ant
27D4 **Lesser Antilles** *Is* Caribbean S
13E1 **Lesser Slave L** Can
55C3 **Lésvos** *I* Greece
58B2 **Leszno** Pol
86C2 **Letha Range** *Mts* Burma
5G5 **Lethbridge** Can
33F3 **Lethem** Guyana
59D3 **Letichev** Ukraine
63D2 **Let Oktyobr'ya** Russian Fed
78B2 **Letong** Indon
46A1 **Le Touquet-Paris-Plage** France
76B2 **Letpadan** Burma
48C1 **Le Tréport** France
47B1 **Leuk** Switz
57A2 **Leuven** Belg
55B3 **Levádhia** Greece
38G6 **Levanger** Nor
47B2 **Levanna** *Mt* Italy
106B2 **Lévêque,C** Aust
46D1 **Leverkusen** Germany
59B3 **Levice** Czech
47D1 **Levico** Italy
110C2 **Levin** NZ
7C5 **Lévis** Can
15D2 **Levittown** USA
55B3 **Lévka ·ri** *Mt* Greece
55B3 **Levkás** Greece
55B3 **Levkás** *I* Greece
54C2 **Levski** Bulg
43E4 **Lewes** Eng
40B2 **Lewis** *I* Scot
16A2 **Lewisburg** USA
111B2 **Lewis P** NZ
8B2 **Lewis Range** *Mts* USA
8B2 **Lewiston** Idaho, USA
10C2 **Lewiston** Maine, USA
8C2 **Lewistown** Montana, USA
15C2 **Lewistown** Pennsylvania, USA
19B3 **Lewisville** USA
11B3 **Lexington** Kentucky, USA
18B2 **Lexington** Missouri, USA
15C3 **Lexington Park** USA
79C3 **Leyte G** Phil
54A2 **Lezhe** Alb
82D3 **Lhasa** China
86B1 **Lhazê** China
70A3 **Lhokseumawe** Indon
86C1 **Lhozhag** China
68B4 **Lhunze** China
Liancourt Rocks = Tok-do
79C4 **Lianga** Phil
72B3 **Liangdang** China
73C5 **Lianjiang** China
73C5 **Lianping** China
73C5 **Lian Xian** China
72D3 **Lianyungang** China
72E1 **Liaoding Bandao** *Pen* China
72E1 **Liaodong Wan** *B* China
72E1 **Liao He** *R* China
72E1 **Liaoning** Province, China
72E1 **Liaoyang** China
72E1 **Liaoyuan** China
74B2 **Liaoyuang** China
4F3 **Liard** *R* Can
4F4 **Liard River** Can
46C2 **Liart** France
98B2 **Libenge** Zaïre
9C3 **Liberal** USA
57C2 **Liberec** Czech
97A4 **Liberia** Republic, Africa
18B2 **Liberty** Missouri, USA
15D2 **Liberty** New York, USA
19B3 **Liberty** Texas, USA
48B3 **Libourne** France
23B2 **Libres** Mexico
98A2 **Libreville** Gabon
95A2 **Libya** Republic, Africa
95B2 **Libyan Desert** Libya
95B1 **Libyan Plat** Egypt
53B3 **Licata** Italy
43D3 **Lichfield** Eng
101C2 **Lichinga** Mozam
101G1 **Lichtenburg** S Africa
14B3 **Licking** *R* USA
22B2 **Lick Observatory** USA
60C3 **Lida** Belorussia
39G7 **Lidköping** Sweden
53B2 **Lido di Ostia** Italy
52A1 **Liechtenstein** Principality, Europe
57B2 **Liège** Belg
58C1 **Lielupe** *R* Latvia
98C2 **Lienart** Zaïre
57C3 **Lienz** Austria
60B2 **Liepāja** Latvia
46C1 **Lier** Belg
47B1 **Liestal** Switz
15C1 **Liévre** *R* Can
57C3 **Liezen** Austria
45C2 **Liffey** *R* Irish Rep
45C1 **Lifford** Irish Rep
107F3 **Lifu** *I* Nouvelle Calédonie
109C1 **Lightning Ridge** Aust
46C2 **Ligny-en-Barrois** France
101C2 **Ligonha** *R* Mozam
47C2 **Liguria** Region, Italy
52A2 **Ligurian** *S* Italy
21C4 **Lihue** Hawaiian Is
100B2 **Likasi** Zaïre
49C1 **Lille** France
39G6 **Lillehammer** Nor
46B1 **Lillers** France
39G7 **Lillestøm** Nor
13C2 **Lillooet** Can
13C2 **Lillooet** *R* Can
101C2 **Lilongwe** Malawi
79B4 **Liloy** Phil
54A2 **Lim** *R* Montenegro/ Serbia, Yugos
32B6 **Lima** Peru
50A1 **Lima** Spain
10B2 **Lima** USA
92B3 **Limassol** Cyprus
45C1 **Limavady** N Ire
34B3 **Limay** *R* Arg
34B3 **Limay Mahuida** Arg
98A2 **Limbe** Cam
101C2 **Limbe** Malawi
57B2 **Limburg** W Gem
31B6 **Limeira** Brazil
45B2 **Limerick** County, Irish Rep
41B3 **Limerick** Irish Rep
56B1 **Limfjorden** *L* Den
106C2 **Limmen Bight** *B* Aust
55C3 **Límnos** *I* Greece
31D3 **Limoeiro** Brazil
48C2 **Limoges** France
25D4 **Limón** Costa Rica
8C3 **Limon** USA
48C2 **Limousin** Region, France
79A3 **Linapacan Str** Phil
29B3 **Linares** Chile
9D4 **Linares** Mexico
50B2 **Linares** Spain
68B4 **Lincang** China
29D2 **Lincoln** Arg
18A1 **Lincoln** California, USA
42D3 **Lincoln** County, Eng
42D3 **Lincoln** Eng
18C1 **Lincoln** Illinois, USA
8D2 **Lincoln** Nebraska, USA
15D2 **Lincoln** New Hampshire, USA
111B2 **Lincoln** NZ
80A **Lincoln** *S* Greenland
20B2 **Lincoln City** USA
14B2 **Lincoln Park** USA
52A2 **L'Incudina** *Mt* Corse
57B3 **Lindau** Germany
33F2 **Linden** Guyana
39F7 **Lindesnes** *C* Nor
99D3 **Lindi** Tanz
98C2 **Lindi** *R* Zaïre
101G1 **Lindley** S Africa
55C3 **Lindos** Greece
15C2 **Lindsay** Can
105J3 **Line Is** Pacific O
72C2 **Linfen** China
76D2 **Lingao** China
79B2 **Lingayen** Phil
56B2 **Lingen** Germany
73C4 **Lingling** China
73B5 **Lingshan** China
72C2 **Lingshi** China
97A3 **Linguère** Sen
73E4 **Linhai** Rhejiang, China
31D5 **Linhares** Brazil
72B1 **Linhe** China
74B2 **Linjiang** China
39H7 **Linköping** Sweden
72D2 **Linqing** China
35B2 **Lins** Brazil
72A2 **Lintao** China
47C1 **Linthal** Switz
68D2 **Linxi** China
72A2 **Linxia** China
57C3 **Linz** Austria
79B3 **Lipa** Phil
53B3 **Lipari** *I* Italy
61E3 **Lipetsk** Russian Fed
54B1 **Lipova** Rom
56B2 **Lippe** *R* Germany
46E1 **Lippstadt** Germany
99D2 **Lira** Uganda
98B3 **Liranga** Congo
98C2 **Lisala** Zaïre
50A2 **Lisboa** Port
Lisbon = Lisboa
45C1 **Lisburn** N Ire
45B2 **Liscannor B** Irish Rep
73D4 **Lishui** China
73C4 **Li Shui** *R* China
60E4 **Lisichansk** Ukraine
48C2 **Lisieux** France
60E3 **Liski** Russian Fed
46B2 **L'Isle-Adam** France
47B1 **L'Isle-sur-le-Doubs** France
107E3 **Lismore** Aust
45B2 **Listowel** Irish Rep
73B5 **Litang** China
94B2 **Lītanī** *R* Leb
33G3 **Litani** *R* Suriname
18C2 **Litchfield** USA
107E4 **Lithgow** Aust
60B2 **Lithuania** Republic, Europe
16A2 **Lititz** USA

69F2 **Litovko** Russian Fed
19A3 **Little** *R* USA
11C4 **Little Abaco** *I* The Bahamas
110C1 **Little Barrier I** NZ
13E2 **Little Bow** *R* Can
25D3 **Little Cayman** *I* Caribbean S
16B3 **Little Egg Harbor** *B* USA
26C2 **Little Inagua** *I* Caribbean S
77A4 **Little Nicobar** *I* Nicobar Is
11A3 **Little Rock** USA
22D3 **Littlerock** USA
13D2 **Little Smoky** Can
13D2 **Little Smoky** *R* Can
16A3 **Littlestown** USA
15D2 **Littleton** New Hampshire, USA
74B2 **Liuhe** China
73B5 **Liuzhou** China
55B3 **Livanátais** Greece
58D1 **Līvāni** Latvia
12E1 **Livengood** USA
17B1 **Live Oak** USA
21A2 **Livermore** USA
7D5 **Liverpool** Can
42C3 **Liverpool** Eng
4E2 **Liverpool B** Can
42C3 **Liverpool B** Eng
6C2 **Liverpool,C** Can
109D2 **Liverpool Range** *Mts* Aust
8B2 **Livingston** Montana, USA
19B3 **Livingston** Texas, USA
44C4 **Livingston** UK
Livingstone = Maramba
19A3 **Livingston,L** USA
52C2 **Livno** Bosnia & Herzegovina, Yugos
60E3 **Livny** Russian Fed
14B2 **Livonia** USA
52B2 **Livorno** Italy
99D3 **Liwale** Tanz
52B1 **Ljubljana** Slovenia
38G6 **Ljungan** *R* Sweden
39G7 **Ljungby** Sweden
39H6 **Ljusdal** Sweden
38H6 **Ljusnan** *R* Sweden
43C4 **Llandeilo** Wales
43C4 **Llandovery** Wales
43C3 **Llandrindod Wells** Wales
42C3 **Llandudno** Wales
43B4 **Llanelli** Wales
43C3 **Llangollen** Wales
9C3 **Llano Estacado** *Plat* USA
Z4D2 **Llanos** Region, Colombia/Ven
30D2 **Llanos de Chiquitos** Region, Bol
Lleida = Lérida
50A2 **Llerena** Spain
43B3 **Lleyn** *Pen* Wales
89E7 **Llorin** Nig
5H4 **Lloydminster** Can
30C3 **Llullaillaco** *Mt* Arg/Chile
30C3 **Loa** *R* Chile
49C2 **Loan** France
98B3 **Loange** *R* Zaïre
100B3 **Lobatse** Botswana
98B2 **Lobaye** *R* CAR
34D3 **Loberia** Arg
100A2 **Lobito** Angola
34D3 **Lobos** Arg
47B2 **Locano** Italy
47C1 **Locarno** Switz
44B3 **Loch Awe** *L* Scot
44A3 **Lochboisdale** Scot
44A3 **Loch Bracadale** *Inlet* Scot
44B3 **Loch Broom** *Estuary* Scot
42B2 **Loch Doon** *L* Scot
44B3 **Loch Earn** *L* Scot
44B2 **Loch Eriboll** *Inlet* Scot
44B3 **Loch Ericht** *L* Scot
48C2 **Loches** France
44B3 **Loch Etive** *Inlet* Scot
44B3 **Loch Ewe** *Inlet* Scot
44B3 **Loch Fyne** *Inlet* Scot
44B3 **Loch Hourn** *Inlet* Scot
44B2 **Lochinver** Scot
44B3 **Loch Katrine** *L* Scot
44C3 **Loch Leven** *L* Scot
44B3 **Loch Linnhe** *Inlet* Scot
44B3 **Loch Lochy** *L* Scot
44B3 **Loch Lomond** *L* Scot
44B3 **Loch Long** *Inlet* Scot
44A3 **Lochmaddy** Scot
44B3 **Loch Maree** *L* Scot
44B3 **Loch Morar** *L* Scot
44C3 **Lochnagar** *Mt* Scot
44B3 **Loch Ness** *L* Scot
44B3 **Loch Rannoch** *L* Scot
44A2 **Loch Roag** *Inlet* Scot
44B3 **Loch Sheil** *L* Scot
44B2 **Loch Shin** *L* Scot
44A3 **Loch Snizort** *Inlet* Scot
44B3 **Loch Sunart** *Inlet* Scot
44B3 **Loch Tay** *L* Scot
44B3 **Loch Torridon** *Inlet* Scot
108A2 **Lock** Aust
42C2 **Lockerbie** Scot
15C2 **Lock Haven** USA
15C2 **Lockport** USA
76D3 **Loc Ninh** Viet
53C3 **Locri** Italy
94B3 **Lod** Israel
108B3 **Loddon** *R* Aust
60D1 **Lodeynoye Pole** Russian Fed
84C3 **Lodhran** Pak
52A1 **Lodi** Italy
21A2 **Lodi** USA
98C3 **Lodja** Zaïre
47B1 **Lods** France
99D2 **Lodwar** Kenya
58B2 **Łódź** Pol
38G5 **Lofoten** *Is* Nor
8B2 **Logan** Utah, USA
4D3 **Logan,Mt** Can
14A2 **Logansport** Indiana, USA
19B3 **Logansport** Louisiana, USA
50B1 **Logroño** Spain
86A2 **Lohārdaga** India
39J6 **Lohja** Fin
76B2 **Loikaw** Burma
39J6 **Loimaa** Fin
48C2 **Loir** *R* France
49C2 **Loire** *R* France
32B4 **Loja** Ecuador
50B2 **Loja** Spain
38K5 **Lokan Tekojärvi** *Res* Fin
46B1 **Lokeren** Belg
99D2 **Lokitaung** Kenya
58D1 **Loknya** Russian Fed
98C3 **Lokolo** *R* Zaïre
98C3 **Lokoro** *R* Zaïre
6D3 **Loks Land** *I* Can
56C2 **Lolland** *I* Den
54B2 **Lom** Bulg
98C3 **Lomami** *R* Zaïre
97A4 **Loma Mts** Sierra Leone/Guinea
47C2 **Lombardia** Region, Italy
71D4 **Lomblen** *I* Indon
78D4 **Lombok** *I* Indon
97C4 **Lomé** Togo
98C3 **Lomela** Zaïre
98C3 **Lomela** *R* Zaïre
60C2 **Lomonosov** Russian Fed
47B1 **Lomont** Region, France
21A3 **Lompoc** USA
58C2 **Łomza** Pol
87A1 **Lonāvale** India
29B3 **Loncoche** Chile
7B5 **London** Can
43D4 **London** Eng
45C1 **Londonderry** County, N Ire
45C1 **Londonderry** N Ire
29B7 **Londonderry** *I* Chile
106B2 **Londonderry,C** Aust
30C4 **Londres** Arg
30F3 **Londrina** Brazil
21B2 **Lone Pine** USA
11C4 **Long** *I* The Bahamas
71F4 **Long** *I* PNG
78C2 **Long Akah** Malay
47E1 **Longarone** Italy
34A3 **Longavi** *Mt* Chile
27H2 **Long B** Jamaica
17C1 **Long B** USA
9B3 **Long Beach** California, USA
15D2 **Long Beach** New York, USA
15D2 **Long Branch** USA
73D5 **Longchuan** China
20C2 **Long Creek** USA
109C4 **Longford** Aust
45C2 **Longford** County, Irish Rep
45C2 **Longford** Irish Rep
44D3 **Long Forties** *Region* N Sea
72D1 **Longhua** China
7C4 **Long I** Can
10C2 **Long I** USA
16C2 **Long Island Sd** USA
7B4 **Longlac** Can
73B5 **Longlin** China
8C2 **Longmont** USA
78D2 **Longnawan** Indon
29B3 **Longquimay** Chile
107D3 **Longreach** Aust
72A2 **Longshou Shan** *Upland* China
42C2 **Longtown** Eng
15D1 **Longueuil** Can
34A3 **Longuimay** Chile
46C2 **Longuyon** France
11A3 **Longview** Texas, USA
8A2 **Longview** Washington, USA
46C2 **Longwy** France
72A3 **Longxi** China
77D3 **Long Xuyen** Viet
73D4 **Longyan** China
73B5 **Longzhou** China
47D2 **Lonigo** Italy
49D2 **Lons-le-Saunier** France
11C3 **Lookout,C** USA
99D3 **Loolmalasin** *Mt* Tanz
13D1 **Loon** *R* Can
45B2 **Loop Hd** *C* Irish Rep
76C3 **Lop Buri** Thai
98A3 **Lopez** *C* Gabon
68B2 **Lop Nur** *L* China
50A2 **Lora del Rio** Spain
10B2 **Lorain** USA
84B2 **Loralai** Pak
90B3 **Lordegān** Iran
107E4 **Lord Howe** *I* Aust
105G5 **Lord Howe Rise** Pacific O
6A3 **Lord Mayor B** Can
9C3 **Lordsburg** USA
35B2 **Lorena** Brazil
47E2 **Loreo** Italy
23A1 **Loreto** Mexico
48B2 **Lorient** France
108B3 **Lorne** Aust
57B3 **Lörrach** Germany
49D2 **Lorraine** *Region* France
9C3 **Los Alamos** USA
34A2 **Los Andes** Chile
29B3 **Los Angeles** Chile
9B3 **Los Angeles** USA
21A2 **Los Banos** USA
34B2 **Los Cerrillos** Arg
21A2 **Los Gatos** USA
52B2 **Lošinj** *I* Croatia
29B3 **Los Lagos** Chile
24B2 **Los Mochis** Mexico
22B3 **Los Olivos** USA
34A3 **Los Sauces** Chile
44C3 **Lossiemouth** Scot
27E4 **Los Testigos** *Is* Ven
29B2 **Los Vilos** Chile
48C3 **Lot** *R* France
34A3 **Lota** Chile
42C2 **Lothian** Region, Scot
99D2 **Lotikipi Plain** Sudan/Kenya
98C3 **Loto** Zaïre
47B1 **Lötschberg Tunnel** Switz
38K5 **Lotta** *R* Fin/Russian Fed
48B2 **Loudéac** France
97A3 **Louga** Sen
41B3 **Lough Allen** *L* Irish Rep
45C2 **Lough Boderg** *L* Irish Rep
43D3 **Loughborough** Eng
45C2 **Lough Bowna** *L* Irish Rep
45C1 **Lough Carlingford** *L* N Ire
41B3 **Lough Conn** *L* Irish Rep
41B3 **Lough Corrib** *L* Irish Rep
41B3 **Lough Derg** *L* Irish Rep
45C2 **Lough Derravaragh** *L* Irish Rep
4H2 **Loughead I** Can
45C2 **Lough Ennell** *L* Irish Rep
41B3 **Lough Erne** *L* N Ire
40B2 **Lough Foyle** *Estuary* N Ire/Irish Rep
40B3 **Lough Neagh** *L* N Ire
45C1 **Lough Oughter** *L* Irish Rep
45B2 **Loughrea** Irish Rep
45C2 **Lough Ree** *L* Irish Rep
45C2 **Lough Sheelin** *L* Irish Rep
42B2 **Lough Strangford** *L* Irish Rep
45C1 **Lough Swilly** *Estuary* Irish Rep
14B3 **Louisa** USA
70C3 **Louisa Reef** *I* S E Asia
12E2 **Louise,L** USA
107E2 **Louisiade Arch** Solomon Is
11A3 **Louisiana** State, USA
17B1 **Louisville** Georgia, USA
11B3 **Louisville** Kentucky, USA
38L5 **Loukhi** Russian Fed
48B3 **Lourdes** France
108C2 **Louth** Aust
45C2 **Louth** County, Irish Rep
42D3 **Louth** Eng
Louvain = Leuven
48C2 **Louviers** France
60D2 **Lovat** *R* Russian Fed
54B2 **Lovech** Bulg
21B1 **Lovelock** USA
52B1 **Lóvere** Italy
9C3 **Lovington** USA
38L5 **Lovozero** Russian Fed
6B3 **Low,C** Can
10C2 **Lowell** Massachusetts, USA
20B2 **Lowell** Oregon, USA
16D1 **Lowell** USA
111B2 **Lower Hutt** NZ
43E3 **Lowestoft** Eng
58B2 **Łowicz** Pol
108B2 **Loxton** Aust
5F4 **Loyd George,Mt** Can
54A2 **Loznica** Serbia, Yugos
23A2 **Loz Reyes** Mexico
65H3 **Lozva** *R* Russian Fed
100B2 **Luacano** Angola
98C3 **Luachimo** Angola
98C3 **Lualaba** *R* Zaïre
100B2 **Luampa** Zambia
100B2 **Luân** Angola

73D3 **Lu'an** China
98B3 **Luanda** Angola
100A2 **Luando** *R* Angola
100B2 **Luanginga** *R* Angola
76C1 **Luang Namtha** Laos
76C2 **Luang Prabang** Laos
98B3 **Luangue** *R* Angola
100C2 **Luangwa** *R* Zambia
72D1 **Luan He** *R* China
72D1 **Luanping** China
100B2 **Luanshya** Zambia
100B2 **Luapula** *R* Zaïre
50A1 **Luarca** Spain
98B3 **Lubalo** Angola
58D2 **L'uban** Belorussia
79B3 **Lubang Is** Phil
100A2 **Lubango** Angola
9C3 **Lubbock** USA
56C2 **Lübeck** Germany
98C3 **Lubefu** Zaïre
98C3 **Lubefu** *R* Zaïre
99C3 **Lubero** Zaïre
98C3 **Lubilash** *R* Zaïre
59C2 **Lublin** Pol
60D3 **Lubny** Ukraine
78C2 **Lubok Antu** Malay
98C3 **Lubudi** Zaïre
98C3 **Lubudi** *R* Zaïre
78A3 **Lubuklinggau** Indon
100B2 **Lubumbashi** Zaïre
98C3 **Lubutu** Zaïre
79B3 **Lucban** Phil
52B2 **Lucca** Italy
42B2 **Luce** *B* Scot
19C3 **Lucedale** USA
79B3 **Lucena** Phil
59B3 **Lucenec** Czech
Lucerne = Luzern
73C5 **Luchuan** China
56C2 **Luckenwalde** Germany
101F1 **Luckhoff** S Africa
86A1 **Lucknow** India
100B2 **Lucusse** Angola
46D1 **Lüdenscheid** Germany
100A3 **Lüderitz** Namibia
84D2 **Ludhiana** India
14A2 **Ludington** USA
43C3 **Ludlow** Eng
54C2 **Ludogorie** *Upland* Bulg
17B1 **Ludowici** USA
54B1 **Luduş** Rom
39H6 **Ludvika** Sweden
57B3 **Ludwigsburg** Germany
57B3 **Ludwigshafen** Germany
56C2 **Ludwigslust** Germany
98C3 **Luebo** Zaïre
98C3 **Luema** *R* Zaïre
98C3 **Luembe** *R* Angola
100A2 **Luena** Angola
100B2 **Luene** *R* Angola
72B3 **Lüeyang** China
73D5 **Lufeng** China
11A3 **Lufkin** USA
60C2 **Luga** Russian Fed
60C2 **Luga** *R* Russian Fed
52A1 **Lugano** Switz
60E4 **Lugansk** Ukraine
101C2 **Lugela** Mozam
101C2 **Lugenda** *R* Mozam
50A1 **Lugo** Spain
54B1 **Lugoj** Rom
72A3 **Luhuo** China
98B3 **Lui** *R* Angola
100B2 **Luiana** Angola
100B2 **Luiana** *R* Angola
Luichow Peninsula = Leizhou Bandao
47C2 **Luino** Italy
98B2 **Luionga** *R* Zaïre
72B2 **Luipan Shan** *Upland* China
100B2 **Luishia** Zaïre
68B4 **Luixi** China
98C3 **Luiza** Zaïre
34B2 **Luján** Arg
34D2 **Luján** Arg
73D3 **Lujiang** China
98B3 **Lukenie** *R* Zaïre
64E4 **Luki** Russian Fed
98B3 **Lukolela** Zaïre
58C2 **Luków** Pol
98C3 **Lukuga** *R* Zaïre
100B2 **Lukulu** Zambia
38J5 **Lule** *R* Sweden
38J5 **Luleå** Sweden
54C2 **Lüleburgaz** Turk
72C2 **Lüliang Shan** *Mts* China
19A4 **Luling** USA
98C2 **Lulonga** *R* Zaïre
Luluabourg = Kananga
100B2 **Lumbala Kaquengue** Angola
11C3 **Lumberton** USA
78D1 **Lumbis** Indon
86C1 **Lumding** India
100B2 **Lumeje** Angola
111A3 **Lumsden** NZ
39G7 **Lund** Sweden
101C2 **Lundazi** Zambia
43B4 **Lundy** *I* Eng
56C2 **Lüneburg** Germany
46D2 **Lunéville** France
100B2 **Lunga** *R* Zambia
86C2 **Lunglei** India
100A2 **Lungue Bungo** *R* Angola
58D2 **Luninec** Belorussia
98B3 **Luobomo** Congo
73B5 **Luocheng** China
73C5 **Luoding** China
72C3 **Luohe** China
72C3 **Luo He** *R* Henan, China
72B2 **Luo He** *R* Shaanxi, China
73C4 **Luoxiao Shan** *Hills* China
72C3 **Luoyang** China
98B3 **Luozi** Zaïre
100B2 **Lupane** Zim
101C2 **Lupilichi** Mozam
Lu Qu = Tao He
30E4 **Luque** Par
45C1 **Lurgan** N Ire
101C2 **Lurio** *R* Mozam
90A3 **Luristan** Region, Iran
100B2 **Lusaka** Zambia
98C3 **Lusambo** Zaïre
55A2 **Lushnjë** Alb
99D3 **Lushoto** Tanz
68B4 **Lushui** China
72E2 **Lüshun** China
43D4 **Luton** Eng
60C3 **Lutsk** Ukraine
99E2 **Luuq** Somalia
99C3 **Luvua** *R* Zaïre
99D3 **Luwegu** *R* Tanz
100C2 **Luwingu** Zambia
71D4 **Luwuk** Indon
46D2 **Luxembourg** Grand Duchy, N W Europe
49D2 **Luxembourg** Lux
73A5 **Luxi** China
95C2 **Luxor** Egypt
61G1 **Luza** Russian Fed
61G1 **Luza** *R* Russian Fed
52A1 **Luzern** Switz
73B5 **Luzhai** China
73B4 **Luzhi** China
73B4 **Luzhou** China
35B1 **Luziânia** Brazil
79B2 **Luzon** *I* Phil
79B1 **Luzon Str** Phil
59C3 **L'vov** Ukraine
44C2 **Lybster** Scot
38H6 **Lycksele** Sweden
100B3 **Lydenburg** S Africa
8B3 **Lyell,Mt** USA
16A2 **Lykens** USA
43C4 **Lyme B** Eng
43C4 **Lyme Regis** Eng
11C3 **Lynchburg** USA
108A2 **Lyndhurst** Aust
15D2 **Lynn** USA
12G3 **Lynn Canal** *Sd* USA
17A1 **Lynn Haven** USA
5H4 **Lynn Lake** Can
5H3 **Lynx L** Can
49C2 **Lyon** France
12G3 **Lyon Canal** *Sd* USA
17B1 **Lyons** Georgia, USA
106A3 **Lyons** *R* Aust
47B2 **Lys** *R* Italy
61J2 **Lys'va** Russian Fed
111B2 **Lyttelton** NZ
13C2 **Lytton** Can
22A1 **Lytton** USA
58D2 **Lyubeshov** Ukraine
60E2 **Lyublino** Russian Fed

M

76C1 **Ma** *R* Viet
94B2 **Ma'agan** Jordan
94B2 **Ma'alot Tarshīha** Israel
92C3 **Ma'an** Jordan
73D3 **Ma'anshan** China
92C2 **Ma'arrat an Nu'mān** Syria
46C1 **Maas** *R* Neth
46C1 **Maaseik** Belg
79B3 **Maasin** Phil
57B2 **Maastricht** Belg
101C3 **Mabalane** Mozam
33F2 **Mabaruma** Guyana
42E3 **Mablethorpe** Eng
101C3 **Mabote** Mozam
58C2 **Mabrita** Belorussia
58D2 **M'adel** Belorussia
35C2 **Macaé** Brazil
9D3 **McAlester** USA
9D4 **McAllen** USA
101C2 **Macaloge** Mozam
33G3 **Macapá** Brazil
35C1 **Macarani** Brazil
32B4 **Macas** Ecuador
31D3 **Macaú** Brazil
73C5 **Macau** Dependency, China
98C2 **M'Bari** *R* CAR
13C2 **McBride** Can
12F2 **McCarthy** USA
13A2 **McCauley I** Can
42C3 **Macclesfield** Eng
6B1 **McClintock B** Can
4H2 **McClintock Chan** Can
16A2 **McClure** USA
22B2 **McClure,L** USA
4G2 **McClure Str** Can
19B3 **McComb** USA
8C2 **McCook** USA
6C2 **Macculloch,C** Can
13C1 **McCusker,Mt** Can
4F4 **McDame** Can
20C2 **McDermitt** USA
13E2 **Macdonald** *R* Can
106C3 **Macdonnell Ranges** *Mts* Aust
50A1 **Macedo de Cavaleiros** Port
55B2 **Macedonia** Republic, Yugos
31D3 **Maceió** Brazil
97B4 **Macenta** Guinea
52B2 **Macerata** Italy
108A2 **Macfarlane,L** Aust
19B3 **McGehee** USA
45B3 **MacGillycuddys Reeks** *Mts* Irish Rep
4C3 **McGrath** USA
35B2 **Machado** Brazil
101C3 **Machaíla** Mozam
99D3 **Machakos** Kenya
32B4 **Machala** Ecuador
101C3 **Machaze** Mozam
87B1 **Mācherla** India
94B2 **Machgharab** Leb
87C1 **Machilīpatnam** India
32C1 **Machiques** Ven
32C6 **Machu-Picchu** *Hist Site* Peru
101C3 **Macia** Mozam
109C1 **MacIntyre** *R* Aust
107D3 **Mackay** Aust
106B3 **Mackay,L** Aust
14C2 **McKeesport** USA
13C1 **Mackenzie** Can
4F3 **Mackenzie** *R* Can
4E3 **Mackenzie B** Can
4G2 **Mackenzie King I** Can
4E3 **Mackenzie Mts** Can
14B1 **Mackinac,Str of** USA
14B1 **Mackinaw City** USA
12D2 **McKinley,Mt** USA
19A3 **McKinney** USA
6C2 **Mackinson Inlet** *B* Can
109D2 **Macksville** Aust
20B2 **Mclaoughlin,Mt** USA
109D1 **Maclean** Aust
100B4 **Maclear** S Africa
5G4 **McLennan** Can
13D2 **McLeod** *R* Can
4G3 **McLeod B** Can
106A3 **McLeod,L** Aust
13C1 **McLeod Lake** Can
4E3 **Macmillan** *R* Can
12H2 **Macmillan P** Can
20B1 **McMinnville** Oregon, USA
112B7 **McMurdo** *Base* Ant
13D2 **McNaughton L** Can
18B1 **Macomb** USA
53A2 **Macomer** Sardegna
101C2 **Macomia** Mozam
49C2 **Mâcon** France
11B3 **Macon** Georgia, USA
18B2 **Macon** Missouri, USA
100B2 **Macondo** Angola
18A2 **McPherson** USA
104F6 **Macquarie** *Is* Aust
109C2 **Macquarie** *R* Aust
109C4 **Macquarie Harbour** *B* Aust
109D2 **Macquarie,L** Aust
17B1 **McRae** USA
112B11 **Mac. Robertson Land** Region, Ant
45B3 **Macroom** Irish Rep
96C1 **M'Sila** Alg
4G3 **McTavish Arm** *B* Can
108A1 **Macumba** *R* Aust
47C2 **Macunaga** Italy
4F3 **McVicar Arm** *B* Can
59B3 **M'yaróvár** Hung
94B3 **Mādabā** Jordan
95A3 **Madadi** *Well* Chad
89J10 **Madagascar** *I* Indian O
95A2 **Madama** Niger
71F4 **Madang** PNG
97C3 **Madaoua** Niger
86C2 **Madaripur** Bang
90B2 **Madau** Turkmenistan
15C1 **Madawaska** *R* Can
96A1 **Madeira** *I* Atlantic O
33E5 **Madeira** *R* Brazil
7D5 **Madeleine, Îsle de la** Can
24B2 **Madera** Mexico
21A2 **Madera** USA
87A1 **Madgaon** India
86B1 **Madhubani** India
86A2 **Madhya Pradesh** State, India
87B2 **Madikeri** India
98B3 **Madimba** Zaïre
98B3 **Madingo Kayes** Congo
98B3 **Madingou** Congo
10B3 **Madison** Indiana, USA
10B2 **Madison** Wisconsin, USA
18C2 **Madisonville** Kentucky, USA
19A3 **Madisonville** Texas, USA
78C4 **Madiun** Indon
99D2 **Mado Gashi** Kenya
47D1 **Madonna Di Campiglio** Italy
87C2 **Madras** India
20B2 **Madras** USA
29A6 **Madre de Dios** *I* Chile
32D6 **Madre de Dios** *R* Bol
50B1 **Madrid** Spain
50B2 **Madridejos** Spain
78C4 **Madura** *I* Indon
87B3 **Madurai** India
75B1 **Maebashi** Japan
76B3 **Mae Khlong** *R* Thai
77B4 **Mae Nam Lunang** *R* Thai

76C2 **Mae Nam Mun** *R* Thai
76B2 **Mae Nam Ping** *R* Thai
101D2 **Maevatanana** Madag
101G1 **Mafeteng** Lesotho
109C3 **Maffra** Aust
99D3 **Mafia** *I* Tanz
101G1 **Mafikeng** S Africa
30G4 **Mafra** Brazil
92C3 **Mafraq** Jordan
32C2 **Magangué** Colombia
34D3 **Magdalena** Arg
24A1 **Magdalena** Mexico
26C4 **Magdalena** *R* Colombia
78D1 **Magdalena,Mt** Malay
56C2 **Magdeburg** Germany
31C6 **Magé** Brazil
78C4 **Magelang** Indon
47C1 **Maggia** *R* Switz
92B4 **Maghâgha** Egypt
45C1 **Magherafelt** N Ire
55A2 **Maglie** Italy
61J3 **Magnitogorsk** Russian Fed
19B3 **Magnolia** USA
101C2 **Magoé** Mozam
15D1 **Magog** Can
23B1 **Magosal** Mexico
13E2 **Magrath** Can
7A3 **Maguse River** Can
76B1 **Magwe** Burma
90A2 **Mahābād** Iran
86B1 **Mahabharat Range** *Mts* Nepal
87A1 **Mahād** India
85D4 **Mahadeo Hills** India
101D2 **Mahajanga** Madag
100B3 **Mahalapye** Botswana
86A2 **Mahānadi** *R* India
101D2 **Mahanoro** Madag
16A2 **Mahanoy City** USA
87A1 **Maharashtra** State, India
86A2 **Māhāsamund** India
76C2 **Maha Sarakham** Thai
101D2 **Mahavavy** *R* Madag
87B1 **Mahbūbnagar** India
96D1 **Mahdia** Tunisia
87B2 **Mahe** India
85D4 **Mahekar** India
101D2 **Mahéli** *I* Comoros
86A2 **Mahendragarh** India
99D3 **Mahenge** Tanz
85C4 **Mahesāna** India
110C1 **Mahia Pen** NZ
85D3 **Mahoba** India
51C2 **Mahón** Spain
12J1 **Mahony L** Can
96D1 **Mahrés** Tunisia
85C4 **Mahuva** India
32C1 **Maicao** Colombia
47B1 **Maîche** France
43E4 **Maidstone** Eng
98B1 **Maiduguri** Nig
86A2 **Maihar** India
86C2 **Maijdi** Bang
76B3 **Mail Kyun** *I* Burma
84A1 **Maimana** Afghan
14B1 **Main Chan** Can
98B3 **Mai-Ndombe** *L* Zaïre
10D2 **Maine** State, USA
48B2 **Maine** *Region* France
44C2 **Mainland** *I* Scot
85D3 **Mainpuri** India
46A2 **Maintenon** France
101D2 **Maintirano** Madag
57B2 **Mainz** Germany
97A4 **Maio** *I* Cape Verde
29C2 **Maipó** *Mt* Arg/Chile
34D3 **Maipú** Arg
32D1 **Maiquetía** Ven
47B2 **Maira** *R* Italy
86C1 **Mairābāri** India
86C2 **Maiskhal I** Bang
107E4 **Maitland** New South Wales, Aust
108A2 **Maitland** S Australia, Aust
112C12 **Maitri** *Base* Ant
74D3 **Maizuru** Japan
70C4 **Majene** Indon
30B2 **Majes** *R* Peru
99D2 **Maji** Eth
72D2 **Majia He** *R* China
Majunga = Mahajanga
70C4 **Makale** Indon
86B1 **Makalu** *Mt* China/Nepal
98B2 **Makanza** Zaïre
52C2 **Makarska** Croatia
61F2 **Makaryev** Russian Fed
Makassar = Ujung Pandang
78D3 **Makassar Str** Indon
61H4 **Makat** Kazakhstan
97A4 **Makeni** Sierra Leone
60E4 **Makeyevka** Ukraine
100B3 **Makgadikgadi** *Salt Pan* Botswana
61G5 **Makhachkala** Russian Fed
99D3 **Makindu** Kenya
88H5 **Makkah** S Arabia
7E4 **Makkovik** Can
59C3 **Makó** Hung
98B2 **Makokou** Gabon
110C1 **Makorako,Mt** NZ
98B2 **Makoua** Congo
85C3 **Makrāna** India
85A3 **Makran Coast Range** *Mts* Pak
96C1 **Makthar** Tunisia
93D2 **Mākū** Iran
98C3 **Makumbi** Zaïre
74C4 **Makurazaki** Japan
97C4 **Makurdi** Nig
79B4 **Malabang** Phil
87A2 **Malabar Coast** India
89E7 **Malabo** Bioko
77C5 **Malacca,Str of** S E Asia
32C2 **Málaga** Colombia
50B2 **Malaga** Spain
101D3 **Malaimbandy** Madag
107F1 **Malaita** *I* Solomon Is
99D2 **Malakal** Sudan
84C2 **Malakand** Pak
78C4 **Malang** Indon
98B3 **Malange** Angola
97C3 **Malanville** Benin
39H7 **Mälaren** *L* Sweden
34B3 **Malargüe** Arg
12F3 **Malaspina Gl** USA
93C2 **Malatya** Turk
101C2 **Malawi** Republic, Africa
Malawi,L = Nyasa,L
79C4 **Malaybalay** Phil
90A3 **Malāyer** Iran
70B3 **Malaysia** Fed, S E Asia
93D2 **Malazgirt** Turk
58B2 **Malbork** Pol
56C2 **Malchin** Germany
18C2 **Malden** USA
83B5 **Maldives Is** Indian O
104B4 **Maldives Ridge** Indian O
29F2 **Maldonado** Urug
47D1 **Male** Italy
85C4 **Malegaon** India
59B3 **Malé Karpaty** *Upland* Czech
101C2 **Malema** Mozam
84B2 **Mālestān** Afghan
38H5 **Malgomaj** *L* Sweden
95B3 **Malha** *Well* Sudan
20C2 **Malheur L** USA
97B3 **Mali** Republic, Africa
78D1 **Malinau** Indon
99E3 **Malindi** Kenya
Malines = Mechelen
40B2 **Malin Head** *Pt* Irish Rep
86A2 **Malkala Range** *Mts* India
85D4 **Malkāpur** India
55C2 **Malkara** Turk
54C2 **Malko Tŭrnovo** Bulg
44B3 **Mallaig** Scot
95C2 **Mallawi** Egypt
47D1 **Málles Venosta** Italy
51C2 **Mallorca** *I* Spain
45B2 **Mallow** Irish Rep
38G6 **Malm** Nor
38J5 **Malmberget** Sweden
46D1 **Malmédy** Germany
43C4 **Malmesbury** Eng
100A4 **Malmesbury** S Africa
39G7 **Malmö** Sweden
61G2 **Malmyzh** Russian Fed
79B3 **Malolos** Phil
15D2 **Malone** USA
101G1 **Maloti Mts** Lesotho
38F6 **Måloy** Nor
28A2 **Malpelo** *I* Colombia
34A2 **Malpo** *R* Chile
85D3 **Mālpura** India
8C2 **Malta** Montana, USA
53B3 **Malta** *Chan* Malta/Italy
53B3 **Malta** *I* Medit S
100A3 **Maltahöhe** Namibia
42D2 **Malton** Eng
39G6 **Malung** Sweden
87A1 **Mālvan** India
19B3 **Malvern** USA
85D4 **Malwa Plat** India
65F5 **Malyy Kavkaz** *Mts* Azerbaijan/Georgia
61G4 **Malyy Uzen'** *R* Kazakhstan
63D2 **Mama** Russian Fed
61H2 **Mamadysh** Russian Fed
99C2 **Mambasa** Zaïre
71E4 **Mamberamo** *R* Indon
98B2 **Mambéré** *R* CAR
98A2 **Mamfé** Cam
33D6 **Mamoré** *R* Bol
97A3 **Mamou** Guinea
101D2 **Mampikony** Madag
97B4 **Mampong** Ghana
94B3 **Mamshit** *Hist Site* Israel
100B3 **Mamuno** Botswana
97B4 **Man** Ivory Coast
21C4 **Mana** Hawaiian Is
101D3 **Manabo** Madag
33E4 **Manacapuru** Brazil
51C2 **Manacor** Spain
71D3 **Manado** Indon
25D3 **Managua** Nic
101D3 **Manakara** Madag
101D2 **Mananara** Madag
101D3 **Mananjary** Madag
111A3 **Manapouri** NZ
111A3 **Manapouri,L** NZ
86C1 **Manas** Bhutan
82C1 **Manas** China
65K5 **Manas Hu** *L* China
86A1 **Manaslu** *Mt* Nepal
16B2 **Manasquan** USA
33F4 **Manaus** Brazil
92B2 **Manavgat** Turk
93C2 **Manbij** Syria
42B2 **Man,Calf of** *I* Eng
87B1 **Mancheral** India
15D2 **Manchester** Connecticut, USA
42C3 **Manchester** Eng
10C2 **Manchester** New Hampshire, USA
16A2 **Manchester** Pennsylvania, USA
69E2 **Manchuria** Hist Region, China
91B4 **Mand** *R* Iran
101C2 **Manda** Tanz
35A2 **Mandaguari** Brazil
39F7 **Mandal** Nor
76B1 **Mandalay** Burma
68C2 **Mandalgovĭ** Mongolia
8C2 **Mandan** USA
14A2 **Mandelona** USA
99E2 **Mandera** Eth
26B3 **Mandeville** Jamaica
101C2 **Mandimba** Mozam
86A2 **Mandla** India
101D2 **Mandritsara** Madag
85D4 **Mandsaur** India
53C2 **Manduria** Italy
85B4 **Māndvi** India
87B2 **Mandya** India
58D2 **Manevichi** Ukraine
42D3 **Manfield** Eng
53C2 **Manfredonia** Italy
98B1 **Manga** *Desert Region* Niger
110C1 **Mangakino** NZ
54C2 **Mangalia** Rom
98B1 **Mangalmé** Chad
87A2 **Mangalore** India
78B3 **Manggar** Indon
68B3 **Mangnia** China
101C2 **Mangoche** Malawi
101D3 **Mangoky** *R* Madag
71D4 **Mangole** *I* Indon
85B4 **Māngral** India
63E2 **Mangui** China
8D3 **Manhattan** USA
31C6 **Manhuacu** Brazil
101D2 **Mania** *R* Madag
101C2 **Manica** Mozam
7D5 **Manicouagan** *R* Can
91A4 **Manifah** S Arabia
79B3 **Manila** Phil
109D2 **Manilla** Aust
97B3 **Maninian** Ivory Coast
86C2 **Manipur** State, India
86C2 **Manipur** *R* Burma
92A2 **Manisa** Turk
41C3 **Man,Isle of** Irish S
14A2 **Manistee** USA
14A2 **Manistee** *R* USA
14A1 **Manistique** USA
5H4 **Manitoba** Province, Can
5J4 **Manitoba,L** Can
13F2 **Manito L** Can
14A1 **Manitou Is** USA
7B5 **Manitoulin** *I* Can
14A2 **Manitowoc** USA
15C1 **Maniwaki** Can
32B2 **Manizales** Colombia
101D3 **Manja** Madag
106A4 **Manjimup** Aust
87B1 **Mānjra** *R* India
10A2 **Mankato** USA
97B4 **Mankono** Ivory Coast
12D2 **Manley Hot Springs** USA
110B1 **Manly** NZ
85C4 **Manmād** India
78A3 **Manna** Indon
108A2 **Mannahill** Aust
87B3 **Mannar** Sri Lanka
87B3 **Mannār,G of** India
87B2 **Mannārgudi** India
57B3 **Mannheim** Germany
13D1 **Manning** Can
17B1 **Manning** USA
108A2 **Mannum** Aust
97A4 **Mano** Sierra Leone
71E4 **Manokwari** Indon
98C3 **Manono** Zaïre
76B3 **Manoron** Burma
75B1 **Mano-wan** *B* Japan
74B2 **Manp'o** N Korea
84D3 **Mānsa** India
100B2 **Mansa** Zambia
6B3 **Mansel I** Can
19B2 **Mansfield** Arkansas, USA
108C3 **Mansfield** Aust
19B3 **Mansfield** Louisiana, USA
16D1 **Mansfield** Massachusetts, USA
10B2 **Mansfield** Ohio, USA
15C2 **Mansfield** Pennsylvania, USA
71E2 **Mansyu Deep** Pacific O
32A4 **Manta** Ecuador
79A4 **Mantalingajan,Mt** Phil
32B6 **Mantaro** *R* Peru
22B2 **Manteca** USA
48C2 **Mantes** France
52B1 **Mantova** Italy
38J6 **Mantta** Fin
61F2 **Manturovo** Russian Fed
35A2 **Manuel Ribas** Brazil
79B4 **Manukan** Phil
110B1 **Manukau** NZ
71F4 **Manus** *I* Pacific O

50B2 **Manzanares** Spain
25E2 **Manzanillo** Cuba
24B3 **Manzanillo** Mexico
63D3 **Manzhouli** China
94C3 **Manzil** Jordan
101C3 **Manzini** Swaziland
98B1 **Mao** Chad
72A2 **Maomao Shan** *Mt* China
73C5 **Maoming** China
101C3 **Mapai** Mozam
71E3 **Mapia** *Is* Pacific O
79A4 **Mapin** *I* Phil
5H5 **Maple Creek** Can
101H1 **Maputo** Mozam
101H1 **Maputo** *R* Mozam
Ma Qu = Huange He
72A3 **Maqu** China
86B1 **Maquan He** *R* China
98B3 **Maquela do Zombo** Angola
29C4 **Maquinchao** Arg
31B3 **Marabá** Brazil
32C1 **Maracaibo** Ven
32D1 **Maracay** Ven
95A2 **Marādah** Libya
97C3 **Maradi** Niger
90A2 **Marāgheh** Iran
99D2 **Maralal** Kenya
107F1 **Maramasike** *I* Solomon Is
100B2 **Maramba** Zambia
90A2 **Marand** Iran
31B2 **Maranhõa** State, Brazil
109C1 **Maranoa** *R* Aust
32B4 **Marañón** *R* Peru
7B5 **Marathon** Can
17B2 **Marathon** Florida, USA
78D2 **Maratua** *I* Indon
23A2 **Maravatio** Mexico
79B4 **Marawi** Phil
34B2 **Marayes** Arg
50B2 **Marbella** Spain
106A3 **Marble Bar** Aust
100B3 **Marblehall** S Africa
16D1 **Marblehead** USA
57B2 **Marburg** Germany
57B2 **Marche** Belg
50A2 **Marchean** Spain
46C1 **Marche-en-Famenne** Belg
32J7 **Marchena** *I* Ecuador
17B2 **Marco** USA
34C2 **Marcos Juárez** Arg
12E2 **Marcus Baker,Mt** USA
15D2 **Marcy,Mt** USA
84C2 **Mardan** Pak
29E3 **Mar del Plata** Arg
93D2 **Mardin** Turk
99D1 **Mareb** *R* Eth
16B1 **Margaretville** USA
43E4 **Margate** Eng
54B1 **Marghita** Rom
109C4 **Maria I** Aust
104F3 **Mariana** *Is* Pacific O
13E1 **Mariana Lake** Can
104F3 **Marianas Trench** Pacific O
86C1 **Mariāni** India
19B3 **Marianna** Arkansas, USA
17A1 **Marianna** Florida, USA
7G4 **Maria Van Diemen,C** NZ
59B3 **Mariazell** Austria
52C1 **Maribor** Slovenia
99C2 **Maridi** Sudan
112B5 **Marie Byrd Land** Region, Ant
27E3 **Marie Galante** *I* Caribbean S
39H6 **Mariehamn** Fin
46C1 **Mariembourg** Belg
33G2 **Marienburg** Surinam
100A3 **Mariental** Namibia
39G7 **Mariestad** Sweden
17B1 **Marietta** Georgia, USA
14B3 **Marietta** Ohio, USA
19A3 **Marietta** Oklahoma, USA
27Q2 **Marigot** Dominica
60B3 **Marijampole** Lithuania
31B6 **Marilia** Brazil
98B3 **Marimba** Angola
79B3 **Marinduque** *I* Phil
10B2 **Marinette** USA
30F3 **Maringá** Brazil
98C2 **Maringa** *R* Zaïre
18B2 **Marion** Arkansas, USA
18C2 **Marion** Illinois, USA
10B2 **Marion** Indiana, USA
10B2 **Marion** Ohio, USA
17C1 **Marion** S Carolina, USA
11B3 **Marion,L** USA
107E2 **Marion Reef** Aust
21B2 **Mariposa** USA
22B2 **Mariposa** *R* USA
22B2 **Mariposa Res** USA
60C5 **Marista** *R* Bulg
60E4 **Mariupol'** Ukraine
61G2 **Mariyskaya Respublika,** Russian Fed
94B2 **Marjayoun** Leb
58D2 **Marjina Gorki** Belorussia
94B3 **Marka** Jordan
99E2 **Marka** Somalia
56C1 **Markaryd** Sweden
43C3 **Market Drayton** Eng
43D3 **Market Harborough** Eng
112A **Markham,Mt** Ant
22C1 **Markleeville** USA
16D1 **Marlboro** Massachusetts, USA
107D3 **Marlborough** Aust
46B2 **Marle** France
19A3 **Marlin** USA
48C3 **Marmande** France
55C2 **Marmara Adi** *I* Turk
92A1 **Marmara,S of** Turk
55C3 **Marmaris** Turk
14B3 **Marmet** USA
52B1 **Marmolada** *Mt* Italy
12D3 **Marmot B** USA
47A1 **Marnay** France
46B2 **Marne** Department, France
46B2 **Marne** *R* France
98B2 **Maro** Chad
101D2 **Maroantsetra** Madag
101C2 **Marondera** Zim
33G3 **Maroni** *R* French Guiana
109D1 **Maroochydore** Aust
98B1 **Maroua** Cam
101D2 **Marovoay** Madag
11B4 **Marquesas Keys** *Is* USA
10B2 **Marquette** USA
46A1 **Marquise** France
109C2 **Marra** *R* Aust
101H1 **Marracuene** Mozam
96B1 **Marrakech** Mor
106C3 **Marree** Aust
19B4 **Marrero** USA
101C2 **Marromeu** Mozam
101C2 **Marrupa** Mozam
95C2 **Marsa Alam** Egypt
99D2 **Marsabit** Kenya
53B3 **Marsala** Italy
49D3 **Marseille** France
12B2 **Marshall** Alaska, USA
14A3 **Marshall** Illinois, USA
14B2 **Marshall** Michigan, USA
18B2 **Marshall** Missouri, USA
11A3 **Marshall** Texas, USA
105G3 **Marshall Is** Pacific O
18B2 **Marshfield** Missouri, USA
26B1 **Marsh Harbour** The Bahamas
19B4 **Marsh I** USA
12H2 **Marsh L** Can
76B2 **Martaban,G of** Burma
78A3 **Martapura** Indon
78C3 **Martapura** Indon
15D2 **Martha's Vineyard** *I* USA
49D2 **Martigny** Switz
59B3 **Martin** Czech
111C2 **Martinborough** NZ
34B3 **Martín de Loyola** Arg
23B1 **Martínez de la Torre** Mexico
27E4 **Martinique** *I* Caribbean S
17A1 **Martin,L** USA
15C3 **Martinsburg** USA
14B2 **Martins Ferry** USA
103G6 **Martin Vaz** *I* Atlantic O
49D3 **Martiques** France
110C2 **Marton** NZ
50B2 **Martos** Spain
78D1 **Marudi** Malay
84B2 **Maruf** Afghan
75A2 **Marugame** Japan
85C3 **Mārwār** India
65H6 **Mary** Turkmenistan
107E3 **Maryborough** Queensland, Aust
108B3 **Maryborough** Victoria, Aust
5F4 **Mary Henry,Mt** Can
10C3 **Maryland** State, USA
42C2 **Maryport** Eng
21A2 **Marysville** California, USA
18A2 **Marysville** Kansas, USA
20B1 **Marysville** Washington, USA
10A2 **Maryville** Iowa, USA
18B1 **Maryville** Missouri, USA
95A2 **Marzuq** Libya
Masada = Mezada
94B2 **Mas'adah** Syria
99D3 **Masai Steppe** *Upland* Tanz
99D3 **Masaka** Uganda
93E2 **Masally** Azerbaijan
74B3 **Masan** S Korea
101C2 **Masasi** Tanz
25D3 **Masaya** Nic
79B3 **Masbate** Phil
79B3 **Masbate** *I* Phil
96C1 **Mascara** Alg
23A1 **Mascota** Mexico
35D1 **Mascote** Brazil
101G1 **Maseru** Lesotho
66C3 **Mashad** Iran
84B2 **Mashaki** Afghan
90C2 **Mashhad** Iran
98B3 **Masi-Manimba** Zaïre
99D2 **Masindi** Uganda
99C3 **Masisi** Zaïre
90A3 **Masjed Soleyman** Iran
101E2 **Masoala** *C* Madag
10A2 **Mason City** USA
91C5 **Masqat** Oman
52B2 **Massa** Italy
10C2 **Massachusetts** State, USA
15D2 **Massachusetts B** USA
98B1 **Massakori** Chad
101C3 **Massangena** Mozam
Massawa = Mits'iwa
15D2 **Massena** USA
98B1 **Massénya** Chad
14B1 **Massey** Can
49C2 **Massif Central** *Mts* France
98B2 **Massif de l'Adamaoua** *Mts* Cam
26C3 **Massif de la Hotte** *Mts* Haiti
101D3 **Massif de l'Isalo** *Upland* Madag
98C2 **Massif des Bongo** *Upland* CAR
49D2 **Massif du Pelvoux** *Mts* France
101D2 **Massif du Tsaratanana** *Mt* Madag
14B2 **Massillon** USA
97B3 **Massina** Region, Mali
101C3 **Massinga** Mozam
101C3 **Massingir** Mozam
61H4 **Masteksay** Kazakhstan
111C2 **Masterton** NZ
74C4 **Masuda** Japan
98B3 **Masuku** Gabon
100C3 **Masvingo** Zim
92C2 **Maşyāf** Syria
98B3 **Matadi** Zaïre
25D3 **Matagalpa** Nic
7C4 **Matagami** Can
9D4 **Matagorda B** USA
110C1 **Matakana I** NZ
100A2 **Matala** Angola
87C3 **Matale** Sri Lanka
97A3 **Matam** Sen
97C3 **Matameye** Niger
24C2 **Matamoros** Mexico
95B2 **Ma'tan as Sarra** *Well* Libya
7D5 **Matane** Can
25D2 **Matanzas** Cuba
34A2 **Mataquito** *R* Chile
87C3 **Matara** Sri Lanka
106A1 **Mataram** Indon
30B2 **Matarani** Peru
51C1 **Mataró** Spain
111A3 **Mataura** NZ
24B2 **Matehuala** Mexico
27L1 **Matelot** Trinidad
53C2 **Matera** Italy
59C3 **Mátészalka** Hung
85D3 **Mathura** India
79C4 **Mati** Phil
78D3 **Matisiri** *I* Indon
43D3 **Matlock** Eng
33F6 **Mato Grosso** Brazil
33F6 **Mato Grosso** State, Brazil
30E2 **Mato Grosso do Sul** State, Brazil
101H1 **Matola** Mozam
91C5 **Matrah** Oman
92A3 **Matrûh** Egypt
74C3 **Matsue** Japan
74E2 **Matsumae** Japan
74D3 **Matsumoto** Japan
74D4 **Matsusaka** Japan
74C4 **Matsuyama** Japan
7B5 **Mattagami** *R* Can
15C1 **Mattawa** Can
52A1 **Matterhorn** *Mt* Italy/Switz
26C2 **Matthew Town** The Bahamas
16C2 **Mattituck** USA
18C2 **Mattoon** USA
84B2 **Matun** Afghan
27L1 **Matura B** Trinidad
33E2 **Maturin** Ven
86A1 **Mau** India
101C2 **Maúa** Mozam
49C1 **Maubeuge** France
108B2 **Maude** Aust
103J8 **Maud Seamount** Atlantic O
21C4 **Maui** *I* Hawaiian Is
34A3 **Maule** *R* Chile
14B2 **Maumee** USA
14B2 **Maumee** *R* USA
100B2 **Maun** Botswana
21C4 **Mauna Kea** *Mt* Hawaiian Is
21C4 **Mauna Loa** *Mt* Hawaiian Is
4F3 **Maunoir** *L* Can
4F3 **Maunoir,L** Can
48C2 **Mauriac** France
96A2 **Mauritania** Republic, Africa
100E3 **Mauritius** *I* Indian O
100B2 **Mavinga** Angola
86C2 **Mawlaik** Burma
112C10 **Mawson** *Base* Ant
78B3 **Maya** *I* Indon
63F2 **Maya** *R* Russian Fed
93D2 **Mayādīn** Syria

11C4 **Mayaguana** *I* The Bahamas
27D3 **Mayagüez** Puerto Rico
97C3 **Mayahi** Niger
98B3 **Mayama** Congo
90C2 **Mayamey** Iran
42B2 **Maybole** Scot
10C3 **May,C** USA
109C4 **Maydena** Aust
46D1 **Mayen** Germany
48B2 **Mayenne** France
13D2 **Mayerthorpe** Can
18C2 **Mayfield** USA
61E5 **Maykop** Russian Fed
65H6 **Maymaneh** Afghan
76B1 **Maymyo** Burma
4E3 **Mayo** Can
45B2 **Mayo** County, Irish Rep
16A3 **Mayo** USA
45B1 **Mayo,Mts of** Irish Rep
79B3 **Mayon** *Mt* Phil
51C2 **Mayor** *Mt* Spain
34C3 **Mayor Buratovich** Arg
110C1 **Mayor I** NZ
30D2 **Mayor P Lagerenza** Par
101D2 **Mayotte** *I* Indian O
27H2 **May Pen** Jamaica
16B3 **May Point,C** USA
47D1 **Mayrhofen** Austria
16B3 **Mays Landing** USA
14B3 **Maysville** USA
98B3 **Mayumba** Gabon
100B2 **Mazabuka** Zambia
84D1 **Mazar** China
94B3 **Mazār** Jordan
53B3 **Mazara del Vallo** Italy
84B1 **Mazar-i-Sharif** Afghan
24B2 **Mazatlán** Mexico
60B2 **Mazeikiai** Lithuania
94B3 **Mazra** Jordan
101C3 **Mbabane** Swaziland
98B2 **Mbaïki** CAR
99D3 **Mbala** Zambia
100B3 **Mbalabala** Zim
99D2 **Mbale** Uganda
98B2 **Mbalmayo** Cam
98B2 **Mbam** *R* Cam
101C2 **Mbamba Bay** Tanz
98B2 **Mbandaka** Zaïre
98B3 **Mbanza Congo** Angola
98B3 **Mbanza-Ngungu** Zaïre
99D3 **Mbarara** Uganda
98B2 **Mbènza** Congo
98B2 **Mbére** *R* Cam
99D3 **Mbeya** Tanz
98B3 **Mbinda** Congo
97A3 **Mbout** Maur
98C3 **Mbuji-Mayi** Zaïre
99D3 **Mbulu** Tanz
96B2 **Mcherrah** Region, Alg
101C2 **Mchinji** Malawi
76D3 **Mdrak** Viet
9B3 **Mead,L** USA
5H4 **Meadow Lake** Can
14B2 **Meadville** USA
7E4 **Mealy Mts** Can
109C1 **Meandarra** Aust
5G4 **Meander River** Can
45C2 **Meath** County, Irish Rep
49C2 **Meaux** France
16C1 **Mechanicville** USA
56A2 **Mechelen** Belg
96B1 **Mecheria** Alg
56C2 **Mecklenburg-Vorpommern** *State* Germany
56C2 **Mecklenburger Bucht** *B* Germany
101C2 **Meconta** Mozam
101C2 **Mecuburi** Mozam
101D2 **Mecufi** Mozam
101C2 **Mecula** Mozam
70A3 **Medan** Indon
34C3 **Medanos** Arg
34D2 **Médanos** Arg
13E2 **Medecine Hat** Can
32B2 **Medellín** Colombia
96D1 **Medenine** Tunisia
8A2 **Medford** USA
54C2 **Medgidia** Rom
34B2 **Media Agua** Arg
54B1 **Mediaş** Rom
20C1 **Medical Lake** USA
5G5 **Medicine Hat** Can
35C1 **Medina** Brazil
80B3 **Medina** S Arabia
50B1 **Medinaceli** Spain
50B1 **Medina del Campo** Spain
50A1 **Medina de Rio Seco** Spain
86B2 **Medinīpur** India
88E4 **Mediterranean S** Europe
13F2 **Medley** Can
61J3 **Mednogorsk** Russian Fed
86D1 **Mêdog** China
98B2 **Medouneu** Gabon
61F3 **Medvedista** *R* Russian Fed
64E3 **Medvezh'yegorsk** Russian Fed
106A3 **Meekatharra** Aust
84D3 **Meerut** India
99D2 **Mēga** Eth
55B3 **Megalópolis** Greece
55B3 **Mégara** Greece
86C1 **Meghālaya** State, India
86C2 **Meghna** *R* Bang
94B2 **Megiddo** *Hist Site* Israel
91B4 **Mehran** *R* Iran
90B3 **Mehriz** Iran
35B1 **Meia Ponte** *R* Brazil
98B2 **Meiganga** Cam
76B1 **Meiktila** Burma
47C1 **Meiringen** Switz
73A4 **Meishan** China
57C2 **Meissen** Germany
73D5 **Mei Xian** China
73D5 **Meizhou** China
30B3 **Mejillones** Chile
98B2 **Mekambo** Gabon
99D1 **Mek'elē** Eth
96B1 **Meknès** Mor
76D3 **Mekong** *R* Camb
97C3 **Mekrou** *R* Benin
77C5 **Melaka** Malay
104F4 **Melanesia** *Region* Pacific O
78C3 **Melawi** *R* Indon
107D4 **Melbourne** Aust
11B4 **Melbourne** USA
9C4 **Melchor Muźguiz** Mexico
61J3 **Meleuz** Russian Fed
98B1 **Melfi** Chad
5H4 **Melfort** Can
96B1 **Melilla** N W Africa
29B4 **Melimoyu** *Mt* Chile
34C2 **Melincué** Arg
34A2 **Melipilla** Chile
60E4 **Melitopol'** Ukraine
6D2 **Meliville Bugt** *B* Greenland
99D2 **Melka Guba** Eth
101H1 **Melmoth** S Africa
34C2 **Melo** Arg
29F2 **Melo** Urug
22B2 **Melones Res** USA
12D1 **Melozitna** *R* USA
47C1 **Mels** Switz
43D3 **Melton Mowbry** Eng
49C2 **Melun** France
5H4 **Melville** Can
27Q2 **Melville,C** Dominica
4F3 **Melville Hills** *Mts* Can
106C2 **Melville I** Aust
4G2 **Melville I** Can
7E4 **Melville,L** Can
6B3 **Melville Pen** Can
45B1 **Melvin,L** Irish Rep
101D2 **Memba** Mozam
106A1 **Memboro** Indon
57C3 **Memmingen** Germany
78B2 **Mempawan** Indon
11B3 **Memphis** Tennessee, USA
19B3 **Mena** USA
43B3 **Menai Str** Wales
97C3 **Ménaka** Mali
14A2 **Menasha** USA
78C3 **Mendawai** *R* Indon
49C3 **Mende** France
99D2 **Mendebo** *Mts* Eth
43C4 **Mendip Hills** *Upland* Eng
20B2 **Mendocino,C** USA
105J2 **Mendocino Seascarp** Pacific O
22B2 **Mendota** California, USA
29C2 **Mendoza** Arg
29C3 **Mendoza** State, Arg
55C3 **Menemen** Turk
46B1 **Menen** Belg
72D3 **Mengcheng** China
78B3 **Menggala** Indon
76B1 **Menghai** China
73A5 **Mengla** China
76B1 **Menglian** China
73A5 **Mengzi** China
107D4 **Menindee** Aust
108B2 **Menindee L** Aust
108A3 **Meningie** Aust
14A1 **Menominee** USA
14A2 **Menomonee Falls** USA
100A2 **Menongue** Angola
51C1 **Menorca** *I* Spain
12F2 **Mentasta Mts** USA
78B3 **Mentok** Indon
14B2 **Mentor** USA
46B2 **Ménu** France
72A2 **Menyuan** China
61H2 **Menzelinsk** Russian Fed
56B2 **Meppen** Germany
78D2 **Merah** Indon
18B2 **Meramec** *R* USA
52B1 **Merano** Italy
71F4 **Merauke** Indon
8A3 **Merced** USA
22B2 **Merced** *R* USA
29B2 **Mercedario** *Mt* Chile
29C2 **Mercedes** Arg
29E2 **Mercedes** Buenos Aires, Arg
30E4 **Mercedes** Corrientes, Arg
29E2 **Mercedes** Urug
110C1 **Mercury B** NZ
110C1 **Mercury Is** NZ
4F2 **Mercy B** Can
6D3 **Mercy,C** Can
99E2 **Meregh** Somalia
76B3 **Mergui** Burma
76B3 **Mergui Arch** Burma
25D2 **Mérida** Mexico
50A2 **Mérida** Spain
32C2 **Mérida** Ven
11B3 **Meridian** USA
109C3 **Merimbula** Aust
108B2 **Meringur** Aust
95C3 **Merowe** Sudan
106A4 **Merredin** Aust
42B2 **Merrick** *Mt* Scot
14A2 **Merrillville** USA
13C2 **Merritt** Can
17B2 **Merritt Island** USA
109D2 **Merriwa** Aust
99E1 **Mersa Fatma** Eth
51B2 **Mers el Kebir** Alg
42C3 **Mersey** *R* Eng
42C3 **Merseyside** Metropolitan County, Eng
92B2 **Mersin** Turk
77C5 **Mersing** Malay
85C3 **Merta** India
43C4 **Merthyr Tydfil** Wales
50A2 **Mertola** Port
99D3 **Meru** *Mt* Tanz
60E5 **Merzifon** Turk
46D2 **Merzig** Germany
9B3 **Mesa** USA
46E1 **Meschede** Germany
93D1 **Mescit Dağ** *Mt* Turk
12C3 **Meshik** USA
99C2 **Meshra Er Req** Sudan
47C1 **Mesocco** Switz
55B3 **Mesolóngion** Greece
19A3 **Mesquite** Texas, USA
101C2 **Messalo** *R* Mozam
53C3 **Messina** Italy
100B3 **Messina** S Africa
55B3 **Messíni** Greece
55B3 **Messiniakós Kólpos** *G* Greece
54B2 **Mesta** *R* Bulg
52B1 **Mestre** Italy
32C3 **Meta** *R* Colombia
60D2 **Meta** *R* Russian Fed
32D2 **Meta** *R* Ven
6C3 **Meta Incognito Pen** Can
19B4 **Metairie** USA
20C1 **Metaline Falls** USA
30D4 **Metán** Arg
101C2 **Metangula** Mozam
53C2 **Metaponto** Italy
44C3 **Methil** Scot
16D1 **Methuen** USA
111B2 **Methven** NZ
12H3 **Metlakatla** USA
18C2 **Metropolis** USA
87B2 **Mettūr** India
49D2 **Metz** France
70A3 **Meulaboh** Indon
46A2 **Meulan** France
46C2 **Meuse** Department, France
49D2 **Meuse** *R* France
19A3 **Mexia** USA
24A1 **Mexicali** Mexico
24B2 **Mexico** Federal Republic, Cent America
24C3 **México** Mexico
23A2 **México** State, Mexico
18B2 **Mexico** USA
24C2 **Mexico,G of** Cent America
94B3 **Mezada** *Hist Site* Israel
23B2 **Mezcala** Mexico
64F3 **Mezen'** Russian Fed
64G2 **Mezhdusharskiy, Ostrov** *I* Russian Fed
85D4 **Mhow** India
23B2 **Miahuatlán** Mexico
11B4 **Miami** Florida, USA
18B2 **Miami** Oklahoma, USA
11B4 **Miami Beach** USA
90A2 **Miandowāb** Iran
101D2 **Miandrivazo** Madag
90A2 **Mīāneh** Iran
84C2 **Mianwali** Pak
73A3 **Mianyang** China
73C3 **Mianyang** China
73A3 **Mianzhu** China
72E2 **Miaodao Qundao** *Arch* China
73B4 **Miao Ling** *Upland* China
61K3 **Miass** Russian Fed
59C3 **Michalovce** Czech
27D3 **Miches** Dom Rep
10B2 **Michigan** State, USA
14A2 **Michigan City** USA
10B2 **Michigan,L** USA
7B5 **Michipicoten I** Can
23A2 **Michoacan** State, Mexico
54C2 **Michurin** Bulg
61F3 **Michurinsk** Russian Fed
104F3 **Micronesia** *Region* Pacific O
78B2 **Midai** *I* Indon
102F4 **Mid Atlantic Ridge** Atlantic O
46B1 **Middelburg** Neth
20B2 **Middle Alkali L** USA
16D2 **Middleboro** USA
100B4 **Middleburg** Cape Province, S Africa

16A2 **Middleburg** Pennsylvania, USA
101G1 **Middleburg** Transvaal, S Africa
16B1 **Middleburgh** USA
15D2 **Middlebury** USA
11B3 **Middlesboro** USA
42D2 **Middlesbrough** Eng
16C2 **Middletown** Connecticut, USA
16B3 **Middletown** Delaware, USA
15D2 **Middletown** New York, USA
14B3 **Middletown** Ohio, USA
16A2 **Middletown** Pennsylvania, USA
96B1 **Midelt** Mor
43C4 **Mid Glamorgan** County, Wales
104B4 **Mid Indian Basin** Indian O
104B4 **Mid Indian Ridge** Indian O
7C5 **Midland** Can
14B2 **Midland** Michigan, USA
9C3 **Midland** Texas, USA
101D3 **Midongy Atsimo** Madag
105G2 **Mid Pacific Mts** Pacific O
20C2 **Midvale** USA
105H2 **Midway Is** Pacific O
18A2 **Midwest City** USA
93D2 **Midyat** Turk
54B2 **Midžor** *Mt* Serbia, Yugos
59B2 **Mielec** Pol
54C1 **Miercurea-Ciuc** Rom
50A1 **Mieres** Spain
16A2 **Mifflintown** USA
75A2 **Mihara** Japan
72D1 **Mijun Shuiku** *Res* China
54B2 **Mikhaylovgrad** Bulg
61F3 **Mikhaylovka** Russian Fed
65J4 **Mikhaylovskiy** Russian Fed
38K6 **Mikkeli** Fin
55C3 **Míkonos** *I* Greece
59B3 **Mikulov** Czech
99D3 **Mikumi** Tanz
74D3 **Mikuni-sammyaku** *Mts* Japan
75B2 **Mikura-jima** *I* Japan
32B4 **Milagro** Ecuador
Milan = Milano
51C2 **Milana** Alg
101C2 **Milange** Mozam
52A1 **Milano** Italy
92A2 **Milas** Turk
107D4 **Mildura** Aust
73A5 **Mile** China
93D3 **Mileh Tharthār** *L* Iraq
107E3 **Miles** Aust
8C2 **Miles City** USA
16C2 **Milford** Connecticut, USA
15C3 **Milford** Delaware, USA
15D2 **Milford** Massachusetts, USA
18A1 **Milford** Nebraska, USA
16B2 **Milford** Pennsylvania, USA
43B4 **Milford Haven** Wales
43B4 **Milford Haven** *Sd* Wales
18A2 **Milford L** USA
111A2 **Milford Sd** NZ
13E2 **Milk River** Can
49C3 **Millau** France
16C2 **Millbrook** USA
17B1 **Milledgeville** USA
12F2 **Miller,Mt** USA
61F4 **Millerovo** Russian Fed
16A2 **Millersburg** USA
108A1 **Millers Creek** Aust
16C1 **Millers Falls** USA
16C2 **Millerton** USA
22C2 **Millerton L** USA
108B3 **Millicent** Aust
109D1 **Millmerran** Aust
45B2 **Milltown Malbay** Irish Rep
22A2 **Mill Valley** USA
15D3 **Millville** USA
6H2 **Milne Land** *I* Greenland
21C4 **Milolii** Hawaiian Is
55B3 **Milos** *I* Greece
107D3 **Milparinka** Aust
16A2 **Milroy** USA
111A3 **Milton** NZ
16A2 **Milton** Pennsylvania, USA
10B2 **Milwaukee** USA
51C2 **Mina** *R* Alg
93E4 **Mīnā' al Ahmadī** Kuwait
91C4 **Mīnāb** Iran
74C4 **Minamata** Japan
78A2 **Minas** Indon
29E2 **Minas** Urug
31B5 **Minas Gerais** State, Brazil
35C1 **Minas Novas** Brazil
25C3 **Minatitlan** Mexico
76A1 **Minbu** Burma
76A1 **Minbya** Burma
34A2 **Mincha** Chile
44A3 **Minch,Little** *Sd* Scot
44A2 **Minch,North** *Sd* Scot
40B2 **Minch,The** *Sd* Scot
12D2 **Minchumina,L** USA
47D2 **Mincio** *R* Italy
79B4 **Mindanao** *I* Phil
19B3 **Minden** Louisiana, USA
56B2 **Minden** Germany
108B2 **Mindona L** Aust
79B3 **Mindoro** *I* Phil
79B3 **Mindoro Str** Phil
45C3 **Mine Hd** *C* Irish Rep
43C4 **Minehead** Eng
30F2 **Mineiros** Brazil
19A3 **Mineola** USA
23B1 **Mineral de Monte** Mexico
16A2 **Minersville** USA
108B2 **Mingary** Aust
72A2 **Minhe** China
87A3 **Minicoy** *I* India
73D4 **Min Jiang** *R* Fujian, China
73A4 **Min Jiang** *R* Sichuan, China
22C2 **Minkler** USA
108A2 **Minlaton** Aust
72A2 **Minle** China
97C4 **Minna** Nig
10A2 **Minneapolis** USA
5J4 **Minnedosa** Can
10A2 **Minnesota** State, USA
50A1 **Miño** *R* Spain
8C2 **Minot** USA
72A2 **Minqin** China
72A3 **Min Shan** *Upland* China
60C3 **Minsk** Belorussia
58C2 **Minsk Mazowiecki** Pol
12E2 **Minto** USA
4G2 **Minto Inlet** *B* Can
7C4 **Minto,L** Can
63B2 **Minusinsk** Russian Fed
72A3 **Min Xian** China
7E5 **Miquelon** Can
22D3 **Mirage L** USA
87A1 **Miraj** India
29E3 **Miramar** Arg
84B2 **Miram Shah** Pak
50B1 **Miranda de Ebro** Spain
47D2 **Mirandola** Italy
84B2 **Mir Bachchen Kūt** Afghan
78D1 **Miri** Malay
96A3 **Mirik,C** Maur
63A1 **Mirnoye** Russian Fed
63D1 **Mirnyy** Russian Fed
112C9 **Mirnyy** *Base* Ant
84C2 **Mirpur** Pak
85B3 **Mirpur Khas** Pak
55B3 **Mirtoan S** Greece
74B3 **Miryang** S Korea
86A1 **Mirzāpur** India
23B2 **Misantla** Mexico
84C1 **Misgar** Pak
14A2 **Mishawaka** USA
12B1 **Misheguk Mt** USA
75A2 **Mi-shima** *I* Japan
107E2 **Misima** *I* Solomon Is
30F4 **Misiones** State, Arg
59C3 **Miskolc** Hung
94C2 **Mismīyah** Syria
71E4 **Misoöl** *I* Indon
95A1 **Misrātah** Libya
7B5 **Missinaibi** *R* Can
20B1 **Mission City** Can
15C2 **Mississauga** Can
11A3 **Mississippi** State, USA
11A3 **Mississippi** *R* USA
19C3 **Mississippi Delta** USA
8B2 **Missoula** USA
96B1 **Missour** Mor
11A3 **Missouri** State, USA
10A2 **Missouri** *R* USA
10C1 **Mistassini,L** Can
30B2 **Misti** *Mt* Peru
109C1 **Mitchell** Aust
8D2 **Mitchell** USA
107D2 **Mitchell** *R* Aust
11B3 **Mitchell,Mt** USA
45B2 **Mitchelstown** Irish Rep
84C3 **Mithankot** Pak
55C3 **Mitilíni** Greece
23B2 **Mitla** Mexico
95C3 **Mits'iwa** Eth
32C3 **Mitu** Colombia
99C3 **Mitumbar** *Mts* Zaïre
98C3 **Mitwaba** Zaïre
98B2 **Mitzic** Gabon
75B1 **Miura** Japan
72C3 **Mi Xian** China
69F3 **Miyake** *I* Japan
75B2 **Miyake-jima** *I* Japan
69E4 **Miyako** *I* Japan
74C4 **Miyakonojō** Japan
74C4 **Miyazaki** Japan
75B1 **Miyazu** Japan
74C4 **Miyoshi** Japan
72D1 **Miyun** China
99D2 **Mīzan Teferi** Eth
95A1 **Mizdah** Libya
45B3 **Mizen Hd** *C* Irish Rep
54C1 **Mizil** Rom
86C2 **Mizo Hills** India
86C2 **Mizoram** Union Territory, India
94B3 **Mizpe Ramon** Israel
112B11 **Mizuho** *Base* Ant
74E3 **Mizusawa** Japan
39H7 **Mjolby** Sweden
100B2 **Mkushi** Zambia
101H1 **Mkuzi** S Africa
57C2 **Mladá Boleslav** Czech
58C2 **Mława** Pol
52C2 **Mljet** *I* Croatia
100B3 **Mmabatho** S Africa
84D2 **Mnadi** India
97A4 **Moa** *R* Sierra Leone
94B3 **Moab** Region, Jordan
9C3 **Moab** USA
98B3 **Moanda** Congo
98B3 **Moanda** Gabon
99C3 **Moba** Zaïre
75C1 **Mobara** Japan
98C2 **Mobaye** CAR
98C2 **Mobayi** Zaïre
10A3 **Moberly** USA
11B3 **Mobile** USA
11B3 **Mobile B** USA
8C2 **Mobridge** USA
101D2 **Moçambique** Mozam
76C1 **Moc Chau** Viet
100B3 **Mochudi** Botswana
101D2 **Mocimboa da Praia** Mozam
32B3 **Mocoa** Colombia
35B2 **Mococa** Brazil
34D2 **Mocoreta** *R* Arg
23B1 **Moctezuma** *R* Mexico
101C2 **Mocuba** Mozam
47B2 **Modane** France
101G1 **Modder** *R* S Africa
52B2 **Modena** Italy
46D2 **Moder** *R* France
8A3 **Modesto** USA
22B2 **Modesto Res** USA
53B3 **Modica** Italy
59B3 **Mödling** Austria
107D4 **Moe** Aust
47C1 **Moesa** *R* Switz
42C2 **Moffat** Scot
84D2 **Moga** India
35B2 **Mogi das Cruzes** Brazil
60C3 **Mogilev** Belorussia
60C4 **Mogilev Podolskiy** Ukraine
35B2 **Mogi-Mirim** Brazil
101D2 **Mogincual** Mozam
47E2 **Mogliano** Italy
34B2 **Mogna** Arg
68D1 **Mogocha** Russian Fed
65K4 **Mogochin** Russian Fed
50A2 **Moguer** Spain
110C1 **Mohaka** *R* NZ
86C2 **Mohanganj** Bang
15D2 **Mohawk** *R* USA
99D3 **Mohoro** Tanz
65J5 **Mointy** Kazakhstan
38G5 **Mo i Rana** Nor
48C3 **Moissac** France
21B2 **Mojave** USA
22D3 **Mojave** *R* USA
9B3 **Mojave Desert** USA
78C4 **Mojokerto** Indon
86B1 **Mokama** India
110B1 **Mokau** *R* NZ
22B1 **Mokelumne Aqueduct** USA
22B1 **Mokelumne Hill** USA
22B1 **Mokelumne North Fork** *R* USA
101G1 **Mokhotlong** Lesotho
96D1 **Moknine** Tunisia
86C1 **Mokokchūng** India
98B1 **Mokolo** Cam
74B4 **Mokp'o** S Korea
61F3 **Moksha** *R* Russian Fed
23B1 **Molango** Mexico
55B3 **Moláoi** Greece
60C4 **Moldavia** Republic, Europe
38F6 **Molde** Nor
54B1 **Moldoveanu** *Mt* Rom
100B3 **Molepolole** Botswana
53C2 **Molfetta** Italy
34A3 **Molina** Chile
30B2 **Mollendo** Peru
60C3 **Molodechno** Belorussia
112C11 **Molodezhnaya** *Base* Ant
21C4 **Molokai** *I* Hawaiian Is
61G2 **Moloma** *R* Russian Fed
109C2 **Molong** Aust
100B3 **Molopo** *R* Botswana
98B2 **Molounddu** Cam
8D1 **Molson L** Can
71D4 **Molucca** *S* Indon
71D4 **Moluccas** *Is* Indon
101C2 **Moma** Mozam
31C3 **Mombaca** Brazil
99D3 **Mombasa** Kenya
98C2 **Mompono** Zaïre
56C2 **Mon** *I* Den
44A3 **Monach** *Is* Scot
49D3 **Monaco** Principality, Europe

44B3 **Monadhliath** *Mts* Scot
45C1 **Monaghan** County, Irish Rep
45C1 **Monaghan** Irish Rep
27D3 **Mona Pass** Caribbean S
13B2 **Monarch Mt** Can
5G4 **Monashee Mts** Can
41B3 **Monastereven** Irish Rep
47B2 **Moncalieri** Italy
31B2 **Monção** Brazil
38L5 **Monchegorsk** Russian Fed
56B2 **Mönchen-gladbach** Germany
24B2 **Monclova** Mexico
7D5 **Moncton** Can
9C4 **Monctova** Mexico
50A1 **Mondego** *R* Port
52A2 **Mondovi** Italy
27H1 **Moneague** Jamaica
14C2 **Monessen** USA
18B2 **Monett** USA
52B1 **Monfalcone** Italy
50A1 **Monforte de Lemos** Spain
98C2 **Monga** Zaïre
98C2 **Mongala** *R* Zaïre
99D2 **Mongalla** Sudan
76D1 **Mong Cai** Viet
98B1 **Mongo** Chad
68B2 **Mongolia** Republic, Asia
100B2 **Mongu** Zambia
21B2 **Monitor Range** *Mts* USA
98C3 **Monkoto** Zaïre
43C4 **Monmouth** Eng
18B1 **Monmouth** USA
13C2 **Monmouth,Mt** Can
97C4 **Mono** *R* Togo
21B2 **Mono L** USA
53C2 **Monopoli** Italy
51B1 **Monreal del Campo** Spain
19B3 **Monroe** Louisiana, USA
14B2 **Monroe** Michigan, USA
20B1 **Monroe** Washington, USA
18B2 **Monroe City** USA
97A4 **Monrovia** Lib
20D3 **Monrovia** USA
56A2 **Mons** Belg
47D2 **Monselice** Italy
16C1 **Monson** USA
58B1 **Mönsterås** Sweden
101D2 **Montagne d'Ambre** *Mt* Madag
96C1 **Montagnes des Ouled Naïl** *Mts* Alg
12E3 **Montague I** USA
49C3 **Mont Aigoual** *Mt* France
48B2 **Montaigu** France
53C3 **Montallo** *Mt* Italy
8B2 **Montana** State, USA
50A1 **Montañas de León** *Mts* Spain
49C2 **Montargis** France
48C3 **Montauban** France
15D2 **Montauk** USA
15D2 **Montauk Pt** USA
49D2 **Montbéliard** France
52A1 **Mont Blanc** *Mt* France/Italy
49C2 **Montceau les Mines** France
51C1 **Montceny** *Mt* Spain
49D3 **Mont Cinto** *Mt* Corse
46C2 **Montcornet** France
48B3 **Mont-de-Marsin** France
48C2 **Montdidier** France
30D2 **Monteagudo** Bol
33G4 **Monte Alegre** Brazil
52B2 **Monte Amiata** *Mt* Italy
47D2 **Monte Baldo** *Mt* Italy
15C1 **Montebello** Can
106A3 **Monte Bello Is** Aust
47E2 **Montebelluna** Italy
49D3 **Monte Carlo** Monaco
35B1 **Monte Carmelo** Brazil
34D2 **Monte Caseros** Arg
52B2 **Monte Cimone** *Mt* Italy
52A2 **Monte Cinto** *Mt* Corse
34B2 **Monte Coman** Arg
52B2 **Monte Corno** *Mt* Italy
27C3 **Montecristi** Dom Rep
52B2 **Montecristo** *I* Italy
23A1 **Monte Escobedo** Mexico
53C2 **Monte Gargano** *Mt* Italy
26B3 **Montego Bay** Jamaica
47D2 **Monte Grappa** *Mt* Italy
47C2 **Monte Lesima** *Mt* Italy
49C3 **Montélimar** France
53B2 **Monte Miletto** *Mt* Italy
50A2 **Montemo-o-Novo** Port
24C2 **Montemorelos** Mexico
26B5 **Montená** Colombia
54A2 **Montenegro** Republic, Yugos
35D1 **Monte Pascoal** *Mt* Brazil
34A2 **Monte Patria** Chile
53C3 **Monte Pollino** *Mt* Italy
101C2 **Montepuez** Mozam
8A3 **Monterey** California, USA
15C3 **Monterey** Virginia, USA
8A3 **Monterey B** USA
32B2 **Montería** Colombia
30D2 **Montero** Bol
47B2 **Monte Rosa** *Mt* Italy/Switz
24B2 **Monterrey** Mexico
31C5 **Montes Claros** Brazil
50B2 **Montes de Toledo** *Mts* Spain
29E2 **Montevideo** Urug
52A2 **Monte Viso** *Mt* Italy
27P2 **Mont Gimie** *Mt* St Lucia
11B3 **Montgomery** Alabama, USA
96C2 **Mont Gréboun** Niger
46C2 **Montherme** France
47B1 **Monthey** Switz
19B3 **Monticello** Arkansas, USA
16B2 **Monticello** New York, USA
9C3 **Monticello** Utah, USA
53A2 **Monti del Gennargentu** *Mt* Sardegna
47D2 **Monti Lessini** *Mts* Italy
53B3 **Monti Nebrodi** *Mts* Italy
7C5 **Mont-Laurier** Can
48C2 **Montluçon** France
7C5 **Montmagny** Can
46C2 **Montmédy** France
49C3 **Mont Mézenc** *Mt* France
46B2 **Montmirail** France
50B2 **Montoro** Spain
49D3 **Mont Pelat** *Mt* France
14B2 **Montpelier** Ohio, USA
10C2 **Montpelier** Vermont, USA
49C3 **Montpellier** France
7C5 **Montréal** Can
48C1 **Montreuil** France
52A1 **Montreux** Switz
47B1 **Mont Risoux** *Mt* France
8C3 **Montrose** Colorado, USA
40C2 **Montrose** Scot
48B2 **Mont-St-Michel** France
96B1 **Monts des Ksour** *Mts* Alg
51C3 **Monts des Ouled Neil** *Mts* Alg
51C2 **Monts du Hodna** *Mts* Alg
27E3 **Montserrat** *I* Caribbean S
10C1 **Monts Otish** *Mts* Can
12B1 **Monument Mt** USA
9B3 **Monument V** USA
98C2 **Monveda** Zaïre
76B1 **Monywa** Burma
52A1 **Monza** Italy
100B2 **Monze** Zambia
101H1 **Mooi** *R* S Africa
101G1 **Mooi River** S Africa
108B1 **Moomba** Aust
109D2 **Moonbi Range** *Mts* Aust
108B1 **Moonda L** Aust
109D1 **Moonie** Aust
109C1 **Moonie** *R* Aust
108A2 **Moonta** Aust
106A4 **Moora** Aust
106A3 **Moore,L** Aust
42C2 **Moorfoot Hills** Scot
8D2 **Moorhead** USA
22C3 **Moorpark** USA
7B4 **Moose** *R* Can
5H4 **Moose Jaw** Can
5H4 **Moosomin** Can
7B4 **Moosonee** Can
16D2 **Moosup** USA
101C2 **Mopeia** Mozam
97B3 **Mopti** Mali
30B2 **Moquegua** Peru
39G6 **Mora** Sweden
31D3 **Morada** Brazil
84D3 **Morādābād** India
35B1 **Morada Nova de Minas** *L* Brazil
101D2 **Morafenobe** Madag
101D2 **Moramanga** Madag
27J2 **Morant Bay** Jamaica
27J2 **Morant Pt** Jamaica
87B3 **Moratuwa** Sri Lanka
59B3 **Morava** *R* Austria/Czech
54B2 **Morava** *R* Serbia, Yugos
90C2 **Moraveh Tappeh** Iran
40C2 **Moray Firth** *Estuary* Scot
47C1 **Morbegno** Italy
85C4 **Morbi** India
93D2 **Mor Dağ** *Mt* Turk
5J5 **Morden** Can
61F3 **Mordovskaya Respublika,** Russian Fed
42C2 **Morecambe** Eng
42C2 **Morecambe B** Eng
107D3 **Moree** Aust
14B3 **Morehead** USA
47C1 **Mörel** Switz
24B3 **Morelia** Mexico
23B2 **Morelos** State, Mexico
85D3 **Morena** India
5E4 **Moresby I** Can
109D1 **Moreton I** Aust
46B2 **Moreuil** France
47B1 **Morez** France
19B4 **Morgan City** USA
22B2 **Morgan Hill** USA
14C3 **Morgantown** USA
101G1 **Morgenzon** S Africa
47B1 **Morges** Switz
46D2 **Morhange** France
74E2 **Mori** Japan
27K1 **Moriatio** Tobago
13B2 **Morice L** Can
13E2 **Morinville** Can
74E3 **Morioka** Japan
109D2 **Morisset** Aust
63D1 **Morkoka** *R* Russian Fed
48B2 **Morlaix** France
27Q2 **Morne Diablotin** *Mt* Dominica
106C2 **Mornington** *I* Aust
85B3 **Moro** Pak
96B2 **Morocco** Kingdom, Africa
79B4 **Moro G** Phil
99D3 **Morogoro** Tanz
23A1 **Moroleon** Mexico
101D3 **Morombe** Madag
26B2 **Morón** Cuba
101D3 **Morondava** Madag
50A2 **Moron de la Frontera** Spain
101D2 **Moroni** Comoros
71D3 **Morotai** *I* Indon
99D2 **Moroto** Uganda
61F4 **Morozovsk** Russian Fed
42D2 **Morpeth** Eng
19B2 **Morrilton** USA
35B1 **Morrinhos** Brazil
110C1 **Morrinsville** NZ
16B2 **Morristown** New Jersey, USA
15C2 **Morristown** New York, USA
16B2 **Morrisville** Pennsylvania, USA
21A2 **Morro Bay** USA
23A2 **Morro de Papanoa** Mexico
23A2 **Morro de Petatlán** Mexico
101C2 **Morrumbala** Mozam
101C3 **Morrumbene** Mozam
61F3 **Morshansk** Russian Fed
47C2 **Mortara** Italy
34C2 **Morteros** Arg
33G6 **Mortes** *R* Mato Grosso, Brazil
35C2 **Mortes** *R* Minas Gerais, Brazil
108B3 **Mortlake** Aust
27L1 **Moruga** Trinidad
109D3 **Moruya** Aust
109C1 **Morven** Aust
44B3 **Morvern** *Pen* Scot
109C3 **Morwell** Aust
76B3 **Moscos Is** Burma
Moscow = Moskva
20C1 **Moscow** Idaho, USA
56B2 **Mosel** *R* Germany
46D2 **Moselle** Department, France
46D2 **Moselle** *R* France
20C1 **Moses Lake** USA
111B3 **Mosgiel** NZ
99D3 **Moshi** Tanz
38G5 **Mosjøen** Nor
63G2 **Moskal'vo** Russian Fed
64E4 **Moskva** Russian Fed
35C1 **Mosquito** *R* Brazil
39G7 **Moss** Nor
98B3 **Mossaka** Congo
100B4 **Mossel Bay** S Africa
98B3 **Mossendjo** Congo
108B2 **Mossgiel** Aust
31D3 **Mossoró** Brazil
57C2 **Most** Czech
96C1 **Mostaganem** Alg
54A2 **Mostar** Bosnia & Herzegovina, Yugos
58C2 **Mosty** Belorussia
93D2 **Mosul** Iraq
39H7 **Motala** Sweden
42C2 **Motherwell** Scot
86A1 **Motihāri** India
51B2 **Motilla del Palancar** Spain
50B2 **Motril** Spain
111B2 **Motueka** NZ
111B2 **Motueka** *R* NZ
47B1 **Moudon** Switz
98B3 **Mouila** Gabon
108B2 **Moulamein** Aust
4G2 **Mould Bay** Can
49C2 **Moulins** France
76B2 **Moulmein** Burma

96B1 **Moulouya** *R* Mor
17B1 **Moultrie** USA
17C1 **Moultrie,L** USA
18C2 **Mound City** Illinois, USA
18A1 **Mound City** Missouri, USA
98B2 **Moundou** Chad
14B3 **Moundsville** USA
12J1 **Mountain** *R* Can
17A1 **Mountain Brook** USA
18B2 **Mountain Grove** USA
18B2 **Mountain Home** Arkansas, USA
22A2 **Mountain View** USA
12B2 **Mountain Village** USA
16A3 **Mount Airy** Maryland, USA
16A2 **Mount Carmel** USA
108A1 **Mount Dutton** Aust
108A2 **Mount Eba** Aust
108B3 **Mount Gambier** Aust
16B3 **Mount Holly** USA
16A2 **Mount Holly Springs** USA
108A2 **Mount Hope** Aust
106C3 **Mount Isa** Aust
108A2 **Mount Lofty Range** *Mts* Aust
12D2 **Mount McKinley Nat Pk** USA
106A3 **Mount Magnet** Aust
108B2 **Mount Manara** Aust
107E3 **Mount Morgan** Aust
19B3 **Mount Pleasant** Texas, USA
20B1 **Mount Rainier Nat Pk** USA
43B4 **Mounts B** Eng
20B2 **Mount Shasta** USA
11B3 **Mount Vernon** Illinois, USA
19A3 **Mount Vernon** Kentucky, USA
20B1 **Mount Vernon** Washington, USA
45C1 **Mourne Mts** N Ire
98B1 **Moussoro** Chad
86B2 **Mouths of the Ganga** India/Bang
85B4 **Mouths of the Indus** Pak
77D4 **Mouths of the Mekong** Viet
97C4 **Mouths of the Niger** Nig
47B1 **Moutier** Switz
47B2 **Moûtiers** France
96C2 **Mouydir** *Mts* Alg
98B3 **Mouyondzi** Congo
46C2 **Mouzon** France
59B3 **M'óvár** Hung
23A1 **Moyahua** Mexico
99D2 **Moyale** Kenya
97A4 **Moyamba** Sierra Leone
96B1 **Moyen Atlas** *Mts* Mor
100B4 **Moyeni** Lesotho
99D2 **Moyo** Uganda
32B5 **Moyobamba** Peru
84D1 **Moyu** China
101C3 **Mozambique** Republic, Africa
101C3 **Mozambique Chan** Mozam/Madag
61H2 **Mozhga** Russian Fed
60C3 **Mozyr'** Belorussia
99D3 **Mpanda** Tanz
101C2 **Mpika** Zambia
99D3 **Mporokosa** Zambia
100B2 **Mposhi** Zambia
99D3 **Mpulungu** Zambia
99D3 **Mpwapwa** Tanz
60E3 **Mtsensk** Russian Fed
101H1 **Mtubatuba** S Africa
101D2 **Mtwara** Tanz
76C2 **Muang Chainat** Thai
76C2 **Muang Chiang Rai** Thai
76C2 **Muang Kalasin** Thai
76C2 **Muang Khon Kaen** Thai
76B2 **Muang Lampang** Thai
76B2 **Muang Lamphun** Thai
76C2 **Muang Loei** Thai
76C2 **Muang Lom Sak** Thai
76C2 **Muang Nakhon Phanom** Thai
76B2 **Muang Nakhon Sawan** Thai
76C2 **Muang Nan** Thai
76C2 **Muang Phayao** Thai
76C2 **Muang Phetchabun** Thai
76C2 **Muang Phichit** Thai
76C2 **Muang Phitsanulok** Thai
76C2 **Muang Phrae** Thai
76C2 **Muang Roi Et** Thai
76C2 **Muang Sakon Nakhon** Thai
76C3 **Muang Samut Prakan** Thai
76C2 **Muang Uthai Thani** Thai
76C2 **Muang Yasothon** Thai
77C5 **Muar** Malay
78C2 **Muara** Brunei
70B4 **Muara** Indon
78A3 **Muaralakitan** Indon
78A3 **Muaratebo** Indon
78C3 **Muaratewah** Indon
78A3 **Muarenim** Indon
76A2 **Muaungmaya** Burma
99D2 **Mubende** Uganda
100C2 **Muchinga** *Mts* Zambia
44A3 **Muck** *I* Scot
109C1 **Muckadilla** Aust
100B2 **Muconda** Angola
35D1 **Mucuri** Brazil
35C1 **Mucuri** *R* Brazil
100B2 **Mucusso** Angola
69E2 **Mudanjiang** China
109C2 **Mudgee** Aust
76B2 **Mudon** Burma
101C2 **Mueda** Mozam
107F3 **Mueo** Nouvelle Calédonie
100B2 **Mufulira** Zambia
73C4 **Mufu Shan** *Hills* China
Mugadishu = Muqdisho
93C4 **Mughayra** S Arabia
92A2 **Muğla** Turk
65G5 **Mugodzhary** *Mts* Kazakhstan
73A3 **Muguaping** China
93D3 **Muhaywir** Iraq
57C3 **Mühldorf** Germany
57C2 **Muhlhausen** Germany
38K6 **Muhos** Fin
77C4 **Mui Bai Bung** *C* Camb
45C2 **Muine Bheag** Irish Rep
100B2 **Mujimbeji** Zambia
59C3 **Mukachevo** Ukraine
78C2 **Mukah** Malay
69G4 **Muko-jima** *I* Japan
86A1 **Muktinath** Nepal
84B2 **Mukur** Afghan
18B2 **Mulberry** USA
12C2 **Mulchatna** *R* USA
34A3 **Mulchén** Chile
56C2 **Mulde** *R* Germany
71F5 **Mulgrave I** Aust
50B2 **Mulhacén** *Mt* Spain
46D1 **Mülheim** Germany
49D2 **Mulhouse** France
73A4 **Muli** China
44B3 **Mull** *I* Scot
87C3 **Mullaitvu** Sri Lanka
109C2 **Mullaley** Aust
106A3 **Mullewa** Aust
16B3 **Mullica** *R* USA
45C2 **Mullingar** Irish Rep
42B2 **Mull of Kintyre** *Pt* Scot
45C1 **Mull of Oa** *C* Scot
109D1 **Mullumbimby** Aust
100B2 **Mulobezi** Zambia
84C2 **Multan** Pak
100B2 **Mumbwa** Zambia
61G4 **Mumra** Russian Fed
71D4 **Muna** *I* Indon
57C3 **München** Germany
14A2 **Muncie** USA
15C2 **Muncy** USA
56B2 **Münden** Germany
109D1 **Mundubbera** Aust
109C1 **Mungallala** Aust
109C1 **Mungallala** *R* Aust
99C2 **Mungbere** Zaïre
86A2 **Mungeli** India
86B1 **Munger** India
109C1 **Mungindi** Aust
Munich = München
14A1 **Munising** USA
29B6 **Muñoz Gomero,Pen** Chile
45B2 **Munster** Region, Irish Rep
47C1 **Münster** Switz
56B2 **Münster** Germany
54B1 **Muntii Apuseni** *Mts* Rom
54B1 **Muntii Călimanilor** *Mts* Rom
54B1 **Muntii Carpaţii Meridionali** *Mts* Rom
54B1 **Muntii Rodnei** *Mts* Rom
54B1 **Muntii Zarandului** *Mts* Rom
100B2 **Munyati** *R* Zim
93C2 **Munzur Silsilesi** *Mts* Turk
64D3 **Muomio** Fin
76C1 **Muong Khoua** Laos
76D3 **Muong Man** Viet
76D2 **Muong Nong** Laos
76C1 **Muong Ou Neua** Laos
76C1 **Muong Sai** Laos
76C2 **Muong Sen** Viet
76C1 **Muong Sing** Laos
76C1 **Muong Son** Laos
38J5 **Muonio** Fin
38J5 **Muonio** *R* Sweden/Fin
99E2 **Muqdisho** Somalia
52B1 **Mur** *R* Austria
74D3 **Murakami** Japan
29B5 **Murallón** *Mt* Arg/Chile
61G2 **Murashi** Russian Fed
93D2 **Murat** *R* Turk
53A3 **Muravera** Sardegna
75C1 **Murayama** Japan
90B3 **Murcheh Khvort** Iran
111B2 **Murchison** NZ
106A3 **Murchison** *R* Aust
51B2 **Murcia** Region, Spain
51B2 **Murcia** Spain
54B1 **Mureş** *R* Rom
46E2 **Murg** *R* Germany
65H6 **Murgab** *R* Turkmenistan
84B2 **Murgha Kibzai** Pak
109D1 **Murgon** Aust
86B2 **Muri** India
35C2 **Muriaé** Brazil
98C3 **Muriege** Angola
64E3 **Murmansk** Russian Fed
61F2 **Murom** Russian Fed
74E2 **Muroran** Japan
50A1 **Muros** Spain
74C4 **Muroto** Japan
75A2 **Muroto-zaki** *C* Japan
20C2 **Murphy** Idaho, USA
22B1 **Murphys** USA
18C2 **Murray** Kentucky, USA
108B2 **Murray** *R* Aust
13C2 **Murray** *R* Can
108A3 **Murray Bridge** Aust
71F4 **Murray,L** PNG
17B1 **Murray,L** USA
105J2 **Murray Seacarp** Pacific O
108B2 **Murrumbidgee** *R* Aust
109C2 **Murrumburrah** Aust
109D2 **Murrurundi** Aust
47B1 **Murten** Switz
108B3 **Murtoa** Aust
110C1 **Murupara** NZ
86A2 **Murwāra** India
109D1 **Murwillimbah** Aust
93D2 **Muş** Turk
54B2 **Musala** *Mt* Bulg
74B2 **Musan** N Korea
91C4 **Musandam** *Pen* Oman
Muscat = Masqat
91C5 **Muscat** Region, Oman
106C3 **Musgrave Range** *Mts* Aust
98B3 **Mushie** Zaïre
14A2 **Muskegon** USA
14A2 **Muskegon** *R* USA
18A2 **Muskogee** USA
15C2 **Muskoka,L** Can
95C3 **Musmar** Sudan
99D3 **Musoma** Tanz
8C2 **Musselshell** *R* USA
100A2 **Mussende** Angola
48C2 **Mussidan** France
55C2 **Mustafa-Kemalpasa** Turk
86A1 **Mustang** Nepal
109D2 **Muswelibrook** Aust
95B2 **Mut** Egypt
101C2 **Mutarara** Mozam
101C2 **Mutare** Zim
101C2 **Mutoko** Zim
101D2 **Mutsamudu** Comoros
100B2 **Mutshatsha** Zaïre
74E2 **Mutsu** Japan
74E2 **Mutsu-wan** *B* Japan
45B2 **Mutton** *I* Irish Rep
72B2 **Mu Us Shamo** *Desert* China
98B3 **Muxima** Angola
63D2 **Muya** Russian Fed
38L6 **Muyezerskiy** Russian Fed
99D3 **Muyinga** Burundi
98C3 **Muyumba** Zaïre
82A1 **Muyun Kum** *Desert* Kazakhstan
84C2 **Muzaffarābad** Pak
84C2 **Muzaffargarh** Pak
84D3 **Muzaffarnagar** India
86B1 **Muzaffarpur** India
64H3 **Muzhi** Russian Fed
82C2 **Muztag** *Mt* China
82B2 **Muztagata** *Mt* China
100C2 **Mvuma** Zim
99D3 **Mwanza** Tanz
98C3 **Mwanza** Zaïre
98C3 **Mweka** Zaïre
98C3 **Mwene Ditu** Zaïre
100C3 **Mwenezi** Zim
99C3 **Mwenga** Zaïre
99C3 **Mweru** *L* Zambia
100B2 **Mwinilunga** Zambia
83D4 **Myanaung** Burma
Myanma = Burma
86D2 **Myingyan** Burma
76B1 **Myingyao** Burma
76B3 **Myinmoletkat** *Mt* Burma
82D3 **Myitkyina** Burma
76B3 **Myitta** Burma
86C2 **Mymensingh** Bang
69F3 **Myojin** *I* Japan
39F6 **Myrdal** Nor
38B2 **Myrdalsjökur** *Mts* Iceland
17C1 **Myrtle Beach** USA
20B2 **Myrtle Creek** USA
39G7 **Mysen** Nor
56C2 **Mysiloborz** Pol
64F3 **Mys Kanin Nos** *C* Russian Fed
59B3 **Myślenice** Pol
69H1 **Mys Lopatka** *C* Russian Fed
87B2 **Mysore** India
60D5 **Mys Sarych** *C* Ukraine

16D2 **Mystic** USA
61H5 **Mys Tyub-Karagan** *Pt* Kazakhstan
63G2 **Mys Yelizavety** *C* Russian Fed
64H2 **Mys Zhelaniya** *C* Russian Fed
77D3 **My Tho** Viet
20B2 **Mytle Point** USA
101C2 **Mzimba** Malawi
101C2 **Mzuzú** Malawi

N

21C4 **Naalehu** Hawaiian Is
39J6 **Naantali** Fin
45C2 **Naas** Irish Rep
75B2 **Nabari** Japan
61H2 **Naberezhnye Chelny** Russian Fed
12F2 **Nabesna** *R* USA
96D1 **Nabeul** Tunisia
94B2 **Nablus** Israel
101D2 **Nacala** Mozam
20B1 **Naches** USA
101C2 **Nachingwea** Tanz
19B3 **Nacogdoches** USA
76A3 **Nacondam** *I* Indian O
24B1 **Nacozari** Mexico
85C4 **Nadiād** India
50B2 **Nador** Mor
90B3 **Nadūshan** Iran
59C3 **Nadvornaya** Ukraine
56C1 **Naestved** Den
95B2 **Nāfūrah** Libya
75A2 **Nagahama** Japan
82D3 **Naga Hills** Burma
75B1 **Nagai** Japan
86C1 **Nāgāland** State, India
74D3 **Nagano** Japan
74D3 **Nagaoka** Japan
87B2 **Nāgappattinam** India
85C4 **Nagar Parkar** Pak
74B4 **Nagasaki** Japan
75B2 **Nagashima** Japan
75A2 **Nagato** Japan
85C3 **Nāgaur** India
87B3 **Nāgercoil** India
85B3 **Nagha Kalat** Pak
84D3 **Nagīna** India
74D3 **Nagoya** Japan
85D4 **Nāgpur** India
82D2 **Nagqu** China
59B3 **Nagykanizsa** Hung
59B3 **Nagykörös** Hung
69E4 **Naha** Japan
8A2 **Nahaimo** Can
84D2 **Nāhan** India
4F3 **Nahanni Butte** Can
94B2 **Nahariya** Israel
90A3 **Nahāvand** Iran
46D2 **Nahe** *R* Germany
72D2 **Nahpu** China
72E1 **Naimen Qi** China
7D4 **Nain** Can
90B3 **Nā'īn** Iran
84D3 **Naini Tai** India
44C3 **Nairn** Scot
99D3 **Nairobi** Kenya
90B3 **Najafābād** Iran
74C2 **Najin** N Korea
75A2 **Nakama** Japan
74E3 **Nakaminato** Japan
75A2 **Nakamura** Japan
75B1 **Nakano** Japan
75A1 **Nakano-shima** *I* Japan
74C4 **Nakatsu** Japan
75B1 **Nakatsu-gawa** Japan
95C3 **Nak'fa** Eth
93E2 **Nakhichevan** Azerbaijan
92B4 **Nakhl** Egypt
74C2 **Nakhodka** Russian Fed
76C3 **Nakhon Pathom** Thai
76C3 **Nakhon Ratchasima** Thai
77C4 **Nakhon Si Thammarat** Thai
12H3 **Nakina** Can
7B4 **Nakina** Ontario, Can
12C3 **Naknek** USA
12C3 **Naknek L** USA
4C4 **Nakrek** USA
39G8 **Nakskov** Den
99D3 **Nakuru** Kenya
13D2 **Nakusp** Can
61F5 **Nal'chik** Russian Fed
87B1 **Nalgonda** India
87B1 **Nallamala Range** *Mts* India
95A1 **Nālūt** Libya
101H1 **Namaacha** Mozam
65G6 **Namak** *L* Iran
90C3 **Namakzar-e Shadad** *Salt Flat* Iran
65J5 **Namangan** Uzbekistan
101C2 **Namapa** Mozam
100A4 **Namaqualand** Region, S Africa
109D1 **Nambour** Aust
109D2 **Nambucca Heads** Aust
77D4 **Nam Can** Viet
82D2 **Nam Co** *L* China
76D1 **Nam Dinh** Viet
101C2 **Nametil** Mozam
74B4 **Namhae-do** *I* S Korea
100A2 **Namib Desert** Namibia
100A2 **Namibe** Angola
100A3 **Namibia** Dependency, Africa
82D3 **Namjagbarwa Feng** *Mt* China
71D4 **Namlea** Indon
109C2 **Namoi** *R* Aust
13D1 **Nampa** Can
20C2 **Nampa** USA
97B3 **Nampala** Mali
76C2 **Nam Phong** Thai
74B3 **Namp'o** N Korea
101C2 **Nampula** Mozam
38G6 **Namsos** Nor
76B1 **Namton** Burma
86D2 **Namtu** Burma
13B2 **Namu** Can
101C2 **Namuno** Mozam
46C1 **Namur** Belg
100A2 **Namutoni** Namibia
74B3 **Namwŏn** S Korea
13C3 **Nanaimo** Can
74B2 **Nanam** N Korea
109D1 **Nanango** Aust
74D3 **Nanao** Japan
75B1 **Nanatsu-jima** *I* Japan
73B3 **Nanbu** China
73D4 **Nanchang** China
73B3 **Nanchong** China
49D2 **Nancy** France
87B1 **Nānded** India
109D2 **Nandewar Range** *Mts* Aust
85C4 **Nandurbar** India
87B1 **Nandyāl** India
98B2 **Nanga Eboko** Cam
84C1 **Nanga Parbat** *Mt* Pak
78C3 **Nangapinoh** Indon
78C3 **Nangatayap** Indon
74B2 **Nangnim Sanmaek** *Mts* N Korea
86C1 **Nang Xian** China
67F3 **Nangzhou** China
87B2 **Nanjangūd** India
72D3 **Nanjing** China
Nanking = Nanjing
75A2 **Nankoku** Japan
73C4 **Nan Ling** Region, China
76D1 **Nanliu** *R* China
73B5 **Nanning** China
6F3 **Nanortalik** Greenland
73A5 **Nanpan Jiang** *R* China
86A1 **Nānpāra** India
73D4 **Nanping** China
6A1 **Nansen Sd** Can
99D3 **Nansio** Tanz
48B2 **Nantes** France
13E2 **Nanton** Can
72E3 **Nantong** China
10C2 **Nantucket** *I* USA
35C1 **Nanuque** Brazil
72C3 **Nanyang** China
72D2 **Nanyang Hu** *L* China
99D2 **Nanyuki** Kenya
74D3 **Naoetsu** Japan
85B4 **Naokot** Pak
22A1 **Napa** USA
12B2 **Napaiskak** USA
15C2 **Napanee** Can
65K4 **Napas** Russian Fed
6E3 **Napassoq** Greenland
76D2 **Nape** Laos
110C1 **Napier** NZ
Naples = Napoli
17B2 **Naples** Florida, USA
19B3 **Naples** Texas, USA
73B5 **Napo** China
32C4 **Napo** *R* Peru/ Ecuador
53B2 **Napoli** Italy
90A2 **Naqadeh** Iran
92C4 **Naqb Ishtar** Jordan
75B2 **Nara** Japan
97B3 **Nara** Mali
107D4 **Naracoorte** Aust
23B1 **Naranjos** Mexico
87C1 **Narasarāopet** India
77C4 **Narathiwat** Thai
86C2 **Narayanganj** Bang
87B1 **Nārāyenpet** India
49C3 **Narbonne** France
84D2 **Narendranagar** India
6C2 **Nares Str** Can
58C2 **Narew** *R* Pol
75C1 **Narita** Japan
85C4 **Narmada** *R* India
84D3 **Nārnaul** India
60E2 **Naro Fominsk** Russian Fed
99D3 **Narok** Kenya
84C2 **Narowal** Pak
107D4 **Narrabri** Aust
109C1 **Narran** *L* Aust
109C1 **Narran** *R* Aust
109C2 **Narrandera** Aust
106A4 **Narrogin** Aust
109C2 **Narromine** Aust
85D4 **Narsimhapur** India
87C1 **Narsīpatnam** India
6F3 **Narssalik** Greenland
6F3 **Narssaq** Greenland
6F3 **Narssarssuaq** Greenland
75C1 **Narugo** Japan
75A2 **Naruto** Japan
60C2 **Narva** Russian Fed
38H5 **Narvik** Nor
84D3 **Narwāna** India
64G3 **Nar'yan Mar** Russian Fed
108B1 **Narylico** Aust
65J5 **Naryn** Kazakhstan
97C4 **Nasarawa** Nig
103D5 **Nasca Ridge** Pacific O
16D1 **Nashua** USA
19B3 **Nashville** Arkansas, USA
11B3 **Nashville** Tennessee, USA
54A1 **Našice** Croatia
85D4 **Nāsik** India
99D2 **Nasir** Sudan
13B1 **Nass** *R* Can
26B1 **Nassau** The Bahamas
16C1 **Nassau** USA
95C2 **Nasser,L** Egypt
39G7 **Nässjö** Sweden
7C4 **Nastapoka Is** Can
100B3 **Nata** Botswana
31D3 **Natal** Brazil
70A3 **Natal** Indon
101H1 **Natal** Province, S Africa
90B3 **Natanz** Iran
7D4 **Natashquan** Can
7D4 **Natashquan** *R* Can
19B3 **Natchez** USA
19B3 **Natchitoches** USA
108C3 **Nathalia** Aust
6H2 **Nathorsts Land** *Region* Greenland
13C1 **Nation** *R* Can
21B3 **National City** USA
75C1 **Natori** Japan
99D3 **Natron** *L* Tanz
106A4 **Naturaliste,C** Aust
47D1 **Nauders** Austria
56C2 **Nauen** Germany
16C2 **Naugatuck** USA
57C2 **Naumburg** Germany
94B3 **Naur** Jordan
105G4 **Nauru** *I* Pacific O
63C2 **Naushki** Russian Fed
23B1 **Nautla** Mexico
9C3 **Navajo Res** USA
50A2 **Navalmoral de la Mata** Spain
29C7 **Navarino** *I* Chile
51B1 **Navarra** Province, Spain
34D3 **Navarro** Arg
19A3 **Navasota** USA
19A3 **Navasota** *R* USA
50A1 **Navia** *R* Spain
34A2 **Navidad** Chile
85C4 **Navlakhi** India
60D3 **Navlya** Russian Fed
24B2 **Navojoa** Mexico
55B3 **Návpaktos** Greece
55B3 **Návplion** Greece
85C4 **Navsāri** India
94C2 **Nawá** Syria
86B2 **Nawāda** India
84B2 **Nawah** Afghan
85B3 **Nawrabshah** Pak
73B4 **Naxi** China
55C3 **Náxos** *I* Greece
23A1 **Nayar** Mexico
90C3 **Nay Band** Iran
91B4 **Nāy Band** Iran
74E2 **Nayoro** Japan
94B2 **Nazareth** Israel
48B2 **Nazay** France
32C6 **Nazca** Peru
92A2 **Nazilli** Turk
63B2 **Nazimovo** Russian Fed
13C2 **Nazko** *R* Can
99D2 **Nazret** Eth
91C5 **Nazwa** Oman
65J4 **Nazyvayevsk** Russian Fed
98B3 **Ndalatando** Angola
98C2 **Ndélé** CAR
98B3 **Ndendé** Gabon
98B1 **Ndjamena** Chad
98B3 **Ndjolé** Gabon
100B2 **Ndola** Zambia
109C1 **Neabul** Aust
108A1 **Neales** *R* Aust
55B3 **Neápolis** Greece
43C4 **Neath** Wales
109C1 **Nebine** *R* Aust
65G6 **Nebit Dag** Turkmenistan
8C2 **Nebraska** State, USA
18A1 **Nebraska City** USA
13C2 **Nechako** *R* Can
19A3 **Neches** *R* USA
34D3 **Necochea** Arg
86C1 **Nêdong** China
9B3 **Needles** USA
14A2 **Neenah** USA
5J4 **Neepawa** Can
46C1 **Neerpelt** Belg
63C2 **Neftelensk** Russian Fed
99D2 **Negelē** Eth
94B3 **Negev** *Desert* Israel
60B4 **Negolu** *Mt* Rom
87B3 **Negombo** Sri Lanka
76A2 **Negrais,C** Burma
32A4 **Negritos** Peru
33E4 **Negro** *R* Amazonas, Brazil
29C4 **Negro** *R* Arg
34D2 **Negro** *R* Urug
79B4 **Negros** *I* Phil
54C2 **Negru Voda** Rom
90D3 **Nehbāndan** Iran
73B4 **Neijiang** China
72B1 **Nei Monggol** Autononous Region, China
32B3 **Neiva** Colombia
99D2 **Nejo** Eth

99D2 **Nek'emtē** Eth
60D2 **Nelidovo** Russian Fed
87B2 **Nellore** India
69F2 **Nel'ma** Russian Fed
13D3 **Nelson** Can
111B2 **Nelson** NZ
7A4 **Nelson** *R* Can
108B3 **Nelson,C** Aust
12B2 **Nelson I** USA
97B3 **Néma** Maur
72A1 **Nemagt Uul** *Mt* Mongolia
54C1 **Nemira** *Mt* Rom
58C1 **Nemunas** *R* Lithuania
74F2 **Nemuro** Japan
63E3 **Nen** *R* China
41B3 **Nenagh** Irish Rep
12E2 **Nenana** USA
12E2 **Nenana** *R* USA
43D3 **Nene** *R* Eng
69E2 **Nenjiang** China
18A2 **Neodesha** USA
18B2 **Neosho** USA
63C2 **Nepa** Russian Fed
82C3 **Nepal** Kingdom, Asia
86A1 **Nepalganj** Nepal
45B1 **Nephin** *Mt* Irish Rep
94B3 **Neqarot** *R* Israel
34A3 **Nequén** State, Arg
68D1 **Nerchinsk** Russian Fed
52C2 **Neretva** *R* Bosnia & Herzegovina, Yugos/ Croatia
71F2 **Nero Deep** Pacific O
38C1 **Neskaupstaður** Iceland
46B2 **Nesle** France
7E5 **Nesleyville** Can
55B2 **Néstos** *R* Greece
94B2 **Netanya** Israel
16B2 **Netcong** USA
56B2 **Netherlands** Kingdom, Europe
3M7 **Netherlands Antilles** *Is* Caribbean S
86C2 **Netrakona** Bang
6C3 **Nettilling L** Can
56C2 **Neubrandenburg** Germany
47B1 **Neuchâtel** Switz
46C2 **Neufchâteau** Belg
48C2 **Neufchâtel** France
46A2 **Neufchâtel-en-Bray** France
56B2 **Neumünster** Germany
52C1 **Neunkirchen** Austria
46D2 **Neunkirchen** Germany
34B3 **Neuquén** Arg
29B4 **Neuquén** State, Arg
34B3 **Neuquén** *R* Arg
56C2 **Neuruppin** Germany
46D1 **Neuss** Germany
46E2 **Neustadt** Germany
56C2 **Neustadt** Germany
56C2 **Neustrelitz** Germany
46D1 **Neuwied** Germany
8B3 **Nevada** State, USA
18B2 **Nevada** USA
34A3 **Nevada de Chillán** *Mts* Arg/Chile
23A2 **Nevada de Collima** Mexico
23B2 **Nevada de Toluca** *Mt* Mexico
94B3 **Nevatim** Israel
60C2 **Nevel'** Russian Fed
49C2 **Nevers** France
109C2 **Nevertire** Aust
27E3 **Nevis** *I* Caribbean S
58D2 **Nevis** *R* Belorussia/ Lithuania
92B2 **Nevşehir** Turk
61K2 **Nev'yansk** Russian Fed
101C2 **Newala** Tanz
14A3 **New Albany** Indiana, USA
19C3 **New Albany** Mississippi, USA
33F2 **New Amsterdam** Guyana
109C1 **New Angledool** Aust
15C3 **Newark** Delaware, USA
10C2 **Newark** New Jersey, USA
14B2 **Newark** Ohio, USA
43D3 **Newark-upon-Trent** Eng
15D2 **New Bedford** USA
13B2 **New Bella Bella** Can
20B1 **Newberg** USA
11C3 **New Bern** USA
17B1 **Newberry** USA
26B2 **New Bight** The Bahamas
14B3 **New Boston** USA
9D4 **New Braunfels** USA
16C2 **New Britain** USA
7D5 **New Brunswick** Province, Can
16B2 **New Brunswick** USA
16B2 **Newburgh** USA
43D4 **Newbury** Eng
16D1 **Newburyport** USA
16C2 **New Canaan** USA
109D2 **Newcastle** Aust
14A3 **New Castle** Indiana, USA
42B2 **Newcastle** N Ire
14B2 **New Castle** Pennsylvania, USA
101G1 **Newcastle** S Africa
8C2 **Newcastle** Wyoming, USA
42D2 **Newcastle upon Tyne** Eng
106C2 **Newcastle Waters** Aust
45B2 **Newcastle West** Irish Rep
84D3 **New Delhi** India
109D2 **New England Range** *Mts* Aust
12B3 **Newenham,C** USA
43D4 **New Forest,The** Eng
7D4 **Newfoundland** Province, Can
7E5 **Newfoundland** *I* Can
102F2 **Newfoundland Basin** Atlantic O
18B2 **New Franklin** USA
42B2 **New Galloway** Scot
107E1 **New Georgia** *I* Solomon Is
7D5 **New Glasgow** Can
71F4 **New Guinea** SE Asia
12D3 **Newhalen** USA
22C3 **Newhall** USA
10C2 **New Hampshire** State, USA
101H1 **New Hanover** S Africa
43E4 **Newhaven** Eng
15D2 **New Haven** USA
13B1 **New Hazelton** Can
19B3 **New Iberia** USA
10C2 **New Jersey** State, USA
7C5 **New Liskeard** Can
16C2 **New London** USA
106A3 **Newman** Aust
22B2 **Newman** USA
43E3 **Newmarket** Eng
45B2 **Newmarket** Irish Rep
15C3 **New Market** USA
9C3 **New Mexico** State, USA
16C2 **New Milford** Connecticut, USA
17B1 **Newnan** USA
109C4 **New Norfolk** Aust
11A3 **New Orleans** USA
16B2 **New Paltz** USA
14B2 **New Philadelphia** USA
110B1 **New Plymouth** NZ
18B2 **Newport** Arkansas, USA
43D4 **Newport** Eng
14B3 **Newport** Kentucky, USA
20B2 **Newport** Oregon, USA
16A2 **Newport** Pennsylvania, USA
15D2 **Newport** Rhode Island, USA
15D2 **Newport** Vermont, USA
43C4 **Newport** Wales
20C1 **Newport** Washington, USA
22D4 **Newport Beach** USA
11C3 **Newport News** USA
26B1 **New Providence** *I* Caribbean S
43B4 **Newquay** Eng
6C3 **New Quebec Crater** Can
45C2 **New Ross** Irish Rep
45C1 **Newry** N Ire
New Siberian Is = Novosibirskye Ostrova
17B2 **New Smyrna Beach** USA
107D4 **New South Wales** State, Aust
12C3 **New Stuyahok** USA
18A2 **Newton** Kansas, USA
16D1 **Newton** Massachusetts, USA
19C3 **Newton** Mississippi, USA
16B2 **Newton** New York, USA
43C4 **Newton Abbot** Eng
45C1 **Newton Stewart** N Ire
42B2 **Newton Stewart** Scot
43C3 **Newtown** Wales
42B2 **Newtownards** N Ire
16A2 **Newville** USA
5F5 **New Westminster** Can
10C2 **New York** State, USA
10C2 **New York** USA
110 **New Zealand** Dominion, SW Pacific O
105G6 **New Zealand Plat** Pacific O
61F2 **Neya** Russian Fed
91B4 **Neyrīz** Iran
90C2 **Neyshābūr** Iran
60D3 **Nezhin** Russian Fed
98B3 **Ngabé** Congo
100B3 **Ngami** *L* Botswana
110C1 **Ngaruawahia** NZ
110C1 **Ngaruroro** *R* NZ
110C1 **Ngauruhoe,Mt** NZ
98B3 **Ngo** Congo
76D2 **Ngoc Linh** *Mt* Viet
98B2 **Ngoko** *R* Cam
68B3 **Ngoring Hu** *L* China
99D3 **Ngorongoro Crater** Tanz
98B3 **N'Gounié** *R* Gabon
98B1 **Nguigmi** Niger
71E3 **Ngulu** *I* Pacific O
97D3 **Nguru** Nig
76D3 **Nha Trang** Viet
108B3 **Nhill** Aust
101H1 **Nhlangano** Swaziland
76D2 **Nhommarath** Laos
106C2 **Nhulunbuy** Aust
97B3 **Niafounké** Mali
14A1 **Niagara** USA
15C2 **Niagara Falls** Can
15C2 **Niagara Falls** USA
70C3 **Niah** Malay
97B4 **Niakaramandougou** Ivory Coast
97C3 **Niamey** Niger
99C2 **Niangara** Zaïre
98C2 **Nia Nia** Zaïre
70A3 **Nias** *I* Indon
25D3 **Nicaragua** Republic, Cent America
53C3 **Nicastro** Italy
49D3 **Nice** France
26B1 **Nicholl's Town** The Bahamas
83D5 **Nicobar Is** Indian O
92B2 **Nicosia** Cyprus
25D3 **Nicoya,Pen de** Costa Rica
58C2 **Nidzica** Pol
46D2 **Niederbronn** France
56B2 **Niedersachsen** State, Germany
99C3 **Niemba** Zaïre
56B2 **Nienburg** Germany
46D1 **Niers** *R* Germany
97B4 **Niete,Mt** Lib
33F2 **Nieuw Amsterdam** Surinam
33F2 **Nieuw Nickerie** Surinam
46B1 **Nieuwpoort** Belg
92B2 **Niğde** Turk
97C3 **Niger** Republic, Africa
97C4 **Niger** *R* Nig
97C4 **Nigeria** Federal Republic, Africa
55B2 **Nigríta** Greece
75C1 **Nihommatsu** Japan
74D3 **Niigata** Japan
74C4 **Niihama** Japan
75B2 **Nii-jima** *I* Japan
75A2 **Niimi** Japan
74D3 **Niitsu** Japan
94B3 **Nijil** Jordan
56B2 **Nijmegen** Neth
64E3 **Nikel'** Russian Fed
97C3 **Nikki** Benin
74D3 **Nikko** Japan
60D4 **Nikolayev** Ukraine
61G4 **Nikolayevsk** Russian Fed
63G2 **Nikolayevsk-na-Amure** Russian Fed
61G2 **Nikol'sk** Russian Fed
61G3 **Nikol'sk** Russian Fed
60D4 **Nikopol** Ukraine
92C1 **Niksar** Turk
91D4 **Nīkshahr** Iran
54A2 **Nikšić** Montenegro, Yugos
71D4 **Nila** *I* Indon
80B3 **Nile** *R* N E Africa
14A2 **Niles** USA
87B2 **Nilgiri Hills** India
85C4 **Nimach** India
49C3 **Nîmes** France
109C3 **Nimmitabel** Aust
99D2 **Nimule** Sudan
83B5 **Nine Degree Chan** Indian O
104C4 **Ninety-East Ridge** Indian O
109C3 **Ninety Mile Beach** Aust
73D4 **Ningde** China
73D4 **Ningdu** China
68B3 **Ningjing Shan** *Mts* China
76D1 **Ningming** China
73A4 **Ningnan** China
72B2 **Ningxia** Province, China
72B2 **Ning Xian** China
73B5 **Ninh Binh** Vietnam
107D1 **Ninigo Is** PNG
12D2 **Ninilchik** USA
8D2 **Niobrara** *R* USA
98B3 **Nioki** Zaïre
97B3 **Nioro du Sahel** Mali
48B2 **Niort** France
5H4 **Nipawin** Can
7B5 **Nipigon** Can
7B5 **Nipigon,L** Can
7B5 **Nipissing** *R* Can
14B1 **Nipissing,L** Can
87B1 **Nirmal** India
86B1 **Nirmāli** India
54B2 **Niš** Serbia, Yugos
81C4 **Nisāb** Yemen
69F4 **Nishino-shima** *I* Japan
75A1 **Nishino-shima** *I* Japan
75A2 **Nishiwaki** Japan
12G2 **Nisling** *R* Can

12H2 **Nisutlin** *R* Can
7C4 **Nitchequon** Can
31C6 **Niterói** Brazil
42C2 **Nith** *R* Scot
59B3 **Nitra** Czech
14B3 **Nitro** USA
78C2 **Niut** *Mt* Malay
46C1 **Nivelles** Belg
49C2 **Nivernais** Region, France
38L5 **Nivskiy** Russian Fed
87B1 **Nizāmābād** India
94B3 **Nizana** *Hist Site* Israel
61J2 **Nizhniye Sergi** Russian Fed
65F4 **Nizhniy Novgorod** Russian Fed
61F3 **Nizhniy Lomov** Russian Fed
65G4 **Nizhniy Tagil** Russian Fed
63B1 **Nizhnyaya Tunguska** *R* Russian Fed
93C2 **Nizip** Turk
100B2 **Njoko** *R* Zambia
99D3 **Njombe** Tanz
98B2 **Nkambé** Cam
101C2 **Nkhata Bay** Malawi
98B2 **Nkongsamba** Cam
97C3 **N'Konni** Niger
86C2 **Noakhali** Bang
12B1 **Noatak** USA
12C1 **Noatak** *R* USA
74C4 **Nobeoka** Japan
47D1 **Noce** *R* Italy
23A1 **Nochistlán** Mexico
23B2 **Nochixtlán** Mexico
19A3 **Nocona** USA
24A1 **Nogales** Sonora, Mexico
9B3 **Nogales** USA
23B2 **Nogales** Veracruz, Mexico
47D2 **Nogara** Italy
75A2 **Nogata** Japan
60E2 **Noginsk** Russian Fed
34D2 **Nogoyá** Arg
34D2 **Nogoyá** *R* Arg
84C3 **Nohar** India
75B2 **Nojima-zaki** *C* Japan
98B2 **Nola** CAR
61G2 **Nolinsk** Russian Fed
16D2 **Nomans Land** *I* USA
12A2 **Nome** USA
46D2 **Nomeny** France
72B1 **Nomgon** Mongolia
5H3 **Nonachol L** Can
76C2 **Nong Khai** Thai
101H1 **Nongoma** S Africa
12B1 **Noorvik** USA
13B3 **Nootka Sd** Can
98B3 **Noqui** Angola
7C5 **Noranda** Can
46B1 **Nord** Department, France
64D2 **Nordaustlandet** *I* Barents S
13D2 **Nordegg** Can
38F6 **Nordfjord** *Inlet* Nor
39F8 **Nordfriesische** *Is* Germany
56C2 **Nordhausen** Germany
56B2 **Nordhrein Westfalen** State, Germany
38J4 **Nordkapp** *C* Nor
6E3 **Nordre** Greenland
38H5 **Nord Stronfjället** *Mt* Sweden
1B9 **Nordvik** Russian Fed
45C2 **Nore** *R* Irish Rep
43E3 **Norfolk** County, Eng
8D2 **Norfolk** Nebraska, USA
11C3 **Norfolk** Virginia, USA
107F3 **Norfolk I** Aust
18B2 **Norfolk L** USA
105G5 **Norfolk Ridge** Pacific O
1C10 **Noril'sk** Russian Fed
18C1 **Normal** USA
19A2 **Norman** USA
48B2 **Normandie** Region, France
107D2 **Normanton** Aust
12J1 **Norman Wells** Can
4B3 **Norne** USA
15C2 **Norristown** USA
39H7 **Norrköping** Sweden
39H6 **Norrsundet** Sweden
39H7 **Norrtälje** Sweden
106B4 **Norseman** Aust
63F2 **Norsk** Russian Fed
102J2 **North** *S* N W Europe
42D2 **Northallerton** Eng
106A4 **Northam** Aust
102E3 **North American Basin** Atlantic O
106A3 **Northampton** Aust
43D3 **Northampton** County, Eng
43D3 **Northampton** Eng
15D2 **Northampton** USA
4G3 **North Arm** *B* Can
17B1 **North Augusta** USA
6D4 **North Aulatsvik** *I* Can
13F2 **North Battleford** Can
7C5 **North Bay** Can
20B2 **North Bend** USA
44C3 **North Berwick** Scot
7D5 **North,C** Can
7G4 **North C** NZ
11B3 **North Carolina** State, USA
20B1 **North Cascade Nat Pk** USA
14B1 **North Chan** Can
42B2 **North Chan** Ire/Scot
8C2 **North Dakota** State, USA
43E4 **North Downs** Eng
14C2 **North East** USA
102H2 **North East Atlantic Basin** Atlantic O
4B3 **Northeast C** USA
40B3 **Northern Ireland** UK
27L1 **Northern Range** *Mts* Trinidad
106C2 **Northern Territory** Aust
44C3 **North Esk** *R* Scot
16C1 **Northfield** Massachusetts, USA
12D2 **North Fork** *R* USA
110B1 **North I** NZ
74B3 **North Korea** Republic, S E Asia
North Land = Severnaya Zemlya
19B3 **North Little Rock** USA
1B4 **North Magnetic Pole** Can
17B2 **North Miami** USA
17B2 **North Miami Beach** USA
8C2 **North Platte** USA
8C2 **North Platte** *R* USA
27R3 **North Pt** Barbados
14B1 **North Pt** USA
40B2 **North Rona** *I* Scot
44C2 **North Ronaldsay** *I* Scot
13F2 **North Saskatchewan** *R* Can
40D2 **North Sea** N W Europe
4D3 **North Slope** *Region* USA
109D1 **North Stradbroke** *I* Aust
110B1 **North Taranaki Bight** *B* NZ
9C3 **North Truchas Peak** *Mt* USA
44A3 **North Uist** *I* Scot
42C2 **Northumberland** County, Eng
107E3 **Northumberland Is** Aust
7D5 **Northumberland Str** Can
20B1 **North Vancouver** Can
43E3 **North Walsham** Eng
12F2 **Northway** USA
106A3 **North West C** Aust
84C2 **North West Frontier** Province, Pak
7D4 **North West River** Can
4F3 **North West Territories** Can
42D2 **North York Moors Nat Pk** Eng
12B2 **Norton B** USA
12B2 **Norton Sd** USA
112B1 **Norvegia,C** Ant
16C2 **Norwalk** Connecticut, USA
14B2 **Norwalk** Ohio, USA
39F6 **Norway** Kingdom, Europe
5J4 **Norway House** Can
6A2 **Norwegian B** Can
102H1 **Norwegian Basin** Norewegian S
64A3 **Norwegian S** N W Europe
16C2 **Norwich** Connecticut, USA
43E3 **Norwich** Eng
16D1 **Norwood** Massachusetts, USA
14B3 **Norwood** Ohio, USA
54C2 **Nos Emine** *C* Bulg
74D2 **Noshiro** Japan
54C2 **Nos Kaliakra** *C* Bulg
44E1 **Noss** *I* Scot
91D4 **Nostrābād** Iran
101D2 **Nosy Barren** *I* Madag
101D2 **Nosy Bé** *I* Madag
101E2 **Nosy Boraha** *I* Madag
101D3 **Nosy Varika** Madag
58B2 **Notéc** *R* Pol
5G4 **Notikeuin** Can
53C3 **Noto** Italy
39F7 **Notodden** Nor
75B1 **Noto-hantō** *Pen* Japan
7E5 **Notre Dams B** Can
43D3 **Nottingham** County, Eng
43D3 **Nottingham** Eng
6C3 **Nottingham** *I* Can
6C3 **Nottingham Island** Can
96A2 **Nouadhibou** Maur
97A3 **Nouakchott** Maur
107F3 **Nouméa** Nouvelle Calédonie
97B3 **Nouna** Burkina
107F3 **Nouvelle Calédonie** *I* S W Pacific O
98B3 **Nova Caipemba** Angola
35A2 **Nova Esperança** Brazil
35C2 **Nova Friburgo** Brazil
100A2 **Nova Gaia** Angola
35B2 **Nova Granada** Brazil
35B2 **Nova Horizonte** Brazil
35C1 **Nova Lima** Brazil
Nova Lisboa = Huambo
35A2 **Nova Londrina** Brazil
101C3 **Nova Mambone** Mozam
47C2 **Novara** Italy
7D5 **Nova Scotia** Province, Can
22A1 **Novato** USA
35C1 **Nova Venécia** Brazil
60D4 **Novaya Kakhovka** Ukraine
64G2 **Novaya Zemlya** *I* Barents S
54C2 **Nova Zagora** Bulg
31C2 **Nove Russas** Brazil
54A1 **Nové Zámky** Czech
60D2 **Novgorod** Russian Fed
47C2 **Novi Ligure** Italy
54C2 **Novi Pazar** Bulg
54B2 **Novi Pazar** Serbia, Yugos
54A1 **Novi Sad** Serbia, Yugos
61J3 **Novoalekseyevka** Kazakhstan
61F3 **Novoanninskiy** Russian Fed
61E4 **Novocherkassk** Russian Fed
60C3 **Novograd Volynskiy** Ukraine
58D2 **Novogrudok** Russian Fed
30F4 **Novo Hamburgo** Brazil
65H5 **Novokazalinsk** Kazakhstan
65K4 **Novokuznetsk** Russian Fed
112B12 **Novolazarevskaya** *Base* Ant
52C1 **Novo Mesto** Slovenia
60E3 **Novomoskovsk** Russian Fed
60E5 **Novorossiysk** Russian Fed
65K4 **Novosibirsk** Russian Fed
1B8 **Novosibirskiye Ostrova** *I* Russian Fed
61J3 **Novotroitsk** Russian Fed
61G3 **Novo Uzensk** Russian Fed
59C2 **Novovolynsk** Ukraine
61G2 **Novo Vyatsk** Russian Fed
60D3 **Novozybkov** Russian Fed
58C2 **Novy Dwór Mazowiecki** Pol
61K2 **Novyy Lyalya** Russian Fed
61H5 **Novyy Port** Russian Fed
61H5 **Novyy Uzen** Kazakhstan
58B2 **Nowa Sól** Pol
18A2 **Nowata** USA
86C1 **Nowgong** India
12D2 **Nowitna** *R* USA
109D2 **Nowra** Aust
90B2 **Now Shahr** Iran
84C2 **Nowshera** Pak
59C3 **Nowy Sącz** Pol
12H3 **Noyes I** USA
46B2 **Noyon** France
97B4 **Nsawam** Ghana
99D1 **Nuba** *Mts* Sudan
81B3 **Nubian Desert** Sudan
34A3 **Nuble** *R* Chile
9D4 **Nueces** *R* USA
5J3 **Nueltin L** Can
26A2 **Nueva Gerona** Cuba
34A3 **Nueva Imperial** Chile
9C4 **Nueva Laredo** Mexico
34D2 **Nueva Palmira** Urug
24B2 **Nueva Rosita** Mexico
26B2 **Nuevitas** Cuba
24B1 **Nuevo Casas Grandes** Mexico
24C2 **Nuevo Laredo** Mexico
99E2 **Nugaal** Region, Somalia
6E2 **Nûgâtsiaq** Greenland
6E2 **Nugssuag** *Pen* Greenland
6E2 **Nûgussaq** *I* Greenland
108A2 **Nukey Bluff** *Mt* Aust
93D3 **Nukhayb** Iraq
65G5 **Nukus** Uzbekistan
12C2 **Nulato** USA
106B4 **Nullarbor Plain** Aust
97D4 **Numan** Nig
75B1 **Numata** Japan
98C2 **Numatinna** *R* Sudan
74D3 **Numazu** Japan
71E4 **Numfoor** *I* Indon
108C3 **Numurkah** Aust
12B2 **Nunapitchuk** USA

84D2 **Nunkun** *Mt* India
53A2 **Nuoro** Sardegna
91B3 **Nurābād** Iran
47C2 **Nure** *R* Italy
108A2 **Nuriootpa** Aust
84C1 **Nuristan** *Upland* Afghan
61H3 **Nurlat** Russian Fed
38K6 **Nurmes** Fin
57C3 **Nürnberg** Germany
108C2 **Nurri,Mt** Aust
93D2 **Nusaybin** Turk
12C3 **Nushagak** *R* USA
12C3 **Nushagak B** USA
12C3 **Nushagak Pen** USA
84B3 **Nushki** Pak
7D4 **Nutak** Can
12F2 **Nutzotin Mts** USA
86A1 **Nuwakot** Nepal
87C3 **Nuwara-Eliya** Sri Lanka
6C3 **Nuyukjuak** Can
16C2 **Nyack** USA
99D2 **Nyahururu** Kenya
108B3 **Nyah West** Aust
4C3 **Nyai** USA
68B3 **Nyainqentanglha Shan** *Mts* China
99D3 **Nyakabindi** Tanz
98C1 **Nyala** Sudan
86B1 **Nyalam** China
98C2 **Nyamlell** Sudan
64F3 **Nyandoma** Russian Fed
101C2 **Nyanga** Zim
98B3 **Nyanga** *R* Gabon
101C2 **Nyasa L** Malawi/Mozam
76B2 **Nyaunglebin** Burma
61J2 **Nyazepetrovsk** Russian Fed
39G7 **Nyborg** Den
39H7 **Nybro** Sweden
64J3 **Nyda** Russian Fed
6D1 **Nyeboes Land** *Region* Can
99D3 **Nyeri** Kenya
101C2 **Nyimba** Zambia
82D3 **Nyingchi** China
59C3 **Nyíregyháza** Hung
99D2 **Nyiru,Mt** Kenya
38J6 **Nykarleby** Fin
39F7 **Nykøbing** Den
39G8 **Nykøbing** Den
39H7 **Nyköping** Sweden
100B3 **Nylstroom** S Africa
109C2 **Nymagee** Aust
39H7 **Nynäshamn** Sweden
109C2 **Nyngan** Aust
47B1 **Nyon** Switz
98B2 **Nyong** *R* Cam
49D3 **Nyons** France
59B2 **Nysa** Pol
20C2 **Nyssa** USA
63D1 **Nyurba** Russian Fed
99D3 **Nzega** Tanz
97B4 **Nzérékore** Guinea
98B3 **N'zeto** Angola

O

6F3 **Oaggsimiut** Greenland
8C2 **Oahe Res** USA
21C4 **Oahu** *I* Hawaiian Is
108B2 **Oakbank** Aust
22B2 **Oakdale** USA
109D1 **Oakey** Aust
21A2 **Oakland** California, USA
20B2 **Oakland** Oregon, USA
14A3 **Oakland City** USA
14A2 **Oak Lawn** USA
22B2 **Oakley** California, USA
20B2 **Oakridge** USA
14C2 **Oakville** Can
111B3 **Oamaru** NZ
112B7 **Oates Land** Region, Ant
109C4 **Oatlands** Aust
23B2 **Oaxaca** Mexico
23B2 **Oaxaca** State, Mexico
65J3 **Ob'** *R* Russian Fed
75B1 **Obama** Japan
111A3 **Oban** NZ
44B3 **Oban** Scot
75C1 **Obanazawa** Japan
47D1 **Oberammergau** Germany
46D1 **Oberhausen** Germany
47D1 **Oberstdorf** Germany
71D4 **Obi** *I* Indon
33F4 **Obidos** Brazil
74E2 **Obihiro** Japan
98C2 **Obo** CAR
99E1 **Obock** Djibouti
58B2 **Oborniki** Pol
60E3 **Oboyan** Russian Fed
20B2 **O'Brien** USA
61H3 **Obshchiy Syrt** *Mts* Russian Fed
64J3 **Obskava Guba** *B* Russian Fed
97B4 **Obuasi** Ghana
17B2 **Ocala** USA
32C2 **Ocana** Colombia
50B2 **Ocaño** Spain
12G3 **Ocean C** USA
15C3 **Ocean City** Maryland, USA
16B3 **Ocean City** New Jersey, USA
5F4 **Ocean Falls** Can
22D4 **Oceanside** USA
19C3 **Ocean Springs** USA
61H2 **Ocher** Russian Fed
44C3 **Ochil Hills** Scot
17B1 **Ochlockonee** *R* USA
27H1 **Ocho Rios** Jamaica
17B1 **Ocmulgee** *R* USA
17B1 **Oconee** *R* USA
14A2 **Oconto** USA
23A1 **Ocotlán** Jalisco, Mexico
23B2 **Ocotlán** Oaxaca, Mexico
97B4 **Oda** Ghana
75A1 **Ōda** Japan
38B2 **Ódáðahraun** Region, Iceland
74E2 **Odate** Japan
74D3 **Odawara** Japan
39F6 **Odda** Nor
50A2 **Odemira** Port
55C3 **Ödemiş** Turk
101G1 **Odendaalsrus** S Africa
39G7 **Odense** Den
56C2 **Oder** *R* Pol/Germany
9C3 **Odessa** Texas, USA
60D4 **Odessa** Ukraine
20C1 **Odessa** Washington, USA
97B4 **Odienné** Ivory Coast
59B2 **Odra** *R* Pol
31C3 **Oeiras** Brazil
53C2 **Ofanto** *R* Italy
94B3 **Ofaqim** Israel
45C2 **Offaly** County, Irish Rep
49D1 **Offenbach** Germany
49D2 **Offenburg** Germany
74D3 **Oga** Japan
99E2 **Ogaden** Region, Eth
74D3 **Ogaki** Japan
8C2 **Ogallala** USA
69G4 **Ogasawara Gunto** *Is* Japan
97C4 **Ogbomosho** Nig
8B2 **Ogden** Utah, USA
15C2 **Ogdensburg** USA
17B1 **Ogeechee** *R* USA
12G1 **Ogilvie** Can
4E3 **Ogilvie Mts** Can
17B1 **Oglethorpe,Mt** USA
47D2 **Oglio** *R* Italy
47B1 **Ognon** *R* France
97C4 **Ogoja** Nig
98A3 **Ogooué** *R* Gabon
58C1 **Ogre** Latvia
96B2 **Oguilet Khenachich** *Well* Mali
52C1 **Ogulin** Croatia
111A3 **Ohai** NZ
110C1 **Ohakune** NZ
96C2 **Ohanet** Alg
111A2 **Ohau,L** NZ
10B2 **Ohio** State, USA
14A3 **Ohio** *R* USA
100A2 **Ohopoho** Namibia
57C2 **Ohre** *R* Czech
55B2 **Ohrid** Macedonia, Yugos
55B2 **Ohridsko Jezero** *L* Macedonia, Yugos/Alb
110B1 **Ohura** NZ
33G3 **Oiapoque** French Guiana
68B2 **Oijiaojing** China
14C2 **Oil City** USA
21B2 **Oildale** USA
46B2 **Oise** Department, France
49C2 **Oise** *R* France
74C4 **Oita** Japan
22C3 **Ojai** USA
24B2 **Ojinaga** Mexico
23B2 **Ojitlán** Mexico
75B1 **Ojiya** Japan
30C4 **Ojos del Salado** *Mt* Arg
23A1 **Ojueloz** Mexico
60E3 **Oka** *R* Russian Fed
100A3 **Okahandja** Namibia
20C1 **Okanagan Falls** Can
13D2 **Okanagan L** Can
20C1 **Okanogan** USA
20C1 **Okanogan** *R* USA
20B1 **Okanogan Range** *Mts* Can/USA
84C2 **Okara** Pak
100A2 **Okavango** *R* Angola/Namibia
100B2 **Okavango Delta** *Marsh* Botswana
74D3 **Okaya** Japan
74C4 **Okayama** Japan
75B2 **Okazaki** Japan
17B2 **Okeechobee** USA
17B2 **Okeechobee,L** USA
17B1 **Okefenokee Swamp** USA
97C4 **Okene** Nig
85B4 **Okha** India
69G1 **Okha** Russian Fed
86B1 **Okhaldunga** Nepal
62J3 **Okhotsk,S of** Russian Fed
69E4 **Okinawa** *I* Japan
69E4 **Okinawa gunto** *Arch* Japan
74C3 **Oki-shoto** *Is* Japan
9D3 **Oklahoma** State, USA
18A2 **Oklahoma City** USA
18A2 **Okmulgee** USA
98B3 **Okondja** Gabon
98B3 **Okoyo** Congo
97C4 **Okpara** *R* Nig
61J4 **Oktyabr'sk** Kazakhstan
61H3 **Oktyabr'skiy** Russian Fed
74D2 **Okushiri-tō** *I* Japan
38A2 **Olafsvik** Iceland
39H7 **Öland** *I* Sweden
108B2 **Olary** Aust
18B2 **Olathe** USA
29D3 **Olavarría** Arg
53A2 **Olbia** Sardegna
12G1 **Old Crow** Can
56B2 **Oldenburg** Niedersachsen, Germany
56C2 **Oldenburg** Schleswig-Holstein, Germany
15C2 **Old Forge** USA
42C3 **Oldham** Eng
12D3 **Old Harbor** USA
41B3 **Old Head of Kinsale** *C* Scot
16C2 **Old Lyme** USA
13E2 **Olds** Can
72B1 **Öldziyt** Mongolia
15C2 **Olean** USA
63E2 **Olekma** *R* Russian Fed
63D1 **Olekminsk** Russian Fed
38L5 **Olenegorsk** Russian Fed
58D2 **Olevsk** Ukraine
69F2 **Ol'ga** Russian Fed
100A3 **Olifants** *R* Namibia
55B2 **Ólimbos** *Mt* Greece
35B2 **Olímpia** Brazil
23B2 **Olinala** Mexico
31E3 **Olinda** Brazil
34C2 **Oliva** Arg
29C2 **Olivares** *Mt* Arg
35C2 **Oliveira** Brazil
13D3 **Oliver** Can
30C3 **Ollague** Chile
30C3 **Ollagüe** *Mt* Bol
18C2 **Olney** USA
68E1 **Olochi** Russian Fed
39G7 **Olofstrom** Sweden
98B3 **Olombo** Congo
59B3 **Olomouc** Czech
60D1 **Olonets** Russian Fed
79B3 **Olongapa** Phil
48B3 **Oloron Ste Marie** France
68D1 **Olovyannaya** Russian Fed
46D1 **Olpe** Germany
58C2 **Olsztyn** Pol
54B2 **Olt** *R* Rom
47B1 **Olten** Switz
20B1 **Olympia** USA
20B1 **Olympic Nat Pk** USA
Olympus = Ólimbos
20B1 **Olympus,Mt** USA
65J4 **Om'** *R* Russian Fed
75B1 **Omachi** Japan
75B2 **Omae-zaki** *C* Japan
45C1 **Omagh** N Ire
18A1 **Omaha** USA
20C1 **Omak** USA
91C5 **Oman** Sultanate, Arabian Pen
91C4 **Oman,G of** UAE
98A3 **Omboué** Gabon
99D1 **Omdurman** Sudan
23B2 **Ometepec** Mexico
99D1 **Om Hājer** Eth
13B1 **Omineca** *R* Can
13B1 **Omineca Mts** Can
75B1 **Omiya** Japan
12H3 **Ommaney,C** USA
4H2 **Ommanney B** Can
99D2 **Omo** *R* Eth
65J4 **Omsk** Russian Fed
74B4 **Omura** Japan
74C4 **Ōmuta** Japan
61H2 **Omutninsk** Russian Fed
78D3 **Onang** Indon
14B1 **Onaping L** Can
100A2 **Oncócua** Angola
100A2 **Ondangua** Namibia
59C3 **Ondava** *R* Czech
68D2 **Öndörhaan** Molgolia
83B5 **One and Half Degree Chan** Indian O
64E3 **Onega** Russian Fed
64E3 **Onega** *R* Russian Fed
15C2 **Oneida L** USA
8D2 **O'Neill** USA
69H2 **Onekotan** *I* Russian Fed
98C3 **Onema** Zaïre
15D2 **Oneonta** USA
54C1 **Oneşti** Rom
64E3 **Onezhskoye Ozero** *L* Russian Fed
100A2 **Ongiva** Angola
74B3 **Ongjin** N Korea
72D1 **Ongniud Qi** China
87C1 **Ongole** India
15C2 **Onieda L** USA
101D3 **Onilahy** *R* Madag
97C4 **Onitsha** Nig
68C2 **Onjüül** Mongolia
75B1 **Ono** Japan
75B2 **Onohara-jima** *I* Japan
74C4 **Onomichi** Japan
106A3 **Onslow** Aust
17C1 **Onslow B** USA

75B1 **Ontake-san** *Mt* Japan
22D3 **Ontario** California, USA
20C2 **Ontario** Oregon, USA
7A4 **Ontario** Province, Can
15C2 **Ontario,L** Can/USA
51B2 **Onteniente** Spain
106C3 **Oodnadatta** Aust
106C4 **Ooldea** Aust
18A2 **Oologah L** USA
46B1 **Oostende** Belg
46B1 **Oosterschelde** *Estuary* Neth
87B2 **Ootacamund** India
13B2 **Ootsa L** Can
69H1 **Opala** Russian Fed
98C3 **Opala** Zaïre
87C3 **Opanake** Sri Lanka
61G2 **Oparino** Russian Fed
59B3 **Opava** Czech
17A1 **Opelika** USA
19B3 **Opelousas** USA
12C2 **Ophir** USA
58D1 **Opochka** Russian Fed
59B2 **Opole** Pol
Oporto = Porto
110C1 **Opotiki** NZ
17A1 **Opp** USA
38F6 **Oppdal** Nor
110B1 **Opunake** NZ
54B1 **Oradea** Rom
38B2 **Oraefajökull** *Mts* Iceland
85D3 **Orai** India
96B1 **Oran** Alg
30D3 **Orán** Arg
109C2 **Orange** Aust
22D4 **Orange** California, USA
49C3 **Orange** France
19B3 **Orange** Texas, USA
100A3 **Orange** *R* S Africa
17B1 **Orangeburg** USA
101G1 **Orange Free State** Province, S Africa
17B1 **Orange Park** USA
14B2 **Orangeville** Can
56C2 **Oranienburg** Germany
79C3 **Oras** Phil
54B1 **Orăstie** Rom
54B1 **Oraviţa** Rom
52B2 **Orbetello** Italy
109C3 **Orbost** Aust
46B1 **Orchies** France
47B2 **Orco** *R* Italy
106B2 **Ord** *R* Aust
106B2 **Ord,Mt** Aust
93C1 **Ordu** Turk
39H7 **Örebro** Sweden
8A2 **Oregon** State, USA
14B2 **Oregon** USA
20B1 **Oregon City** USA
39H6 **Oregrund** Sweden
60E2 **Orekhovo Zuyevo** Russian Fed
60E3 **Orel** Russian Fed
61H3 **Orenburg** Russian Fed
34D3 **Orense** Arg
50A1 **Orense** Spain
56C1 **Oresund** *Str* Den/Sweden
111A3 **Oreti** *R* NZ
55C3 **Orhaneli** *R* Turk
68C2 **Orhon Gol** *R* Mongolia
23B2 **Oriental** Mexico
108B1 **Orientos** Aust
51B2 **Orihuela** Spain
15C2 **Orillia** Can
33E2 **Orinoco** *R* Ven
86A2 **Orissa** State, India
53A3 **Oristano** Sardegna
38K6 **Orivesi** *L* Fin
33F4 **Oriximina** Brazil
23B2 **Orizaba** Mexico
35B1 **Orizona** Brazil
44C2 **Orkney** *I* Scot
35B2 **Orlândia** Brazil
17B2 **Orlando** USA
48C2 **Orléanais** *Region* France
48C2 **Orléans** France
63B2 **Orlik** Russian Fed
82A3 **Ormara** Pak
79B3 **Ormoc** Phil
17B2 **Ormond Beach** USA
46C2 **Ornain** *R* France
47B1 **Ornans** France
48B2 **Orne** *R* France
38H6 **Örnsköldsvik** Sweden
32C3 **Orocué** Colombia
94B3 **Oron** Israel
Orontes = 'āṣī
79B4 **Oroquieta** Phil
59C3 **Orosháza** Hung
21A2 **Oroville** California, USA
20C1 **Oroville** Washington, USA
47B1 **Orsières** Switz
65G4 **Orsk** Russian Fed
38F6 **Ørsta** Nor
48B3 **Orthez** France
50A1 **Ortigueira** Spain
47D1 **Ortles** *Mts* Italy
27L1 **Ortoire** *R* Trinidad
93E2 **Orūmīyeh** Iran
30C2 **Oruro** Bol
61J2 **Osa** Russian Fed
18B2 **Osage** *R* USA
75B1 **Osaka** Japan
25D4 **Osa,Pen de** Costa Rica
18C2 **Osceola** Arkansas, USA
18B1 **Osceola** Iowa, USA
20C2 **Osgood Mts** USA
15C2 **Oshawa** Can
75B2 **O-shima** *I* Japan
10B2 **Oshkosh** USA
97C4 **Oshogbo** Nig
7B5 **Oshosh** USA
98B3 **Oshwe** Zaïre
54A1 **Osijek** Croatia
65K5 **Osinniki** Russian Fed
58D2 **Osipovichi** Belorussia
18B1 **Oskaloosa** USA
60A2 **Oskarshamn** Sweden
39G7 **Oslo** Nor
92C2 **Osmaniye** Turk
56B2 **Osnabrück** Germany
30F4 **Osório** Brazil
29B4 **Osorno** Chile
50B1 **Osorno** Spain
20C1 **Osoyoos** Can
13C1 **Ospika** *R* Can
107D5 **Ossa,Mt** Aust
16C2 **Ossining** USA
60D2 **Ostashkov** Russian Fed
Ostend = Oostende
38G6 **Østerdalen** *V* Nor
38G6 **Östersund** Sweden
56B2 **Ostfriesische Inseln** *Is* Germany
39H6 **Östhammär** Sweden
53B2 **Ostia** Italy
47D2 **Ostiglia** Italy
59B3 **Ostrava** Czech
58B2 **Ostróda** Pol
58B2 **Ostroleka** Pol
60C2 **Ostrov** Russian Fed
64J2 **Ostrov Belyy** *I* Russian Fed
64H1 **Ostrov Greem Bell** *I* Barents S
64F3 **Ostrov Kolguyev** *I* Russian Fed
74F2 **Ostrov Kunashir** *I* Russian Fed
64F2 **Ostrov Mechdusharskiy** *I* Barents S
90B2 **Ostrov Ogurchinskiy** *I* Turkmenistan
64G1 **Ostrov Rudol'fa** *I* Barents S
64G2 **Ostrov Vaygach** *I* Russian Fed
1B7 **Ostrov Vrangelya** *I* Russian Fed
58B2 **Ostrów** Pol
59C2 **Ostrowiec** Pol
58C2 **Ostrów Mazowiecka** Pol
50A2 **Osuna** Spain
15C2 **Osweg** USA
15C2 **Oswego** USA
43C3 **Oswestry** Eng
59B2 **Oświęcim** Pol
75B1 **Ota** Japan
111B3 **Otago Pen** NZ
110C2 **Otaki** NZ
74E2 **Otaru** Japan
32B3 **Otavalo** Ecuador
100A2 **Otavi** Namibia
75C1 **Otawara** Japan
20C1 **Othello** USA
55B3 **Óthris** *Mt* Greece
16C1 **Otis** Massachusetts, USA
16B2 **Otisville** USA
100A3 **Otjiwarongo** Namibia
72B2 **Otog Qi** China
110C1 **Otorohanga** NZ
55A2 **Otranto** Italy
55A2 **Otranto,Str of** *Chan* Italy/Alb
14A2 **Otsego** USA
75B1 **Otsu** Japan
39F6 **Otta** Nor
39F7 **Otta** *R* Nor
15C1 **Ottawa** Can
18A2 **Ottawa** Kansas, USA
15C1 **Ottawa** *R* Can
7B4 **Ottawa Is** Can
7B4 **Otter Rapids** Can
6B1 **Otto Fjord** Can
101G1 **Ottosdal** S Africa
18B1 **Ottumwa** USA
46D2 **Ottweiler** Germany
97C4 **Oturkpo** Nig
32B5 **Otusco** Peru
108B3 **Otway,C** Aust
58C2 **Otwock** Pol
47D1 **Ötz** Austria
47D1 **Otzal** *Mts* Austria
76C1 **Ou** *R* Laos
19B3 **Ouachita** *R* USA
19B3 **Ouachita,L** USA
19B3 **Ouachita Mts** USA
96A2 **Ouadane** Maur
98C2 **Ouadda** CAR
98C1 **Ouaddai** *Desert Region* Chad
97B3 **Ouagadougou** Burkina
97B3 **Ouahigouya** Burkina
98C2 **Ouaka** CAR
97C3 **Oualam** Niger
96C2 **Ouallen** Alg
98C2 **Ouanda Djallé** CAR
96A2 **Ouarane** Region, Maur
96C1 **Ouargla** Alg
98C2 **Ouarra** *R* CAR
96B1 **Ouarzazate** Mor
51C2 **Ouassel** *R* Alg
98B2 **Oubangui** *R* Congo
46B1 **Oudenaarde** Belg
100B4 **Oudtshoorn** S Africa
51B2 **Oued Tlělat** Alg
96B1 **Oued Zem** Mor
98B2 **Ouesso** Congo
96B1 **Ouezzane** Mor
98B2 **Ouham** *R* Chad
97C4 **Ouidah** Benin
96B1 **Oujda** Mor
38J6 **Oulainen** Fin
38K5 **Oulu** Fin
38K6 **Oulu** *R* Fin
38K6 **Oulujärvi** *L* Fin
95B3 **Oum Chalouba** Chad
98B1 **Oum Hadjer** Chad
95B3 **Oum Haouach** *Watercourse* Chad
38K5 **Ounas** *R* Fin
95B3 **Ounianga Kébir** Chad
46D1 **Our** *R* Germany
46B2 **Ourcq** *R* France
Ourense = Orense
31C3 **Ouricurí** Brazil
35B2 **Ourinhos** Brazil
35C2 **Ouro Prêto** Brazil
46C1 **Ourthe** *R* Belg
42D2 **Ouse** *R* Eng
43E3 **Ouse** *R* Eng
40B2 **Outer Hebrides** *Is* Scot
22C4 **Outer Santa Barbara** *Chan* USA
100A3 **Outjo** Namibia
38K6 **Outokumpu** Fin
108B3 **Ouyen** Aust
47C2 **Ovada** Italy
34A2 **Ovalle** Chile
100A2 **Ovamboland** Region, Namibia
61H5 **Ova Tyuleni** *Is* Kazakhstan
38J5 **Övertorneå** Sweden
50A1 **Oviedo** Spain
60C3 **Ovruch** Ukraine
63E2 **Ovsyanka** Russian Fed
111A3 **Owaka** NZ
75B2 **Owase** Japan
11B3 **Owensboro** USA
21B2 **Owens L** USA
14B2 **Owen Sound** Can
107D1 **Owen Stanley Range** *Mts* PNG
97C4 **Owerri** Nig
97C4 **Owo** Nig
14B2 **Owosso** USA
20C2 **Owyhee** *R* USA
20C2 **Owyhee Mts** USA
32B6 **Oxapampa** Peru
39H7 **Oxelösund** Sweden
43D4 **Oxford** County, Eng
43D4 **Oxford** Eng
16D1 **Oxford** Massachusetts, USA
19C3 **Oxford** Mississippi, USA
45B1 **Ox Mts** Irish Rep
22C3 **Oxnard** USA
74D3 **Oyama** Japan
13E2 **Oyen** Can
98B2 **Oyem** Gabon
44B3 **Oykel** *R* Scot
39F6 **Øyre** Nor
109C4 **Oyster B** Aust
79B4 **Ozamiz** Phil
17A1 **Ozark** USA
18B2 **Ozark Plat** USA
18B2 **Ozarks,L of the** USA
59C3 **Ózd** Hung
65K5 **Ozero Alakol** *L* Kazakhstan/Russian Fed
65J5 **Ozero Balkhash** *L* Kazakhstan
63C2 **Ozero Baykal** *L* Kazakhstan
65J4 **Ozero Chany** *L* Russian Fed
69F1 **Ozero Chukchagirskoye** Russian Fed
69F1 **Ozero Evoron** Russian Fed
60C2 **Ozero Chudskoye** *L* Russian Fed
60D2 **Ozero Il'men** *L* Russian Fed
38L5 **Ozero Imandra** *L* Russian Fed
82B1 **Ozero Issyk Kul'** *L* Kirgizia
69F2 **Ozero Khanka** *L* China/Russian Fed
38L5 **Ozero Kovdozero** *L* Russian Fed
38L5 **Ozero Kuyto** *L* Russian Fed
38L5 **Ozero Pyaozero** *L* Russian Fed
65H4 **Ozero Tengiz** *L* Kazakhstan
38L5 **Ozero Topozero** *L* Russian Fed
65K5 **Ozero Zaysan** Kazakhstan
23B1 **Ozuluama** Mexico

P

100A4 **Paarl** S Africa
44A3 **Pabbay** *I* Scot

58B2 **Pabianice** Pol
86B2 **Pabna** Bang
58D2 **Pabrade** Lithuania
32B5 **Pacasmayo** Peru
23B1 **Pachuca** Mexico
105K6 **Pacific-Antarctic Ridge** Pacific O
22B2 **Pacific Grove** USA
78C4 **Pacitan** Indon
35C1 **Pacuí** *R* Brazil
70B4 **Padang** Indon
56B2 **Paderborn** Germany
5J3 **Padlei** Can
86C2 **Padma** *R* Bang
47D2 **Padova** Italy
9D4 **Padre I** USA
43B4 **Padstow** Eng
108B3 **Padthaway** Aust
Padua = Padova
14A3 **Paducah** Kentucky, USA
11B3 **Paducah** USA
38L5 **Padunskoye More** *L* Russian Fed
74A3 **Paengnyŏng-do** *I* S Korea
110C1 **Paeroa** NZ
100C3 **Pafuri** Mozam
52B2 **Pag** *I* Croatia
79B4 **Pagadian** Phil
70B4 **Pagai Selatan** *I* Indon
70B4 **Pagai Utara** *I* Indon
71F2 **Pagan** *I* Pacific O
78D3 **Pagatan** Indon
55C3 **Pagondhas** Greece
110C2 **Pahiatua** NZ
21C4 **Pahoa** Hawaiian Is
17B2 **Pahokee** USA
39K6 **Päijänna** *L* Fin
21C4 **Pailola Chan** Hawaiian Is
14B2 **Painesville** USA
9B3 **Painted Desert** USA
42B2 **Paisley** Scot
32A5 **Paita** Peru
38J5 **Pajala** Sweden
80E3 **Pakistan** Republic, Asia
76C2 **Pak Lay** Laos
86D2 **Pakokku** Burma
13E2 **Pakowki L** Can
52C1 **Pakrac** Croatia
54A1 **Paks** Hung
76C2 **Pak Sane** Laos
76D2 **Pakse** Laos
99D2 **Pakwach** Uganda
98B2 **Pala** Chad
52C2 **Palagruža** *I* Croatia
46B2 **Palaiseau** France
78C3 **Palangkaraya** Indon
87B2 **Palani** India
85C4 **Palanpur** India
100B3 **Palapye** Botswana
17B2 **Palatka** USA
71E3 **Palau Is** Pacific O
76B3 **Palaw** Burma
79A4 **Palawan** *I* Phil
79A4 **Palawan Pass** Phil
87B3 **Palayankottai** India
39J7 **Paldiski** Estonia
78A3 **Palembang** Indon
50B1 **Palencia** Spain
94A1 **Paleokhorio** Cyprus
53B3 **Palermo** Italy
94B3 **Palestine** Region, Israel
19A3 **Palestine** USA
86C2 **Paletwa** Burma
87B2 **Pālghāt** India
85C3 **Pāli** India
85C4 **Pālitāna** India
87B3 **Palk Str** India/ Sri Lanka
61G3 **Pallasovka** Russian Fed
38J5 **Pallastunturi** *Mt* Fin
111B2 **Palliser B** NZ
111C2 **Palliser,C** NZ
101D2 **Palma** Mozam
51C2 **Palma de Mallorca** Spain
31D3 **Palmares** Brazil
26A5 **Palmar Sur** Costa Rica
97B4 **Palmas,C** Lib
26B2 **Palma Soriano** Cuba
17B2 **Palm Bay** USA
17B2 **Palm Beach** USA
22C3 **Palmdale** USA
31D3 **Palmeira dos Indos** Brazil
12E2 **Palmer** USA
112C3 **Palmer** *Base* Ant
112C3 **Palmer Arch** Ant
112B3 **Palmer Land** *Region* Ant
111B3 **Palmerston** NZ
110C2 **Palmerston North** NZ
16B2 **Palmerton** USA
17B2 **Palmetto** USA
53C3 **Palmi** Italy
32B3 **Palmira** Colombia
107D2 **Palm Is** Aust
21B3 **Palm Springs** USA
18B2 **Palmyra** Missouri, USA
16A2 **Palmyra** Pennsylvania, USA
86B2 **Palmyras Pt** India
22A2 **Palo Alto** USA
78B2 **Paloh** Indon
99D1 **Paloích** Sudan
21B3 **Palomar Mt** USA
70D4 **Palopo** Indon
70C4 **Palu** Indon
93C2 **Palu** Turk
84D3 **Palwal** India
97C3 **Pama** Burkina
78C4 **Pamekasan** Indon
78B4 **Pameungpeuk** Indon
48C3 **Pamiers** France
82B2 **Pamir** *Mts* China
65J6 **Pamir** *R* Russian Fed
11C3 **Pamlico Sd** USA
9C3 **Pampa** USA
34B2 **Pampa de la Salinas** *Salt pan* Arg
34B3 **Pampa de la Varita** *Plain* Arg
32C2 **Pamplona** Colombia
50B1 **Pamplona** Spain
18C2 **Pana** USA
54B2 **Panagyurishte** Bulg
87A1 **Panaji** India
32B2 **Panamá** Panama
32A2 **Panama** Republic, Cent America
26B5 **Panama Canal** Panama
17A1 **Panama City** USA
21B2 **Panamint Range** *Mts* USA
21B2 **Panamint V** USA
47D2 **Panaro** *R* Italy
79B3 **Panay** *I* Phil
54B2 **Pancevo** Serbia, Yugos
79B3 **Pandan** Phil
87B1 **Pandharpur** India
108A1 **Pandie Pandie** Aust
58C1 **Panevežys** Lithuania
65K5 **Panfilov** Kazakhstan
76B1 **Pang** *R* Burma
99D3 **Pangani** Tanz
99D3 **Pangani** *R* Tanz
98C3 **Pangi** Zaïre
78B3 **Pangkalpinang** Indon
6D3 **Pangnirtung** Can
76B1 **Pangtara** Burma
79B4 **Pangutaran Group** *Is* Phil
84D3 **Panipat** India
84B2 **Panjao** Afghan
74B3 **P'anmunjŏm** N Korea
86A2 **Panna** India
35A2 **Panorama** Brazil
53B3 **Pantelleria** *I* Medit S
23B1 **Pantepec** Mexico
23B1 **Panuco** Mexico
23B1 **Pánuco** *R* Mexico
73A4 **Pan Xian** China
53C3 **Paola** Italy
18B2 **Paola** USA
14A3 **Paoli** USA
59B3 **Pápa** Hung
110B1 **Papakura** NZ
23B2 **Papaloapan** *R* Mexico
23B1 **Papantla** Mexico
44E1 **Papa Stour** *I* Scot
110B1 **Papatoetoe** NZ
44C2 **Papa Westray** *I* Scot
107D1 **Papua,G of** PNG
107D1 **Papua New Guinea** Republic, S E Asia
34A2 **Papudo** Chile
76B2 **Papun** Burma
33G4 **Para** State, Brazil
31B2 **Pará** *R* Brazil
106A3 **Paraburdoo** Aust
32B6 **Paracas,Pen de** Peru
35B1 **Paracatu** Brazil
35B1 **Paracatu** *R* Brazil
108A2 **Parachilna** Aust
84C2 **Parachinar** Pak
54B2 **Paracin** Serbia, Yugos
35C1 **Pará de Minas** Brazil
21A2 **Paradise** California, USA
18B2 **Paragould** USA
33E6 **Paraguá** *R* Bol
33E2 **Paragua** *R* Ven
30E2 **Paraguai** *R* Brazil
30E4 **Paraguari** Par
30E3 **Paraguay** Republic, S America
30E3 **Paraguay** *R* Par
31D3 **Paraiba** State, Brazil
35B2 **Paraiba** *R* Brazil
35C2 **Paraíba do Sul** *R* Brazil
97C4 **Parakou** Benin
108A2 **Parakylia** Aust
87B3 **Paramakkudi** India
33F2 **Paramaribo** Surinam
69H1 **Paramushir** *I* Russian Fed
30F3 **Paraná** State, Brazil
34C2 **Paraná** Urug
29E2 **Paraná** *R* Arg
31B4 **Paranã** *R* Brazil
35A2 **Paraná** *R* Brazil
30G4 **Paranaguá** Brazil
35A1 **Paranaiba** Brazil
35A1 **Paranaiba** *R* Brazil
35A2 **Paranapanema** *R* Brazil
35A2 **Paranavai** Brazil
79B4 **Parang** Phil
35C1 **Paraope** *R* Brazil
110B2 **Paraparaumu** NZ
87B1 **Parbhani** India
94B2 **Pardes Hanna** Israel
34D3 **Pardo** Arg
35D1 **Pardo** *R* Bahia, Brazil
35A2 **Pardo** *R* Mato Grosso do Sul, Brazil
35B1 **Pardo** *R* Minas Gerais, Brazil
35B2 **Pardo** *R* Sao Paulo, Brazil
59B2 **Pardubice** Czech
69F4 **Parece Vela** *Reef* Pacific O
10C2 **Parent** Can
70C4 **Parepare** Indon
34C3 **Parera** Arg
70B4 **Pariaman** Indon
33E1 **Paria,Pen de** Ven
48C2 **Paris** France
14B3 **Paris** Kentucky, USA
19A3 **Paris** Texas, USA
14B3 **Parkersburg** USA
109C2 **Parkes** Aust
16B3 **Parkesburg** USA
14A2 **Park Forest** USA
20B1 **Parksville** Can
87B1 **Parli** India
47D2 **Parma** Italy
14B2 **Parma** USA
31C2 **Parnaiba** Brazil
31C2 **Parnaiba** *R* Brazil
55B3 **Párnon Óros** *Mts* Greece
60B2 **Pärnu** Estonia
86B1 **Paro** Bhutan
108B1 **Paroo** *R* Aust
108B2 **Paroo Channel** *R* Aust
55C3 **Páros** *I* Greece
47B2 **Parpaillon** *Mts* France
34A3 **Parral** Chile
109D2 **Parramatta** Aust
9C4 **Parras** Mexico
6B3 **Parry B** Can
4G2 **Parry Is** Can
7C5 **Parry Sd** Can
14B1 **Parry Sound** Can
57C3 **Parsberg** Germany
5F4 **Parsnip** *R* Can
18A2 **Parsons** Kansas, USA
14C3 **Parsons** West Virginia, USA
48B2 **Parthenay** France
53B3 **Partinico** Italy
74C2 **Partizansk** Russian Fed
33G4 **Paru** *R* Brazil
101G1 **Parys** S Africa
19A4 **Pasadena** Texas, USA
22C3 **Pasadena** California, USA
78D3 **Pasangkayu** Indon
76B2 **Pasawing** Burma
19C3 **Pascagoula** USA
54C1 **Paşcani** Rom
20C1 **Pasco** USA
46B1 **Pas-de-Calais** Department, France
39G8 **Pasewalk** Germany
91C4 **Pashū'īyeh** Iran
106B4 **Pasley,C** Aust
29E2 **Paso de los Toros** Urug
29B4 **Paso Limay** Arg
21A2 **Paso Robles** USA
45B3 **Passage West** Irish Rep
16B2 **Passaic** USA
57C3 **Passau** Germany
30E4 **Passo de los Libres** Arg
47D1 **Passo di Stelvio** *Mt* Italy
30F4 **Passo Fundo** Brazil
35B2 **Passos** Brazil
47B2 **Passy** France
32B4 **Pastaza** *R* Peru
34C3 **Pasteur** Arg
5H4 **Pas,The** Can
32B3 **Pasto** Colombia
12B2 **Pastol B** USA
47D2 **Pasubio** *Mt* Italy
78C4 **Pasuruan** Indon
58C1 **Pasvalys** Lithuania
85C4 **Pātan** India
86B1 **Patan** Nepal
108B3 **Patchewollock** Aust
110B1 **Patea** NZ
111B2 **Patea** *R* NZ
53B3 **Paterno** Italy
16B2 **Paterson** USA
111A3 **Paterson Inlet** *B* NZ
84D2 **Pathankot** India
84D2 **Patiāla** India
32B6 **Pativilca** Peru
55C3 **Pátmos** *I* Greece
86B1 **Patna** India
93D2 **Patnos** Turk
63D2 **Patomskoye Nagor'ye** *Upland* Russian Fed
31D3 **Patos** Brazil
35B1 **Patos de Minas** Brazil
34B2 **Patquia** Arg
55B3 **Pátrai** Greece
35B1 **Patrocinio** Brazil
99E3 **Patta** *I* Kenya
78D4 **Pattallasang** Indon
77C4 **Pattani** Thai
22B2 **Patterson** California, USA
19B4 **Patterson** Louisiana, USA
12H2 **Patterson,Mt** Can
22C2 **Patterson Mt** USA
13B1 **Pattullo,Mt** Can
31D3 **Patu** Brazil
86C2 **Patuakhali** Bang

25D3 **Patuca** *R* Honduras
23A2 **Patzcuaro** Mexico
48B3 **Pau** France
4F3 **Paulatuk** Can
31C3 **Paulistana** Brazil
101H1 **Paulpietersburg** S Africa
19A3 **Pauls Valley** USA
76B2 **Paungde** Burma
84D2 **Pauri** India
38H5 **Pauskie** Nor
35C1 **Pavão** Brazil
47C2 **Pavia** Italy
65J4 **Pavlodar** Kazakhstan
61J2 **Pavlovka** Russian Fed
61F2 **Pavlovo** Russian Fed
61F3 **Pavlovsk** Russian Fed
78C3 **Pawan** *R* Indon
18A2 **Pawhuska** USA
16D2 **Pawtucket** USA
47B1 **Payerne** Switz
20C2 **Payette** USA
7C4 **Payne,L** Can
34D2 **Paysandu** Urug
46A2 **Pays-de-Bray** Region, France
54B2 **Pazardzhik** Bulg
13D1 **Peace** *R* Can
17B2 **Peace** *R* USA
13D1 **Peace River** Can
43D3 **Peak District Nat Pk** Eng
108A1 **Peake** *R* Aust
109C2 **Peak Hill** Aust
71E4 **Peak Mandala** *Mt* Indon
42D3 **Peak,The** *Mt* Eng
19B3 **Pearl** *R* USA
21C4 **Pearl City** Hawaiian Is
21C4 **Pearl Harbor** Hawaiian Is
4H2 **Peary Chan** Can
101C2 **Pebane** Mozam
54B2 **Peć** Serbia, Yugos
35C1 **Peçanha** Brazil
19B4 **Pecan Island** USA
38L5 **Pechenga** Russian Fed
64F3 **Pechora** *R* Russian Fed
64G3 **Pechorskoye More** *S* Russian Fed
53C3 **Pecoraro** *Mt* Italy
9C3 **Pecos** USA
9C3 **Pecos** *R* USA
59B3 **Pécs** Hung
108A1 **Pedirka** Aust
35C1 **Pedra Azul** Brazil
35B2 **Pedregulho** Brazil
26B3 **Pedro Cays** *Is* Caribbean S
30C3 **Pedro de Valdivia** Chile
30E3 **Pedro Juan Caballero** Par
34C3 **Pedro Luro** Arg
23B1 **Pedro Mentova** Mexico
87C3 **Pedro,Pt** Sri Lanka
108B2 **Peebinga** Aust
42C2 **Peebles** Scot
17C1 **Pee Dee** *R* USA
16C2 **Peekskill** USA
42B2 **Peel** Eng
12H1 **Peel** *R* Can
4J2 **Peel Sd** Can
108A1 **Peera Peera Poolanna** *L* Aust
13E1 **Peerless L** Can
71E4 **Peg Arfak** *Mt* Indon
111B2 **Pegasus B** NZ
83D4 **Pegu** Burma
78A3 **Pegunungan Barisan** *Mts* Indon
78C2 **Pegunungan Iran** *Mts* Malay/Indon
71E4 **Pegunungan Maoke** *Mts* Indon
78D3 **Pegunungan Meratus** *Mts* Indon
78C2 **Pegunungan Muller** *Mts* Indon
78C3 **Pegunungan Schwanet** *Mts* Indon
78A3 **Pegunungan Tigapuluh** *Mts* Indon
76B2 **Pegu Yoma** *Mts* Burma
34C3 **Pehuajó** Arg
39K7 **Péipsi Järve** *L* Estonia
39K7 **Peipus, Lake** Estonia/Russian Fed
35A2 **Peixe** *R* Sao Paulo, Brazil
72D3 **Pei Xian** China
78B4 **Pekalongan** Indon
77C5 **Pekan** Malay
78A2 **Pekanbaru** Indon
18C1 **Pekin** USA
Peking = Beijing
77C5 **Pelabohan Kelang** Malay
78D4 **Pelau Pelau Kangean** *Is* Indon
78C4 **Pelau Pelau Karimunjawa** *Arch* Indon
78D4 **Pelau Pelau Postilyon** *Is* Indon
54B1 **Peleaga** *Mt* Rom
63D2 **Peleduy** Russian Fed
14B2 **Pelee I** Can
71D4 **Peleng** *I* Indon
12G3 **Pelican** USA
69F1 **Peliny Osipenko** Russian Fed
34C3 **Pellegrini** Arg
38J5 **Pello** Fin
12H2 **Pelly** *R* Can
6A3 **Pelly Bay** Can
12G2 **Pelly Crossing** Can
12H2 **Pelly Mts** Can
30F5 **Pelotas** Brazil
30F4 **Pelotas** *R* Brazil
47B2 **Pelvoux** Region, France
78B4 **Pemalang** Indon
78A3 **Pematang** Indon
101D2 **Pemba** Mozam
99D3 **Pemba** *I* Tanz
13C2 **Pemberton** Can
13D2 **Pembina** *R* Can
15C1 **Pembroke** Can
17B1 **Pembroke** USA
43B4 **Pembroke** Wales
34A3 **Pemuco** Chile
78D2 **Pemambo Range** *Mts* Malay
35A2 **Penápolis** Brazil
50A2 **Peñarroya** Spain
51B1 **Penarroya** *Mt* Spain
50A1 **Peña Trevina** *Mt* Spain
98B2 **Pende** *R* Chad
12J3 **Pendelton,Mt** Can
20C1 **Pendleton** USA
20C1 **Pend Oreille** *R* USA
31D4 **Penedo** Brazil
85D5 **Penganga** *R* India
73D5 **P'eng-hu Lieh-tao** *Is* Taiwan
72E2 **Penglai** China
73B4 **Pengshui** China
71E4 **Pengunungan Maoke** *Mts* Indon
26C4 **Península de la Guajiri** *Pen* Colombia
27E4 **Península de Paria** *Pen* Ven
77C5 **Peninsular Malaysia** Malay
10D2 **Peninsule de Gaspé** *Pen* Can
23A1 **Penjamo** Mexico
87B2 **Penner** *R* India
42C2 **Pennine Chain** *Mts* Eng
16B3 **Penns Grove** USA
10C2 **Pennsylvania** State, USA
6D3 **Penny Highlands** *Mts* Can
108B3 **Penola** Aust
106C4 **Penong** Aust
42C2 **Penrith** Eng
11B3 **Pensacola** USA
112A **Pensacola Mts** Ant
78D1 **Pensiangan** Malay
13D3 **Penticton** Can
44C2 **Pentland Firth** *Chan* Scot
42C2 **Pentland Hills** Scot
61G3 **Penza** Russian Fed
43B4 **Penzance** Eng
10B2 **Peoria** USA
78A3 **Perabumulih** Indon
77C5 **Perak** *R* Malay
78A2 **Perawang** Indon
32B3 **Pereira** Colombia
35A2 **Pereira Barreto** Brazil
61F4 **Perelazovskiy** Russian Fed
12D3 **Perenosa B** USA
34C2 **Pergamino** Arg
7C4 **Peribonca** *R* Can
48C2 **Périqueux** France
25E4 **Perlas Arch de** *Is* Panama
61J2 **Perm'** Russian Fed
Pernambuco = Recife
31D3 **Pernambuco** State, Brazil
108A2 **Pernatty Lg** Aust
54B2 **Pernik** Bulg
46B2 **Péronne** France
23B2 **Perote** Mexico
49C3 **Perpignan** France
22D4 **Perris** USA
17B1 **Perry** Florida, USA
17B1 **Perry** Georgia, USA
18A2 **Perry** Oklahoma, USA
4H3 **Perry River** Can
14B2 **Perrysburg** USA
12C3 **Perryville** Alaska, USA
18C2 **Perryville** Missouri, USA
106A4 **Perth** Aust
15C2 **Perth** Can
44C3 **Perth** Scot
16B2 **Perth Amboy** USA
32C6 **Peru** Republic, S America
18C1 **Peru** USA
103E5 **Peru-Chile Trench** Pacific O
52B2 **Perugia** Italy
52C2 **Perušic** Croatia
93D2 **Pervari** Turk
61F3 **Pervomaysk** Russian Fed
60D4 **Pervomaysk** Ukraine
61J2 **Pervoural'sk** Russian Fed
52B2 **Pesaro** Italy
22A2 **Pescadero** USA
Pescadores = P'eng-hu Lieh-tao
52B2 **Pescara** Italy
47D2 **Peschiera** Italy
84C2 **Peshawar** Pak
54B2 **Peshkopi** Alb
14A1 **Peshtigo** USA
60E2 **Pestovo** Russian Fed
94B2 **Petah Tiqwa** Israel
21A2 **Petaluma** USA
46C2 **Pétange** Lux
23A2 **Petatlán** Mexico
101C2 **Petauke** Zambia
108A2 **Peterborough** Aust
15C2 **Peterborough** Can
43D3 **Peterborough** Eng
44D3 **Peterhead** Scot
6D1 **Petermann Gletscher** *Gl* Greenland
106B3 **Petermann Range** *Mts* Aust
29B3 **Peteroa** *Mt* Arg/Chile
13F1 **Peter Pond L** Can
12H3 **Petersburg** Alaska, USA
85C4 **Petlād** India
23B2 **Petlalcingo** Mexico
25D2 **Peto** Mexico
63D2 **Petomskoye Nagor'ye** *Upland* Russian Fed
34A2 **Petorca** Chile
14B1 **Petoskey** USA
31C3 **Petrolina** Brazil
65H4 **Petropavlovsk** Kazakhstan
35C2 **Petrópolis** Brazil
61G3 **Petrovsk** Russian Fed
68C1 **Petrovsk Zabaykal'skiy** Russian Fed
64E3 **Petrozavodsk** Russian Fed
101G1 **Petrus** S Africa
101G1 **Petrusburg** S Africa
1B7 **Pevek** Russian Fed
46D2 **Pfälzer Wald** Region, Germany
57B3 **Pforzheim** Germany
84D2 **Phagwara** India
85C3 **Phalodi** India
46D2 **Phalsbourg** France
87A1 **Phaltan** India
77B4 **Phangnga** Thai
76C3 **Phanom Dang** *Mts* Camb
76D3 **Phan Rang** Viet
76D3 **Phan Thiet** Viet
17A1 **Phenix City** USA
76B3 **Phet Buri** Thai
76D3 **Phiafay** Laos
19C3 **Philadelphia** Mississippi, USA
16B2 **Philadelphia** Pennsylvania, USA
Philippeville = Skikda
46C1 **Philippeville** Belg
71D2 **Philippine S** Pacific O
71D2 **Philippines** Republic, S E Asia
104E3 **Philippine Trench** Pacific O
15C2 **Philipsburg** Pennsylvania, USA
12E1 **Philip Smith Mts** USA
79B2 **Phillipine S** Phil
6B1 **Phillips B** Can
16B2 **Phillipsburg** New Jersey, USA
6B2 **Philpots Pen** Can
76C3 **Phnom Penh** Camb
9B3 **Phoenix** Arizona, USA
16B2 **Phoenixville** USA
76C1 **Phong Saly** Laos
Phra Nakhon = Bangkok
76C2 **Phu Bia** *Mt* Laos
76D3 **Phu Cuong** Viet
77B4 **Phuket** Thai
86A2 **Phulbāni** India
76C2 **Phu Miang** *Mt* Thai
76D2 **Phu Set** *Mt* Laos
76D1 **Phu Tho** Viet
77D4 **Phu Vinh** Viet
47C2 **Piacenza** Italy
109C2 **Pian** *R* Aust
52B2 **Pianosa** *I* Italy
52C2 **Pianosa** *I* Italy
58C2 **Piaseczno** Pol
54C1 **Piatra-Neamţ** Rom
31C3 **Piaui** State, Brazil
47E2 **Piave** *R* Italy
99D2 **Pibor** *R* Sudan
99D2 **Pibor Post** Sudan
46B1 **Picardie** Region, France
19C3 **Picayune** USA
47B2 **Pic de Rochebrune** *Mt* France
34A2 **Pichilemu** Chile
34C3 **Pichi Mahuida** Arg
42D2 **Pickering** Eng
7A4 **Pickle Lake** Can
96A1 **Pico** *I* Açores
47C1 **Pico Bernina** *Mt* Switz
51C1 **Pico de Anito** *Mt* Spain
24B3 **Pico del Infiernillo** *Mt* Mexico

27C3 **Pico Duarte** *Mt* Dom Rep
31C3 **Picos** Brazil
50B1 **Picos de Europa** *Mt* Spain
109D2 **Picton** Aust
111B2 **Picton** NZ
95A2 **Pic Toussidé** *Mt* Chad
35B2 **Piedade** Brazil
22C2 **Piedra** USA
24B2 **Piedras Negras** Mexico
38K6 **Pieksämäki** Fin
38K6 **Pielinen** *L* Fin
47B2 **Piemonte** Region, Italy
8C2 **Pierre** USA
59B3 **Pieštany** Czech
101H1 **Pietermaritzburg** S Africa
100B3 **Pietersburg** S Africa
101H1 **Piet Retief** S Africa
60B4 **Pietrosu** *Mt* Rom
47E1 **Pieve di Cadore** Italy
13E2 **Pigeon L** Can
18B2 **Piggott** USA
34C3 **Pigüé** Arg
7A4 **Pikangikum L** Can
8C3 **Pikes Peak** USA
100A4 **Piketberg** S Africa
6F3 **Pikintaleq** Greenland
82B2 **Pik Kommunizma** *Mt* Tajikistan
98B2 **Pikounda** Congo
82C1 **Pik Pobedy** *Mt* China/Kirgizia
34D3 **Pila** Arg
58B2 **Pila** Pol
30E4 **Pilar** Par
30D3 **Pilcomayo** *R* Arg/Par
84D3 **Pīlībhīt** India
59B2 **Pilica** *R* Pol
109C4 **Pillar,C** Aust
55B3 **Pílos** Greece
12C3 **Pilot Point** USA
12B2 **Pilot Station** USA
19C3 **Pilottown** USA
33F4 **Pimenta** Brazil
77C4 **Pinang** *I* Malay
26A2 **Pinar del Rio** Cuba
34B2 **Pinas** Arg
46C1 **Pinche** Belg
13E2 **Pincher Creek** Can
31B2 **Pindaré** *R* Brazil
55B3 **Píndhos** *Mts* Greece
19B3 **Pine Bluff** USA
106C2 **Pine Creek** Aust
22C1 **Pinecrest** USA
22C2 **Pinedale** California, USA
22C2 **Pine Flat Res** USA
64F3 **Pinega** *R* Russian Fed
16A2 **Pine Grove** USA
17B2 **Pine Hills** USA
17B2 **Pine I** USA
19B3 **Pineland** USA
17B2 **Pinellas Park** USA
5G3 **Pine Point** Can
47B2 **Pinerolo** Italy
19B3 **Pines,Lo'the** USA
19B3 **Pineville** USA
72C3 **Pingdingshan** China
73B5 **Pingguo** China
72B2 **Pingliang** China
72B2 **Pingluo** China
73D4 **Pingtan Dao** *I* China
73E5 **P'ing tung** Taiwan
72A3 **Pingwu** China
73B5 **Pingxiang** Guangxi, China
73C4 **Pingxiang** Jiangxi, China
31B2 **Pinheiro** Brazil
70A3 **Pini** *I* Indon
55B3 **Piniós** *R* Greece
106A4 **Pinjarra** Aust
13C1 **Pink Mountain** Can
108B3 **Pinnaroo** Aust
Pinos,I de, I = Isla de la Juventud
21A2 **Pinos,Pt** USA
23B2 **Pinotepa Nacional** Mexico
70C4 **Pinrang** Indon
60C3 **Pinsk** Belorussia
32J7 **Pinta** *I* Ecuador
61G1 **Pinyug** Russian Fed
8B3 **Pioche** USA
52B2 **Piombino** Italy
6H3 **Piórsá** Iceland
59B2 **Piotrków Trybunalski** Pol
44E2 **Piper** *Oilfield* N Sea
21B2 **Piper Peak** *Mt* USA
10C2 **Pipmuacan Res** Can
14B2 **Piqua** USA
35B1 **Piracanjuba** Brazil
35B2 **Piracicaba** Brazil
35B2 **Piraçununga** Brazil
35B2 **Piraí do Sul** Brazil
55B3 **Piraiévs** Greece
35B2 **Pirajui** Brazil
35A1 **Piranhas** Brazil
35C1 **Pirapora** Brazil
35B1 **Pirenópolis** Brazil
35B1 **Pires do Rio** Brazil
55B3 **Pírgos** Greece
Pirineos = Pyrénees
31C2 **Piripiri** Brazil
46D2 **Pirmasens** Germany
54B2 **Pirot** Serbia, Yugos
84C2 **Pīr Panjāl Range** *Mts* Pak
71D4 **Piru** Indon
22C3 **Piru Creek** *R* USA
49E3 **Pisa** Italy
32B6 **Pisco** Peru
57C3 **Písek** Czech
84B2 **Pishin** Pak
30C4 **Pissis** *Mt* Arg
49E3 **Pistoia** Italy
50B1 **Pisuerga** *R* Spain
20B2 **Pit** *R* USA
32B3 **Pitalito** Colombia
105K5 **Pitcairn** *I* Pacific O
38H5 **Pite** *R* Sweden
38J5 **Piteå** Sweden
54B2 **Piteşti** Rom
63B2 **Pit Gorodok** Russian Fed
38L6 **Pitkyaranta** Russian Fed
44C3 **Pitlochry** Scot
34A3 **Pitrutquén** Chile
13B2 **Pitt I** Can
22B1 **Pittsburg** California, USA
18B2 **Pittsburg** Kansas, USA
14C2 **Pittsburgh** USA
18B2 **Pittsfield** Illinois, USA
16C1 **Pittsfield** Massachusetts, USA
109D1 **Pittsworth** Aust
86A1 **Piuthan** Nepal
47D1 **Pizzo Redorta** *Mt* Italy
38B2 **Pjórsá** Iceland
32A5 **Pjura** Peru
7E5 **Placentia B** Can
22B1 **Placerville** USA
46B1 **Plaine des Flandres** *Plain* Belg/France
96C2 **Plaine du Tidikelt** *Desert* Region
9C3 **Plainview** Texas, USA
22B2 **Planada** USA
30F2 **Planalto de Mato Grosso** *Plat* Brazil
31D3 **Planalto do Borborema** *Plat* Brazil
32A1 **Planalto do Mato Grosso** *Mts* Brazil
19A3 **Plano** USA
17B2 **Plantation** USA
17B2 **Plant City** USA
50A1 **Plasencia** Spain
61K3 **Plast** Russian Fed
69F2 **Plastun** Russian Fed
96C2 **Plateau du Tademait** Alg
46D2 **Plateau Lorrain** *Plat* France
48C2 **Plateaux de Limousin** *Plat* France
51C2 **Plateaux du Sersou** *Plat* Alg
26C5 **Plato** Colombia
65G5 **Plato Ustyurt** *Plat* Kazakhstan
8C2 **Platte** *R* USA
15D2 **Plattsburgh** USA
18A1 **Plattsmouth** USA
57C2 **Plauen** Germany
60E3 **Plavsk** Russian Fed
23A2 **Playa Azul** Mexico
32A4 **Playas** Ecuador
23B2 **Playa Vicente** Mexico
50A1 **Plaza de Moro Almanzor** *Mt* Spain
22B2 **Pleasanton** California, USA
16B3 **Pleasantville** USA
14A3 **Pleasure Ridge Park** USA
76D3 **Pleiku** Viet
110C1 **Plenty,B of** NZ
58B2 **Pleszew** Pol
7C4 **Pletipi,L** Can
54B2 **Pleven** Bulg
54A2 **Pljevlja** Montenegro, Yugos
52C2 **Ploče** Bosnia & Herzegovina, Yugos
58B2 **Płock** Pol
48B2 **Ploërmel** France
54C2 **Ploieşti** Rom
60B3 **Płońsk** Pol
54B2 **Plovdiv** Bulg
20C1 **Plummer** USA
12C2 **Plummer,Mt** USA
100B3 **Plumtree** Zim
22B1 **Plymouth** California, USA
43B4 **Plymouth** Eng
14A2 **Plymouth** Indiana, USA
16D2 **Plymouth** Massachusetts, USA
15C2 **Plymouth** Pennsylvania, USA
43B4 **Plymouth Sd** Eng
43C3 **Plynlimon** *Mt* Wales
57C3 **Plzeň** Czech
58B2 **Pniewy** Pol
38K6 **Pnyäselkä** *L* Fin
97B3 **Pô** Burkina
47E2 **Po** *R* Italy
97C4 **Pobé** Benin
69G2 **Pobedino** Russian Fed
8B2 **Pocatello** USA
15C3 **Pocomoke City** USA
35B2 **Pocos de Caldas** Brazil
47D2 **Po di Volano** *R* Italy
63B1 **Podkamennaya** *R* Russian Fed
60E2 **Podol'sk** Russian Fed
59D3 **Podol'skaya Vozvyshennost'** *Upland* Ukraine
60D1 **Podporozh'ye** Russian Fed
61F1 **Podyuga** Russian Fed
100A3 **Pofadder** S Africa
74B3 **P'ohang** S Korea
112C9 **Poinsett,C** Ant
108C2 **Point** Aust
27E3 **Pointe-à-Pitre** Guadeloupe
48B2 **Pointe de Barfleur** *Pt* France
98B3 **Pointe Noire** Congo
98A2 **Pointe Pongara** *Pt* Gabon
108B3 **Point Fairy** Aust
27L1 **Point Fortin** Trinidad
4B3 **Point Hope** USA
4G3 **Point L** Can
12B1 **Point Lay** USA
16B2 **Point Pleasant** New Jersey, USA
14B3 **Point Pleasant** W Virginia, USA
47B2 **Point St Bernard** *Mt* France
48C2 **Poitiers** France
48B2 **Poitou** Region, France
46A2 **Poix** France
85C3 **Pokaran** India
109C1 **Pokataroo** Aust
63E1 **Pokrovsk** Russian Fed
58B2 **Poland** Republic, Europe
92B2 **Polatli** Turk
78D3 **Polewali** Indon
47A1 **Poligny** France
55B2 **Políyiros** Greece
87B2 **Pollāchi** India
79B3 **Polollo Is** Phil
59D2 **Polonnye** Ukraine
58D1 **Polotsk** Russian Fed
60D4 **Poltava** Russian Fed
52C1 **Pölten** Austria
64F3 **Poluostrov Kanin** *Pen* Russian Fed
61H5 **Poluostrov Mangyshlak** *Pen* Kazakhstan
38L5 **Poluostrov Rybachiy** *Pen* Russian Fed
64H2 **Poluostrov Yamal** *Pen* Russian Fed
38L5 **Polyarnyy** Murmansk, Russian Fed
1B8 **Polyarnyy** Yakutskaya, Russian Fed
105H3 **Polynesia** *Region* Pacific O
32B5 **Pomabamba** Peru
35C2 **Pomba** *R* Brazil
22D3 **Pomona** USA
18A2 **Pomona Res** USA
17B2 **Pompano Beach** USA
16B2 **Pompton Lakes** USA
18A2 **Ponca City** USA
27D3 **Ponce** Puerto Rico
17B2 **Ponce de Leon B** USA
87B2 **Pondicherry** India
6C2 **Pond Inlet** Can
50A1 **Ponferrade** Spain
98C2 **Pongo** *R* Sudan
101H1 **Pongola** *R* S Africa
87B2 **Ponnāni** India
86C2 **Ponnyadoung Range** *Mts* Burma
13E2 **Ponoka** Can
64F3 **Ponoy** Russian Fed
48B2 **Pons** France
35D1 **Ponta da Baleia** *Pt* Brazil
96A1 **Ponta Delgada** Açores
98B3 **Ponta do Padrão** *Pt* Angola
35C2 **Ponta dos Búzios** *Pt* Brazil
30F4 **Ponta Grossa** Brazil
35B2 **Pontal** Brazil
46D2 **Pont-à-Mousson** France
30E3 **Ponta Pora** Brazil
49D2 **Pontarlier** France
19B3 **Pontchartrain,L** USA
52B2 **Pontedera** Italy
52A2 **Ponte Leccia** Corse
50A1 **Pontevedra** Spain
18C1 **Pontiac** Illinois, USA
14B2 **Pontiac** Michigan, USA
78B3 **Pontianak** Indon
48B2 **Pontivy** France
46B2 **Pontoise** France
19C3 **Pontotoc** USA
43C4 **Pontypool** Wales
43C4 **Pontypridd** Wales
43D4 **Poole** Eng
Poona = Pune
108B2 **Pooncarie** Aust
108B2 **Poopelloe,L** *L* Aust
12C2 **Poorman** USA
32B3 **Popayán** Colombia
46B1 **Poperinge** Belg

108B2 **Popilta L** Aust
18B2 **Poplar Bluff** USA
19C3 **Poplarville** USA
107D1 **Popndetta** PNG
23B2 **Popocatepetl** *Mt* Mexico
98B3 **Popokabaka** Zaïre
71F4 **Popondetta** PNG
54C2 **Popovo** Bulg
85B4 **Porbandar** India
13A2 **Porcher I** Can
12F1 **Porcupine** *R* Can/ USA
52B1 **Poreč** Croatia
35A2 **Porecatu** Brazil
39J6 **Pori** Fin
111B2 **Porirua** NZ
38H5 **Porjus** Sweden
69G2 **Poronaysk** Russian Fed
47B1 **Porrentruy** Switz
38K4 **Porsangen** *Inlet* Nor
39F7 **Porsgrunn** Nor
45C1 **Portadown** N Ire
8D2 **Portage la Prairie** Can
13C3 **Port Alberni** Can
50A2 **Portalegre** Port
9C3 **Portales** USA
100B4 **Port Alfred** S Africa
13B2 **Port Alice** Can
19B3 **Port Allen** USA
20B1 **Port Angeles** USA
26B3 **Port Antonio** Jamaica
45C2 **Portarlington** Irish Rep
19B4 **Port Arthur** USA
108A2 **Port Augusta** Aust
26C3 **Port-au-Prince** Haiti
14B2 **Port Austin** USA
108B3 **Port Campbell** Aust
86B2 **Port Canning** India
7D5 **Port Cartier** Can
111B3 **Port Chalmers** NZ
17B2 **Port Charlotte** USA
16C2 **Port Chester** USA
15C2 **Port Colborne** Can
15C2 **Port Credit** Can
109C4 **Port Davey** Aust
26C3 **Port-de-Paix** Haiti
77C5 **Port Dickson** Malay
100C4 **Port Edward** S Africa
35C1 **Porteirinha** Brazil
14B2 **Port Elgin** Can
100B4 **Port Elizabeth** S Africa
27N2 **Porter Pt** St Vincent
21B2 **Porterville** USA
107D4 **Port Fairy** Aust
98A3 **Port Gentil** Gabon
19B3 **Port Gibson** USA
12D3 **Port Graham** USA
20B1 **Port Hammond** Can
89E7 **Port Harcourt** Nig
13B2 **Port Hardy** Can
7D5 **Port Hawkesbury** Can
106A3 **Port Hedland** Aust
Port Heiden = Meshik
43B3 **Porthmadog** Wales
7E4 **Port Hope Simpson** Can
22C3 **Port Hueneme** USA
14B2 **Port Huron** USA
50A2 **Portimão** Port
109D2 **Port Jackson** *B* Aust
16C2 **Port Jefferson** USA
16B2 **Port Jervis** USA
109D2 **Port Kembla** Aust
14B2 **Portland** Indiana, USA
10C2 **Portland** Maine, USA
109C2 **Portland** New South Wales, Aust
20B1 **Portland** Oregon, USA
108B3 **Portland** Victoria, Aust
27H2 **Portland Bight** *B* Jamaica
43C4 **Portland Bill** *Pt* Eng
109C4 **Portland,C** Aust
13A1 **Portland Canal** Can/ USA
110C1 **Portland I** NZ
27H2 **Portland Pt** Jamaica
45C2 **Port Laoise** Irish Rep
108A2 **Port Lincoln** Aust
97A4 **Port Loko** Sierra Leone
101E3 **Port Louis** Mauritius
108B3 **Port MacDonnell** Aust
13B2 **Port McNeill** Can
109D2 **Port Macquarie** Aust
12B3 **Port Moller** USA
107D1 **Port Moresby** PNG
100A3 **Port Nolloth** S Africa
16B3 **Port Norris** USA
89E7 **Port Novo** Benin
50A1 **Porto** Port
30F5 **Pôrto Alegre** Brazil
33F6 **Pôrto Artur** Brazil
30F3 **Pôrto E Cunha** Brazil
52B2 **Portoferraio** Italy
27E4 **Port of Spain** Trinidad
47D2 **Portomaggiore** Italy
97C4 **Porto Novo** Benin
20B1 **Port Orchard** USA
20B2 **Port Orford** USA
96A1 **Porto Santo** *I* Medeira
31D5 **Pôrto Seguro** Brazil
53A2 **Porto Torres** Sardegna
53A2 **Porto Vecchio** Corse
33E5 **Pôrto Velho** Brazil
111A3 **Port Pegasus** *B* NZ
108B3 **Port Phillip B** Aust
108A2 **Port Pirie** Aust
44A3 **Portree** Scot
20B1 **Port Renfrew** Can
27J2 **Port Royal** Jamaica
17B1 **Port Royal Sd** USA
45C1 **Portrush** N Ire
92B3 **Port Said** Egypt
17A2 **Port St Joe** USA
100B4 **Port St Johns** S Africa
7E4 **Port Saunders** Can
100C4 **Port Shepstone** S Africa
13A2 **Port Simpson** Can
27Q2 **Portsmouth** Dominica
43D4 **Portsmouth** Eng
14B3 **Portsmouth** Ohio, USA
11C3 **Portsmouth** Virginia, USA
109D2 **Port Stephens** *B* Aust
95C3 **Port Sudan** Sudan
19C3 **Port Sulphur** USA
38K5 **Porttipahdan Tekojärvi** *Res* Fin
50A2 **Portugal** Republic, Europe
14A2 **Port Washington** USA
77C5 **Port Weld** Malay
32D6 **Porvenir** Bol
39K6 **Porvoo** Fin
30E4 **Posadas** Arg
50A2 **Posadas** Spain
47D1 **Poschiavo** Switz
6B2 **Posheim Pen** Can
90C3 **Posht-e Badam** Iran
71D4 **Poso** Indon
58D1 **Postavy** Belorussia
14B2 **Post Clinton** USA
100B3 **Postmasburg** S Africa
52B1 **Postojna** Slovenia
74C2 **Pos'yet** Russian Fed
101G1 **Potchetstroom** S Africa
19B2 **Poteau** USA
53C2 **Potenza** Italy
100B3 **Potgietersrus** S Africa
97D3 **Potiskum** Nig
20C1 **Potlatch** USA
15C3 **Potomac** *R* USA
30C2 **Potosi** Bol
30C4 **Potrerillos** Chile
56C2 **Potsdam** Germany
16B2 **Pottstown** USA
16A2 **Pottsville** USA
16C2 **Poughkeepsie** USA
35B2 **Pouso Alegre** Brazil
110C1 **Poverty B** NZ
61F3 **Povorino** Russian Fed
7C4 **Povungnituk** Can
8C2 **Powder** *R* USA
106C2 **Powell Creek** Aust
9B3 **Powell,L** USA
13C3 **Powell River** Can
8C2 **Power** *R* USA
43C3 **Powys** County, Wales
73D4 **Poyang Hu** *L* China
92B2 **Pozantı** Turk
23B1 **Poza Rica** Mexico
58B2 **Poznań** Pol
30E3 **Pozo Colorado** Par
53B2 **Pozzuoli** Italy
97B4 **Pra** *R* Ghana
76C3 **Prachin Buri** Thai
76B3 **Prachuap Khiri Khan** Thai
59B2 **Praděd** *Mt* Czech
49C3 **Pradelles** France
35D1 **Prado** Brazil
Prague = Praha
57C2 **Praha** Czech
97A4 **Praia** Cape Verde
33E5 **Prainha** Brazil
18B2 **Prairie Village** USA
76C3 **Prakhon Chai** Thai
35B1 **Prata** Brazil
35B1 **Prata** *R* Brazil
Prates = Dongsha Qundao
49E3 **Prato** Italy
16B1 **Prattsville** USA
17A1 **Prattville** USA
48B1 **Prawle Pt** Eng
78D4 **Praya** Indon
47D1 **Predazzo** Italy
63B2 **Predivinsk** Russian Fed
58C2 **Pregolyu** *R* Russian Fed
76D3 **Prek Kak** Camb
56C2 **Prenzlau** Germany
76A3 **Preparis** *I* Burma
76A2 **Preparis North Chan** Burma
59B3 **Přerov** Czech
23A2 **Presa del Infiernillo** Mexico
9B3 **Prescott** Arizona, USA
19B3 **Prescott** Arkansas, USA
15C2 **Prescott** Can
30D4 **Presidencia Roque Sáenz Peña** Arg
35A2 **Presidente Epitácio** Brazil
112C2 **Presidente Frei** *Base* Ant
23B2 **Presidente Migúel Aleman** *L* Mexico
35A2 **Presidente Prudente** Brazil
35A2 **Presidente Venceslau** Brazil
59C3 **Prešov** Czech
55B2 **Prespansko Jezero** *L* Macedonia, Yugos
10D2 **Presque Isle** USA
42C3 **Preston** Eng
8B2 **Preston** Idaho, USA
18B2 **Preston** Missouri, USA
42B2 **Prestwick** Scot
31B6 **Prêto** Brazil
35B1 **Prêto** *R* Brazil
101G1 **Pretoria** S Africa
55B3 **Préveza** Greece
76D3 **Prey Veng** Camb
8B3 **Price** USA
13B2 **Price I** Can
60D4 **Prichernomorskaya Nizmennost'** *Lowland* Ukraine
27M2 **Prickly Pt** Grenada
58C1 **Priekule** Lithuania
100B3 **Prieska** S Africa
20C1 **Priest L** USA
20C1 **Priest River** USA
61G4 **Prikaspiyskaya Nizmennost'** *Region* Kazakhstan
55B2 **Prilep** Macedonia, Yugos
60D3 **Priluki** Ukraine
34C2 **Primero** *R* Arg
39K6 **Primorsk** Russian Fed
60E4 **Primorsko-Akhtarsk** Russian Fed
13F2 **Primrose L** Can
5H4 **Prince Albert** Can
4F2 **Prince Albert,C** Can
4G2 **Prince Albert Pen** Can
4G2 **Prince Albert Sd** Can
6C3 **Prince Charles I** Can
112B10 **Prince Charles Mts** Ant
7D5 **Prince Edward I** Can
13C2 **Prince George** Can
4H2 **Prince Gustaf Adolp** *S* Can
5E4 **Prince of Wales** *I* USA
71F5 **Prince of Wales I** Aust
4H2 **Prince of Wales I** Can
4G2 **Prince of Wales Str** Can
4F2 **Prince Patrick I** Can
6A2 **Prince Regent Inlet** *Str* Can
13A2 **Prince Rupert** Can
107D2 **Princess Charlotte B** Aust
13B2 **Princess Royal I** Can
27L1 **Princes Town** Trinidad
13C3 **Princeton** Can
18C2 **Princeton** Kentucky, USA
18B1 **Princeton** Missouri, USA
16B2 **Princeton** New Jersey, USA
4D3 **Prince William** USA
12E2 **Prince William Sd** USA
97C4 **Principe** *I* W Africa
20B2 **Prineville** USA
12E1 **Pringle,Mt** USA
6F3 **Prins Christian Sund** *Sd* Greenland
112B12 **Prinsesse Astrid Kyst** Region, Ant
112B12 **Prinsesse Ragnhild Kyst** Region, Ant
64B2 **Prins Karls Forland** *I* Barents S
25D3 **Prinzapolca** Nic
58D2 **Pripyat'** *R* Belorussia
54B2 **Priština** Serbia, Yugos
56C2 **Pritzwalk** Germany
61F3 **Privolzhskaya Vozvyshennost'** *Upland* Russian Fed
54B2 **Prizren** Serbia, Yugos
78C4 **Probolinggo** Indon
5G5 **Procatello** USA
87B2 **Proddatūr** India
25D2 **Progreso** Mexico
20B2 **Project City** USA
61F5 **Prokhladnyy** Russian Fed
65K4 **Prokop'yevsk** Russian Fed
61F4 **Proletarskaya** Russian Fed
64G2 **Proliv Karskiye Vorota** *Str* Russian Fed
83D4 **Prome** Burma
31D4 **Propriá** Brazil
20B2 **Prospect** Oregon, USA

107D3 **Prosperine** Aust
59B3 **Prostĕjov** Czech
6E2 **Prøven** Greenland
49D3 **Provence** Region, France
16D2 **Providence** USA
15D2 **Provincetown** USA
49C2 **Provins** France
8B2 **Provo** USA
13E2 **Provost** Can
4D2 **Prudhoe Bay** USA
6D2 **Prudhoe Land** Greenland
58C2 **Pruszkow** Pol
60C4 **Prut** *R* Romania/ Moldavia
60C4 **Prutul** *R* Romania
58C2 **Pruzhany** Belorussia
18A2 **Pryor** USA
59C3 **Przemys'l** Pol
55C3 **Psará** *I* Greece
60C2 **Pskov** Russian Fed
58D2 **Ptich** *R* Belorussia
55B2 **Ptolemaïs** Greece
32C5 **Pucallpa** Peru
73D4 **Pucheng** China
34A3 **Pucón** Chile
38K5 **Pudasjärvi** Fin
87B2 **Pudukkottai** India
23B2 **Puebla** Mexico
23B2 **Puebla** State, Mexico
50A1 **Puebla de Sanabria** Spain
50A1 **Puebla de Trives** Spain
9C2 **Pueblo** USA
34B3 **Puelches** Arg
34B3 **Puelén** Arg
23A2 **Puenta Ixbapa** Mexico
34B2 **Puente del Inca** Arg
32A5 **Puerta Aguja** Peru
30B2 **Puerta Coles** Peru
34B2 **Puerta de los Llanos** Arg
31D3 **Puerta do Calcanhar** *Pt* Brazil
32C1 **Puerta Gallinas** Colombia
23B2 **Puerta Maldonado** *Pt* Mexico
32A2 **Puerta Mariato** Panama
29C5 **Puerta Médanosa** *Pt* Arg
23A2 **Puerta Mongrove** Mexico
25E4 **Puerta San Blas** *Pt* Panama
23A2 **Puerta San Telmo** Mexico
29B5 **Puerto Aisén** Chile
25D4 **Puerto Armuelles** Panama
33F6 **Puerto Artur** Brazil
32B3 **Puerto Asis** Colombia
32D2 **Puerto Ayacucho** Ven
25D3 **Puerto Barrios** Guatemala
32C2 **Puerto Berrio** Colombia
32D1 **Puerto Cabello** Ven
25D3 **Puerto Cabezas** Nic
32D2 **Puerto Carreño** Colombia
25D4 **Puerto Cortes** Costa Rica
25D3 **Puerto Cortés** Honduras
96A2 **Puerto del Rosario** Canary Is
30F3 **Puerto E Cunha** Brazil
32C1 **Puerto Fijo** Ven
31B3 **Puerto Franco** Brazil
32D6 **Puerto Heath** Bol
25D2 **Puerto Juarez** Mexico
33E1 **Puerto la Cruz** Ven
50B2 **Puertollano** Spain
27C4 **Puerto Lopez** Colombia
29D4 **Puerto Madryn** Arg
32D6 **Puerto Maldonado** Peru
23B2 **Puerto Marquéz** Mexico
29B4 **Puerto Montt** Chile
30E3 **Puerto Murtinho** Brazil
29B6 **Puerto Natales** Chile
24A1 **Puerto Peñasco** Mexico
29D4 **Puerto Pirámides** Arg
27C3 **Puerto Plata** Dom Rep
79A4 **Puerto Princesa** Phil
32B3 **Puerto Rico** Colombia
27D3 **Puerto Rico** *I* Caribbean S
27D3 **Puerto Rico Trench** Caribbean S
23A2 **Puerto San Juan de Lima** Mexico
33G4 **Puerto Santanga** Brazil
30E2 **Puerto Suárez** Bol
24B2 **Puerto Vallarta** Mexico
29B4 **Puerto Varas** Chile
30D2 **Puerto Villarroel** Bol
61G3 **Pugachev** Russian Fed
84C3 **Pugal** India
51C1 **Puigcerdá** Spain
111B2 **Pukaki,L** *L* NZ
74B2 **Pukch'ŏng** N Korea
110B1 **Pukekobe** NZ
111B2 **Puketeraki Range** *Mts* NZ
52B2 **Pula** Croatia
15C2 **Pulaski** New York, USA
71E4 **Pulau Kolepom** *I* Indon
70A4 **Pulau Pulau Batu** *Is* Indon
58C2 **Pulawy** Pol
87C2 **Pulicat,L** India
84B1 **Pul-i-Khumri** Afghan
87B3 **Puliyangudi** India
20C1 **Pullman** USA
71E3 **Pulo Anna Merir** *I* Pacific O
79B2 **Pulog,Mt** Phil
38L5 **Pulozero** Russian Fed
58C2 **Pultusk** Pol
30C4 **Puna de Atacama** Arg
86B1 **Punakha** Bhutan
84C2 **Punch** Pak
87A1 **Pune** India
23A2 **Punéper** Mexico
98C3 **Punia** Zaïre
34A2 **Punitaqui** Chile
84C2 **Punjab** Province, Pak
84D2 **Punjab** State, India
30B2 **Puno** Peru
24A2 **Punta Abreojos** *Pt* Mexico
53C3 **Punta Alice** *Pt* Italy
34C3 **Punta Alta** Arg
29B6 **Punta Arenas** Chile
24A2 **Punta Baja** *Pt* Mexico
34A2 **Punta Curaumilla** *Pt* Chile
100A2 **Punta da Marca** *Pt* Angola
101C3 **Punta de Barra Falsa** *Pt* Mozam
29F2 **Punta del Este** Urug
24A2 **Punta Eugenia** *Pt* Mexico
25D3 **Punta Gorda** Belize
17B2 **Punta Gorda** USA
34A3 **Punta Lavapié** *Pt* Chile
34A2 **Punta Lengua de Vaca** *Pt* Chile
53B2 **Punta Licosa** *Pt* Italy
34A1 **Punta Poroto** *Pt* Chile
9B4 **Punta San Antonia** *Pt* Mexico
34A2 **Punta Topocalma** Chile
73C4 **Puqi** China
64J3 **Pur** *R* Russian Fed
19A2 **Purcell** USA
12C1 **Purcell Mt** USA
13D2 **Purcell Mts** Can
34A3 **Purén** Chile
86B2 **Puri** India
87B1 **Pūrna** India
86B1 **Pūrnia** India
76C3 **Pursat** Camb
23A1 **Puruandro** Mexico
33E4 **Purus** *R* Brazil
19C3 **Purvis** USA
78B4 **Purwokerto** Indon
78C4 **Purworejo** Indon
85D5 **Pusad** India
74B3 **Pusan** S Korea
60D2 **Pushkin** Russian Fed
58D1 **Pustoshka** Russian Fed
82D3 **Puta** Burma
34A2 **Putaendo** Chile
110C1 **Putaruru** NZ
73D4 **Putian** China
16D2 **Putnam** USA
87B3 **Puttalam** Sri Lanka
56C2 **Puttgarden** Germany
32B4 **Putumayo** *R* Ecuador
78C2 **Putussibau** Indon
38K6 **Puulavesl** *L* Fin
20B1 **Puyallup** USA
49C2 **Puy de Sancy** *Mt* France
111A3 **Puysegur Pt** NZ
99C3 **Pweto** Zaïre
43B3 **Pwllheli** Wales
76B2 **Pyapon** Burma
61F5 **Pyatigorsk** Russian Fed
74B3 **P'yŏngyang** N Korea
108B3 **Pyramid Hill** Aust
21B1 **Pyramid L** USA
111A2 **Pyramid,Mt** NZ
48B3 **Pyrénées** *Mts* France
58D1 **Pytalovo** Russian Fed
76B2 **Pyu** Burma

Q

94B2 **Qabatiya** Israel
94C3 **Qā'el Hafīra** *Mud Flats* Jordan
94C3 **Qa'el Jinz** *Mud Flats* Jordan
68B3 **Qaidam Pendi** *Salt Flat* China
94C2 **Qa Khanna** *Salt Marsh* Jordan
99D1 **Qala'en Nahl** Sudan
84B2 **Qalat** Afghan
94C1 **Qal'at al Hisn** Syria
81C3 **Qal'at Bīshah** S Arabia
93E3 **Qal'at Sālih** Iraq
68B3 **Qamdo** China
99E1 **Qandala** Somalia
99E2 **Qardho** Somalia
95B2 **Qara** Egypt
90A3 **Qaṛe Shīrīn** Iran
91A4 **Qaryat al Ulyā** S Arabia
94C3 **Qasr el Kharana** Jordan
91D4 **Qasr-e-Qand** Iran
95B2 **Qasr Farafra** Egypt
94C2 **Qaṭana** Syria
91B4 **Qatar** Emirate, Arabian Pen
94C3 **Qatrāna** Jordan
95B2 **Qattāra Depression** Egypt
90C3 **Qāyen** Iran
90A2 **Qazvīn** Iran
95C2 **Qena** Egypt
90A2 **Qeydār** Iran
91B4 **Qeys** *I* Iran
94B3 **Qeziot** Israel
73B5 **Qian Jiang** *R* China
72E1 **Qian Shan** *Upland* China
72E3 **Qidong** China
73B4 **Qijiang** China
84B2 **Qila Saifullah** Pak
72A2 **Qilian** China
68B3 **Qilian Shan** China
72B3 **Qin'an** China
72E2 **Qingdao** China
72A2 **Qinghai** Province, China
68B3 **Qinghai Hu** *L* China
72D3 **Qingjiang** Jiangsu, China
73D4 **Qingjiang** Jiangxi, China
72B3 **Qing Jiang** *R* China
72C2 **Qingshuihe** China
72B2 **Qingshui He** *R* China
72B2 **Qingtonxia** China
72B2 **Qingyang** China
74B2 **Qingyuan** Liaoning, China
73D4 **Qingyuan** Zhejiang, China
82C2 **Qing Zang** *Upland* China
72D2 **Qinhuangdao** China
72B3 **Qin Ling** *Mts* China
73B5 **Qinzhou** China
76E2 **Qionghai** China
73A3 **Qionglai Shan** *Upland* China
76D1 **Qiongzhou Haixia** *Str* China
69E2 **Qiqihar** China
94B2 **Qiryat Ata** Israel
94B3 **Qiryat Gat** Israel
94B2 **Qiryat Shemona** Israel
94B2 **Qiryat Yam** Israel
94B2 **Qishon** *R* Israel
63A3 **Qitai** China
73C4 **Qiyang** China
72B1 **Qog Qi** China
90B2 **Qolleh-ye Damavand** *Mt* Iran
90B3 **Qom** Iran
90B3 **Qomisheh** Iran
Qomolangma Feng = Everest,Mt
94C1 **Qornet es Saouda** *Mt* Leb
6E3 **Qôrnoq** Greenland
90A2 **Qorveh** Iran
91C4 **Qotābad** Iran
16C1 **Quabbin Res** USA
16B2 **Quakertown** USA
77C3 **Quam Phu Quoc** *I* Viet
76D2 **Quang Ngai** Viet
76D2 **Quang Tri** Viet
77D4 **Quan Long** Viet
73D5 **Quanzhou** Fujian, China
73C4 **Quanzhou** Guangxi, China
5H4 **Qu' Appelle** *R* Can
91C5 **Quarayyāt** Oman
13B2 **Quatsino Sd** Can
90C2 **Quchan** Iran
109C3 **Queanbeyan** Aust
15D1 **Québec** Can
7C4 **Quebec** Province, Can
35B1 **Quebra-Anzol** *R* Brazil
34D2 **Quebracho** Urug
30F4 **Quedas do Iguaçu** Brazil/Arg
16A3 **Queen Anne** USA
13B2 **Queen Bess,Mt** Can
5E4 **Queen Charlotte** *Is* Can
13B2 **Queen Charlotte Sd** Can
13B2 **Queen Charlotte Str** Can
4H1 **Queen Elizabeth Is** Can
112B9 **Queen Mary Land** Region, Ant
4H3 **Queen Maud G** Can
112A **Queen Maud Mts** Ant
16C2 **Queens** Borough, New York, USA
108B3 **Queenscliff** Aust

107D3 **Queensland** State, Aust
109C4 **Queenstown** Aust
111A3 **Queenstown** NZ
100B4 **Queenstown** S Africa
16A3 **Queenstown** USA
98B3 **Quela** Angola
101C2 **Quelimane** Mozam
34C3 **Quemuquemú** Arg
13C2 **Quensel L** Can
34D3 **Quequén** Arg
34D3 **Quequén** *R* Arg
23A1 **Querétaro** Mexico
23A1 **Queretaro** *State* Mexico
13C2 **Quesnel** Can
84B2 **Quetta** Pak
25C3 **Quezaltenango** Guatemala
79B3 **Quezon City** Phil
100A2 **Quibala** Angola
98B3 **Quibaxe** Angola
32B2 **Quibdó** Colombia
48B2 **Quiberon** France
98B3 **Quicama Nat Pk** Angola
73A4 **Quijing** China
34A2 **Quilima** Chile
34C2 **Quilino** Arg
32C6 **Quillabamba** Peru
30C2 **Quillacollo** Bol
48C3 **Quillan** France
5H4 **Quill L** Can
5H4 **Quill Lakes** Can
34A2 **Quillota** Chile
Quilon = Kollam
108B1 **Quilpie** Aust
34A2 **Quilpué** Chile
98B3 **Quimbele** Angola
48B2 **Quimper** France
48B2 **Quimperlé** France
21A2 **Quincy** California, USA
10A3 **Quincy** Illinois, USA
16D1 **Quincy** Massachusetts, USA
34B2 **Quines** Arg
12B3 **Quinhagak** USA
76D3 **Qui Nhon** Viet
50B2 **Quintanar de la Orden** Spain
34A2 **Quintero** Chile
34C2 **Quinto** *R* Arg
34A3 **Quirihue** Chile
100A2 **Quirima** Angola
109D2 **Quirindi** Aust
101D2 **Quissanga** Mozam
101C3 **Quissico** Mozam
32B4 **Quito** Ecuador
31D2 **Quixadá** Brazil
108A2 **Quorn** Aust
95C2 **Quseir** Egypt
6E3 **Qutdligssat** Greenland
Quthing = Moyeni
73B3 **Qu Xian** Sichuan, China
73D4 **Qu Xian** Zhejiang, China
76D2 **Quynh Luu** Viet
72C2 **Quzhou** China
86C1 **Qüzü** China

R

38J6 **Raahe** Fin
44A3 **Raasay** *I* Scot
44A3 **Raasay,Sound of** *Chan* Scot
99F1 **Raas Caseyr** *C* Somalia
52B2 **Rab** *I* Croatia
78D4 **Raba** Indon
59B3 **Rába** *R* Hung
96B1 **Rabat** Mor
94B3 **Rabba** Jordan
80B3 **Rabigh** S Arabia
47B2 **Racconigi** Italy
7E5 **Race,C** Can
94B2 **Rachaya** Leb
57C3 **Rachel** *Mt* Germany
76D3 **Rach Gia** Viet
14A2 **Racine** USA
59D3 **Rădăuţi** Rom
85C4 **Radhanpur** India
27L1 **Radix,Pt** Trinidad
58C2 **Radom** Pol
59B2 **Radomsko** Pol
58C1 **Radviliškis** Lithuania
4G3 **Rae** Can
86A1 **Rāe Bareli** India
6B3 **Rae Isthmus** Can
4G3 **Rae L** Can
110C1 **Raetihi** NZ
34C2 **Rafaela** Arg
94B3 **Rafah** Egypt
98C2 **Rafai** CAR
93D3 **Rafhā Al Jumaymah** S Arabia
91C3 **Rafsanjān** Iran
98C2 **Raga** Sudan
27R3 **Ragged Pt** Barbados
53B3 **Ragusa** Italy
99D1 **Rahad** *R* Sudan
84C3 **Rahimyar Khan** Pak
90B3 **Rāhjerd** Iran
34D2 **Raíces** Arg
87B1 **Rāichur** India
86A2 **Raigarh** India
108B3 **Rainbow** Aust
17A1 **Rainbow City** USA
20B1 **Rainier** USA
20B1 **Rainier,Mt** USA
10A2 **Rainy L** Can
12D2 **Rainy P** USA
10A2 **Rainy River** Can
86A2 **Raipur** India
87C1 **Rājahmundry** India
78C2 **Rajang** *R* Malay
84C3 **Rajanpur** Pak
87B3 **Rājapālaiyam** India
85C3 **Rājasthan** State, India
84D3 **Rājgarh** India
85D4 **Rājgarh** State, India
85C4 **Rājkot** India
86B2 **Rājmahāl Hills** India
86A2 **Raj Nāndgaon** India
85C4 **Rājpīpla** India
86B2 **Rajshahi** Bang
85D4 **Rajur** India
111B2 **Rakaia** *R* NZ
78B4 **Rakata** *I* Indon
82C3 **Raka Zangbo** *R* China
59C3 **Rakhov** Ukraine
100B3 **Rakops** Botswana
58D2 **Rakov** Belorussia
11C3 **Raleigh** USA
7A5 **Ralny L** Can
94B2 **Rama** Israel
94B3 **Ramallah** Israel
87B3 **Rāmanāthapuram** India
69G3 **Ramapo Deep** Pacific O
94B2 **Ramat Gan** Israel
46A2 **Rambouillet** France
86B2 **Rāmgarh** Bihar, India
85C3 **Rāmgarh** Rajosthan, India
90A3 **Rāmhormoz** Iran
94B3 **Ramla** Israel
91C5 **Ramlat Al Wahibah** Region, Oman
21B3 **Ramona** USA
84D3 **Rāmpur** India
85D4 **Rāmpura** India
90B2 **Rāmsar** Iran
42B2 **Ramsey** Eng
16B2 **Ramsey** USA
43B4 **Ramsey I** Wales
43E4 **Ramsgate** Eng
94C2 **Ramtha** Jordan
71F4 **Ramu** *R* PNG
34A2 **Rancagua** Chile
86B2 **Rānchi** India
86A2 **Rānchi Plat** India
101G1 **Randburg** S Africa
39G7 **Randers** Den
101G1 **Randfontein** S Africa
15D2 **Randolph** Vermont, USA
111B3 **Ranfurly** NZ
86C2 **Rangamati** Bang
111B2 **Rangiora** NZ
110C1 **Rangitaiki** *R* NZ
111B2 **Rangitate** *R* NZ
110C1 **Rangitikei** *R* NZ
76B2 **Rangoon** Burma
86B1 **Rangpur** India
87B2 **Rānībennur** India
8A2 **Ranier,Mt** *Mt* USA
86B2 **Rānīganj** India
109C2 **Rankins Springs** Aust
6A3 **Ranklin Inlet** Can
85B4 **Rann of Kachchh** *Flood Area* India
77B4 **Ranong** Thai
70A3 **Rantauparapat** Indon
18C1 **Rantoul** USA
49D3 **Rapallo** Italy
34A2 **Rapel** *R* Chile
6D3 **Raper,C** Can
8C2 **Rapid City** USA
14A1 **Rapid River** USA
15C3 **Rappahannock** *R* USA
47C1 **Rapperswil** Switz
16B2 **Raritan B** USA
95C2 **Ras Abu Shagara** *C* Sudan
93D2 **Ra's al 'Ayn** Syria
91C5 **Ra's al Hadd** *C* Oman
91C4 **Ras al Kaimah** UAE
91C4 **Ras-al-Kuh** *C* Iran
81D4 **Ra's al Madrakah** *C* Oman
91A4 **Ra's az Zawr** *C* S Arabia
95C2 **Rās Bânas** *C* Egypt
94A3 **Ras Burûn** *C* Egypt
99D1 **Ras Dashan** *Mt* Eth
90A3 **Ra's-e-Barkan** *Pt* Iran
92A3 **Râs el Kenâyis** *Pt* Egypt
81D4 **Ra's Fartak** *C* Yemen
95C2 **Râs Ghârib** Egypt
99D1 **Rashad** Sudan
94B3 **Rashādīya** Jordan
92B3 **Rashîd** Egypt
90A2 **Rasht** Iran
91C5 **Ra's Jibish** *C* Oman
99E1 **Ras Khanzira** *C* Somalia
84B3 **Ras Koh** *Mt* Pak
95C2 **Râs Muhammad** *C* Egypt
96A2 **Ras Nouadhibou** *C* Maur
69H2 **Rasshua** *I* Russian Fed
61F3 **Rasskazovo** Russian Fed
91A4 **Ra's Tanāqib** *C* S Arabia
91B4 **Ra's Tannūrah** S Arabia
57B3 **Rastatt** Germany
Ras Uarc = Cabo Tres Forcas
99F1 **Ras Xaafuun** *C* Somalia
84C3 **Ratangarh** India
76B3 **Rat Buri** Thai
85D3 **Rath** India
56C2 **Rathenow** Germany
45B2 **Rathkeale** Irish Rep
45C1 **Rathlin** *I* N Ire
45B2 **Ráth Luirc** Irish Rep
85D4 **Ratlām** India
87A1 **Ratnāgiri** India
87C3 **Ratnapura** Sri Lanka
58C2 **Ratno** Ukraine
47D1 **Rattenberg** Austria
39H6 **Rättvik** Sweden
12H3 **Ratz,Mt** Can
34D3 **Rauch** Arg
110C1 **Raukumara Range** *Mts* NZ
35C2 **Raul Soares** Brazil
39J6 **Rauma** Fin
86A2 **Raurkela** India
90A3 **Ravānsar** Iran
90C3 **Rāvar** Iran
59C2 **Rava Russkaya** Ukraine
16C1 **Ravena** USA
52B2 **Ravenna** Italy
57B3 **Ravensburg** Germany
107D2 **Ravenshoe** Aust
42E2 **Ravenspurn** *Oilfield* N Sea
84C2 **Ravi** *R* Pak
84C2 **Rawalpindi** Pak
93D2 **Rawāndiz** Iraq
58B2 **Rawicz** Pol
106B4 **Rawlinna** Aust
8C2 **Rawlins** USA
29C4 **Rawson** Arg
78C3 **Raya** *Mt* Indon
87B2 **Rāyadurg** India
94C2 **Rayak** Leb
7E5 **Ray,C** Can
91C4 **Rāyen** Iran
22C2 **Raymond** California, USA
20B1 **Raymond** Washington, USA
109D2 **Raymond Terrace** Aust
12D1 **Ray Mts** USA
23B1 **Rayon** Mexico
90A2 **Razan** Iran
54C2 **Razgrad** Bulg
54C2 **Razim** *L* Rom
43D4 **Reading** Eng
16B2 **Reading** USA
4G3 **Read Island** Can
16C1 **Readsboro** USA
34B2 **Real de Padre** Arg
34C3 **Realicó** Arg
95B2 **Rebiana** *Well* Libya
95B2 **Rebiana Sand Sea** Libya
38L6 **Reboly** Russian Fed
106B4 **Recherche,Arch of the** *Is* Aust
31E3 **Recife** Brazil
107F2 **Récifs D'Entrecasteaux** Nouvelle Calédonie
46D1 **Recklinghausen** Germany
30E4 **Reconquista** Arg
19B3 **Red** *R* USA
77C4 **Redang** *I* Malay
16B2 **Red Bank** New Jersey, USA
21A1 **Red Bluff** USA
42D2 **Redcar** Eng
13E2 **Redcliff** Can
109D1 **Redcliffe** Aust
108B2 **Red Cliffs** Aust
13E2 **Red Deer** Can
13E2 **Red Deer** *R* Can
20B2 **Redding** USA
10A2 **Red L** USA
7A4 **Red Lake** Can
22D3 **Redlands** USA
16A3 **Red Lion** USA
20B2 **Redmond** USA
18A1 **Red Oak** USA
48B2 **Redon** France
22C4 **Redondo Beach** USA
12D2 **Redoubt V** USA
73B5 **Red River Delta** Vietnam
80B3 **Red Sea** Africa/ Arabian Pen
13E2 **Redwater** Can
22A2 **Redwood City** USA
14A2 **Reed City** USA
22C2 **Reedley** USA
20B2 **Reedsport** USA
111B2 **Reefton** NZ
93C2 **Refahiye** Turk
35D1 **Regência** Brazil
57C3 **Regensburg** Germany
96C2 **Reggane** Alg
53C3 **Reggio di Calabria** Italy
47D2 **Reggio Nell'Emilia** Italy
54B1 **Reghin** Rom
5H4 **Regina** Can
100A3 **Rehoboth** Namibia
15C3 **Rehoboth Beach** USA
94B3 **Rehovot** Israel
32D1 **Reicito** Ven
43D4 **Reigate** Eng
46C2 **Reims** France
5H4 **Reindeer** *R* Can

50B1 **Reinosa** Spain
16A3 **Reisterstown** USA
101G1 **Reitz** S Africa
4H3 **Reliance** Can
108A2 **Remarkable,Mt** Aust
78C4 **Rembang** Indon
91C4 **Remeshk** Iran
46D1 **Remscheid** Germany
18C2 **Rend,L** USA
56B2 **Rendsburg** Germany
15C1 **Renfrew** Can
78A3 **Rengat** Indon
34A2 **Rengo** Chile
59D3 **Reni** Ukraine
99D1 **Renk** Sudan
6H2 **Renland** *Pen* Greenland
108B2 **Renmark** Aust
107F2 **Rennell** *I* Solomon Is
48B2 **Rennes** France
21B2 **Reno** USA
47D2 **Reno** *R* Italy
15C2 **Renovo** USA
16C1 **Rensselaer** USA
20B1 **Renton** USA
70D4 **Reo** Indon
35B2 **Reprêsa de Furnas** *Dam* Brazil
30E3 **Reprêsa Ilha Grande** *Dam* Brazil
30E3 **Reprêsa Itaipu** *Dam* Brazil
35A2 **Reprêsa Porto Primavera** *Dam* Brazil
35B1 **Reprêsa Três Marias** *Dam* Brazil
20C1 **Republic** USA
41B3 **Republic of Ireland** NW Europe
6B3 **Repulse Bay** Can
15C1 **Réservoir Baskatong** *Res* Can
10C1 **Réservoir de la Grande 2** *Res* Can
10C1 **Réservoir de la Grande 3** *Res* Can
7C4 **Réservoir de la Grande 4** *Res* Can
7C5 **Réservoire Cabonga** *Res* Can
7C5 **Réservoire Gouin** *Res* Can
10D1 **Réservoire Manicouagan** *Res* Can
90B2 **Reshteh-ye Alborz** *Mts* Iran
72A2 **Reshui** China
30E4 **Resistencia** Arg
54B1 **Resita** Rom
6A2 **Resolute** Can
111A3 **Resolution I** NZ
6D3 **Resolution Island** Can
101H1 **Ressano Garcia** Mozam
34B2 **Retamito** Arg
46C2 **Rethel** France
55B3 **Réthimnon** Greece
89K10 **Reunion** *I* Indian O
51C1 **Reus** Spain
47C1 **Reuss** *R* Switz
47D1 **Reutte** Austria
61K3 **Revda** Russian Fed
13D2 **Revelstoke** Can
24A3 **Revillagigedo** *Is* Mexico
12H3 **Revillagigedo I** USA
46C2 **Revin** France
94B3 **Revivim** Israel
86A2 **Rewa** India
84D3 **Rewari** India
8B2 **Rexburg** USA
38A2 **Reykjavik** Iceland
24C2 **Reynosa** Mexico
48B2 **Rezé** France
58D1 **Rezekne** Latvia
61K2 **Rezh** Russian Fed
47C1 **Rhätikon** *Mts* Austria/Switz
94B1 **Rhazīr** Republic, Leb
56B2 **Rhein** *R* W Europe
56B2 **Rheine** Germany
47B1 **Rheinfielden** Switz
49D2 **Rheinland Pfalz** Region, Germany
47C1 **Rheinwaldhorn** *Mt* Switz
Rhine = Rhein
16C2 **Rhinebeck** USA
10B2 **Rhinelander** USA
47C2 **Rho** Italy
15D2 **Rhode Island** State, USA
16D2 **Rhode Island Sd** USA
Rhodes = Ródhos
49C3 **Rhône** *R* France
43C3 **Rhyl** Wales
31D4 **Riachão do Jacuipe** Brazil
50A1 **Ria de Arosa** *B* Spain
50A1 **Ria de Betanzos** *B* Spain
50A1 **Ria de Corcubion** *B* Spain
50A1 **Ria de Lage** *B* Spain
50A1 **Ria de Sta Marta** *B* Spain
50A1 **Ria de Vigo** *B* Spain
84C2 **Riāsi** Pak
50A1 **Ribadeo** Spain
35A2 **Ribas do Rio Pardo** Brazil
101C2 **Ribauè** Mozam
42C3 **Ribble** *R* Eng
35B2 **Ribeira** Brazil
35B2 **Ribeirão Prêto** Brazil
32D6 **Riberalta** Bol
15C2 **Rice L** Can
10A2 **Rice Lake** USA
101H1 **Richard's Bay** S Africa
19A3 **Richardson** USA
12G1 **Richardson Mts** Can
8B3 **Richfield** USA
20C1 **Richland** USA
22A2 **Richmond** California, USA
101H1 **Richmond** Natal, S Africa
109D2 **Richmond** New South Wales, Aust
111B2 **Richmond** NZ
107D3 **Richmond** Queensland, Aust
10C3 **Richmond** Virginia, USA
111B2 **Richmond Range** *Mts* NZ
15C2 **Rideau,L** Can
17B1 **Ridgeland** USA
15C2 **Ridgway** USA
27D4 **Riecito** Ven
47D1 **Rienza** *R* Italy
57C2 **Riesa** Germany
29B6 **Riesco** *I* Chile
101F1 **Riet** *R* S Africa
52B2 **Rieti** Italy
50B2 **Rif** *Mts* Mor
58C1 **Riga** Latvia
60B2 **Riga,G of** Estonia/Latvia
91C4 **Rīgān** Iran
20C1 **Riggins** USA
7E4 **Rigolet** Can
39J6 **Riihimaki** Fin
52B1 **Rijeka** Croatia
13E2 **Rimbey** Can
39H7 **Rimbo** Sweden
52B2 **Rimini** Italy
54C1 **Rîmnicu Sărat** Rom
54B1 **Rîmnicu Vîlcea** Rom
10D2 **Rimouski** Can
23A1 **Rincón de Romos** Mexico
39F7 **Ringkøbing** Den
98A2 **Rio Benito** Eq Guinea
32D5 **Rio Branco** Brazil
24B1 **Rio Bravo del Norte** *R* Mexico/USA
32C1 **Riochacha** Colombia
35B2 **Rio Claro** Brazil
27L1 **Rio Claro** Trinidad
34C3 **Rio Colorado** Arg
34C2 **Rio Cuarto** Arg
31D4 **Rio de Jacuipe** Brazil
35C2 **Rio de Janeiro** Brazil
35C2 **Rio de Janeiro** State, Brazil
29E3 **Rio de la Plata** *Est* Arg/Urug
29C6 **Rio Gallegos** Arg
29C6 **Rio Grande** Arg
30F5 **Rio Grande** Brazil
26A4 **Rio Grande** Nic
25D3 **Rio Grande** *R* Nic
24B2 **Rio Grande** *R* Mexico/USA
23A1 **Rio Grande de Santiago** Mexico
31D3 **Rio Grande do Norte** State, Brazil
30F4 **Rio Grande do Sul** State, Brazil
103G6 **Rio Grande Rise** Atlantic O
26C4 **Riohacha** Colombia
49C2 **Riom** France
32B4 **Riombamba** Ecuador
30C2 **Rio Mulatos** Bol
29C3 **Río Negro** State, Arg
30F4 **Rio Pardo** Brazil
34C2 **Rio Tercero** Arg
33E6 **Rio Theodore Roosevelt** *R* Brazil
29B6 **Rio Turbio** Arg
35A1 **Rio Verde** Brazil
23A1 **Rio Verde** Mexico
14B3 **Ripley** Ohio, USA
14B3 **Ripley** West Virginia, USA
42D2 **Ripon** Eng
22B2 **Ripon** USA
94B3 **Rishon le Zion** Israel
16A3 **Rising Sun** USA
39F7 **Risør** Nor
6E2 **Ritenberk** Greenland
22C2 **Ritter,Mt** USA
20C1 **Ritzville** USA
34B2 **Rivadavia** Arg
34A1 **Rivadavia** Chile
34C3 **Rivadavia Gonzalez Moreno** Arg
47D2 **Riva de Garda** Italy
34C3 **Rivera** Arg
29E2 **Rivera** Urug
22B2 **Riverbank** USA
97B4 **River Cess** Lib
16C2 **Riverhead** USA
108B3 **Riverina** Aust
111A3 **Riversdale** NZ
22D4 **Riverside** USA
13B2 **Rivers Inlet** Can
111A3 **Riverton** NZ
8C2 **Riverton** USA
17B2 **Riviera Beach** USA
7C4 **Rivière aux Feuilles** *R* Can
7D4 **Rivière de la Baleine** *R* Can
7D4 **Rivière du Petit Mècatina** *R* Can
46C2 **Rivigny-sur-Ornain** France
93D1 **Rize** Turk
72D2 **Rizhao** China
Rizhskiy Zaliv = Riga,G of
39F7 **Rjukan** Nor
6B2 **Roanes Pen** Can
49C2 **Roanne** France
17A1 **Roanoke** Alabama, USA
11C3 **Roanoke** Virginia, USA
11C3 **Roanoke** *R* USA
45B3 **Roaringwater B** Irish Rep
38J6 **Robertsforz** Sweden
19B2 **Robert S Kerr Res** USA
97A4 **Robertsport** Lib
7C5 **Roberval** Can
30H6 **Robinson Crusoe** *I* Chile
108B2 **Robinvale** Aust
13D2 **Robson,Mt** Can
24A3 **Roca Partida** *I* Mexico
103G5 **Rocas** *I* Atlantic O
31E2 **Rocas** *I* Brazil
29F2 **Rocha** Urug
42C3 **Rochdale** Eng
48B2 **Rochefort** France
5G3 **Rocher River** Can
108B3 **Rochester** Aust
7C5 **Rochester** Can
43E4 **Rochester** Eng
10A2 **Rochester** Minnesota, USA
15D2 **Rochester** New Hampshire, USA
10C2 **Rochester** New York, USA
10B2 **Rockford** USA
11B3 **Rock Hill** USA
10A2 **Rock Island** USA
108B3 **Rocklands Res** Aust
17B2 **Rockledge** USA
8C2 **Rock Springs** Wyoming, USA
110B2 **Rocks Pt** NZ
109C3 **Rock,The** Aust
16C2 **Rockville** Connecticut, USA
14A3 **Rockville** Indiana, USA
16A3 **Rockville** Maryland, USA
14B1 **Rocky Island L** Can
13E2 **Rocky Mountain House** Can
8B1 **Rocky Mts** Can/USA
12B2 **Rocky Pt** USA
56C2 **Rødbyhavn** Den
34B2 **Rodeo** Arg
49C3 **Rodez** France
55C3 **Ródhos** Greece
55C3 **Ródhos** *I* Greece
52C2 **Rodi Garganico** Italy
54B2 **Rodopi Planina** *Mts* Bulg
106A3 **Roebourne** Aust
46C1 **Roermond** Neth
46B1 **Roeselare** Belg
6B3 **Roes Welcome Sd** Can
18B2 **Rogers** USA
14B1 **Rogers City** USA
20B2 **Rogue** *R* USA
85B3 **Rohn** Pak
84D3 **Rohtak** India
58C1 **Roja** Latvia
35A2 **Rolândia** Brazil
18B2 **Rolla** USA
109C1 **Roma** Aust
52B2 **Roma** Italy
47C2 **Romagnano** Italy
17C1 **Romain,C** USA
54C1 **Roman** Rom
103H5 **Romanche Gap** Atlantic O
71D4 **Romang** *I* Indon
60B4 **Romania** Republic, E Europe
17B2 **Romano,C** USA
49D2 **Romans sur Isère** France
79B3 **Romblon** Phil
Rome = Roma
17A1 **Rome** Georgia, USA
15C2 **Rome** New York, USA
49C2 **Romilly-sur-Seine** France
15C3 **Romney** USA
60D3 **Romny** Ukraine
56B1 **Rømø** *I* Den
47B1 **Romont** Switz
48C2 **Romoratin** France
50A2 **Ronda** Spain
33E6 **Rondônia** Brazil
24F6 **Rondônia** State, Brazil
30F2 **Rondonópolis** Brazil
73B4 **Rong'an** China
73B4 **Rongchang** China
72E2 **Rongcheng** China
73B4 **Rongjiang** China
73B4 **Rong Jiang** *R* China
76A1 **Rongklang Range** *Mts* Burma
39G7 **Rønne** Den
39H7 **Ronneby** Sweden

112B2 **Ronne Ice Shelf** Ant
46B1 **Ronse** Belg
46A1 **Ronthieu** Region, France
9C3 **Roof Butte** *Mt* USA
84D3 **Roorkee** India
46C1 **Roosendaal** Neth
112B6 **Roosevelt I** Ant
106C2 **Roper** *R* Aust
33E3 **Roraima** State, Brazil
33E2 **Roraime** *Mt* Ven
38G6 **Røros** Nor
47C1 **Rorschach** Switz
38G6 **Rørvik** Nor
27Q2 **Rosalie** Dominica
22C3 **Rosamond L** USA
34C2 **Rosario** Arg
31C2 **Rosário** Brazil
34D2 **Rosario del Tala** Arg
48B2 **Roscoff** France
45B2 **Roscommon** County, Irish Rep
41B3 **Roscommon** Irish Rep
45C2 **Roscrea** Irish Rep
27E3 **Roseau** Dominica
109C4 **Rosebery** Aust
20B2 **Roseburg** USA
19A4 **Rosenberg** USA
57C3 **Rosenheim** Germany
13F2 **Rosetown** Can
54B2 **Roşiori de Vede** Rom
39G7 **Roskilde** Den
60D3 **Roslavl'** Russian Fed
61E2 **Roslyatino** Russian Fed
111B2 **Ross** NZ
12H2 **Ross** *R* Can
40B3 **Rossan** *Pt* Irish Rep
53C3 **Rossano** Italy
19C3 **Ross Barnet Res** USA
15C1 **Rosseau L** *L* Can
107E2 **Rossel** *I* Solomon Is
112A **Ross Ice Shelf** Ant
20B1 **Ross L** USA
13D3 **Rossland** Can
45C2 **Rosslare** Irish Rep
111C2 **Ross,Mt** NZ
97A3 **Rosso** Maur
43C4 **Ross-on-Wye** Eng
60E4 **Rossosh** Russian Fed
4E3 **Ross River** Can
112B6 **Ross S** Ant
91B4 **Rostāq** Iran
56C2 **Rostock** Germany
Rostov = Rostov-na-Donu
61E4 **Rostov-na-Donu** Russian Fed
17B1 **Roswell** Georgia, USA
9C3 **Roswell** New Mexico, USA
71F2 **Rota** Pacific O
56B2 **Rotenburg** Niedersachsen, Germany
46E1 **Rothaar-Geb** *Region* Germany
112C3 **Rothera** *Base* Ant
42D3 **Rotherham** Eng
42B2 **Rothesay** Scot
71D5 **Roti** *I* Indon
108C2 **Roto** Aust
111B2 **Rotoiti,L** NZ
111B2 **Rotoroa,L** NZ
110C1 **Rotorua** NZ
110C1 **Rotorua,L** NZ
56A2 **Rotterdam** Neth
46B1 **Roubaix** France
48C2 **Rouen** France
42E3 **Rough** *Oilfield* N Sea
Roulers = Roeselare
101E3 **Round I** Mauritius
109D2 **Round Mt** Aust
8C2 **Roundup** USA
44C2 **Rousay** *I* Scot
48C3 **Roussillon** Region, France
10C2 **Rouyn** Can
38K5 **Rovaniemi** Fin
47D2 **Rovereto** Italy
47D2 **Rovigo** Italy
52B1 **Rovinj** Croatia
59D2 **Rovno** Ukraine
90A2 **Row'ān** Iran
109C1 **Rowena** Aust
6C3 **Rowley I** Can
106A2 **Rowley Shoals** Aust
79A3 **Roxas** Palawan, Phil
79B3 **Roxas** Panay, Phil
111A3 **Roxburgh** NZ
45C2 **Royal Canal** Irish Rep
43D3 **Royal Leamington Spa** Eng
14B2 **Royal Oak** USA
43E4 **Royal Tunbridge Wells** Eng
48B2 **Royan** France
46B2 **Roye** France
43D3 **Royston** Eng
59C3 **Rožňava** Czech
46B2 **Rozoy** France
61F3 **Rtishchevo** Russian Fed
99D3 **Ruaha Nat Pk** Tanz
110C1 **Ruahine Range** *Mts* NZ
110C1 **Ruapehu,Mt** NZ
65D3 **Rub al Khālī** *Desert* S Arabia
44A3 **Rubha Hunish** Scot
35A2 **Rubinéia** Brazil
65K4 **Rubtsovsk** Russian Fed
12C2 **Ruby** USA
91C4 **Rudan** Iran
90A2 **Rūdbār** Iran
69F2 **Rudnaya Pristan'** Russian Fed
54B2 **Rudoka Planina** *Mt* Macedonia, Yugos
72E3 **Rudong** China
14B1 **Rudyard** USA
46A1 **Rue** France
48C2 **Ruffec** France
99D3 **Rufiji** *R* Tanz
34C2 **Rufino** Arg
97A3 **Rufisque** Sen
100B2 **Rufunsa** Zambia
43D3 **Rugby** Eng
39G8 **Rügen** *I* Germany
56B2 **Ruhr** *R* Germany
73D4 **Ruijin** China
54B2 **Rujen** *Mt* Bulg/ Macedonia, Yugos
99D3 **Rukwa** *L* Tanz
44A3 **Rum** *I* Scot
54A1 **Ruma** Serbia, Yugos
91A4 **Rumāh** S Arabia
98C2 **Rumbek** Sudan
26C2 **Rum Cay** *I* Caribbean S
47A2 **Rumilly** France
106C2 **Rum Jungle** Aust
101C2 **Rumphi** Malawi
111B2 **Runanga** NZ
110C1 **Runaway,C** NZ
100C3 **Rundi** *R* Zim
100A2 **Rundu** Namibia
99D3 **Rungwa** Tanz
99D3 **Rungwa** *R* Tanz
99D3 **Rungwe** *Mt* Tanz
82C2 **Ruoqiang** China
68C2 **Ruo Shui** *R* China
54C1 **Rupea** Rom
7C4 **Rupert** *R* Can
46D1 **Rur** *R* Germany
32D6 **Rurrenabaque** Bol
101C2 **Rusape** Zim
54C2 **Ruse** Bulg
18B1 **Rushville** Illinois, USA
108B3 **Rushworth** Aust
19A3 **Rusk** USA
17B2 **Ruskin** USA
110B1 **Russell** NZ
18B2 **Russellville** Arkansas, USA
18C2 **Russellville** Kentucky, USA
21A2 **Russian** *R* USA
62C3 **Russian Fed** Asia/ Europe
93E1 **Rustavi** Georgia
101G1 **Rustenburg** S Africa
19B3 **Ruston** USA
99C3 **Rutana** Burundi
46E1 **Rüthen** Germany
23B2 **Rutla** Mexico
15D2 **Rutland** USA
84D2 **Rutog** China
Ruvu = Pangani
101D2 **Ruvuma** *R* Tanz/ Mozam
99D2 **Ruwenzori Range** *Mts* Uganda/Zaïre
101C2 **Ruya** *R* Zim
59B3 **Ružomberok** Czech
99C3 **Rwanda** Republic, Africa
60E3 **Ryazan'** Russian Fed
61F3 **Ryazhsk** Russian Fed
60E2 **Rybinsk** Russian Fed
60E2 **Rybinskoye Vodokhranilishche** *Res* Russian Fed
13D1 **Rycroft** Can
43D4 **Ryde** Eng
43E4 **Rye** Eng
20C2 **Rye Patch Res** USA
60D3 **Ryl'sk** Russian Fed
61G4 **Ryn Peski** *Desert* Kazakhstan
74D3 **Ryōtsu** Japan
59D3 **Ryskany** Moldavia
69E4 **Ryūkyū Retto** *Arch* Japan
59C2 **Rzeszów** Pol
60D2 **Rzhev** Russian Fed

S

91B3 **Sa'ādatābād** Iran
56C2 **Saale** *R* Germany
47B1 **Saanen** Switz
46D2 **Saar** *R* Germany
46D2 **Saarbrücken** Germany
46D2 **Saarburg** Germany
39J7 **Saaremaa** *I* Estonia
46D2 **Saarland** State, Germany
46D2 **Saarlouis** Germany
34C3 **Şaavedra** Arg
54A2 **Šabac** Serbia, Yugos
51C1 **Sabadell** Spain
75B1 **Sabae** Japan
78D1 **Sabah** State, Malay
26C4 **Sabanalarga** Colombia
70A3 **Sabang** Indon
87C1 **Sabari** *R* India
94B2 **Sabastiya** Israel
30C2 **Sabaya** Bol
93C3 **Sab'Bi'ār** Syria
94C2 **Sabhā** Jordan
95A2 **Sabhā** Libya
24B2 **Sabinas** Mexico
24B2 **Sabinas Hidalgo** Mexico
19A3 **Sabine** *R* USA
19B4 **Sabine L** USA
91B5 **Sabkhat Maţţi** *Salt Marsh* UAE
94A3 **Sabkhet El Bardawîl** *Lg* Egypt
79B3 **Sablayan** Phil
7D5 **Sable,C** Can
17B2 **Sable,C** USA
7D5 **Sable I** Can
90C2 **Sabzevār** Iran
20C1 **Sacajawea Peak** USA
10A1 **Sachigo** *R* Can
57C2 **Sachsen** State, Germany
56C2 **Sachsen-Anhalt** State, Germany
4F2 **Sachs Harbour** Can
47B1 **Säckingen** Germany
22B1 **Sacramento** USA
22B1 **Sacramento** *R* USA
21A1 **Sacramento** *V* USA
9C3 **Sacramento Mts** USA
81C4 **Sa'dah** Yemen
54B2 **Sadanski** Bulg
82D3 **Sadiya** India
50A2 **Sado** *R* Port
74D3 **Sado-shima** *I* Japan
85C3 **Sādri** India
Safad = Zefat
84A2 **Safed Koh** *Mts* Afghan
39G7 **Saffle** Sweden
92C3 **Safi** Jordan
96B1 **Safi** Mor
90D3 **Safidabeh** Iran
94C1 **Şāfītā** Syria
93E3 **Şafwān** Iraq
75A2 **Saga** Japan
76B1 **Sagaing** Burma
75B2 **Sagami-nada** *B* Japan
85D4 **Sāgar** India
16C2 **Sag Harbor** USA
14B2 **Saginaw** USA
14B2 **Saginaw B** USA
26B2 **Sagua de Tánamo** Cuba
26B2 **Sagua la Grande** Cuba
7C5 **Saguenay** *R* Can
51B2 **Sagunto** Spain
94C3 **Sahāb** Jordan
50A1 **Sahagún** Spain
96C2 **Sahara** *Desert* N Africa
84D3 **Saharanpur** India
84C2 **Sahiwal** Pak
93D3 **Şahrā al Hijārah** *Desert Region* Iraq
23A1 **Sahuayo** Mexico
107D1 **Saibai I** Aust
96C1 **Saïda** Alg
94B2 **Saïda** Leb
91C4 **Sa'īdabad** Iran
51B2 **Saidia** Mor
86B1 **Saidpur** India
84C2 **Saidu** Pak
75A1 **Saigō** Japan
Saigon = Ho Chi Minh
86C2 **Saiha** India
68D2 **Saihan Tal** China
75A2 **Saijo** Japan
74C4 **Saiki** Japan
42C2 **St Abb's Head** *Pt* Scot
43D4 **St Albans** Eng
15D2 **St Albans** Vermont, USA
14B3 **St Albans** West Virginia, USA
43C4 **St Albans Head** *C* Eng
13E2 **St Albert** Can
46B1 **St Amand-les-Eaux** France
48C2 **St Amand-Mont Rond** France
17A2 **St Andrew B** USA
44C3 **St Andrews** Scot
17B1 **St Andrew Sd** USA
27H1 **St Ann's Bay** Jamaica
7E4 **St Anthony** Can
108B3 **St Arnaud** Aust
17B2 **St Augustine** USA
43B4 **St Austell** Eng
46D2 **St-Avold** France
42C2 **St Bees Head** *Pt* Eng
47B2 **St-Bonnet** France
43B4 **St Brides B** Wales
48B2 **St-Brieuc** France
15C2 **St Catharines** Can
27M2 **St Catherine,Mt** Grenada
17B1 **St Catherines I** USA
43D4 **St Catherines Pt** Eng
49C2 **St Chamond** France
18B2 **St Charles** Missouri, USA
14B2 **St Clair** USA
14B2 **St Clair,L** Can/USA
14B2 **St Clair Shores** USA
49D2 **St Claud** France
10A2 **St Cloud** USA
47B1 **Ste Croix** Switz
27E3 **St Croix** *I* Caribbean S
43B4 **St Davids Head** *Pt* Wales
46B2 **St Denis** France
101E3 **St Denis** Réunion
46C2 **St Dizier** France
12F2 **St Elias,Mt** USA

12G2 **St Elias Mts** Can
48B2 **Saintes** France
49C2 **St Étienne** France
18B2 **St Francis** *R* USA
100B4 **St Francis,C** S Africa
47C1 **St Gallen** Switz
48C3 **St-Gaudens** France
109C1 **St George** Aust
17B1 **St George** South Carolina, USA
9B3 **St George** Utah, USA
17B2 **St George I** Florida, USA
20B2 **St George,Pt** USA
15D1 **St-Georges** Can
27E4 **St George's** Grenada
45C3 **St George's Chan** Irish Rep/Wales
46A2 **St Germain-en-Laye** France
47B2 **St-Gervais** France
47C1 **St Gotthard** *P* Switz
43B4 **St Govans Head** *Pt* Wales
22A1 **St Helena** USA
103H5 **St Helena** *I* Atlantic O
100A4 **St Helena B** S Africa
17B1 **St Helena Sd** USA
109C4 **St Helens** Aust
42C3 **St Helens** Eng
20B1 **St Helens** USA
20B1 **St Helens,Mt** USA
48B2 **St Helier** Jersey
47B1 **St Hippolyte** France
46C1 **St-Hubert** Belg
7C5 **St-Hyacinthe** Can
14B1 **St Ignace** USA
43B4 **St Ives** Eng
18B2 **St James** Missouri, USA
5E4 **St James,C** Can
15D1 **St Jean** Can
48B2 **St Jean-d'Angely** France
47B2 **St-Jean-de-Maurienne** France
10C2 **St Jean,L** Can
15D1 **St-Jérôme** Can
20C1 **St Joe** *R* USA
7D5 **Saint John** Can
7E5 **St John's** Can
14B2 **St Johns** Michigan, USA
17B2 **St Johns** *R* USA
15D2 **St Johnsbury** USA
15D1 **St-Joseph** Can
19B3 **St Joseph** Louisiana, USA
14A2 **St Joseph** Michigan, USA
18B2 **St Joseph** Missouri, USA
27L1 **St Joseph** Trinidad
14B2 **St Joseph** *R* USA
14B1 **St Joseph I** Can
7A4 **St Joseph,L** Can
47B1 **St Julien** France
48C2 **St-Junien** France
46B2 **St-Just-en-Chaussée** France
4B2 **St Kilda** *I* Scot
27E3 **St Kitts-Nevis** *Is* Caribbean S
47A1 **St-Laurent** France
7D5 **St Lawrence** *R* Can
7D5 **Saint Lawrence,G of** Can
4A3 **St Lawrence I** USA
15C2 **St Lawrence Seaway** Can/USA
48B2 **St Lô** France
97A3 **St Louis** Sen
11A3 **St Louis** USA
27E4 **St Lucia** *I* Caribbean S
101H1 **St Lucia,L** S Africa
44E1 **St Magnus** *B* Scot
48B2 **St Malo** France
20C1 **St Maries** USA
27E3 **St Martin** *I* Caribbean S
108A2 **St Mary Peak** *Mt* Aust
109C4 **St Marys** Aust
15C2 **St Marys** USA
17B1 **St Marys** *R* USA
46C2 **Ste-Menehould** France
12B2 **St Michael** USA
16A3 **St Michaels** USA
47B2 **St-Michel** France
46C2 **St-Mihiel** France
47C1 **St Moritz** Switz
48B2 **St-Nazaire** France
46C1 **St-Niklaas** Belg
46B1 **St-Omer** France
13E2 **St Paul** Can
10A2 **St Paul** Minnesota, USA
97A4 **St Paul** *R* Lib
17B2 **St Petersburg** USA
7E5 **St Pierre** Can
15D1 **St Pierre,L** Can
46B1 **St-Pol-Sur-Ternoise** France
59B3 **St Pölten** Austria
46B2 **St Quentin** France
49D3 **St Raphaël** France
101D2 **St Sébastien** *C* Madag
17B1 **St Simons I** USA
17B1 **St Stephen** USA
14B2 **St Thomas** Can
49D3 **St-Tropez** France
46C1 **St Truiden** Belg
46A1 **St-Valéry-sur-Somme** France
27E4 **St Vincent** *I* Caribbean S
108A2 **St Vincent,G** Aust
46D1 **St-Vith** Germany
46D2 **St Wendel** Germany
71F2 **Saipan** *I* Pacific O
84B2 **Saiydabad** Afghan
30C2 **Sajama** *Mt* Bol
74D4 **Sakai** Japan
75A2 **Sakaidi** Japan
75A1 **Sakaiminato** Japan
93D4 **Sakākah** S Arabia
10C1 **Sakami,L** Can
100B2 **Sakania** Zaïre
101D3 **Sakaraha** Madag
60D5 **Sakarya** *R* Turk
58C1 **Sakasleja** Latvia
74D3 **Sakata** Japan
97C4 **Saketél** Benin
69G1 **Sakhalin** *I* Russian Fed
69E4 **Sakishima gunto** *Is* Japan
97A4 **Sal** *I* Cape Verde
61F4 **Sal** *R* Russian Fed
39H7 **Sala** Sweden
34D3 **Saladillo** Arg
34C2 **Saladillo** *R* Arg
34D3 **Salado** *R* Buenos Aires, Arg
34B3 **Salado** *R* Mendoza/San Luis, Arg
30D4 **Salado** *R* Sante Fe, Arg
97B4 **Salaga** Ghana
76C3 **Sala Hintoun** Camb
98B1 **Salal** Chad
81D4 **Şalālah** Oman
34A2 **Salamanca** Chile
23A1 **Salamanca** Mexico
50A1 **Salamanca** Spain
15C2 **Salamanca** USA
98B2 **Salamat** *R* Chad
71F4 **Salamaua** PNG
15C2 **Salamonica** USA
78D1 **Salang** Indon
38H5 **Salangen** Nor
30C3 **Salar de Arizaro** Arg
30C3 **Salar de Atacama** *Salt Pan* Chile
30C2 **Salar de Coipasa** *Salt Pan* Bol
30C3 **Salar de Uyuni** *Salt Pan* Bol
47C2 **Salasomaggiore** Italy
61J3 **Salavat** Russian Fed
70D4 **Salayar** Indon
105L5 **Sala y Gomez** *I* Pacific O
34C3 **Salazar** Arg
48C2 **Salbris** France
12E2 **Salcha** *R* USA
100A4 **Saldanha** S Africa
94C2 **Saldhad** Syria
34C3 **Saldungaray** Arg
58C1 **Saldus** Latvia
109C3 **Sale** Aust
18C2 **Salem** Illinois, USA
87B2 **Salem** India
16D1 **Salem** Massachusetts, USA
16B3 **Salem** New Jersey, USA
20B2 **Salem** Oregon, USA
78C4 **Salembu Besar** *I* Indon
39G6 **Salen** Sweden
53B2 **Salerno** Italy
42C3 **Salford** Eng
54A1 **Salgót** Hung
59B3 **Salgótarjan** Hung
31D3 **Salgueiro** Brazil
55C3 **Salihli** Turk
101C2 **Salima** Malawi
39K6 **Salimaa** *L* Fin
18A2 **Salina** Kansas, USA
53B3 **Salina** *I* Italy
23B2 **Salina Cruz** Mexico
30C3 **Salina de Arizato** Arg
34B3 **Salina Grande** *Salt pan* Arg
34B2 **Salina La Antigua** *Salt pan* Arg
35C1 **Salinas** Brazil
22B2 **Salinas** USA
22B2 **Salinas** *R* USA
34B3 **Salinas de Llancaneb** *Salt Pan* Arg
34B2 **Salinas Grandes** *Salt Pan* Arg
19B3 **Saline** *R* Arkansas, USA
27M2 **Salines,Pt** Grenada
31B2 **Salinópolis** Brazil
47A1 **Salins** France
Salisbury = Harare
43D4 **Salisbury** Eng
15C3 **Salisbury** Maryland, USA
6C3 **Salisbury I** Can
43D4 **Salisbury Plain** Eng
38K5 **Salla** Fin
47B2 **Sallanches** France
18B2 **Sallisaw** USA
6C3 **Salluit** Can
86A1 **Sallyana** Nepal
93D2 **Salmas** Iran
38L6 **Salmi** Russian Fed
20C1 **Salmo** Can
8B2 **Salmon** USA
13D2 **Salmon Arm** Can
8B2 **Salmon River Mts** USA
39J6 **Salo** Fin
47D2 **Salò** Italy
49D3 **Salon-de-Provence** France
Salonica = Thessaloníki
54B1 **Salonta** Rom
38K6 **Salpausselka** Region, Fin
34B2 **Salsacate** Arg
61F4 **Sal'sk** Russian Fed
94B2 **Salt** Jordan
30C3 **Salta** Arg
30C3 **Salta** State, Arg
24B2 **Saltillo** Mexico
8B2 **Salt Lake City** USA
34C2 **Salto** Arg
34D2 **Salto** Urug
32C3 **Salto Angostura** *Waterfall* Colombia
35D1 **Salto da Divisa** Brazil
33E2 **Salto del Angel** *Waterfall* Ven
30E3 **Salto del Guaira** *Waterfall* Brazil
32C4 **Salto Grande** *Waterfall* Colombia
84C2 **Salt Range** *Mts* Pak
27H2 **Salt River** Jamaica
17B1 **Saluda** USA
47B2 **Saluzzo** Italy
31D4 **Salvador** Brazil
19B4 **Salvador,L** USA
23A1 **Salvatierra** Mexico
91B5 **Salwah** Qatar
76B1 **Salween** *R* Burma
93E2 **Sal'yany** Azerbaijan
57C3 **Salzburg** Austria
56C2 **Salzgitter** Germany
56C2 **Salzwedel** Germany
68B1 **Samagaltay** Russian Fed
79B4 **Samales Group** *Is* Phil
27D3 **Samaná** Dom Rep
92C2 **Samandaği** Turk
84B1 **Samangan** Afghan
79C3 **Samar** *I* Phil
65G4 **Samara** Russian Fed
107E2 **Samarai** PNG
78D3 **Samarinda** Indon
80E2 **Samarkand** Uzbekistan
93D3 **Sāmarrā'** Iraq
79B3 **Samar S** Phil
86A2 **Sambalpur** India
78B2 **Sambas** Indon
101E2 **Sambava** Madag
84D3 **Sambhal** India
78D3 **Samboja** Indon
59C3 **Sambor** Ukraine
46B1 **Sambre** *R* France
74B3 **Samch'ŏk** S Korea
99D3 **Same** Tanz
47C1 **Samedan** Switz
46A1 **Samer** France
100B2 **Samfya** Zambia
76B1 **Samka** Burma
76C1 **Sam Neua** Laos
55C3 **Sámos** *I* Greece
55C2 **Samothráki** *I* Greece
34C2 **Sampacho** Arg
78D3 **Sampaga** Indon
78C3 **Sampit** Indon
78C3 **Sampit** *R* Indon
19B3 **Sam Rayburn Res** USA
76C3 **Samrong** Camb
56C1 **Samsø** *I* Den
92C1 **Samsun** Turk
97B3 **San** Mali
76D3 **San** *R* Camb
59C2 **San** *R* Pol
81C4 **Şan'ā'** Yemen
98B2 **Sanaga** *R* Cam
29C2 **San Agustín** Arg
79C4 **San Agustin,C** Phil
90A2 **Sanandaj** Iran
22B1 **San Andreas** USA
25C3 **San Andrés Tuxtla** Mexico
9C3 **San Angelo** USA
53A3 **San Antioco** Sardegna
53A3 **San Antioco** *I* Medit S
34A2 **San Antonio** Chile
9C3 **San Antonio** New Mexico, USA
79B2 **San Antonio** Phil
9D4 **San Antonio** *R* Texas, USA
51C2 **San Antonio Abad** Spain
25D2 **San Antonio,C** Cuba
26A2 **San Antonio de los Banos** Cuba
22D3 **San Antonio,Mt** USA
29C4 **San Antonio Oeste** Arg
34D3 **San Augustin** Arg
34B2 **San Augustin de Valle Féril** Arg
85D4 **Sanawad** India
23A1 **San Bartolo** Mexico
24A3 **San Benedicto** *I* Mexico
22B2 **San Benito** *R* USA
22B2 **San Benito Mt** USA
22D3 **San Bernardino** USA
34A2 **San Bernardo** Chile
17A2 **San Blas,C** USA
34A3 **San Carlos** Chile
32A1 **San Carlos** Nic
79B2 **San Carlos** Phil

29B4 **San Carlos de Bariloche** Arg
69E4 **San-chung** Taiwan
61G2 **Sanchursk** Russian Fed
34A3 **San Clemente** Chile
22D4 **San Clemente** USA
21B3 **San Clemente I** USA
34C2 **San Cristóbal** Arg
25C3 **San Cristóbal** Mexico
32C2 **San Cristóbal** Ven
32J7 **San Cristóbal** *I* Ecuador
107F2 **San Cristobal** *I* Solomon Is
25E2 **Sancti Spíritus** Cuba
78C3 **Sandai** Indon
70C3 **Sandakan** Malay
44C2 **Sanday** *I* Scot
9C3 **Sanderson** USA
13F1 **Sandfly L** Can
21B3 **San Diego** USA
92B2 **Sandikli** Turk
86A1 **Sandīla** India
39F7 **Sandnes** Nor
38G5 **Sandnessjøen** Nor
98C3 **Sandoa** Zaïre
59C2 **Sandomierz** Pol
38D3 **Sandoy** Føroyar
20C1 **Sandpoint** USA
49D2 **Sandrio** Italy
18A2 **Sand Springs** USA
106A3 **Sandstone** Aust
73C4 **Sandu** China
14B2 **Sandusky** USA
39H6 **Sandviken** Sweden
7A4 **Sandy L** Can
34C2 **San Elcano** Arg
9B3 **San Felipe** Baja Cal, Mexico
34A2 **San Felipe** Chile
23A1 **San Felipe** Guanajuato, Mexico
27D4 **San Felipe** Ven
51C1 **San Feliu de Guixols** Spain
28A5 **San Felix** *I* Pacific O
34A2 **San Fernando** Chile
79B2 **San Fernando** Phil
79B2 **San Fernando** Phil
50A2 **San Fernando** Spain
27E4 **San Fernando** Trinidad
22C3 **San Fernando** USA
32D2 **San Fernando** Ven
17B2 **Sanford** Florida, USA
12F2 **Sanford,Mt** USA
34C2 **San Francisco** Arg
27C3 **San Francisco** Dom Rep
22A2 **San Francisco** USA
22A2 **San Francisco B** USA
24B2 **San Francisco del Oro** Mexico
23A1 **San Francisco del Rincon** Mexico
22D3 **San Gabriel Mts** USA
85C5 **Sangamner** India
18C2 **Sangamon** *R* USA
71F2 **Sangan** *I* Pacific O
87B1 **Sangāreddi** India
78D4 **Sangeang** *I* Indon
22C2 **Sanger** USA
72C2 **Sanggan He** *R* China
78C2 **Sanggau** Indon
98B2 **Sangha** *R* Congo
85B3 **Sanghar** Pak
76B2 **Sangkhla Buri** Thai
78D2 **Sangkulirang** Indon
87A1 **Sāngli** India
98B2 **Sangmélima** Cam
9B3 **San Gorgonio Mt** USA
9C3 **Sangre de Cristo** *Mts* USA
34C2 **San Gregorio** Arg
22A2 **San Gregorio** USA
84D2 **Sangrūr** India
30E4 **San Ignacio** Arg
79B3 **San Isidro** Phil
32B2 **San Jacinto** Colombia
21B3 **San Jacinto Peak** *Mt* USA
34A3 **San Javier** Chile
34D2 **San Javier** Sante Fe, Arg
74D3 **Sanjō** *I* Japan
31C6 **San João del Rei** Brazil
22B2 **San Joaquin** *R* USA
22B2 **San Joaquin Valley** USA
32A1 **San José** Costa Rica
25C3 **San José** Guatemala
79B2 **San Jose** Luzon, Phil
79B3 **San Jose** Mindoro, Phil
22B2 **San Jose** USA
9B4 **San José** *I* Mexico
30D2 **San José de Chiquitos** Bol
34D2 **San José de Feliciano** Arg
34B2 **San José de Jachal** Arg
34C2 **San José de la Dormida** Arg
31B6 **San José do Rio Prêto** Brazil
24B2 **San José del Cabo** Mexico
34B2 **San Juan** Arg
27D3 **San Juan** Puerto Rico
34B2 **San Juan** State, Arg
27L1 **San Juan** Trinidad
32D2 **San Juan** Ven
26B2 **San Juan** *Mt* Cuba
8C3 **San Juan** *Mts* USA
34B2 **San Juan** *R* Arg
23B2 **San Juan** *R* Mexico
25D3 **San Juan** *R* Nic/ Costa Rica
23B2 **San Juan Bautista** Mexico
30E4 **San Juan Bautista** Par
22B2 **San Juan Bautista** USA
25D3 **San Juan del Norte** Nic
27D4 **San Juan de los Cayos** Ven
23A1 **San Juan de loz Lagoz** Mexico
23A1 **San Juan del Rio** Mexico
25D3 **San Juan del Sur** Nic
20B1 **San Juan Is** USA
23B2 **San Juan Tepozcolula** Mexico
29C5 **San Julián** Arg
34C2 **San Justo** Arg
60D2 **Sankt-Peterburg** Russian Fed
98C3 **Sankuru** *R* Zaïre
22A2 **San Leandro** USA
93C2 **Şanlıurfa** Turk
32B3 **San Lorenzo** Ecuador
34C2 **San Lorenzo** Arg
22B2 **San Lucas** USA
34B2 **San Luis** Arg
34B2 **San Luis** State, Arg
23A1 **San Luis de la Paz** Mexico
21A2 **San Luis Obispo** USA
23A1 **San Luis Potosi** Mexico
22B2 **San Luis Res** USA
53A3 **Sanluri** Sardegna
33D2 **San Maigualida** *Mts* Ven
34D3 **San Manuel** Arg
34A2 **San Marcos** Chile
23B2 **San Marcos** Mexico
52B2 **San Marino** Republic, Europe
34B2 **San Martin** Mendoza, Arg
112C3 **San Martin** *Base* Ant
47D1 **San Martino di Castroza** Italy
23B2 **San Martin Tuxmelucan** Mexico
22A2 **San Mateo** USA
30E2 **San Matias** Bol
72C3 **Sanmenxia** China
25D3 **San Miguel** El Salvador
22B3 **San Miguel** *I* USA
23A1 **San Miguel del Allende** Mexico
34D3 **San Miguel del Monte** Arg
30C4 **San Miguel de Tucumán** Arg
73D4 **Sanming** China
9B3 **San Nicolas** *I* USA
34C2 **San Nicolás de los Arroyos** Arg
101G1 **Sannieshof** S Africa
97B4 **Sanniquellie** Lib
59C3 **Sanok** Pol
26B5 **San Onofore** Colombia
22D4 **San Onofre** USA
79B3 **San Pablo** Phil
22A1 **San Pablo B** USA
34D2 **San Pedro** Buenos Aires, Arg
97B4 **San Pédro** Ivory Coast
30D3 **San Pedro** Jujuy, Arg
30E3 **San Pedro** Par
22C4 **San Pedro Chan** USA
9C4 **San Pedro de los Colonias** Mexico
25D3 **San Pedro Sula** Honduras
53A3 **San Pietro** *I* Medit S
24A1 **San Quintin** Mexico
34B2 **San Rafael** Arg
22A2 **San Rafael** USA
22C3 **San Rafael Mts** USA
49D3 **San Remo** Italy
34D2 **San Salvador** Arg
26C2 **San Salvador** *I* Caribbean S
32J7 **San Salvador** *I* Ecuador
30C3 **San Salvador de Jujuy** Arg
51B1 **San Sebastian** Spain
53C2 **San Severo** Italy
30C2 **Santa Ana** Bol
25C3 **Santa Ana** Guatemala
22D4 **Santa Ana** USA
22D4 **Santa Ana Mts** USA
34A3 **Santa Bárbara** Chile
24B2 **Santa Barbara** Mexico
22C3 **Santa Barbara** USA
22C4 **Santa Barbara** *I* USA
22B3 **Santa Barbara Chan** USA
22C3 **Santa Barbara Res** USA
22C4 **Santa Catalina** *I* USA
22C4 **Santa Catalina,G of** USA
30F4 **Santa Catarina** State, Brazil
26B2 **Santa Clara** Cuba
22B2 **Santa Clara** USA
22C3 **Santa Clara** *R* USA
29C6 **Santa Cruz** Arg
30D2 **Santa Cruz** Bol
34A2 **Santa Cruz** Chile
79B3 **Santa Cruz** Phil
29B5 **Santa Cruz** State, Arg
22A2 **Santa Cruz** USA
22C4 **Santa Cruz** *I* USA
35D1 **Santa Cruz Cabrália** Brazil
22C3 **Santa Cruz Chan** USA
96A2 **Santa Cruz de la Palma** Canary Is
26B2 **Santa Cruz del Sur** Cuba
96A2 **Santa Cruz de Tenerife** Canary Is
100B2 **Santa Cruz do Cuando** Angola
35B2 **Santa Cruz do Rio Pardo** Brazil
22A2 **Santa Cruz Mts** USA
34D2 **Santa Elena** Arg
33E3 **Santa Elena** Ven
34C2 **Santa Fe** Arg
34C2 **Santa Fe** State, Arg
9C3 **Santa Fe** USA
35A1 **Santa Helena de Goiás** Brazil
73B3 **Santai** China
29B6 **Santa Inés** *I* Chile
34B3 **Santa Isabel** La Pampa, Arg
34C2 **Santa Isabel** Sante Fe, Arg
107E1 **Santa Isabel** *I* Solomon Is
21A2 **Santa Lucia** *Ra* USA
21A2 **Santa Lucia Range** *Mts* USA
97A4 **Santa Luzia** *I* Cape Verde
9B4 **Santa Margarita** *I* Mexico
22D4 **Santa Margarita** *R* USA
30F4 **Santa Maria** Brazil
26C4 **Santa Maria** Colombia
21A3 **Santa Maria** USA
96A1 **Santa Maria** *I* Açores
23B1 **Santa Maria** *R* Queretaro, Mexico
23A1 **Santa Maria del Rio** Mexico
32C1 **Santa Marta** Colombia
22C3 **Santa Monica** USA
22C4 **Santa Monica B** USA
29E2 **Santana do Livramento** Brazil
32B3 **Santander** Colombia
50B1 **Santander** Spain
51C2 **Santañy** Spain
22C3 **Santa Paula** USA
31C2 **Santa Quitéria** Brazil
33G4 **Santarem** Brazil
50A2 **Santarém** Port
22A1 **Santa Rosa** California, USA
25D3 **Santa Rosa** Honduras
34C3 **Santa Rosa** La Pampa, Arg
34B2 **Santa Rosa** Mendoza, Arg
34B2 **Santa Rosa** San Luis, Arg
22B3 **Santa Rosa** *I* USA
24A2 **Santa Rosalía** Mexico
20C2 **Santa Rosa Range** *Mts* USA
31D3 **Santa Talhada** Brazil
35C1 **Santa Teresa** Brazil
53A2 **Santa Teresa di Gallura** Sardegna
22B3 **Santa Ynez** *R* USA
22B3 **Santa Ynez Mts** USA
17C1 **Santee** *R* USA
47C2 **Santhia** Italy
34A2 **Santiago** Chile
27C3 **Santiago** Dom Rep
32A2 **Santiago** Panama
79B2 **Santiago** Phil
32B4 **Santiago** *R* Peru
50A1 **Santiago de Compostela** Spain
26B2 **Santiago de Cuba** Cuba
30D4 **Santiago del Estero** Arg
30D4 **Santiago del Estero** State, Arg
22D4 **Santiago Peak** *Mt* USA
31C5 **Santo** State, Brazil
35A2 **Santo Anastatácio** Brazil
30F4 **Santo Angelo** Brazil
97A4 **Santo Antão** *I* Cape Verde
35A2 **Santo Antonio da Platina** Brazil
27D3 **Santo Domingo** Dom Rep
35B2 **Santos** Brazil

35C2 **Santos Dumont** Brazil
30E4 **Santo Tomé** Arg
29B5 **San Valentin** *Mt* Chile
34A2 **San Vicente** Chile
98B3 **Sanza Pomba** Angola
30E4 **São Borja** Brazil
35B2 **São Carlos** Brazil
33G5 **São Félix** Mato Grosso, Brazil
35C2 **São Fidélis** Brazil
35C1 **São Francisco** Brazil
31D3 **São Francisco** *R* Brazil
30G4 **São Francisco do Sul** Brazil
35B1 **São Gotardo** Brazil
99D3 **Sao Hill** Tanz
35C2 **São João da Barra** Brazil
35B2 **São João da Boa Vista** Brazil
35C1 **São João da Ponte** Brazil
35C2 **São João del Rei** Brazil
35B2 **São Joaquim da Barra** Brazil
96A1 **São Jorge** *I* Açores
35B2 **São José do Rio Prêto** Brazil
35B2 **São José dos Campos** Brazil
31C2 **São Luis** Brazil
35B1 **São Marcos** *R* Brazil
35C1 **São Maria do Suaçui** Brazil
35D1 **São Mateus** Brazil
35C1 **São Mateus** *R* Brazil
96A1 **São Miguel** *I* Açores
49C2 **Saône** *R* France
97A4 **São Nicolau** *I* Cape Verde
35B2 **São Paulo** Brazil
35A2 **São Paulo** State, Brazil
31C3 **São Raimundo Nonato** Brazil
35B1 **São Romão** Brazil
35B2 **São Sebastia do Paraiso** Brazil
35A1 **São Simão** Goias, Brazil
35B2 **São Simão** Sao Paulo, Brazil
97A4 **São Tiago** *I* Cape Verde
97C4 **São Tomé** *I* W Africa
97C4 **São Tomé and Principe** Republic, W Africa
96B2 **Saoura** *Watercourse* Alg
35B2 **São Vicente** Brazil
97A4 **São Vincente** *I* Cape Verde
55C2 **Sápai** Greece
78D4 **Sape** Indon
97C4 **Sapele** Nig
74E2 **Sapporo** Japan
53C2 **Sapri** Italy
18A2 **Sapulpa** USA
90A2 **Saqqez** Iran
10C2 **Saquenay** *R* Can
90A2 **Sarāb** Iran
54A2 **Sarajevo** Bosnia & Herzegovina, Yugos
90D2 **Sarakhs** Iran
61J3 **Saraktash** Russian Fed
63A2 **Sarala** Russian Fed
15D2 **Saranac L** USA
15D2 **Saranac Lake** USA
55B3 **Sarandë** Alb
79C4 **Sarangani Is** Phil
61G3 **Saransk** Russian Fed
61H2 **Sarapul** Russian Fed
17B2 **Sarasota** USA
54C1 **Sarata** Ukraine
15D2 **Saratoga Springs** USA
78C2 **Saratok** Malay
61G3 **Saratov** Russian Fed
61G3 **Saratovskoye Vodokhranilishche** *Res* Russian Fed
67F4 **Sarawak** State, Malay
92A2 **Saraykoy** Turk
90C3 **Sarbīsheh** Iran
47D1 **Sarca** *R* Italy
95A2 **Sardalas** Libya
90A2 **Sar Dasht** Iran
52A2 **Sardegna** *I* Medit S
Sardinia = Sardegna
38H5 **Sarektjåkkå** *Mt* Sweden
84C2 **Sargodha** Pak
98B2 **Sarh** Chad
90B2 **Sārī** Iran
94B2 **Sarida** *R* Isreal
93D1 **Sarikamiş** Turk
107D3 **Sarina** Aust
47B1 **Sarine** *R* Switz
84B1 **Sar-i-Pul** Afghan
95B2 **Sarīr** Libya
95A2 **Sarir Tibesti** *Desert* Libya
74B3 **Sariwŏn** N Korea
48B2 **Sark** *I* UK
92C2 **Sarkišla** Turk
71E4 **Sarmi** Indon
29C5 **Sarmiento** Arg
39G6 **Särna** Sweden
47C1 **Sarnen** Switz
14B2 **Sarnia** Can
58D2 **Sarny** Ukraine
6E2 **Saroaq** Greenland
84B2 **Sarobi** Afghan
78A3 **Sarolangun** Indon
55B3 **Saronikós Kólpos** *G* Greece
47C2 **Saronno** Italy
55C2 **Saros Körfezi** *B* Turk
39G7 **Sarpsborg** Nor
46D2 **Sarralbe** France
46D2 **Sarrebourg** France
46D2 **Sarreguemines** France
46D2 **Sarre-Union** France
51B1 **Sarrion** Spain
85B3 **Sartanahu** Pak
53A2 **Sartène** Corse
48B2 **Sarthe** *R* France
61H4 **Sarykamys** Kazakhstan
65H5 **Sarysu** *R* Kazakhstan
86A2 **Sasarām** India
74B4 **Sasebo** Japan
5H4 **Saskatchewan** Province, Can
5H4 **Saskatchewan** *R* Can
13F2 **Saskatoon** Can
101G1 **Sasolburg** S Africa
61F3 **Sasovo** Russian Fed
97B4 **Sassandra** Ivory Coast
97B4 **Sassandra** *R* Ivory Coast
53A2 **Sassari** Sardegna
56C2 **Sassnitz** Germany
47D2 **Sassuolo** Italy
34C2 **Sastre** Arg
87A1 **Sātāra** India
4G2 **Satellite B** Can
78D4 **Satengar** *Is* Indon
39H6 **Säter** Sweden
17B1 **Satilla** *R* USA
61J2 **Satka** Russian Fed
84D2 **Satluj** *R* India
86A2 **Satna** India
85C4 **Sātpura Range** *Mts* India
54B1 **Satu Mare** Rom
34D2 **Sauce** Arg
39F7 **Sauda** Nor
80C3 **Saudi Arabia** Kingdom, Arabian Pen
46D2 **Sauer** *R* Germany/ Lux
46D1 **Sauerland** Region, Germany
38B1 **Sauðárkrókur** Iceland
14A2 **Saugatuck** USA
16C1 **Saugerties** USA
13B2 **Saugstad,Mt** Can
7B5 **Sault Sainte Marie** Can
14B1 **Sault Ste Marie** Can
14B1 **Sault Ste Marie** USA
71E4 **Saumlaki** Indon
48B2 **Saumur** France
98C3 **Saurimo** Angola
27M2 **Sauteurs** Grenada
54A2 **Sava** *R* Serbia, Yugos
97C4 **Savalou** Benin
17B1 **Savannah** Georgia, USA
17B1 **Savannah** *R* USA
76C2 **Savannakhet** Laos
26B3 **Savanna la Mar** Jamaica
7A4 **Savant Lake** Can
76D2 **Savarane** Laos
97C4 **Savé** Benin
101C3 **Save** *R* Mozam
90B3 **Sāveh** Iran
46D2 **Saverne** France
47B2 **Savigliano** Italy
46B2 **Savigny** France
49D2 **Savoie** *Region* France
49D3 **Savona** Italy
38K6 **Savonlinna** Fin
4A3 **Savoonga** USA
38K5 **Savukoski** Fin
71D4 **Savu S** Indon
76A1 **Saw** Burma
85D3 **Sawai Mādhopur** India
78A2 **Sawang** Indon
76B2 **Sawankhalok** Thai
75C1 **Sawara** Japan
12E1 **Sawtooth Mt** USA
106B2 **Sawu** *I* Indon
97C3 **Say** Niger
84B1 **Sayghan** Afghan
91B5 **Sayhūt** Yemen
61G4 **Saykhin** Kazakhstan
68D2 **Saynshand** Mongolia
61H5 **Say-Utes** Kazakhstan
16C2 **Sayville** USA
13B2 **Sayward** Can
57C3 **Sázava** *R* Czech
51C2 **Sbisseb** *R* Alg
42C2 **Scafell Pike** *Mt* Eng
44E1 **Scalloway** Scot
44C2 **Scapa Flow** *Sd* Scot
15C2 **Scarborough** Can
42D2 **Scarborough** Eng
27E4 **Scarborough** Tobago
44A2 **Scarp** *I* Scot
45B2 **Scarriff** Irish Rep
52A1 **Schaffhausen** Switz
57C3 **Scharding** Austria
46D1 **Scharteberg** *Mt* Germany
7D4 **Schefferville** Can
46B1 **Schelde** *R* Belg
10C2 **Schenectady** USA
47D2 **Schio** Italy
46D1 **Schleiden** Germany
56B2 **Schleswig** Germany
56B2 **Schleswig Holstein** State, Germany
16B1 **Schoharie** USA
71F4 **Schouten** *Is* PNG
7B5 **Schreiber** Can
21B2 **Schurz** USA
16A2 **Schuykill Haven** USA
16B2 **Schuylkill** *R* USA
57B3 **Schwabische Alb** *Upland* Germany
57B3 **Schwarzwald** *Upland* Germany
12C1 **Schwatka Mts** USA
47D1 **Schwaz** Austria
57C2 **Schweinfurt** Germany
101G1 **Schweizer Reneke** S Africa
56C2 **Schwerin** Germany
47C1 **Schwyz** Switz
53B3 **Sciacca** Italy
14B3 **Scioto** *R* USA
109D2 **Scone** Aust
6H2 **Scoresby Sd** Greenland
103F7 **Scotia Ridge** Atlantic O
103F7 **Scotia S** Atlantic O
44B3 **Scotland** Country, UK
112B7 **Scott** *Base* Ant
13B2 **Scott,C** Can
9C2 **Scott City** USA
112C6 **Scott I** Ant
6C2 **Scott Inlet** *B* Can
20B2 **Scott,Mt** USA
106B2 **Scott Reef** Timor S
8C2 **Scottsbluff** USA
17A1 **Scottsboro** USA
109C4 **Scottsdale** Aust
10C2 **Scranton** USA
47D1 **Scuol** Switz
Scutari = Shkodër
5J4 **Seal** *R* Can
108B3 **Sea Lake** Aust
18B2 **Searcy** USA
22B2 **Seaside** California, USA
20B1 **Seaside** Oregon, USA
16B3 **Seaside Park** USA
20B1 **Seattle** USA
22A1 **Sebastopol** USA
58D1 **Sebez** Russian Fed
17B2 **Sebring** USA
111A3 **Secretary I** NZ
18B2 **Sedalia** USA
46C2 **Sedan** France
111B2 **Seddonville** NZ
94B3 **Sede Boqer** Israel
94B3 **Sederot** Israel
97A3 **Sédhiou** Sen
94B3 **Sedom** Israel
100A3 **Seeheim** Namibia
111B2 **Sefton,Mt** NZ
77C5 **Segamat** Malay
51B2 **Segorbe** Spain
97B3 **Ségou** Mali
Segovia = Coco
50B1 **Segovia** Spain
51C1 **Segre** *R* Spain
97B4 **Séguéla** Ivory Coast
96A2 **Seguia el Hamra** *Watercourse* Mor
34C2 **Segundo** *R* Arg
78D2 **Seguntur** Indon
50B2 **Segura** *R* Spain
85B3 **Sehwan** Pak
46D2 **Seille** *R* France
38J6 **Seinäjoki** Fin
48C2 **Seine** *R* France
46B2 **Seine-et-Marne** Department, France
99D3 **Sekenke** Tanz
99D1 **Sek'ot'a** Eth
20B1 **Selah** USA
71E4 **Selaru** *I* Indon
78D4 **Selat Alas** *Str* Indon
78B3 **Selat Bangka** *Str* Indon
78A3 **Selat Berhala** *B* Indon
71E4 **Selat Dampier** *Str* Indon
78B3 **Selat Gaspar** *Str* Indon
78D4 **Selat Lombok** *Str* Indon
78D4 **Selat Sape** *Str* Indon
78B4 **Selat Sunda** *Str* Indon
71D4 **Selat Wetar** *Chan* Indon
12B1 **Selawik** USA
12C1 **Selawik** *R* USA
12B1 **Selawik L** USA
42D3 **Selby** Eng
55C3 **Selçuk** Turk
12D3 **Seldovia** USA
100B3 **Selebi Pikwe** Botswana
6H3 **Selfoss** Iceland
95B2 **Selima Oasis** Sudan
5J4 **Selkirk** Can
42C2 **Selkirk** Scot
13D2 **Selkirk Mts** Can

22C2 **Selma** California, USA
50B2 **Selouane** Mor
12H2 **Selous,Mt** Can
78B3 **Selta Karimata** *Str* Indon
32C5 **Selvas** Region, Brazil
107D3 **Selwyn** Aust
4E3 **Selwyn Mts** Can
78C4 **Semarang** Indon
61E2 **Semenov** Russian Fed
12C3 **Semidi Is** USA
60E3 **Semiluki** Russian Fed
19A2 **Seminole** Oklahoma, USA
17B1 **Seminole,L** USA
65K4 **Semipalatinsk** Kazakhstan
79B3 **Semirara Is** Phil
90B3 **Semirom** Iran
78C2 **Semitau** Indon
90B2 **Semnān** Iran
46C2 **Semois** *R* Belg
23B2 **Sempoala** Hist Site, Mexico
32D5 **Sena Madureira** Brazil
100B2 **Senanga** Zambia
19C3 **Senatobia** USA
74E3 **Sendai** Honshū, Japan
74C4 **Sendai** Kyūshū, Japan
85D4 **Sendwha** India
15C2 **Seneca Falls** USA
97A3 **Senegal** Republic, Africa
97A3 **Sénégal** *R* Maur Sen
101G1 **Senekal** S Africa
31D4 **Senhor do Bonfim** Brazil
52B2 **Senigallia** Italy
52C2 **Senj** Croatia
69E4 **Senkaku Gunto** *Is* Japan
46B2 **Senlis** France
99D1 **Sennar** Sudan
7C5 **Senneterre** Can
49C2 **Sens** France
54A1 **Senta** Serbia, Yugos
98C3 **Sentery** Zaïre
13C2 **Sentinel Peak** *Mt* Can
85D4 **Seoni** India
Seoul = Soul
110B2 **Separation Pt** NZ
76D2 **Sepone** Laos
7D4 **Sept-Iles** Can
95A2 **Séquédine** Niger
21B2 **Sequoia** Nat Pk, USA
71D4 **Seram** *I* Indon
78B4 **Serang** Indon
78B2 **Serasan** *I* Indon
54A2 **Serbia** Republic, Yugos
61F3 **Serdobsk** Russian Fed
77C5 **Seremban** Malay
99D3 **Serengeti Nat Pk** Tanz
100C2 **Serenje** Zambia
59D3 **Seret** *R* Ukraine
61G2 **Sergach** Russian Fed
65H3 **Sergino** Russian Fed
31D4 **Sergipe** State, Brazil
78C2 **Seria** Brunei
78C2 **Serian** Malay
55B3 **Sérifos** *I* Greece
47C2 **Serio** *R* Italy
95B2 **Serir Calanscio** *Desert* Libya
46C2 **Sermaize-les-Bains** France
71D4 **Sermata** *I* Indon
61H3 **Sernovodsk** Russian Fed
65H4 **Serov** Russian Fed
100B3 **Serowe** Botswana
50A2 **Serpa** Port
60E3 **Serpukhov** Russian Fed
35B2 **Serra da Canastra** *Mts* Brazil
50A1 **Serra da Estrela** *Mts* Port
35B2 **Serra da Mantiqueira** *Mts* Brazil
35A1 **Serra da Mombuca** Brazil
35C1 **Serra do Cabral** *Mt* Brazil
33F5 **Serra do Cachimbo** *Mts* Brazil
35A1 **Serra do Caiapó** *Mts* Brazil
35A2 **Serra do Cantu** *Mts* Brazil
35C2 **Serra do Caparaó** *Mts* Brazil
31C5 **Serra do Chifre** Brazil
35C1 **Serra do Espinhaço** *Mts* Brazil
35B2 **Serra do Mar** *Mts* Brazil
35A2 **Serra do Mirante** *Mts* Brazil
33G3 **Serra do Navio** Brazil
35B2 **Serra do Paranapiacaba** *Mts* Brazil
33F6 **Serra dos Caiabis** *Mts* Brazil
35A2 **Serra dos Dourados** *Mts* Brazil
33E6 **Serra dos Parecis** *Mts* Brazil
35B1 **Serra dos Pilões** *Mts* Brazil
35A1 **Serra Dourada** *Mts* Brazil
33F6 **Serra Formosa** *Mts* Brazil
55B2 **Sérrai** Greece
25D3 **Serrana Bank** *Is* Caribbean S
51B1 **Serrana de Cuenca** *Mts* Spain
35A1 **Serranópolis** Brazil
33E3 **Serra Pacaraima** *Mts* Brazil/Ven
33E3 **Serra Parima** *Mts* Brazil
33G3 **Serra Tumucumaque** Brazil
46B2 **Serre** *R* France
34B2 **Serrezuela** Arg
31D4 **Serrinha** Brazil
6G3 **Serrmilik** Greenland
35C1 **Serro** Brazil
35A2 **Sertanópolis** Brazil
72A3 **Sêrtar** China
78C3 **Seruyan** *R* Indon
100A2 **Sesfontein** Namibia
100B2 **Sesheke** Zambia
47B2 **Sestriere** Italy
74D2 **Setana** Japan
49C3 **Sète** France
35C1 **Sete Lagoas** Brazil
96C1 **Sétif** Alg
75B1 **Seto** Japan
75A2 **Seto Naikai** *S* Japan
96B1 **Settat** Mor
42C2 **Settle** Eng
5G4 **Settler** Can
50A2 **Sêtúbal** Port
93E1 **Sevan,Oz** *L* Armenia
60D5 **Sevastopol'** Ukraine
7B4 **Severn** *R* Can
43C3 **Severn** *R* Eng
1B9 **Severnaya Zemlya** *I* Russian Fed
63C2 **Severo-Baykalskoye Nagorye** *Mts* Russian Fed
60E4 **Severo Donets** Ukraine
64E3 **Severodvinsk** Russian Fed
64H3 **Severo Sos'va** *R* Russian Fed
8B3 **Sevier** *R* USA
8B3 **Sevier L** USA
50A2 **Sevilla** Spain
Seville = Sevilla
54C2 **Sevlievo** Bulg
97A4 **Sewa** *R* Sierra Leone
12E2 **Seward** Alaska, USA
18A1 **Seward** Nebraska, USA
12A1 **Seward Pen** USA
13D1 **Sexsmith** Can
89K8 **Seychelles** *Is* Indian O
38C1 **Seyðisfjörður** Iceland
92C2 **Seyhan** Turk
60E3 **Seym** *R* Russian Fed
108C3 **Seymour** Aust
16C2 **Seymour** Connecticut, USA
14A3 **Seymour** Indiana, USA
46B2 **Sézanne** France
96D1 **Sfax** Tunisia
54C1 **Sfînto Gheorghe** Rom
56A2 **'s-Gravenhage** Neth
72B3 **Shaanxi** Province, China
98C3 **Shabunda** Zaïre
82B2 **Shache** China
112C9 **Shackleton Ice Shelf** Ant
85B3 **Shadadkot** Pak
91B3 **Shādhām** *R* Iran
43C4 **Shaftesbury** Eng
29G8 **Shag Rocks** *Is* South Georgia
90A3 **Shāhabād** Iran
94C2 **Shahbā** Syria
91C3 **Shahdap** Iran
86A2 **Shahdol** India
90A2 **Shāhīn Dezh** Iran
90C3 **Shāh Kūh** Iran
91C3 **Shahr-e Bābak** Iran
Shahresa = Qomisheh
90B3 **Shahr Kord** Iran
87B1 **Shājābād** India
84D3 **Shājahānpur** India
85D4 **Shājāpur** India
61F4 **Shakhty** Russian Fed
61G2 **Shakhun'ya** Russian Fed
97C4 **Shaki** Nig
12B2 **Shaktoolik** USA
61J2 **Shamary** Russian Fed
99D2 **Shambe** Sudan
16A2 **Shamokin** USA
16B1 **Shandaken** USA
72D2 **Shandong** Province, China
73C5 **Shangchuan Dao** *I* China
72C1 **Shangdu** China
73E3 **Shanghai** China
72C3 **Shangnan** China
100B2 **Shangombo** Zambia
73D4 **Shangra** China
73B5 **Shangsi** China
72C3 **Shang Xian** China
41B3 **Shannon** *R* Irish Rep
72D3 **Shanqiu** China
74B2 **Shansonggang** China
63F2 **Shantarskiye Ostrova** *I* Russian Fed
73D5 **Shantou** China
72C2 **Shanxi** Province, China
72D3 **Shan Xian** China
73C5 **Shaoguan** China
73E4 **Shaoxing** China
73C4 **Shaoyang** China
44C2 **Shapinsay** *I* Scot
94C2 **Shaqqā** Syria
72A1 **Sharhulsan** Mongolia
90C2 **Sharifābād** Iran
91C4 **Sharjah** UAE
106A3 **Shark B** Aust
90C2 **Sharlauk** Turkmenistan
94B2 **Sharon,Plain of** Israel
61G2 **Sharya** Russian Fed
99D2 **Shashemanē** Eth
73C3 **Shashi** China
20B2 **Shasta L** USA
20B2 **Shasta,Mt** USA
93E3 **Shaṭṭ al Gharrat** *R* Iraq
94B3 **Shaubak** Jordan
13F3 **Shaunavon** Can
22C2 **Shaver L** USA
16B2 **Shawangunk Mt** USA
15D1 **Shawinigan** Can
19A2 **Shawnee** Oklahoma, USA
73D4 **Sha Xian** China
106B3 **Shay Gap** Aust
94C2 **Shaykh Miskīn** Syria
99E1 **Shaykh 'Uthmān** Yemen
60E3 **Shchekino** Russian Fed
60E3 **Shchigry** Russian Fed
60D3 **Shchors** Ukraine
65J4 **Shchuchinsk** Kazakhstan
99E2 **Shebele** *R* Eth
14A2 **Sheboygan** USA
98B2 **Shebshi** *Mts* Nig
12F1 **Sheenjek** *R* USA
45C1 **Sheep Haven** *Estuary* Irish Rep
43E4 **Sheerness** Eng
94B2 **Shefar'am** Israel
42D3 **Sheffield** Eng
84C2 **Shekhupura** Pak
13B1 **Shelagyote Peak** *Mt* Can
16C1 **Shelburne Falls** USA
14A2 **Shelby** Michigan, USA
8B2 **Shelby** Montana, USA
14A3 **Shelbyville** Indiana, USA
12H2 **Sheldon,Mt** Can
12D3 **Shelikof Str** USA
109D2 **Shellharbour** Aust
111A3 **Shelter Pt** NZ
20B1 **Shelton** USA
93E1 **Shemakha** Azerbaijan
18A1 **Shenandoah** USA
15C3 **Shenandoah** *R* USA
15C3 **Shenandoah Nat Pk** USA
97C4 **Shendam** Nig
95C2 **Shendi** Sudan
72C2 **Shenmu** China
72E1 **Shenyang** China
73C5 **Shenzhen** China
85D3 **Sheopur** India
59D2 **Shepetovka** Ukraine
108C3 **Shepparton** Aust
6B2 **Sherard,C** Can
43C4 **Sherborne** Eng
97A4 **Sherbro I** Sierra Leone
15D1 **Sherbrooke** Can
85C3 **Shergarh** India
19B3 **Sheridan** Arkansas, USA
8C2 **Sheridan** Wyoming, USA
19A3 **Sherman** USA
56B2 **s-Hertogenbosh** Neth
12H3 **Sheslay** Can
40C1 **Shetland** *Is* Scot
61H5 **Shevchenko** Kazakhstan
91B4 **Sheyk Sho'eyb** *I* Iran
69H2 **Shiashkotan** *I* Russian Fed
84B1 **Shibarghan** Afghan
74D3 **Shibata** Japan
95C1 **Shibin el Kom** Egypt
75B1 **Shibukawa** Japan
72C2 **Shijiazhuang** China
84B3 **Shikarpur** Pak
67G3 **Shikoku** *I* Japan
75A2 **Shikoku-sanchi** *Mts* Japan
86B1 **Shiliguri** India
68D1 **Shilka** Russian Fed
68D1 **Shilka** *R* Russian Fed
16B2 **Shillington** USA
86C1 **Shillong** India
61F3 **Shilovo** Russian Fed
75A2 **Shimabara** Japan
75B2 **Shimada** Japan
69E1 **Shimanovsk** Russian Fed

74D3 **Shimizu** Japan
75B2 **Shimoda** Japan
87B2 **Shimoga** India
74C4 **Shimonoseki** Japan
75B1 **Shinano** *R* Japan
91C5 **Shināş** Oman
74D4 **Shingū** Japan
75C1 **Shinjō** Japan
74D3 **Shinminato** Japan
94C1 **Shinshār** Syria
99D3 **Shinyanga** Tanz
74E3 **Shiogama** Japan
75B2 **Shiono-misaki** *C* Japan
73A5 **Shiping** China
16A2 **Shippensburg** USA
72B3 **Shiquan** China
75C1 **Shirakawa** Japan
75B1 **Shirane-san** *Mt* Japan
75B1 **Shirani-san** *Mt* Japan
91B4 **Shīraz** Iran
90B3 **Shīr Kūh** Iran
75B1 **Shirotori** Japan
90C2 **Shirvān** Iran
12A1 **Shishmaref** USA
12A1 **Shishmaref Inlet** USA
4B3 **Shishmaret** USA
72B2 **Shitanjing** China
14A3 **Shively** USA
85D3 **Shivpuri** India
94B3 **Shivta** *Hist Site* Israel
101C2 **Shiwa Ngandu** Zambia
72C3 **Shiyan** China
72B2 **Shizuishan** China
75B1 **Shizuoka** Japan
54A2 **Shkodër** Alb
109D2 **Shoalhaven** *R* Aust
75A2 **Shobara** Japan
87B2 **Shoranūr** India
87B1 **Shorāpur** India
21B2 **Shoshone Mts** USA
60D3 **Shostka** Ukraine
19B3 **Shreveport** USA
43C3 **Shrewsbury** Eng
43C3 **Shropshire** County, Eng
72E1 **Shuanglia** China
69F2 **Shuangyashan** China
61J4 **Shubar-Kuduk** Kazakhstan
72D2 **Shu He** *R* China
73A4 **Shuicheng** China
84C3 **Shujaabad** Pak
85D4 **Shujālpur** India
68B2 **Shule He** China
54C2 **Shumen** Bulg
61G2 **Shumerlya** Russian Fed
73D4 **Shuncheng** China
12C1 **Shungnak** USA
72C2 **Shuo Xian** China
91C4 **Shūr Gaz** Iran
100B2 **Shurugwi** Zim
13D2 **Shuswap L** Can
61F2 **Shuya** Russian Fed
12D3 **Shuyak I** USA
82D3 **Shwebo** Burma
76B2 **Shwegyin** Burma
84A2 **Siah Koh** *Mts* Afghan
84C2 **Sialkot** Pak
Sian = Xi'an
79C4 **Siarao** *I* Phil
79B4 **Şiaton** Phil
58C1 **Šiauliai** Lithuania
65G4 **Sibay** Russian Fed
101H1 **Şibayi L** S Africa
52C2 **Šibenik** Croatia
70A4 **Siberut** *I* Indon
84B3 **Sibi** Pak
68C1 **Sibirskoye** Russian Fed
98B3 **Sibiti** Congo
99D3 **Sibiti** *R* Tanz
54B1 **Sibiu** Rom
70A3 **Sibolga** Indon
86C1 **Sibsāgār** India
78C2 **Sibu** Malay
79B4 **Sibuguay B** Phil
98B2 **Sibut** CAR
79B3 **Sibuyan** *I* Phil
79B3 **Sibuyan S** Phil
73A3 **Sichuan** Province, China
53B3 **Sicilia** *I* Medit S
53B3 **Sicilian** *Chan* Italy/Tunisia
Sicily = Sicilia
32C6 **Sicuani** Peru
85C4 **Siddhapur** India
87B1 **Siddipet** India
86A2 **Sidhi** India
95B1 **Sidi Barrani** Egypt
96B1 **Sidi Bel Abbès** Alg
96B1 **Sidi Kacem** Mor
44C3 **Sidlaw Hills** Scot
112B5 **Sidley,Mt** Ant
20B1 **Sidney** Can
8C2 **Sidney** Nebraska, USA
15C2 **Sidney** New York, USA
14B2 **Sidney** Ohio, USA
17B1 **Sidney Lanier,L** USA
Sidon = Säida
58C2 **Siedlce** Pol
46D1 **Sieg** *R* Germany
46D1 **Siegburg** Germany
46D1 **Siegen** Germany
76C3 **Siem Reap** Camb
52B2 **Siena** Italy
58B2 **Sierpc** Pol
23B2 **Sierra Andrés Tuxtla** Mexico
34B3 **Sierra Auca Mahuida** *Mts* Arg
9C3 **Sierra Blanca** USA
51B1 **Sierra de Albarracin** *Mts* Spain
50B2 **Sierra de Alcaraz** *Mts* Spain
34B2 **Sierra de Cordoba** *Mts* Arg
50A1 **Sierra de Gredos** *Mts* Spain
50A2 **Sierra de Guadalupe** *Mts* Spain
50B1 **Sierra de Guadarrama** *Mts* Spain
51B1 **Sierra de Guara** *Mts* Spain
51B1 **Sierra de Gudar** *Mts* Spain
23B2 **Sierra de Juárez** Mexico
34C3 **Sierra de la Ventana** *Mts* Arg
51C1 **Sierra del Codi** *Mts* Spain
34B2 **Sierra del Morro** *Mt* Arg
34B3 **Sierra del Nevado** *Mts* Arg
24B2 **Sierra de los Alamitos** *Mts* Mexico
50B2 **Sierra de los Filabres** Spain
23A1 **Sierra de los Huicholes** Mexico
23B2 **Sierra de Miahuatlán** Mexico
23A1 **Sierra de Morones** *Mts* Mexico
50A2 **Sierra de Ronda** *Mts* Spain
34B2 **Sierra de San Luis** *Mts* Arg
50B2 **Sierra de Segura** *Mts* Spain
50B1 **Sierra de Urbion** *Mts* Spain
34B2 **Sierra de Uspallata** *Mts* Arg
34B2 **Sierra de Valle Fértil** *Mts* Arg
23B2 **Sierra de Zongolica** Mexico
34C2 **Sierra Grande** *Mts* Arg
97A4 **Sierra Leone** Republic, Africa
97A4 **Sierra Leone,C** Sierra Leone
79B2 **Sierra Madre** *Mts* Phil
23A2 **Sierra Madre del Sur** *Mts* Mexico
24B2 **Sierra Madre Occidental** *Mts* Mexico
24C2 **Sierra Madre Oriental** *Mts* Mexico
34B2 **Sierra Malanzan** *Mts* Arg
9C4 **Sierra Mojada** Mexico
50A2 **Sierra Morena** *Mts* Spain
50B2 **Sierra Nevada** *Mts* Spain
21A2 **Sierra Nevada** *Mts* USA
32C1 **Sierra Nevada de Santa Marta** *Mts* Colombia
34B2 **Sierra Pié de Palo** *Mts* Arg
47B1 **Sierre** Switz
55B3 **Sífnos** *I* Greece
59C3 **Sighetu Marmaţiei** Rom
54B1 **Sighişoara** Rom
38B1 **Siglufjörður** Iceland
50B1 **Sigüenza** Spain
97B3 **Siguiri** Guinea
85E4 **Sihora** India
93D2 **Siirt** Turk
68B3 **Sikai Hu** *L* China
85D3 **Sikar** India
84B2 **Sikaram** *Mt* Afghan
97B3 **Sikasso** Mali
18C2 **Sikeston** USA
55C3 **Síkinos** *I* Greece
55B3 **Sikionía** Greece
86B1 **Sikkim** State, India
50A1 **Sil** *R* Spain
47D1 **Silandro** Italy
23A1 **Silao** Mexico
79B3 **Silay** Phil
86C2 **Silchar** India
96C2 **Silet** Alg
86A1 **Silgarhi** Nepal
92B2 **Silifke** Turk
82C2 **Siling Co** *L* China
54C2 **Silistra** Bulg
39F7 **Silkeborg** Den
47E1 **Sillian** Austria
18B2 **Siloam Springs** USA
19B3 **Silsbee** USA
95A3 **Şiltou** *Well* Chad
58C1 **Šilute** Lithuania
93D2 **Silvan** Turk
35B1 **Silvania** Brazil
85C4 **Silvassa** India
21B2 **Silver City** Nevada, USA
9C3 **Silver City** New Mexico, USA
20B2 **Silver Lake** USA
16A3 **Silver Spring** USA
13B2 **Silverthrone Mt** Can
108B2 **Silverton** Aust
47C1 **Silvretta** *Mts* Austria/Switz
78C2 **Simanggang** Malay
76C1 **Simao** China
90A3 **Simareh** *R* Iran
55C3 **Simav** Turk
55C3 **Simav** *R* Turk
15C2 **Simcoe,L** Can
70A3 **Simeulue** *I* Indon
60D5 **Simferopol'** Ukraine
55C3 **Sími** *I* Greece
84D2 **Simla** India
46D1 **Simmern** Germany
13B2 **Simoon Sound** Can
49D2 **Simplon** *Mt* Switz
47C1 **Simplon** *P* Switz
4C2 **Simpson,C** USA
106C3 **Simpson Desert** Aust
6B3 **Simpson Pen** Can
39G7 **Simrishamn** Sweden
69H2 **Simushir** *I* Russian Fed
99E2 **Sina Dhaqa** Somalia
92B4 **Sinai** *Pen* Egypt
32B2 **Sincelejo** Colombia
17B1 **Sinclair,L** USA
85D3 **Sind** *R* India
85B3 **Sindh** Region, Pak
55C3 **Sindirği** Turk
86B2 **Sindri** India
50A2 **Sines** Port
99D1 **Singa** Sudan
77C5 **Singapore** Republic, S E Asia
77C5 **Singapore,Str of** S E Asia
78D4 **Singaraja** Indon
99D3 **Singida** Tanz
78B2 **Singkawang** Indon
109D2 **Singleton** Aust
78A3 **Singtep** *I* Indon
76B1 **Singu** Burma
53A2 **Siniscola** Sardgena
93D2 **Sinjár** Iraq
84B2 **Sinkai Hills** *Mts* Afghan
95C3 **Sinkat** Sudan
82C1 **Sinkiang** Autonomous Region, China
33G2 **Sinnamary** French Guiana
92C1 **Sinop** Turk
54B1 **Sîntana** Rom
78C2 **Sintang** Indon
50A2 **Sintra** Port
32B2 **Sinú** *R* Colombia
74A2 **Sinŭiju** N Korea
59B3 **Siofok** Hung
47B1 **Sion** Switz
8D2 **Sioux City** USA
8D2 **Sioux Falls** USA
10A2 **Sioux Lookout** Can
79B4 **Sipalay** Phil
27L1 **Siparia** Trinidad
69E2 **Siping** China
112B3 **Siple** *Base* Ant
112B5 **Siple I** Ant
79B3 **Sipocot** Phil
70A4 **Sipora** Indon
79B4 **Siquijor** *I* Phil
87B2 **Sira** India
53C3 **Siracusa** Italy
86B2 **Sirajganj** Bang
13C2 **Sir Alexander,Mt** Can
91B5 **Sīr Banī Yās** *I* UAE
106C2 **Sir Edward Pellew Group** *Is* Aust
54C1 **Siret** *R* Rom
12J2 **Sir James McBrien,Mt** Can
87B2 **Sir Kālahasti** India
13D2 **Sir Laurier,Mt** Can
93D2 **Şirnak** Turk
85C4 **Sirohi** India
87B1 **Sironcha** India
85D4 **Sironj** India
55B3 **Síros** *I* Greece
91B4 **Sirri** *I* Iran
84D3 **Sirsa** India
13D2 **Sir Sandford,Mt** Can
87A2 **Sirsi** India
95A1 **Sirte Desert** Libya
95A1 **Sirte,G of** Libya
52C1 **Sisak** Croatia
76C2 **Sisaket** Thai
76C3 **Sisophon** Camb
46B2 **Sissonne** France
90D3 **Sistan** Region, Iran/Afghan
49D3 **Sisteron** France
63B2 **Sistig Khem** Russian Fed
86A1 **Sītāpur** India
55C3 **Sitía** Greece
4E4 **Sitka** USA
12D3 **Sitkalidak I** USA
12D3 **Sitkinak** *I* USA
76B2 **Sittang** *R* Burma
46C1 **Sittard** Neth
86C2 **Sittwe** Burma
78C4 **Situbondo** Indon
92C2 **Sivas** Turk
93C2 **Siverek** Turk
92B2 **Sivrihisar** Turk
95B2 **Siwa** Egypt

84D2 **Siwalik Range** *Mts* India
86A1 **Siwalik Range** *Mts* Nepal
72D3 **Siyang** China
56C1 **Sjaelland** *I* Den
39G7 **Skagen** Den
39F7 **Skagerrak** *Str* Nor/Den
20B1 **Skagit** *R* USA
20B1 **Skagit Mt** Can
4E4 **Skagway** USA
39G7 **Skara** Sweden
59C2 **Skarzysko-Kamlenna** Pol
5F4 **Skeena** *R* Can
13B1 **Skeena Mts** Can
4D3 **Skeenjek** *R* USA
42E3 **Skegness** Eng
38H5 **Skellefte** *R* Sweden
38J6 **Skellefteå** Sweden
55B3 **Skíathos** *I* Greece
45B3 **Skibbereen** Irish Rep
5E4 **Skidegate** Can
58C2 **Skiemiewice** Pol
39F7 **Skien** Nor
96C1 **Skikda** Alg
74C4 **Skikoku** *I* Japan
42D3 **Skipton** Eng
55B3 **Skíros** *I* Greece
39F7 **Skive** Den
56B1 **Skjern** Den
6F3 **Skjoldungen** Greenland
14A2 **Skokie** USA
55B3 **Skópelos** *I* Greece
54B2 **Skopje** Macedonia, Yugos
39G7 **Skövde** Sweden
63E2 **Skovorodino** Russian Fed
4C3 **Skwentna** USA
58B2 **Skwierzyna** Pol
40B2 **Skye** *I* Scot
39G7 **Slagelse** Den
45C2 **Slaney** *R* Irish Rep
54B2 **Slatina** Rom
78C4 **Slaung** Indon
5G3 **Slave** *R* Can
13E1 **Slave Lake** Can
65J4 **Slavgorod** Russian Fed
59D2 **Slavuta** Ukraine
60E4 **Slavyansk** Ukraine
44B3 **Sleat,Sound of** *Chan* Scot
12C2 **Sleetmute** USA
45C2 **Sleeve Bloom** *Mts* Irish Rep
19C3 **Slidell** USA
16B2 **Slide Mt** USA
45B1 **Sligo** County, Irish Rep
41B3 **Sligo** Irish Rep
41B3 **Sligo** *B* Irish Rep
54C2 **Sliven** Bulg
54C2 **Slobozia** Rom
13D3 **Slocan** Can
58D2 **Slonim** Belorussia
43D4 **Slough** Eng
22B2 **Slough** *R* USA
52B1 **Slovenia** Republic, Europe
59B3 **Slovensko** Region, Czech
56C2 **Slubice** Pol
59D2 **Sluch'** *R* Ukraine
58B2 **Słupsk** Pol
58D2 **Slutsk** Belorussia
58D2 **Slutsk** *R* Belorussia
41A3 **Slyne Head** *Pt* Irish Rep
63C2 **Slyudyanka** Russian Fed
7D4 **Smallwood Res** Can
54B2 **Smederevo** Serbia, Yugos
54B2 **Smederevska Palanka** Serbia, Yugos
60D4 **Smela** Ukraine
15C2 **Smethport** USA
13E1 **Smith** Can
4F3 **Smith Arm** *B* Can
13B2 **Smithers** Can
7C3 **Smith I** Can
13B2 **Smith Sd** Can
15C2 **Smiths Falls** Can
109C4 **Smithton** Aust
13D1 **Smoky** *R* Can
109D2 **Smoky C** Aust
13E2 **Smoky Lake** Can
38F6 **Smøla** *I* Nor
60D3 **Smolensk** Russian Fed
55B2 **Smólikas** *Mt* Greece
54B2 **Smolyan** Bulg
58D2 **Smorgon'** Belorussia
16B3 **Smyrna** Delaware, USA
17B1 **Smyrna** Georgia, USA
42B2 **Snaefell** *Mt* Eng
38B2 **Snafell** *Mt* Iceland
8B2 **Snake** *R* USA
8B2 **Snake River Canyon** USA
56B2 **Sneek** Neth
45B3 **Sneem** Irish Rep
22B2 **Snelling** USA
59B2 **Sněžka** *Mt* Pol/Czech
38F6 **Snøhetta** *Mt* Nor
20B1 **Snohomish** USA
20B1 **Snoqualmie P** USA
76D3 **Snoul** Camb
43B3 **Snowdon** *Mt* Wales
43B3 **Snowdonia Nat Pk** Wales
4G3 **Snowdrift** Can
5H4 **Snow Lake** Can
108A2 **Snowtown** Aust
109C3 **Snowy Mts** Aust
9C3 **Snyder** USA
74B4 **Soan-kundo** *I* S Korea
99D2 **Sobat** *R* Sudan
31C2 **Sobral** Brazil
58C2 **Sochaczew** Pol
61E5 **Sochi** Russian Fed
9C3 **Socorro** USA
24A3 **Socorro** *I* Mexico
34A2 **Socos** Chile
81D4 **Socotra** *I* Yemen
38K5 **Sodankylä** Fin
39H6 **Soderhamn** Sweden
39H7 **Södertälje** Sweden
99C1 **Sodiri** Sudan
99D2 **Sodo** Eth
46E1 **Soest** Germany
101C2 **Sofala** Mozam
Sofia = Sofiya
54B2 **Sofiya** Bulg
69G4 **Sofu Gan** *I* Japan
32C2 **Sogamoso** Colombia
39F6 **Sognefjorden** *Inlet* Nor
82D2 **Sog Xian** China
95C2 **Sohâg** Egypt
84D3 **Sohīpat** India
46B1 **Soignies** Belg
46B2 **Soissons** France
85C3 **Sojat** India
74A3 **Sŏjosŏn-man** *B* N Korea
92A2 **Söke** Turk
97C4 **Sokodé** Togo
61E2 **Sokol** Russian Fed
58C2 **Sokołka** Pol
97B3 **Sokolo** Mali
6H3 **Søkongens Øy** *I* Greenland
99D1 **Sokota** Eth
97C3 **Sokoto** Nig
97C3 **Sokoto** *R* Nig
111A3 **Solander I** NZ
79B2 **Solano** Phil
87B1 **Solapur** India
47D1 **Solbad Hall** Austria
47D1 **Sölden** Austria
12D2 **Soldotna** USA
26C4 **Soledad** Colombia
43D4 **Solent** *Sd* Eng
46B1 **Solesmes** France
58D2 **Soligorsk** Belorussia
61J2 **Solikamsk** Russian Fed
32C4 **Solimões** *R* Peru
46D1 **Solingen** Germany
38H6 **Sollefteå** Sweden
61H3 **Sol'lletsk** Russian Fed
70B4 **Solok** Indon
105G4 **Solomon** *Is* Pacific O
47B1 **Solothurn** Switz
39F8 **Soltau** Germany
22B3 **Solvang** USA
42C2 **Solway Firth** *Estuary* Eng/Scot
100B2 **Solwezi** Zambia
75C1 **Sōma** Japan
55C3 **Soma** Turk
81C5 **Somalia** Republic, E Africa
54A1 **Sombor** Serbia, Yugos
107D2 **Somerset** Aust
43C4 **Somerset** County, Eng
16D2 **Somerset** Massachusetts, USA
15C2 **Somerset** Pennsylvania, USA
100B4 **Somerset East** S Africa
6A2 **Somerset I** Can
16B3 **Somers Point** USA
16B2 **Somerville** USA
19A3 **Somerville Res** USA
54B1 **Somes** *R* Rom
46B2 **Somme** Department, France
46B2 **Somme** *R* France
46C2 **Sommesous** France
86A2 **Son** *R* India
74A3 **Sonch'ŏn** N Korea
39F8 **Sønderborg** Den
6E3 **Søndre Strømfjord** Greenland
47C1 **Sondrio** Italy
76D3 **Song Ba** *R* Viet
76D3 **Song Cau** Viet
101C2 **Songea** Tanz
73E3 **Songjiang** China
77C4 **Songkhla** Thai
74B3 **Songnim** N Korea
77C5 **Sông Pahang** *R* Malay
72A3 **Songpan** China
72C1 **Sonid Youqi** China
76C1 **Son La** Viet
85B3 **Sonmiani** Pak
85B3 **Sonmiani Bay** Pak
22A1 **Sonoma** USA
22B2 **Sonora** California, USA
24A2 **Sonora** *R* Mexico
9B3 **Sonoran Desert** USA
22C1 **Sonora P** USA
25D3 **Sonsonate** El Salvador
71E3 **Sonsorol** *I* Pacific O
10B2 **Soo Canals** Can/USA
13C3 **Sooke** Can
58B2 **Sopot** Pol
59B3 **Sopron** Hung
22B2 **Soquel** USA
53B2 **Sora** Italy
94B3 **Sored** *R* Israel
15D1 **Sorel** Can
109C4 **Sorell** Aust
92C2 **Sorgun** Turk
50B1 **Soria** Spain
38J5 **Sørkjosen** Nor
64C2 **Sørksop** *I* Barents S
61H4 **Sor Mertvyy Kultuk** *Plain* Kazakhstan
35B2 **Sorocaba** Brazil
61H3 **Sorochinsk** Russian Fed
71F3 **Soroi** *I* Pacific O
60C4 **Soroki** Moldavia
71E4 **Sorong** Indon
71E4 **Sorong** Province, Indon
99D2 **Soroti** Uganda
38J4 **Sørøya** *I* Nor
53B2 **Sorrento** Italy
38K5 **Sorsatunturi** *Mt* Fin
38H5 **Sorsele** Sweden
79B3 **Sorsogon** Phil
38L6 **Sortavala** Russian Fed
74B3 **Sŏsan** S Korea
59B2 **Sosnowiec** Pol
65H4 **Sos'va** Russian Fed
98B2 **Souanké** Congo
97B4 **Soubré** Ivory Coast
16B2 **Souderton** USA
27P2 **Soufrière** St Lucia
27N2 **Soufrière** *V* St Vincent
48C3 **Souillac** France
96C1 **Souk Ahras** Alg
74B3 **Soul** S Korea
51C2 **Soummam** *R* Alg
Sour = Tyr
101G1 **Sources,Mt aux** Lesotho
31D3 **Sousa** Brazil
96D1 **Sousse** Tunisia
100B4 **South Africa** Republic, Africa
16B2 **South Amboy** USA
14B2 **Southampton** Can
43D4 **Southampton** Eng
16C2 **Southampton** USA
6B3 **Southampton I** Can
28F6 **South Atlantic O**
7D4 **South Aulatsivik I** Can
106C3 **South Australia** State, Aust
104E5 **South Australian Basin** Indian O
19C3 **Southaven** USA
17B2 **South Bay** USA
14B1 **South Baymouth** Can
14A2 **South Bend** Indiana, USA
20B1 **South Bend** Washington, USA
16D1 **Southbridge** USA
South Cape = Ka Lae
11B3 **South Carolina** State, USA
70C2 **South China S** S E Asia
8C2 **South Dakota** State, USA
16C1 **South Deerfield** USA
43D4 **South Downs** Eng
109C4 **South East C** Aust
111A2 **Southen Alps** *Mts* NZ
5H4 **Southend** Can
43E4 **Southend-on-Sea** Eng
111A2 **Southern Alps** *Mts* NZ
106A4 **Southern Cross** Aust
5J4 **Southern Indian L** Can
27H2 **Southfield** Jamaica
105G5 **South Fiji Basin** Pacific O
12D2 **South Fork** *R* Alaska, USA
22B1 **South Fork** *R* California, USA
28F8 **South Georgia** *I* S Atlantic O
43C4 **South Glamorgan** County, Wales
14A2 **South Haven** USA
5J3 **South Henik L** Can
104F3 **South Honshu Ridge** Pacific O
111A2 **South I** NZ
16C2 **Southington** USA
74B3 **South Korea** Republic, S E Asia
21A2 **South Lake Tahoe** USA
112C8 **South Magnetic Pole** Ant
17B2 **South Miami** USA
16A3 **South Mt** USA
4F3 **South Nahanni** *R* Can
26G1 **South Negril Pt** Jamaica
103F8 **South Orkney** *Is* Atlantic O
8C2 **South Platte** *R* USA
80E **South Pole** Ant
42C3 **Southport** Eng

27R3 **South Pt** Barbados
16B2 **South River** USA
44C2 **South Ronaldsay** *I* Scot
103G7 **South Sandwich Trench** Atlantic O
22A2 **South San Francisco** USA
5H4 **South Saskatchewan** *R* Can
42D2 **South Shields** Eng
110B1 **South Taranaki Bight** *B* NZ
44A3 **South Uist** *I* Scot
South West Africa = Namibia
107D5 **South West C** Aust
105J5 **South West Pacific Basin** Pacific O
103D5 **South West Peru Ridge** Pacific O
43D3 **South Yorkshire** County, Eng
58C1 **Sovetsk** Russian Fed
61G2 **Sovetsk** Russian Fed
101G1 **Soweto** S Africa
98B3 **Soyo Congo** Angola
60D3 **Sozh** *R* Belorussia
46C1 **Spa** Belg
50A1 **Spain** Kingdom
Spalato = Split
43D3 **Spalding** Eng
14B1 **Spanish** *R* Can
26B3 **Spanish Town** Jamaica
21B2 **Sparks** USA
11B3 **Spartanburg** USA
55B3 **Spartí** Greece
69F2 **Spassk Dal'niy** Russian Fed
27R3 **Speightstown** Barbados
12E2 **Spenard** USA
14A3 **Spencer** Indiana, USA
8D2 **Spencer** Iowa, USA
6A3 **Spencer Bay** Can
108A3 **Spencer,C** Aust
108A2 **Spencer G** Aust
6C3 **Spencer I** Can
111B2 **Spenser Mts** NZ
45C1 **Sperrin** *Mts* N Ire
44C3 **Spey** *R* Scot
57B3 **Speyer** Germany
27K1 **Speyside** Tobago
47B1 **Spiez** Switz
12F1 **Spike Mt** USA
20C1 **Spirit Lake** USA
5G4 **Spirit River** Can
Spitsbergen = Svalbard
64C2 **Spitsbergen** *I* Barents S
57C3 **Spittal** Austria
38F6 **Spjelkavik** Nor
52C2 **Split** Croatia
47C1 **Splügen** Switz
20C1 **Spokane** USA
55C3 **Sporádhes** *Is* Greece
20C2 **Spray** USA
56C2 **Spree** *R* Germany
100A3 **Springbok** S Africa
18B2 **Springdale** USA
10B3 **Springfield** Illinois, USA
10C2 **Springfield** Massachusetts, USA
18B2 **Springfield** Missouri, USA
14B3 **Springfield** Ohio, USA
20B2 **Springfield** Oregon, USA
15D2 **Springfield** Vermont, USA
100B4 **Springfontein** S Africa
101G1 **Springs** S Africa
41D3 **Spurn Head** *Pt* Eng
13C3 **Squamish** Can
60E3 **Sredne-Russkaya Vozvyshennost** *Upland* Russian Fed
63B1 **Sredne Sibirskoye Ploskogorve** *Tableland* Russian Fed
61J2 **Sredniy Ural** *Mts* Russian Fed
76D3 **Srepok** *R* Camb
68D1 **Sretensk** Russian Fed
76C3 **Sre Umbell** Camb
83C5 **Sri Lanka** Republic, S Asia
84C2 **Srīnagar** Pak
87A1 **Srīvardhan** India
58B2 **Sroda** Pol
30H6 **Sta Clara** *I* Chile
32J7 **Sta Cruz** *I* Ecuador
56B2 **Stade** Germany
44A3 **Staffa** *I* Scot
43C3 **Stafford** County, Eng
43C3 **Stafford** Eng
16C2 **Stafford Springs** USA
Stalingrad = Volgograd
6A1 **Stallworthy,C** Can
59C2 **Stalowa Wola** Pol
32J7 **Sta Maria** *I* Ecuador
16C2 **Stamford** Connecticut, USA
16B1 **Stamford** New York, USA
100A3 **Stampriet** Namibia
101G1 **Standerton** S Africa
14B2 **Standish** USA
101H1 **Stanger** S Africa
22B2 **Stanislaus** *R* USA
54B2 **Stanke Dimitrov** Bulg
109C4 **Stanley** Aust
29E6 **Stanley** Falkland Is
87B2 **Stanley Res** India
Stanleyville = Kisangani
25D3 **Stann Creek** Belize
63E2 **Stanovoy Khrebet** *Mts* Russian Fed
47C1 **Stans** Switz
109D1 **Stanthorpe** Aust
59C2 **Starachowice** Pol
54B2 **Stara Planiná** *Mts* Bulg
60D2 **Staraya Russa** Russian Fed
54C2 **Stara Zagora** Bulg
58B2 **Stargard** Pol
19C3 **Starkville** USA
57C3 **Starnberg** Germany
58B2 **Starogard Gdanski** Pol
59D3 **Starokonstantinov** Ukraine
43C4 **Start Pt** Eng
60E3 **Staryy Oskol** Russian Fed
15C2 **State College** USA
16B2 **Staten I** USA
17B1 **Statesboro** USA
15C3 **Staunton** USA
39F7 **Stavanger** Nor
46C1 **Stavelot** Belg
61F4 **Stavropol'** Russian Fed
108B3 **Stawell** Aust
58B2 **Stawno** Pol
20B2 **Stayton** USA
12B2 **Stebbins** USA
12F2 **Steele,Mt** Can
16A2 **Steelton** USA
20C2 **Steens Mt** USA
6E2 **Steenstrups Gletscher** *Gl* Greenland
4H2 **Stefansson I** Can
101H1 **Stegi** Swaziland
47D1 **Steinach** Austria
8D2 **Steinback** Can
38G6 **Steinkjer** Nor
13C2 **Stein Mt** Can
23B2 **Stemaco** Mexico
46C2 **Stenay** France
56C2 **Stendal** Germany
110B2 **Stephens,C** NZ
108B2 **Stephens Creek** Aust
14A1 **Stephenson** USA
12H3 **Stephens Pass** USA
7E5 **Stephenville** Can
100B4 **Sterkstroom** S Africa
8C2 **Sterling** Colorado, USA
14B2 **Sterling Heights** USA
61J3 **Sterlitamak** Russian Fed
13E2 **Stettler** Can
14B2 **Steubenville** USA
4D3 **Stevens Village** USA
13B1 **Stewart** Can
21B2 **Stewart** USA
12G2 **Stewart** *R* Can
12G2 **Stewart Crossing** Can
111A3 **Stewart I** NZ
107F1 **Stewart Is** Solomon Is
4E3 **Stewart River** Can
16A3 **Stewartstown** USA
101G1 **Steyn** S Africa
57C3 **Steyr** Austria
12G3 **Stika** USA
12H3 **Stikine** *R* Can
12H3 **Stikine Ranges** *Mts* Can
18A2 **Stillwater** Oklahoma, USA
21B2 **Stillwater Range** *Mts* USA
108A2 **Stirling** Aust
44C3 **Stirling** Scot
16C1 **Stockbridge** USA
59B3 **Stockerau** Austria
39H7 **Stockholm** Sweden
42C3 **Stockport** Eng
22B2 **Stockton** California, USA
42D2 **Stockton** Eng
18B2 **Stockton L** USA
43C3 **Stoke-on-Trent** Eng
38A2 **Stokkseyri** Iceland
38G5 **Stokmarknes** Nor
39K8 **Stolbtsy** Belorussia
58D2 **Stolin** Belorussia
16B3 **Stone Harbor** USA
44C3 **Stonehaven** Scot
19A3 **Stonewall** USA
12D2 **Stony** *R* USA
38H5 **Storavan** *L* Sweden
38G6 **Støren** Nor
109C4 **Storm B** Aust
44A2 **Stornoway** Scot
59D3 **Storozhinets** Ukraine
16C2 **Storrs** USA
38G6 **Storsjön** *L* Sweden
38H5 **Storuman** Sweden
16D1 **Stoughton** USA
43E3 **Stowmarket** Eng
45C1 **Strablane** N Ire
109C4 **Strahan** Aust
56C2 **Stralsund** Germany
38F6 **Stranda** Nor
39H7 **Strängnäs** Sweden
42B2 **Stranraer** Scot
49D2 **Strasbourg** France
15C3 **Strasburg** USA
14B2 **Stratford** Can
16C2 **Stratford** Connecticut, USA
110B1 **Stratford** NZ
43D3 **Stratford-on-Avon** Eng
108A3 **Strathalbyn** Aust
42B2 **Strathclyde** Region, Scot
13E2 **Strathmore** Can
18C1 **Streator** USA
47C2 **Stresa** Italy
53C3 **Stretto de Messina** *Str* Italy/Sicily
38D3 **Streymoy** Føroyar
53C3 **Stroboli** *I* Italy
6E3 **Strømfjord** Greenland
44C2 **Stromness** Scot
18A1 **Stromsburg** USA
38H6 **Stromsund** Sweden
38G6 **Ströms Vattudal** *L* Sweden
44C2 **Stronsay** *I* Scot
43C4 **Stroud** Eng
16B2 **Stroudsburg** USA
54B2 **Struma** *R* Bulg
43B3 **Strumble Head** *Pt* Wales
55B2 **Strumica** Macedonia, Yugos
59C3 **Stryy** Ukraine
59C3 **Stryy** *R* Ukraine
108B1 **Strzelecki Creek** *R* Aust
17B2 **Stuart** Florida, USA
13C2 **Stuart** *R* Can
12B2 **Stuart I** USA
13C2 **Stuart L** Can
47D1 **Stubaier Alpen** *Mts* Austria
76D3 **Stung Sen** Camb
76D3 **Stung Treng** Camb
52A2 **Stura** *R* Italy
112C7 **Sturge I** Ant
14A2 **Sturgeon Bay** USA
14C1 **Sturgeon Falls** Can
18C2 **Sturgis** Kentucky, USA
14A2 **Sturgis** Michigan, USA
106B2 **Sturt Creek** *R* Aust
108B1 **Sturt Desert** Aust
100B4 **Stuttemeim** S Africa
19B3 **Stuttgart** USA
57B3 **Stuttgart** Germany
38A1 **Stykkishólmur** Iceland
59D2 **Styr'** *R* Ukraine
35C1 **Suaçuí Grande** *R* Brazil
81B4 **Suakin** Sudan
73E5 **Su-ao** Taiwan
34C2 **Suardi** Arg
78B2 **Subi** *I* Indon
54A1 **Subotica** Serbia, Yugos
60C4 **Suceava** Rom
45B2 **Suck** *R* Irish Rep
30C2 **Sucre** Bol
35A1 **Sucuriú** *R* Brazil
98C1 **Sudan** Republic, Africa
14B1 **Sudbury** Can
43E3 **Sudbury** Eng
99C2 **Sudd** *Swamp* Sudan
33F2 **Suddie** Guyana
98C2 **Sue** *R* Sudan
4H2 **Suerdrup Is** Can
92B4 **Suez** Egypt
92B3 **Suez Canal** Egypt
92B4 **Suez,G of** Egypt
16B2 **Suffern** USA
43E3 **Suffolk** County, Eng
109D2 **Sugarloaf Pt** Aust
91C5 **Suhār** Oman
68C1 **Sühbaatar** Mongolia
84B3 **Sui** Pak
72C2 **Suide** China
69E2 **Suihua** China
73B3 **Suining** China
46C2 **Suippes** France
41B3 **Suir** *R* Irish Rep
73C3 **Sui Xian** China
72E1 **Suizhong** China
85C3 **Sujāngarh** India
78B4 **Sukabumi** Indon
78C3 **Sukadana** Borneo, Indon
78B4 **Sukadana** Sumatra, Indon
74E3 **Sukagawa** Japan
78C3 **Sukaraya** Indon
60E3 **Sukhinichi** Russian Fed
61F2 **Sukhona** *R* Russian Fed
61F5 **Sukhumi** Georgia
6E3 **Sukkertoppen** Greenland
6E3 **Sukkertoppen** *L* Greenland
38L6 **Sukkozero** Russian Fed
85B3 **Sukkur** Pak
87C1 **Sukma** India
95A2 **Sūknah** Libya
100A3 **Sukses** Namibia
75A2 **Sukumo** Japan

13C1 **Sukunka** *R* Can
60E3 **Sula** *R* Russian Fed
84B3 **Sulaiman Range** *Mts* Pak
70C4 **Sulawesi** *I* Indon
93E3 **Sulaymānīyah** Iraq
54C1 **Sulina** Rom
38H5 **Sulitjelma** Nor
32A4 **Sullana** Peru
18B2 **Sullivan** USA
13B2 **Sullivan Bay** Can
13E2 **Sullivan L** Can
52B2 **Sulmona** Italy
19B3 **Sulphur** Louisiana, USA
19A3 **Sulphur** Oklahoma, USA
19A3 **Sulphur Springs** USA
86A1 **Sultānpur** India
79B4 **Sulu Arch** Phil
70C3 **Sulu S** Philip
30D4 **Sumampa** Arg
70B4 **Sumatera** *I* Indon
70C4 **Sumba** *I* Indon
78D4 **Sumbawa** *I* Indon
78D4 **Sumbawa Besar** Indon
99D3 **Sumbawanga** Tanz
100A2 **Sumbe** Angola
44E2 **Sumburgh Head** *Pt* Scot
78C4 **Sumenep** Indon
69G3 **Sumisu** *I* Japan
13D3 **Summerland** Can
5F4 **Summit Lake** Can
21B2 **Summit Mt** USA
111B2 **Sumner,L** NZ
75A2 **Sumoto** Japan
17B1 **Sumter** USA
60D3 **Sumy** Ukraine
16A2 **Sunbury** USA
34C2 **Sunchales** Arg
74B3 **Sunch'ŏn** N Korea
74B4 **Sunch'ŏn** S Korea
86A2 **Sundargarh** India
86B2 **Sunderbans** *Swamp* India
42D2 **Sunderland** Eng
13E2 **Sundre** Can
15C1 **Sundridge** Can
38H6 **Sundsvall** Sweden
38D3 **Suduroy** Føroyar
78D3 **Sungaianyar** Indon
78A3 **Sungaisalak** Indon
20C1 **Sunnyside** USA
21A2 **Sunnyvale** USA
63D1 **Suntar** Russian Fed
97B4 **Sunyani** Ghana
75A2 **Suō-nada** *B* Japan
38K6 **Suonejoki** Fin
86B1 **Supaul** India
18A1 **Superior** Nebraska, USA
10A2 **Superior** Wisconsin, USA
10B2 **Superior,L** Can/USA
76C3 **Suphan Buri** Thai
93D2 **Süphan Dağ** Turk
71E4 **Supiori** *I* Indon
93E3 **Suq ash Suyukh** Iraq
72D3 **Suqian** China
Suqutra = Socotra
91C5 **Sūr** Oman
61G3 **Sura** *R* Russian Fed
78C4 **Surabaya** Indon
75B2 **Suraga-wan** *B* Japan
78C4 **Surakarta** Indon
109C1 **Surat** Aust
85C4 **Sūrat** India
84C3 **Sūratgarh** India
77B4 **Surat Thani** Thai
85C4 **Surendranagar** India
16B3 **Surf City** USA
64J3 **Surgut** Russian Fed
87B1 **Suriāpet** India
49D2 **Sürich** Switz
79C4 **Surigao** Phil
76C3 **Surin** Thai
33F3 **Surinam** Republic, S America
43D4 **Surrey** County, Eng
47C1 **Sursee** Switz
95A1 **Surt** Libya
38A2 **Surtsey** *I* Iceland
78A3 **Surulangan** Indon
47B2 **Susa** Italy
75A2 **Susa** Japan
75A2 **Susaki** Japan
21A1 **Susanville** USA
47D1 **Süsch** Switz
12E2 **Susitna** *R* USA
16A3 **Susquehanna** *R* USA
16B2 **Sussex** USA
43D4 **Sussex West** Eng
13B1 **Sustut Peak** *Mt* Can
100B4 **Sutherland** S Africa
84C2 **Sutlej** *R* Pak
21A2 **Sutter Creek** USA
14B3 **Sutton** USA
12C3 **Sutwik I** USA
74D3 **Suwa** Japan
58C2 **Suwałki** Pol
17B2 **Suwannee** *R* USA
94B2 **Suweilih** Jordan
74B3 **Suwŏn** S Korea
72D3 **Su Xian** China
75B1 **Suzaka** Japan
73E3 **Suzhou** China
74D3 **Suzu** Japan
75B2 **Suzuka** Japan
75B1 **Suzu-misaki** *C* Japan
64C2 **Svalbard** *Is* Barents S
59C3 **Svalyava** Ukraine
38G5 **Svartisen** *Mt* Nor
76D3 **Svay Rieng** Camb
38G6 **Sveg** Sweden
39G7 **Svendborg** Den
6A1 **Sverdrup Chan** Can
69F2 **Svetlaya** Russian Fed
58C2 **Svetlogorsk** Russian Fed
39K6 **Svetogorsk** Russian Fed
54B2 **Svetozarevo** Serbia, Yugos
54C2 **Svilengrad** Bulg
58D2 **Svir'** Belorussia
59B3 **Švitavy** Czech
69E1 **Svobodnyy** Russian Fed
38G5 **Svolvaer** Nor
107E3 **Swain Reefs** Aust
17B1 **Swainsboro** USA
100A3 **Swakopmund** Namibia
42D2 **Swale** *R* Eng
70C3 **Swallow Reef** *I* S E Asia
87B2 **Swāmihalli** India
25D3 **Swan** *I* Honduras
43D4 **Swanage** Eng
108B3 **Swan Hill** Aust
13D2 **Swan Hills** Can
13D2 **Swan Hills** *Mts* Can
26A3 **Swan I** Caribbean S
5H4 **Swan River** Can
43C4 **Swansea** Wales
43C4 **Swansea B** Wales
101G1 **Swartruggens** S Africa
Swatow = Shantou
101H1 **Swaziland** Kingdom, S Africa
39G7 **Sweden** Kingdom, N Europe
20B2 **Sweet Home** USA
9C3 **Sweetwater** USA
100B4 **Swellendam** S Africa
59B2 **Świdnica** Pol
58B2 **Świdwin** Pol
58B2 **Świebodzin** Pol
58B2 **Świecie** Pol
5H4 **Swift Current** Can
43D4 **Swindon** Eng
45B2 **Swinford** Irish Rep
56C2 **Świnoujście** Pol
49D2 **Switzerland** Federal Republic, Europe
45C2 **Swords** Irish Rep
109D2 **Sydney** Aust
7D5 **Sydney** Can
64G3 **Syktyvkar** Russian Fed
17A1 **Sylacauga** USA
38G6 **Sylarna** *Mt* Sweden
86C2 **Sylhet** Bang
56B1 **Sylt** *I* Germany
14B2 **Sylvania** USA
112C11 **Syowa** *Base* Ant
Syracuse = Siracusa
15C2 **Syracuse** USA
65H5 **Syrdar'ya** *R* Kazakhstan
93C2 **Syria** Republic, S W Asia
61J2 **Sysert'** Russian Fed
61G3 **Syzran'** Russian Fed
56C2 **Szczecin** Pol
58B2 **Szczecinek** Pol
58C2 **Szczytno** Pol
59C3 **Szeged** Hung
59B3 **Székesfehérvar** Hung
59B3 **Szekszard** Hung
59B3 **Szolnok** Hung
59B3 **Szombathely** Hung
58B2 **Szprotawa** Pol

T

90C3 **Tabas** Iran
23A1 **Tabasco** Mexico
32D4 **Tabatinga** Brazil
96B2 **Tabelbala** Alg
76C3 **Tabeng** Camb
13E2 **Taber** Can
79B3 **Tablas** *I* Phil
100A4 **Table Mt** S Africa
12F1 **Table Mt** USA
18B2 **Table Rock Res** USA
78B3 **Taboali** Indon
57C3 **Tábor** Czech
99D3 **Tabora** Tanz
97B4 **Tabou** Ivory Coast
90A2 **Tabrīz** Iran
92C4 **Tabūk** S Arabia
23A2 **Tacámbaro** Mexico
82C1 **Tacheng** China
79C3 **Tacloban** Phil
30B2 **Tacna** Peru
8A2 **Tacoma** USA
99E1 **Tadjoura** Djibouti
87B2 **Tādpatri** India
74B3 **Taebaek Sanmaek** *Mts* S Korea
74B3 **Taegu** S Korea
74B4 **Taehŭksan** *I* S Korea
74B3 **Taejŏn** S Korea
51B1 **Tafalla** Spain
96C2 **Tafasaset** *Watercourse* Alg
43C4 **Taff** *R* Wales
94B3 **Tafila** Jordan
60E4 **Taganrog** Ukraine
97A3 **Tagant** Region, Maur
79B4 **Tagbilaran** Phil
96B2 **Taguenout Hagguerete** *Well* Maur
107E2 **Tagula** *I* Solomon Is
79C4 **Tagum** Phil
Tagus = Tejo
96C2 **Tahat** *Mt* Alg
105J4 **Tahiti** *I* Pacific O
18A2 **Tahlequah** USA
21A2 **Tahoe City** USA
21A2 **Tahoe,L** USA
97C3 **Tahoua** Niger
71D3 **Tahuna** Indon
72D2 **Tai'an** China
72B3 **Taibai Shan** *Mt* China
72D1 **Taibus Qi** China
73E5 **T'ai-chung** Taiwan
111B3 **Taieri** *R* NZ
72C2 **Taihang Shan** China
110C1 **Taihape** NZ
72E3 **Tai Hu** *L* China
108A3 **Tailem Bend** Aust
44B3 **Tain** Scot
73E5 **T'ai-nan** Taiwan
35C1 **Taiobeiras** Brazil
73E5 **T'ai pei** Taiwan
77C5 **Taiping** Malay
75C1 **Taira** Japan
78A3 **Tais** Indon
75A1 **Taisha** Japan
29B5 **Taitao,Pen de** Chile
73E5 **T'ai-tung** Taiwan
38K5 **Taivelkoski** Fin
69E4 **Taiwan** Republic, China
Taiwan Haixia = Formosa Str
72C2 **Taiyuan** China
72D3 **Taizhou** China
81C4 **Ta'izz** Yemen
82A2 **Tajikistan** Republic, Asia
50B1 **Tajo** *R* Spain
76B2 **Tak** Thai
74D3 **Takada** Japan
75A2 **Takahashi** Japan
110B2 **Takaka** NZ
74C4 **Takamatsu** Japan
74D3 **Takaoka** Japan
110B1 **Takapuna** NZ
74D3 **Takasaki** Japan
75B1 **Takayama** Japan
74D3 **Takefu** Japan
70A3 **Takengon** Indon
76C3 **Takeo** Camb
75A2 **Takeo** Japan
Take-shima = Tok-do
90A2 **Takestān** Iran
75A2 **Taketa** Japan
4G3 **Takjvak L** Can
99D1 **Takkaze** *R* Eth
13B1 **Takla L** Can
13B1 **Takla Landing** Can
12B2 **Takslesluk L** USA
12H2 **Taku Arm** *R* Can
23A1 **Tala** Mexico
59B3 **Talabanya** Hung
84C2 **Talagang** Pak
34A2 **Talagante** Chile
87B3 **Talaimannar** Sri Lanka
97C3 **Talak** *Desert* Region, Niger
78A3 **Talangbetutu** Indon
32A4 **Talara** Peru
50B2 **Talavera de la Reina** Spain
34A3 **Talca** Chile
34A3 **Talcahuano** Chile
86B2 **Tālcher** India
82B1 **Taldy Kurgan** Kazakhstan
71D4 **Taliabu** Indon
84B1 **Taligan** Afghan
99D2 **Tali Post** Sudan
78D4 **Taliwang** Indon
12D2 **Talkeetna** USA
12E2 **Talkeetna Mts** USA
17A1 **Talladega** USA
93D2 **Tall 'Afar** Iraq
17B1 **Tallahassee** USA
94C1 **Tall Bīsah** Syria
60B2 **Tallinn** Estonia
92C3 **Tall Kalakh** Syria
19B3 **Tallulah** USA
60D4 **Tal'noye** Ukraine
58C2 **Talpaki** Russian Fed
30B4 **Taltal** Chile
109C1 **Talwood** Aust
78D1 **Tamabo Range** *Mts* Malay
97B4 **Tamale** Ghana
96C2 **Tamanrasset** Alg
96C2 **Tamanrasset** *Watercourse* Alg
16B2 **Tamaqua** USA
Tamatave = Toamasina
23A2 **Tamazula** Jalisco, Mexico
23B2 **Tamazulapán** Mexico
23B1 **Tamazunchale** Mexico
97A3 **Tambacounda** Sen
61F3 **Tambov** Russian Fed
50A1 **Tambre** *R* Spain
98C2 **Tambura** Sudan
97A3 **Tamchaket** Maur
50A1 **Tamega** *R* Port
23B1 **Tamiahua** Mexico
87B2 **Tamil Nādu** State, India
76D2 **Tam Ky** Viet
17B2 **Tampa** USA
17B2 **Tampa B** USA
39J6 **Tampere** Fin
23B1 **Tampico** Mexico

68D2 **Tamsagbulag** Mongolia
86C2 **Tamu** Burma
23B1 **Tamuis** Mexico
109D2 **Tamworth** Aust
43D3 **Tamworth** Eng
38K4 **Tana** Nor
99D1 **Tana** *L* Eth
99E3 **Tana** *R* Kenya
38K5 **Tana** *R* Nor/Fin
75B2 **Tanabe** Japan
38K4 **Tanafjord** *Inlet* Nor
78D3 **Tanahgrogot** Indon
71E4 **Tanahmerah** Indon
12D1 **Tanana** USA
12E2 **Tanana** *R* USA
Tananarive = Antananarivo
47C2 **Tanaro** *R* Italy
74B2 **Tanch'ŏn** N Korea
34D3 **Tandil** Arg
78B2 **Tandjong Datu** *Pt* Indon
71E4 **Tandjung d'Urville** *C* Indon
78D3 **Tandjung Layar** *C* Indon
78B3 **Tandjung Lumut** *C* Indon
78D2 **Tandjung Mangkalihet** *C* Indon
78C3 **Tandjung Sambar** *C* Indon
78C2 **Tandjung Sirik** *C* Malay
71E4 **Tandjung Vals** *C* Indon
85B3 **Tando Adam** Pak
85B3 **Tando Muhammad Khan** Pak
108B2 **Tandou L** Aust
87B1 **Tāndūr** India
110C1 **Taneatua** NZ
76B2 **Tanen Range** *Mts* Burma/Thai
96B2 **Tanezrouft** *Desert Region* Alg
91C4 **Tang** Iran
99D3 **Tanga** Tanz
60E4 **Tanganrog** Russian Fed
99C3 **Tanganyika,L** Tanz/Zaïre
96B1 **Tanger** Mor
82C2 **Tanggula Shan** *Mts* China
Tangier = Tanger
78A2 **Tangjungpinang** Indon
82C2 **Tangra Yumco** *L* China
72D2 **Tangshan** China
79B4 **Tangub** Phil
63C2 **Tanguy** Russian Fed
79B4 **Tanjay** Phil
101D3 **Tanjona Ankaboa** *C* Madag
101D2 **Tanjona Babaomby** *C* Madag
101D2 **Tanjona Vilanandro** *C* Madag
101D3 **Tanjona Vohimena** *C* Madag
78C4 **Tanjong Bugel** *C* Indon
78B4 **Tanjong Cangkuang** *C* Indon
78C3 **Tanjong Puting** *C* Indon
78C3 **Tanjong Selatan** *C* Indon
78D3 **Tanjung** Indon
70A3 **Tanjungbalai** Indon
78A3 **Tanjung Jabung** *Pt* Indon
78B3 **Tanjungpandan** Indon
78B4 **Tanjung Priok** Indon
78D2 **Tanjungredeb** Indon
78D2 **Tanjungselor** Indon
84C2 **Tank** Pak
68B1 **Tannu Ola** *Mts* Russian Fed
97B4 **Tano** *R* Ghana
97C3 **Tanout** Niger
23B1 **Tanquián** Mexico
73E4 **Tan-shui** Taiwan
86A1 **Tansing** Nepal
95C1 **Tanta** Egypt
96A2 **Tan-Tan** Mor
4B3 **Tanunak** USA
99D3 **Tanzania** Republic, Africa
72A3 **Tao He** *R* China
72B2 **Taole** China
96B1 **Taourirt** Mor
60C2 **Tapa** Estonia
25C3 **Tapachula** Mexico
33F4 **Tapajós** *R* Brazil
34C3 **Tapalquén** Arg
70B4 **Tapan** Indon
111A3 **Tapanui** NZ
32D5 **Tapauá** *R* Brazil
85D4 **Tapi** *R* India
86B1 **Taplejung** Nepal
111B2 **Tapuaeniku** *Mt* NZ
35B2 **Tapuaritinga** Brazil
79B4 **Tapul Group** *Is* Phil
33E4 **Tapurucuara** Brazil
109D1 **Tara** Aust
65J4 **Tara** Russian Fed
65J4 **Tara** *R* Russian Fed
54A2 **Tara** *R* Bosnia & Herzegovina/Montenegro, Yugos
97D4 **Taraba** *R* Nig
30D2 **Tarabuco** Bol
Tarābulus = Tripoli
50B1 **Taracón** Spain
110C1 **Taradale** NZ
78D2 **Tarakan** Indon
44A3 **Taransay** *I* Scot
53C2 **Taranto** Italy
32B5 **Tarapoto** Peru
49C2 **Tarare** France
110C2 **Tararua Range** *Mts* NZ
96C2 **Tarat** Alg
110C1 **Tarawera** NZ
51B1 **Tarazona** Spain
44C3 **Tarbat Ness** *Pen* Scot
84C2 **Tarbela Res** Pak
42B2 **Tarbert** Strathclyde, Scot
44A3 **Tarbert** Western Isles, Scot
48C3 **Tarbes** France
106C4 **Tarcoola** Aust
109C2 **Tarcoon** Aust
109D2 **Taree** Aust
96A2 **Tarfaya** Mor
95A1 **Tarhūnah** Libya
91B5 **Tarīf** UAE
30D3 **Tarija** Bol
87B2 **Tarikere** India
81C4 **Tarīm** Yemen
99D3 **Tarime** Tanz
82C1 **Tarim He** *R* China
82C2 **Tarim Pendi** *Basin* China
84B2 **Tarin Kut** Afghan
18A1 **Tarkio** USA
79B2 **Tarlac** Phil
32B6 **Tarma** Peru
49C3 **Tarn** *R* France
59C2 **Tarnobrzeg** Pol
59C3 **Tarnów** Pol
107D3 **Taroom** Aust
51C1 **Tarragona** Spain
109C4 **Tarraleah** Aust
51C1 **Tarrasa** Spain
16C2 **Tarrytown** USA
92B2 **Tarsus** Turk
44D2 **Tartan** *Oilfield* N Sea
47D2 **Tartaro** *R* Italy
60C2 **Tartu** Estonia
92C3 **Tartūs** Syria
35C1 **Tarumirim** Brazil
70A3 **Tarutung** Indon
52B1 **Tarvisio** Italy
80D1 **Tashauz** Turkmenistan
86C1 **Tashigang** Bhutan
82A1 **Tashkent** Uzbekistan
65K4 **Tashtagol** Russian Fed
63A2 **Tashtyp** Russian Fed
78B4 **Tasikmalaya** Indon
94B2 **Tasīl** Syria
6E2 **Tasiussaq** Greenland
95A3 **Tasker** *Well* Niger
110B2 **Tasman B** NZ
107D5 **Tasmania** *I* Aust
111B2 **Tasman Mts** NZ
109C4 **Tasman Pen** Aust
107E4 **Tasman S** NZ Aust
92C1 **Taşova** Turk
96C2 **Tassili du Hoggar** *Desert* Region, Alg
96C2 **Tassili N'jjer** *Desert* Region, Alg
96B2 **Tata** Mor
96D1 **Tataouine** Tunisia
65J4 **Tatarsk** Russian Fed
61G2 **Tatarskaya Respublika,** Russian Fed
69G2 **Tatarskiy Proliv** *Str* Russian Fed
75B1 **Tateyama** Japan
5G3 **Tathlina L** Can
12E2 **Tatitlek** USA
13C2 **Tatla Lake** Can
59B3 **Tatry** *Mts* Pol/Czech
75A2 **Tatsuno** Japan
85B4 **Tatta** Pak
35B2 **Tatuí** Brazil
93D2 **Tatvan** Turk
31C3 **Tauá** Brazil
35B2 **Taubaté** Brazil
110C1 **Taumarunui** NZ
101F1 **Taung** S Africa
76B2 **Taungdwingyi** Burma
76B1 **Taung-gyi** Burma
76A2 **Taungup** Burma
84C2 **Taunsa** Pak
43C4 **Taunton** Eng
16D2 **Taunton** USA
46E1 **Taunus** Region, Germany
110C1 **Taupo** NZ
110C1 **Taupo,L** NZ
58C1 **Taurage** Lithuania
110C1 **Tauranga** NZ
110C1 **Tauranga Harbour** *B* NZ
110B1 **Tauroa Pt** NZ
7A3 **Tavani** Can
7A3 **Tavani** Can
65H4 **Tavda** *R* Russian Fed
43B4 **Tavistock** Eng
76B3 **Tavoy** Burma
76B3 **Tavoy Pt** Burma
92A2 **Tavsanli** Turk
111B2 **Tawa** NZ
19A3 **Tawakoni,L** USA
14B2 **Tawas City** USA
70C3 **Tawau** Malay
98C1 **Taweisha** Sudan
79B4 **Tawitawi** *I* Phil
79B4 **Tawitawi Group** *Is* Phil
23B2 **Taxco** Mexico
23B2 **Taxcoco** Mexico
44C3 **Tay** *R* Scot
78C3 **Tayan** Indon
12B1 **Taylor** Alaska, USA
13C1 **Taylor** Can
14B2 **Taylor** Michigan, USA
19A3 **Taylor** Texas, USA
18C2 **Taylorville** USA
80B3 **Taymā'** S Arabia
63B1 **Taymura** *R* Russian Fed
76D3 **Tay Ninh** Viet
63B2 **Tayshet** Russian Fed
68B2 **Tayshir** Mongolia
44C3 **Tayside** Region, Scot
79A3 **Taytay** Phil
90D3 **Tayyebāt** Iran
96B1 **Taza** Mor
95B2 **Tazirbu** Libya
12E2 **Tazlina L** USA
64J3 **Tazovskiy** Russian Fed
65F5 **Tbilisi** Georgia
98B3 **Tchibanga** Gabon
95A2 **Tchigai,Plat du** Niger
97C3 **Tchin Tabaradene** Niger
98B2 **Tchollíré** Cam
58B2 **Tczew** Pol
111A3 **Te Anau** NZ
111A3 **Te Anau,L** NZ
110C1 **Te Aroha** NZ
110C1 **Te Awamutu** NZ
96C1 **Tébessa** Alg
23A2 **Teboman** Mexico
23A2 **Tecailtlān** Mexico
21B3 **Tecate** Mexico
61K2 **Techa** *R* Russian Fed
23A1 **Tecolotlán** Mexico
23A2 **Tečpan** Mexico
54C1 **Tecuci** Rom
18A1 **Tecumseh** USA
80E2 **Tedzhen** Turkmenistan
65H6 **Tedzhen** *R* Turkmenistan
42D2 **Tees** *R* Eng
33E4 **Tefé** Brazil
78B4 **Tegal** Indon
78B4 **Tegineneng** Indon
25D3 **Tegucigalpa** Honduras
21B3 **Tehachapi Mts** USA
21B2 **Tehachapi P** USA
4J3 **Tehek L** Can
90B2 **Tehrān** Iran
23B2 **Tehuacán** Mexico
23B2 **Tehuantepec** Mexico
23B2 **Tehuitzingo** Mexico
43B3 **Teifi** *R* Wales
50A2 **Tejo** *R* Port
23A2 **Tejupilco** Mexico
111B2 **Tekapo,L** NZ
82B1 **Tekeli** Kazakhstan
92A1 **Tekirdağ** Turk
55C2 **Tekir Dağlari** *Mts* Turk
86C2 **Teknaf** Bang
110C1 **Te Kuiti** NZ
25D3 **Tela** Honduras
94B2 **Tel Aviv Yafo** Israel
34B3 **Telén** Arg
21B2 **Telescope Peak** *Mt* USA
33F5 **Teles Pires** *R* Brazil
47D1 **Telfs** Austria
63A2 **Teli** Russian Fed
94B3 **Tell el Meise** *Mt* Jordan
12A1 **Teller** USA
87B2 **Tellicherry** India
77C5 **Telok Anson** Malay
78D2 **Tĕlok Darvel** Malay
71E4 **Tĕlok Flamingo** *B* Indon
78C3 **Tĕlok Kumai** *B* Indon
78B4 **Tĕlok Pelabuanratu** *B* Indon
78D4 **Tĕlok Saleh** *B* Indon
78C3 **Tĕlok Sampit** *B* Indon
78B3 **Tĕlok Sukadona** *B* Indon
23B2 **Teloloapán** Mexico
64G3 **Tel'pos-iz** *Mt* Russian Fed
58C1 **Telšiai** Lithuania
78C3 **Telukbatang** Indon
71E4 **Teluk Berau** *B* Indon
78B4 **Telukbetung** Indom
70D4 **Teluk Bone** *B* Indon
71E4 **Teluk Cendrawasih** *B* Indon
78D3 **Teluk Mandar** *B* Indon
71D4 **Teluk Tolo** *B* Indon
70D3 **Teluk Tomini** *B* Indon
71D3 **Tĕluk Weda** *B* Indon
14B1 **Temagami,L** Can
23B2 **Temascal** Mexico
78A3 **Tembesi** *R* Indon
78A3 **Tembilahan** Indon
27E5 **Temblador** Ven
77C5 **Temerloh** Malay
65G5 **Temir** Kazakhstan
65J4 **Temirtau** Kazakhstan
15C1 **Temiscaming** Can
109C2 **Temora** Aust

9B3 **Tempe** USA
19A3 **Temple** USA
45C2 **Templemore** Irish Rep
23B1 **Tempoal** Mexico
34A3 **Temuco** Chile
111B2 **Temuka** NZ
32B4 **Tena** Ecuador
87C1 **Tenāli** India
23B2 **Tenancingo** Mexico
76B3 **Tenasserim** Burma
43B4 **Tenby** Wales
99E1 **Tendaho** Eth
83D5 **Ten Degree Chan** Indian O
98B1 **Ténéré** *Desert Region* Niger
96A2 **Tenerife** *I* Canary Is
76B1 **Teng** *R* Burma
78D3 **Tenggarong** Indon
72A2 **Tengger Shamo** *Desert* China
112C2 **Teniente Jubany** *Base* Ant
112C2 **Teniente Rodolfo Marsh Martin** *Base* Ant
87B3 **Tenkāsi** India
100B2 **Tenke** Zaïre
97B3 **Tenkodogo** Burkina
106C2 **Tennant Creek** Aust
11B3 **Tennessee** State, USA
18C2 **Tennessee** *R* USA
34A2 **Teno** Chile
78D1 **Tenom** Malay
25C3 **Tenosique** Mexico
109D1 **Tenterfield** Aust
17B2 **Ten Thousand Is** USA
23A1 **Teocaltiche** Mexico
35C1 **Teófilo Otôni** Brazil
23B2 **Teotihiucan** Hist Site, Mexico
23B2 **Teotitlan** Mexico
23A1 **Tepatitlan** Mexico
24B2 **Tepehuanes** Mexico
23B2 **Tepeji** Mexico
23A1 **Tepic** Mexico
57C2 **Teplice** Czech
110C1 **Te Puke** NZ
23A1 **Tequila** Mexico
23B2 **Tequistepec** Mexico
51C1 **Ter** *R* Spain
97C3 **Téra** Niger
75B1 **Teradomari** Japan
52B2 **Teramo** Italy
96A1 **Terceira** *I* Açores
59D3 **Terebovlya** Ukraine
31C3 **Teresina** Brazil
35C2 **Teresópolis** Brazil
92C1 **Terme** Turk
80E2 **Termez** Uzbekistan
52B2 **Termoli** Italy
71D3 **Ternate** Indon
52B2 **Terni** Italy
59D3 **Ternopol** Ukraine
13B2 **Terrace** Can
53B2 **Terracina** Italy
100B3 **Terrafirma** S Africa
112C8 **Terre Adélie** Region, Ant
19B4 **Terre Bonne B** USA
14A3 **Terre Haute** USA
19A3 **Terrell** USA
56B2 **Terschelling** *I* Neth
51B1 **Teruel** Spain
4C2 **Teshekpuk** USA
4C2 **Teshekpuk L** USA
74E2 **Teshio** *R* Japan
68B2 **Tesiyn Gol** *Mts* Mongolia
12H2 **Teslin** Can
12H3 **Teslin** *R* Can
12H2 **Teslin L** Can
63B3 **Teslyn Gol** *R* Mongolia
96C2 **Tessalit** Mali
97C3 **Tessaoua** Niger
101C2 **Tete** Mozam
23A2 **Tetela** Mexico
96B1 **Tetouan** Mor
61G2 **Tetyushi** Russian Fed
30D3 **Teuco** *R* Arg
23A1 **Teúl de Gonzalez Ortega** Mexico
71D4 **Teun** *I* Indon
52B2 **Tevere** *R* Italy
42C2 **Teviot** *R* Scot
65J4 **Tevriz** Russian Fed
111A3 **Te Waewae B** NZ
78C3 **Tewah** Indon
109D1 **Tewantin** Aust
72A3 **Têwo** China
19B3 **Texarkana** USA
19B3 **Texarkana,L** USA
109D1 **Texas** Aust
9C3 **Texas** State, USA
19B4 **Texas City** USA
56A2 **Texel** *I* Neth
19A3 **Texoma,L** USA
101G1 **Teyateyaneng** Lesotho
23B2 **Teziutlán** Mexico
86C1 **Tezpur** India
76C1 **Tha** Laos
101G1 **Thabana Ntlenyana** *Mt* Lesotho
101G1 **Thaba Putsoa** *Mt* Lesotho
76B3 **Thagyettaw** Burma
76D1 **Thai Binh** Viet
76C2 **Thailand** Kingdom, S E Asia
76C3 **Thailand,G of** Thai
76D1 **Thai Nguyen** Viet
76C2 **Thakhek** Laos
84C2 **Thal** Pak
77C4 **Thale Luang** *L* Thai
109C1 **Thallon** Aust
110C1 **Thames** NZ
43E4 **Thames** *R* Eng
76D2 **Thanh Hoah** Viet
87B2 **Thanjavur** India
85C3 **Thar Desert** India
108B1 **Thargomindah** Aust
55B2 **Thásos** *I* Greece
76B2 **Thaton** Burma
76B2 **Thayetmyo** Burma
5F5 **The Dalles** USA
91B4 **The Gulf** S W Asia
4H3 **Thelon** *R* Can
107E3 **Theodore** Aust
9B3 **Theodore Roosevelt L** USA
55B2 **Thermaïkós Kólpos** *G* Greece
8C2 **Thermopolis** USA
4F2 **Thesiger B** Can
14B1 **Thessalon** Can
55B2 **Thessaloníki** Greece
43E3 **Thetford** Eng
15D1 **Thetford Mines** Can
101G1 **Theunissen** S Africa
19B4 **Thibodaux** USA
5J4 **Thicket Portage** Can
8D2 **Thief River Falls** USA
20B2 **Thielsen,Mt** USA
49C2 **Thiers** France
97A3 **Thiès** Sen
99D3 **Thika** Kenya
86B1 **Thimphu** Bhutan
49D2 **Thionville** France
55C3 **Thíra** *I* Greece
42D2 **Thirsk** Eng
87B3 **Thiruvananthapuram** India
39F7 **Thisted** Den
55B3 **Thívai** Greece
48C2 **Thiviers** France
17B1 **Thomaston** Georgia, USA
45C2 **Thomastown** Irish Rep
17B1 **Thomasville** Georgia, USA
6A2 **Thom Bay** Can
5J4 **Thompson** Can
18B1 **Thompson** *R* USA
4G3 **Thompson Landing** Can
13C2 **Thompson R** Can
16C2 **Thompsonville** USA
17B1 **Thomson** USA
107D3 **Thomson** *R* Aust
76C3 **Thon Buri** Thai
76B2 **Thongwa** Burma
47B1 **Thonon-les-Bains** France
42C2 **Thornhill** Scot
48B2 **Thouars** France
15C2 **Thousand Is** Can/USA
13E2 **Three Hills** Can
7G4 **Three Kings Is** NZ
76B2 **Three Pagodas P** Thai
14A2 **Three Rivers** Michigan, USA
20B2 **Three Sisters** *Mt* USA
6D2 **Thule** Greenland
47B1 **Thun** Switz
10B2 **Thunder Bay** Can
47B1 **Thuner See** *L* Switz
77B4 **Thung Song** Thai
47C1 **Thur** *R* Switz
57C2 **Thüringen** State, Germany
57C2 **Thüringen Wald** *Upland* Germany
45C2 **Thurles** Irish Rep
71F5 **Thursday I** Aust
44C2 **Thurso** Scot
112B4 **Thurston I** Ant
47C1 **Thusis** Switz
108B1 **Thylungra** Aust
73B5 **Tiandong** China
73B5 **Tian'e** China
72D2 **Tianjin** China
73B5 **Tianlin** China
82C1 **Tiân Shan** *Mts* C Asia
72B3 **Tianshui** China
72A2 **Tianzhu** China
96C1 **Tiaret** Alg
35A2 **Tibagi** *R* Brazil
94B2 **Tiberias** Israel
94B2 **Tiberias,L** Israel
Tiber,R = Tevere,R
95A2 **Tibesti** *Mountain Region* Chad
82C2 **Tibet** Autonomous Region, China
108B1 **Tibooburra** Aust
86A1 **Tibrikot** Nepal
24A2 **Tiburón** *I* Mexico
97B3 **Tichitt** Maur
96A2 **Tichla** Mor
47C2 **Ticino** *R* Italy/Switz
15D2 **Ticonderoga** USA
25D2 **Ticul** Mexico
97A3 **Tidjikja** Maur
47C1 **Tiefencastel** Switz
74A2 **Tieling** China
46B1 **Tielt** Belg
46C1 **Tienen** Belg
65J5 **Tien Shan** *Mts* China/Kirgizia
72D2 **Tientsin** China
39H6 **Tierp** Sweden
23B2 **Tierra Blanca** Mexico
23B2 **Tierra Colorada** Mexico
29C6 **Tierra del Fuego** Territory, Arg
28C8 **Tierra del Fuego** *I* Arg/Chile
35B2 **Tietê** Brazil
35A2 **Tiete** *R* Brazil
14B2 **Tiffin** USA
17B1 **Tifton** USA
32B4 **Tigre** *R* Peru
33E2 **Tigre** *R* Ven
93E3 **Tigris** *R* Iraq
23B1 **Tihuatlán** Mexico
21B3 **Tijuana** Mexico
85D4 **Tikamgarh** India
60D2 **Tikhin** Russian Fed
61F4 **Tikhoretsk** Russian Fed
93D3 **Tikrīt** Iraq
1B8 **Tiksi** Russian Fed
46C1 **Tilburg** Neth
43E4 **Tilbury** Eng
30C3 **Tilcara** Arg
108B1 **Tilcha** Aust
76A1 **Tilin** Burma
97C3 **Tillabéri** Niger
20B1 **Tillamook** USA
97C3 **Tillia** Niger
55C3 **Tílos** *I* Greece
108B2 **Tilpa** Aust
32B3 **Tiluá** Colombia
64G3 **Timanskiy Kryazh** *Mts* Russian Fed
111B2 **Timaru** NZ
60E4 **Timashevsk** Russian Fed
55B3 **Timbákion** Greece
19B4 **Timbalier B** USA
97B3 **Timbédra** Maur
Timbuktu = Tombouctou
97B3 **Timétrine Monts** *Mts* Mali
97C3 **Timia** Niger
96C2 **Timis** *R* Rom
54B1 **Timişoara** Rom
10B2 **Timmins** Can
106B1 **Timor** *I* Indon
106B2 **Timor S** Aust/Indon
34C3 **Timote** Arg
79C4 **Tinaca Pt** Phil
27D5 **Tinaco** Ven
87B2 **Tindivanam** India
96B2 **Tindouf** Alg
96B2 **Tinfouchy** Alg
96C2 **Tin Fouye** Alg
6F3 **Tingmiarmiut** Greenland
32B5 **Tingo Maria** Peru
97B3 **Tingrela** Ivory Coast
86B1 **Tingri** China
71F2 **Tinian** Pacific O
30C4 **Tinogasta** Arg
55C3 **Tínos** *I* Greece
43B4 **Tintagel Head** *Pt* Eng
96C2 **Tin Tarabine** *Watercourse* Alg
108B3 **Tintinara** Aust
96C2 **Tin Zaouaten** Alg
22C2 **Tioga P** USA
77C5 **Tioman** *I* Malay
47D1 **Tione** Italy
45C2 **Tipperary** County, Irish Rep
41B3 **Tipperary** Irish Rep
18B2 **Tipton** Missouri, USA
87B2 **Tiptūr** India
23A2 **Tiquicheo** Mexico
55A2 **Tiranë** Alb
47D1 **Tirano** Italy
60C4 **Tiraspol** Moldavia
87B2 **Tirchchirāppalli** India
55C3 **Tire** Turk
93C1 **Tirebolu** Turk
44A3 **Tiree** *I* Scot
54C2 **Tîrgovişte** Rom
54B1 **Tîrgu Jiu** Rom
54B1 **Tîrgu Mureş** Rom
84C1 **Tirich Mir** *Mt* Pak
96A2 **Tiris** Region, Mor
61J3 **Tirlyanskiy** Russian Fed
54B1 **Tîrnăveni** Rom
55B3 **Tírnavos** Greece
85D4 **Tirodi** India
47D1 **Tirol** Province, Austria
53A2 **Tirso** *R* Sardegna
87B3 **Tiruchchendūr** India
87B3 **Tirunelveli** India
87B2 **Tirupati** India
87B2 **Tiruppattūr** India
87B2 **Tiruppur** India
87B2 **Tiruvannamalai** India
19A3 **Tishomingo** USA
94C2 **Tisīyah** Syria
59C3 **Tisza** *R* Hung
86A2 **Titlagarh** India
54A2 **Titograd** Montenegro, Yugos
54B2 **Titova Mitrovica** Serbia, Yugos
54A2 **Titovo Užice** Serbia, Yugos
52C1 **Titovo Velenje** Slovenia
54B2 **Titov Veles** Macedonia, Yugos
98C2 **Titule** Zaïre
17B2 **Titusville** USA
43C4 **Tiverton** Eng

52B2 **Tivoli** Italy
23B2 **Tixtla** Mexico
99E2 **Tiyeglow** Somalia
23B2 **Tizayuca** Mexico
25D2 **Tizimin** Mexico
96C1 **Tizi Ouzou** Alg
96B2 **Tiznit** Mor
23A1 **Tizpan el Alto** Mexico
23B2 **Tlacolula** Mexico
23B2 **Tlacotalpan** Mexico
23A2 **Tlalchana** Mexico
23B2 **Tlalnepantla** Mexico
23B2 **Tlalpan** Mexico
23A1 **Tlaltenango** Mexico
23B2 **Tlancualpicán** Mexico
23B2 **Tlapa** Mexico
23B2 **Tlapacoyan** Mexico
23A1 **Tlaquepaque** Mexico
23B2 **Tlaxcala** Mexico
23B2 **Tlaxcala** State, Mexico
23B2 **Tlaxiaco** Mexico
96B1 **Tlemcem** Alg
101D2 **Toamasina** Madag
34C3 **Toay** Arg
75B2 **Toba** Japan
84B2 **Toba and Kakar Ranges** *Mts* Pak
27E4 **Tobago** *I* Caribbean S
13C2 **Toba Inlet** *Sd* Can
71D3 **Tobelo** Indon
14B1 **Tobermory** Can
44A3 **Tobermory** Scot
71E3 **Tobi** *I* Pacific O
21B1 **Tobin,Mt** USA
65H4 **Tobol** *R* Kazakhstan
70D4 **Toboli** Indon
65H4 **Tobol'sk** Russian Fed
Tobruk = Tubruq
31B2 **Tocantins** *R* Brazil
17B1 **Toccoa** USA
47C1 **Toce** *R* Italy
30B3 **Tocopilla** Chile
30C3 **Tocorpuri** *Mt* Chile
32D1 **Tocuyo** *R* Ven
85D3 **Toda** India
47C1 **Tödi** *Mt* Switz
75A1 **Todong** S Korea
9B4 **Todos Santos** Mexico
13E2 **Tofield** Can
13B3 **Tofino** Can
12B3 **Togiak** USA
12B3 **Togiak B** USA
97C4 **Togo** Republic, Africa
72C1 **Togtoh** China
12F2 **Tok** USA
74E2 **Tokachi** *R* Japan
75B1 **Tokamachi** Japan
95C3 **Tokar** Sudan
69E4 **Tokara Retto** *Arch* Japan
92C1 **Tokat** Turk
74B3 **Tŏkchŏk-kundo** *Arch* S Korea
75A1 **Tok-do** *I* S Korea
82B1 **Tokmak** Kirgizia
110C1 **Tokomaru Bay** NZ
12H3 **Toku** *R* Can/USA
78C3 **Tokung** Indon
69E4 **Tokuno** *I* Japan
74C4 **Tokushima** Japan
75A2 **Tokuyama** Japan
74D3 **Tōkyō** Japan
110C1 **Tolaga Bay** NZ
101D3 **Tôlañaro** Madag
30F3 **Toledo** Brazil
50B2 **Toledo** Spain
14B2 **Toledo** USA
19B3 **Toledo Bend Res** USA
101D3 **Toliara** Madag
23B1 **Toliman** Mexico
32B3 **Tolina** *Mt* Colombia
51B1 **Tolosa** Spain
29B3 **Toltén** Chile
23B2 **Toluca** Mexico
61G3 **Tol'yatti** Russian Fed
74E2 **Tomakomai** Japan
78D1 **Tomani** Malay
58C2 **Tomaszów Mazowiecka** Pol
11B3 **Tombigbee** *R* USA
98B3 **Tomboco** Angola
35C2 **Tombos** Brazil
97B3 **Tombouctou** Mali
100A2 **Tombua** Angola
34A3 **Tomé** Chile
50B2 **Tomelloso** Spain
50A2 **Tomer** Port
106B3 **Tomkinson Range** *Mts* Aust
63E2 **Tommot** Russian Fed
55B2 **Tomorrit** *Mt* Alb
65K4 **Tomsk** Russian Fed
16B3 **Toms River** USA
25C3 **Tonalá** Mexico
20C1 **Tonasket** USA
15C2 **Tonawanda** USA
105H4 **Tonga** *Is* Pacific O
101H1 **Tongaat** S Africa
73D3 **Tongcheng** China
72B2 **Tongchuan** China
72A2 **Tongde** China
46C1 **Tongeren** Belg
76E2 **Tonggu Jiao** *I* China
73A5 **Tonghai** China
74B2 **Tonghua** China
74B3 **Tongjosŏn-man** N Korea
76D1 **Tongkin,G of** China/Viet
72E1 **Tonglia** China
73D3 **Tongling** China
108B2 **Tongo** Aust
34A2 **Tongoy** Chile
73B4 **Tongren** Guizhou, China
72A2 **Tongren** Qinghai, China
86C1 **Tongsa** Bhutan
76B1 **Tongta** Burma
68B3 **Tongtian He** *R* China
44B2 **Tongue** Scot
72D2 **Tong Xian** China
72B2 **Tongxin** China
73B4 **Tongzi** China
9C4 **Tonich** Mexico
99C2 **Tonj** Sudan
85D3 **Tonk** India
18A2 **Tonkawa** USA
76C3 **Tonle Sap** *L* Camb
21B2 **Tonopah** USA
12E2 **Tonsina** USA
8B2 **Tooele** USA
109D1 **Toogoolawah** Aust
108B1 **Toompine** Aust
109D1 **Toowoomba** Aust
22C1 **Topaz L** USA
18A2 **Topeka** USA
9C4 **Topolobampo** Mexico
20B1 **Toppenish** USA
99D2 **Tor** Eth
55C3 **Torbali** Turk
90C2 **Torbat-e-Heydarīyeh** Iran
90D2 **Torbat-e Jām** Iran
12D2 **Torbert,Mt** USA
50A1 **Tordesillas** Spain
56C2 **Torgau** Germany
46B1 **Torhout** Belg
69G3 **Tori** *I* Japan
47B2 **Torino** Italy
99D2 **Torit** Sudan
35A1 **Torixoreu** Brazil
50A1 **Tormes** *R* Spain
13E2 **Tornado Mt** Can
38J5 **Torne** *L* Sweden
38H5 **Torneträsk** Sweden
7D4 **Torngat** *Mts* Can
38J5 **Tornio** Fin
34C3 **Tornquist** Arg
15C2 **Toronto** Can
60D2 **Toropets** Russian Fed
99D2 **Tororo** Uganda
92B2 **Toros Dağlari** *Mts* Turk
43C4 **Torquay** Eng
22C4 **Torrance** USA
50A2 **Torrão** Port
51C1 **Torreblanca** Spain
53B2 **Torre del Greco** Italy
50B1 **Torrelavega** Spain
50B2 **Torremolinos** Spain
108A2 **Torrens,L** Aust
24B2 **Torreón** Mexico
47B2 **Torre Pellice** Italy
107D2 **Torres Str** Aust
50A2 **Torres Vedras** Port
16C2 **Torrington** Connecticut, USA
8C2 **Torrington** Wyoming, USA
9C4 **Torrón** Mexico
38D3 **Tórshavn** Føroyar
47C2 **Tortona** Italy
51C1 **Tortosa** Spain
90C2 **Torūd** Iran
58B2 **Toruń** Pol
40B2 **Tory** *I* Irish Rep
60D2 **Torzhok** Russian Fed
75A2 **Tosa** Japan
74C4 **Tosa-shimizu** Japan
74C4 **Tosa-wan** *B* Japan
75B2 **To-shima** *I* Japan
60D2 **Tosno** Russian Fed
75A2 **Tosu** Japan
92B1 **Tosya** Turk
61F1 **Tot'ma** Russian Fed
43C4 **Totnes** Eng
33F2 **Totness** Surinam
23B2 **Totolapan** Mexico
51B2 **Totona** Spain
109C2 **Tottenham** Aust
74C3 **Tottori** Japan
97B4 **Touba** Ivory Coast
97A3 **Touba** Sen
96B1 **Toubkal** *Mt* Mor
97B3 **Tougan** Burkina
96C1 **Touggourt** Alg
97A3 **Tougué** Guinea
46C2 **Toul** France
49D3 **Toulon** France
48C3 **Toulouse** France
97B4 **Toumodi** Ivory Coast
76B2 **Toungoo** Burma
46B1 **Tourcoing** France
96A2 **Tourine** Maur
46B1 **Tournai** Belg
48C2 **Tours** France
74E2 **Towada** Japan
74E2 **Towada-ko** *L* Japan
15C2 **Towanda** USA
107D2 **Townsville** Aust
16A3 **Towson** USA
43C4 **Towy** *R* Wales
74D3 **Toyama** Japan
75B1 **Toyama-wan** *B* Japan
75B2 **Toyohashi** Japan
75B2 **Toyonaka** Japan
75A1 **Toyooka** Japan
74D3 **Toyota** Japan
96C1 **Tozeur** Tunisia
46D2 **Traben-Trarbach** Germany
93C1 **Trabzon** Turk
22B2 **Tracy** California, USA
34A3 **Traiguén** Chile
13D3 **Trail** Can
41B3 **Tralee** Irish Rep
45B2 **Tralee B** Irish Rep
45C2 **Tramore** Irish Rep
39G7 **Tranås** Sweden
77B4 **Trang** Thai
71E4 **Trangan** *I* Indon
109C2 **Trangie** Aust
12E2 **Transalaskan Pipeline** USA
100B3 **Transvaal** Province, S Africa
Transylvanian Alps = Muntii Carpaţii Meridionali
53B3 **Trapani** Italy
109C3 **Traralgon** Aust
97A3 **Trarza** Region, Maur
76C3 **Trat** Thai
108B2 **Traveller's** *L* Aust
56C2 **Travemünde** Germany
14A2 **Traverse City** USA
12C1 **Traverse Peak** *Mt* USA
111B2 **Travers,Mt** NZ
47C2 **Trebbia** *R* Italy
59B3 **Třebíč** Czech
54A2 **Trebinje** Bosnia & Herzegovina, Yugos
57C3 **Trebon** Czech
29F2 **Treinta y Tres** Urug
29C4 **Trelew** Arg
39G7 **Trelleborg** Sweden
43B3 **Tremadog B** Wales
15D1 **Tremblant,Mt** Can
13C2 **Trembleur L** Can
16A2 **Tremont** USA
59B3 **Trenčin** Czech
34C3 **Trenque Lauquén** Arg
43D3 **Trent** *R* Eng
47D1 **Trentino** Region, Italy
47D1 **Trento** Italy
15C2 **Trenton** Can
18B1 **Trenton** Missouri, USA
16B2 **Trenton** New Jersey, USA
7E5 **Trepassey** Can
34C3 **Tres Arroyos** Arg
35B2 **Tres Corações** Brazil
30F3 **Três Lagoas** Brazil
34C3 **Tres Lomas** Arg
22B2 **Tres Pinos** USA
35C2 **Três Rios** Brazil
47C2 **Treviglio** Italy
47E2 **Treviso** Italy
47C2 **Trezzo** Italy
87B2 **Trichūr** India
108C2 **Trida** Aust
46D2 **Trier** Germany
52B1 **Trieste** Italy
45C2 **Trim** Irish Rep
87C3 **Trincomalee** Sri Lanka
33E6 **Trinidad** Bol
29E2 **Trinidad** Urug
9C3 **Trinidad** USA
34C3 **Trinidad** *I* Arg
27E4 **Trinidad** *I* Caribbean S
103G6 **Trindade** *I* Atlantic O
27E4 **Trinidad & Tobago** *Republic* Caribbean S
19A3 **Trinity** USA
9D3 **Trinity** *R* USA
7E5 **Trinity B** Can
12D3 **Trinity Is** USA
17A1 **Trion** USA
94B1 **Tripoli** Leb
95A1 **Tripoli** Libya
55B3 **Trípolis** Greece
86C2 **Tripura** State, India
103H6 **Tristan da Cunha** *Is* Atlantic O
Trivandrum = Thiruvananthapuram
59B3 **Trnava** Czech
107E1 **Trobriand Is** PNG
15D1 **Trois-Riviéres** Can
65H4 **Troitsk** Russian Fed
39G7 **Trollhättan** Sweden
38F6 **Trollheimen** *Mt* Nor
89K9 **Tromelin** *I* Indian O
38H5 **Tromsø** Nor
38G6 **Trondheim** Nor
38G6 **Trondheimfjord** *Inlet* Nor
42B2 **Troon** Scot
102J3 **Tropic of Cancer**
103J6 **Tropic of Capricorn**
96B2 **Troudenni** Mali
7A4 **Trout L** Ontario, Can
17A1 **Troy** Alabama, USA
16C1 **Troy** New York, USA
14B2 **Troy** Ohio, USA
54B2 **Troyan** Bulg
49C2 **Troyes** France
91B5 **Trucial Coast** Region, UAE
21A2 **Truckee** *R* USA
25D3 **Trujillo** Honduras
32B5 **Trujillo** Peru
50A2 **Trujillo** Spain
32C2 **Trujillo** Ven
109C2 **Trundle** Aust
7D5 **Truro** Can
43B4 **Truro** Eng

71E3 **Trust Territories of the Pacific Is** Pacific O
68B2 **Tsagaan Nuur** *L* Mongolia
68B1 **Tsagan-Tologoy** Russian Fed
101D2 **Tsaratanana** Madag
100B3 **Tsau** Botswana
99D3 **Tsavo** Kenya
99D3 **Tsavo Nat Pk** Kenya
65J4 **Tselinograd** Kazakhstan
100A3 **Tses** Namibia
68C2 **Tsetserleg** Mongolia
97C4 **Tsévié** Togo
100B3 **Tshabong** Botswana
100B3 **Tshane** Botswana
98B3 **Tshela** Zaïre
98C3 **Tshibala** Zaïre
98C3 **Tshikapa** Zaïre
98C3 **Tshuapa** *R* Zaïre
101D3 **Tsihombe** Madag
61F4 **Tsimlyanskoye Vodokhranilishche** *Res* Russian Fed
Tsinan = Jinan
Tsingtao = Qingdao
101D2 **Tsiroanomandidy** Madag
13B2 **Tsitsutl Peak** *Mt* Can
58D2 **Tsna** *R* Belorussia
72B1 **Tsogt Ovoo** Mongolia
68C2 **Tsomog** Mongolia
75B2 **Tsu** Japan
75B1 **Tsubata** Japan
74E3 **Tsuchira** Japan
74E2 **Tsugaru-kaikyō** *Str* Japan
100A2 **Tsumeb** Namibia
100A3 **Tsumis** Namibia
75B1 **Tsunugi** Japan
74D3 **Tsuruga** Japan
74D3 **Tsuruoka** Japan
75B1 **Tsushima** Japan
74B4 **Tsushima** *I* Japan
74C3 **Tsuyama** Japan
50A1 **Tua** *R* Port
45B2 **Tuam** Irish Rep
60E5 **Tuapse** Russian Fed
111A3 **Tuatapere** NZ
30G4 **Tubarão** Brazil
94B2 **Tubas** Israel
79A4 **Tubbataha Reefs** *Is* Phil
57B3 **Tübingen** Germany
95B1 **Tubruq** Libya
16B3 **Tuckerton** USA
9B3 **Tucson** USA
30C4 **Tucumán** State, Arg
34B2 **Tucunuco** Arg
33E2 **Tucupita** Ven
51B1 **Tudela** Spain
93C3 **Tudmur** Syria
101H1 **Tugela** *R* S Africa
109D2 **Tuggerah** *L* Aust
12D3 **Tugidak** *I* USA
79B2 **Tuguegarao** Phil
63F2 **Tugur** Russian Fed
72D2 **Tuhai He** *R* China
4E3 **Tuktoyaktuk** USA
58C1 **Tukums** Latvia
99D3 **Tukuyu** Tanz
84B1 **Tukzar** Afghan
60E3 **Tula** Russian Fed
23B1 **Tulancingo** Mexico
78A3 **Tulangbawang** *R* Indon
32B3 **Tulcán** Colombia
60C5 **Tulcea** Rom
100B3 **Tuli** Zim
94B2 **Tulkarm** Israel
48C2 **Tulle** France
19B3 **Tullos** USA
45C2 **Tullow** Irish Rep
18A2 **Tulsa** USA
93C3 **Tulūl ash Shāmīyah** *Desert Region* Syria/ S Arabia
63C2 **Tulun** Russian Fed
78C4 **Tulungagung** Indon
32B3 **Tumaco** Colombia
109C3 **Tumbarumba** Aust
32A4 **Tumbes** Ecuador
108A2 **Tumby Bay** Aust
74B2 **Tumen** China
87B2 **Tumkūr** India
77C4 **Tumpat** Malay
85D4 **Tumsar** India
97B3 **Tumu** Ghana
109C3 **Tumut** Aust
109C3 **Tumut** *R* Aust
27L1 **Tunapuna** Trinidad
93C2 **Tunceli** Turk
99D3 **Tunduma** Zambia
101C2 **Tunduru** Tanz
54C2 **Tundzha** *R* Bulg
87B1 **Tungabhadra** *R* India
68D4 **Tung-Chiang** Taiwan
38B2 **Tungnafellsjökull** *Mts* Iceland
12J2 **Tungsten** Can
63B1 **Tunguska** *R* Russian Fed
87C1 **Tuni** India
96D1 **Tunis** Tunisia
88E4 **Tunisia** Republic, N Africa
32C2 **Tunja** Colombia
12B2 **Tuntutuliak** USA
12B2 **Tununak** USA
34B2 **Tunuyán** Arg
34B2 **Tunuyán** *R* Arg
73D4 **Tunxi** China
22C2 **Tuolumne Meadows** USA
35A2 **Tupã** Brazil
35B1 **Tupaciguara** Brazil
19C3 **Tupelo** USA
30C3 **Tupiza** Bol
15D2 **Tupper Lake** USA
34B2 **Tupungato** Arg
29C2 **Tupungato** *Mt* Arg
86C1 **Tura** India
63C1 **Tura** Russian Fed
61K2 **Tura** *R* Russian Fed
90C2 **Turān** Iran
63B2 **Turan** Russian Fed
93C3 **Turayf** S Arabia
80E3 **Turbat** Pak
32B2 **Turbo** Colombia
54B1 **Turda** Rom
63A3 **Turfan Depression** China
65H4 **Turgay** Kazakhstan
63B3 **Turgen Uul** *Mt* Mongolia
54C2 **Turgovishte** Bulg
92A2 **Turgutlu** Turk
92C1 **Turhal** Turk
39K7 **Türi** Estonia
51B2 **Turia** *R* Spain
Turin = Torino
61K2 **Turinsk** Russian Fed
69F2 **Turiy Rog** Russian Fed
99D2 **Turkana,L** Kenya/Eth
80E1 **Turkestan** Region, C Asia
82A1 **Turkestan** Kazakhstan
92C2 **Turkey** Republic, W Asia
80D1 **Turkmenistan** Republic, Asia
90B2 **Turkmenskiy Zaliv** *B* Turkmenistan
27C2 **Turks Is** Caribbean S
39J6 **Turku** Fin
99D2 **Turkwel** *R* Kenya
22B2 **Turlock** USA
22B2 **Turlock L** USA
110C2 **Turnagain,C** NZ
25D3 **Turneffe I** Belize
16C1 **Turners Falls** USA
46C1 **Turnhout** Belg
13F1 **Turnor L** Can
54B2 **Turnu Măgurele** Rom
63A3 **Turpan** China
26B2 **Turquino** *Mt* Cuba
80E1 **Turtkul'** Uzbekistan
18A2 **Turtle Creek Res** USA
13F2 **Turtle L** Can
63A1 **Turukhansk** Russian Fed
68C1 **Turuntayevo** Russian Fed
35A1 **Turvo** *R* Goias, Brazil
35B2 **Turvo** *R* São Paulo, Brazil
58C2 **Tur'ya** *R* Ukraine
19C3 **Tuscaloosa** USA
18C2 **Tuscola** USA
90C3 **Tusharík** Iran
Tutera = Tudela
87B3 **Tuticorin** India
54C2 **Tutrakan** Bulg
57B3 **Tuttlingen** Germany
68C2 **Tuul Gol** *R* Mongolia
105G4 **Tuvalu** *Is* Pacific O
63B2 **Tuvinskaya Respublika,** Russian Fed
23A2 **Tuxpan** Jalisco, Mexico
24B2 **Tuxpan** Nayarit, Mexico
23B1 **Tuxpan** Veracruz, Mexico
23B2 **Tuxtepec** Mexico
25C3 **Tuxtla Gutiérrez** Mexico
50A1 **Túy** Spain
76D3 **Tuy Hoa** Viet
92B2 **Tuz Gölü** *Salt L* Turk
93D3 **Tuz Khurmātū** Iraq
54A2 **Tuzla** Bosnia & Herzegovina, Yugos
60E2 **Tver'** Russian Fed
42C2 **Tweed** *R* Eng/Scot
109D1 **Tweed Heads** Aust
42C2 **Tweedsmuir Hills** Scot
7E5 **Twillingate** Can
8B2 **Twin Falls** USA
111B2 **Twins,The** *Mt* NZ
14A2 **Two Rivers** USA
63E2 **Tygda** Russian Fed
19A3 **Tyler** USA
65K3 **Tym** *R* Russian Fed
69G1 **Tymovskoye** Russian Fed
42D2 **Tyne** *R* Eng
42D2 **Tyne and Wear** Metropolitan County, Eng
42D2 **Tynemouth** Eng
38G6 **Tynset** Nor
12D3 **Tyonek** USA
94B2 **Tyr** Leb
Tyre = Tyr
45C1 **Tyrone** County, N Ire
108B3 **Tyrrell,L** Aust
53B2 **Tyrrhenian S** Italy
65H4 **Tyumen'** Russian Fed
43B3 **Tywyn** Wales
55B3 **Tzoumérka** *Mt* Greece

U

99E2 **Uarsciek** Somalia
35C2 **Ubá** Brazil
35C1 **Ubaí** Brazil
98B2 **Ubangi** *R* CAR
47B2 **Ubaye** *R* France
75A2 **Ube** Japan
50B2 **Ubeda** Spain
6E2 **Ubekendt Ejland** *I* Greenland
35B1 **Uberaba** Brazil
35B1 **Uberlândia** Brazil
76C2 **Ubon Ratchathani** Thai
58D2 **Ubort** *R* Belorussia
98C3 **Ubundi** Zaïre
32C5 **Ucayali** *R* Peru
84C3 **Uch** Pak
63F2 **Uchar** *R* Russian Fed
74E2 **Uchiura-wan** *B* Japan
63B2 **Uda** *R* Russian Fed
85C4 **Udaipur** India
86B1 **Udaipur Garhi** Nepal
34D3 **Udaquoila** Arg
39G7 **Uddevalla** Sweden
38H5 **Uddjaur** *L* Sweden
87B1 **Udgir** India
84D2 **Udhampur** India
61H2 **Udmurtskaya Respublika,** Russian Fed
76C2 **Udon Thani** Thai
63F2 **Udskaya Guba** *B* Russian Fed
87A2 **Udupi** India
75B1 **Ueda** Japan
99C2 **Uele** *R* Zaïre
56C2 **Uelzen** Germany
98C2 **Uere** *R* Zaïre
61J3 **Ufa** Russian Fed
61J2 **Ufa** *R* Russian Fed
100A3 **Ugab** *R* Namibia
99D3 **Ugaila** *R* Tanz
12D3 **Ugak B** USA
99D2 **Uganda** Republic, Africa
12C3 **Ugashik B** USA
12C3 **Ugashik L** USA
47B2 **Ugine** France
69G2 **Uglegorsk** Russian Fed
60E2 **Uglich** Russian Fed
60E3 **Ugra** *R* Russian Fed
44A3 **Uig** Scot
98B3 **Uige** Angola
61H4 **Uil** Kazakhstan
8B2 **Uinta Mts** USA
100B4 **Uitenhage** S Africa
59C3 **Ujfehértó** Hung
75B2 **Uji** Japan
99C3 **Ujiji** Tanz
30C3 **Ujina** Chile
85D4 **Ujjain** India
70C4 **Ujung Pandang** Indon
99D3 **Ukerewe** *I* Tanz
86C1 **Ukhrul** India
21A2 **Ukiah** California, USA
20C1 **Ukiah** Oregon, USA
58C1 **Ukmerge** Lithuania
60C4 **Ukraine** Republic, Europe
68C2 **Ulaanbaatar** Mongolia
68B2 **Ulaangom** Mongolia
72C1 **Ulaan Uul** Mongolia
82C1 **Ulangar Hu** *L* China
68C1 **Ulan Ude** Russian Fed
68B3 **Ulan Ul Hu** *L* China
34B2 **Ulapes** Arg
74B3 **Ulchin** S Korea
54A2 **Ulcinj** Montenegro, Yugos
68D2 **Uldz** Mongolia
68B2 **Uliastay** Mongolia
58D1 **Ulla** Lithuania
109D3 **Ulladulla** Aust
44B3 **Ullapool** Scot
38H5 **Ullsfjorden** *Inlet* Nor
42C2 **Ullswater** *L* Eng
74C3 **Ullung-do** *I* S Korea
57C3 **Ulm** Germany
108A1 **Uloowaranie,L** Aust
74B3 **Ulsan** S Korea
45C1 **Ulster** Region, N Ire
65K5 **Ulungur He** *R* China
65K5 **Ulungur Hu** *L* China
44A3 **Ulva** *I* Scot
42C2 **Ulverston** Eng
109C4 **Ulverstone** Aust
63G2 **Ulya** *R* Russian Fed
61G3 **Ul'yanovsk** Russian Fed
60D4 **Uman** Ukraine
6E2 **Umanak** Greenland
86A2 **Umaria** India
85B3 **Umarkot** Pak
108A1 **Umaroona,L** Aust
20C1 **Umatilla** USA
38L5 **Umba** Russian Fed
99D3 **Umba** *R* Tanz
38H6 **Ume** *R* Sweden
38J6 **Umea** Sweden
101H1 **Umfolozi** *R* S Africa
4C3 **Umiat** USA
91C4 **Umm al Qaiwain** UAE
91C5 **Umm as Samīm** *Salt Marsh* Oman
99C1 **Umm Bell** Sudan

98C1 **Umm Keddada** Sudan
99D1 **Umm Ruwaba** Sudan
91B5 **Umm Sa'id** Qatar
20B2 **Umpqua** *R* USA
85D4 **Umred** India
100B4 **Umtata** S Africa
35A2 **Umuarama** Brazil
52C1 **Una** *R* Bosnia & Herzegovina, Yugos/ Croatia
35B1 **Unai** Brazil
12B2 **Unalakleet** USA
80C3 **Unayzah** S Arabia
16C2 **Uncasville** USA
101G1 **Underberg** S Africa
60D3 **Unecha** Russian Fed
94B3 **Uneisa** Jordan
7D4 **Ungava B** Can
30F4 **União de Vitória** Brazil
34B3 **Unión** Arg
18B2 **Union** Missouri, USA
17B1 **Union** S Carolina, USA
14C2 **Union City** Pennsylvania, USA
17A1 **Union Springs** USA
15C3 **Uniontown** USA
91B5 **United Arab Emirates** Arabian Pen
36C3 **United Kingdom** Kingdom, W Europe
2H4 **United States of America**
6B1 **United States Range** *Mts* Can
13F2 **Unity** Can
20C2 **Unity** USA
46D1 **Unna** Germany
86A1 **Unnão** India
44E1 **Unst** *I* Scot
13A1 **Unuk** *R* USA
92C1 **Ünye** Turk
61F2 **Unzha** *R* Russian Fed
33E2 **Upata** Ven
98C3 **Upemba Nat Pk** Zaïre
6E2 **Upernavik** Greenland
22D3 **Upland** USA
100B3 **Uplington** S Africa
14B2 **Upper Arlington** USA
13D2 **Upper Arrow L** Can
111C2 **Upper Hutt** NZ
20B2 **Upper Klamath L** USA
20B2 **Upper L** USA
45C1 **Upper Lough Erne** *L* N Ire
27L1 **Upper Manzanilla** Trinidad
39H7 **Uppsala** Sweden
72B1 **Urad Qianqi** China
91A4 **Urairah** S Arabia
61H3 **Ural** *R* Kazakhstan
109D2 **Uralla** Aust
61H3 **Ural'sk** Kazakhstan
65G4 **Uralskiy Khrebet** *Mts* Russian Fed
5H4 **Uranium City** Can
75B1 **Urawa** Japan
18C1 **Urbana** Illinois, USA
14B2 **Urbana** Ohio, USA
52B2 **Urbino** Italy
42C2 **Ure** *R* Eng
61G2 **Uren'** Russian Fed
80E1 **Urgench** Uzbekistan
84B2 **Urgun** Afghan
55C3 **Urla** Turk
54B2 **Uroševac** Serbia, Yugos
31B4 **Uruaçu** Brazil
23A2 **Uruapan** Mexico
35B1 **Urucuia** *R* Brazil
30E4 **Uruguaiana** Brazil
29E2 **Uruguay** Republic, S America
29E2 **Uruguay** *R* Urug
82C1 **Ürümqi** China
69H2 **Urup** *I* Russian Fed
84B2 **Uruzgan** Afghan
61F3 **Uryupinsk** Russian Fed
61H2 **Urzhum** Russian Fed
54C2 **Urziceni** Rom
82C1 **Usa** China
75A2 **Usa** Japan
64G3 **Usa** *R* Russian Fed
92A2 **Uşak** Turk
100A3 **Usakos** Namibia
99D3 **Ushashi** Tanz
65J5 **Ush Tobe** Kazakhstan
29C6 **Ushuaia** Arg
63E2 **Ushumun** Russian Fed
43C4 **Usk** *R* Wales
92A1 **Üsküdar** Turk
63C2 **Usolye Sibirskoye** Russian Fed
34B2 **Uspallata** Arg
69F2 **Ussuriysk** Russian Fed
47C1 **Uster** Switz
53B3 **Ustica** *I* Italy
57C2 **Ústi nad Labem** Czech
65J4 **Ust'Ishim** Russian Fed
58B2 **Ustka** Pol
65K5 **Ust'-Kamenogorsk** Kazakhstan
63B2 **Ust Karabula** Russian Fed
61J2 **Ust'Katav** Russian Fed
63C2 **Ust'-Kut** Russian Fed
61E4 **Ust Labinsk** Russian Fed
63F1 **Ust'Maya** Russian Fed
1C8 **Ust'Nera** Russian Fed
63E2 **Ust'Nyukzha** Russian Fed
63C2 **Ust'Ordynskiy** Russian Fed
64G3 **Ust'Tsil'ma** Russian Fed
63F2 **Ust'Umal'ta** Russian Fed
75A2 **Usuki** Japan
25C3 **Usumacinta** *R* Guatemala/Mexico
101H1 **Usutu** *R* Swaziland
8B3 **Utah** State, USA
8B2 **Utah L** USA
58D1 **Utena** Russian Fed
85B3 **Uthal** Pak
10C2 **Utica** USA
51B2 **Utiel** Spain
13D1 **Utikuma L** Can
56B2 **Utrecht** Neth
101H1 **Utrecht** S Africa
50A2 **Utrera** Spain
38K5 **Utsjoki** Fin
74D3 **Utsunomiya** Japan
76C2 **Uttaradit** Thai
86A1 **Uttar Pradesh** State, India
65H4 **Uval** Russian Fed
107F3 **Uvéa** *I* Nouvelle Calédonie
99D3 **Uvinza** Tanz
99C3 **Uvira** Zaïre
6E2 **Uvkusigssat** Greenland
39J6 **Uvsikaupunki** Fin
68B1 **Uvs Nuur** *L* China
74C4 **Uwajima** Japan
72B2 **Uxin Qi** China
63B2 **Uyar** Russian Fed
30C3 **Uyuni** Bol
80E1 **Uzbekistan** Republic, Asia
48C2 **Uzerche** France
59C3 **Uzhgorod** Ukraine
60E3 **Uzlovaya** Russian Fed
92A1 **Uzunköprü** Turk

V

101F1 **Vaal** *R* S Africa
101G1 **Vaal Dam** *Res* S Africa
100B3 **Vaalwater** S Africa
38J6 **Vaasa** Fin
59B3 **Vác** Hung
30F4 **Vacaria** Brazil
35C1 **Vacaria** *R* Minas Gerais, Brazil
21A2 **Vacaville** USA
85C4 **Vadodara** India
38K4 **Vadsø** Nor
47C1 **Vaduz** Leichtenstein
38D3 **Vágar** Føroyar
29E3 **Va Gesell** Arg
59B3 **Váh** *R* Czech
87B2 **Vaigai** *R* India
65K3 **Vakh** *R* Russian Fed
60B4 **Vâlcea** Rom
29C4 **Valcheta** Arg
47D2 **Valdagno** Italy
60D2 **Valday** Russian Fed
60D2 **Valdayskaya Vozvyshennost'** *Upland* Russian Fed
32D2 **Val de la Pascua** Ven
50B2 **Valdepeñas** Spain
12E2 **Valdez** USA
29B3 **Valdivia** Chile
46B2 **Val d'Oise** *Department* France
17B1 **Valdosta** USA
20C2 **Vale** USA
13D2 **Valemount** Can
31D4 **Valença** Bahia, Brazil
35C2 **Valença** Rio de Janeiro, Brazil
49C3 **Valence** France
51B2 **Valencia** Region, Spain
51B2 **Valencia** Spain
32D1 **Valencia** Ven
45A3 **Valencia** *I* Irish Rep
50A2 **Valencia de Alcantara** Spain
46B1 **Valenciennes** France
47C2 **Valenza** Italy
32C2 **Valera** Ven
39K7 **Valga** Estonia
54A2 **Valjevo** Serbia, Yugos
39J6 **Valkeakoski** Fin
25D2 **Valladolid** Mexico
50B1 **Valladolid** Spain
47B2 **Valle d'Aosta** Region, Italy
27D5 **Valle de la Pascua** Ven
23A1 **Valle de Santiago** Mexico
47B2 **Valle d'Isére** France
32C1 **Valledupar** Colombia
97C3 **Vallée de l'Azaouak** *V* Niger
97C3 **Vallée Tilemis** *V* Mali
30D2 **Valle Grande** Bol
22A1 **Vallejo** USA
30B4 **Vallenar** Chile
53B3 **Valletta** Malta
8D2 **Valley City** USA
20B2 **Valley Falls** USA
15D1 **Valleyfield** Can
13D1 **Valleyview** Can
47E2 **Valli di Comacchio** *Lg* Italy
51C1 **Valls** Spain
58D1 **Valmiera** Latvia
35A2 **Valparaiso** Brazil
34A2 **Valparaiso** Chile
23A1 **Valparaiso** Mexico
17A1 **Valparaiso** USA
101G1 **Vals** *R* S Africa
85C4 **Valsād** India
60E3 **Valuyki** Russian Fed
50A2 **Valverde del Camino** Spain
38J6 **Vammala** Fin
93D2 **Van** Turk
63C1 **Vanavara** Russian Fed
18B2 **Van Buren** Arkansas, USA
13C3 **Vancouver** Can
20B1 **Vancouver** USA
5F5 **Vancouver I** Can
12G2 **Vancouver,Mt** Can
18C2 **Vandalia** Illinois, USA
14B3 **Vandalia** Ohio, USA
13C2 **Vanderhoof** Can
106C2 **Van Diemen G** *Gulf* Aust
39G7 **Vänern** *L* Sweden
39G7 **Vänersborg** Sweden
101D3 **Vangaindrano** Madag
93D2 **Van Gölü** *Salt L* Turk
76C2 **Vang Vieng** Laos
9C3 **Van Horn** USA
15C1 **Vanier** Can
1C6 **Vankarem** Russian Fed
38H6 **Vännäs** Sweden
48B2 **Vannes** France
47B2 **Vanoise** *Mts* France
100A4 **Vanrhynsdorp** S Africa
6B3 **Vansittart I** Can
105G4 **Vanuatu** *Is* Pacific O
14B2 **Van Wert** USA
47C2 **Varallo** Italy
90B2 **Varāmīn** Iran
86A1 **Vārānasi** India
38K4 **Varangerfjord** *Inlet* Nor
38K4 **Varangerhalvøya** *Pen* Nor
52C1 **Varazdin** Croatia
39G7 **Varberg** Sweden
39F7 **Varde** Den
38L4 **Vardø** Nor
58C2 **Varéna** Lithuania
47C2 **Varenna** Italy
47C2 **Varese** Italy
35B2 **Varginha** Brazil
38K6 **Varkaus** Fin
54C2 **Varna** Bulg
39G7 **Värnamo** Sweden
17B1 **Varnville** USA
35C1 **Várzea da Palma** Brazil
47C2 **Varzi** Italy
50B1 **Vascongadas** Region, Spain
60D3 **Vasil'kov** Ukraine
14B2 **Vassar** USA
39H7 **Västerås** Sweden
39H7 **Västervik** Sweden
52B2 **Vasto** Italy
65J4 **Vasyugan** *R* Russian Fed
38B2 **Vatnajökull** *Mts* Iceland
38A1 **Vatneyri** Iceland
54C1 **Vatra Dornei** Rom
39G7 **Vättern** *L* Sweden
9C3 **Vaughn** USA
32C3 **Vaupés** *R* Colombia
13E2 **Vauxhall** Can
87C3 **Vavunija** Sri Lanka
39G7 **Växjö** Sweden
64G2 **Vaygach, Ostrov** *I* Russian Fed
34C2 **Vedia** Arg
38G5 **Vega** *I* Nor
13E2 **Vegreville** Can
50A2 **Vejer de la Frontera** Spain
39F7 **Vejle** Den
52C2 **Velebit** *Mts* Croatia
35C1 **Velhas** *R* Brazil
39K7 **Velikaya** *R* Russian Fed
60D2 **Velikiye Luki** Russian Fed
61G1 **Velikiy Ustyug** Russian Fed
54C2 **Veliko Tŭrnovo** Bulg
97A3 **Vélingara** Sen
87B2 **Vellore** India
61F1 **Vel'sk** Russian Fed
87B3 **Vembanad L** India
34C2 **Venado Tuerto** Arg
35B2 **Vençeslau Braz** Brazil
49C2 **Vendôme** France
12E1 **Venetie** USA
47D2 **Veneto** Region, Italy
47E2 **Venezia** Italy
32D2 **Venezuela** Republic, S America
87A1 **Vengurla** India
12C3 **Veniaminof V** USA
Venice = Venezia
87B2 **Venkatagiri** India
56B2 **Venlo** Neth
58C1 **Venta** *R* Latvia

101G1 **Ventersburg** S Africa
58C1 **Ventspils** Latvia
32D3 **Ventuari** *R* Ven
22C3 **Ventura** USA
60D1 **Vepsovskaya Vozvyshennost'** *Upland* Russian Fed
30D4 **Vera** Arg
51B2 **Vera** Spain
23B2 **Veracruz** Mexico
23B1 **Veracruz** State, Mexico
85C4 **Verāval** India
47C2 **Verbania** Italy
47C2 **Vercelli** Italy
35A1 **Verde** *R* Goias, Brazil
23A1 **Verde** *R* Jalisco, Mexico
35A1 **Verde** *R* Mato Grosso do Sul, Brazil
23B2 **Verde** *R* Oaxaca, Mexico
Verde,C = Cap Vert
35C1 **Verde Grande** *R* Brazil
34C3 **Verde,Pen** Arg
49D3 **Verdon** *R* France
46C2 **Verdun** France
101G1 **Vereeniging** S Africa
61H2 **Vereshchagino** Russian Fed
97A3 **Verga,C** Guinea
34D3 **Vergara** Arg
50A1 **Verin** Spain
63D2 **Verkh Angara** *R* Russian Fed
61J3 **Verkhneural'sk** Russian Fed
63E1 **Verkhnevilyuysk** Russian Fed
1C8 **Verkhoyansk** Russian Fed
35A1 **Vermelho** *R* Brazil
13E2 **Vermilion** Can
10C2 **Vermont** State, USA
22B2 **Vernalis** USA
13D2 **Vernon** Can
46A2 **Vernon** France
9D3 **Vernon** USA
17B2 **Vero Beach** USA
54B2 **Veroia** Greece
47D2 **Verolanuova** Italy
47D2 **Verona** Italy
46B2 **Versailles** France
101H1 **Verulam** S Africa
46C1 **Verviers** Belg
46B2 **Vervins** France
46C2 **Vesle** *R* France
49D2 **Vesoul** France
38G5 **Vesterålen** *Is* Nor
38G5 **Vestfjorden** *Inlet* Nor
38A2 **Vestmannaeyjar** Iceland
53B2 **Vesuvio** *Mt* Italy
59B3 **Veszprém** Hung
39H7 **Vetlanda** Sweden
61F2 **Vetluga** *R* Russian Fed
46B1 **Veurne** Belg
47B1 **Vevey** Switz
46A2 **Vexin** Region, France
47A2 **Veynes** France
50A1 **Viana do Castelo** Port
Viangchan = Vientiane
49E3 **Viareggio** Italy
39F7 **Viborg** Den
53C3 **Vibo Valentia** Italy
Vic = Vich
112C2 **Vicecomodoro Marambio** *Base* Ant
52B1 **Vicenza** Italy
51C1 **Vich** Spain
32D3 **Vichada** *R* Colombia
61F2 **Vichuga** Russian Fed
49C2 **Vichy** France
19B3 **Vicksburg** USA
35C2 **Vicosa** Brazil
106C4 **Victor Harbour** Aust
34C2 **Victoria** Arg
13C3 **Victoria** Can
34A3 **Victoria** Chile
78D1 **Victoria** Malay
108B3 **Victoria** State, Aust
9D4 **Victoria** USA
106C2 **Victoria** *R* Aust
26B2 **Victoria de las Tunas** Cuba
100B2 **Victoria Falls** Zambia/Zim
4G2 **Victoria I** Can
108B2 **Victoria,L** Aust
99D3 **Victoria,L** C Africa
112B7 **Victoria Land** Region, Ant
86C2 **Victoria,Mt** Burma
99D2 **Victoria Nile** *R* Uganda
111B2 **Victoria Range** *Mts* NZ
106C2 **Victoria River Downs** Aust
4H3 **Victoria Str** Can
15D1 **Victoriaville** Can
100B4 **Victoria West** S Africa
34B3 **Victorica** Arg
21B3 **Victorville** USA
34A2 **Vicuña** Chile
34C2 **Vicuña Mackenna** Arg
17B1 **Vidalia** USA
54C2 **Videle** Rom
54B2 **Vidin** Bulg
85D4 **Vidisha** India
58D1 **Vidzy** Belorussia
29D4 **Viedma** Arg
26A4 **Viéjo** Costa Rica
Vielha = Viella
51C1 **Viella** Spain
Vienna = Wien
18C2 **Vienna** Illinois, USA
14B3 **Vienna** W Virginia, USA
49C2 **Vienne** France
48C2 **Vienne** *R* France
76C2 **Vientiane** Laos
47C1 **Vierwaldstätter See** *L* Switz
48C2 **Vierzon** France
53C2 **Vieste** Italy
70B2 **Vietnam** Republic, S E Asia
76D1 **Vietri** Viet
27P2 **Vieux Fort** St Lucia
79B2 **Vigan** Phil
47C2 **Vigevano** Italy
48B3 **Vignemale** *Mt* France
50A1 **Vigo** Spain
87C1 **Vijayawāda** India
55A2 **Vijosë** *R* Alb
38B2 **Vik** Iceland
54B2 **Vikhren** *Mt* Bulg
13E2 **Viking** Can
38G6 **Vikna** *I* Nor
101C2 **Vila da Maganja** Mozam
101C2 **Vila Machado** Mozam
101C3 **Vilanculos** Mozam
Vilanova i la Geltrú = Villanova-y-Geltrú
50A1 **Vila Real** Port
101C2 **Vila Vasco da Gama** Mozam
35C2 **Vila Velha** Brazil
58D2 **Vileyka** Belorussia
38H6 **Vilhelmina** Sweden
33E6 **Vilhena** Brazil
60C2 **Viljandi** Estonia
101G1 **Viljoenskroon** S Africa
9C3 **Villa Ahumada** Mexico
34B2 **Villa Atuel** Arg
50A1 **Villaba** Spain
23A2 **Villa Carranza** Mexico
52B1 **Villach** Austria
34B2 **Villa Colon** Arg
34C2 **Villa Constitución** Arg
34C1 **Villa de Maria** Arg
23A1 **Villa de Reyes** Mexico
34B2 **Villa Dolores** Arg
47D2 **Villafranca di Verona** Italy
34C2 **Villa General Mitre** Arg
34B2 **Villa General Roca** Arg
34D2 **Villaguay** Arg
25C3 **Villahermosa** Mexico
23A1 **Villa Hidalgo** Mexico
34C2 **Villa Huidobro** Arg
34C3 **Villa Iris** Arg
34C2 **Villa Maria** Arg
30D3 **Villa Montes** Bol
23A1 **Villaneuva** Mexico
50A1 **Villa Nova de Gaia** Port
50A2 **Villanueva de la Serena** Spain
51C1 **Villanueva-y-Geltrú** Spain
34B3 **Villa Regina** Arg
51B2 **Villarreal** Spain
29B3 **Villarrica** Chile
30E4 **Villarrica** Par
50B2 **Villarrobledo** Spain
34D2 **Villa San José** Arg
34C2 **Villa Valeria** Arg
32C3 **Villavicencio** Colombia
49C2 **Villefranche** France
7C5 **Ville-Marie** Can
51B2 **Villena** Spain
46B2 **Villeneuve-St-Georges** France
48C3 **Villeneuve-sur-Lot** France
19B3 **Ville Platte** USA
46B2 **Villers-Cotterêts** France
49C2 **Villeurbanne** France
101G1 **Villiers** S Africa
87B2 **Villupuram** India
58D2 **Vilnius** Lithuania
63D1 **Vilyuy** *R* Russian Fed
63E1 **Vilyuysk** Russian Fed
34A2 **Viña del Mar** Chile
51C1 **Vinaroz** Spain
14A3 **Vincennes** USA
38H5 **Vindel** *R* Sweden
85D4 **Vindhya Range** *Mts* India
16B3 **Vineland** USA
16D2 **Vineyard Haven** USA
76D2 **Vinh** Viet
76D3 **Vinh Cam Ranh** *B* Viet
77D4 **Vinh Loi** Viet
77D3 **Vinh Long** Viet
18A2 **Vinita** USA
54A1 **Vinkovci** Croatia
60C4 **Vinnitsa** Ukraine
112B3 **Vinson Massif** *Upland* Ant
100A3 **Vioolsdrift** S Africa
47D1 **Vipiteno** Italy
79B3 **Virac** Phil
87B2 **Virddhāchalam** India
100A2 **Virei** Angola
35C1 **Virgem da Lapa** Brazil
101G1 **Virginia** S Africa
10C3 **Virginia** State, USA
10A2 **Virginia** USA
21B2 **Virginia City** USA
27E3 **Virgin Is** Caribbean S
52C1 **Virovitica** Croatia
46C2 **Virton** Belg
87B3 **Virudunagar** India
52C2 **Vis** *I* Croatia
21B2 **Visalia** USA
79B3 **Visayan S** Phil
39H7 **Visby** Sweden
4H2 **Viscount Melville Sd** Can
54A2 **Višegrad** Bosnia & Herzegovina, Yugos
50A1 **Viseu** Port
83C4 **Vishākhapatnam** India
47B1 **Visp** Switz
49C1 **Vissingen** Neth
21B3 **Vista** USA
Vistula = Wisla
57C3 **Vitavia** *R* Czech
87A1 **Vite** India
60D2 **Vitebsk** Belorussia
52B2 **Viterbo** Italy
50A1 **Vitigudino** Spain
63D2 **Vitim** *R* Russian Fed
50B1 **Vitora** Spain
31C6 **Vitória** Brazil
31C4 **Vitória da Conquista** Brazil
48B2 **Vitré** France
46C2 **Vitry-le-Francois** France
38J5 **Vittangi** Sweden
53B3 **Vittoria** Italy
47E2 **Vittorio Veneto** Italy
69H2 **Vityaz Depth** Pacific O
50A1 **Vivero** Spain
63B1 **Vivi** *R* Russian Fed
34D3 **Vivorata** Arg
63C2 **Vizhne-Angarsk** Russian Fed
83C4 **Vizianagaram** India
54B1 **Vlădeasa** *Mt* Rom
61F5 **Vladikavkaz** Russian Fed
65F4 **Vladimir** Russian Fed
59C2 **Vladimir Volynskiy** Ukraine
74C2 **Vladivostok** Russian Fed
56A2 **Vlieland** *I* Neth
46B1 **Vlissingen** Neth
55A2 **Vlorë** Alb
57C3 **Vöcklabruck** Austria
76D3 **Voeune Sai** Camb
47C2 **Voghera** Italy
101D2 **Vohibinany** Madag
101E2 **Vohimarina** Madag
99D3 **Voi** Kenya
97B4 **Voinjama** Lib
49D2 **Voiron** France
54A1 **Vojvodina** *Aut Republic* Serbia, Yugos
26A5 **Volcán Baru** *Mt* Panama
23B2 **Volcán Citlaltepetl** *Mt* Mexico
30C3 **Volcán Lullaillaco** *Mt* Chile
34A3 **Volcáno Copahue** *Mt* Chile
34A3 **Volcáno Domuyo** *Mt* Arg
Volcano Is = Kazan Retto
29B3 **Volcáno Lanin** *Mt* Arg
30C3 **Volcán Ollagüe** *Mt* Chile
34A3 **Volcáno Llaima** *Mt* Chile
34B2 **Volcáno Maipo** *Mt* Arg
34A3 **Volcáno Peteroa** *Mt* Chile
34B3 **Volcáno Tromen** *V* Arg
23A2 **Volcán Paracutin** *Mt* Mexico
32B3 **Volcán Puraće** *Mt* Colombia
34A2 **Volcán Tinguiririca** *Mt* Arg/Chile
61J2 **Volchansk** Russian Fed
61G4 **Volga** *R* Russian Fed
61F4 **Volgodonsk** Russian Fed
61F4 **Volgograd** Russian Fed
61G3 **Volgogradskoye Vodokhranilishche** *Res* Russian Fed
60D2 **Volkhov** Russian Fed
60D2 **Volkhov** *R* Russian Fed
58C2 **Volkovysk** Belorussia
101G1 **Volksrust** S Africa
61F2 **Vologda** Russian Fed

48B2 **Volognes** France
55B3 **Vólos** Greece
61G3 **Vol'sk** Russian Fed
22B2 **Volta** USA
97B3 **Volta Blanche** *R* Burkina
97B4 **Volta,L** Ghana
97B3 **Volta Noire** *R* Burkina
35C2 **Volta Redonda** Brazil
97B3 **Volta Rouge** *R* Burkina
61F4 **Volzhskiy** Russian Fed
12D2 **Von Frank Mt** USA
6J3 **Vopnafjörður** Iceland
47C1 **Voralberg** Province, Austria
47C1 **Vorder Rhein** *R* Switz
56C1 **Vordingborg** Den
64H3 **Vorkuta** Russian Fed
39G6 **Vorma** *R* Nor
60E3 **Voronezh** Russian Fed
38M5 **Voron'ya** *R* Russian Fed
39K7 **Võru** Estonia
49D2 **Vosges** *Mt* France
39F6 **Voss** Nor
63B2 **Vostochnyy Sayan** *Mts* Russian Fed
112B9 **Vostok** *Base* Ant
61H2 **Votkinsk** Russian Fed
46C2 **Vouziers** France
60D4 **Voznesensk** Ukraine
54B2 **Vranje** Serbia, Yugos
54B2 **Vratsa** Bulg
54A1 **Vrbas** Serbia, Yugos
52C2 **Vrbas** *R* Serbia, Yugos
52B1 **Vrbovsko** Bosnia & Herzegovina, Yugos
101G1 **Vrede** S Africa
33F2 **Vreed en Hoop** Guyana
54B1 **Vršac** Serbia, Yugos
52C2 **Vrtoče** Bosnia & Herzegovina, Yugos
100B3 **Vryburg** S Africa
101H1 **Vryheid** S Africa
54A1 **Vukovar** Croatia
13E2 **Vulcan** Can
53B3 **Vulcano** *I* Italy
77D3 **Vung Tau** Viet
38J5 **Vuollerim** Sweden
38L6 **Vyartsilya** Russian Fed
61H2 **Vyatka** *R* Russian Fed
69F2 **Vyazemskiy** Russian Fed
60D2 **Vyaz'ma** Russian Fed
61F2 **Vyazniki** Russian Fed
60C1 **Vyborg** Russian Fed
64G3 **Vym'** *R* Russian Fed
43C3 **Vyrnwy** *R* Wales
60D2 **Vyshiy Volochek** Russian Fed
59B3 **Vyškov** Czech
60E1 **Vytegra** Russian Fed

W

97B3 **Wa** Ghana
13E1 **Wabasca** Can
5G4 **Wabasca** *R* Can
13E1 **Wabasca L** Can
14A2 **Wabash** USA
14A3 **Wabash** *R* USA
5J4 **Wabowden** Can
7D4 **Wabush** Can
17B2 **Waccasassa B** USA
16D1 **Wachusett Res** USA
19A3 **Waco** USA
85B3 **Wad** Pak
95A2 **Waddān** Libya
5F4 **Waddington,Mt** Can
93E4 **Wadi al Bātin** *Watercourse* Iraq
93D3 **Wadi al Ghudāf** *Watercourse* Iraq
94C2 **Wadi al Harīr** *V* Syria
93D3 **Wadi al Mirah** *Watercourse* Iraq/ S Arabia
93D3 **Wadi al Ubayyid** *Watercourse* Iraq
93D3 **Wadi Ar'ar** *Watercourse* S Arabia
91A5 **Wadi as Hsabā'** *Watercourse* S Arabia
92C3 **Wadi as Sirhān** *V* Jordan/S Arabia
94C2 **Wadi az Zaydi** *V* Syria
94C3 **Wadi edh Dhab'i** *V* Jordan
94A3 **Wadi el 'Arish** *V* Egypt
94C3 **Wadi el Ghadaf** *V* Jordan
94B3 **Wadi el Hasa** *V* Jordan
94C3 **Wadi el Janab** *V* Jordan
94B3 **Wadi el Jeib** *V* Israel/ Jordan
95B3 **Wadi el Milk** *Watercourse* Sudan
92A3 **Wadi el Natrun** *Watercourse* Egypt
94B3 **Wadi es Sir** Jordan
94B3 **Wadi Fidan** *V* Jordan
94B3 **Wadi Hareidin** *V* Egypt
93D3 **Wadi Hawrān** *R* Iraq
95B3 **Wadi Howa** *Watercourse* Sudan
98C1 **Wadi Ibra** *Watercourse* Sudan
94C2 **Wadi Luhfi** *Watercourse* Jordan
94B3 **Wadi Mujib** *V* Jordan
94B3 **Wadi Qîtaiya** *V* Egypt
80B3 **Wadi Sha'it** *Watercourse* Egypt
99D1 **Wad Medani** Sudan
93E4 **Wafra** Kuwait
6B3 **Wager B** Can
6A3 **Wager Bay** Can
109C3 **Wagga Wagga** Aust
106A4 **Wagin** Aust
95A2 **Wāḥa** Libya
21C4 **Wahaiwa** Hawaiian Is
18A1 **Wahoo** USA
8D2 **Wahpeton** USA
87A1 **Wai** India
111B2 **Waiau** NZ
111A3 **Waiau** *R* NZ
111B2 **Waiau** *R* NZ
71E3 **Waigeo** *I* Indon
110C1 **Waihi** NZ
110C1 **Waikaremoana,L** NZ
110C1 **Waikato** *R* NZ
108A2 **Waikerie** Aust
111B3 **Waikouaiti** NZ
21C4 **Wailuku** Hawaiian Is
111B2 **Waimakariri** *R* NZ
111B2 **Waimate** NZ
21C4 **Waimea** Hawaiian Is
106B1 **Waingapu** Indon
13E2 **Wainwright** Can
4B2 **Wainwright** USA
111B2 **Waipara** NZ
110C2 **Waipukurau** NZ
111C2 **Wairarapa,L** NZ
111B2 **Wairau** *R* NZ
110C1 **Wairoa** NZ
110C1 **Wairoa** *R* NZ
111B2 **Waitaki** *R* NZ
110B1 **Waitara** NZ
110C1 **Waitomo** NZ
110B1 **Waiuku** NZ
75B1 **Wajima** Japan
99E2 **Wajir** Kenya
75B1 **Wakasa-wan** *B* Japan
111A3 **Wakatipu,L** NZ
74D4 **Wakayama** Japan
42D3 **Wakefield** Eng
27H1 **Wakefield** Jamaica
16D2 **Wakefield** Rhode Island, USA
76B2 **Wakema** Burma
69G2 **Wakkanai** Japan
108B3 **Wakool** *R* Aust
59B2 **Walbrzych** Pol
109D2 **Walcha** Aust
58B2 **Walcz** Pol
46D1 **Waldbröl** Germany
16B2 **Walden** USA
43C3 **Wales** Country, UK
12A1 **Wales** USA
6B3 **Wales I** Can
109C2 **Walgett** Aust
112B4 **Walgreen Coast** Region, Ant
99C3 **Walikale** Zaïre
21B2 **Walker** *L* USA
14B2 **Walkerton** Can
8B2 **Wallace** USA
108A2 **Wallaroo** Aust
109C3 **Walla Walla** Aust
20C1 **Walla Walla** USA
16C2 **Wallingford** USA
105H4 **Wallis and Futuna** *Is* Pacific O
20C1 **Wallowa** USA
20C1 **Wallowa Mts** *Mts* USA
109C1 **Wallumbilla** Aust
18B2 **Walnut Ridge** USA
110C1 **Walouru** NZ
43D3 **Walsall** Eng
9C3 **Walsenburg** USA
9C3 **Walsenburgh** USA
17B1 **Walterboro** USA
17A1 **Walter F George Res** USA
16D1 **Waltham** USA
100A3 **Walvis Bay** S Africa
103J6 **Walvis Ridge** Atlantic O
97C4 **Wamba** Nig
98B3 **Wamba** *R* Zaïre
18A2 **Wamego** USA
84B2 **Wana** Pak
108B1 **Wanaaring** Aust
111A2 **Wanaka** NZ
111A2 **Wanaka,L** NZ
14B1 **Wanapitei L** Can
109C1 **Wandoan** Aust
108B3 **Wanganella** Aust
110C1 **Wanganui** NZ
110C1 **Wanganui** *R* NZ
109C3 **Wangaratta** Aust
99E2 **Wanle Weyne** Somalia
76E2 **Wanning** China
87B1 **Wanparti** India
73B3 **Wanxian** China
73B3 **Wanyuan** China
13D2 **Wapiti** *R* Can
18B2 **Wappapello,L** USA
16C2 **Wappingers Falls** USA
87B1 **Warangal** India
109C4 **Waratah** Aust
108C3 **Waratah B** Aust
108C3 **Warburton** Aust
108A1 **Warburton** *R* Aust
109C1 **Ward** *R* Aust
101G1 **Warden** S Africa
99E2 **Warder** Eth
85D4 **Wardha** India
111A3 **Ward,Mt** NZ
5F4 **Ware** Can
16C1 **Ware** USA
16D2 **Wareham** USA
109D1 **Warialda** Aust
76C2 **Warin Chamrap** Thai
100B3 **Warmbad** S Africa
16B2 **Warminster** USA
21B2 **Warm Springs** USA
56C2 **Warnemünde** Germany
20B2 **Warner Mts** USA
17B1 **Warner Robins** USA
108B3 **Warracknabeal** Aust
108A1 **Warrandirinna,L** Aust
107D3 **Warrego** *R* Aust
19B3 **Warren** Arkansas, USA
109C2 **Warren** Aust
16D2 **Warren** Massachusetts, USA
14B2 **Warren** Ohio, USA
15C2 **Warren** Pennsylvania, USA
45C1 **Warrenpoint** N Ire
18B2 **Warrensburg** USA
101F1 **Warrenton** S Africa
15C3 **Warrenton** USA
97C4 **Warri** Nig
108A1 **Warrina** Aust
42C3 **Warrington** Eng
108B3 **Warrnambool** Aust
Warsaw = Warszawa
58C2 **Warszawa** Pol
59B2 **Warta** *R* Pol
109D1 **Warwick** Aust
43D3 **Warwick** County, Eng
43D3 **Warwick** Eng
16B2 **Warwick** New York, USA
16D2 **Warwick** Rhode Island, USA
8B3 **Wasatch Range** *Mts* USA
101H1 **Wasbank** S Africa
21B2 **Wasco** USA
4H2 **Washburn L** Can
85D4 **Wāshīm** India
10C3 **Washington** District of Columbia, USA
17B1 **Washington** Georgia, USA
14A3 **Washington** Indiana, USA
18B2 **Washington** Missouri, USA
16B2 **Washington** New Jersey, USA
14B2 **Washington** Pennsylvania, USA
8A2 **Washington** State, USA
14B3 **Washington Court House** USA
6D1 **Washington Land** Can
15D2 **Washington,Mt** USA
43E3 **Wash,The** Eng
85A3 **Washuk** Pak
12E2 **Wasilla** USA
7C4 **Waskaganish** Can
26A4 **Waspán** Nic
70D4 **Watampone** Indon
16C2 **Waterbury** USA
45C2 **Waterford** County, Irish Rep
41B3 **Waterford** Irish Rep
45C2 **Waterford Harbour** Irish Rep
46C1 **Waterloo** Belg
10A2 **Waterloo** USA
15C2 **Watertown** New York, USA
101H1 **Waterval-Boven** S Africa
10D2 **Waterville** Maine, USA
16C1 **Watervliet** USA
5G4 **Waterways** Can
43D4 **Watford** Eng
15C2 **Watkins Glen** USA
8C1 **Watrous** Can
99C2 **Watsa** Zaïre
12J2 **Watson Lake** Can
22B2 **Watsonville** USA
71F4 **Wau** PNG
99C2 **Wau** Sudan
7B5 **Waua** Can
109D2 **Wauchope** Aust
17B2 **Wauchula** USA
14A2 **Waukegan** USA
10B2 **Wausau** USA
14A2 **Wauwatosa** USA
106C2 **Wave Hill** Aust
43E3 **Waveney** *R* Eng
14B3 **Waverly** Ohio, USA
46C1 **Wavre** Belg
10B2 **Wawa** Can
95A2 **Wāw Al Kabīr** Libya
95A2 **Wāw an Nāmūs** *Well* Libya
22C2 **Wawona** USA

19A3 **Waxahachie** USA
17B1 **Waycross** USA
17B1 **Waynesboro** Georgia, USA
19C3 **Waynesboro** Mississippi, USA
16A3 **Waynesboro** Pennsylvania, USA
15C3 **Waynesboro** Virginia, USA
18B2 **Waynesville** Missouri, USA
84B2 **Wazi Khwa** Afghan
43E4 **Weald,The** *Upland* Eng
42C2 **Wear** *R* Eng
19A3 **Weatherford** Texas, USA
20B2 **Weaverville** USA
14B1 **Webbwood** Can
16D1 **Webster** USA
18B2 **Webster Groves** USA
29D6 **Weddell I** Falkland Is
112C2 **Weddell S** Ant
13C2 **Wedge Mt** Can
20B2 **Weed** USA
101H1 **Weenen** S Africa
109C2 **Wee Waa** Aust
72D1 **Weichang** China
57C3 **Weiden** Germany
72D2 **Weifang** China
72E2 **Weihai** China
72C3 **Wei He** *R* Henan, China
72C2 **Wei He** *R* Shaanxi, China
109C1 **Weilmoringle** Aust
73A4 **Weining** China
107D2 **Weipa** Aust
14B2 **Weirton** USA
20C2 **Weiser** USA
72D3 **Weishan Hu** *L* China
57C2 **Weissenfels** Germany
17A1 **Weiss L** USA
99D1 **Weldiya** Eth
101G1 **Welkom** S Africa
15C2 **Welland** Can
43D3 **Welland** *R* Eng
106C2 **Wellesley Is** Aust
12G2 **Wellesley L** Can
43D3 **Wellingborough** Eng
109C2 **Wellington** Aust
18A2 **Wellington** Kansas, USA
111B2 **Wellington** NZ
6A2 **Wellington Chan** Can
13C2 **Wells** Can
43C4 **Wells** Eng
110B1 **Wellsford** NZ
106B3 **Wells,L** Aust
57C3 **Wels** Austria
43C3 **Welshpool** Wales
13D1 **Wembley** Can
7C4 **Wemindji** Can
20B1 **Wenatchee** USA
20C1 **Wenatchee** *R* USA
97B4 **Wenchi** Ghana
72E2 **Wenden** China
73E4 **Wenling** China
32J7 **Wenman** *I* Ecuador
73A5 **Wenshan** China
107D4 **Wenthaggi** Aust
108B2 **Wentworth** Aust
72A3 **Wen Xian** China
73E4 **Wenzhou** China
73C4 **Wenzhu** China
101G1 **Wepener** S Africa
12G1 **Wernecke Mts** Can
57C2 **Werra** *R* Germany
109D2 **Werris Creek** Aust
56B2 **Wesel** Germany
56B2 **Weser** *R* Germany
106C2 **Wessel Is** Aust
14A2 **West Allis** USA
104C4 **West Australian Basin** Indian O
104C5 **West Australian Ridge** Indian O
19C3 **West B** USA
86B2 **West Bengal** State, India
43D3 **West Bromwich** Eng
16B3 **West Chester** USA
46D1 **Westerburg** Germany
56B2 **Westerland** Germany
16D2 **Westerly** USA
106A3 **Western Australia** State, Aust
87A1 **Western Ghats** *Mts* India
44A3 **Western Isles** Scot
96A2 **Western Sahara** Region, Mor
105H4 **Western Samoa** *Is* Pacific O
46B1 **Westerschelde** *Estuary* Neth
46D1 **Westerwald** Region, Germany
49D1 **Westfalen** Region, Germany
29D6 **West Falkland** *I* Falkland Is
16C1 **Westfield** Massachusetts, USA
15C2 **Westfield** New York, USA
18C2 **West Frankfort** USA
109C1 **Westgate** Aust
43C4 **West Glamorgan** County, Wales
102E3 **West Indies** *Is* Caribbean S
13E2 **Westlock** Can
14B2 **West Lorne** Can
45C2 **Westmeath** County, Irish Rep
18B2 **West Memphis** USA
43D3 **West Midlands** County, Eng
43D4 **Westminster** Eng
16A3 **Westminster** Maryland, USA
17B1 **Westminster** S Carolina, USA
100B3 **West Nicholson** Zim
78D1 **Weston** Malay
14B3 **Weston** USA
43C4 **Weston-super-Mare** Eng
17B2 **West Palm Beach** USA
18B2 **West Plains** USA
22B1 **West Point** California, USA
19C3 **West Point** Mississippi, USA
16C2 **West Point** New York, USA
12F2 **West Point** *Mt* USA
45B2 **Westport** Irish Rep
111B2 **Westport** NZ
40C2 **Westray** *I* Scot
13C2 **West Road** *R* Can
42E3 **West Sole** *Oilfield* N Sea
11B3 **West Virginia** State, USA
22C1 **West Walker** *R* USA
109C2 **West Wyalong** Aust
42D3 **West Yorkshire** County, Eng
71D4 **Wetar** *I* Indon
13E2 **Wetaskiwin** Can
99D3 **Wete** Tanz
46E1 **Wetzlar** Germany
Wevok = Cape Lisburne
71F4 **Wewak** PNG
19A2 **Wewoka** USA
45C2 **Wexford** County, Irish Rep
45C2 **Wexford** Irish Rep
5H5 **Weyburn** Can
43C4 **Weymouth** Eng
16D1 **Weymouth** USA
110C1 **Whakatane** NZ
110C1 **Whakatane** *R* NZ
44E1 **Whalsay** *I* Scot
110B1 **Whangarei** NZ
42D3 **Wharfe** *R* Eng
19A4 **Wharton** USA
111B2 **Whataroa** NZ
16A3 **Wheaton** Maryland, USA
8B3 **Wheeler Peak** *Mt* Nevada, USA
9C3 **Wheeler Peak** *Mt* New Mexico, USA
14B2 **Wheeling** USA
13C3 **Whistler** Can
15C2 **Whitby** Can
42D2 **Whitby** Eng
18B2 **White** *R* Arkansas, USA
12F2 **White** *R* Can
14A3 **White** *R* Indiana, USA
8C2 **White** *R* S Dakota, USA
7E4 **White B** Can
108B2 **White Cliffs** Aust
40C2 **White Coomb** *Mt* Scot
13D2 **Whitecourt** Can
14A1 **Whitefish Pt** USA
7D4 **Whitegull L** Can
15D2 **Whitehall** New York, USA
16B2 **Whitehall** Pennsylvania, USA
42C2 **Whitehaven** Eng
12G2 **Whitehorse** Can
110C1 **White I** NZ
19B4 **White L** USA
109C4 **Whitemark** Aust
21B2 **White Mountain Peak** *Mt* USA
12E1 **White Mts** Alaska, USA
15D2 **White Mts** New Hampshire, USA
99D1 **White Nile** *R* Sudan
16C2 **White Plains** USA
7B5 **White River** Can
15D2 **White River Junction** USA
White S = Beloye More
13B2 **Whitesail L** Can
20B1 **White Salmon** USA
17C1 **Whiteville** USA
97B4 **White Volta** *R* Ghana
42B2 **Whithorn** Scot
17B1 **Whitmire** USA
21B2 **Whitney,Mt** USA
12E2 **Whittier** Alaska, USA
22C4 **Whittier** California, USA
5H3 **Wholdia L** Can
108A2 **Whyalla** Aust
14B2 **Wiarton** Can
18A2 **Wichita** USA
9D3 **Wichita Falls** USA
44C2 **Wick** Scot
45C2 **Wicklow** County, Irish Rep
45C2 **Wicklow** Irish Rep
45C2 **Wicklow** *Mts* Irish Rep
109C1 **Widgeegoara** *R* Aust
46D1 **Wied** *R* Germany
59B2 **Wielun** Pol
59B3 **Wien** Austria
59B3 **Wiener Neustadt** Austria
58C2 **Wieprz** *R* Pol
46E1 **Wiesbaden** Germany
42C3 **Wigan** Eng
19C3 **Wiggins** USA
42B2 **Wigtown** Scot
42B2 **Wigtown B** Scot
47C1 **Wil** Switz
20C1 **Wilbur** USA
108B2 **Wilcannia** Aust
21B2 **Wildcat Peak** *Mt* USA
47B1 **Wildhorn** *Mt* Switz
13E2 **Wild Horse** Can
47D1 **Wildspitze** *Mt* Austria
17B2 **Wildwood** Florida, USA
16B3 **Wildwood** New Jersey, USA
101G1 **Wilge** *R* S Africa
56B2 **Wilhelmshaven** Germany
15C2 **Wilkes-Barre** USA
112B8 **Wilkes Land** Ant
13F2 **Wilkie** Can
20B2 **Willamette** *R* USA
108B2 **Willandra** *R* Aust
20B1 **Willapa B** USA
9C3 **Willcox** USA
27D4 **Willemstad** Curaçao
108A1 **William Creek** Aust
108B3 **William,Mt** Aust
21A2 **Williams** California, USA
13C2 **Williams Lake** Can
15C2 **Williamsport** USA
16C1 **Williamstown** Massachusetts, USA
14B3 **Williamstown** W Virginia, USA
16C2 **Willimantic** USA
16B2 **Willingboro** USA
13D2 **Willingdon,Mt** Can
107E2 **Willis Group** *Is* Aust
17B2 **Williston** Florida, USA
100B4 **Williston** S Africa
13C1 **Williston L** Can
8D2 **Willmar** USA
108A3 **Willoughby,C** Aust
13C2 **Willow** *R* Can
20B2 **Willow Ranch** USA
21A2 **Willows** USA
18B2 **Willow Springs** USA
108A2 **Wilmington** Aust
16B3 **Wilmington** Delaware, USA
17C1 **Wilmington** N Carolina, USA
7A5 **Wilnona** USA
11C3 **Wilson** USA
108B1 **Wilson** *R* Aust
6B3 **Wilson,C** Can
22C3 **Wilson,Mt** California, USA
20B1 **Wilson,Mt** Oregon, USA
109C3 **Wilsons Promontory** *Pen* Aust
43D4 **Wiltshire** County, Eng
46C2 **Wiltz** Lux
106B3 **Wiluna** Aust
14A2 **Winamac** USA
101G1 **Winburg** S Africa
16C1 **Winchendon** USA
15C1 **Winchester** Can
43D4 **Winchester** Eng
16C1 **Winchester** New Hampshire, USA
15C3 **Winchester** Virginia, USA
42C2 **Windermere** Eng
100A3 **Windhoek** Namibia
107D3 **Windorah** Aust
8C2 **Wind River Range** *Mts* USA
109D2 **Windsor** Aust
16C2 **Windsor** Connecticut, USA
43D4 **Windsor** Eng
7D5 **Windsor** Nova Scotia, Can
14B2 **Windsor** Ontario, Can
15D1 **Windsor** Quebec, Can
17B1 **Windsor Forest** USA
16C2 **Windsor Locks** USA
27E4 **Windward Is** Caribbean S
26C3 **Windward Pass** Caribbean S
13E1 **Winefred L** Can
18A2 **Winfield** Kansas, USA
109D2 **Wingham** Aust
34C3 **Winifreda** Arg
7B4 **Winisk** *R* Can
7B4 **Winisk L** Can
76B2 **Winkana** Burma
20B1 **Winlock** USA
97B4 **Winneba** Ghana
14A2 **Winnebago,L** USA
20C2 **Winnemucca** USA
19B3 **Winnfield** USA

5J4 **Winnipeg** Can
5J4 **Winnipeg,L** Can
5J4 **Winnipegosis** Can
4J4 **Winnipegosis,L** Can
15D2 **Winnipesaukee,L** USA
10A2 **Winona** Minnesota, USA
19C3 **Winona** Mississippi, USA
15D2 **Winooski** USA
9B3 **Winslow** USA
16C2 **Winsted** USA
11B3 **Winston-Salem** USA
46E1 **Winterberg** Germany
17B2 **Winter Garden** USA
17B2 **Winter Park** USA
22B1 **Winters** USA
47C1 **Winterthur** Switz
107D3 **Winton** Aust
111A3 **Winton** NZ
43E3 **Wisbech** Eng
10B2 **Wisconsin** State, USA
7B5 **Wisconsin Rapids** USA
12D1 **Wiseman** USA
58B2 **Wisla** *R* Pol
56C2 **Wismar** Germany
33F2 **Witagron** Surinam
101G1 **Witbank** S Africa
9D3 **Witchita Falls** USA
43D3 **Witham** *R* Eng
42E3 **Withernsea** Eng
43D4 **Witney** Eng
46D1 **Witten** Germany
56C2 **Wittenberg** Germany
106A3 **Wittenoom** Aust
46D1 **Wittlich** Germany
58B2 **Wladyslawowo** Pol
58B2 **Włocławek** Pol
58C2 **Włodawa** Pol
109C3 **Wodonga** Aust
47C1 **Wohlen** Switz
71E4 **Wokam** Indon
43D4 **Woking** Eng
71F3 **Woleai** *I* Pacific O
20B2 **Wolf Creek** USA
8C2 **Wolf Point** USA
57C3 **Wolfsberg** Austria
56C2 **Wolfsburg** Germany
5H4 **Wollaston L** Can
5H4 **Wollaston Lake** Can
4G3 **Wollaston Pen** Can
109D2 **Wollongong** Aust
101G1 **Wolmaransstad** S Africa
59B2 **Wolow** Pol
108B3 **Wolseley** Aust
43C3 **Wolverhampton** Eng
16A2 **Womelsdorf** USA
109D1 **Wondai** Aust
74B3 **Wŏnju** S Korea
108B2 **Wonominta** *R* Aust
13C1 **Wonowon** Can
74B3 **Wŏnsan** N Korea
108C3 **Wonthaggi** Aust
108A2 **Woocalla** Aust
16B3 **Woodbine** USA
15C3 **Woodbridge** USA
5G4 **Wood Buffalo Nat Pk** Can
109D1 **Woodburn** Aust
20B1 **Woodburn** USA
16B3 **Woodbury** USA
12F1 **Woodchopper** USA
21A2 **Woodland** California, USA
20B1 **Woodland** Washington, USA
107E1 **Woodlark** *I* PNG
106C4 **Woodmera** Aust
106C3 **Woodroffe,Mt** Aust
14B2 **Woodstock** Ontario, Can
16B3 **Woodstown** USA
110C2 **Woodville** NZ
19B3 **Woodville** USA
108A2 **Woomera** Aust
15D2 **Woonsocket** USA
14B2 **Wooster** USA
43C3 **Worcester** Eng
100A4 **Worcester** S Africa
16D1 **Worcester** USA
47E1 **Wörgl** Austria
42C2 **Workington** Eng
8C2 **Worland** USA
46E2 **Worms** Germany
43B4 **Worms Head** *Pt* Wales
43D4 **Worthing** Eng
8D2 **Worthington** USA
71D4 **Wowoni** *I* Indon
12H3 **Wrangell** USA
12H3 **Wrangell I** USA
12F2 **Wrangell Mts** USA
40B2 **Wrath,C** Scot
43C3 **Wrexham** Wales
17B1 **Wrightsville** USA
22D3 **Wrightwood** USA
4F3 **Wrigley** Can
59B2 **Wrocław** Pol
58B2 **Wrzésnia** Pol
69E2 **Wuchang** China
76E1 **Wuchuan** China
72E2 **Wuda** China
72C2 **Wuding He** *R* China
72A3 **Wudu** China
73C4 **Wugang** China
72B2 **Wuhai** China
73C3 **Wuhan** China
73D3 **Wuhu** China
73D5 **Wuhua** China
84D2 **Wüjang** China
72B1 **Wujia He** *R* China
73B4 **Wu Jiang** *R* China
97C4 **Wukari** Nig
73B4 **Wuling Shan** *Mts* China
97D4 **Wum** Cam
73A4 **Wumeng Shan** *Upland* China
46D1 **Wuppertal** Germany
72B2 **Wuqi** China
72D2 **Wuqing** China
57B3 **Würzburg** Germany
57C2 **Wurzen** Germany
72C2 **Wutai Shan** *Mt* China
71F4 **Wuvulu** *I* Pacific O
72A2 **Wuwei** China
73E3 **Wuxi** China
73E3 **Wuxing** China
72C2 **Wuyang** China
73D4 **Wuyi Shan** *Mts* China
72B1 **Wuyuan** China
76D2 **Wuzhi Shan** *Mts* China
72B2 **Wuzhong** China
73C5 **Wuzhou** China
14B2 **Wyandotte** USA
109C1 **Wyandra** Aust
43C4 **Wye** *R* Eng
43C4 **Wylye** *R* Eng
43E3 **Wymondham** Eng
106B2 **Wyndham** Aust
18B2 **Wynne** USA
4G2 **Wynniatt B** Can
109C4 **Wynyard** Aust
8C2 **Wyoming** State, USA
14A2 **Wyoming** USA
109D2 **Wyong** Aust

X

84D1 **Xaidulla** China
72D1 **Xai Moron He** *R* China
101C3 **Xai Xai** Mozam
23B2 **Xaltinguis** Mexico
100A2 **Xangongo** Angola
46D1 **Xanten** Germany
55B2 **Xánthi** Greece
100B3 **Xau,L** Botswana
14B3 **Xenia** USA
68B4 **Xiaguan** China
72A2 **Xiahe** China
73D5 **Xiamen** China
72B3 **Xi'an** China
73B4 **Xianfeng** China
73C3 **Xiangfan** China
73C4 **Xiang Jiang** *R* China
73C4 **Xiangtan** Province, China
73C4 **Xianning** China
72B3 **Xianyang** China
73C4 **Xiao Shui** *R* China
73D4 **Xiapu** China
73A4 **Xichang** China
23B1 **Xicotepec** Mexico
76C2 **Xieng Khouang** Laos
73B4 **Xifeng** China
86B1 **Xigazê** China
72A1 **Xi He** *R* China
72B2 **Xiji** China
73C5 **Xi Jiang** *R* China
72E1 **Xiliao He** *R* China
73B5 **Xilin** China
23B1 **Xilitla** Mexico
73D4 **Xinfeng** China
72C1 **Xinghe** China
73D5 **Xingning** China
73B4 **Xingren** China
72C2 **Xingtai** China
33G4 **Xingu** *R* Brazil
68B2 **Xingxingxia** China
73A4 **Xingyi** China
72A2 **Xining** China
72E2 **Xinjin** Liaoning, China
73A3 **Xinjin** Sichuan, China
72D2 **Xinwen** China
72C2 **Xin Xian** China
72C2 **Xinxiang** China
73C3 **Xinyang** China
73C5 **Xinyi** Guangdong, China
72D3 **Xinyi** Jiangsu, China
72D1 **Xi Ujimqin Qi** China
74A2 **Xiuyan** China
23B2 **Xochimilco** Mexico
73D3 **Xuancheng** China
73B3 **Xuanhan** China
72D1 **Xuanhua** China
73A4 **Xuanwei** China
72C3 **Xuchang** China
99E2 **Xuddur** Somalia
72A2 **Xunhua** China
73C5 **Xun Jiang** *R* China
69E2 **Xunke** China
73D5 **Xunwu** China
73C4 **Xupu** China
76E1 **Xuwen** China
73B4 **Xuyong** China
72D3 **Xuzhou** China

Y

73A4 **Ya'an** China
108B3 **Yaapeet** Aust
98B2 **Yabassi** Cam
68C1 **Yablonovyy Khrebet** *Mts* Russian Fed
94C2 **Yabrūd** Syria
20B2 **Yachats** USA
30D3 **Yacuiba** Bol
87B1 **Yādgīr** India
95A1 **Yafran** Libya
23A1 **Yahualica** Mexico
98C2 **Yahuma** Zaïre
75B1 **Yaita** Japan
75B2 **Yaizu** Japan
73A4 **Yajiang** China
20B1 **Yakima** USA
20B1 **Yakima** *R* USA
97B3 **Yako** Burkina
98C2 **Yakoma** Zaïre
74E2 **Yakumo** Japan
12G3 **Yakutat** USA
12G3 **Yakutat B** USA
63E1 **Yakutsk** Russian Fed
77C4 **Yala** Thai
23B2 **Yalalag** Mexico
98C2 **Yalinga** CAR
109C3 **Yallourn** Aust
68B3 **Yalong** *R* China
73A4 **Yalong Jiang** *R* China
54C2 **Yalova** Turk
60D5 **Yalta** Ukraine
74B2 **Yalu Jiang** *R* China
74D3 **Yamagata** Japan
74C4 **Yamaguchi** Japan
68D1 **Yamarovka** Russian Fed
109D1 **Yamba** New S Wales, Aust
108B2 **Yamba** S Australia, Aust
99C2 **Yambio** Sudan
54C2 **Yambol** Bulg
71E4 **Yamdena** *I* Indon
Yam Kinneret = Tiberias,L
108B1 **Yamma Yamma,L** Aust
97B4 **Yamoussoukro** Ivory Coast
85D3 **Yamuna** *R* India
86C1 **Yamzho Yumco** *L* China
63F1 **Yana** *R* Russian Fed
108B3 **Yanac** Aust
75A2 **Yanagawa** Japan
87C1 **Yanam** India
72B2 **Yan'an** China
80B3 **Yanbu'al Bahr** S Arabia
108B2 **Yancannia** Aust
72E3 **Yancheng** China
72B2 **Yanchi** China
108B1 **Yandama** *R* Aust
98C2 **Yangambi** Zaïre
72C1 **Yang He** *R* China
73C5 **Yangjiang** China
Yangon = Rangoon
72C2 **Yangquan** China
73C5 **Yangshan** China
73C3 **Yangtze Gorges** China
72E3 **Yangtze,Mouths of the** China
72D3 **Yangzhou** China
73B4 **Yanhe** China
74B2 **Yanji** China
108C3 **Yanko** *R* Aust
8D2 **Yankton** USA
68A2 **Yanqqi** China
72D1 **Yan Shan** *Hills*
108B1 **Yantabulla** Aust
72E2 **Yantai** China
72D2 **Yanzhou** China
98B2 **Yaoundé** Cam
71E4 **Yapen** *I* Indon
71E3 **Yap Is** Pacific O
24B2 **Yaqui** *R* Mexico
61G2 **Yaransk** Russian Fed
32C3 **Yari** *R* Colombia
74D3 **Yariga-dake** *Mt* Japan
82B2 **Yarkant He** *R* China
86C1 **Yarlung Zangbo Jiang** *R* China
7D5 **Yarmouth** Can
94B2 **Yarmūk** *R* Syria/Jordan
61E2 **Yaroslavl'** Russian Fed
94B2 **Yarqon** *R* Israel
109C3 **Yarram** Aust
109D1 **Yarraman** Aust
109C3 **Yarrawonga** Aust
60D2 **Yartsevo** Russian Fed
63B1 **Yartsevo** Russian Fed
32B2 **Yarumal** Colombia
97C3 **Yashi** Nig
97C4 **Yashikera** Nig
61F4 **Yashkul'** Russian Fed
84C1 **Yasin** Pak
59C3 **Yasinya** Ukraine
109C2 **Yass** Aust
109C2 **Yass** *R* Aust
75A1 **Yasugi** Japan
18A2 **Yates Center** USA
98C2 **Yatolema** Zaïre
74C4 **Yatsushiro** Japan
94B3 **Yatta** Israel
32C4 **Yavari** Peru
85D4 **Yavatmāl** India
74C4 **Yawatahama** Japan
76D2 **Ya Xian** China
90B3 **Yazd** Iran
90B3 **Yazd-e Khvāst** Iran
19B3 **Yazoo** *R* USA
19B3 **Yazoo City** USA
76B2 **Ye** Burma
59D3 **Yedintsy** Moldavia
108A2 **Yeelanna** Aust
60E3 **Yefremov** Russian Fed
61F4 **Yegorlyk** *R* Russian Fed
99D2 **Yei** Sudan

65H4 **Yekaterinburg** Russian Fed
60E3 **Yelets** Russian Fed
44E1 **Yell** *I* Scot
87C1 **Yellandu** India
Yellow = Huang He
8B1 **Yellowhead P** Can
4G3 **Yellowknife** Can
5G4 **Yellowmead P** Can
109C2 **Yellow Mt** Aust
69E3 **Yellow Sea** China/ Korea
8C2 **Yellowstone** *R* USA
8B2 **Yellowstone L** USA
6B1 **Yelverton B** Can
97C3 **Yelwa** Nig
81C4 **Yemen** Republic, Arabian Pen
76C1 **Yen Bai** Viet
97B4 **Yendi** Ghana
76B1 **Yengan** Burma
63B2 **Yeniseysk** Russian Fed
63B1 **Yeniseyskiy Kryazh** *Ridge* Russian Fed
64J2 **Yeniseyskiy Zal** *B* Russian Fed
12D2 **Yentna** *R* USA
43C4 **Yeo** *R* Eng
109C2 **Yeoval** Aust
43C4 **Yeovil** Eng
63C1 **Yerbogachen** Russian Fed
65F5 **Yerevan** Armenia
21B2 **Yerington** USA
21B3 **Yermo** USA
69E1 **Yerofey-Pavlovich** Russian Fed
94B3 **Yeroham** Israel
61G3 **Yershov** Russian Fed
Yerushalayim = Jerusalem
92C1 **Yeşil** *R* Turk
94B2 **Yesud Hama'ala** Israel
109D1 **Yetman** Aust
96B2 **Yetti** Maur
93E1 **Yevlakh** Azerbaijan
60D4 **Yevpatoriya** Ukraine
72E2 **Ye Xian** China
60E4 **Yeysk** Russian Fed
55B2 **Yiannitsá** Greece
73A4 **Yibin** China
73C3 **Yichang** China
69E2 **Yichun** China
72B2 **Yijun** China
54C2 **Yildiz Dağlari** *Upland* Turk
92C2 **Yıldızeli** Turk
73A5 **Yiliang** China
72B2 **Yinchuan** China
72D3 **Ying He** *R* China
72E1 **Yingkou** China
73D3 **Yingshan** Hubei, China
72B3 **Yingshan** Sichuan, China
73D4 **Yingtan** China
82C1 **Yining** China
72B1 **Yin Shan** *Upland* China
99D2 **Yirga Alem** Eth
99D2 **Yirol** Sudan
63D3 **Yirshi** China
73B5 **Yishan** China
72D2 **Yishui** China
55B3 **Yíthion** Greece
38J6 **Yivieska** Fin
73C4 **Yiyang** China
38K5 **Yli-Kitka** *L* Fin
38J5 **Ylilornio** Sweden
19A4 **Yoakum** USA
23B2 **Yogope** Mexico
78C4 **Yogyakarta** Indon
13D2 **Yoho Nat Pk** Can
98B2 **Yokadouma** Cam
75B2 **Yokkaichi** Japan
75B1 **Yokohama** Japan
75B1 **Yokosuka** Japan
74C3 **Yonago** Japan
74E3 **Yonezawa** Japan
73D4 **Yong'an** China
72A2 **Yongchang** China
74B3 **Yŏngch'on** S Korea
73B4 **Yongchuan** China
72A2 **Yongdeng** China
73D5 **Yongding** China
72D2 **Yongding He** *R* China
74B3 **Yŏngdŏk** S Korea
74B3 **Yŏnghŭng** N Korea
74B3 **Yongju** S Korea
72B2 **Yongning** China
16C2 **Yonkers** USA
49C2 **Yonne** *R* France
42D3 **York** Eng
18A1 **York** Nebraska, USA
16A3 **York** Pennsylvania, USA
107D2 **York,C** Aust
108A2 **Yorke Pen** Aust
108A3 **Yorketown** Aust
7A4 **York Factory** Can
41C3 **Yorkshire Moors** *Moorland* Eng
42D2 **Yorkshire Wolds** *Upland* Eng
5H4 **Yorkton** Can
22B2 **Yosemite L** USA
22C1 **Yosemite Nat Pk** USA
75A2 **Yoshii** *R* Japan
75A2 **Yoshino** *R* Japan
61G2 **Yoshkar Ola** Russian Fed
74B4 **Yŏsu** S Korea
41B3 **Youghal** Irish Rep
45C3 **Youghal Harb** Irish Rep
73B5 **You Jiang** *R* China
109C2 **Young** Aust
34D2 **Young** Urug
111A2 **Young Range** *Mts* NZ
13E2 **Youngstown** Can
14B2 **Youngstown** Ohio, USA
22A1 **Yountville** USA
73B4 **Youyang** China
92B2 **Yozgat** Turk
20B2 **Yreka** USA
39G7 **Ystad** Sweden
43C3 **Ystwyth** *R* Wales
44C3 **Ythan** *R* Scot
73C4 **Yuan Jiang** *R* Hunan, China
73A5 **Yuan Jiang** *R* Yunnan, China
73A4 **Yuanmu** China
72C2 **Yuanping** China
21A2 **Yuba City** USA
74E2 **Yūbari** Japan
25D3 **Yucatan** *Pen* Mexico
25D2 **Yucatan Chan** Mexico/Cuba
72C2 **Yuci** China
63F2 **Yudoma** *R* Russian Fed
73D4 **Yudu** China
73A4 **Yuexi** China
73C4 **Yueyang** China
54A2 **Yugoslavia** Republic, Europe
73B5 **Yu Jiang** *R* China
12C2 **Yukon** *R* Can/USA
4E3 **Yukon Territory** Can
76E1 **Yulin** Guangdong, China
73C5 **Yulin** Guangxi, China
72B2 **Yulin** Shaanxi, China
9B3 **Yuma** USA
68B3 **Yumen** China
72D2 **Yunan** China
34A3 **Yungay** Chile
73C5 **Yunkai Dashan** *Hills* China
108A2 **Yunta** Aust
72C3 **Yunxi** China
72C3 **Yun Xian** China
73B3 **Yunyang** China
32B5 **Yurimaguas** Peru
73E5 **Yu Shan** *Mt* Taiwan
38L6 **Yushkozero** Russian Fed
82D2 **Yushu** Tibet, China
73A5 **Yuxi** China
74F2 **Yuzhno-Kuril'sk** Russian Fed
69G2 **Yuzhno-Sakhalinsk** Russian Fed
61J3 **Yuzh Ural** *Mts* Russian Fed
46A2 **Yvelines** Department, France
47B1 **Yverdon** Switz

Z

56A2 **Zaandam** Neth
93D2 **Zāb al Babir** *R* Iraq
93D2 **Zāb as Şaghīr** *R* Iraq
68D2 **Zabaykal'sk** Russian Fed
59B3 **Zabreh** Czech
59B2 **Zabrze** Pol
23A2 **Zacapu** Mexico
24B2 **Zacatecas** Mexico
23B2 **Zacatepec** Morelos, Mexico
23B2 **Zacatepec** Oaxaca, Mexico
23B2 **Zacatlan** Mexico
23A1 **Zacoalco** Mexico
23B1 **Zacualtipan** Mexico
52C2 **Zadar** Croatia
76B3 **Zadetkyi** *I* Burma
50A2 **Zafra** Spain
95C1 **Zagazig** Egypt
96B1 **Zagora** Mor
60E2 **Zagorsk** Russian Fed
52C1 **Zagreb** Croatia
91D4 **Zāhedān** Iran
94B2 **Zahle** Leb
51C2 **Zahrez Chergui** *Marshland* Alg
61H2 **Zainsk** Russian Fed
98C3 **Zaïre** Republic, Africa
98B3 **Zaïre** *R* Zaïre/Congo
54B2 **Zaječār** Yugos
68C1 **Zakamensk** Russian Fed
93D2 **Zakho** Iraq
55B3 **Zákinthos** *I* Greece
59B3 **Zakopane** Pol
59B3 **Zalaegerszeg** Hung
54B1 **Zalău** Rom
56C2 **Zalew Szczeciński** *Lg* Pol
98C1 **Zalingei** Sudan
63F2 **Zaliv Akademii** *B* Russian Fed
65G5 **Zaliv Kara-Bogaz Gol** *B* Turkmenistan
74C2 **Zaliv Petra Velikogo** *B* Russian Fed
69G2 **Zaliv Turpeniya** *B* Russian Fed
95A2 **Zaltan** Libya
89H9 **Zambesi** *R* Mozam
100B2 **Zambezi** Zambia
100B2 **Zambezi** *R* Zambia
100B2 **Zambia** Republic, Africa
79B4 **Zamboanga** Phil
79B4 **Zamboanga Pen** Phil
58C2 **Zambrów** Pol
32B4 **Zamora** Ecuador
23A2 **Zamora** Mexico
50A1 **Zamora** Spain
59C2 **Zamość** Pol
72A3 **Zamtang** China
98B3 **Zanaga** Congo
50B2 **Záncara** *R* Spain
84D2 **Zanda** China
14B3 **Zanesville** USA
84D2 **Zangla** India
90A2 **Zanjān** Iran
34B2 **Zanjitas** Arg
34B2 **Zanjon** *R* Arg
99D3 **Zanzibar** Tanz
99D3 **Zanzibar** *I* Tanz
96C2 **Zaouatallaz** Alg
72D3 **Zaozhuang** China
93D2 **Zap** *R* Turk
39K7 **Zapadnaja Dvina** *R* Russian Fed
65H3 **Zapadno-Sibirskaya Nizmennost'** *Lowland* Russian Fed
63B2 **Zapadnyy Sayan** *Mts* Russian Fed
34A3 **Zapala** Arg
60E4 **Zaporozh'ye** Ukraine
93C2 **Zara** Turk
23A1 **Zaragoza** Mexico
50B1 **Zaragoza** Spain
90B2 **Zarand** Iran
90C3 **Zarand** Iran
80E2 **Zaranj** Afghan
33D2 **Zarara** Ven
58D1 **Zarasai** Lithuania
34D2 **Zárate** Arg
90B3 **Zard Kuh** *Mt* Iran
12H3 **Zarembo I** USA
84B2 **Zarghun Shahr** Afghan
84B2 **Zargun** *Mt* Pak
97C3 **Zaria** Nig
92C3 **Zarqa** Jordan
94B2 **Zarqa** *R* Jordan
32B4 **Zaruma** Ecuador
58B2 **Zary** Pol
96D1 **Zarzis** Tunisia
84D2 **Zāskār** *Mts* India
84D2 **Zāskār** *R* India
94C2 **Zatara** *R* Jordan
Zatoka Gdańska = Gdańsk,G of
69E1 **Zavitinsk** Russian Fed
59B2 **Zawiercie** Pol
63C2 **Zayarsk** Russian Fed
65K5 **Zaysan** Kazakhstan
82D3 **Zayü** China
68B4 **Zayü** *Mt* China
58B2 **Zduńska Wola** Pol
46B1 **Zeebrugge** Belg
94B3 **Zeelim** Israel
101G1 **Zeerust** S Africa
94B2 **Zefat** Israel
97C3 **Zegueren** *Watercourse* Mali
99E1 **Zeila** Somalia
57C2 **Zeitz** Germany
72A2 **Zekog** China
61G2 **Zelenodol'sk** Russian Fed
39K6 **Zelenogorsk** Russian Fed
47D1 **Zell** Austria
98C2 **Zemio** CAR
64F1 **Zemlya Aleksandry** *I* Barents S
64F2 **Zemlya Frantsa Iosifa** *Is* Barents S
64F1 **Zemlya Georga** *I* Barents S
64H1 **Zemlya Vil'cheka** *I* Barents S
73B4 **Zenning** China
47B1 **Zermatt** Switz
63E2 **Zeya** Russian Fed
63E2 **Zeya** *Res* Russian Fed
50A1 **Zézere** *R* Port
94B1 **Zghorta** Leb
58B2 **Zgierz** Pol
72D1 **Zhangjiakou** China
73D4 **Zhangping** China
72D2 **Zhangwei He** *R* China
72E1 **Zhangwu** China
72A2 **Zhangye** China
73D5 **Zhangzhou** China
73C5 **Zhanjiang** China
73A4 **Zhanyi** China
73C5 **Zhaoqing** China
73A4 **Zhaotong** China
72D2 **Zhaoyang Hu** *L* China
61J4 **Zharkamys** Russian Fed
63E1 **Zhatay** Russian Fed
73D4 **Zhejiang** Province, China
67F3 **Zhengou** China
72C3 **Zhengzhou** China
72D3 **Zhenjiang** China
73A4 **Zhenxiong** China
73B4 **Zhenyuan** China
61F3 **Zherdevka** Russian Fed
73C3 **Zhicheng** China
68C1 **Zhigalovo** Russian Fed
73B4 **Zhijin** China

58D2 **Zhitkovichi** Belorussia
60C3 **Zhitomir** Ukraine
60D3 **Zhlobin** Belorussia
60C4 **Zhmerinka** Ukraine
84B2 **Zhob** Pak
58D2 **Zhodino** Latvia
72B2 **Zhongning** China
112C10 **Zhongshan** *Base* Ant
73C5 **Zhongshan** China
72B2 **Zhongwei** China
68B4 **Zhougdian** China
73E3 **Zhoushan Quandao** *Arch* China
72E2 **Zhuanghe** China
72A3 **Zhugqu** China
73C3 **Zhushan** China
73C4 **Zhuzhou** China
72D2 **Zibo** China
106C3 **Ziel,Mt** Aust
58B2 **Zielona Gora** Pol
76A1 **Zigaing** Burma
73A4 **Zigong** China
97A3 **Ziguinchor** Sen
23A2 **Zihuatanejo** Mexico
94B2 **Zikhron Ya'aqov** Israel
59B3 **Žilina** Czech
95A2 **Zillah** Libya
47D1 **Ziller** *R* Austria
47D1 **Zillertaler Alpen** *Mts* Austria
58D1 **Zilupe** Russian Fed
63C2 **Zima** Russian Fed
23B1 **Zimapan** Mexico
23B2 **Zimatlan** Mexico
100B2 **Zimbabwe** Republic, Africa
94B3 **Zin** *R* Israel
23B2 **Zinacatepec** Mexico
23A2 **Zinapécuaro** Mexico
97C3 **Zinder** Niger
73C4 **Zi Shui** China
23A2 **Zitácuaro** Mexico
57C2 **Zittau** Germany
72D2 **Ziya He** *R* China
72A3 **Ziyang** China
61J2 **Zlatoust** Russian Fed
59B3 **Zlin** Czech
65K4 **Zmeinogorsk** Russian Fed
58B2 **Znin** Pol
59B3 **Znoimo** Czech
100B3 **Zoekmekaar** S Africa
47B1 **Zofinger** Switz
72A3 **Zoigê** China
59D3 **Zolochev** Ukraine
101C2 **Zomba** Malawi
98B2 **Zongo** Zaïre
92B1 **Zonguldak** Turk
97B4 **Zorzor** Lib
96A2 **Zouerate** Maur
54B1 **Zrenjanin** Serbia, Yugos
47C1 **Zug** Switz
47D1 **Zugspitze** *Mt* Germany
50A2 **Zújar** *R* Spain
100C2 **Zumbo** Mozam
23B2 **Zumpango** Mexico
97C4 **Zungeru** Nig
73B4 **Zunyi** China
76D1 **Zuo** *R* China
73B5 **Zuo Jiang** *R* China
47C1 **Zürich** Switz
47C1 **Zürichsee** *L* Switz
95A1 **Zuwārah** Libya
95A2 **Zuwaylah** Libya
61H2 **Zuyevka** Russian Fed
100B4 **Zvishavane** Zim
59B3 **Zvolen** Czech
54A2 **Zvornik** Bosnia & Herzegovina, Yugos
97B4 **Zwedru** Lib
46D2 **Zweibrücken** Germany
47B1 **Zweisimmen** Switz
57C2 **Zwickau** Germany
56B2 **Zwolle** Neth
58C2 **Zyrardów** Pol
65K5 **Zyryanovsk** Kazakhstan
59B3 **Żywiec** Pol
94A1 **Zyyi** Cyprus